The Toad and the Donkey

An Anthology of Norman Literature
from the Channel Islands

The Toad and the Donkey

An Anthology of Norman literature
from the Channel Islands

Edited by
Geraint Jennings and Yan Marquis

Francis
Boutle
Publishers

First published by Francis Boutle Publishers
272 Alexandra Park Road
London N22 7BG
Tel/Fax: 020 8889 7744
Email: info@francisboutle.co.uk
www.francisboutle.co.uk

Lesser Used Languages of Europe series editor: Alan M. Kent

ISBN 978 1 903427 61 3
Printed in Malta at Melita Press

Acknowledgments

The editors would like to thank the Guernsey and Jersey authors and their families for the use of their texts in this collection.

Thanks to *Le Don Balleine* and L'Assembliée d'Jèrriais and La Société Guernesiaise for permission to use material originally published by them; to the Lord Coutanche Library, Société Jersiaise, the Priaulx Library and the Island Archives (Guernsey); to Ted Vibert for permission to use material from *Jersey Topic* magazine and for information provided; to Ken Hill whose transcriptions and translations of works by Marjorie Ozanne and Denys Corbet we have consulted.

Contents

Foreword

Language is a living medium through which communication is exchanged, either in groups or on a one to one basis. Therefore languages such as Jèrriais, Guernesiais and Sercquiais are vital and must be spoken to appreciate the richness and diversity of their prose as well as the written word for prosperity.

Trees can only grow into longevity by both their root action as well as the new leaves they produce each spring. I use this analogy to compare this book as being an essential read not only for the beginner learning Jèrriais or Guernesiais but also for the seasoned practitioner of our mother tongues.

For me, learning Jèrriais falls into two categories. Firstly there are those of us who learnt it like my sisters and I did at our parent's knee and grew up to speak it from the heart, way before we could read anything, let alone Jèrriais. Living in a household where it surrounded you on a daily basis, where the neighbours spoke it to one another and where a child asking for another slice of bread and butter at tea time was all communicated in Jèrriais. This was the only language we knew. The very fact it surrounded you was a joy, it was your own communication and it was, and remains, special.

Secondly there are those who have to learn it from worthy scholars who pass their knowledge on. Present day students, whether young or mature, may have an advantage in reading and writing it much more than we did, but the communication of its learning finishes at the end of the lesson.

The Jèrriais, Guernesiais and Sercquiais of our yesterdays are spoken amongst ourselves less than they were, as we move forward into a cosmopolitan age. Perhaps they are moving from their autumn to the stillness of winter. But what is essential? Publications of this quality and magnitude are clearly not only a labour of love but of vital importance for our languages' survival. So, dear reader, like the seasons of time, please remember that, after the still of winter, the leaves of spring emerge with abundance and flourish into summer. Let this worthy tome be a springboard and help you on your way to partake, share and preserve our mother tongues. I strongly recommend it.

E. Winston Le Brun
Président, L'Assembliée d'Jèrriais

Introduction

To many outside onlookers the Channel Islands, possessions of the British Crown nestled between the peninsulas of northwestern France, seem a unit, a singular archipelago. And yet across and between these islands call different peoples with different languages, having lived under different laws and governments for centuries. And though the Channel tides that have kept them insular for so long are being overborne by waves of internationalisation and population change fuelled by changing economies, still the voices of the donkey and the toad call back and forth between the Bailiwicks and can be heard on neighbouring shores through the influence of their literatures.

From the ninth century, Vikings started settling the coasts of Normandy and heading upstream and inland. In 911AD the King of France recognised the claims of the Norse settlers to control territory centred around the meanders of the Seine and along the Channel coast. With the annexation in 933AD of territories to the west, the Cotentin peninsula and the Channel Islands, the extent of what was known as the Duchy of Normandy became recognisable. The majority of the indigenous population in the lands now controlled by the Norsemen spoke varieties of Gallo-Romance language descended from Latin. This Romance speech was influenced by the Germanic language of the rulers as the Norsemen adopted the language of the ruled. The presence of words of Norse origin is one of the distinguishing features of Norman. In 1066, William of Normandy sealed his claim to the throne of England and for a time the Duchy of Normandy and the Kingdom of England existed in what has been described as an Anglo-Norman commonwealth. Normandy was divided after 1204, when the King of France incorporated the continental possessions of the Duchy into his Kingdom and the Channel Islands remained under the control of the King of England according to his claim of Duke. However, into the twentieth century a majority of Channel Islanders still spoke varieties of Norman language descended from the language of William the Conqueror and related to the Norman language spoken in neighbouring mainland Normandy.

Some of the Norman speaking Channel Islanders have been concerned not only to speak their languages and to continue speaking them despite the competition from two dominant languages, French and English, but also to develop literatures that reflect the lives and concerns of their fellows. Although Jersey produced a major poet of Anglo-Norman literature in the person of Wace, it was only at the end of the eighteenth century that, with Romanticism's interest in regional cultures and the rise of European nationalism, conscious efforts were made to use the vernaculars of the Islands for serious literature. Matthew Le Geyt at the end of the eighteenth century was the first of the wave of Jersey writers; George Métivier's astonishing career started in the early nineteenth century. They were followed by other poets and prose writers who kept up streams of commentary on life in the Islands and overseas, even as the proportion of Norman speakers started a long decline, and English grew in importance. No vernacular novels have been produced; immediacy and topicality were prized. Poems and short stories appeared in newspapers and almanacs, occasionally being collected in pamphlets and books. Although Guernsey and Jersey followed separate paths towards standardisation, contacts and exchanges between the writers of the Islands influenced their respective literatures. Texts reproduced in this collection retain their original spelling – this reflects the variety of dialects and influences across the historical range. Modern Jèrriais has a standard writing system as used in schools and media; the situation for Guernesiais is less settled.

The press freedom in the Islands, compared to the political upheavals in France during the nineteenth century, meant that French language Channel Island newspapers were eagerly distributed along the neighbouring coasts. Norman language writers in the Cotentin were inspired by the vernacular literature produced by Channel Island writers, sparking the Norman literary revival of the mid-nineteenth century. Writers such as Alfred Rossel and Louis Beuve owed a debt to the authors of the Islands. Contacts between the literatures continue as adaptations are made from one variety of Norman to another, helping to cross-fertilise the literatures.

The vernacular literatures of the Islands have been open to outside influences. As will be seen in this selection, Island writers have travelled and written outside the archipelago – sometimes on the other side of the world. Émigré writers have contributed to the literatures; and visitors have left their imprints in the Islands.

Roger-Jean Lebarbenchon, in his study of the vernacular literatures of the Channel Islands *La Grève de Lecq*, describes the Jersey author Philippe Le Sueur Mourant as having the gift of a satirical gaze. If the toad and the donkey may sometimes eye each other with sibling rivalry from their respective coasts they also turn their satirical gaze on the people, customs, politics and lives of their own Islands.

The Languages of the Islands

There are three extant Norman languages in the Islands – Auregnais, the language of Alderney, became extinct in the twentieth century.

In Jersey, Jèrriais is most easily identifiable by its characteristic "th", a feature most evident in the North-Western dialect. Some of the smaller dialects died out in the twentieth century (although leaving behind them some literary output as a record of their existence), leaving the main distinctions in accent and vocabulary between the dialects of the West and those of the East. The dialect of Saint Helier, as the first to disappear under encroaching anglicisation, has left behind a scanty record in literature. The main literary dialect is that of Saint Ouen, the basis of the modern standard writing system.

In Guernsey, Guernesiais can be divided into the dialects of the Haut Pas, the Higher Parishes on the raised terrain of the South and West, and those of the Bas Pas, the Lower Parishes on the flat terrain of the North (the most striking contrast lies in the vowel-sounds). Most Guernesiais literature has been produced by writersof the Bas Pas. To the outside ear, perhaps the most distinctive feature of Guernesiais is its strong diphthongs (this is a feature shared by Eastern dialects of Jèrriais, Guernesiais also shares strong palatalisation of consonants with Jèrriais).

In Sark, a small number of speakers of Sercquiais remain. Sark has not produced a written literature of its own, although some of its oral tradition has been preserved by writers from outside. Although Sark is part of the Bailiwick of Guernsey, the Island was settled in the sixteenth century by families from Saint Ouen in Jersey. The vernacular of Sark, therefore retains some dialectal features particular to Saint Ouen (although the typical 'th' has never developed here). Sercquiais has preserved some features such as pronunciation of final consonants and palatalisation of consonants is less advanced.

All the vernacular languages have been influenced by contact with French, and their literatures by the prestige model offered by French literature. The influence of English language and literature has increased with ever greater rapidity since the mid-nineteenth century.

Toads and Donkeys

An unititiated visitor watching the annual Channel Island football final might wonder why some of the more boisterous Jersey fans customarily throw carrots onto the pitch for the Guernsey players. And strolling round Jersey's capital, Saint Helier, the sight of a sculpted toad on a stone column might set such a visitor wondering.

Traditional animal nicknames are attributed to each major island, and often borne with pride by the islanders in question: the toad for Jersey and the donkey for Guernsey are well known, while the crow for Sark and the rabbit for Alderney are almost forgotten nowadays by most people.

Why toads? Some might maintain that Saint Samson of Dol, evangeliser of Guernsey, cast out the snakes and toads from that island and sent them to Jersey, where he had, according to legend, received a less welcoming reception; naturalists would point to the fact that Jersey and Guernsey became islands at different periods, thereby leaving a different heritage of fauna trapped as the Channel waters rose about eight millennia ago.

Why donkeys? The two capitals, Saint Peter Port and Saint Helier, differ in their terrain. While Saint Peter Port clings to the steep terrain overlooking its natural harbour, Saint Helier has sprawled across a marshy basin between higher ground and the dunes of the sweeping bay where ships were beached. Unloading and loading cargoes was done on the flat in Saint Helier, while donkeys were used to transport goods up and down the steep winding streets of Saint Peter Port.

The donkeys have long been replaced, in Guernsey, by the car, the lorry and the van; and in Jersey, the toad has been in retreat as development and urbanisation affects his habitats. But the nicknames live on.

A traditional rhyme (here given in a Jèrriais version) encapsulates the sort of neighbourly digs the Islanders have long taken pleasure in.

Traditional (Jèrriais)

Dgèrnésiais au Jèrriais:–

J'crai qu'j'éthons d'la plyie,
car j'vai qu'les crapauds sont sortis!

Jèrriais au Dgèrnésiais:–

J'n'ai pas d'peine à l'craithe,
car j'entends les ânes braithe!

Translation

The Guernseyman to the Jerseyman:–

I think we'll have rain,
for I see that the toads have come out!

The Jerseyman to the Guernseyman:–

I don't have any trouble believing it,
for I can hear the donkeys braying!

The following skit ascribes various qualities to different Islanders. Jersey is a bailiwick in itself; its dependent islets and reefs being generally uninhabited. The bailiwick of Guernsey includes not only Guernsey, but the other inhabited islands as well as various uninhabited rocks. It is true today that Guernsey has more of a reputation for traditional dance than Jersey – but this may not be connected with any supposed four-leggedness among Guernsey dancers. The poem is ascribed to Jean Dorey of Jersey, but an alternative story claims that it is the result of poetic banter between Sir Robert Pipon Marett (who wrote, according to the source, the main body of the little poem) and the father of the Rev Philip Ahier (who wrote, according to the source, the footnote).

Attributed to Jean Dorey

Eune Hinprovisation Satirique èt Farcico-Coumique sus les Divers Nationnaux d'la Manche, *1867* (Jèrriais)

Lé JERRIAIS couor quand i veux donné assistanc',
Lé *Guernésiais* lèv' *tous* ses dguérets quand i danc',⋆
L'Aur'gnais accatte ordinair'ment quand i dêpens,'
Lé *Serquais* bé un verr' quand i-l-en a la chanc',

L'Hermais est hardi court dé pé quand nou l'offens',
Et lé *Jétouais* s'en souv'ain bain quand i-l-y pens'!!!

UN GNIOLEUX.

★Qué nos vaîsins aient *quatr' dguérets*,
Ou mêm' qu'i cri'nt "Hi-hans!"
J'voudrais savé tchès qu'i-l-en est,
Pourvé qu'i saient d'brav's gens.

A Satirical and Farcically Comical Himprovisation on the Different Nationalities of the Channel, *1867*

The Jerseyman runs when he wants to lend a hand,
The Guernseyman lifts *all* his legs up when he dances,★
The Alderneyman usually buys when he spends,
The Sarkee has a drink when he gets the chance,
The Herm man is very touchy when you offend him,
And the Jéthou man can well remember when he thinks about it!

A Joker

★So what, if our neighbours have four legs,
or even if they cry "Hee-haw!"
I'd like to know what's wrong with that,
seeing what fine fellows they are.

Philippe Falle, Rector of Saint Saviour, found, when sent to London in the late seventeenth century to petition for Jersey's interests, that ruling circles in England were uninformed about the constitution and history of the Channel Islands. He wrote his 'Account' to educate the British about all aspects of Jersey – he left the job of standing up for Guernsey to anyone who wanted to write a similar book. Nobody did.

Philippe Falle

From An Account of the Island of Jersey, *1694*

The only blemish and disgrace of the Island (as 'tis by some accounted) is the great multitude of Toads which swarm in it, and are chiefly seen in Summer and moist Weather. It must be owned they are no very agreeable Sight, though many of them have their Skins finely speckled and variegated. 'Tis commonly said, *Poisonous as a Toad*; but where that Poison lurks, or in what manner it operates, we are yet to find.

They neither bite, nor sting. They lye in our sweet Water, and among our best Fruit when it falls on the Ground; and 'tis not known that ever any Man received any injury from their doing so. The notion our People have of them, is, that they draw out what is noxious and impure in the Elements, and thereby contribute to health; and this they pretend to prove by the contrary example of *Guernezey*, which will not suffer a Toad to live in it, and yet is thought not so healthy as JERSEY. However that he, these and others such unsightly Creatures, found both on the Land and in the Waters, seem wisely contrived and designed by the Almighty Creator, as foils to set off the Beauty of his other Works.

This poem by Guernseyman Denys Corbet, probably written to the Jerseyman Charles Picot who served as Anglican clergyman for many years in Guernsey and who was himself a writer of stories in Jèrriais, provides us with a brief tour round the parishes of Guernsey and the nicknames associated with the inhabitants of each parish. Just like their Islands, the people of Jersey and Guernsey would find themselves labelled according to their origins.

Denys Corbet ('Bad'lagoule')

À un Rév. Crapaud – sàns r'preuche, *1889* (Guernesiais)

Séyiz l'bienv'nu, moussieu l'crapaud,
Ilo dans la vieille île ès ânes;
Vou savaïz qu'leus tout pus grànd d'faut
Est l'hôrriblle entrìnn'tai d'leus crânes:
Eh bien, s'ou' corrigîz chunna
Vou s'raïz, brâment, l'prumier d'vot' dra'.

Vou savaïz qu'tout âne est têtu;
Mais l's-uns un amas pus que l's-autres;
Si bien qu'aût'feis v'là qu'a valu
Pus d'un bien joli titre ès nôtres,
Suivànt l'érague, où qu'un châcun
S'mourtrait d'bouan ou d'maivais aigrun.

En tout prumier ll'a les *cllichards*,
Qui sont, nou dit, l's-ânes d'la ville;
D'long, rapalis, faillis cracards,
Maladifs, attaquis d'la bile;
Terjous pllaintuchànt – v'là qu'j'ai oui –
Terjous malade', et n'mouarànt pouit.

L'âne d'vient *raïne* à Saint Sàmson,
Et ch'est dans les praîs qu'i s'herbige;
Dans l'douït, dans marais, en d'muchon
Tout' les sortes d'pertus s'érige:
Nou dit qu'en Guernesy n'y-a ieû
Jamais un pus fichu crâqueux.

L'âne *ann'ton* du Valle est l'natif:
Dans l'Cllos i dâte un p'tit d'la *raïne* –
Exeptaï qu'il est mouens craintif –
Mais adret squître à la vingtaïne:
Dans l'fouaïllage i bourdonne au ser,
Et s'rait ékerbot s'il' tait ner.

L'Càt'lain est l'*âne au tout pur sàng*;
Es superbes qualitais d'race;
Espritu, long d'oreille et d'fllànc;
Ossìn d's-admiraïr jamais n'lasse,
D'nobllesse i s'pique étou bouan frais;
Prend d's-airs de prìnce, et n'est pouit niais.

D'Saint Sauveux l'âne est *fouarmillon*,
Et meut coum un vier cat en pouque;
Peuplle étou, cordingue! à fouéson;
Tout entouar d'li boul'verse et bouque:
Fait des monquiaux, ma fé, de rien,
Et s'approvisiounne, et fait bien.

L'âne d'Saint Pierre est *l'ékerbot*,
Et ch'est l'pus au ser qu'i' s'réville;
Fort de tête, et d'êtchine, et d'co,
Il est de tout pertu la gu'ville,
Et pâss'rait bien jour après jour
En cour – j'entends dans l'mouaché d'cour.

Qu'est qu'en est du cien d'Torteva'?
Où, tout douach'ment, piâ-n-piâ, j'arrive;
Nou dit qu'ch'est l'*âne à pid de ch'va*,
Qui jamais cavalier n'déhouive:
Pâtient, et doux coum un agné,
De tous ch'est l'pus docile, j'cré.

Pour quânt à l'âne app'laï *bourdon*,
Ch'est la Fouarêt qu'est sa pâresse;
Coum l'aïsse i porte un aiguillon,
Et tout en bourdonnànt vou blesse;
Mais pour chu qu'est d'sen produit d'miel,
I' l'mettrait tout dans sen couain d'iel.

A Saint Martin, si bien j'comprends,
L'âne est biaûcoup pus paisson qu'viànde,
D'pis qu'nou l'dit d'l'érâgue ès *dravans* –
Ichìn s'la raison nou me d'mànde –
J'réponds qu'j'ai oui qu'aût' feis, d'méquier.
Ch'tait, dame, un fàmaeux païssonnier.

D'Saint André l's-ânesse' et l's-ânons
Sont les tous pus l'giers à la course,
Chu qui leus valit l'nom d'*crainchons*,
Titre i parait bien qu'aeut la source
Dans l'fait qu'dans l'crible d'notre îlot
I' sont coupé, coquette et fllot.

V'là tout, moussieu l'crapaud, entouar
L's-ânes d'cîz nou et leus pernagues,
Et j'm'attends qu'ou' m'diraïz, en r'touar
D'combein d'crapauds ill' a d'éragues
Cîz vou; mais, surtout, s'll'en a ieû
A coue. Ah! v'là qu'jamais j'n'ai seû.

To a Rev. Toad – sans reproche, *1889*

Welcome to you, Mr. Toad,
over here on old donkey island;
you know that their greatest flaw
is the awful stubbornness of their skulls:
well, if you're able to put this right
you'll be the very first man of your cloth to do so.

You know that every donkey is stubborn;
but some a lot more than others;
so much so that in the past ours
earned themselves pretty little nicknames,
according to their kind, where each and every one
would demonstrate their good or bad breeding.

First off there are the *spurters*
which are, so they say, the town donkeys.
Dawdling, pale, poor chatterers,
sickly, bilious;
always whingeing – that's what I've heard –
always ill, but never dying.

The donkey becomes a *frog* in St. Sampson,
and it's in the water meadows that he lives:
in the stream, in the marsh, surreptitiously
building all sorts of holes for himself:
they say that in Guernsey there's
never been a worse damned croaking chatterbox.

The *cockchafer* is the native donkey of the Vale:
in the Clos he's a little like the frog –
except that he's less timid –
but quite cunning at the Vingtaine:
in the bracken he buzzes in the evening,
and would be a beetle if he were black.

The Castel donkey is a *thoroughbred*;
with all the breed's best qualities;
spirited, long ears and flanks;
and so he never tires of admiring himself,
he feels he's very much honour-bound too;
takes princely airs, and is no fool.

The St. Saviour's donkey is an *ant*,
and wriggles like an old cat in a bag (a pig in a poke);
my goodness, there's an infinite amount of them as well;
everything around him, he topples and crumples:
makes mountains, my word, out of ant-hills,
and provides for himself, and does well.

The St. Peter's donkey is a *beetle*,
and he's more likely to wake in the evening;
with a strong head, and spine, and neck.
He's the round peg to every hole,
and would happily spend day after day
in court – I mean, in the courtyard manure heap.

What about the one from Torteval?
Which, very slowly, plodding along, I eventually get to.
They say that this is the *donkey with horse's hooves*,
that never leads its rider astray:
patient, and as gentle as a lamb,
of them all he's the most docile, I think.

As for the donkey called the *bumble bee*,
the Forest is his parish;
like the honey bee he has a sting,
and buzzes about as he injures you;
but as for his product of honey,
he would keep it all in the corner of his eye.

In St. Martin's, if I understand aright,
the donkey is much more fish than meat,
as they say that his species is that of the *thornback ray*.
Here if you ask me the reason –
I'll tell you that I heard that once, as for work,
he was a really excellent fisherman.

In St. Andrew's the female donkeys and the foals
are the most lightweight in the race,
which has earned them the name of *'the siftings'*,
a soubriquet which clearly seems to have its origins
in the fact that in our islet's sieve
they're tips, undeveloped grain, and fannings.

That's all, Mr. Toad, about
the donkeys round where we live and their antics.
And I expect that you'll tell me, in return,
how many sorts of toads there are
where you come from; but, above all, if there are any
with tails. Ah! that I've never known.

George Métivier, called during his lifetime Guernsey's national poet, the Guernsey Burns and the Guernsey bard, is a towering figure in the history of the development of the literatures of the Channel Islands, and of mainland Normandy. His antiquarian and philological approach to poetry, full of allusions and high-flown Romanticism, has meant a fall from favour in current-day literary appreciation in Guernsey. This poem was published in Métivier's 1831 collection *Rimes guernesiaises*.

Midsummer celebrations (at the feast of Saint John) were formerly the occasion of sometimes riotous gatherings. In Jersey the States banned the midsummer fair in the parish of Saint John in 1797 in an attempt to impose public order. The tradition of rowing round a rock, called Lé J'va Dgillaume (the William horse), in the bay at Bonne Nuit in Saint John at Midsummer continued however. The rock was supposedly a shapeshifting spirit which had taken the form of a horse and then been turned to stone by a curse. With the suppression of the fair in Jersey, many Jersey people in the nineteenth century made alternative arrangements by setting sail for Guernsey where the Midsummer fair was held near the Castel church. Métivier refers to the circumnavigation of Lé J'va Dgillaume and the Jersey legend of the dragon of La Hougue Bie, slain by the Seigneur of Hambie, from mainland Normandy. Alexandre's was a popular tavern in Saint Saviour, Guernsey.

George Métivier

St. Jean et ses Crapauds, *1831* (Guernesiais)

Hélas mon dou, tous ches Crapauds que vlò!
Est-che qu'i sont v'nus pour goûtaïr not baguiau?
Est-che qu'i sont v'nus pour écuraïr nos aires?
J'crâïns qu'i n'défoncent nos navires à caûguières!
Dame, il en plieut! chiers amis, j'en avon
Coum de raïnequaux cie le roué Faraon.
S'la grand couleuvre était acouore en vie
Qui l's énaquait du tems du vier Hambie,
J'dirion, vraîment qu'a veurt en faire une fin,
Et qu'i sont v'nus sauvaîr leux couâne ichin.

Auve sa bouane cotte, sa doncelle, et sa pipe,
Et ses longues brayes d'nanquine, véyous Maîte Flipe!
Autefais, mordingue, i s'contentait brâment
De faire le touar de la roque au bouan Saint Jean,
De jouaïr sa gamme de raflle-bord ou ses cartes,
Supaïr sen dram, ou buvotaïr sa quarte;
Fier coum un crax et vif coum un ribé,
A-ch-t-heure le v'là qui fait d'sen Quéripé,
Qui chante, rit, niolle et danse auve sa mouissette,
De Saint Aubin la pus fieffaïe grisette!
En v'là qui roulent, et prennent tout leux pllaisi',
Coum des messiûs, dans les chaises de Mêssi –
La cargaison s'en va cies Alissandre,
Vée si la chair de not volaille est tendre;
I n'liqu'ront pas leux barbe, au jour qu'il est,
De couâne rouaître, cidre aigre, et gros durs peis,

De congre au sail, d'piécho d'vaque éragie –
I f'ront ripaille ... une paure feis dans leux vie!

I ll'y-en a menu coum saûtrillons dans l'faïn –
Pour me j'sies fier coum un roué d'vée l'essaïm;
La maïre en bouit, et toute l'île en est pliaïne –
Bienv'nus, messiûs, cousins-germâïns des raïnes!
Honneur es ânes et salut ès crapauds –
La pllie nous manque, et j'en érons tantôt!

Midsummer and its toads, *1831*

Alas my goodness, just look at all the Toads we've got here!
Have they come to taste our cherries?
Have they come to scrub our floors?
I fear that they'll sink our steamships!
There's a downright downpour of toads! Dear friends, we have as
                                        many of them
as there were frogs in the kingdom of the Pharaoh.
If the great snake was still alive
that devoured them in old Hambie's days,
we'd say, that it really wants to finish them off,
and so they've come here to save their skins.

With his good coat, his girlfriend, and his pipe,
and his long nankeen trousers, look at Mr. Philip!
Time past, he was quite content
just circumnavigating the rock in good old Saint John,
playing his game of raffle-board or cards,
supping his dram, or drinking his quart;
happy as a stonechat and lively as a wren.
Now there he is showing off,
singing, laughing, fooling around and dancing with his hen-bird,
the downiest bird in Saint Aubin!
And off they go, and find all of their pleasure,
like gentry, in gentlemen's carriages,
the cargo is off to Alexandre's,
to see if the flesh of our poultry is tender.
They won't be licking their lips, on this day,
at rancid rind, sour cider, and big hard beans,
at salt conger, and humble pie.
They'll live it up ... for once in their miserable lives!

There are some scattered like grasshoppers in the hay.
As for me I'm glad as a king to see the swarm;
the sea is boiling with them, and the whole island is full of them.
Welcome, gentlemen, first cousins of frogs!
Praise to the donkeys and greetings to the toads!
We've been lacking rain, and now there's some on its way!

This donkey's-eye view of the customs of the people of Jersey brought forth a response in verse from Jean Sullivan (or John Sullivan, who also published as 'Oméga'). A roguish and self-promoting Jerseyman, Sullivan was convinced that Jèrriais literature could be lofty, noble and inspiring – although that never stopped him descending into the gutter if he felt like it. The mix of Jèrriais, Guernesiais and English in this poem, along with its footnotes in French, give a flavour of a multi-lingual holiday outing in nineteenth century Jersey – and if anyone still wants to celebrate similarly, the Peirson and Cock and Bottle pubs are still open for business in the Royal Square today.

Jean (John) Sullivan ('Oméga')

A Song for the Races, *1867* (English, Jèrriais, & Guernesiais)

A Song for the Races!
Hurrah!! Hurrah!!!

Who's for the Races? Hie! Who's for Gorey?
Hie? Who's for Gorey?
Who's for the Races?
Jump on the Busses!
Come Swains and lasses!
Oh! do come and see!
The racing at Gorey!!
Qu'est qui veux v'nin sus la qu'meune de Grouville,
Vais les Jockeys et tous lus biaux p'tits ch'vaux,
Et tout chu monde essaimai de tout' l'Ile,
Qui vat et vaint et par monts et par vaux.
Allons garçons, v'nais dan vais les racès!
Ne v'là des cab's, des vans et des queriots,
De biaux spring carts et des omnibécès,
Sautons dedans et levons les ergots.
Now – Who's for Gorey?
Hie! Who's for a spree?
Come my dear Nellie!

Do jump up with me!
And then we shall see!
The racing at Gorey!

Houras! allons, v'nais vais chut assembliage,
Qui par flioquets dansent sus le gazon,
Chest bain curioeux, v'nais vais tout l'estalage,
D'pis Saint-Hélï jusqu'à l'avarizon.
Montais garçons, v'nais don vais les racès,
Né v'là des cabs, des vans et des queriots!
Des wheelbarrows et des omnibécès,
Garçons et fille, oh! levons les ergots!
Now, who's for Gorey?
Who's for the Races?
Come Swains and lasses!
Jump on the busses!
Oh! do come and see!
The racing at Gorey!!

Nos v'là rendus – chest l'Derby d'Anglieterre;
Viyis l'grand stand, décorai de couleurs;
Ah! chest superbe! oh! qui biau grand parterre,
Chest un gardin, chest un gaszon en flieurs.
D'scendais garçons, et vous jennes fillettes,
V'nais au sounnoeux, sautons-y z-en flioquets,
Car j'y dans'sons des gigs et des rislettes,
Garçons et fille y lèv'ront les guérets.
Now for the races!
See the swift horses!
Come Swains and lasses!!
Fill up your glasses!
Let us have a spree!
Now we're at Gorey!!

Les steam est v'nu z-auve un' carquaison d'asnes ★
De Guernezi, pour battre les crapauds! †
Viyis les tous coum' i sont fiers et crasnes!
Il ont bain l'air d'un flioquet d'asnichauds.
Nico vient don ov tes jeun's a-szinettes,
V'nais bère un dram sis Jemmy des Marets.
V'nais jouer l'ergot ov nos douoches drinettes!
M'ais r'gardais bien com' ou l'vais les guérets.
Now for the races!

See the *suift* asses!
Kick at the horses!
What a jolly spree!
Oh! do come and see!
The Donkeys at Gorey!!

Pliachous en rang; car v'là v'nni Ph'lip Guidasnes,
Il a san fouet – oyious – silenche – obéiseis!
Pas d'vos i-hans, et pas d'vos cops d'pids d'asnes,
Back – as you were – et siyis tous rassis.
Now – en avaunt – qu'menchis bien du pid gauche
Chest un faux start – allons – erquémenchis –
Gniéra pouint d'fin – prend tan whip don Ph'lip Bauche.
Et slash mé-les – i sont endémenchis.
What a stubborn sett
They are not plac'd yet
Will you take a bet
The cup they'll not get.
They'll have an *ass*-iet,
That is all they'll get.

Les vlo startais – high – z-en avant Geannette!
Vlà Nico sus but – erlèv' té dan Martin!
Long-Ourillon dévaunch'ra la Brunette!
Nick vient d'boltaï jusqu'au dout d'Saint-Martin.
Bravo Brunette, a quache au coïn ès-asnes –
Aliboran – bravo – Brunette est des pu crasnes
Oulle a gangni – chest bien pour iel' le prix!
Oh! the Donkey races!
Are so very funny!
Hurrah for the asses!!
They're so wery bonny!
Fill up your glasses!
And drink to the Asses!!

Au mast d'cocangne, ah! vait t'en z-y man Ph'lippe,
Nico viens z-y et siyons compangnions,
Prend du toubac, un p'tit dram et ta pipe,
Houras – Bravo pour crapauds et asnons!
Man vier Nico quand tu f'ras une feste
J'irons vos vais – tu verras les crapauds,
Ovec mait' Ph'lip et sa musique en teste!
Fraternisai – z ovec les asnichauds.

Oh! what a pretty sight!
Dear sweet hearts and graces!!
With crapauds and asses!!
Are all at the races!
All a little bit tight!
Hurras – Nico – all's right!

(*Prononcez en patois Guernesiais*)
Now viers garçons ertouosnons viers la ville,
Oquor un dram, et siyons bouans éfaunts
J'avons bien ri tout le jour à Grouille,
Chest bien le pais des pliaisirs innocaunts.
Houras Gesriais – houras pour les races!
Montons en vans, en cars, ou en kériots!
V'là les couleurs sus les omnibécès,
Garçons houras – houras pour les crapauds.
Now – Now – hourah my boys!
Hurrah! for the races!
Come do fill your glasses,
Do, drink to the lasses!
For they are pretty toys!!
Hurrah – hurrah, my boys!!!

Nos v'là z-en route – ah! qui tas de vétures –
Vait dan Nico chu que chest que Gezzy!
Vait ses besquiaux et ses belles pastures,
Avous ditait dans vouot p'tit Guernezy?
Houras – Houras – j'apperchons de la ville
Nico Ihan – entend tu les chansons?
Chest fête angniet, chest un spree pour tout' l'Ile,
Houras – houras – bravo mes viers garçons!
Now – Now – hurrah my boys!
Hurrah for the races!
Now, do fill your glasses!
And drink to the Graces!
For they are pretty toys!!
Hurrah – hurrah, my boys!

Nos v'là rendus – v'nais dans lé Royal-Square,
Au Peirson-Inn, ou z-au Cock and Bottel
J'osrons la band, en prannant un p'tit verre
J'irons disner au vier Union Hotel!
Houras, bravo, – qui sublièsme musique!

Fliuste et tambours resjouissent le coeur!
Allons garçons donnais nous un cantique!
Chantons Gerry, chantons-le tous en choeur!
Now – now – hurrah my boys!
Hurrah for the music,
Take a little *physic*!
And fill up your glasses,
And drink to the Graces,
For they are pretty toys!
Hurrah! for them my boys!
Hurrah for the races!

★Notre cher et estimable ami, LE RIMOEUX DU CASTÉ, en l'Isle de Guernesey, le spirituel et érudit Poète, Auteur des "Rimes Guernesiaises" se prit d'idée un "bouan matin" de berner les crapauds (soubriquet donné aux jersiais par nos amis de Guernesey, qui en retout du compliment furent nommés par nous, des "Anes") dans une pièce intitulée SAINT-JEAN ET SES CRAPAUDS inspirée à la vue d'un grand nombre de jersiais qui mettaient pied à terre à Guernesey pour prendre part aux fêtes de la Saint-Jean – alors *nous, nous avons voulu nos desgrouter en viyant v'nin par flioquets bel et bien de ches quadrupèdes à longues ouoreilles, qui sont angniet à brouster des querdons sus la qu'meune de Grouille et qui sont la dans l'but bain esvident d'esprouver à attraper doeux trois de nos pus belles coupes! Va-t-en vais si vainnent Martin?*

Notre petite satire aura sans doute le même effet sur nos voisins que celle de notre ami eut sus *les pouors crapauds, qui risrent a s'en d'pichir les costais une bouanne fais en lus vie*, en liésant san spirituel espitre.

† Chose étrange les Crapauds ne vivent pas dans l'Ile de Guernesey, l'on en a souvent porté d'ici qui sont morts peu de temps après leur arrivée.

Le patois Gerriais de ce chant est celui que l'on parle à St. Hélier.

A Song for the Races!, *1867*

A Song for the Races
Hurrah! Hurrah!! Hurrah!!!

Who's for the Races? Hie! Who's for Gorey?
Hie? Who's for Gorey?
Who's for the Races?
Jump on the Buses!
Come Swains and lasses!
Oh! do come and see!

The racing at Gorey!!
Who wants to come to Grouville common,
to see the jockeys and all their fine horses,
and all those people swarming from all over the Island,
coming and going up hill and down dale.
Let's go, lads, come and see the races!
There are cabs, vans and wagons,
fine spring-carts and omnibuses.
Jump in and shake a leg
Now – Who's for Gorey?
Hie! Who's for a spree?
Come my dear Nellie!
Do jump up with me!
And then we shall see!
The racing at Gorey!

Hooray! let's go, come and see this crowd
dancing on the turf in large groups.
It's most curious, come and see the whole display
from Saint Helier as far as Seymour Tower.
Climb up, lads, come and see the races!
There are cabs, vans and wagons,
wheelbarrows and omnibuses.
Lads and lasses, oh! let's shake a leg!
Now, who's for Gorey?
Who's for the Races?
Come Swains and lasses!
Jump on the buses!
Oh! do come and see!
The racing at Gorey!!

We've arrived – it's like the Derby in England;
see the grandstand, decorated with flags;
Ah! it's superb! oh! what a fine large lawn,
It's a garden, it's lawn edged with bedding.
Get down, lads, and you young lasses,
come to the dance, let's jump to it in large groups,
for there we'll dance jigs and reels,
Lads and lasses will lift their legs there.
Now for the races!
See the swift horses!
Come Swains and lasses!!
Fill up your glasses!

Let us have a spree!
Now we're at Gorey!!

The steamer's arrived with a cargo of donkeys *
from Guernsey, to beat the toads! †
See how proud they all are and up for it!
They look like a load of real jackasses,
Come on, Nick, bring your young jennies,
Come and have a drink at Jemmy des Marets' place.
Come and kick up your heels with our pretty girls!
But watch out for where you're kicking.
Now for the races!
See the *swift* asses!
Kick at the horses!
What a jolly spree!
Oh! do come and see!
The Donkeys at Gorey!!

Get lined up; for here's Phil Donkey-driver,
he's got his whip – listen up – silence – obey!
None of your hee-hawing, and none of your donkey kicks,
Back – as you were – and settle back down.
Now – off you go – start on the left foot
That's a false start – let's go – start over again –
We'll never get going – take your whip Phil Bauche
and whip them for me – they're tricky.
What a stubborn set
They are not placed yet
Will you take a bet
The cup they'll not get.
They'll have a plate,
That is all they'll get.

They're off – hey – go Janet!
There's Nick standing up – get up Martin!
Long-Ear will overtake Brunette!
Nick's just bolted for the Saint Martin brook.
Well done Brunette, she's off to New Cut –
Aliboran – well done – Brunette is really up for it
She's won – it's her who's got the prize!
Oh! the Donkey races!
Are so very funny!
Hurrah for the asses!!

They're so very bonny!
Fill up your glasses!
And drink to the Asses!!

Come on, Phil, let's go see the greasy pole,
come on, Nick, and let's be mates,
have some tobacco, a drop of drink and your pipe,
Hooray – well done, toads and donkeys!
Nick, my old friend, when you have a festival
we'll go and see you – you'll see the toads,
led by Mr Phil and his band!
Rubbing shoulders with the jackasses.
Oh! what a pretty sight!
Dear sweet hearts and graces!!
With toads and asses!!
Are all at the races!
All a little bit tight!
Hurras – Nico – all's right!

(*To be pronounced in Guernsey lingo*)
Now, old mates, let's go back to town,
another drink, and let's behave ourselves
We've had a good laugh all day at Grouville,
it's really the country of innocent pleasures.
Hooray Jerseymen – hooray for the races!
Let's climb into vans, traps and wagons!
Look at the flags on the omnibuses,
Hooray lads – hooray for the toads
Now – Now – hourah my boys!
Hurrah! for the races!
Come do fill your glasses,
Do, drink to the lasses!
For they are pretty toys!!
Hurrah – hurrah, my boys!!!

We're on our way – ah! what a lot of carriages –
Look, Nick, and see what Jersey's like!
See its cattle and its fine pastures,
have you got anything similar in your little Guernsey?
Hooray, hooray, we're coming into town
Hee-haw Nick – can you hear the singing?
It's a holiday today, the whole Island's on a spree,
Hooray, hooray, well done, my old mates!

Now – Now – hurrah my boys!
Hurrah for the races!
Now, do fill your glasses!
And drink to the Graces!
For they are pretty toys!!
Hurrah – hurrah, my boys!

We've arrived – come into the Royal Square,
to the Peirson inn or to the Cock and Bottle
We'll hear the band, while having a little drink
we'll go and dine at the old Union Hotel!
Hooray, well done, – what sublime music!
The flute and drums lift one's heart!
Come on, lads, give us a hymn!
Let's sing, Jersey, let's sing all together!
Now – now – hurrah my boys!
Hurrah for the music,
Take a little *physic*!
And fill up your glasses,
and drink to the Graces,
For they are pretty toys!
Hurrah! for them my boys!
Hurrah for the races!

*Our dear and esteemed friend, The Poet of the Castel, in the Island of Guernsey, the wise and learned poet, author of the "Rimes Guernesiaises" (George Métivier) took it into his head one fine day to lampoon the toads (a nickname given to Jerseymen by our Guernsey friends, who by way of returning the compliment were dubbed by us, the Donkeys) in a piece entitled "Midsummer and its toads" inspired by the sight of a large number of Jersey folk who set foot in Guernsey to take part in the midsummer festivities – so we decided to get our own back when we saw loads of those very quadrupeds with long ears coming, who are now nibbling thistles on Grouville common and who are here with the obvious intention of trying to nab a couple of our finest cups! Go and see if they're coming, Martin.

Our little satire will doubtless have the same effect on our neighbours as that of our friend had on the poor toads who practically cracked a rib laughing, in reading his witty epistle.

† Strangely, toads don't live in the Island of Guernsey. They've often been taken over from here, but have died soon after their arrival.

The Jersey lingo of this song is that spoken in St Helier.

As we will see, the literatures of the Channel Islands have not been restricted to the Islands themselves. The importance of fishing has led many Jersey people abroad, and many have sought opportunities around the world. Writers too have travelled, and it is an interesting thing that the man generally recognised as the pre-eminent Jèrriais prose writer of the twentieth century spent most of his life as a citizen of the United States and lived most of his life in North America. George F. Le Feuvre, best known to readers as George d'la Forge (George from the smithy), produced hundreds of articles in Jèrriais for newspapers in Jersey. Most were written in the form of letters from abroad, mixing reminiscences of his youth in Jersey and comments on international news and goings-on in Jersey. Some, like this one, were written during his visits back to Jersey in later years.

George F. Le Feuvre ('George d'la Forge')

Les crapauds à quat' pattes!, *1967* (Jèrriais)

Le Ménage ès Feuvres
St. Ouën
Lé 16 dé septembre, 1967

Moussieu l'Rédacteu,
Ieune des choses qué j'ai r'mèrtchi d'pis qué j'passe partie dé m's êtés en Jèrri, est qu'nou n'vait pon d'crapauds par les c'mîns. Tch'est tch'en est dév'nu? Est-che tch'il ont 'té tellement êcrâsés par les motos en crouaîsant les routes qué la race dispathaît? Ch'est bein danmage si ch'est d'même. Chu bouan vièr crapaud avait même donné san nom au genre humain Jèrriais! Et j'vouos asseûthe qué j'aime mus êt' appelé un crapaud qu'eune âne ou un corbîn ou un lapîn!

Quand j'tais mousse nou-s-en viyait partout. Y'en avait dans les pits. J'ai veu ma m'mèe en ramonter dans l'sieau bein des fais quand ou' halait d'l'ieau! I' m'sembl'ye qué j'la vai acouo prandre eune broque à châque main et touanner l'gîndas jusqu'à que l'sieau vînsse en veue. S'i' y'avait un crapaud ou deux d'dans quand ou' lé m'ttait bas, ou' m'ttait sa main d'ssous et l'env'yait douochement s'prom'ner dans l'gardîn. Ou' nouos disait tréjous tch'i' n'fallait pon lus faithe dé ma car il' 'taient des Jèrriais, et tch'il' avaient d'la valeu dans les gardîns et mangeaient d's însectes tchi dêtruisaient les lédgeunmes. "Mais les Jèrriais n'ont qu'deux pids!" j'li dis eune fais. "Eh bein, véthe," ou' m'dit, "mais l'Bouan Dgieu peut tout faithe, et Il en a donné quatre à ches'là!"

Ch'n'est pon rein d'bé, qu'un crapaud. Mais i' faut penser tch'i' n'est pon laid pour sa janne fille car les crapauds du temps pâssé d'vaient lus mathier et aver d'grand' fanmiles, et l's anciens disaient qu'l'Île en 'tait remplyie! Ch'est d'autant pus tchuthieux pour mé d'vaie tch'i' dispathaissent en même temps qu'les Jèrriais dispathaîssent dé Jèrri étout!

J'mé r'souveins tch'i' y'en avait un tas parmi les patates quand les gens 'taient à dêfoui, et s'i' y'avait des jannes filles et des jannes hommes à gliainer, j'ai souvent veu iun d's hommes env'yer un crapaud parmi les patates en d'vant d'la janne fille dans la rande à côté d'li. V'la tchi la faîsait faithe des cris et sauter houors dé sa rande! Pour tchique raison les filles pathaîssaient en aver peux des crapauds. Malheutheusement, i' s'adonnait tchiquesfais qué l'dêfoueux né viyait pon l'cra-paud parmi les vîngnes, sustout s'i' dêfouissait dêliément et i' li pâssait iun des dé d'sa frouque lé travèrs du corps par accident. L'pouorre crapaud! V'là tchi m'faîsait chose dé l'vaie souffri un martythe dé même, mais i' faut avouer qu'en général lé dêfoueux n'lé faîsait pon par exprès.

Y'en avait même tant dans l'Île y'a septante ans qué ch'tait rare qué nou n'en viyait pon iun l'long d'tchique vièr fossé en allant ou r'vénant d'l'êcole, sustout auprès eune achie d'plyie. Ch'tait à pid qu'nou-s-allait à l'êcole dans chu temps-là, et sachant qu'les filles en 'taient êffritées, les garçons en m'ttaient iun dans lus pouchettes pour lé mettre sus lus êpaules ou dans lus j'veux. Ch'là n'avait qué d'touanner les sangs ès pouorres filles!

Eune chose tch'est bein cèrtaine: L'bouan vièr crapaud Jèrriais né faisait pon d'ma à pèrsonne, et les jannes dé man temps l'savaient bein, ouaithe qué les touos-anciens criyaient tch'il' êclyichaient du v'lîn. Mais y'avait tchiquesfais des mauvais sujets tchi lus faisaient du ma, ès crapauds. Ch'tait d'habitude des jannes hommes tchi 'taient grands assez pour saver mus, mais tch'est qu'ou' voulez, bouannes gens – y'a ieu d'la cruauté d'tout temps! Y'en avait tch'attrapaient un pouorre dgiâtre d'crapaud, et pis il' alleunmaient eune cigarette et la fouôrraient dans sa bouoche pour lé faithe heunmer et avaler la feunmée et s'gonflier jusqu'à tch'i' s'êtoufîsse!

Four-footed toads!, *1967*

Le Ménage ès Feuvres
St Ouen
16 September 1967

Dear Mr Editor,
One of the things that I've noticed since I've been spending part of my summers in Jersey, is that you don't see any toads around. What's become of them? Is it that they've been run over so often by cars while crossing the roads that the species has died out? It's a real pity if so. That good old toad had even given his name to the Jersey human being! And I can tell you that I'd rather be called a toad than a don-key or a crow or a rabbit!

When I was a boy, you saw them everywhere. There were some in the wells. I've seen my mum hauling them up in the bucket many times when she was fetching water! I can still seem to see her taking a handle in each hand and turning the wind-lass until the bucket came into view. If there was a toad or two inside when she put it down, she put her hand underneath and slowly set it off to wander round the gar-den. She always told us that we mustn't harm them because they were Jersey folk, and that they did good work in the gardens and ate insects that destroyed the vegetables. "But Jersey folk only have two feet!" I said to her once. "Well, yes," she told me, "but the Lord can accomplish anything, and He's given them four!"

He's not really handsome, a toad. But you have to think that he's not ugly for his girlfriend for toads, time past, must have got married and had large families, and the old folks said that the Island was full of them! Which makes it all the more puzzling for me to see that they're disappearing at the same time that Jersey folk are also disappearing from Jersey!

I remember that there were a lot of them among the potatoes when folks were digging, and if young women and young men were gleaning, I've often seen one of the men chuck a toad among the potatoes in front of the young woman in the next furrow to him. And that made her scream and jump out of her furrow! For some reason girls seemed to be afraid of toads. Unfortunately, it so happened sometimes that the digger didn't see the toad amid the haulms, especially if he was digging hastily and he'd stick one of the tines of his fork through the toad's body by accident. Poor toad! It gave me a turn to see him being tortured like that, but I have to say that in general the digger didn't do it on purpose.

There were even so many in the Island seventy years ago that it was rare not to see one along some old hedgerow going to or coming back from school, especially after a shower of rain. We all walked to school in those days, and knowing that the girls were frightened of them, boys would put one in their pockets so as to put it on their shoulders or in their hair. That was enough to scare the poor girls silly!

One thing is quite certain: the good old toad did no harm to anyone, and the young folks of my time knew that well, although the old folk from way back believed that they spat venom. But there were sometimes louts who maltreated toads. It was usually young men who were old enough to know better, but what can one do about it, folks – there has always been cruelty around! Some of them would catch a poor old toad, and then they would light a cigarette and would stick in its mouth to make it inhale and swallow down the smoke and swell up until it choked!

Denys Corbet was contributor to the newspaper *Le Bailliage* (The Bailiwick), and under the pen-name Bad'lagoule (Chatterbox) wrote weekly articles and stories. This extract describes the custom of rough music as practised, with the help of the ever-present donkeys, in Guernsey.

Denys Corbet ('Bad'lagoule')

La Draïne Courrie d'Ânes, *1893* (Guernesiais)

(...) la s'maïne draïne nos galbouantemps d'garçons s'mirent en tête de c'menchier les séraïes d'hiver par unn' courrie d'ânes – vou savaïz tous qu'est qu'ch'est, sàns doute; et coum nos grànds pères, et grànds-grànds-pères pour quiq chentaïnes d'aunnâïes ont gén'râll'ment manifestaï leus pllaisi ou putôt leus dépllaisi par des courrier d'ânes. Par exàmple, Pierro hànte-t-i l'amouaraeuse de Paul? eh! bien, ll'aira unn' courrie d'ânes pour chunna. Missis Jenséqui baille-t-alle à soupaïr au ser à quànd s'n-homme est gav'laï au liet? ll'y-aira courrie d'ânes! C. et B. d'meurent-i ensemblle sàns aver étaï à l'Egllise? il est saeur d'y-aver unn' courrie d'ânes; mais ch'est surtout s'un homme et sa femme s'ent' jaffent ou s'ent' quérellent qu'la courrie d'ânes est à la mode.

Chès courries d'ânes là s'font d'pus d'unn' manière: quiq feis ch'est d's-ânes à quat' pids, l'aût' feis d's-ânes à daeux pids; mais l'pus souvent ll'y-en a des daeux éragues. En des temps sou-s-y tire des chents traits d'armes. d'aût' caoups nou-s-a une âne à quat' pids sus l'dos de qui nou-s-a fixaï une effigies r'sembllànt pus ou moins à la personne en l'honneur de qui la fête a llu. D'aût' fais nou-s-a des lànternes et des torches; mais dans toutes ill-y a des cocluches, des cornes, des tabouarins, des cauguères, des sâcepen, des basshins, des cannes à lait, des suffllets, cornêts, et j'vous d'mànde s'l'affaire y-écauffe. Et pis donc, d'auv tout chunna il y-a des ha! has! des crieries, des sufflleries, des chànsons; et pîs tout s'akeuve par un biaû discours, prononçaï par le millaeux orateur d'la guiaine qui va s'pllàntaï dret d'vànt la maison où d'meurent cheux de qui nou veur se moquer, et là i heurle de tout' la forche d'ses poumons tout chu qu'i lî passes de millaeux et d'pus à propos à travers d'la tête. V'là chu qu'ch'est des courries d'ânes, leurs origine et leus pratique à St. Martin, du moins, d'pîs un temps immémorial et bien d'vànt que j'vinsse au monde.

The Last Donkey Serenade, *1893*

(...) last week our hedonistic boys decided to kick off the winter evenings with a donkey serenade – you all probably know what that is; and as our grandfathers, and great grandfathers for hundreds of years have in general shown their pleasure or rather their displeasure through donkey serenades. For example, is Pete seeing Paul's girlfriend? well then! he'll have a donkey serenade for that. Is Mrs I. Dunno having supper with someone in the evening when her husband is collapsed in bed? There will be a donkey serenade! Are C. and B. living in sin? There will surely be a donkey serenade; but it is above all if a husband and his wife smack each other about or quarrel between themselves that the donkey serenade is all the rage.

These donkey serenades are done in more ways than one: sometimes it involves four-legged donkeys, others two-legged donkeys; but more often there are the two kinds. Sometimes we fire some hundreds of gun shots. Other times we have a four-legged donkey with an effigy which resembles more-or-less the person for whom the event has been held. Other times we have lanterns and torches; but in all of them there are conch shells, horns, drums, kettles, saucepans, big brass bachins, milk cans,whistles, cornets, and that's when things start hotting up, I can tell you! And then, with all of that there is laughing, shouting, whistling, songs; and then things culminate with a fine speech, given by the best speaker in the gang who goes and plants himself right in front of the house of those that they intend to make fun of, and shouts with all of the force of his lungs all the best and most appropriate of what enters into his head. This is what donkey serenades are, their origin and how they take place in St. Martin's, at least, since time immemorial and long before I came into the world.

Tam Lenfestey was born in Castel, Guernsey, in 1813 and farmed there all his life. Compared to Métivier's and Corbet's intellectual ambitions for Guernesiais literature, Lenfestey's aims were simpler: to record and celebrate rural life in language that could be appreciated by ordinary folk. He has been called the bard of rustic life in Guernsey, and his work does not strive for the satirical gaze of so many other writers. As evidence of that, in this poem he even goes so far as to state that he likes Guernsey's government.

Tam Lenfestey

Guernesy, *1876* (Guernesiais)

Ah! Guernesy; auve tous tes d'fauts,
Je t'aime hardi, et j'aime accore,
A ouit tes fins, à ouit tes gniaux,
Chu q'tas de bouan terjous j'honore,
J'aime t'en Gouvernement l's'Etats,
Justiciers, terriens, Ministres,
Et à ouit tous leux p'tits débats,
Qui rejouiraient l'coeur pu des tristes.

Ah! Guernesy; j'aime ta libertaï,
Pour ta Gazette, et pour la plieumme,
Q'écrit d'qué bouan, la veritaï,
Sans la salir atou sa flieumme,
Et j'aime tes taxes, et ta pientaï,
Corps sans argent est corps sans âme,
Jusqu'à mes chents ils ont taxaï
Mais i'n faut qu'aucun je blâme.

Ah! Guernesy; j'aime le bouan temps,
A travaillier, t'nit les querrues,
A me r'posaï quand il est temps,
A m'pourmenaï le long d'tes rues,
A meditaï l'temps d'ichin-d'vant,
A gnolaï auve tes jolies filles,

A ouit l'camas de tes effants,
A d'meurraï seul, ou en familles.

Ah! Guernesy l'ia du jaune burre
D'la merqueresse si bien merqui
Et pour m'aigié à faire ma lure,
Nou peut en accataï Sam'di.
L'ia des patates, d'la belle grappe,
Et nou s'y vet toutes sortes de frit
L'ia du gibier s'nou s'en attrappe
Et du paisson par su l'marchi.

Ah! Guernesy! j'aime tes soudards,
Et l's'officiers de la milice,
Les Guernesiais n'sont pas couards
Et i nont pas souvent d'malice.
Et l'Gouverneux qui veux du feü,
Pourrait contaï su leux braveure,
I s'deffendront terjous sis ieüx,
Et en tous temps, et à toute heure.

Ah! Guernesy! j'aime tes garçons,
Tes belles flieurs, tes jolies filles,
Tes bouans cantiques, et tes chansons
Le bouan accord dans tes familles,
Quand pères et mères, et tous les gens,
Sons tous heureuts, et sans défiance
Et qu'un chaqun à du bouan sens,
Et à la paix, en jouissance.

Guernsey, *1876*

Ah! Guernsey; with all your faults,
I love you a lot, and I love you still,
to hear your finest, to hear your fools,
I honour what you have that is good,
I love your government, the States,
Jurats, farmers, Ministers,
and to hear all their little debates,
which would cheer the pure hearts of the wobegone.

Ah! Guernsey; I love your freedom,
for your press, and for the pen,

which writes good things, the truth,
without soiling it with its phlegm,
and I love your taxes, and your abundance,
body without money is body without soul,
they have taxed me down to my last hundredweight
but I must not blame anyone.

Ah! Guernsey; I love the good times,
working, guiding the ploughs,
resting when it is time,
walking along your roads,
contemplating bygone times,
joking with your pretty girls,
hearing the sound of your children,
living alone, or with a family.

Ah! Guernsey there is yellow butter
with the butter-stamp so well they mark it
(and this helps me versify my tale),
we can buy it at the Saturday market.
There are potatoes, beautiful grapes,
and you can see all kinds of fruit.
There is game if you catch it
and fish into the bargain.

Ah! Guernsey! I love your soldiers,
and officers of the militia,
Guernsey folk are no cowards
and their intentions are usually honourable.
and any Governor who wants gunfire,
could count on their bravery,
they will always defend themselves at home,
at all times, and at all hours.

Ah! Guernsey! I love your boys,
your beautiful flowers, and your pretty girls,
your fine hymns, and songs
the harmony in your families,
when fathers and mothers, and all folk,
are all happy, and without distrust
and that each and everyone has good sense,
and peaceful enjoyment.

Philippe Langlois came from Saint Lawrence in Jersey – hence his pen-name of 'Un St.-Louorenchais' (a man from Saint Lawrence). This poem would seem to be based on the Normandy anthem 'Ma Normandie', written by Frédéric Bérat (1801–1855) and used for many years as Jersey's national anthem when 'God Save the Queen' is not available. It uses the same form as 'Ma Normandie', and the second verse contains particular similarities with the second verse of 'Ma Normandie', but Philippe Langlois takes the theme of patriotic comparisons and adapts it specifically to Jersey and finally to his own parish.

Philippe Langlois ('Un St.-Louorenchais')

Jêrri, *1872* (Jèrriais)

Il y-a des gens qui sembllent craire
Que che n'est rein qu'le ptit Jerri;
Qui n'y trouvent rein à lus pllaire,
Mais bein de qui a mesprisi:
N'faut pas qu'ils aient grand connaissance
Les cheins qu'nou ouait conter d'itai;
Mal pâler du llieu d'sa naissance
Est et sera tréjous bein laid.

J'ai veu l'Angleterre et la France,
L'Italie, la Suisse et ses monts;
Qui qu'nouz en dise et qu'nouz en pense,
J'aime mux Jerri et ses vallons:
Nou pâle de lacs et de montangnes,
Nou pâle de vingne et d'orangiers;
Rein n'est pus bé que nouos campangnes,
Rein n'est pus bé que nouos pommiers.

Qu'est-che qu'une orange aupres des pommes?
Qu'est-che qu'un lac aupres d'la mer?
Je sommes bein comme je sommes,
J'n'avons vrainment rein à envier:
J'n'avons pas d'craie mais de bouanne terre
Pas d'riviere et d'inondations,
Que nouz ait la paix ou la guerre,
Je souffrons mains qu'les grands nations.

N'y-a pon caleu ni d'fredure
A comparer es grands pays;
Le pus rude hiver nou l'endure,

Et l'êtè nou n'est pon havis:
Les biaux vallons de qui nou dvise,
Les gardins, côtis et russiaux,
Tout jusqu'à la pour' vieille église,
Me paraissent tréjous pus biaux.

L'Cidre est un excellent breuvage
S'il est de bouanne qualitè;
Si nou le fait d'un bouan pommage,
S'il est etou bein apprêtè:
J'ai oui qu'un Ministre d'campangne,
Pus avisè que cheux qu'j'avons,
Faisait passer pour du champangne
De fameux prè de sa faichon.

A prendre Jerri tout ensemblle,
Souos tout le touannant du solèi
I'n'y-a pas de pllaiche qui m'semblle
Préférablle d'aucun côtè:
St. Louorains, ma vieille pâraisse,
Tu m'pllais pus qu'nulle autre en Jêrri,
De men cœur tu reste maitresse
Je t'aimerai jusqu'au drain soupi.

Jersey, *1872*

There are people who seem to believe
that little Jersey is nothing at all;
who don't find anything about it to please them,
but plenty to despise:
they can't have any great knowledge,
those who you hear talking like that;
to speak ill of one's place of birth
is and always will be despicable.

I've seen England and France,
Italy, Switzerland and its mountains;
whatever you say and whatever you think,
I prefer Jersey and its valleys:
you can speak of lakes and mountains,
you can speak of vines and orange trees;
nothing's more beautiful than our countryside,
nothing's more beautiful than our apple trees.

What is an orange compared to apples?
What is a lake compared to the sea?
We are well-off as we are,
we haven't really got anything to be envious of:
we haven't got any chalk but good earth,
no river and no floods,
whether we have peace or war,
we suffer less than big nations.

There's neither heat nor cold
to compare with big countries;
we can withstand the harshest winter,
and we're not scorched in summer:
the beautiful valleys of which we speak,
gardens, côtils and streams,
everything up to the humble old church
always seems more beautiful to me.

Cider is an excellent drink
if it's of good quality;
if it's made from a good apple harvest,
if it's also well made:
I've heard that a country priest,
cleverer than the ones we've got,
passed off his home-made perry
as champagne.

Taking Jersey as a whole,
there's no other place under the sun
that seems to me
preferable however you look at it
Saint Lawrence, my old parish,
you please me better than any other in Jersey,
you remain mistress of my heart
I will love you to my last breath.

The Mists of Time

The twelfth-century Jersey-born author Wace is the earliest writer we know of from the Islands. Nineteenth-century writers trying to develop a vernacular literary tradition looked back to Wace as a founding father. In the same way that to French speakers, French is 'the language of Molière' and English is 'the language of Shakespeare', they referred to Jèrriais as the 'language of Wace'.

Vikings controlled or settled parts of the Islands even before the Duchy of Normandy annexed the Islands along with the Cotentin in 933AD. Place names preserve the names of Norse chieftains and many rocks and coastal features show linguistic evidence of the importance to this maritime people of the Islands' coasts. It was the incorporation of the Islands within the Duchy of Normandy that implanted the Norman language in the Islands. The division of Normandy in 1204 when the continental territories were lost to the King of France meant that the Islands continued to develop in political independence, while retaining the Norman cultural links.

The prehistoric sites that dot the islands have inspired writers. Folk tradition saw the dolmens as belonging to the often malevolent fairy folk, or in the case of the prehistoric burial mound of La Hougue Bie in Jersey as being connected to the slaying of a dragon. In Guernsey, the Catioroc dolmen was believed to be the gathering place of witches. The Jèrriais word *pouquelaye* (dolmen) turns up in Falle's 'Account' – and the Romantic fascination with the horror of human sacrifice and druidic rituals seems to have affected Victor Hugo.

Rev Philip Falle
From An Account of the Island of Jersey, *1694*

There are still to be seen in this Island some Old Monuments of Paganism. They are great flat Rag-Stones, of vast bulk and weight, raised three or four foot from the ground, and born up by others of a less size. We call them *Poquelayes*, a Word I can hear of no where else, and therefore take it to be purely local. (...) They are found more or less in all these Parts of the World, where the Superstition of the *Druids* those famous Priests among the ancient *Celts* and *Britons*, obtained before the days of Christianity; and are the Altars whereon Sacrifices were offered by them, not of Beasts only, but of Living Men also, as *Caesar*, *Tacitus*, and all Historians bear witness. Now, because in this Island, these *Poquelayes* or *Cromlechs* are generally erected on eminences near the Sea, I was inclined to think them dedicated to the Divinities of the Ocean. But herein I stand corrected by Mr. *Toland*, who having seen my Book, observes, that the Culture of the inland Parts is the reason that few *Poquelayes* are left, besides those on the barren rocks and hills on the Seaside; nor is that Situation alone sufficient for entitling them to the Marine Powers, there being proper Marks to distinguish such wheresoever situated. I must own this animadversion to be just, being apprized that here and there in this Island, one meets with a Field, or enclosed ground, bearing the name of *le Clos de la Poquelaye*, an evident sign and token that on the same Spot, there formerly stood one of those Altars, since removed and carried away to make room for the plough. (...) I would only add, that the Sight of those Barbarous Altars, which have so often been besmeared and seen smoking with Human Blood, should remind us and others among whom they still subsist, of God's infinite grace and mercy, in extinguishing so hellish a Superstition by the Gospel of his Son. (...)

Near *Mont Orgueil Castle*, there is one on five Supporters which exceeds the rest, being fifteen foot in length, ten and a half in breadth, three and a half in thickness. With its weight it has made the Supporters sink so deep in the earth, that one must creep to go under it.

La Pouquelaye de Faldouët is an impressive dolmen that stands on a promontory on the west coast of Jersey, just above Mont Orgueil, and is also depicted on the Jersey ten pence coin. Victor Hugo arrived in exile in Jersey and settled in Saint Clement. He came to know some, at least, of the vernacular writers. Philippe Asplet, the writer 'L'Amin Flip', was a political supporter of Hugo and the other French proscrits in exile. Despite having such an important figure of French literature in their midst, it is not clear that any of the vernacular writers were influenced, although they were encouraged and must have been inspired, by Hugo. In fact, it seems that the influences may have been in the other direction. Hugo conversed with the fishermen of the coast, just by his Saint Clement home, and it is there that he must have heard on regular occasions the word *pieuvre* (octopus), an impression which was reinforced when he was forced to move to Guernsey where the Guernesiais speakers also spoke of *pieuvres* and where he wrote *The Toilers of the Sea* with its famous description of the 'pieuvre', the monstrous octopus that so inspired readers in France that 'pieuvre' was adopted as the usual word in French for octopus. Roger-Jean Lebarbenchon also noted certain similarities between Robert Pipon Marett's poem about a mother and son and one of Hugo's poems and suggests that Hugo would have been familiar with the Jèrriais poem before working on his own. Hugo referred to Métivier's *Dictionnaire franco-normand* (1870) during the writing of his last novel *Quatrevingt-treize*. Although the action of the novel does not take place in Guernsey, but is set against the background of the war in the Vendée during the French revolutionary period, Hugo used expressions and their corresponding definitions from Métivier's dictionary of Guernesiais to furnish supposed local colour for action taking place in Brittany. He went so far as to quote a line from a Guernesiais poem by Métivier, but attributed it to an ancient manuscript. In 1793, the year the novel is set, Métivier was only three years old.

Victor Hugo

Nomen, Numen, Lumen, *1855* (translated from French)

> When he had finished, when the scattered suns,
> dazzling, rising from the chaos on all sides,
> had all been set in the depths of their places,
> he felt the need to name himself to the world;
> and the formidable and serene being rose up;
> he drew himself up on the shadows and cried: JEHOVAH!
> and these seven letters fell into the vastness;
> and are, in the heavens reflected in our eyes,
> above our foreheads trembling beneath their rays,
> the seven giant stars of the northern blackness.

> Midnight, at the dolmen of Faldouet, March 1855.

Denys Corbet's 'L'Touar de Guernesy' is a picaresque tour of Guernsey in verse that takes up over 200 pages of *Les Chànts du Draïn Rimeux* (published in 1884) – it takes the reader on an, at times, nostalgic and quirky journey round the parishes, commenting on the sights and customs of the Island, notable personalities, and even mermaids. This short extract refers to the dolmen de Déhus in the Vale, and the images summoned up by a visit to a dolmen are less lofty than Victor Hugo's.

Denys Corbet ('Bad'lagoule')

Les Chants du Draïn Rimeaux, *1884* (Guernesiais)

From L' Touar de Guernesy

> Nou v'là, palfràndìngue arroutaïs,
> Et n'pouvon brìn nou-s-arrêtaïr;
> Pouit seul'ment pour render visite

A l'autel du D'hus, ou d'l'ermite
Du deruide, ou chu qu'nou voudra,
Et qu'à daeux pas d'nou, la haut, v'là
Chu qu'était la maison d'perière,
Egllise et chapelle et chimquière
D la pâreisse, ou d'l'île, ichìn d'vànt;
Ch'est-à-dire ill' a daeux mille àns
Tànt pus qu'du moins; caêr, à vrai dire,
Non n'peut pronaîr, ni mìme écrire
Rien d'certain sus chu sujet là.
Pourtànt, tout incounneû qu'le v'là,
Ch'est l'endret où j'ai l'pus jouaï, p't-être,
P'tit crâgnon; caêr, j'n'étais pouit pètre
D'ma paine, et quànté Margotton,
Nico, Racho, Gllaume et Suson
J'y-aï trigalaï, quànd j'étais janne.

From The Tour of Guernsey

We have, by Jove, begun,
and can't stop off at all;
not even to pay a visit
to the altar of Le Déhus, or of the druid's
hermitage, or what you will,
and a stone's throw from us, up there, there's
what was the house of prayer,
church and chapel and cemetery
of the parish, or of the Island, in bygone days;
that's to say two thousand years ago,
perhaps more, perhaps less; as, to tell the truth,
none can hold forth, nor write
anything certain on that subject.
And yet, as unfathomable as it is,
it is the place where I have played the most, maybe,
as a little child; as I was not at all backward
in coming forward, and along with Maggie,
Nick, Rachel, Will and Susie,
I frolicked there, when I was young.

It is not only the prehistoric monuments of Guernsey and Jersey that have inspired Channel Island writers. The Jersey-born Wace wove the legends surrounding Stonehenge in England into his verse chronicle of the origins of the British. The idea that the stones were moved by giants and by magic would not have been strange even to more recent Islanders. The traditional belief in the Islands was that the dolmens were the home of *les p'tits faîtchieaux* (in Jèrriais) or *les faiquiaoux* (in Guernesiais) – the little people, or fairies – and they were also capable of moving building materials that threatened to encroach on their dwelling places. Saint Brelade's parish church in Jersey owes its eccentric beachside location, so tradition has it, to the intervention of the little people who objected to the site originally chosen and repeatedly transported the builders' materials down to the beach until the humans gave in.

Wace

From **Roman de Brut,** *12th century* **(Old Norman)**

> Quant Bretun furent desarmé
> E bien se furent reposé,
> Merlin, ki ert en la compaine,
> Les mena en une muntaine
> U la carole esteit assise
> As gaianz, qu'il aveient quise.
> Killomar li munz aveit nun
> U la carole esteit en su
> Cil unt les pieres esguardees
> Assez les unt environees;
> E li uns ad a l'altre dit,
> Ki unches mais tel ovre vit
> 'Cument sunt ces pieres levees
> E cument serunt remuees?'
> 'Seinurs, dist Merlin, assaiez
> Se par vertu ke vus aiez
> Purrez ces pieres remuer,
> E si vus les purrez porter.'
> Cil se sunt as pieres aërs
> Detriés, devant e de travers;
> Bien unt enpeint e bien buté
> E bien retraite bien crollé;
> Unches par force a la ment
> Ne porent faire prendre ut
> 'Traiez vus, dist Merlin, en sus
> Ja par force nen ferez plus.
> Or verrez engin e saveir
> Mielz que vertu de cors valeir.'
> Dunc ala avant si s'estut,
> Entur guarda, les levres mut

Comë huem ki dit oreisun;
Ne sai s'il dist preiere u nun.
Dunc ad les Bretuns rapelez:
'Venez avant, dist il, venez!
Or poëz les pieres baillier,
A voz nefs porter e chargier.'
Si come Merlin enseinna,
Si cum il dist e enginna,
Unt li Bretun les pieres prises,
As nés portees e enz mises.
En Engleterre les menerent,
A Ambresbire les porterent
En la champaine illuec dejuste.
Li reis i vint a Pentecuste;
Ses evesques e ses abez
E ses baruns ad tuz mandez;
Altre gent mult i assembla,
Feste tint si se coruna.
Treis jurs tint grant feste e al quart
Duna croces par grant esguart
A saint Dubriz de Karlion
E d'Everwic a saint Sanson.
Andui erent de grant clergie
E andui mult de sainte vie.
E Merlin les pieres dreça,
En lur ordre les raloa;
Bretun les suelent en bretanz
Apeler carole as gaianz,
Stanhenges unt nun en engleis,
Pieres pendues en franceis.

From The Story of Brutus, *12th century*

When the Britons had laid down their arms
and taken their rest,
Merlin, who accompanied them,
led them to a mountain
where the giants' stone circle sat
which they had sought.
The mountain was called Kildare
and the stone circle was on top of it.
They looked at the stones
and walked round them

and said to each other
that they'd never seen anything built like it.
"How were these stones set up
and how can they be transported?"
"My lords," said Merlin, "try
with all the might you possess
and see if you can move these stones
and if you can carry them."
They took hold of the stones,
grappling them from every angle,
pushed and pulled,
and tried to rock them loose;
but no amount of force
could make them move at all.
"Work away," said Merlin, "but
if force cannot prevail,
you'll see that skill and knowledge
is worth more than bodily strength."
So forward he stepped, looked round,
his lips moving like a man saying prayers,
but whether he was praying or not, I can't say.
"Come forward," he said, "come!
Now you'll be able to take these stones,
carry them to your ships and load them."
So as Merlin instructed them
and as he told them and directed them
the Britons lifted the stones,
carried them to their ships and put them aboard.
They took them to England,
and carried them to Avebury
and set them down in the countryside.
The king arrived at Pentecost;
his bishops and abbots
and his barons had been summoned;
many other people assembled.
He held a feast and crowned himself.
The great feast lasted three days, and on the fourth
he magnanimously conferred bishops' crosses:
that of Caerleon to Saint Dubricius
and that of York to Saint Samson.
Both were great clergymen
and both of very holy life.
And Merlin set up the stones

and arranged them in their order.
The Britons are accustomed to call them in the British language
the Giants' Dance;
they're called Stonehenge in English,
and the Hanging Stones in French.

The Church in the Middle Ages used Latin, and it is in Latin that the earliest versions of the legend of Saint Helier have come down to us. Helier, a wanderer seeking a solitary life of prayer after having fled his home in the town of Tongeren (in present-day Belgium), arrived in the Cotentin and was sent to Jersey – it is he who is credited with bringing Christianity to Jersey in the sixth century. The traditional date of his martyrdom is 555AD. The details of the description of the Hermitage Rock, cut off at high tide, and the hollow in it reputed to be Saint Helier's Bed, suggest that someone who was familiar with the geography and tides of the bay contributed at some point in the compilation of this version of the life of the saint – since a monastery was founded on the neighbouring tidal islet where Elizabeth Castle was later built, it is not improbable that the monks had a hand in it.

From **The Martyrdom of Saint Helier,** *c. 11th century* **(translated from Latin)**

At the beginning of the fourth month, Saint Marculf gave Saint Helier permission to live as a hermit, and so he could lead such a life, indicated to him a suitable place called Jersey. He also granted him a guide for the journey called Romard, who became his companion and friend. Romard and Saint Helier travelled their path until they arrived at a certain place called Genêts, where they set off, under the protection of the Lord, in a small boat for the island called Jersey. The population of this island consisted of no more than about thirty inhabitants of both sexes. They saw numerous rocks, and on one of these rocks the blessed Helier came across a crippled man, called Anquetil, with twisted legs. He cured him by means of a prayer and a blessing. To this day, reminders of this miracle are shown in these rocks. There was also another rock surrounded by the sea on all sides, where the holy man found himself a sleeping-place. This was no fine bed, decked with embroidered cloths, but a hollow in the rock itself. That is where he lived, giving a few moments of rest every day to his body. In the third year after Saint Helier arrived in the island, Saint Marculf came to visit him. He found him so worn out and haggard from his vigils and fasts that he could scarcely recognise him. When they saw each other, they wept with joy, and as they embraced each other at length, their faces were flooded with tears.

While Saint Marculf was staying with Saint Helier, pirates came from Orkney to Jersey; their ships were about thirty in number. When Saint Helier's follower spotted them, he ran to his master and said: "Do you realise that we are surrounded by pirates?"

The blessed Helier raised his head and opened his eyes, which were tired from his keeping vigil. He saw the pirate fleet approaching. So he went to the blessed Marculf and asked him what they should do. The saint replied that the barbarians would be brought to naught by the weapons of prayer. The two blessed men prostrated themselves in prayer, and begged the Lord to see fit to deliver them and the inhabitants of the island from the pirates. The wrath of heaven descended on the pirates in such force that they fell upon one another, and the killing among them was such that out of thirty thousand, not one was left to carry the news of this defeat back to their homeland. The two saints finished their prayer, stood up, and seeing themselves delivered from their enemies, thanked the Lord who does not abandon those who place their trust in him. Three days after the deliverance of the island, Saint Marcouf and the good Romard parted from Saint Helier, who they were never to see again in this life. He remained alone with his follower, serving God day and night. To mortify his flesh, he only ate once a week, just enough to sustain himself to honour the Lord. But he was so weakened that, in the course of a day, he was unable to walk even a stone's throw. After he had lived in the island for fifteen years, Our Lord appeared to him and said: "Come to me, my well-beloved; in three days' time you will leave this earth with a martyr's crown."

At low tide the next day, and before dawn, the servant came, as was his custom, to find the saint, who told him what he had heard. The follower was distraught at the news. The following day, a great fleet of ships appeared, blown by the north wind, and Vandals invaded the whole island. Saint Helier hid himself, not because he feared death but because of his lack of physical strength. Nevertheless, the twittering of birds, by God's will, betrayed his hiding place, and the Vandals seized him, believing him to be a madman, and one of them drew his sword and cut off his head. Traces of his blood can still be seen on the rocks and will endure as long as the stone survives. The pirates withdrew after having ravaged the island. The follower came to the shore and found his master decapitated, and holding his head in his arms. In this manner, he had carried it the sixth part of a half-mile from the rock to the land.

Geoffrey of Monmouth's *History of the Kings of Britain* was used as a source by Wace for his Roman de Brut, a history of the kings of Britain. In Geoffrey's account, as in Wace's, Cadwalla arrives in Guernsey. The city of Kidaleta mentioned is Aleth, later Saint-Servan, neighbouring Saint Malo on the coast of Brittany.

Geoffrey of Monmouth

From History of the Kings of Britain, *12th century* (translated from Latin)

Cadwalla, not knowing what to do, was almost in despair of ever returning. At last it occurred to him to go to Salomon, king of the Armorican Britons, and ask his assistance and advice as to how to return to his kingdom. And so, as he was steering towards Armorica, a strong tempest suddenly arose, which scattered the ships of his companions, and in a short time left no two in sight of one another. The pilot of the king's ship was seized immediately with such fear, that quitting the rudder, he left the vessel to the fates; so that all that night it was tossed up and down in great danger by the raging waves. The next morning they arrived at a certain island called Guernsey, where with great difficulty they got ashore. Cadwalla was immediately overcome with such grief for the loss of his companions, that for a whole three days and nights he refused to eat, but lay sick upon his bed. The fourth day he was taken with a very great longing for some venison, and causing Brian to be called, told him what he craved. Whereupon Brian took his bow and quiver, and went through the island, so that should he come across any wild beast, he might bag it. But having walked over the whole island without finding what he was seeking, he was extremely concerned that he would not succeed in satisfying his master's desire; and was afraid his sickness would prove mortal if his longing were not satisfied. He, therefore, hit upon a plan, and cut a piece of flesh out of his own thigh, which he roasted upon a spit, and carried to the king, claiming it to be venison. The king, took it for real venison, began to eat it to get his strength back, admiring the sweetness of it, which in his opinion exceeded any meat he ever had tasted before. At last, when he had fully satisfied his appetite, he became more cheerful, and in three days was perfectly well again. With the wind now favourable, he readied his ship, they hoisted sail, set off again, and arrived at the city of Kidaleta.

Amelia Perchard, from Saint Martin in Jersey, was active in organising performances of plays and readings of poetry, as well as writing plays herself, adapting songs into Jèrriais and witing poems – especially for children. This piece was written in 1966 against the background of the celebrations of the 900th anniversary of the Norman Conquest of England – when, of course, the Channel Islanders were on the winning side, and proud of it too.

Amelia Perchard
Not' Destinnée, *1966* (Jèrriais)

> Dgilliaume lé Contchéthant – en mille souoxante-six,
> En mille quatre-vîngt sept, ch'tait Dgilliaume san fis;
> Henri, lé préchain sus l'trône en onze chents,
> Fut suivi d'eune liste deux fais longue coumme lé bras
> D'rouais et d'reines qui fallait qu'nou-s-apprînsse par tchoeu,
> Qu'nou répétaît en rînme pour s'en ramémouaither,
> Quand nou-s-'tait a l'école – hélas, tchille embête!
> Janmais jé n'pus, mé, les fouôrrer dans ma tête,

Sinon Dgilliaume, brave Duc dé Normandîe,
Qui d'vînt Rouai d'Angliéterre en mille souoxante-six.

J'avais raison d'm'en rappeler, j'vai bein a ch't heu,
Dé Dgilliaume et s'n armée qui crouaîsitent la mé,
D'St. Valéry dans dgiex-sept chents batchieaux dgerre,
Pour lus battre dans l'pays êtrange d'Angliéterre;
Car n'y'a pas d'învention dans tout l'monde entchi,
Dans la scienche, l'ingîn'nie, ou n'împorte tchi,
Qu'a tant changi l'cours dé not' vie, jé dithais –
Bieau que j'ayons tréjous resté bouans Jèrriais –
Coumme la victouaithe dé Dgilliaume et dé s'n armée,
Lé quatorze d'octobre, y'a neu' chents ans ch't' année!

Où'est qu'jé s'saîmes, jé n'sai; av'ous pensé à ch'la?
Mais pus important, tch'est qu'jé s'saîmes, don, ah ça?
Ch's'sait-i' Français ou Normands? J'mé d'mande tchiquefais
N'y'a rein d'garanti qué j's'saîmes même des Jèrriais! –
Si Dgilliaume n'avait pas entréprîns la tâche,
D'envahi chu pays d'l'autre côté d'la Manche.
Jé s'saîmes pe't-être Allemands d'pis la dèrnié dgerre,
Si j'n'avaîmes pas 'té alliés a l'Angliêterre,
Et qu'les Îles n'avaient pas ch't hounneu mangnifique
D'être preunmiéthes a faithe part d'l'Empire Britannique.

Combein d'autres tchestchions qué nou pouôrrait d'mander
Si nou restait tchîques minnutes à y penser!
Aniet, don, par exemplye, tch'est qu'jé s'saîmes à faithe,
Au lîeu d'être ichîn tous, en trains d'nos distraithe?
J'éthaîmes-t'i' not' libèrté, et lé drouait d'vouaix,
D'êcrithe des lettres à la Gazette, s'i' nos plîaît?
Sans doute, nou trouv'thait sans peine tchique caractéthe
Prêt a entrinner qu'nou n'pouôrrait pas être piéthe!
Ch'est p'têtre aussi bein qué jé n'lé savons pas –
N'y'a pon trop a r'dithe des dèrnié neu' chents ans!

Tchi changements qu'i' y'a ieu, d'pis mille souoxante-six!
S'il allait r'vénîn, Dgilliaume dé Normandie,
Il éthait bouane raison d'être êpouvanté
Par les choses modèrnes qui rempl'yent la vie aniet.
Tout cheîn qui nos reste avaû l's années, j'dîthais,
Et qu'i' pouôrrait comprendre, est not' vièr Jèrriais,
Mais n'faut pas oublier qué j'soummes cheîn qué j'soummes

À cause d'la hardgièche, y'a neu' chents ans, d'un houmme
Quî changit l'cours d'not' vie! Ch'tait not' destinnée
Et, par lé Duc Dgilliaume ou fut asseûthée.

Our Destiny, *1966*

William the Conqueror – in 1066,
in 1087, it was William his son;
Henry, the next on the throne in 1100,
was followed by a list twice as long as your arm
of kings and queens that we had to learn by heart,
that we repeated in rhyme to remember them,
when we were at school – oh dear, what a nuisance!
I never could manage to stuff them into my head,
except for William, brave Duke of Normandy,
who became King of England in 1066.

I was right to recall, I can see that clearly now,
William and his army who crossed the sea,
from Saint-Valéry in 1,700 warships
to fight in England's foreign land;
for there's no invention in the whole world,
in science, engineering, or anything,
that has so changed the course of our lives, I'd say –
although we've always remained good Jersey people –
as the victory of William and his army,
on the 14th of October, 900 years ago this year!

Where would we be, I don't know; have you thought of that?
But more importantly, what would we be then, indeed?
Would we be French or Norman? I sometimes ask myself
if there'd be any guarantee that we'd even be Jersey people!
If William hadn't undertaken the task
of invading that country the other side of the Channel.
Perhaps we'd have been German since the last war
if we hadn't been allied to England,
and if the Islands hadn't had the magnificent honour
of being the first ones to be part of the British Empire.

How many other questions one could ask
if one took a few minutes to think about it!
So today, for example, what would we be doing
instead of being here entertaining ourselves?

Would we, I ask you, have our freedom, and right to vote,
and to write letters to the Evening Post?
You could doubtless find some character easily enough
ready to insist that we couldn't be worse off!
It's perhaps just as well that we don't know –
we haven't had too much to complain about over the last nine
hundred years!

How many changes there have been since 1066!
If William of Normandy were to return,
he'd had good reason to be frightened
by the modern things that fill life today.
All that remains to us across the years, I'd say,
that he'd be able to understand, is our old Jersey language,
but we mustn't forget that we are what we are
thanks to the bravery, nine hundred years ago, of one man
who changed the course of our life! It was our destiny
and it was assured by Duke William.

Wace was born in Jersey, but it is unknown which parish can claim him as its own, probably at the beginning of the twelfth century (possibly at the very end of the eleventh century). He was not therefore a contemporary of William the Conqueror, although he tells us that his father described Duke William's invasion fleet to him, implying that his father was an eyewitness to the preparations. As far as we know, Wace never wrote anything in Jersey – he only learned to write once he'd been sent away to Caen – and his Norman is not yet what is familiar to us as Jèrriais.

Wace

From **Roman de Rou,** *12th century* **(Old Norman)**

Toute rien se tourne en declin,
Tout chiet, tout meurt, tout vait à fin;
Hom meurt, fer use, fust pourrist,
Tour font, mur chiet, rose flaistrist,
Cheval trebuche, drap vieillist,
Toute oevre faite o mains perist.
Bien entent et conois et sai
Que tuit mourront, et clerc et lai,
Et moult avra lor renomee
Apres lor mort courte duree,
Se par clerc nen est mise en livre:

Ne puet par et durer ne vivre
Mult soleient estre onuré
e mult preisé e mult amé
cil ki les gestes escriveient
e ki les estoires treiteient;
suvent aveient des baruns
e des nobles dames beaus duns,
pur mettre lur nuns en estoire,
que tuz tens mais fust de eus memoire.
Mais or(e) puis jeo lunges penser,
livres escrire e translater,
faire rumanz e serventeis,
tart truverai tant seit curteis
ki tant me duinst e mette en mein
dunt jeo aie un meis un escrivein,
ne ki nul autre bien me face
fors tant: "Mult dit bien Maistre Wace;
vus devrïez tuz tens escrire,
ki tant savez bel e bien dire."
A ceo me tienc e a ceo mus;
ja de plusurs ne en avrai plus.
Jeo parouc a la riche gent,
ki unt les rentes e le argent,
kar pur eus sunt li livre fait
e bon dit fait e bien retrait.

From The Story of Rollo, *12th century*

Everything turns to decline,
everything falls, everything dies, everything comes to an end;
man dies, iron wears out, wood rots,
tower collapses, wall falls, rose wilts,
horse stumbles, cloth ages,
every work of men's hands perishes.
I've heard and know well
that everyone will die, both clergy and lay people,
and the fame of many
will not last long after their death,
unless a cleric puts it down in a book.
It cannot live or last otherwise.
Those who wrote tales
and chronicled histories
used to be honoured

and highly prized and loved;
they often used to receive fine gifts
from barons and noble ladies,
in return for putting their names into literature
so that memory of them would remain for all time.
But now I can think for a long time,
write books and translate,
write in the vernacular and write skits,
all without finding anyone courteous enough
to give me and hand over
enough for me to employ a scribe for a month,
or who'd do anything else for me,
except say: "Master Wace expresses this very well;
you ought to write all the time,
since you can express yourself so well and so eloquently."
That satisfies me and stirs me;
I would not receive as much from most people.
I speak to rich people
who possess property income and silver,
because they are the people who get books made
and good deeds recorded and properly set down.

Jean Sullivan would never have dreamed of letting the obvious lack of biographical detail about Wace stand in the way of overblown literary speculation. In this 1864 poem, he lets his imagination run wild in a mediaevalist fantasy about Wace and the church of Saint Brelade – his belief that Wace deserves the highest honours in his native Island reflects his view of the importance and value of Jèrriais and Jèrriais writers. He also takes the opportunity to boost other notable Jersey heroes: Philippe Falle, author of the *Account of the Island of Jersey* and founder of the Jersey Library; Major Francis Peirson, hero of the Battle of Jersey in 1781; Charles Le Geyt, hero of the Battle of Minden 1759 and Jersey's first postmaster; Daniel Dumaresq, educational reformer and adviser to Catherine the Great of Russia; François Jeune, Dean of Jersey, Master of Pembroke College, Oxford, and Bishop of Peterborough; Jean Le Capelain, Romantic artist; John Everett Millais, Pre-Raphaelite artist, President of the Royal Academy and portraitist of Lillie Langtry with whom he spoke Jèrriais; and General George Don, Lieutenant-Governor of Jersey during the Napoleonic Wars.

Jean (John) Sullivan ('Oméga')

L'Eglise dé St.-Brelade et Maistre Wace, *1864* (Jèrriais)

Salut, bieau vièr Cliochir!
Salut, ô vieille Eglise!
Jé sis v'nu té cherchir,
Pour qu'un ségret tu m'dise:
As-tu veu z-un esfant
Sur les fonts du bastêsme,
A l'yi z esbliouissant,
Au r'gard noble et suprêsme?

L'as-tu veu v'nin pus tard,
S'ag'nouillir à la messe:
L'as-tu veu par hasard
A la main du vier Wace?
Sa prumieth' commugnion,
Chu pas béastifique,
Du Ciel le lumignon,
L'fist-ti souos tan portique?

Pus tard en r'venant d'Caen,
Quand ti v'nait vais sa mèthe,
V'nait-ti d'un coeur ardent
T'adrèchir sa prièthe?
V'nait-ti z-a tan austet,
Condit par iun des prestres,
Ov un chant solemnet,
Prier pour ses anchestres?

I r'chut le saint bastême
D'un vier prestre pesquoeur,
Sa commugnion du mêsme,
Mais z-il tait esfant d'choeur,
En r'touonant du colège,
I r'venait avec feu,
Ch'tait pour baillir un pliège
A m'n austel, à san Gieu.

I vint ov un' couronne
De louothi sus san front,
Ov l'air que Succès donne
Au fils stugioeux, profond,

De la fest' solemnelle
I r'vint, chergi de prix,
R'mercier Gui z-ovec zèle
Au pid du crucifix!

Quand-ti fut consacrai,
Quand-ti d'vint un bouan prêstre,
A tan temple sacrai
Vint-ti pour t'erconnaître?
Sa mèthe au coeu joyioeux,
Vint ovec san chier pèthe
Quand-ti chantait es Cioeux
Sa messe et sa prièthe.

Quand Henri le grand Roy
Le minst au pid d'san trosne,
Le fist chanter sa foy,
Son payïs, sa couronne,
Ah! Gerry tressailli:
Et dist que: "Gieu le garde!"
Et i s'esnorguillit
De san fils dév'nu Barde.

Quand-ti fut de Bayeux
Consacrai grand Canoine,
I vint dans tes saints lioeux
Donner la sainte scène,
I vint tout décothai
Dans ses habits de Prince,
Et i fut procliasmai
Le Roy de la Province.

La p'tite Isle en enquir
De s'nesfant orguilloeuse,
Vint-alle t'invoqui
D'unne ardeu génétheuse?
Oui! z-ou vint d'un bouan coeur,
Dans ses hardes de faste,
Mettre à san fils vainquoeur,
Un Louothi sus la teste.

Ché fut un jour glouothioeux,
Pour notre Isle, sa Mèthe,

Qui dans chu jour joyoeux
Le surnommit Homèthe.
V'là qui resjouït l'coeur
Quand un fils de noutre Ile,
Par talent, par laboeur,
Devaint un grand Virgile!

Pus tard i vint en Barde,
Ovec sa Lyre en màin,
Invoquir Saint-Brolarde,
Li baillir z'un refrain.
I vint r'mercier san Gui,
Quand san âsme ravie
Vint chanter san agui
D'vant quitter chutte vie.

I laissit un grand r'nom
Bain merqui dans l'histouaithe,
Henry gravit san nom
Au temple de mémouaithe!
Le Rou, san grand roman,
Son Brut De l'Anglieterre,
Sont un ramémoithement
De nouotre grand Trouvère.

Esl'vons un monueusment
Et gravons, tant que j'sommes,
Sus un bel ornement
Les noms de nouos grands hommes.
WACE et FALLE et PIERSON,
LE GEYT, DUMARESQ, JEUNE,
CAP'LAIN, MILLAIS et DON,
F'ront l'honnoeu d'nouot quémeune.

Allons, Gerriais, m'sesfants,
Donnons à nouot jennesse
Des conseils incessants,
Instruisons-là sans cesse.
Chessa pour nouot payis
Un honnoeu, z-une glouaithe,
Pour parents et ammis
Une grande victouaithe.

The Church of Saint Brelade and Master Wace, *1864*

Hail, fine old steeple!
Hail, o ancient church!
I have come to seek you out
so you can tell me a secret:
Have you seen a child
at the baptismal font,
with glittering eye
and noble and lofty gaze?

Have you seen him come later
to kneel at mass:
have you by chance seen him
held by the elder Wace?
Did he take his first communion,
that blessed step,
the light of heaven,
under your portico?

Later, returning from Caen
when he came to see his mother,
did he come with heart aflame
to address his prayer to you?
Did he come to your altar,
led by one of the priests,
with a joyous song,
to pray for his ancestors?

He received holy baptism
from an old fisherman priest,
his communion from the same,
but he was a choirboy,
returning from the college,
he came back with fire,
to give a pledge
to my altar, to his God.

He came with a wreath of laurels on his forehead,
with the manner that Success gives
to a deeply studious son,
from the joyous festival
he came back, loaded with prizes,

to thank God with zeal
at the foot of the crucifix!

When he was ordained,
when he became a good priest,
did he come to your sacred temple
to recognise you?
His mother with a joyful heart
came with his dear father
when he sang to heaven
his mass and his prayer.

When the great king Henry
set him at the foot of his throne,
bade him sing of his faith,
his country, his crown,
Ah! Jersey thrilled
and said "May God keep him safe!"
and grew in pride
of its son become Bard.

When he was ordained
great Canon of Bayeux,
He came to your holy places
to give the holy scene,
he came all decked
in the clothes of a Prince,
and he was proclaimed
the King of the Province.

Did the whole little Island,
proud of its offspring,
come to invoke you
with generous ardour?
Yes! It came in good heart
in its best clothes
to place laurels on the head
of its conquering son.

It was a glorious day
for our Island, his Mother,
who that joyous day
dubbed him Homer.

It lifts one's heart
when a son of our Island,
through talent and toil,
becomes a great Virgil!

Later he came as Bard,
with his lyre in hand,
to invoke Saint Brelade,
to offer him a refrain.
He came to thank his God,
when his rapt soul
came to sing his farewell
before leaving this life.

He left a great renown
graven in history,
Henry carved his name
in the temple of memory!
His great story of Rollo,
his Brutus of England,
are a reminder
of our great troubador.

Let us raise a monument
and carve, while we are about it,
on some fine ornament
the names of our great men.
Wace and Falle and Peirson,
Le Geyt, Dumaresq, Jeune,
Le Capelain, Millais and Don,
will honour our society.

Go, people of Jersey, my children,
let us offer to our young
constant advice,
let us instruct them unceasingly.
It will be for our country
an honour, a glory,
for family and friends,
a great victory.

In 1372 Owain Lawgoch, also known as Yvain de Galles, soldier and claimant to the Principality of Wales, having set sail from Honfleur, attacked Guernsey with an army of Aragonese troops. The story of the 'Descente des Aragousai' has left traces in Guernsey folklore, not only in placenames linked to the legendary battle (such as La Rouage Rue – the red road) but also in the belief that the Guernsey people are descended from fairies. Folk memory in Guernsey seems to have equated the invading alien soldiers with the little people, leading to a belief that Islanders descended from the offspring of the conquering fairies from overseas and Guernseywomen. Jersey people, on the other hand, have never believed they were of fairy ancestry. Jean Le Tocq, whose early morning arrival became proverbial, is mentioned in Tam Lenfestey's *La Matinaïe*. Sarnia is the traditional Latin name for Guernsey (just as Jersey's is Caesarea, which is Gallicised as 'Césarée', a term we will meet later on). The story of Owen's attack is recorded in a French ballad, surviving in various versions to which a later, and entirely fictitious, ending was added, depicting Owain getting his come-uppance. George Métivier compiled a text from seven mutilated manuscript copies. An English verse translation was published in the Guernsey newspaper *L'Indépendance* in February 1824. There is reason to believe that this is Métivier's own translation from the French.

Translation from French attributed to George Métivier

Owen of Wales, or the Invasion of Guernsey, in the reigns of Edward III of England and Charles V of France. – January 5th, 1372 (*translated from French 1824, original 14th–15th century*)

> O listen, listen, gentles all,
> My tale's not over long:
> And whether ye be great or small,
> Attend well to my song.

> I sing of Owen, prince of Wales,
> A chief of Royal blood;
> He loves a dance in whistling gales
> Far oe'r the briny flood.

> His merrymen grown old in sin, –
> For plunder is their duty, –
> Cut, slash and dash thro' thick and thin,
> Wherever there is booty.

> Norman, French, Arragonian, Turk,
> They're of all sorts and sizes;

Black and white villains of all work
Like rogues at the assizes.

Charles, whom they style The Wise, de France,
With very little grace,
Once sent them on a wild-goose dance;
I should have said a chase.

They landed in a Tuesday morn
On VÂZON's happy shore,
Threat'ning to mow us down as corn,
And drench the land with gore.

Dames, had ye heard each blackamoor
Your heads to Allah vow! –
His first attack is like the roar
Of winds at Brécon-Mow.

What time the lonely bird of night
Had ceas'd her plaintive lay,
With the cold blush of orient light,
JOHN LÉTO rose that day.

All slept – not e'en a zephyr broke
The silence of the deep;
And the swain hasten'd ere they woke
To count his silly sheep.

With that intent he wound his way
Where Vâzon's waters flow,
And view'd, alas! in fierce array,
The power of the foe!

The yeoman caught a fiery steed,
And many a weary mile,
He rode the stranger-horse full speed
O'er all the Blessed Ile.

He rode, like one distracted quite,
And with a dreadful voice,
"Arouse," he cried, "for ye must fight!
To arms, to arms, my boys!"

"For I have seen, at Vâzon bay,
A multitude! a host! –
Stir up, my lads, arouse, I say,
Or all the land is lost!"

"Hazard your lives, while they are yours,
And then ye need not fear:
The brave may die – their fall secures
A blessing and a tear!"

"Alert! – Or ye shall die the death
Of rascals and of knaves!
Sarnia must curse, with her last breath,
THE FATHERS OF HER SLAVES!"

"Our wives and small ones claim our aid
'Gainst yon infernal crew!
Go, try the temper of each blade,
Cut down, and run them thro'!"

Soon as they heard the sad report,
All from their couches leapt:
The ladies of St. Peter's-Port,
Lamented, pray'd and wept!

Owen of Wales, of royal kin,
The leader of the foe,
Sigh'd for new laurels, in the din
Of carnage and of woe.

Dangers the hero lov'd and dar'd,
By disappointment vext;
No peril of this world he fear'd
Nor car'd he for the next.

Yet, in our isle, he found, I ween,
A garter on his thigh:
'Twas neither silk, nor velvet sheen,
Though scarlet was the die.

For, nigh the Mill of LA CARRIÈRE,
As the rash leader came,

Stout RICHARD gash'd him with a spear
That never miss'd its aim.

Then whirl'd in air a trusty brand,
And felt his bosom glow,
Yet only back'd SIR OWEN's hand
With a tremendous blow.

And tho' good Richard, fearless youth,
Carried the palm away,
TOUMIN LE LORREUR was in sooth
Our Captain in the fray.

RALPH HOLLAND, in the battle's heat,
Fair signs of valor gave –
The traitor foe smit of his feet,
And Sarnia deck'd his grave.

The foemen climb sweet houguette-hill,
And trample on the dead;
They wade through blood, they die, they kill;
The path is hence call'd RED.

Hard blows fall to the right and left
As thick as rattling hail;
Heads fly apace, and skulls are cleft,
And dead men strew the vale.

Steel clashing steel as lightning gleams,
And from Guernesian veins,
Blood flows, alas! like mountain streams
Swell'd with autumnal rains.

A deadly weapon strongly bent,
And shot against the foe,
Many a renegado sent
To the dark realms of woe.

Eighty good English Merchant-men,
Arrived at close of day,
And old King Charles's merrymen,
For mercy 'gan to pray.

They knew resistence was all vain,
'Gainst English hearts of oak:
Bordage is cover'd with the slain,
That fall at every stroke.

To CORNET-ISLE these Gallic slaves
Rush'd o'er the seas moist bed:
Our jolly men pursu'd the knaves,
And slew them as they fled.

They storm at once the goodly fort,
Where Owen's banner floats;
And drive him from this last resort
With scandal to his boats.

While the French navy tack'd again,
Many an arrow flew
From the stout bows of Guernseymen,
And pierc'd a foeman through.

At LA CORBIÈRE they fain would land,
And try their fates once more;
Our peasants make a noble stand,
And drive them from the shore.

They catch anew, like men perplext,
The breezes as they rise,
Gnashing their teeth, and sorely vext,
To forfeit such a prize.

Nettled with rage at this defeat,
Sir Owen, full of cares,
Now gave the word – the hostile fleet,
To Sampson's harbour steers.

Then to St. Michael's Priory,
Ellen his lady fair,
Hasten'd in all her bravery,
And found sweet welcome there.

Sir Owen woo'd the lovely dame
In Gravelle's wealthy land;

Proud heiress of a noble name,
She claim'd a prince's hand.

Now, thou shrew'd Abbot of the Vale,
Secure thy little fold,
When tears, and beads, and masses fail,
With omnipotent gold!

The rascal Gauls, in fierce array,
The Castle wall surround;
Our Guernseymen, as bold as they,
Though few, were faithful found.

"God and St. Michael," cried OLD ROSE,
His arms then proudly hit,
"Head, limb, and chattels, I may lose,
I never can SUBMIT."

Once the Normans had enforced their dynastic claim in England following 1066, they interested themselves in the history of the territory. In his *Roman de Brut* from 1155, Wace provided a vernacular account of the British foundation myth, weaving from his sources (mainly Geoffrey of Monmouth's Latin history) a tale of the origins of the British people in the exile of Brutus the Trojan and his companions, through the rise of King Arthur to the arrival of the Saxons and the establishment of a Christian English kingdom. To the existing Arthurian material, Wace added and elaborated elements. He was the first writer to mention the Round Table. This may have been an invention of his own, or a detail picked up and enhanced from some part of the tradition, perhaps oral, now lost to us. Wace was familiar with the Arthurian traditions of Brittany and Great Britain; with Jersey situated between the two, one wonders whether he had heard Arthurian stories told in his childhood – speculation which might be 'neither wholly falsehood, nor wholly truth'.

Wace

From Roman de Brut, *12th century* (Old Norman)

Duze anz puis cel repairement
Regna Artur paisiblement,
Ne nuls guerreier ne l'osa
Ne il altre ne guereia.
Par sei, senz altre enseinement,
Emprist si grant afaitement
E se cuntint tant noblement,

Tant bel e tant curteisement,
N'esteit parole de curt d'ume,
Neis de l'empereür de Rome.
N'oeit parler de chevalier
Ki alques feïst a preisier,
Ki de sa maisnee ne fust,
Pur ço qu'il aveir le peüst;
Si pur aveir servir vulsist,
Ja pur aveir ne s'en partist.
Pur les nobles baruns qu'il out,
Dunt chescuns mieldre estre quidout,
Chescuns se teneit al meillur,
Ne nuls n'en saveit le peiur,
Fist Artur la Runde Table
Dunt Bretun dient mainte fable.
Illuec seeient li vassal
Tuit chevalment e tuit egal;
A la table egalment seeient
E egalment servi esteient;
Nul d'els ne se poeit vanter
Qu'il seïst plus hait de sun per,
Tuit esteient assis meain,
Ne n'i aveit nul de forain.
N'esteit pas tenuz pur curteis
Escot ne Bretun ne Franceis,
Normant, Angevin ne Flamenc
Ne Burguinun ne Loherenc,
De ki que il tenist sun feu,
Des occident jesqu'a Muntgeu,
Ki a la curt Artur n'alout
E ki od lui ne sujurnout,
E ki n'en aveit vesteüre
E cunuissance e armeüre
A la guise que cil teneient
Ki en la curt Artur serveient.
De plusurs terres i veneient
Cil ki pris e enur quereient,
Tant pur oïr ses curteisies,
Tant pur veeir ses mananties,
Tant pur cunuistre ses baruns,
Tant pur aveir ses riches duns.
De povres humes ert amez
E des riches mult enurez.

Li rei estrange l'envioent
Kar mult cremeient e dutoent
Que tuit le munde cunquesist
E lur digneté lur tolist.
Que pur amur de sa largesce,
Que pur poür de sa prüesce,
En cele grant pais ke jo di,
Ne sai si vus l'avez oï,
Furent les merveilles pruvees
E les aventures truvees
Ki d'Artur sunt tant recuntees
Ke a fable sunt aturnees:
Ne tut mençunge, ne tut veir,
Ne tut folie ne tut saveir.
Tant unt li cunteür cunté
E li fableür tant flablé
Pur lur cuntes enbeleter,
Que tut unt fait fable sembler.

From The Story of Brutus, *12th century*

So for twelve contented years
Arthur reigned in peace.
No one made war on him
and he made war on no one.
On his own account, without need of advice,
he gained such accomplishments
and bore himself so nobly,
so fine and in such a courtly manner,
no one spoke so of any other court,
not even that of the emperor of Rome.
no knight could be spoken of
by anyone in terms of praise,
whom he did not bring into his household
provided he could obtain him.
If recompense were required,
no one went away unrewarded.
For his noble barons,
each of whom held himself better than anyone else,
each of whom held himself the best,
none of them was believed to be the worst,
Athur made the Round Table
about which the Britons tell many stories.

The vassals sat there,
all in knightly honour and all equal.
At the table they sat equally
and were served equally
None of them could boast
that he sat higher than his peer.
All sat in the midst of their fellows
and none was below the salt.
No one was held to be of courtly status
whether Scot, Briton, Frenchman,
Norman, Angevin, Fleming,
Burgundian or Lorrain,
no matter from whom he held his fief,
from the West to the Saint Bernard Pass,
who didn't go to Arthur's court
and didn't stay with him,
and didn't put on the livery,
the emblem and the armour
in the manner of those
who served in Arthur's court.
They came from many lands,
those seeking rewards and honour,
some to hear of his courtly deeds,
some to see his estate,
some to make acquaintance of his barons,
some to receive rich gifts from him;
he was loved by poor men,
and greatly honoured by the rich.
Foreign kings envied him
because they feared him and suspected
that he would conquer the whole world
and deprive them of their realms.
Whether for love of his beneficence
or for fear of his prowess,
during that great peace I've spoken of,
I don't know if you've heard about it,
wonders occurred
and adventures sought out
which have so often been told about Arthur
that they've been turned into fabulous stories:
neither wholly falsehood, nor wholly truth,
nor wholly silliness, nor wholly fact.
Storytellers have told so many stories

and spinners of yarns have spun so many yarns
to embellish their tales
that they've made it all seem like a fairy-story.

The English author Michael Drayton's *Poly-Olbion* is a long topographical poem that describes England, Wales and associated islands, published in 1612, with a revised and expanded edition appearing in 1622. In this passage, Jersey, Guernsey, Lihou, Sark, Jéthou and Alderney appear. Notable for their absence among animals mentioned are the donkey and the toad. Jersey's multi-horned sheep became extinct as the wool trade lost its economic importance – Manx Loaghten sheep have recently been introduced in order to revive the heritage. No attempt has been made, however, to reintroduce sea-nymphs.

Michael Drayton

Poly-Olbion, *1612*

Thus scarcely said the Muse, but hovering while she hung
Upon the Celtic wastes, the Sea-Nymphs loudly sung:
O ever-happy Isles, your heads so high that bear,
By nature strongly fenc'd, which never need to fear
On Neptune's wat'ry realms when Eolus raiseth wars.
And ev'ry billow bounds, as though to quench the stars:
Fair Jersey first of these here scatt'red in the deep.
Peculiarly that boast'st thy double-horned sheep:
Inferior nor to thee, thou Jernsey, bravely crown'd
With rough-imbattl'd rocks, whose venom-hating ground
The hard'ned emeril hath, which thou abroad dost send:
Thou Ligon, her belov'd, and Serk, that dost attend
Her pleasure ev'ry hour; as Jethow, them at need,
With pheasants, fallow deer, and conies, that dost feed:
Ye Seven small sister Isles, and Sorlings, which to see
The half-sunk seaman joys, whatsoe'er you be,
From fruitful Aurney, near the ancient Celtic shore.
To Ushant, and the Seams, whereas those Nuns of yore
Gave answers from their caves, and took what shapes they please
Ye happy Islands set within the British Seas,
With shrill and jocund shouts, th' unmeasur'd deeps awake,
And let the Gods of sea their secret bow'rs forsake,
Whilst our industrious Muse great Britain forth shall bring,
Crown'd with those glorious wreaths that beautify the Spring;
And whilst green Thetis' Nymphs, with many an amorous lay
Sing our invention safe unto her long-wish'd Bay.

At Sea, Beside the Sea

The people of the Channel Islands have naturally enough been influenced by the sea – whether collecting *vraic* (seaweed) for fertilising the fields, fishing in local waters, or setting up in North America to exploit the cod fisheries, or promoting the seaside charms of the Islands for tourism, the livelihoods of Islanders have often depended on the sea. It is therefore not surprising to find aspects of the sea in the literatures of the Islands and of visitors to their shores.

The dramatic tidal range around the Islands has also shaped their traditional cultures and their literatures. Low-water fishing and collecting limpets, whelks, ormers and razor-fish helped keep Island households – sometimes half-farmer, half-fisherman – above subsistence level.

Philippe Le Sueur Mourant enjoyed great success with his character of Bram Bilo, a pompous innocent abroad. However he killed off his most popular character and launched a new series of stories about the Pain (Payn) family, who move from Jersey's still rural and Jèrriais-speaking countryside in the years before the First World War to the now-Anglicised and bustling town of Saint Helier with its modern entertainments and attractions. Here, however, we have a description of a stint in the Jersey-controlled cod fisheries of Quebec in the latter half of the nineteenth century. The account, farcical and exaggerated though it may be, contains some valuable descriptions of the work and working conditions of the time.

Philippe Le Sueur Mourant ('Bram Bilo', 'Piteur Pain', etc)
How Mister Piteur had good times in his youth, *1912* (Jèrriais)

J'disais y'a tchiq' temps que j'fut forgi un viage à la Côte pour les Messieux Collas. J'nos en fûmes de Jerri a bord du Boadicea, de tchi Captaine La Forge était maître chu viage la. Y'avait eunne douzaine ou d'viers de passagièrs dans la Chambre:

Moussieu Pain, Moussieu Le Couteur, Mess Trachy, Mess Gaudin, et deus-très clérques. Je n'tais pon d'la djingue de l'arrièthe. Mé, un forgeux, ou comprennez, n'tait pon d'hantîse ov la squad du quartchi-pont; j'tais du châté, ov l'estchipage, et y m'mîntes sus l'quart a Jim smith, l'preumi contre maître.

Chose èstrange! ny'eut personne de niet en nos n'allant: et si ch'n'est que l'lard 'tait rouetre, l'bistchuit magotté, l'beurre sallé, la graisse mouesie, et l'cook enteuthé, n'y'avait pon trop a s'piendre. Quand l'cook brulait sa soupe de paids, ou n'roussissait pon assez l'lobscouse, ou n'tchuisait pon l'duff, ou n'dèssallait pon la mouothue, j'lis fichaimes la tête dans eune bouq'tee d'ieau-d'mé, et l'affaithe amendait pou tchiq' jours.

La terre 'té oquo couerte de mé quand j'arrivîmes a la Pointe: les graviers 'taient a nivlé l'gravi sis tchi qu'nou met la mouothue s'tchi. Les tcherpentchiers 'taient a r'graie et peindre les berges de pêque, ou a tîlé la membreuse d'un navithe sus les choutchets – le Warrior j'cré –; y'avait du monde a faithe des vigneaux sus tchi qu'nhou signe la mouothue en sortant du piclye. John Du Feu 'tait a martellé des grapins dans la forge, les clèrques 'taient, coumme d'amord, a s'entre èsprouvé à tchi en fthait l'mains dans la boutique, et Moussieu Sam Collas 'tait dans l'office a mertchi bas les comptes – car, a la Côte coumme partout – ch'est la mérquethie qui sauve.

Et ch'fut là qué j'passi mes djix huit mais a forgi d'la féthalle de navithe, des grapins, des gaffes, – et èsmoudre les coutieaux des trancheurs. L'navithe fut lanchi au S'tembre: toutes les femmes et filles de pètcheurs vintent sus l'run, en crinolines les clèrques touônaient alentou d'ieux coumme des bourdons a l'entou d'un pre-unnyi, et la clioche sounni pour "all hands grog-oh" deux fais dans la r'levée. L'temps s'mint squalleux quand vint l'sé, et l'navithe qui v'nait d'être lanchi faillyi couôrre au plien dans Lance Cove. "All hands and the cook" passîtes eune partie d'la niet a porté s'cours, et l'navithe s'mint a l'abri au Bachin – mais l'bourgeais avait yeu peux! j'vos certifie.

Jammais n'roublièthai l'hivé que j'passi là! Ou paslez d'né! Ch'est par la qui faut allé pour en vaie, d'la né. V'la tchi qu'menche, fin Octobre, et nou ne r'vé pon la terre d'vant l'mais d'Mai en r'venant. J'en ai veu jusqu'a tchinze pids a des bords! J'ai veu des temps qu'en s'levant l'matin, nou n'pouait sorti par l'hue: fallait sauté d'hort par eune f'nêtre de chambre ov des pelles, et s'mettre a fouî la né pour dèbarassé la porte et les f'nêtres de bas! Et d'la fret! Ch'est par là que, quand nou pasle dehort dans la foret, les patholles gellent, et ch'n'est qu'au Printemps, quand l'Solet qu'menche a caufé, qu'nou peut oué ch'q'ua était dit en hivé! Ch'fut là qu'j'eu l'nez j'lé, eune niet qu'j'avait 'té a un "shake-down" siez Patrick Maloney; j'avais resté trop longtemps souôs l'portico a dithe good-bye a sa fille. Et ch'est de mème qu'oquo au jour d'anniét man nez est pus-a-co enfié du bu, et jaunit par les vents d'Nord-Ouès.

Ch'fut ch't'hivé qu'deus-très d'nous jouimes eune trique a "fat Annie," la veuve qui lavait l'linge du cookroom. Ou d'meuthait toute seule, sus Stone Point, dans eune p'tite maison en bouais ov rin qu'eune porte et eune f'nêtre a quatre ozennes. Eunne néthe niet qu'ou dormait, j'lis tathîmes ses ozennes et j'djem-mimes sa porte ov des pitchelles. Natuthellement, ou n'y viyait pon quand vint l'matin, et ou resti au liet eunne partie du jour attendant sinnette de matin. A la fin, ou se l'vit en s'en fut pour ouvri la porte. Pas moyen! Ch'en fut qué l'surlendmain qu'un pétcheux entendit sa capuchchie et qu'nou vint lis porté s'cour. Les clerques fudrent soupcounnées d'avé fait l'coup, et l'Agent les mnichi d'lus r'ténnin un mais d'gages. Nou creut qué p't'ètre ch'tait les tcherpentchiers – a cause de la tathe – et l'Reverend Moulpied en pasli l'Dinmanche en r'venant d'la tchaise, et prèchi sus les siens qu'opprimènt la veuve et l'orphelin.

Mais "fat Annie" n'en mouothi pon; et quand ou vint cherchi l'linge sale a la cook room, j'lis baillimes un gros gobbin d'lard pour la consolé.

How Mr Peter had good times in his youth, *1912*

As I was saying a while back, I was a blacksmith on a voyage to the Gaspé for the Collas company. We set off from Jersey aboard the Boadicea, under Captain La Forge on that journey, it was. There were a dozen passengers or thereabouts in the berths: Mr Payn, Esq., Mr Le Couteur, Esq., Mr Trachy, Mr Gaudin, and a couple of clerks. I wasn't one of that lot at the stern of the ship. Me, as a blacksmith, you understand, I wasn't hobnobbing with that crowd on the quarterdeck, I was with the crew, one of the foc'sle lot, and they put me on the watch of Jim Smith, the first mate.

Strangely enough, nobody got drowned on the voyage out; and if it wasn't for the rancid pork, the maggotty hard-tack, the salty butter, the mouldy lard and the filthy cook, there wasn't much to complain about. When the cook burned his bean soup, or didn't brown the lobscouse enough, or didn't cook the duff, or didn't soak the dried cod enough, we'd stick his head in a bucket of sea-water, and things would go better for a few days.

The ground was still covered by the sea when we arrived at the Point: the cod-driers were levelling off the shingle on which the dried cod is put. The carpenters were fixing up and painting the fishing barges, or taking an adze to the ribs of a ship on chocks – I think it was the Warrior – there were people making the racks on which the cod is dried when it comes out of the pickling brine. John du Feu was hammering rakes in the smithy, the clerks were, as usual, competing with each other as to who could do least work in the office, and Mr Sam Collas, Esq. was in the accounts office tallying the accounts – for, in the Gaspé as everywhere else – it's the tallying that counts.

And there it was that I spent my eighteen months smithing iron for ships, rakes, boat-hooks – and grinding the knives of the fish-gutters. The ship was launched in Autumn: all the wives and daughters of the fishermen came to the "room" in crinolines. The clerks hovered around them like bumblebees round a plum tree, and the bell rang for "all hands grog-oh" twice that afternoon. The weather turned squally by evening, and the ship that had just been launched nearly ran aground in

Lance Cove. "All hands and the cook" spent part of the night on the rescue, and the ship came into shelter in the Basin – but the shipowner had had a fright, I can tell you!

I'll never forget the winter I spent there! Talk about snow! If you want to see snow, that's where you'll want to go. It starts at the end of October, and you don't get to see the ground again before the following May. I've seen it up to fifteen feet in places! I've seen times when you'd get up in the morning and you couldn't get out the door: you had to jump out through the bedroom window with shovels, and set to digging the snow to clear the door and the ground floor windows! And the cold! It's up there that, when you're speaking outside in the forest, your words freeze, and it's only come Spring, when the sun starts to heat up, that you can hear what's been said in the Winter! It was there that I got my nose frozen, one night when I'd been to a shake-down at Patrick Maloney's. I'd stayed too long under the portico, saying goodbye to his daughter. And so it is still nowadays that the tip of my nose is rather swollen and jaundiced by the nor'-westerlies.

That was the winter that a couple of us played a trick on "fat Annie", the widow who did the cookroom laundry. She lived alone on Stone Point in a little wooden house with only one door and a four-paned window. One dark night while she was asleep, we daubed her windowpanes with pitch and jammed her door with stakes. Naturally, she couldn't see anything come morning, and she stayed in bed for part of the day waiting for dawn. Finally, she got up and went to open the door. No way! It was only two days later that a fisherman heard her knocking and they came to her rescue. The clerks were suspected of having pulled it off, and the Agent threatened to dock them a month's pay. It was thought that it might have been the carpenters, on account of the pitch, and the Reverend Moulpied spoke from the pulpit about it on Sunday, and preached on those who oppress the widow and orphan.

But "fat Annie" got over it; and when she came to fetch the dirty laundry from the cookhouse, we gave her a big chunk of pork to make her feel better.

This poem by George Métivier has somewhat of the feeling of a sea shanty, as it cheerfully glamorises the life of the fisherman.

George Métivier

J'n'iron pus à la maïre (Chanson St. Martinaise), *1845* (Guernesiais)

> L'soleil fait l'amour à la terre,
> L'cieil est doux, l'air séraïn;
> À Sâïnt la maïre est coum' ùn verre,
> A' bat déjà sen pllaïn:
> L'voûs, car il est haut temps, Jean, Pierre,
> Marguerite et Mad'lon!

Not' fortune est dans not' galère,
A' va coum' ùn mouisson!
Quànd les houmards, sangllottànt d'fret,
S'hébergeront sus l's âtres,
Quànd l's ormers grimp'ront sus l'Béquet,
J'n'iron pus ès banâtres,
Ès banâtres,
J'n'iron pus ès banâtres!

Bllûe, ou verte coum' de la plise,
L'cher mireux du soleil,
Qu'l'iaue rouâne ou rouablle, nère ou grise,
Que l'temps seit laid ou bel, –
Bllànc coum' la née, où l'berouet joue,
M'nichànt quiq' malin caoup,
J'navigue et j'ris, parmi la broue,
De Roc-Dôvre à Lihaou!
Quànd les Frànçais f'ront viraïr d'bord
Nos murs de coeur de quêne,
Quànd j'haïss'teron leur tricolor,
J'n'iron pus à la sênne,
À la sênne,
J'n'iron pus à la sènne!

L'état du terrien ne m'pllaît guère
Car il est triste adret, –
Baillies-mé nos roquers pour douaire,
Pour demeure ùn baté!
Baillies-mé l'càmp, où la quérue
Jamais n'tourne motté!
Baillies-mé l'turbot, la mouarue,
La sole et l'gris mulet!
Auve les vèles en berdelle ès mâts,
Si j'ronfllon dàns la câle, –
Quànd les dravàns craïndront les vracs,
J'n'iron pus à la tralle,
À la tralle,
J'n'iron pus à la tralle!

L'jeur creît, fai-d'ver, l'vent suffle et crie,
Il enflle not' can'vas!
V'là Pierre et Jean sus la caûchie,
Éfànts, à vot' travas!

Ah! vou r'viendraïz brâment, vos quatre,
Soupaïr, fiers et goguets,
D'vànt not' raguer, les pids sus l'âtre,
Chàntànt coum' des coquets!
Quànd not' soleil aira perdu
Sa lueur brillànte et cllaïre,
Quànd j's'ron tous à la gar de Gu,
J'n'iron pus à la maïre,
À la maïre,
J'n'iron pus à la maïre!

We'll go no more to sea (a song from St. Martin), *1845*

The sun woos the earth,
the sky is fair, the air calm;
at Saints the sea is like glass,
it's already reaching high-water:
get up, for it's high time, John, Peter,
Margaret and Maddie!
Our fortune's in our galley,
she flies like a bird!
When lobsters, sobbing from cold,
huddle on hearths,
when ormers climb up onto Le Becquet,
then we'll go no more to the lobster pots,
to the lobster pots,
we'll go no more to the lobster pots!

Blue, or green as sea-grass,
the dear mirror of the sun,
whether the water wracks or rages, black or grey,
whether the weather is foul or fair, –
white as snow, where the surf foams,
from the Roches Douvres to Lihou!
When the Frenchmen force aside
our walls of hearts of oak,
when we hoist their tricolor,
then we'll go no more to the draw-net,
to the draw-net,
we'll go no more to the draw-net!

The life of a farmer doesn't attract me
for it's fairly sad –

give me our rocks as dower,
as dwelling, a boat!
Give me the field where the plough
has never yet turned a clod!
Give me the turbot, the cod,
the sole and the grey mullet!
With sails in tatters on the masts,
if we're snoring away in the hold, –
when thornback rays are afraid of wrasse,
then we'll go no more trawling,
trawling,
we'll go no more trawling!

Day is breaking, indeed, the wind whistles and moans,
it fills our canvas!
There are Peter and John on the quayside,
lads, to work!
Ah! you'll come back promptly, you four,
for supper, proud and swaggering,
in front of our blazing fire, feet on the hearth,
crowing like cocks!
When our sun has lost
its brilliant clear light,
when we're all in the keeping of God,
then we'll go no more to sea,
to sea,
we'll go no more to sea!

A rather less idealised picture of boats and life afloat is offered by this extract from a Jèrriais story. In 1890 a statue of Queen Victoria was unveiled in Saint Helier. Jersey had intended to mark the Golden Jubilee of 1887 with an appropriate statue, but government delays and budgetary wrangles had delayed getting anything done in good time. A booklet appeared giving a comical account of the festivities surrounding the unveiling of the statue on 3 September 1890 and this story recounts the visit of Captain Jan d'la Maze (de la Mare, i.e. 'from the bay', specifically Saint Catherine's Bay) and his wife Jeanneton who decide to travel round the coast to St. Helier by sea in order to attend the unveiling. A newly-wed English-speaking couple, Mr and Mrs Fish, hitch a ride with the Captain and his wife back to Town. The story is in Jèrriais apart from snatches of conversation in English, with a distinct Jersey accent, transcribed into the author's own Jèrriais spelling. Transcriptions of English phrases also crop up in the second half of the story which is set in majority English-speaking Saint Helier. Jan d'la Maze is an author who wrote stories published in the almanacs as well as commentaries in the form of letters in the newspapers. The dialect of these texts, with their style and their distinctive spelling, seems identical to that used under other names by the Rev. Charles Picot. Since these sailor stories are so much saltier and much less respectable than one might expect a clergyman to publish, perhaps it would not be surprising if he concealed his identity behind an undeclared pseudonym.

'Jan d'la Maze' (possibly Rev. Charles Picot)

From Lé Dêcouvrement d'la Statue, *1890* (Jèrriais)

Ou' pouvèz pânsé que chutte feis je n'bailli pas l'bras à Micice Fiche…

V'nus au yatte n'ou s'ambèrtchi tous bein vite. Janneton s'mint lavant pour souogni d'la djibbe, mé à la bârre, et l'janne couplle s'assît dans l'mitan oprès l'mât.

– Unne belle petite brîse de tèrre, les velles trimèes, et nos v'là en route pour not' petit

VIAGE EN MÉ.

"*Aoûe naïce, caiptunne,*" s'faîsait Micice Fiche. J'pânsi daeûsse-treis feis: je n'sai' s'tu dizâs aoûe naïce tréjous – j'vèrron' bétôt.

J'sortîmmes de charme d'la baie, par un p'tit vent arriéze; n'ou doubllit la pointe de l'Artchézondé, et n'ou pâssi d'vant Aoûne-Port sans avâzies. Dans unne heuze j'étion' endrait l'Vièr-Châté, Et tchi belle veûe, mes chiézes gens! il 'tait tout êluminé par le solèt l'vant. Janmais d'votte vie n'avèz veu rein d'pûs bé! Janneton, tch'a veu chonna des feis sans nombre, n'y prennait pas d'avis; mais nos daeûx pâssagier' ne s'en cônt'naiont pas d'jouaîe. La p'tite janne famme, partitchuliézement, tapait dans ses p'tites pattes en as-tu en veur-tu, et criyait toutes les minutes:

"*Louque, Fredde, aoûe pretti; louque, louque!*"

En êffet, ch'tait supèrbement bé.

Pâssè l'Châté, i' k'menchi a y-avei un ptit d'cllapotée. I' nos faillit prendre un rîs dans la grand' velle, et couôrre en d'hor', et lovié – le vent avait un miot changi.

Je r'mèrtchi bétôt qu'nos pâssagier' étaient toués les daeûx trantchilles. Micice Fiche n'avait pon grosse mînne, vraînment. Ou'm'avait l'air bein jaoûne. Oul' avait la tête app'yè sûs l'êpaûle à sân Fredde, tchi n'avait pon n'tou l'air bein dîguânt. La brîse s'accrut un p'tit, à m'suz que j'prenion' l'large – *la Belle Bèrgère* filait et saoûticotait d'pllaîsi – ch'tait coume unne héronde!

J'avais l's'yièr' sûs Micice Fiche, tchi m'pazaîssait touânné sûs l'vèrt. Janneton n'viyait rein – oul' tait otchupèe lavant à souogni l's'êcoutes.

Tout d'un coup la pouôrre petite Micice Fiche fut prinse du hitchèt et à sué à d'goûts.

J'creu tch'il tait temps, et j'criyi: "Janneton, ma garce, ergarde, j't'en prie, ramâsse dôn la toube, et vain-t'en vite veis entouôre Micice Fiche." Ma famme comprînt bain; ou' s'en vînt vite atou la toube à assisté la pouôrre petite janne famme tch'était, en êffèt, bain malade: le tcheu lî cratchait coume un tas d'cannibottes, et pîs…

J'dîs à s'n'houme d'allé prendre la pièche à Janneton quândi qu'ou' prendrait la sienne. Le pouôrre pend'loque en s'n'allant s'êtravelit je n'sai combein d'feis à qua-tre pattes dans l'fond du baté. Il avait bein d'la painne à se r'mâté touôs les coups qui tchiyait.

La pouôrre petite Micice Fiche en avait-alle dans l'estouma! – Dans un temps ou' s'trouvit si malade qu'ou' s'mînt à miaoûné coume unne êfant. Mais oprès tout, che n'tait djéze qu'unne êfant, unne toute janne garce, tch'ézait deu être occouo à l'êcole, à la pièche d'être embâtée d'un houme.

Mais à-ch't'heu i' n'y-a pûs d'avèr!

La préchainne chôse, ou' s'mînt à criyé des cris piteur': "*Mémèe, aï ouantce tou gô tou maï mémèe! Fredde, têke mi tou maï mémèe!*"

Quand j'la ouï, j'pânsi: n'ou n'peut pas alloué d'itèt gnolin à bor', i' faoût r'vizé et faize un p'tit miot d'combat.

J'mîns la bârre dessous et j'm'êcriyi "Louque aoûte, ioû faredde! Lèt gô de djibbe-shîte, lèt gô de djibbe-shîte."

Mistré Fiche se r'touânnit à me r'gardé coume un innocent – i' n' comprennait pas unne mie.

– "*Lèt gô de djibbe-shîte, lèt gô de frannete sêle rôpe*, tchan d'annima!" – Chutte feis ichin i' comprînt et lâtchi l'êcoute, et je r'vizion d'charme.

Quand l'baté fut pas bouannement rabattu, j'criyi: "*Drâ de djibbe-shîte tâte, Mistré Fiche.*"

Sav-ous tch'est que ch't'ouézé-là allait faize? I' s'mînt à hallé sûs l'êcoute au vent; dans un cllin-d'yi l'baté arrive, et s'en' va erprendre l'vent d'l'aoûtre bor' – un pouce de pûs et j'ézîmmes tè tous caipsaïzès! J'tais-ti mârri! J'lî baîlli 'un p'tit miot d'mân' bréviaize, à Mistré Fiche; j'lî dis: "*Lèt gô, ioû foûle, lèt gô, t'chan d'annima, lèt gô. Ioû lainnede-sheurke, di odeur, poule di odeur, poule di odeur djibbe-shîte!*

"*For shême, ôlde mainne,*" se m'fît Micice Fiche, "*ouate fore saie shîte sô motche é-bôrde é bôte?*"

Je n'tais pûs *Caip'tunne*, ou' viyîz bein. Dans ma coléze, j'sai bein qu'j'lî rêpouni' rupêment: "*Maïne yeûre siquenesse, mèdemme; maïne yeurselfe.*" Ou' s'teut et ne r'dît pûs mot.

Il en' tait temps èttou; car l'êffort qu'oul' avait fait pour me pâlé si bein, lî r'baîllit l'hitchèt; et lî-en fît dêgôrré du stoffe – i'y-en eut unne fèrre toubèe chu coup-là.

Ma famme, tchi faîsait d'hôriblles grimaches et teurtait l'néz assèz à se d'dêtil-bouêtchi, envyit bein vite la toubêe hor' bor'. J'la ouï dize "Tch'est don qu'ou peut avei mângi, chutte famme pour qu'il infecte tant!"

Mistré Fiche était acclutchi dans le d'vant et ne s'gênait pas fort de sa micice. Le pouôre cor était èttou bein vèrt.

From The Unveiling of the Statue, *1890*

You can imagine that this time I didn't offer my arm to Mrs Fish...

When we got to the yacht, we all went aboard quickly. Joan went forward to take care of the jib, me on the tiller, and the young couple sat amidships behind the mast.

A nice little land breeze, sails trimmed, and off we go on our little sea voyage.

"How nice, captain," said Mrs Fish. I thought on a couple of occasions: I don't know as how you'll carry on saying "how nice" – we'll soon see.

We left the bay fine, with a little wind astern; we doubled the point of Archirondel, and passed Anne Port without incident. In an hour we were off Mont Orgueil, and what a fine view of the castle, folks! It was all lit up by the sunrise. You've never seen anything more beautiful in your life! Joan, who's seen that countless times, paid no attention; but our two passengers couldn't contain their joy. The little young woman in particular clapped her little hands like mad, and cried out by the minute: "Look, Fred, how pretty, look, look!"

Well, it was absolutely splendid.

Past the Castle, it started to get a little choppy. We had to take in a reef in the mainsail, and run out and tack about – the wind had changed a bit.

I soon noticed that our passengers were both quiet. Mrs Fish was really looking a bit sick. She seemed rather yellowish to me. She had her head on her Fred's shoulder, and he didn't look too good either. The breeze got up a bit as we headed offshore – the "Belle Bèrgère" ran and skipped with pleasure – she was like a swallow!

I had my eyes on Mrs Fish who seemed to be turning green. Joan didn't see anything – she was busy forward taking care of the sheets. Suddenly poor little Mrs Fish got the hiccups and started pouring with sweat.

I thought it was time so I shouted, "Joan, my girl, look, get the tub please, and go and see to Mrs Fish." My wife understood perfectly; she came down quickly with the tub to help the poor little young woman who was really ill: she was retching violently and...

I told her husband to go and take Joan's place while she took his. The poor lubber managed to end up I don't know how many times on the way flat on his hands and knees in the bottom of the boat. He had great trouble getting up again every time he fell down.

Didn't poor little Mrs Fish have something to get off her chest! After a while she got so sick that she started to mewl like a child. But after all, she was barely more than a child, a very young girl who ought to have been at school, instead of being hitched to a husband. But now, this wasn't child's play!

The next thing, she started to wail piercingly: "Mummy, I wants to go to my mummy! Fred, take me to my mummy!"

When I heard her, I thought we can't be having any of that nonsense aboard, we'll have to tack about again and fight our way through it a bit.

I put the tiller under and cried out: "Look out, you forward! Let go the jib-sheet, let go the jib-sheet!"

Mr Fish turned to look at me like an innocent – he didn't understand at all.

"Let go the jib-sheet, let go the front sail rope, you dog!" This time he understood and released the sheet and we tacked back perfectly.

When the boat had pulled back enough, I called out "Draw the jib-sheet tight, Mr Fish."

Do you know what that lummox went and did? He started hauling on the windward sheet; in a blink the boat headed against the wind and went to take the wind from the other side – an inch more and we'd all have been capsized! How angry I was! I gave Mr Fish a right talking-to, I said to him: "Let go, you fool, let go, you dog, let go. You land-shark, the other, pull the other, pull the other jib-sheet!"

"For shame, old man," Mrs Fish said to me, "what for say shit so much aboard a boat?"

I wasn't "Captain" any more, you notice. I was so angry that I answered her high-handedly: "Mind your sickness, madam, mind yourself." She shut up and didn't say another word.

And about time too, for the effort she'd made to speak to me like that had given her the hiccups again, and got her puking up some stuff – there was a fair tubful that came up that time.

My wife was making horrible faces and screwing up her nose enough to put it out of joint, and she quickly threw that tubful overboard. I heard her say, "What could that woman have eaten to make it stink so!"

Mr Fish was squatting in the bows and wasn't caring about his wife. The poor soul was also looking very green.

This sailor's yarn, written by the otherwise landlubberly Denys Corbet and published in December 1884, tells the story of Sam who runs away to sea in 1804 at the age of 16 as a cabin boy on a merchant ship, and as a result of the adventure in the slave trade recounted in this extract, is captured and falls in with pirates, before retiring and investing his ill-gotten gains in a farm back in his native Guernsey.

Denys Corbet ('Bad'lagoule')

From **Coum' est que l'vier Sam d'vint pirate,** *1884* **(Guernesiais)**

Palaïz d'tounnerre et d'écllairs! jamais vou n'en vitent, ni n'en verraïz d'vànt qu'd'être attrapaïs d'une squâle dans la rivière Pllatte. J'ai veû autànt coum 4 différentes sortes d'écllairs tout en mìme temps, et du tounnerre qu'nou n'pouvait s'entre ouïr d'visaïr. J'ai étaï dans toutes sertes d'tormentes, mais pour d'l'entrinn'-taï j'nai veû rien coum chett' là. L'cap'taïne, l'daeuxième contre-maître, et 4 hommes coulirent d'auv la brigue. J'avais 40 dalleurs en or dans une chaìnture autouar de mé, et quànd j'vîmes à Montévido, 4 d'non s'engagirent à bord d'une barque *Angllaique* pour Rio, où j'arrivîmes dans 40 jours. Une niétie qu'j'étais assis dans un p'tit racouain qu'j'avais découvert, où j'beuvais un verre de grag et fumais un pipâie, un curiaeux mâbet étrangier, mainti marinier, mainti terrien, s'trouvì d'vant mé, et après aver r'gardaï autouar d'li, i' s'assiévìt oprès d'mé, et m'dit tout d'un caoup:– Men garçon, ten grag est fini, prend-n'en un autre verre à mes frais et d'vîson un p'tit. "Ma fé, oui guia," j'lî dît, "et d'un frànc cueur." Eh bien, j'prîmes plusieurs crâstâies ensemblle, et dans p'tit d'temps j'vîmes à nou-s-entre entendre. Après que j'y-aeut racontaï m'histouaire, i' m'dìt:

"Coum'est qu'tu-aîm'rais à v'nir à houichba pour du ner gibier?" "Qu'est qu'ch'est chunna," j'lî dît.

"Bah, à la côte de Guinée pour des nègres," s'fît-i' tout d'un caoup; caêr vou savaïz que ch'tait la mode à chu temps là. Ll'ya d'gros marchànts en Amérique qui c'menchirent coum chunna. Est-che pouit drôle qu'chu qu'est bouan à faire aniet s'ra mauvais d'main?

"Quaï gages?" j'lî d'màndì.

"100 dalleurs par meis, et 5 dalleurs pour tous les nègres prins en vie," s'tî.

"J'îrai," j'repounni tout court, "et tu peux m'trouvaïr ichin d'main au ser à 8 heures."

"Eh bien," s'tî, "tu m'as dit qu'tu-avaïs daeux camarades à Rio, s'tu peux l's-am'-naïr, j'vou dounn'rai 25 dalleurs chacun d'prim."

J'n'aeus pouit d'païne à l's-aver, et j'nous-n-allîmes tous à Pernàmbuco, où j'trouvimes la brigue *Ecllair*, Cap'taïne Liénard, pour la côte de Guinée. Ch'tait un grànd et bel engin, bâti en Espengne, et qu'allait raide. Al' avait 40 hommes et 6 canons, 3 d'chaque bord, et un long canon sus pivot au milli. 40 jours après quittaïr Perrnàmbuco, j'avion à bord 500 jolis nègres et négresses, et couarion sous toute not' teile pour le Berzil. Tout fut bien jusqu'au 9e jour, à quànd l'cien d'à haut keryi: "Un navire en veu."

"Eyou?" s'fît l'Cap'taïne.

"Dret par su la bô du vent," s'fît l'autre.

"A qu'est qui r'semblle?" s'fît l'Cap'taïne.

"Ch'est une grànd' brigue, la tête en ichìn," s'fît l'cien d'à haut. J'couarion dret vouest, et avion l'vent du su'est, tandis qu'l'étràngier v'nait d'vent large et à flleur de course. Dans une dem'yheure i' n'tait pas pus d'à 2 milles de non. J'vis qu'il arrivait terjoûs coum pour nou copaïr le ch'mìn. J'étais à la barre, et j'prins la liber-taï d'dire au Cap'taïne:–

"J'cré mé, moussieu," j'lî dîs, "qu'll'ya quiq chose entouar de ch't-anima là qui n'me pllait qu'moyen."

"Qu'est qu'ch'est?" s'tî.

"Quànd il est v'nu prumièrement en veue," m'fît-ju, "il avait l'naïz au nord'est, et à persent i' cueurt du nord au vouest biaû que l'vent n'a miette en tout chàngi."

Là d'sus l'Cap'taïne attrapi sa longue veue, et après l'aver examinaï, i' keryi:–

"Loffaïz, et mettaïz l'navire dret d'vènt l'vent, auv toutes les veiles à haut."

Mais ch'fut tout en vain, l'étràngier nou siévit et nou-s-attrapi dans p'tit d'temps.

A huit chents verges d'nou, i nou-s-env'yi un coupple d'balles qui firent des bûquettes d'not' grànd mât d'heune, et qu'amnît tout patafllâs sus l'pont. En même temps i haïstì la nère couleur auv la tête de mort et l's-os crouaisis. Il avait 12 long canons d'douze livres, et un 32 sus pivot. Sen pont était couvert d'hommes; mais j'décidìmes d'nou battre à la draïne extrêmitaï. L's-écoutiles furent lachies et tous les nègres enfrumaïs, les canons préparaïs, l'amunition servie, et les balles mises à roulaïr. Ch'tait ma prumière bataille, mais pas la draïne par un grànd compte. J'nou battìmes tout chu que paeûmes; mais l'pirate éplluquait sa dinstànce et nou mit en miettes. Pus d'la mainti d'l'équipage fut tuaï, d'côte une tapâie d'blessaïs, l'Captaïne pour un. I' n'y-avait pus rien à faire qu'a d'valaïr la couleur et s'rendre. Vou d'vaïz vou r'souv'nir, mesdames et messiûs, qu'chunchìn s'arrivit ll'ya pus d'75 àns, à quànd l'escllavage était considéraï quâsiment un bouan coummerce et à quànd les maïrs d'Espengne bouaillaient d'pirates.

From How old Sam became a pirate, 1884

Talk about thunder and lightning! You've never seen and never will see anything like it until you've been caught in a squall in the River Plate. I've seen as many as four different sorts of lightning all at the same time, and thunder so you couldn't hear each other speaking. I've been in all sorts of storms, but for persistence I've never seen anything like that. The captain, the second mate, and four men went down with the brig. I had forty dollars in gold in a belt around my waist, and when we came to Montevideo, four of us signed on an English barque for Rio, where we arrived forty days later. One night when I was seated in a little secluded corner I'd discovered, where I was drinking a glass of grog and smoking a pipe, a strange foreign fellow, half sailor, half landlubber, came and stood in front of me, and having looked around himself, sat down next to me, and said to me all of a sudden:– My lad, your grog's gone, have another glass on me and let's have a talk. "Goodness, yes indeed," I said to him, "and willingly." Well, we had several drinks together, and soon we were getting along nicely. After I'd told him my story, he said to me:

"How'd you like to come batfowling for black game?" "What's that?" I asked.

"You know, on the Guinea coast for negroes," he said suddenly; for as you know that was the custom in those days. There are important traders in America who got their start that way. Isn't it strange how something that is quite acceptable today will be unacceptable tomorrow?

"How much for wages?" I asked him.

"A hundred dollars a month, and five dollars for each negro taken alive," he said.

"I'll go," I said, just like that, "and you can find me here tomorrow evening at 8 o'clock."

"Well," he said, "you told me you had two companions in Rio. If you bring them along, I'll give you 25 dollars commission for each of them."

I had no problem getting them along, and off we all went to Pernambuco, where we found the brig, the *Ecllair*, under Captain Leonard bound for the Guinea coast. It was a fine large ship, built in Spain, and with a good speed on her. She had forty men and six cannon, three on each side, and a long swivel gun amidships. Forty days after leaving Pernambuco, we had five hundred fine negroes and negresses on board, and were running under full sail for Brazil. Everything was going well until the ninth day, when we heard the lookout call from up top: "Ship ahoy."

"Where?" said the Captain.

"Straight to windward" replied the other.

"What does it look like?" asked the Captain.

"It's a large brig, bow for'ard," said the lookout. We were running due west, and had a south-easterly, while the other ship was coming with the wind at full speed. In half an hour it was no more than two miles away from us. I saw that it was always trying to head us off. I was at the wheel, and I took the liberty of saying to the Captain:–

"I think, sir," I said to him, "that there's something odd about that critter which I don't like much."

"What is it?" he said.

"When it first came into view," I said, "it was heading nor'east, and now it's running north by west even though the wind hasn't changed at all."

Thereupon the Captain grabbed his telescope and, having examined it, he shouted:–

"Luff, and set the ship before the wind, with all sails set."

But it was all in vain, the other ship followed us and soon caught us up.

At eight hundred yards from us, it fired a couple of shots at us which reduced our top-mast to firewood, and made a mess of the deck. At the same time, it hoisted the black flag with the skull and crossbones. It had 12 long twelve-pounders, and a thirty-two-pounder swivel gun. Its deck was covered with men; but we decided to fight to the bitter end. The hatches were battened and all the negroes stowed, the cannon readied, ammunition handed out, and the cannonballs set rolling. It was my first fight, but not the last by long way. We fought as hard as we can; but the pirate ship picked its range and blew us to pieces. Over half the crew were killed, besides a large number of wounded, among whom the Captain. There was nothing left to do but haul down the colours and surrender. You must remember, ladies and gentlemen, that this happened over seventy five years ago, when slavery was considered an almost respectable trade and when the Spanish Main seethed with pirates.

Closer to home, this poem by George Métivier shows a rather positive view of the life of those whose livelihoods depended on the sea and the harvest of the shore. The appearance of the octopus amid the bucolic high-jinks of the young workers provides suitable Romantic frisson. The poem is dated 1809, and was published in 1873. Métivier also composed a variation on the theme in English written in 1817, revised in 1840 and published in *Fantaisies Guernesiaises* in 1866.

George Métivier

From Fantaisies Guernesiaises, *1866* (Guernesiais)

La Peurve, *1809*

Vlà qui'est bien seur, d'vànt que l'soleil
S'héberge à Lihaou, rouage et bel,
J'écharderon nos bergerettes;
Oui, nou mettra sous leur colrettes
Quiqu' limache ou quiqu' hérichon,
Loche, ou cabot, ou brin d'lànchen.
Oyous Louison? A' plleure, a' crie;
Qu'est donc qu'alle a, la chère amie?
Alle a piqui d'sen faûcillon
Un monstre pus laid que l'démon,
Dans l'vrec la vieille était muchie;
Nou dit qu'a' saque une éclluchie
Pour égaluaïr quiqu' sot païsson,
Et pis à l'énaque en d'muchon.
Nou crâint sen r'gard, sa d'marche est lente,
Sen bec est dur, et, que j'n'en mente,
Ses huit longs pids sont des serpents.
Est-che un avorton des krakans?
La crabe, à r'culons, passe, et vite,
D'ùn saut, d'ùn bond, l'hydre maudite,
En ùn môment, en un cllin d'ieil,
Coumm' le trait d'faeu qui sort du cieil,
La saîsit, l'émacllit, l'avale;
Car alle a terjous la faïm vâle,
Et, coumm' disait Charles Mollet,
Alle est l'Tamerlan d'Portelet.

The Octopus, *1809*

Of course, that's what we'll do, before the sun
settles over Lihou, red and handsome,
we'll tease our shepherdesses;
yes, we'll slip under their neckerchiefs
some sea-hare or some urchin,
groundling, blenny, or sand-eel.
Can you hear Louisa? She cries, she squeals;
what's the matter with her, the little darling?

She's pricked with her sickle
a monster uglier than the devil,
in the vraic the old thing was hidden;
they say that it lets off a squirt
to bamboozle some foolish fish,
and then devours it surreptitiously.
People are afraid of its gaze, its progress is slow,
its beak is hard and, I tell no lie,
its eight long feet are snakes.
Is it some monster of the krakens?
The crab, walking backwards, passes quickly,
in one leap, in one bound, the accursed hydra,
in an instant, in the blink of an eye,
like a bolt of lightning from the sky,
seizes it, crushes it, swallows it;
because it's always hungry,
and, as Charles Mollet used to say,
it's the Tamburlaine of Portelet.

Those Channel Islanders who did not go to sea in ships, would still have depended on the sea and its harvest. Competition in the fishing grounds around the Islands are still sometimes hotly contested with fishermen from mainland Normandy and Brittany; cultivation of mussels and oysters is an economic resource; but the tidal range daily uncovers stretches of beach for those who like to catch razor-fish and other creatures of the coasts, such as the sand eel (Ammodytes tobianus). Sand-eel-ing used to be the occasion for large parties to venture out by moonlight at low tide to dig the fish out from the sand in which they had buried themselves. In the seventeenth century, the Jerseyman Jean Poingdestre wrote in his book *Caesarea* that 'it was wont to be a great pastime, for yong people who flocked to it, not soe much for the fish, as for divertisment and many times for debauchery', but by the time Marjorie Ozanne described a twentieth century sand-eeling party in Guernsey, things were slightly less debauched, but hardly decorous.

The traditional song 'Jean, Gros Jean' is known in various versions, some less ribald than others – but none of them polite, across the Islands. The song was so popular in Guernsey that it gained a reputation as Guernsey's national song and led to a diplomatic incident in 1817: Prince William Frederick, Duke of Gloucester, a nephew of George III, visited the Islands, arriving in Saint Peter Port on 18th September. Unfortunately, someone had had the bright idea that, as a gesture to the people of Guernsey, the Duke should disembark to a traditional air played by the military band. When the assembled crowd saw the royal visitor making his entrance to the tune of 'Jean, Gros Jean', they sang the utterly unsuitable words, to much general laughter – and private mystification on the part of the visiting dignitaries. The Duke did not get a more respectful reception in Jersey, though, on the 20 September. Saint Helier, unlike Saint Peter Port, has no natural harbour, and the royal party arrived at low tide. The Duke transferred to shore in a small boat, but was obliged to scramble on his hands and knees over wet rocks to where the Lieutenant-Governor was waiting, sensibly enough, to greet him. The Duke arrived covered in seaweed.

Marjorie Ozanne

La Grënmaire va au Lënshon, *1949* (Guernesiais)

Ils avaient decidai d'allaï à la Gravette. La maire s'n' allait être basse deviar enne haure et d'mie, qui fait i s'n-allaient sorti dans les dix haures et d'mie. Comme die le Toumas, "il faut dounnaï du temps, parce que la juman c'mënche à viailli et a n'peut pas allaï aussi vite comme a soulait."

En effet, deviar dix haures et d'mie, v'la la rabias qui monte dans l'queriot. Le Toumas était assis su le d'vent, comme casheux. Le Georges montit le prumier pour hallaï su la viaille faume, et la Marguerite restit dans la rue pour poussaï d'su. "Aussa," s'fie Georges, "Vaiyous, Grënmaire, Whoops!" et'i la print pas sous les bras, et la Marguerite poussait par derriaire. "Secours d'la vie," die la Marguerite. "mais y'a d'la b'senteux. Y'a autens païne comme a montai en plâ sue les lattes."

La Grënmaire etait trop en affaire pour leux faire auqueune réponse. Al' tait là, éperqui su l'derriaire du quériot, et i n'pouvait pas la bougier.

Mais tous d'en caoup le Georges dounit enne volas d'captoïne et v'la la viaille dans l'fond du queriot ses bottes à lastic qui pointaïent drait endviar les étaïlles. Par le temps qui l'avaient rammassas et mise le bouan but en haut, ils taient en route. Pour enne ravision, a n'fut pas gergie, et a riait comme enne perdue de pensaï comme a l'avait etaï mise dans l'queriot.

Le Georges etait assis su l'cotai, et la Marguerite et la Grënmaire à chu – piâ dans l'font du queriot.

L'affaire allaient justemënt bian, i faisait biaux fin, et pis entou d'frat. La juman avait bouan pi étou. Il avaient tout leux tripo dans l'aire, leux fourques, pauniais, et ën lentairne ou daü pour si la leune se mushait. La viaille avait étout enne p'tite goute d'y'eaux d'vie 'pour gardaï hors le frat.'

Quën i vinrent le long des Lendes la Grënmaire se trouvait si fiaire qu'a s'mie à shentaï. Par le temps qui vinrent ès Grëns Marais, i shentaïent tous (P'taitre qu'ils avaient déja goutaï y'eaux d'vie).

"Jean gros Jean marie sa fille
Grosse et grasse et bian habile" s'fient les shenteux.

"Roum-toum, roum-toum," s'fie l'queriot.

"Quioupe-et quioupe, quioupe-quioupe," s'fient les pies d'la jumént.

"Radinguette et radingot," s'fient les shenteux, et en mesme temps, v'la le 'tip-stick' qui sort de sa pieche, v'la l'queriot qui mâte et les v'la tous bas en mouochaï dans la rue.

Mais le camas qu'yaü!

"Oo donc," s'fit l'Georges, "me v'la tuaï!"

"Waiqu'est ma pipe?" criyit le Toumas.

"J'ense-tai donc, Marguerite," criyit la Grënmaire, "t'es assise su mën ventre. J'sie piatte comme enne craipe." Su la fin i s'ramassirent, et les r'vla dans l'queriot. Su la fin les v'la su la bënque.

Quën la maire fut basse assaï pour passaï à la Gravette, les v'la allaï et i leux mirent à foui bouan raide.

Tout fut bian pour en p'ti, mais tout d'en caü le Toumas dounnit en broyon. "Il avait etaï piqui d'enne martaene. Vous eraite deux le vais densaï."

Bientot, s'fait le Georges, "Avous r'merquie qu'la viaille n'a pas d'pannier? J'pense qu'a la laissi dans la rue quën j'avons quais hors du queriot."

"Faut pouit dire mot," repounit la Marguerite, "faut la laissier tandis qu'a l'est trenquille. A n'era poui grën lënshon. A n'est pas vivre assaï pour les attrapaï."

Bientot la maire c'mënshi à montaï et le Toumas die, "I faura aussi bien s'entournaï. Waiqu'est la viaille faume?"

"Oh," repounit la Marguerite," a s'en est allas y'a deviar en quart d'aen haure. Al'dit qu'a nous vairrai dans l'queriot."

En effet, la Grënmaire etait bian comfortabyemënt assise quën ils arrivirent.

"Eh bian," s't-alle, "en avous eux du lënshons?"

"Pas mal," repounirent les autres, "et vous?" "J'en au justemënt en bouan frico," a die, toute fiaire.

"Mais dans quique vous l'avais mis," d'mëndit la Marguerite, "vous n'avaites pas de paunier?"

"Eh bian, j'm'envais te dire. J'ai hallaï mes brais, amarraï les guerais et mis le lënshon dedans."

En effet a n'avait justemënt enne bouanne paique.

Mais le Toumas ouï quiqu'a l'avait dit et i die, "Ma-fé, i n' s'ra pas d'mequier que le 'tip-stick' sorte en nous r'tournent.

I peut mënquier si veurt," repounit la viaille, "v'la qui n'me jainera pas. J'en avais mis daüx pâres pour ne prendre pas d'frat, qui fait l'affaire est bian!" Quën maime le queriot tipprait v'la qui n'me frai pas de rian."

Granny goes sand-eeling, *1949*

They'd decided to go to La Gravette. It was going to be low tide at about half past one, which meant that they'd be leaving around half past ten. As Tom said, "We have to take our time, because the mare's getting on and she can't go as fast as she used to."

So, around half past ten, the mob was there, climbing into the cart. Tom was sat up front as driver. George climbed up first to pull the old woman up, and Margaret stayed in the road to push her. "Hup," said George, "There you go, Granny. Whoops!" And he took her under the arms, and Margaret pushed from behind.

"Gracious me," said Margaret, "but that's some weight. It's as heavy as getting a pig's carcase up on the rack."

Granny was too occupied to answer them back. There she was straddling the rear of the cart, and they couldn't budge her.

But suddenly George gave her a thump and there was the old woman in the bottom of the cart with her wellies pointing straight up to the stars. By the time they'd picked her up and set her the right way up, they were on their way. Surprisingly enough, she wasn't bothered, and she laughed like anything to think how they'd got her into the cart.

George was sitting on the side, and Margaret and Granny were sat down in the bottom of the cart.

Everything was going well; it was a moonlit night, and cold. The mare was stepping well too. They had all their stuff on the floor, their forks, baskets, and a couple of lanterns in case the moon went in. The old woman also had a little drop of spirits "to keep the cold out".

When they came along Les Landes, Granny was so merry that she began to sing. By the time they got to les Grands Marais, they were all singing (perhaps they were already under the influence of the spirits).

"John, fat John,
married off his daughter
who was big and fat
and good at housework," sang the singers.

"Rum-ti-tum," went the cart.

"Clip-clop, clip-clop," went the hooves of the mare.

"Radindgette and radingo," sang the singers, and it was just then that the tipstick came loose, the cart tipped up, and they all fell down in a heap in the road.

What a racket they made!

"Oh my," said George, "I've been killed!"

"Where's my pipe gone?" shouted Tom.

"Budge yourself, Margaret," cried Granny, "you're sitting on my stomach. I'm as flat as a pancake."

Eventually they picked themselves up and got back in the cart, and eventually they arrived at the beach.

When the tide was out enough to get to La Gravette, off they went and they quickly set about digging.

Everything went well for a while, but suddenly Tom gave a shout, He'd been stung by a weaver fish. You should have seen the way he danced about.

Soon George spoke up. "Have you noticed that the old woman hasn't got a basket? I think she left it in the road when we fell out of the cart."

"Don't say anything," replied Margaret, "let her be while she's quiet. She's not going to catch many sand-eels, because she isn't quick enough."

Soon the tide started to come in and Tom said, "We might as well be getting back. Where's the old woman?"

"Oh," replied Margaret, "she went off about a quarter of an hour ago. She said she'd see us back at the cart."

And when they got there, that's where Granny was, sat nice and comfortable.

"Well," she said, "got any sand-eels, then?"

"Quite a lot," the others replied, "and how about you?" "Oh, I caught enough for a fine feed," she said proudly.

"But what did you put them in?" asked Margaret. "You didn't have a basket."

"Well I'll tell you. I took off my bloomers, tied off the legs and that's what I put the sand-eels in."

And really she'd got herself a nice haul.

But Tom heard what she'd said, and he said, "Gracious me, a fine thing it'll be if the tipstick comes out while we're going back."

"It can come loose if it likes," replied the old lady, "that won't bother me at all. I'd put two pairs on so as not to catch cold, so that's alright after all! Even if the cart does tip up, it won't matter to me at all."

The ormer, or abalone, is a mollusc (Haliotis tuberculata) much prized as a delicacy. Formerly, it was common: it is recorded that, on an exceptionally good ormering tide on 9 March 1841 in Guernsey, 20,000 ormers were caught on one day alone. The present-day scarceness of the shellfish means that restrictions are placed, by law, on ormer fishing. This does not put off the aficionados; neither does the need to tenderise the meat of the ormer before cooking – although few go as far as recommended by Piteur Pain.

Here we have two texts on the lengths people will go to for ormers: one from Guernsey by Thomas Alfred Grut, and the other by Philippe Le Sueur Mourant.

Thomas Alfred Grut ('T.A.G.')

Les Ormars, *1926* (Guernesiais)

A l'Editeur d'la "Gazette."

Oy'ous Mess Editeur, aim'ous l's ormars? Ch'est donc d'quet bouen quànd i' sont bien cuites, mais ch'est qu'i' faut saver les trimeï.

I' faut les battre dur, pour les faire dev'nir molles, (justement comme nous battrait les crâgnons quànd i' sont d'sobéissants) et p'is les "steweï" ou les fricachier. J'l's aïme bien mues que l'dindon ou l'poulet; biaux que ch'n'est qu'à Noué qu'-nous en goûte.

J'ai grand' envie d'une bouane plliatlaïe d'ormars, caer j'n'en ai jamais ieûe qu'un caoup d'p'is qu'la loué disait qu'i' n'fallait poui d'autre allaï en trachier.

Men viel hômme, Eliazar, est d'la Chapelle, et n'voulait poui allaï en trachier comme tous les vaïsins faisaient, et quand i' r'venaient d'la bànque, la panraïe était toute couverte de fyies, pour faire la meine que n'y'avait que des fyies.

Unn' serraïe j'alli ciz not vaïsin, Paul Berton, pour vée s'i' m'invitrait à soupeï, caer j'l'avais rencontreï d'vier tres haeures atout sa panraïe d'ormars; mais quànd j'tappi à l'us, les poures Bertons quâsi mouorrirent d'effret, caer i'crêyais que ch'-tait les "policemenne," et que quiq'un avait délattaï contre le poure Paul.

Quànd j'c'menchi à crieï que ch'tait seul'ment mé, Nancy Ferbrache, ils ouvrirent l'us, et m'invitirent à soupeï d'leux fricot. J'vous assaeure qu'i' n'eurent pouï à me d'màndeï le daeuxième caoup, caer j'en mouorrais d'envie.

J'n'étais guère de r'touor à la maison, quand Eliâzar r'vînt de s'n assembllaïe et était tout prêt pour sen soupeï. J'avais mangi tànt d'ormars ciz les Bertons, qu'i' m'était impossiblle de mangier, et j'eu à dire à mn hômme que j'avais mal à l'estoumà, et que j'creyais que ch'tait la soupe que j'avaimes ieue au méjeu qu'était trop grasse.

Si Eliâzar était comme un autre hômme, j'erraimes ieue d's ormars à châque grànde maraïe, mais nennin. Eliâzar à unn' pus délicate conschienche qu'aucuen chrêquien, et jamais n'vouli y' allaï.

Si m'n hômme mouorrait, jamais je n'en r'prendrais ieun qui s'rait Econôme à la Chapelle, ou collecteur à l'egllise; mais Eliâzar esʈ fort et robuste comme un ch'và, et têtu comme une âne, et j'n'errais jamais la chànce de m'en debarassaï, caer i' n'mourrà jamais d'unn' mort naturelle, et men seul espoir est qu'la "bosse" que và pour Plleinmont, l'assoum'ra quiq' serraïe.

D'vànt que d'acceptaï un daeuxième hômme, j'le f'rais promettre d'avànche qu'i' m'obéirai terjoûs, et irai ès ormars quànd j'l'i c'màndrais, pour que j'errais men fricot.

Ch'est "alright" de faire unn loué, si tous la gârde, mais j'n'aïme pouï à passaï les maisons ouêsque i' sont à les fricachier, et qu'ma shâre s'rà seul'ment à sentir et pouï gouteï.

J'espère qu'men perchain hômme s'rà un policemenne, et p'is i' n'errà pouï à allaï ès ormars, mais il errà seul'ment à prendre les paniers des cheux qui y' ont àtaï; et n'errà qu'à s'muchier derière la brecque d'la bànque, et pourrà gardeï ses pids et ses brées sec.

Je d'meure votre humblle servànte,
Nancy Ferbrache

Ormers, *1926*

To the Editor of the "Gazette"

Well now Mr. Editor, do you like ormers? They're very good when they are cooked well, but you need to know how to prepare them.

You must beat them to soften them (just like you would beat the children, little blighters, when they're disobedient) and then stew or fry them. I like them more than turkey or chicken; even though we only get to taste them at Christmas.

I crave a good plateful of ormers, as I have only had them once since the law came in which said that we could no longer go after them.

My old man, Eliâzar, is a chapel goer, and certainly didn't want to go gathering them the way all the neighbours were doing, which when they came back from the beach, their basketfuls were all covered in limpets, to make out that there were nothing but limpets in there.

One evening I went to see our neighbour, Paul Breton, to see if he would invite me to supper as I'd met him at around three o'clock with his basketful of ormers, but when I knocked on the door the poor Bretons almost died of fright because they thought that it was the police and that someone had informed on poor Paul.

When I began to call out that it was only me, Nancy Ferbrache, they opened the door and invited me to their feast of a supper. I assure you that they certainly didn't have have to ask me twice as I was dying to try it.

I had hardly arrived back at home when Eliâzar arrived back from his meeting and was all ready for his supper. I had eaten so many ormers at the Bretons' that it was impossible for me to eat, and I had to tell my husband that I had indigestion, and that I thought that the soup that we had had at midday was too rich.

If Eliâzar was like other men we would have had ormers at every spring tide, but no. Eliâzar has a more tender conscience than any other Christian, and never wanted to go.

If my husband were to die, I would never take another that is a steward at Chapel, or sidesman at the church; but Eliâzar is as fit and strong as a horse, and as stubborn as a donkey, and I'll never have the chance to rid myself of him, as he'll never die a natural death, and my only hope is that the bus that goes to Pleinmont, knocks him down one evening.

Before taking on a second husband, I'd make him promise in advance that he would always obey me, and go ormering when I ordered him to so that I would have my feast.

It's all well and good making a law if everyone keeps it, but I really don't care for passing by houses where they're cooking them, and my share is only to smell and not taste.

I hope that my next husband will be a policeman, and then he won't go ormering, but will only need to take baskets off those that have been and he'll just need to hide behind the entrance to the beach and he'll be able to keep his feet and trousers dry.

I remain your humble servant,
Nancy Ferbrache

Philippe Le Sueur Mourant ('Bram Bilo', 'Piteur Pain', etc)

How to Prepare and Cook Ormers, *1913* (Jèrriais)

S'ou sentez l'odeu' d'main, en passant souôs nos f'nètres – ch'est d's ormers. J'en accati un cabot Sam'di – des Jerriais. Pètchis souos la Pulente par un houmme qui s'ait man bieau-frèthe sinon qu'ma soeu l'trouvait trop èslindji. J'en payi un èstchu seul'ment: et j'sis pour r'touôné l's èscalles; y'a un marchand d'guano qui l's accate chi pour les cliutté sus l'portico d'un cottage qu'il est a faithe bâti a La Rocque pour allé y passé les Dinmanches quand i' f'tha bé.

Ch'est pour not' diné de d'main, a ma fille et mé, ov des poummes-de-terre. Et y'étha des domplinnes après et un gobin d'fromage qu'j'accati bouan marchi Sam'di passé, viyant qui r'muait. Sitot rentré siez nous, j'le couli dans un saucepan et j'mint bin vite eunne brique sus l'couérclye. Il est là oquo, et rin n'a bouogi sinon que l'couérclye se souolève parfais coumme si y'avait tchiq'chose a mitounné d'dans.

J'ai idée qu'nos ormers éthont du gout: et j'conte que v'la tchi s'en va être ten-dre coumme d'la mouélle. J'avons prins toutes les precautions: Lonore et mé avons travaillyi bin d's heuthes désus. Ch'fut mé qui les èscalli avec eunne pathe de cisieaux a Laizé. J'passi l'pus bé d'la matinée d'Lundi a les lavé. J'vos les scrobbi, lavi, rinchi: rinchi, scrobbi, lavi, dans assez d'ieau et d'soda pour se bannié d'dans. J'm'ettais mins a la qu'minze, bras r'troussés, braies r'troussées, et un vier gris fro a Laizé coumme d'vanté. J'les lavi a grand ieau, et Lonore se plaignit qu'j'avais èscli-atchi toute la vaisselle sus l'drecheux. Si chutte fille là n'amende, ou vindra rouâblieuse coumme sa chiéthe méthe qu'est au liet – sus du grué.

Eunne fais bin lavés, i' s'agissait d'bin les battre. Y'a du monde qui battent lus ormers ov eunne mailloche, d'autres avec le dos d'eunne bringe a dents, d'autres avec la palette a tcherbon, et j'counnais un St. Pierrais qui prétend qu'i' n'y'a pas devent l'steam-roller. Mé, j'les batti ov eunne s'melle d'un pètcheux. "Tchui con-tre tchui, qu'i' m'avait dit, n'y'a pas miyeu." Ch'est-tan-tchi, j'mint mes bottes, Lonore mint eunne pathe de chabots, j'èstendimes l's ormers sus l'aithe de la tchuizinne: et nos v'la a sauté d'sus a pis joints, qu'la sueu en rouôlait. Après avé travaillyi d'sus pour un coupye d'heuthes, j'bumes du tée, pour en r'avé eunne bor-dée d'vant que d'nos couochi; et pis, Mardi matin, j'lus en ballyi oquo eunne bor-dée tandi qu'Lonore 'tait a grée l'dèsjeunné. Après cheunna, j'agni l'fricot ov un râté, j'le mint dans eunne traisie d'ieau et j'les ouatchinni longtemps ov un g'nèts. M'n' idée est que che s'a eunne mouelle!

La préchenne chose a faithe a ch't'heu, ch'est d'fricachi du gras lard – du lard nouôri sus du gliand, s'nou peut – et eunne tête ou deux d'héthan pour dounné un p'tit gout de r'vas'y. Et pis, quand tout s'a bin roussi, nous les èstuiv'tha a p'tit feu, ov oquo du lard, yeunne ou deux poules, du timbre, du pérsi, eunne démié fielle de louothi, eunne carotte et eunne boutelle ou deux d'Oxo – et l'cook d'un hotel m'a dit que s'nou veurt, nou peut y'ajouôté eunne démié boutelle d'Madère.

J'n'avons pon invité persounne a diné pour chu jour là. Ma femme est au liet – sus du grué; et Lonore a l's ésprits bas d'avé 'té jouée par chu pend'loque la d'l'autre jour. Mais i'n'en couôta rin d'en v'nin senti l'parfum souos nos f'nètres.

How to Prepare and Cook Ormers, *1913*

If you smell anything tomorrow while passing beneath our windows – that'll be ormers. I bought a cabot of them on Saturday – Jersey ones. Fished below La Pulente by a man who would've been my brother-in-law, only my sister found him too lanky. I only paid half-a-crown for them, and I have to give back the shells. There's a guano merchant who pays a high price for them so as to stick them on the portico of a cottage he's building at La Rocque to spend his Sundays in when the weather's good.

It's for our dinner tomorrow, for my daughter and me, with potatoes. And there's going to be dumplings afterwards and a piece of cheese that I bought cheaply last Saturday because it was on the move. As soon as I got back home, I poured it into a saucepan and quickly put a brick on the lid. It's still there, and nothing's budged since except that the lid lifts itself up occasionally as though there was something simmering away inside.

I think our ormers will be tasty, and I'm betting they'll be as tender as marrow. We've taken all the precautions: Ellie and I have spent hours working on them. I shelled them using a pair of Liza's scissors. I spent the best part of Monday morning washing them. You see, I scrubbed them, washed them, rinsed them: rinsed, scrubbed, washed, in enough water and soda to swim in. I set to it in my shirtsleeves with my sleeves and trouser legs rolled up, and with an old grey dress of Liza's as an apron. I washed them in plenty of water, and Ellie complained that I'd splashed all the china on the dresser. If that girl doesn't watch herself she'll become as much of a nag as her dear mother who's in bed on a diet of gruel.

Once they'd been washed, they had to be tenderised. There are people who beat their ormers with a mallet, others with the back of a toothbrush, others with the coal shovel, and I know one man from Saint Peter who claims that nothing beats a steamroller. Me, I beat them with the sole of a fisherman's boot. "Leather against leather," that's what he told me, "there's nothing better." So I put on my boots, Ellie put on a pair of clogs, we laid out the ormers on the kitchen floor: and we jumped up and down on them until the sweat was pouring off us. After having worked on them for a couple of hours, we drank some tea, so we could have another go before going to bed; and then on Tuesday morning, I gave them another going-over while Ellie was getting breakfast ready. After that, I scraped up the feast with a rake, I put them into a troughful of water and gave them a good scrubbing with a broom. I think they're really going to melt in the mouth!

The next thing to do now, is to fry some fatty pork – pork raised on acorns, if possible – and a head of herring or two to make it really tasty. And then when everything's been well browned, you stew them over a low flame, with more pork, a chicken or two, some thyme, parsley, half a bayleaf, a carrot and a bottle or two of Oxo – and a hotel chef has told me that if you want you can add half a bottle of madeira.

We haven't invited anyone for dinner that day. My wife's in bed on a diet of gruel; and Ellie is a bit down after having been thrown over by that fool the other day. But it won't cost you anything to come and smell the odour beneath our windows.

Conger was a staple of the diet of Channel Islanders. This did not escape the notice of a member of the German occupying forces during the Second World War. Just as some Islanders turned to literature as a distraction or an expression of independent identity and intellectual liberty, so the German propaganda newspapers published morale-boosting poems as well as amused observations from amongst the soldiers stationed in the Islands.

Anonymous

The Conger line, *c.1942-1944* (translated from German)

Can you see the boat there on the waves?
It's turning in the wrong direction, and it's coming this way!
It's surely about to crash into the Martello tower,
unless it immediately pulls up its conger line...

I can see that the captain frantically waving his arms –
Damning and blasting because something's wrong!
However, the boat will not sink before arriving at the port,
but is the conger line garlanded full of fish?

I know that the captain is a bold sea-rover,
He even comes from my company.
The Guernsey fisherman has known him for longer
and he's at home with the creatures of the deep!

Twenty times over, heil, Petri, heil!
The food cares of today have disappeared.
You've set out your conger rope
and snared something like a small whale!

Hail to you worthy, brave man
You're not concerned by the dangers of the oceans,
You're not held back by the gale,
when you're seeking food for others!

All praise and honour to the conger line,
channelled between the swelling waves ...
You're not just for show,
but the biggest fish are your hangers-on!

Aha, now I see, the man over there at the mast
is signalling me in Morse code:
"I am turning green at gills,
and feeling pretty seasick!"

The fisherman's haul must be landed and sold. George Métivier gives us a pungent insight into what must have been a lively scene in the days when the steep and narrow streets of Saint Peter Port were filled with fishwives, their wares and their customers. Purpose-built market stalls might have been more hygienic but perhaps progress was less picturesque. In *Redstone's Guernsey and Jersey Guide* (1843), Louisa Lane Clarke compared the market of Saint Helier with its counterpart in Saint Peter Port: "Fish abounds here as well as in Guernsey, though the market-place does not show it off to such advantage. Off the rocks, at Jersey, immense numbers of the conger eel are caught, some of them six feet in length; they are in great demand by the lower class, who salt them for winter use."

George Métivier

L'Palais d'Neptune, *date unknown* (Guernesiais)

Jadis, ma bouane femme de grànd'mère
Acatait sen vrac ou sen lu,
(Car les turbots n'la tentaient guère,)
Dans la Grànd'-Rue, à quiq pas d'u:
Là, étalaïs sus leux brìns d'fouaille,
Congre, sarde, llottìn, macré,
Rais et dravans – les rien-qui-vailles! –
S'miraient – je n'mens pas – dans l'canné.

Ùn jour, Mess Bouanamy la chique
Dit à Aune Clliq, "Ten païsson pu'!"
Dame Aune Clliq aussitôt llî r'pllique,
"Mussieu, vou-z en avaïz mentu!"
I vét sus l'pavaï, l'ba-d'la-goule,
Ùn dravan gros coum' ùn pourpeis,
Llî fourre sen but d'pid dans la goule,
Et y lâque daeux ou treis orteis.

Bientôt Mesdames les congrières,
De Rocquaïne frànc jusqu'au Mont-Cuét,
Vinrent sous l'Grâïe, au pid du chìmquère,
Nou-z écàntaïr auve leux caquet:

J'y veyaimes les chàncres à leur aise,
Broûe au muset, et grìns en haut,
D'leux bâve érousaïr les g'rgeîses,
Haeûlìns, houmards et crabe-à-côs.

Mais, pourtànt, les digdis d'Neptune,
Par trop frillaeuses, à chu que j'cré,
Malgré l'ongllie, faisànt fortune,
Sous l'Grâïe – v'là qu'est seur – mouaraient d'fréd;
Et l'pus biaû marchi du royaume,
Grâce à leur orteis délicats,
Ès assuâïes, et au Gallet-Hiaume,
Leux fut fourni par les États.

M'est avis qu'une bouane cardinale
Nou-z airait saûvaï bien des fraix;
Car la J'nouillon (à Gyu seit-alle!)
S'abrîtait d'une vieille pâre de braies;
Et, si ch'n'était que l'monde empière,
Verrait-nou l'vrac, à St. Pierre-Port,
D'nos belles tablles de marbre faire –
Le tout-en-travers! – sen lliét d'mort?

The Palace of Neptune, *date unknown*

My good old grandmother used to
buy her wrasse or her whiting,
(because she didn't much care for turbot,)
in the High Street, a few doors down:
there, laid out on their bracken,
conger, red bream, small pollack whiting, mackerel,
rays and thornback rays – good-for-nothings! –
gazed on each other – no lie – in the gutter.

One day, weedy Mr Bonamy
said to Urchin Annie, "Your fish stinks!"
Mistress Urchin Annie came right back at him,
"Mister, that's a lie!"
He sees on the cobbles, the gobby fool,
a thornback as large as a porpoise,
he sticks the end of his foot into its mouth,
and leaves behind two or three of his toes.

Soon the lady conger-mongers,
from Rocquaine right as far as Mont Cuet,
came to the Graie at the foot of the cemetery
to entertain us with their patter:
we saw chancres lazing about there,
foaming at the mouth, with pincers raised,
spraying the lady crabs,
the spider crabs and crayfish with their slobber.

However, Neptune's lovelies,
being rather particular, as I understand,
despite numb fingers, making a fortune
under the Graie – and that's a fact – were freezing to death;
and the finest market in the kingdom,
thanks to their delicate toes,
in the buffets of the south-easterlies, and at Gallet Heaume,
was provided for them by the States.

I think a decent scarlet cloak
would have saved a lot of expense;
For J'nouillon (God rest her)
wrapped herself up in an old pair of trousers;
and if it wasn't that the world is going to wrack and ruin,
would we see the wrasse, in St Peter Port,
making of our fine marble tables –
the little bleeder – his deathbed?

The extreme tidal range around the Islands leaves large areas of intertidal zone uncovered. And like the tides around Mont Saint Michel, they come in quickly – but not quite as legend has it, at the speed of a galloping horse. The unwary, and the unsober, can be caught, and these occurrences have provided themes for Island writers. Few characters manage such cynical calculation as Bram Bilo's good-for-nothing son, Laiësse, as shown in this extract by.

Philippe Le Sueur Mourant ('Bram Bilo', 'Piteur Pain', etc)

From Chu Pouore Laiësse, 1899 (Jèrriais)

Pépée et mémmée n'buogent pon d'lus Havre-des-Pas. Y s'font viers, nos pathents, et l'âge et les infirmitées l'z'empêchent dé v'né nos vaie trop souvent. Ch'n'est pon qui m'gênent, bén au contraithe, mais enfin, a lus âge, nou n'dé pon t'né à la terre, et, coumme j'lus dit toutes les faies qué j'les vé, jé s'sai eunne grande délivrance pour yeux d'être tchitte de toutes les minsèthe et infiermitées de chutte vie aussi vite que possib' ... et mé, j'n'éthais pon d'autre a lus payi d'fermage.

Pépée va quasi toutes les mathées basiotté parmi les rotchiers dé par là ... J'ai oui dithe qu'la mathée est traitre, des fais, et qu'a bon d'vielles gens coumme pépée ont tai happés par les cuothants tchi tcheuthent autouôre des rotchiers ... J'dit tréjous a pépée dé n'mantchi pon d'nos envié des bennis souvent, et qu'les miyeurs sont tréjous au pus bas d'l'ieau.

Laïësse Bilo

From Poor Elias, *1899*

Dad and mum don't stir from where they are at Havre des Pas. Our parents are getting on a bit, and age and infirmity prevent them from coming to see us too often. It's not that I'm fed up with them, far from it, but, you know, at their age one shouldn't be clinging on to this world, and, as I tell them every time I see them, it'll be a great deliverance for them to be rid of all the miseries and infirmities of this life as quickly as possible ... and then I won't have to pay them farm rent any longer.

Dad goes low-water fishing on practically every tide down there ... I've heard say that the tide is sometime treacherous, and that a lot of old folks like Dad have been caught by the current which race round the rocks ... I always tell Dad not to forget to sent us limpets often, and that the best ones are always right down at the low-water mark.

Elias Billot

Earth and Hearth

The production of wool and the export of knitted products made the Islands prosperous, and contributed the names of guernseys and jerseys to the vocabulary of clothing. The raising of sheep and the tending of apple orchards yielded in importance, as the centuries passed, to the dairy industry, to greenhouses and tomatoes, to potatoes, and to flowers for export – changing the agricultural landscape and the rhythms of rural life. These varied rhythms also sounded in the literature that described the work of the fields and the work of the home.

For many years, cider was a mainstay of agriculture in the Islands, both for domestic consumption and export. Cider exports from Jersey declined from the 1840s, perhaps due to a rise in the popularity of beer in destination markets, and had dwindled away by the late 1870s. Culturally, the production of cider for domestic consumption remained important and today's small-scale production remains a focus for poetry and traditional song. Métivier's poem has also been adapted to be sung in mainland Norman.

George Métivier ('Un Câtelain')
La Chànsaön du Prînseux, *1831* (Guernesiais)

> À l'hounneu du meïs d'octaöbre
> Not' Jâmes qu'est bragi coumm' aen sac
> Hurle en puchànt dans l'entrebac:
> – Malheur ès ouvrièrs saöbres!
> – Allaöns, teïs ta goule et beïs
> Vive la cuve et vive l'émet!
>
> Leï lé cidre qui pure dans l'auge
> L'affaire craque et m'est avis,

Mes bouans vièrs garçaöns tch'est qu'a dit:
Qu'nou s'abreuve ou qu'nou s'en auge
– Allaöns, teïs ta goule et beïs
Vive la cuve et vive l'émet!

J'avaöns trop sué à la barre
Pour nos s'enfie à maïntchi plloïns
– Tch'est qu'enne bârrique pus ou moïns?
S'fait vièl haömme dé La Poumare:
– Allaöns, teïs ta goule et beïs
Vive la cuve et vive l'émet!

Qu'nou veït sortir les fllamèques
D'nos ièrs coumme des syins d'aen nièr cat:
Ocouo aen p'tit fortificat
À la sàntaï dé toute la pèque!
– Allaöns, teïs ta goule et beïs
Vive la cuve et vive l'émet!

Et si tchique vielle émittaïe rouàne
Et dit qu' j'en avaöns iaou traöp,
Ou s'lève sa tchuillère à pot;
J'lli diraöns:– v'là ta totaïe!
– Allaöns, teïs ta goule et beïs
Vive la cuve et vive l'émet!

Chànsaön faite dé par mé,
Aen loyal sujet du rouai
Qu'oïme à vaie la faönd d'la jutte
Et qui beit coumme enne alputre:
– Allaöns, teïs ta goule et beïs
Vive la cuve et vive l'émet!

The song of the cider press, *1831*

In honour of the first cider of the season,
our James who's as drunk as a sack
yells whilst drawing from the underback:
"Down with sober workers!
Well now, shut up and drink:
Long live the vat and long live the cider press!"

I can hear the cider flowing into the trough.
It's all creaking and speaking, and what I think is this:
Well my old mates, what's it saying?
"Either drink up or leave.
Well now, shut up and drink:
Long live the vat and long live the cider press!"

We have sweated too much working the bar
to leave off in a hurry and half cut.
"What's a barrel more or less?"
says the old man from La Pomare:
"Well now, shut up and drink:
Long live the vat and long live the cider press!"

Even if they see sparks coming out
of our eyes like a black cat's:
"How about one for the road
to the health of all those present?
Well now, shut up and drink:
Long live the vat and long live the cider press!"

And if some old bag of a killjoy grumbles
and says that we have had too much,
or if she brandishes her ladle;
we'll say to her: "Have one on us!
Well now, shut up and drink:
Long live the vat and long live the cider press!"

A song written by me,
a loyal subject of the king,
that loves to see the bottom of his tankard
and drinks like a sea loach.
Well now, shut up and drink:
Long live the vat and long live the cider press!

The champagne-swilling English evoked in this poem are the stereotypical well-off
retired English settlers who, attracted by low taxes and a low cost of living, flooded
into Jersey in the decades after the end of the Napoleonic wars. Besides his other
activities, Augustus Asplet Le Gros became secretary of the Royal Jersey
Agricultural and Horticultural Society in 1865.

Augustus Asplet Le Gros ('A.A.L.G.')

Lé cidre, *c.1874* (Jèrriais)

Le cidre est buon, emplle ta canne;
J'aime en aveir à tuos mes r'pas;
Si j'n'en ai pon, dévrai, j'enhanne;
D'itè breuvage i n'y-en a pas.
Qu'i' gardent leux bière en Allemagne,
Et leux *whisky* les Irlandais;
Je laisse es Anglleis leux champagne:
Le cidre est pour les vièrs Jerriais.

Baille m'en un lermin dans men mogue;
Chu cidre ichin a du piquèt;
Je n'veurs pon chein qui n'est que drogue;
Je veurs qu'il ait un p'tit d'surèt.
Et même j'l'aime sus sa llie:
Si n'y-a pon d'sur avec le doux,
Qu'est donc que ch'est que notre vie:
Un miot d'aîgrin est buon pour tous.

Du cidre coeuru dans sen verre,
Du buon pain d'bllè sus sen râclli,
Un' vaque-à-laît, deux-treis camps d'terre,
Du fein tout pllein dans sen solii,
Du jambon et du lard en paine:
Ne v'lo d'quei faire un houme heureux.
Maugrè le travas qui l'enchaîne,
La vie est duoche au labuoreux.

Cider, *c.1874*

Cider is good, fill your can;
I like to have it with all my meals;
I really suffer if I don't have it,
there's no drink like it.
Let them keep their beer in Germany,
and the Irish, their whiskey;
I leave to the English their champagne:
Cider is for old Jerseymen.

Give me a drop in my mug.
This cider is sharp;

I don't want any that is low quality;
I want it to have a bit of a sharp taste.
And I even like it cloudy with the dregs:
If there wasn't any sharp with the sweet,
what would our life be like?
A bit of sharpness is good for everyone.

Strong cider in its glass,
good bread on its rack,
a dairy cow, a couple of fields of land,
hay filling the loft,
ham and bacon flitch,
that's something to make a man happy.
Despite the work that chains him,
life is sweet for the labourer.

By the time E. J. Luce wrote this poem in Jèrriais, potatoes and tomatoes had displaced the orchards and the cider industry was well into its decline.

E. J. Luce ('Elie')
La mort de la Reine La Poumme, *1914* (Jèrriais)

Du pays qu'est noummê Gardin
La Poumme aut'fais était la Reine.
Belle, innocente, et bouanne, enfin,
Mais l'jaloux Fèrmi fut prins d'haine!

Dans chu temps là, Fèrmi s'disait
D'la Terre être un Propriêtaithe!
Tout ch'qu'était bon, tout ch'qui r'lîsait,
Lis servait, – souvent pour mal faithe!

La Poumme, erlîsant tout l'êtè,
Dev'nait d'pus en pus grosse et tendre;
Mais s'n innocence et sa bieautè
N'pouvaient pas du Fèrmi la d'fendre.

L'solei' brûlant, en sitchant l'fain,
Faisait rouogi san bieau visage,
Mais sus san trône ou s'pliaîsait bein;
Et n'pensait pon à s'mettre en viage.

Au S'tembre, un jour, le Fèrmi vint
L'assonmmer à grands coups d'ravaulle
Le peûle! I' l'agni souos ses grins
En riant ét hautchissant l's'êpaules!

Sus la terre ou' resti longtemps,
L'Vêpre ét la Grive, et la Limache
Se ruant sus l'yi, vivant d'san sang,
Et lis dêfidguthant la fache.

Un bathi lis servi pus tard
De coffre! Et, sans cérémonie,
Oprès qu'oulle eut passè l'Hôgard
La Reine était bétôt finie.

Nou l'enterri la tête en bas!
Sa tombe était bein fraidde et duthe,
Etraite et ronde et mucre... Hélas!
Et jamais n'y craissait d'verduthe!

Mais l'Fèrmi n'tait pas satisfait
Sa haine allait pus lliain qu'la vie.
Et souos sa meule, affreux forfait!
La Poumme eut sa chair êgliammie...

I' voulit même occouo' la nier.
D'peux qu'ou se s'rait rêssuscitèe; –
Et, sus l'cadâvre, i' fut envier
De l'iuau d'la pompe à grand' bouq'têes.

Avec sa pelle, un p'tit pus tard,
Nou l'vit puchi le corps sans forme;
Nou l'vit l'êtreindre en un vrai mar'
Souos un êtau qu'était ênorme!

Dans un grand tchuai, le sang d'goutti,
I' l'transvâsi dans sa barrique –
I' l'bouoll'yi raidde – et pis l'gouôtti
Et dit que ch'tait d'tchi magnifique!

I' l'bait ach'teuthe à tout instant
Pour satisfaithe occouo sa haine;

Et convie, à longs jours, les gens
A baithe ov li le sang d'la Reine!

The Death of the Apple Queen, *1914*

The Apple was once the Queen
of the country called Garden.
Beautiful, innocent and good as she was,
the jealous Farmer was overcome with hate!

At that time the Farmer presumed
to be Owner of the Earth!
All that was good, all that shone,
was used by him – often to evil purpose!

The Apple, shining all summer long,
became plumper and plumper and more and more tender;
but her innocence and her beauty
could not defend her from the Farmer.

The burning sun, as it dried the hay,
made her lovely face blush,
but on her throne she was quite content;
and had no thought of setting off on a journey.

One day in Autumn, the Farmer came
to strike her down with great blows of his harvesting pole.
The wretch! He pulled her towards him with his claws
laughing and shrugging his shoulders!

She lay on the ground for a long time,
the Wasp and the Thrush and the Slug
rushed upon her, living off her blood,
and scarring her face.

A barrel was later used for
her coffin! and unceremoniously
having passed the stackyard
the Queen was soon finished.

She was buried head down!
Her tomb was very cold and hard,

narrow and round and damp... alas!
And no greenery grew there at all!

But the Farmer was not satisfied;
his hatred pursued her after death.
And under the wheel of the apple-crusher, alas!
the Apple had her flesh crushed.

He even wanted to drown her,
fearing that she would be ressuscitated;
and he had poured over her corpse
great bucketfuls of water from the pump.

With his shovel, a little later,
her formless body was seen being scooped up,
and spread out in a layer of pulp
under an enormous vice!

Into a large vat, the blood dripped out,
he transferred it into his vat –
he fermented it strongly – and then tasted it
and said that it was excellent!

He drinks it now all the time
still to satisfy his hatred;
and invites at length, people
to drink with him the blood of the Queen!

Tam Lenfestey's butter-churning poem has gained the status almost of a Guernsey folksong and can be found in different versions.

Tam Lenfestey

La Chansaon de la Ribotresse, *1871* (Guernesiais)

Les berbillettes, l'asphodel,
Les flleurs dé treflle, pimpernelles,
Toutes les flleurs de nos courtis,
Que no vacquottes ont bian mangis.

Ecoutair tous ma belle chanson,
Et ribottons – ton – ton – ton – ton.

En ribottant j'airons du burre,
En ribottant j'vous compte ma lure,
Le ciel est bllu, et tout le jaeur,
J'airon d'la brise des contes d'amour.

Les berbillettes sont sus les fries,
Les pacrolles sont sous nos pids,
J'airon du burre, jaune coum' de l'or,
Et d'biau argent, du tout pus fort.

Le burre sé fait, j'airon du burre,
Le ribot marche, et j'fais ma lure,
D'moin à la ville Marion ira,
Lé vier cheva l'y portera.

Milk-Maid's Song, *1871*

Daisies, asphodels,
clover flowers, scarlet pimpernels,
all the flowers of our fields,
that our cows have eaten.

Listen everyone to my beautiful song,
and let's churn.

By churning, we'll make butter.
Whilst churning I'll tell my tale.
The sky is blue, and all day long
we'll have in the breeze tales of love.

The daisies are in the meadows,
the primroses are under our feet,
we'll have butter, yellow as gold,
and best of all fine silver too.

The butter is forming, we'll have butter,
the churn is on the go, and I tell my tale.
Tomorrow to town, Marion will go,
and the old horse will carry her.

Prince Peter Kropotkin, the Russian anarchist theorist, visited the Channel Islands on at least three occasions – 1890, 1896 and 1903. He was impressed by the productivity and self-suffiency of agriculture in the Islands – and saw them as an eventual model for the self-governing communes of workers that could replace the exploitation of the state and the ruling economic class.

Peter Kropotkin

From Fields, Factories and Workshops, *1912*

Another illustration of this sort may be taken from the Channel Islands, whose inhabitants have happily not known the blessings of Roman law and landlordism, as they still live under the common law of Normandy. The small island of Jersey, eight miles long and less than six miles wide, still remains a land of open-field culture; but, although it comprises only 28,707 acres, rocks included, it nourishes a population of about two inhabitants to each acre, or 1,300 inhabitants to the square mile, and there is not one writer on agriculture who, after having paid a visit to this island, did not praise the well-being of the Jersey peasants and the admirable results which they obtain in their small farms of from five to twenty acres – very often less than five acres – by means of a rational and intensive culture.

Most of my readers will probably be astonished to learn that the soil of Jersey, which consists of decomposed granite, with no organic matter in it, is not at all of astonishing fertility, and that its climate, though more sunny than the climate of these isles, offers many drawbacks on account of the small amount of sun-heat during the summer and of the cold winds in spring. But so it is in reality, and at the beginning of the nineteenth century the inhabitants of Jersey lived chiefly on imported food. The successes accomplished lately in Jersey are entirely due to the amount of labour which a dense population is putting in the land; to a system of land-tenure, land-transference and inheritance very different from those which prevail elsewhere; to freedom from State taxation; and to the fact that communal institutions have been maintained, down to quite a recent period, while a number of communal habits and customs of mutual support, derived therefrom, are alive to the present time. As to the fertility of the soil, it is made partly by the sea-weeds gathered free on the sea-coast, but chiefly by artificial manure fabricated at Blaydon-on-Tyne, out of all sorts of refuse – inclusive of bones shipped from Plevna and mummies of cats shipped from Egypt.

It is well known that for the last thirty years the Jersey peasants and farmers have been growing early potatoes on a great scale, and that in this line they have attained most satisfactory results. Their chief aim being to have the potatoes out as early as possible, when they fetch at the Jersey Weigh-Bridge as much as £17 and £20 the ton, the digging out of potatoes begins, in the best sheltered places, as early as the first days of May, or even at the end of April. Quite a system of potato-culture, beginning with the selection of tubers, the arrangements for making them germinate, the selection of properly sheltered and well situated plots of ground, the choice of proper manure, and ending with the box in which the potatoes germinate and which has so many other useful applications, – quite a system of culture has been worked out in the island for that purpose by the collective intelligence of the peasants.

In the last weeks of May and in June, when the export is at its height, quite a fleet, of steamers runs between the small island of Jersey and various ports of England and Scotland. Every day eight to ten steamers enter the harbour of St. Hélier, and in twenty-four hours they are loaded with potatoes and steer for London, Southampton, Liverpool, Newcastle, and Scotland.

The admirable condition of the meadows and the grazing land in the Channel Islands has often been described, and although the aggregate area which is given in Jersey to green crops, grasses under rotation, and permanent pasture – both for hay and grazing – is less than 11,000 acres, they keep in Jersey over 12,300 head of cattle and over 2,300 horses solely used for agriculture and breeding.

Moreover, about 100 bulls and 1,600 cows and heifers are exported every year, so that by this time, as was remarked in an American paper, there are more Jersey cows in America than in Jersey Island. Jersey milk and butter have a wide renown, as also the pears which are grown in the open air, but each of which is protected on the tree by a separate cap, and still more the fruit and vegetables which are grown in the hothouses. In a word, it will suffice to say that on the whole they obtain agricultural produce to the value of £50 to each acre of the aggregate surface of the island.

The demand for labour involved in agriculture in the Islands has attracted influxes of seasonal workers. In the nineteenth century and much of the twentieth, Breton and mainland Norman peasants provided much of the additional workforce required for planting and harvest. Later, English, Welsh and Irish workers responded to demand, and more recently Portuguese, Latvian and Polish people have contributed to the continuing cycle of agricultural labour. No doubt, the motivation for many of them was economic necessity rather than the cheerful devotion to work portrayed by George Métivier in this poem.

George Métivier

La Chànson du terrien, *1845* (Guernesiais)

> Une bêque, une hâche, une tille,
> Ùn serpé, ùn picouais,
> Faux émoulu, dard ou faucille,
> Ebllaîteux, fourque ou fllais!
> Et v'chìn la maïn d'ùn houme
> Qu'est tout pour le travas –
> Fort et dispos, jamais i n'choume,
> Mais touche à flleur de bras!

Pour d'sertaïr vos jagnières,
Néquaïr douït ou bara,
Quéruaïr l'frie ou fumaïr les terres,
I' s'offre à qui l'voudra!
Pour guerbaïr, au vrai terme,
Vot' bllaï, v'chìn ùn gaillard,
Ou pour bâtir, solide et ferme,
Ùn tas dàns vot' haûgard!

Quànd j'ai fait ma journâïe,
L'cabaret ne m'pllaît brìn;
J'aime à senti' l'fumet d'ma fouâie,
Et à couayer men ch'lìn;
A vée, auprès d'leux mère,
M's éfàns, l'tabouarìn pllaïn,
Dorâïe au bec, trottànt dàns l'aire,
Autouar de not' villiaïn!

Une bêque, une hâche, une tille,
Ùn serpé, ùn picouais,
Faux émoulu, dard ou faucille,
Eblliaîteux, fourque ou fllais!
L'bllaï qu'je l'batte, et qu'j'épile
L's ormes qu'en ont besoin!
Vot' frit qu'je l'gllane, et que je l'pille,
Car l'exercice est saïn!

Satisfait d'men salaire,
J'n'ai pour bien qu'daeux forts bras;
Ma sueur est m'houneur et ma glouaire,
Men pllaisir men travas!
Pour le profit d'la ferme,
Tôt l'vaï et couachi tard,
Me r'fûs'roûs d'pur cidre ma lerme,
Men p'tit ragoût d'gras d'lard?

The song of the farmer, *1845*

A spade, an axe, an adze,
a billhook, a pick-axe,
sharpened scythe, serrated sickle or sickle,
clod-smasher, fork or flail!
And here's the hand of a man

who's ready for work –
strong and capable, he never shirks,
but sets to it with all his strength!

To clear furzebrakes,
clean out brooks and drains,
plough pasture or manure land,
he offers himself to anyone who'll take him!
To bind wheatsheaves properly
he's the lad for you,
or to build, solid and strong,
a stack in your stackyard!

When my day's work is done,
I don't care for the pub at all;
I like to smell my fire,
and save my shilling;
to see, next to their mother,
my children, with full bellies,
and a mouthful of sandwich, trotting on the floor,
around our cresset stand.

A spade, an axe, an adze,
a billhook, a pick-axe,
sharpened scythe, serrated sickle or sickle,
clod-smasher, fork or flail!
Let me thresh the wheat, and let me trim
the elms that need it!
Let me pick your fruit, and let me press it,
for exercise is healthy!

Satisfied with my wages,
all I've got to show is two strong arms;
my sweat is my honour and my glory,
my pleasure is my work!
For the profit of the farm,
getting up early and going to bed late,
would you refuse me my drop of good cider,
and my little stew of fatty pork?

To prepare the ground for deep cultivation for root crops, a particularly deep plough was traditionally used in the Islands. This plough and the associated social customs are called *la Grànd Tchérue*, in Guernesiais, and, in Jèrriais, *la Grande Tchéthue*. In Jersey English, it is referred to as the Big Plough, while in Guernsey it is the Deep Plough. The plough itself, by whatever name it went, was pulled by eight, ten or even sixteen horses or oxen, accompanied by a team of diggers. The resources and manpower required meant that whole neighbourhoods turned out to help each other in turn during the ploughing season. The host farm ensured that the Big Plough was a social occasion, with a supper and entertainment at the end of the long strenuous day. There would be music and dancing, along with the inevitable flirtation. Nico Guilbert's description of the Deep Plough in Guernsey makes one wonder what today's health and safety régime might have made of such working practices.

Nicholas Guilbert

Les Grànd's-Quérues, *1856* (Guernesiais)

> Vlo la saison, vlo l'temps des Grànd's-Quérues;
> Partout i' jouent: quànd nou-s est l'long des rues,
> Nou n'ot q'des "jaue," des "l'avànt," des jourgnieux,
> Leux bêque en l'air, qui font lànchiér des beux.
> Le câgnon crie, l'frie s'enfeut, la raie s'cànte,
> Tout va si bien q'l'elet en suffle et chànte,
> Et q'la lav'resse, en l'vànt la coue en l'air,
> Sautique et joue l'long d'la raie d'un pid l'gier.
> "Mais faut se r'prendre, et vée ès crocs, ès bougues,
> "Saquer du faêu, et caressaïr les djougues;
> "L'monde en un jour ne fut pas tout bâti,"
> S'font les quérueux, en se r'derchànt un p'tit.
> Les v'lo brâment tous assis sus la haie,
> Un des bouans viers, les pids sus l'bord d'la raie,
> R'corde à la guéne une égullie de d'vis,
> Les charmànt tous d'ses pllans et d'ses avis.
> Sti: "Un gosier trop r'squi n'y a rien pière;
> "Si en quéruànt l'terrien oubllie à bère
> "Un gorgeon d'cidre, et un p'tit dram parfais,
> "L'terraïn n'produit q'bien faillies panais!"
> Les r'velo d'but, fiers comme de p'tits prophètes,
> La quérue r'va, les bêqueux n'font q'des jouettes,
> L'vànt des bêquies coum d's étoupons à fouor,
> En fouànt ès buts tànt qu'la quérue fait l'touor.
> Ll'y'a mu, ll'y'a bu; mais faut que l'jour s'en passe;

V'la Jean caudin, mais Aberhan l'surpasse;
Chun'na n'fait rien, ils ont l'travas à cœur,
I' font leur coins acouore à leux honneur...
"Mais vlo l'draïn touor, i' faut tous s'entre entendre,
"Et s'érousaïr devànt que d'l'entreprendre,
"Pour affermir l'pouagnet sus les panchons,
"Et gràïe l'fossaï jus'qu'ès colimâchons!"
V'la un garçon fort ouaidre ès vertesvelles,
Treis l'giers cacheux, un dur t'neux qu'en faites belles,
Gouvernànt l'soc jusque parmi l's orviaux,
Griànt l'fossaï tout long jusq'ès corbiaux.
Tout s'est passaï dans les sou'aits, et, mordingue!
N'y'en a pas iun qui lovie ni bordìngue!
Tous sont déguiaïs et drets coum des piquets,
En dejoigniànt, et fouànt coins et rûquets.
A la maison nos jolies ménagières,
Coum leux quérueux, d'màndaïz-mé s'i sont fières!
Au chànt des crax i sont l'vâïes au matin,
R'brachies au coûte à épliuquér l'raisin,
Graissier les pllats, preparaïr la grànd' tabllle;
Et d'màndaïz-mé s'leux t'nue est agriabllle
En cruquiànt l's'eux, haguiànt l'si, caufânt l'fouor,
Parbouillânt l'riss, écurânt tout atouar,
Les pllats d'étaim et la grànd jute à cidre,
Et pôquiànt l'faeû sous l'jambon qu'est à bouidre?
A leux honneur, dame! i' font leux dévouer!
Mais ch'n'est rien d'jeur, enprès chu q'ch'est au ser,
Quànd des quérueux la respectabllle armaïe
Autouar d'la tabllle est joyaeusement formâïe,
A jouaïr du coute et exerçaïr leux dents;
Et à s'rondir l'tabouarin, coum j'entends,
D'beu et d'jambon où l'graivi en purotte,
D'tendre légume et d'superbe houichepotte.
Ah! ch'est là l'temps q'not biau sexe a l'pid l'gier,
Les bras alliànts, le'ziers fins, le r'gard fier;
Dame! i' sont gaies! ils ont d'l'air, i' sont drètes;
L'bouan frocq à pique à haut, les corles faites,
L'd'vànté ferraï, et la couêffe à riban,
I' charmeraient prélat, pape ou sultan!
Jusqu'à migniét (s'i'n'tait mort) l'roué des sages,
S'frait un hounneur de m'suraïr leux corsages,
Assis d'vànt l'faeû, l'verre en main, au ras d'aeux,
A toubaquér un p'tit fumet ou daeux.

Heuraeux l'terrien qu'en possède une itaille,
Cis li sus l'dun, sus l'âtre ou sus la fouaille!
Qu'i' n'oubllie pas, tout en la caressànt,
D'en avé l'cœur à Gu bien r'counissànt!

The Deep Ploughs, *1856*

Here comes the season, here comes the time of the Big Ploughs
they are in action everywhere, when you're going down the road,
all you hear is day labourers saying "giddy-up" and "walk on"
 with their spades aloft, making bullocks press on.
The screw-plate creaks, the turf is turned, the furrows lie straight,
everything is going so well that the axle whistles and sings;
and the wagtail, lifting her tail in the air,
skips and plays with nimble feet along the furrow.
"But we must rest a little now, and see to the hooks and yoke-bows,
"light up, and embrace the jug;
The world was not built in a day:"
say the ploughmen, as they straighten up a bit.
There they are all sitting right along the plough beam,
one old fellow, his feet on the edge of the furrow,
spins to the gang a measure of chat,
delighting them with his plans and opinions.
Says he: "There's nothing worse than a throat too dry,
if while ploughing the farmer should forget to drink
a swig of cider and a wee dram from time to time,
the land will only produce very poor parsnips!"
Then up they get, pleased as punch,
the plough is on its way again, the diggers seem to be merely playing,
lifting spadefuls like oven-stoppers,
In digging up the furrows' ends while the plough turns.
There's tip-top work and tipsy work, but that's how the day goes;–
John's getting merry, but Abraham outdoes him,
but still, they do their work with care,
and dig their corners in a way that does them credit.
"But here's the final round, let's understand each other,
"and have a drink before we start on it;
"to strengthen the wrists upon the plough handles
"and clear the hedgerow right up to the snails!"
there's a strong sulky lad on the plough hinges;
Three active drivers, as tough a ploughman as you might want to meet,
steering the sock right among the slow-worms
clearing along the hedgerow up to the rooks

everything's gone to plan, and blimey,
not one of them drifts off course or lurches,
But all are dedicated, and straight as a die,
When they unharness, and finish digging corners and perimeter furrow!
Our pretty housewives are at home,
and like their ploughmen, how cheerful they are!
They were up this morning to the song of the stonechat,
with sleeves turned up to their elbows, picking out raisins,
greasing the dishes and preparing the big table;
and isn't their manner delightful!
Cracking eggs, chopping suet, heating the oven,
parboiling the rice, polishing
the pewter plates and big cider jug,
and stoking the fire under the boiling ham!
They really are to be admired for the way they carry out their duties!
But the daytime's nothing, compared with what the evening's like,
when that respectable army of ploughmen,
are joyfully seated around the table,
elbows jostling and teeth in action;
and rounding out their bellies, so I hear,
with beef and ham simply dripping gravy,
with vegetables cooked just right and wonderful puddings!
Ah, this is the time when the fairer sex are nimble on their feet,
with active arms, sparkling eyes, a happy air!
My goodness, how merry they are! they have a way about them, they are
                                        turned out nicely
in smart, peak-waisted dresses, with curls in place,
their aprons ironed, caps trimmed up with ribbons,
they'd charm a bishop, a pope or a sultan!
If he wasn't dead, the king of wise men – up until midnight –,
would have considered it an honour to have put his arm round their waists,
sitting in front of the fire, with a glass in his hand, right beside them,
and smoking a little puff or two.
Happy is the labourer who has such a woman,
at home in bed, beside the hearth or on the green bed.
But he must never forget, even as he embraces her,
To give heartfelt thanks to God!

Nicholas Bott was born in Alderney in 1797, but lived much of his life in Jersey, and is the only self-professed poet of Auregnais that we know of – although he wrote in Guernesiais and Jèrriais, sometimes somewhat Gallicised, as well. The tradition of vraicking – collecting seaweed and using it as fertiliser – is still practised on a small scale, but not to the extent that used to be the case. The vraicking season was regulated by law and custom, and the languages reflected the importance of vraic to the economy in the terminology of seaweed, tools and action. This poem in Jèrriais avoids the technicalities and presents a jollier picture of vraicking than would often be experienced, waist-deep in cold seawater, pitching heavy forkfuls of dripping seaweed into carts among the rocks. Simple fruit buns, called *des galettes à vrai* – 'vraic buns' – would be baked to take out to eat at work.

Nicholas Bott

Chanson la pèche du vraic et pendant la grande Charue, *1868* (Jèrriais)

Fermiers v'chin la saison
Qui faut tous préparer
Nos quesriots pour aller pésqui l'vraic
Ramase chaque faucillion
Et la meule vient tourner
Pour ben ésmoudre et qui n reste pon d'brec

Le vraic, le vraic pour engraissi la terre
Pour nous fermiers est l'article prémiere
Au clios y donne la verdure
Et aux bestiaux la pâture
Vive le tems quand nou va pésqui l'vraic

Tandis que j'préparon
Quesriot fourque et faucille
Nos femmes trimousse à faire de la gallette
Manon, Goton, Fanchon
Tréjous gaies et docille
De lus fort bras ont r'troussai la manchette

Le vraic, le vraic pour engraissi la terre
Pour nous fermiers est l'article prémiere
Au clios y donne la verdure
Et aux bestiaux la pâture
Vive le tems quand nou va pésqui l'vraic

La bouanne femme caufe le fou
Tandis que les hardelles
Pétrisse la pâte en forme rondelette
Elles en ont jus-qu-au coude

A qui fras les pus belles
Et v'la une bouanne provision de gallette

Le vraic, le vraic pour engraissi la terre
Pour nous fermiers est l'article prémiere
Au clios y donne la verdure
Et aux bestiaux la pâture
Vive le tems quand nou va pésqui l'vraic

Y faut nous décider
Y-ronge à la Sansbue
Coper le vraic aux roquiés d'Saint Clement
Ou ben j'pourrions aller
S'ou creyies que j'fron mue
A la Pulente dans la bayé de Saint Ouen

Le vraic, le vraic pour engraissi la terre
Pour nous fermiers est l'article prémiere
Au clios y donne la verdure
Et aux bestiaux la pâture
Vive le tems quand nou va pésqui l'vraic

Comme ch'est le mois de mars
Et la pus grande maraies
Si je prennions du côtai d'Saint Clement
Mais dam mes Effants gars
Si ch'est dans l'eslavaies
Car le passage est dangereux souvent

Le vraic, le vraic pour engraissi la terre
Pour nous fermiers est l'article prémiere
Au clios y donne la verdure
Et aux bestiaux la pâture
Vive le tems quand nou va pésqui l'vraic

Nous v'la bien àrivaies
Et du vraic à foison
Garçons et filles copais à touors de bras
J'faison une bouanne maraies
Et le quesriot j'cherjon
La cherge est lourde mais y ne rompra pas

Le vraic, le vraic pour engraissi la terre
Pour nous fermiers est l'article prémiere
Au clios y donne la verdure
Et aux bestiaux la pâture
Vive le tems quand nou va pésqui l'vraic

Effants dépèschons nous
Car v'la la mé qui r'monte
Filles fillais l'avant pour n'etre pas trop mouollie
Ecoutez comme les roues
Sous le poids du vraic gronde
Mais j'passons les brachets sans exposer not vie

Le vraic, le vraic pour engraissi la terre
Pour nous fermiers est l'article prémiere
Au clios y donne la verdure
Et aux bestiaux la pâture
Vive le tems quand nou va pésqui l'vraic

Nos v'la touos remontais
Sains et sauf en terre ferme
Allons Effants mangeons une becquie
Une dram si vous voulais
Et pie cache pour la ferme
Ove de bouans j-eh-vaux la quesriere est aisie

Le vraic, le vraic pour engraissi la terre
Pour nous fermiers est l'article prémiere
Au clios y donne la verdure
Et aux bestiaux la pâture
Vive le tems quand nou va pésqui l'vraic

Une faiés de r'tou siéz sé
Chacun va se changi
Un bouan souper est prèts à la maison
Avec une franche gaiété
Et un bouan appeti
Après souper nou chante la bouanne chanson

Le vraic, le vraic pour engraissi la terre
Pour nous fermiers est l'article prémiere
Au clios y donne la verdure

Et aux bestiaux la pâture
Vive le tems quand nou va pésqui l'vraic

The Song of vraic gathering and the Big Plough, *1868*

Farmers, here's the season
for everyone to make ready
our carts to go gathering vraic.
Bring out every sickle
and get the whetstone turning
so as to grind out the last nicks.

Vraic, vraic to fertilise the earth
is the thing above all for us farmers.
It gives greenery to the fields
and pasture to the cattle.
Long live vraic-gathering time.

While we make ready
carts, forks and sickles,
our wives bustle about making buns.
Molly, Maggie and Fanny,
always cheerful and even-tempered
have rolled up their sleeves to get stuck in.

The housewife heats up the oven
while the girls
knead the dough into rounds.
They are giving it some elbow grease,
competing as to whose will be best,
and so we're well provided with buns.

We have to decide:
shall we go to La Sambue
and cut vraic among the rocks of Saint Clement,
or, if you think we'd do better,
we could go
to La Pulente in Saint Ouen's Bay.

As it's the month of March
and the largest tides,
what about going round Saint Clement?
But watch out, lads and lasses,

if it's in Les Êlavées
for the passage is often dangerous.

Here we are, we've arrived
and there's vraic a-plenty.
Boys and girls, cut in swathes.
We'll get a good tide's harvest
and we'll load up the cart.
The load is heavy, but it won't break.

Lads and lasses, let's hurry
for the tide is coming in.
Girls, get a move on so you don't get too wet.
Listen how the wheels
creak under the weight of the vraic,
but we get past Les Bratchets without risking our lives.

Here we are all back
safe and sound on dry land.
Lads and lasses, let's have a snack
and a nip of drink if you want
and then off for the farm.
With good horses, the cart-track is easy.

Once back home
everyone gets changed.
A good supper is ready in the house,
with open hearts
and a good appetite
after supper we sing the good old song.

The horses and carts have long since been replaced by tractors and trailers. The old ploughing customs have given way to machinery, but there are still some people around who remember the old farming ways. In 1999, Ted Syvret, now retired from farming in Saint Ouen, imagined how an old spade might recount its own experience of digging and planting techniques – along with the special words and expressions no longer heard in today's mechanised fields.

Ted Syvret

L'Histouaithe dé la bêque, *1999* (Jèrriais)

Au s'tembre l'année pâssée j'clièrgis eune p'tite carre ichîn dans iun d'nos clios – eune carre un mio à l'ombre sans grand solé éyou qu'eune brousse dé dgèrrue c'menchait a s'êtablyi. J'n'aime pon fort lé dgèrrue et, acouo, jé n'sis pas iun d'ches-là tchi n'veurt pon en vaie du tout car j'ai grand pliaîsi quand veint chutte saison-chîn dé dgetter la pâcienche d'un meîl'ye ou d'eune grive à bétchi, à plieine couôtuthe, à même les pourpres graines d'restées sus tchique touffe dé dgèrrue. Ch'est, sans doute, pour sé remplyi la fale et l'estonma d'vant la niet, tchiquefais quand tout l'tou d'ieux, tout est blianc et crêp'lé.

Bein seux, jé n'vis pon d'né au s'tembre; oui, eune vêpriéthe et tout pliein d'vêpres, et la p'tite carre avait gardé un aut' ségret pour mé – eune vielle bêque, toute rouie, dêmanchie et oubliée dans tchique pose, car ou n'tait pon usée assez pour l'env'yer horte. J'la tapis douochement un coupl'ye d'fais sus l'but d'ma botte et l'mio d'manche tchi restait finnit en sno par tèrre. S'oulle 'tait pour èrtravailli, la vielle bêque, i' lî faudrait un nouviau manche. J'trouvis un neu manche l'aut' sémaine quand j'fus acater eune pathe dé sécateurs, et ch'tait quand la vielle bêque et l'neu manche 'taient bein êtreints dans l'êtau siez nous – pour lus mettre les deux rivets pour garder bêque et manche ensembl'ye – qué j'c'menchis à m'înmaginner d's histouaithes qué la vielle bêque pouôrrait raconté au neu manche entouor san temps pâssé. Entouor san temps en côti châque année, au mais d'Dézembre, à foui rande auprès rande, pèrque auprès pèrque dé tèrrain, foui à chutte saison-là pour sé faithe seûse qu'la bouleûse es'sait bein et toute cottie d'vant la pliant'tie d'patates au mais d'Févri, et en même temps, qu'la fraîche tèrre bêtchie était eune bouonne trempeuse dé plyie d'vant Noué, si pôssibl'ye, auprès qu'la tèrre était s'tchi et blianchi un mio en la fouissant.

Pas foui à la franche bêque, chennechîn, mais à la manniéthe Jèrriaise éyou qu'la bouleuse 'tait plichie ou boulée dans l'fond d'la rande ouvèrte auve la bêque ou p't-être auve eune becque – d'vant s'mettre à foui, bêtchie par bêtchie 'la mie' – eune belle finne, propre tèrre au d'ssus d'la bouleuse dé moutarde ofûche, p'tit blianc navet p't-être, ou l'restant d'eune couoche dé vrai ramâssé et tchéthié dé d'ssus ieune dé nos grèves et êtendu au s'tembre comme graîsse.

Lé tou d'Noué et d'la Nouvelle Année, un moment pus trantchille, espéciale-ment si l'temps touônnait au mouoilli – comme au c'menchement dé ch't' année. Temps pour foui un gardîn ou tchique carre dé clios; p't-être plianter, en fouissant châque rande, lé restant des pliantes dé chours. Et pis, êtout, lé moment pour garder pour graine un coupl'ye dé douzaines dé navets, arrachis et chouaîsis en pliein clios et entèrrés d'nouvé dans la fraîche rande, auve les fielles pathées et copées quat' ou chînq pouces en d'ssus d'yi et laîssis monter en graine au r'nouvé. Et don, i' 'taient pendus à s'tchi au bieau solé d'vant qu'la graine fûsse sauvée pour èrs'mer et récolter pour lé bestchias pus tard duthant l'année.

Auprès lé preunmié jour dé l'an, dgia, châque jour comptait poudrer eune raie, dréchi un fôssé, foui eune carre ou deux, sans pâler dé touos les pitchages à foui et les dépitchages à rabilyi duthant la touônn'nie. Et pis i' n'fallait pon laîssi un p'tit flias souotre lé pitchage – bein aîsi à faithe – ou d'bosse au dépitchage, ou bein y'éthait d'la houongnie pus tard quand la tchéthue à plianter, lé préchain mais, n'piqu'thait pas bein ou l'talon n'èrportéthait pon d'l'aut' but ni n'tout.

Au mains, nou 'tait portés à chu moment-là, du pitchage au dépitchage, et au contraithe étout, tout du long d'la fouoyéthe, sus l'épaule au foueux; i' pouvait marchi des milles à chutte saison-chîn. As-tu ouï l'vièr diton 'mangi comme un foueux'? Tu'es trop janne Mess manche! I' lî fallait eune bouonne pathe dé bottes étout, au foueux, pas seulement à cause dé toute sa marchéthie, mais pour sé garder les pids cauds comme un mouosson et en tout cas tch'i' f'thait sèrvi san pid pour enfoncer la pouôrre bêque contre san d'si dans d'la tèrre un mio duthe, ou p't-être pour coper travèrs eune rachinne d'orme en appraichant d'un fôssé, – y'en avait acouo, d's ormes, dans ches temps-là. P't-être eune pièrre souos l'but d'la bêque ou du grupé sus l'fond, – tchi sait? Tchiquefais, ch'tait un mio pus séthieux, dgia, un but d'féthaille ou eune vielle patte dé griffon – pèrdue dans tchique temps. Acouo piéthe, un païsson et but d'chaîne d'un lian à vaque, oublié et d'resté dans un betchet d'cruéthe, et muchi parmi toute la crîngne.

"Hélas", s'fit-t-alle, la bêque, – (y'avait acouothe un mio d'mauvaîtchi dans lyi) – "si foueux né s'mêfier pas, i' pouvait rompre un manche dé bêque en rein d'temps." "Tu m'fais peux", rêponnit l'manche, tout peûtheux, comme j'c'menchis à dêvisser l'êtau pour examinner man travas. "Né t'gêne pon", s'èrfit la bêque, "la vie a changi tellement d'pis mes jannes jours – châque jour aniet est comme un jour dé vacance – tu pâsses à maîntchi d'tan temps pendu sus un cliou, à ch't heu!"

The Spade's story, 1999

In Autumn last year I cleared a small corner here in one of our fields – a bit of a shady corner that doesn't get much sun where an ivy thicket was starting to get established. I don't much like ivy but there again, I'm not one of those who can't bear to see it at all for I get great pleasure when this season comes, watching the patience of a blackbird or of a thrush pecking off, as fast as possible, all the purple seeds left on a clump of ivy. It must be to fill their stomach and belly before night-fall, when sometimes all around them, everything is white and icy.

Of course, I don't see snow in Autumn; yes, a wasps' nest and lots of wasps, and the small corner had kept another secret for me – an old spade, all rusty, with no handle and forgotten about some time back, for it wasn't worn enough to chuck out. I knocked it slowly a couple of times with my boot and the bit of handle that was left crumbled away on the ground. If she was ever to work again, that old spade, she'd need a new handle. I found a new handle the other week when I went to buy a pair of secateurs, and it was when the old spade and the new handle were nice and tight in the vice at home – to put the two rivets into them to keep the spade and handle together – that I began to imagine the stories that the old spade could tell the new handle about her past. About her time on the côtils every year in December, digging furrow after furrow, perch after perch of ground, digging at that season so as to make sure that the layer of green mulch would be well rotted down before the potato planting in February, and at the same time, that the freshly dug soil would get a good soaking of rain before Christmas, if possible, after the soil had dried and blanched a bit from being dug.

But that's not digging by turning each spadeful upside-down in the same hole, that's digging in the Jersey way where the green mulch was sliced off and placed in the bottom of the open furrow with the spade or perhaps with a mattock – before getting down to digging the soil underneath, fine, clean soil – and digging this soil spadeful by spadeful on top of the green mulch, maybe mustard, perhaps small white turnip, or the remains of a layer of vraic collected and carted from one of our beaches and spread out in autumn as fertiliser.

Around Christmas and New Year, a quieter time, especially if the weather turned wet – like at the start of this year. Time to dig a garden or the corner of some field or other; perhaps planting, digging each furrow, the rest of the cabbage plants. And then it was time, too, to keep for seed a couple of dozen turnips, pulled up and chosen out in the field and buried again in the fresh furrow, with leaves trimmed and cut back to four or five inches above and left to go to seed in the Spring. So then they were hung up to dry in the sunshine before the seed was saved to be resown and harvested for the livestock later in the year.

So after New Year's Day every day was busy opening a preliminary furrow, building up a bank, digging a corner or two, not to mention all the starts of furrows that needed a few spadefuls dug to help the plough and the ends of furrow that needed levelling out during the ploughing season. You you mustn't leave a little hollow after the start of the furrow – very easily done – or a hump at the end of the furrow, or else there'd be grumbling later on the following month when the planting plough didn't dig in well or the upright didn't pick up soil at the other end either.

At least then we'd be carried from start of furrow to end of furrow and back again, all along the headland, on the digger's shoulder; he could walk miles during the season. Have you heard the old saying "to eat like a digger"? You're too young, Mr Handle! He needed a good pair of boots too, did the digger, not only because of all the walking, but to keep his feet warm and snug and anyway so that he could use his foot to push the poor spade down against her will into fairly hard ground, or perhaps to cut through an elm root near a bank, – there were still elms around in those days. Perhaps a stone under the edge of the spade or stony ground beneath, – who knows? Sometimes, it was a bit more serious, with a piece of scrap iron or an old tooth of a harrow, lost some time back. Even worse, a peg and length of cattle tether chain, lost and lying about in a patch of pasture, and hidden among the long tangled grass.

"Oh dear, oh dear," said the spade (she still had a bit of mischief in her), "if the digger didn't watch out, he could break a spade handle just like that." "You're scaring me," replied the handle, very afraid, as I began to open the vice to examine my work. "Don't worry," said the spade, "life's changed so much since I was young – every day today is like a holiday – you spend half your time hung up on a nail now!"

The Jersey cow, a breed developed in Jersey following the banning of the import of cattle into Jersey in the 1780s, has become a symbol of the Island. The Guernsey cow is different, although both breeds descend from the Norman cow, which itself, so it has been posited, has inherited genes from the cattle brought with the Viking settlers in the earliest development of what became the Duchy of Normandy. The selective breeding for the improvement of bloodlines and milk yields in the nineteenth century entailed herd books, cattle shows and the judging of animals. Prize cattle could command high prices for export, and competition was fierce among farmers to win sales from buyers across the world. The cow's view of this intensive breeding might have been different. In this extract from a long poem published in 1913, E. J. Luce gives us a sensitive and sympathetic, if anthropomorphic, view of a cattle show from a Jersey cow's point of view. In the very end of the poem, the cow is sold to an American buyer, to be separated from her calf and shipped overseas, never to see Jersey or her calf again.

E. J. Luce ('Elie')
From La Compliainte d'une Vaque, *1913* (Jèrriais)

Cruautè et Injustice

Je n'fu' pas traite le ser de d'vant
L'exposition. – La nièt, j'fus mal à m'n'aise
Man lait sembliait p'ser d'pus en pus
L'piécho m'craissait en londgheur et en laize
Mes trans se mindrent à m'pitchi du,
I' grossissaient et dev'naient duèrs et raiddes
Je piétinais mais à tchi bon?
A man malaise, 'n'yavait qu'un seul èrmièdde –
Je l'savais bein et d'vant longtemps
Je n'pouvais pus y t'nin, je m'mins à braithe...
J'mé l'vi' d'pus bouanne heuthe que d'amor
Espéthant qu'maître ou valèt veindraient m'traithe
Sus l'matin, j'les vi' bein s'en v'nin
Avec couleux d'vanté canne et s'cabelle...
J'pensais qu'i' s'en v'naient m'soulagi
Mais j'oubliais qu'faut souffrir pour être belle
Les filles et femmes le savent ètou

Dans lus habits qui l's'empêchent d'aller vite,
Avec lus corps si raidde êtreint
Et lus pouorres pi'ds dans des bottes bein trop p'tites!
Et quand i' mettent ches grands chapieaux,
Aussi grands comme les roeux de tchique chiviéthe,
Et les font t'nin ov de long clious
I' daivent pus tard, j'sis seux, en être de pièthe!
Mé, qu'avais l'piécho piéthe que pliain,
Qui m'en trouvais déjà toute minzéthabl'ye,
Man tou' n'vint pas: j'plieuthais d'dêpièd
En viyant traithe toutes les autres dans l'êtabl'ye.
Je fu bringie et em'nèe d'hors
Nou m'fit marchi une terribl'ye distance;
Sus le qu'min mes chabos bûchaient;
Si je n'les perdit pon, ch'est qu'j'eu d'la chance!!
J'souffrais-t'i' sus chu trajèt-là...
J'trouvais qu'la route est bein autrement duthe
Que notr' valette et notr' grand prè,
Avec lus frais tapis de riche verduthe!
Ov sept autres bêtes nou m'fit marchi
Dans un grand' tou' endrait un fliotchèt d'monde
Tandis qu'des juges lus abusaient
A nos pinchi la couenne toutes les secondes!
I' voulaient vaie châtchun d'nos points,
Et s'asseuther d'la grosseu' d'notr' lumiéthe,
Saver si nos trans 'taient beins mins.
Et si j'avions d'bieaux quartchèrs de driéthe!
J'tais si lassèe oprès tout ch'là,
Que quand nou m'mins le prix pardessus toutes
Je n'y prins pon autchun pliaisi
J'pensais tout l'temps à mes deux milles de route!
Et m'en r'venant, ov le valèt,
Ma tête ornée d'ribans, je m'trouvais triste.
Le maître, li, 'tait au dîner
Et il avait pus d'vingt pliats sus sa liste!
Pour nous, hélas! le sort est du,
J'gangnons les prix, mais ch'est d'autres qu'en amendent
J'enhannons pour faithe profiter
Des gens qui tout d'un coup nos vendent!
Tout l'long du qu'min en m'en r'venant
Je m'trouvais bête et p'sante coumme une baleine
Toute êcallèe et tout d'travers
Je n'gabathais qu'avec la pus grand peine.

Man pouorre piécho, tout gros enfliê,
M'faisait souffrir d'véthitabl'yes tortuthes
Et goutte à goutte j'perdais man lait
Car nou n'peut pas s'mettre au d'sus d'la natuthe.
Quand j'fu' r'venue, enfin, siez nous,
J'tais certain'ment bein pus morte qu'vivante
Et j'n'avais pus le tchoeu d'penser
Au premié prix de tchi que j'tais gagnante!
Nou m'fliatti quand j'passi dans l'bèl
Et pis je r'fu' condite à ma vielle stalle,
Nou s'mins à m'traithe – et pas trop tôt –
Car à mié-morte, je m'rouolli sus ma pâlle.
Nou m'baillit d'ieau dans un boutchêt
Et nou m'fliantchi une brachie d'grain d'Espagne,
Ch'tait là tout chein qu'y'avait pour mai
Mais l'maître, ailleurs, avalait du champagne!
Viy'ous l'contraste entre nos deux,
N'tait-che pon à mé que v'naient les rêcompenses?
Mais l'maître, hélas, mé gobait tout.
Ah, si j'osais vos dithe tout chein qu'j'en pense!!

From The Lament of a Cow, *1913*

Cruelty and injustice

I wasn't milked the evening before
the show. During the night I was uncomfortable
My milk seemed to weigh heavier and heavier
My udder grew in length and width
my teats started to give me sharp pains,
they swelled up and became hard and stiff.
I stamped my feet but to what use?
For my discomfort there was only one cure –
I knew it well and before long
I could no longer stand it and I started to bray...
I got up earlier than usual
waiting for my master or the farmhand to come and milk me
in the morning, indeed I saw them come along
with strainer, milking can and stool...
I thought they were coming to relieve me
but I'd forgotten that one must suffer for the sake of beauty
Girls and women know that as well
in their clothes that prevent them from walking quickly,

with their corsets so tightly drawn in
and their poor feet in boots much too small!
And when they put on those large hats,
as big as the wheels of some wheelbarrow or other,
and fix them in place with long nails
they must, I'm sure, be much the worse for it later on!
As for me, who had overfilled udders,
who was already feeling utterly miserable,
my turn didn't come; I wept in frustration
seeing all the others being milked in the shed.
I was combed and brought outside
They made me walk a terribly long way;
my hooves were breaking on the road;
it's only by luck that I didn't lose them altogether!
How I suffered on that journey...
I found the road much harder
than our little valley and our large water-meadow,
with their fresh carpet of rich greenery!
With seven other cows they made me walk
in a big circle in front of a crowd of people
while judges had their fun
pinching our hides by the second!
They wanted to see each of our features,
checking out the size of our milk ducts,
finding out if our teats were well set,
and if we had beautiful hindquarters!
I was so worn out after all that
that when I was awarded top prize
I didn't take any pleasure in it.
I was thinking all the time of the two mile trip I'd have to make!
And returning home with the farmhand,
my head decorated with rosettes, I was saddened.
As for the master, he was out to dinner
and he had more than twenty dishes on the menu!
For us, alas, fate is hard,
we win prizes, but others benefit from it.
We suffer to make profits for those
who can sell us at a moment's notice!
All the way back home
I felt dull and heavy as a whale,
turned over and inside out,
I could only stagger with difficulty.
My poor udder, large and swollen,

made me suffer real torment
and drop by drop I lost my milk
for you can't hold out against nature.
When I had at last got back home
I was surely more dead than alive
and I could no longer think
of the first prize I'd won!
They patted me as I passed through the yard
and then I was led back to my old stall,
They started to milk me – and not before time –
for half-dead, I rolled on my straw.
They gave me water in a bucket
and threw me a measure of corn,
that was all there was for me
while my master was somewhere else drinking down champagne!
Can you see the contrast between the two of us,
wasn't it to me that the rewards were given?
But my master, alas, took everything away from me.
Ah, if only I dared tell you what I thought of him!

In contrast to Elie's sympathetic characterisation of a Jersey cow and her unsentimental owner, Marjorie Ozanne presents a whimsical picture of how a farmer can be far more deeply affectionate of his cow than of his sister-in-law. This piece won first prize for composition in the Guernsey Eisteddfod in 1928.

Marjorie Ozanne

La Vaque à Nico, *1928* (Guernesiais)

Nous a oui pâlaï d'la jument qu'aimait tent sen pouloin, qu'a l'mangit. Eh bien, Nico, men vié y'homme, était quâsi aussi mal autouor sa vielle vaque. Vraiment, il en créyait quâsi autent d'quai comme de mai. A l'avait nom Marto. "La vielle Marto" comme y l'applait terjous.

J'avaiment ënne ferme, ichain d'vënt et huit vaques, Marto en etënt yeune. Nico n'en créyait pas pu d'quai qu'chenâ, en prumier, mais j'm'en-vais vous dire comme qui qu'a devint ënne favorite.

Enne journâs, je r'chu ënne lettre de ma soeur Louise, me d'mëndënt si a pouvait v'ni passaï quiques semaines dauve nous. Nico n'pouvait pas la souffri, et en disènt la veritaï, al'tait ënne drôle de pie. Al'avait étaï en service à la même pièche pour trente ëns. Sen vier maître v'nait d'mouori, et y avait laissi dix shlîns la s'maine. Al'avait sauvî ën bouan lot, et était avâre comme tout. Comme a die su sa lettre, a pensait qu'a prendrait ën p'tit holidais, mais al'esperait qu'erait pas d'mauvais goûts d'vaques. "Bran donc," s'fit Nico, qu'ën j'l'y lu la lettre, "y faudra bien i'y dire qu'a peut v'ni. Ch'n'est pas qu'nous la veur, mais p'taitre qu'a nous laissra quique chose dans sens testament, s'nous la graisse bien." "Tais-té donc" j'l'y die. Mais pour dire la veritaï, j'n'étais pas trop ënquette d'lavé mé-même.

La s'maine env'nënt, la Louise se trouvit, dauve trais grëndes câses, et ënne valise, et y r'sembiait qu'a s'n'allait restaï dauve nous pour le restënt d'sa vie. Nico vit du temps. Mais, ën bouan jour il 'tait à fauchiai dans ën courtit, et les vaques étaient dans l'perchain. Bientôt, y vit ma soeur v'ni l'travers du courtit où les vaques étaient, et qu'ën a vint a passaï la vielle Marto (y n'a jaumais seux pourqui), a l'erachi sen paison, et prins la fouite souvantre de y'elle. "Et," s'fit Nico, en m' le racontënt enauprès, "allaient-y. J'n'erais jaumais creux qu'la Louise pouvait coure aussi vite. A t'nait ses cotiyons en d'sus d'ses genouâs, et ses talons n'avaient que d' l'y touchier le derrière d'la tête. Je riais tent, que je n'pouvais pas allaï y'aïguai. A voli par dessus l'perco, comme si l'vier nar la cachait." Auprès chena, la Louise entrit, s'enfut ahaut, paqui ses câses, et s'enfut, et jaumais n'la r'vaüe depie. "Bouanne debâte," s'fit Nico "et bouanne ville Marto," et il a terjous creux mirron d'la vaque depie.

Qu'ën j'vaimes trop viers pour gardaï la ferme, nous vendi le bétail, mais Nico gardit la vielle Marto, et ën courtit pour y'elle, et tous l's ëns y l'y faisait ën ptit tâs d'foin.

Eune journâs, qu'ën l'papier angiais vînt, j'lu ën ptit morcé qui m'fit piaisi. Y' avait quiqu'uns qui trouvaient que s'nous sounait d'la musique es vaques tandis qu'nous les tréyait, qui dauneraient pus d'lat, j'fut niaise assaï que d'le dire à Nico. "Eh bien bon," s'fit-y, mais j'n'y r'pensait pas. Le l'ondemain au ser, qu'ën s'vint lé temps pour traire la vaque, j'étais assise a ramendaï enne pâre de brais d'fûtoine, y s'trouvit dans la cuisaine. "Aû-tu, Judi," y m'die, "la p'tite organette, saune t'alle acore?" "J'pense que oui," j'l'y repounit, "pourqui?" "Eh bien," s'fit-y, paraissënt tout niais, "viendrais-tu la sounaï dans l'étable tandis que j'trait la vielle Marto?" Pour en dire la veritaï, j'avais rombiaï tout antouor le papier angiais, et vraiment j' pensais qu'il était troubiaï. "Tu saïs bien" dit Nico, "chu q'tu m'lu su l'papier hier." Je r'vint à y pensaï, et j'l'y die, "Mais absolument tu n'le crait pas?" "O bien, faut y'éprouvaï," y m'repounit. J'pensit, "faut l'humeuraï," et j'prins la p'tite organette, et Nico sa caune, et nous v'là allaï pour l'étable. En arrivënt, Nico s'assievit au cotaï d'la vielle Marto, et mit sa caune bas. J'mit l'organette su ën scabai, et qu'ën Nico cmanchi à traire, j'cmanchi à sounaï. J'affaire fut bien pour quique minutes, mais je n'saï pas si la musique irritit les nerfs de la vaque, ou si enne mouque la piquit pu dur que d'couteume, mais tout d'ën caü, j'ouis en terrible fiâs, et v'là Nico bas, et la caunâs d'lat tournâs. La vaque prins la fouite par l'us, capsënt l'organette en passënt, et m'évitënt par ën miraque. Nico se r'butit, jurënt comme ën eracheux de dents, dauve ën l'empain gros comme en oeuf su' l'derrière d'la tête, et s'mit à coure souvantre la vaque. L'rond et l'rond du courtit ils allaient, et su' la fin, y l'attrapit, et la r'amnit dans l'étable. Y suait comme ën beu, et rouâbiait. "Chais aussi mal comme qu'ën a cachit la Louise," j'l'y die, pensënt le mettre dans ënne bouanne humeur, "je n'crait pas qu'a l'aime la musique." "Ch'n'est pas chena," s'fit Nico, "chais la

mauniaire que t'as sounaï l'organette. Tu y'as fait peux." "Bon" j'l'y die, "la perchaine fais, tu la sounras té-même." mais, enfin, j'n'en oui jaumais d'autre rian.

Y'a quique temps, y vint ën homme à la maison, ën mauniaire de travleux pour
le wireless. Y voulait nous en vendre y'un, et éprouvit à toutes forches à nous faire
en acataï, "Vous seraï jusque caï sorte de temps qui s'enva faire" s'fit le poupain.
"Nous saï tout chena sëns l'wireless," dit Nico, "la vielle Marto, notre vaque est
ënne bouanne prophète. Qu'ën y s'en-va faire bal, a l'est aisie et tranquille, qu'ën
y'a ënne tormente en v'nënt, a joue, et qu'ën y s'enva tounaï a bré. Qui qu'nous
veurt de pus?" Sus chena, le piëns, s'butit, et die qui fallait qui s'enfusse. J'pense qui
pensit, "Le paure homme n'est pas bien d'la tête, vaudra aussi bien s'en allaï."
Qu'ën y fut partit, Nico die, acore ënne fais, "Bouanne debâte."

Qu'ën le rouai s'env'nait, Nico vint tout gênai, et pour des jours, y n'disait pas
grëns choses. Sus la fin, j'l'y d'mëndit qui qu'il avait. "Sh'nais pas rien, vraiment," y
m'die. Si j'te dit tu t'moqueras d'mai." "Pourtënt," j'l'y repounit, "je n's'y pas dans
l'habitude de faire de même." "Eh bien, pie que tu veur savai, chais comme chen-
chain. V'là le rouai qui s'envian, et je ouis qui s'envont l'y donnaï ënne vaque. Cré-
tu qui voudront l'y dounaï la vielle Marto?" "Nénain sëns doute," j'l'y die, "tu n'as
pas qu'faire de t'gênaï. Y n'ont chuaisi yenne. Il est su l'papier d'asaisai. Ecoute," et
j'l'y lut l'acconte. Y fut bien consolé, et chëngit de tout en tout.

Mais y vian ën temps qui faut perdre jusqu' les animaux que nous aimes, et ënne
journâs, la vielle Marto fut prainse malade, et biauque nous mëndit l'docteur, et
que Nico restit l'vaï niat et jour à la soigner, la paure bête mouorit. Nico fut terri-
blement adoulaï, et l'y fit ënne fosse grénde assaï pour enfoui la maison. Vraiment,
il érait aimaï à y piëntai des fieurs, mais y n'osait pas. La s'maine auprès, la Louise
mouorit étout, et nous laissit chainquënte billes qui fait, j'pense, qu'a nous par-
dounnit pour l'espié d'la vaque. J'gauniaimes jusqu'à Londres pour ën p'tit holidais, et v'là qu'aiguit à passaï la douleur qu'avait settlaï sus la maison, et sus nous
depie la mort d'la "vaque à Nico."

Nick's Cow, 1928

You'll have heard about the mare that loved her foal so much that she ate it. Well
Nick, my old man, was almost as bad with regard to his old cow. Really, he almost
thought as much of her as of me. Her name was Marto. "Old Marto" as he always
called her.

In the past we had a farm and eight cows, Marto was one of them. Nick didn't
think more than that, to begin with, but I'm going to tell you how she became his
favourite.

One day I received a letter from my sister Louise, asking me if she could come
and spend a few weeks with us. Nick couldn't stand her, and to tell the truth, she
was a strange bird. She had been in service at the same place for thirty years. Her
old boss had just died and had left her 10 shillings a week. She had saved a good
amount and was as tightfisted as anything. As she said in her letter, she thought that

she would take a little holiday, but hoped that there wouldn't be bad farmyard smells. "Well there's nothing for it," said Nick, when I read the letter to him. "You'll have to tell her that she can come. It's not that we want her, but maybe she'll leave us something in her will, if we butter her up nicely." "Now be quiet," I said to him. But to tell you the truth, I wasn't so keen on having her myself.

The following week, Louise arrived, with three big boxes, and a suitcase, and it looked like she was going to stay with us for the rest of her life. Nick bided his time. But, one fine day he was mowing in a field, and the cows were in the next. After a short while, he saw my sister coming through the field where the cows were, and when she came to pass by old Marto (he never knew why), she pulled up her tether's peg, and raced off after her. "And," said Nick as he told me about it afterwards, "didn't they go. I would never have believed that Louise could run so fast. She had her petticoats above her knees, and her heels were practically touching the back of her head. I laughed so much, that I couldn't go to help her. She flew over the bar across the entrance to the field as if the devil was chasing her." After that, Louise came in, went upstairs, packed her boxes, and off she went, and we never saw her again after that. "Good riddance," said Nick, "and good old Marto" and ever since he has always believed the cow to be amazing.

When we grew too old to keep the farm, we sold the animals, but Nick kept old Marto, and a field for her, and every year he made a small haystack for her.

One day when the English paper arrived, I read a short piece that amused me. There was someone who had discovered that if you played music to cows whilst milking them, they gave more milk. I was silly enough to tell Nick. "Well now," he said, but I thought no more of it. The following day in the evening, when it was time to milk the cow, I was sitting mending a pair of fustian trousers, he appeared in the kitchen "Oh Judi, my dear," he said to me, "the little organ, does it still work?" "I think so," I replied. "Why?" "Well," he said, looking sheepish, "would you come and play it in the stable whilst I milk old Marto?" To tell you the truth I had forgotten all about the English paper, and I really thought he'd gone loopy. "You know," said Nick. "What you read me out of the paper yesterday." It all came back to me and I said to him, "But you honestly don't believe it?" "Well, might as well try," he replied. I thought, "I have to humour him," and took the little organ, and Nick took his milking can, and off we go to the stable. On arriving, Nick sat down beside old Marto and put his can down. I placed the little organ on a stool, and when Nick began to milk, I began to play. All went well for a few minutes, but I don't know if the music got on the cow's nerves, or if a fly bit her harder than usual, but all of a sudden, I heard a terrible crash, and Nick was on the floor, and the canful of milk was knocked over. The cow fled off through the door, knocking over the little organ as she passed, missing me by some miracle. Nick stood up, swearing like a tooth puller, had a lump on the back of his head as big as an egg, and ran off after the cow. Round and round the field they went, in the end he caught her and brought her back to the stable. He was sweating like an ox, and was grumbling. "It's as bad as when she chased Louise," I said to him, thinking that this would put him in a better mood. "I don't think that she likes music." "It's not that," said Nick, "it's the way that you played the little organ. You frightened her." "Well," I said, "the next time, you can play it yourself." But, however, I never heard any more about it.

Some time ago, a man came to the house, a sort of wireless salesman. He wanted to sell us one, and tried as hard as he could to make us buy one. "You'll even know what the weather will be like." said the fellow. "We know all that without the wireless." Nick said, "old Marto, our cow, is a good prophet, when it's going to be fine, she is calm and easy, when a storm is coming, she plays, and when there's thunder on the way, she moos. What more do we want?" With that, the guy stood up, and said that he needed to go. I think that he thought, "The old boy is not right in the head, best leave." When he had gone, Nick said once again, "Good riddance".

When the King was coming, Nick grew worried, and for days he didn't say much. In the end I asked him what was up. "It really isn't much," he said to me, "if I tell you, you'll laugh at me." "Why?" I replied, "I'm not in the habit of doing that." "Well since you want to know, it's like this. The King is coming, and I heard that they're going to give him a cow, do you think that they will want to give him old Marto?" "I doubt it," I said to him, "You needn't worry. They have chosen one and it is in this evening's paper. Listen." and I read the article to him. He was relieved and much the better for that.

But the time comes when we have to even bear the loss of animals that we love, and one day old Marto was taken ill, and despite calling the doctor, and Nick stayed up with her all night and all day caring for her, the poor animal died. Nick was terribly sad, and dug her a grave big enough to bury the house in. He would really have liked to plant some flowers, but didn't dare go so far. The following week, Louise died as well, and she left us fifty pounds, so I think she forgave us for the cow's exploit. We went all the way to London for a little holiday, and that helped relieve the sadness that had settled upon the house, and upon us, since the death of "Nick's Cow".

In 1880, a Jersey farmer, Hugh de la Haye, discovered that a curiously-shaped potato produced an especially tasty crop. The exports of what became known as Jersey Royal potatoes became a vital part of the Island's economy, just as tomatoes became typical of Guernsey agriculture. This poem cheerfully encapsulates the enthusiasm for the potato and the prosperity it brought. We do not know the identity of the author, hidden behind the pseudonym, but from the variety of language, the author was evidently from the east of the Island, and most probably from Saint Martin.

'Agricola' (identity unknown)

La Patate, *1889* (Jèrriais)

Oh! si en d'Guèrnezi i' font craître à gogo
La radich', le vèrjûs et la belle toumate,
Nous, en Jêrri, j'avons – à tize-larigo,
De tchi pûs nouôrissant, – ch'est la bouanne patate!
Fiche d'la radiche, du vêrjûs, d'la toumate;
Pour de mé, chein tchi m'faoût, ch'est ma chiéze patate!
Où-est qu'n'ou z-îzait, dit'-mé, pour trouvé rein d'pûs sain?
Mangîz-en, d'la patate, et bétôt la bédainne
Tout' ronde vos vaindra, ou' f'sèz vite du rain,
Du sang, d'la chai', des nér', – vot' bàrique s'sa plliainne.
Fiche d'la radiche, du vèrjûs, d'la toumate;
Pour de mé, chein tchi m'faoût, ch'est ma chiéze patate!

Voul-ous vos rigalé, et faize un bouân fricot?
Ov' le lar', ov' le boeu', la patate a sa pièche.
(Faoût chouaîzi, à l'av' nin, la ciènne à Mess Vigot:
N'ou n'sézait la bouoyi, en l'heuze oul' est en méche).
Ch'est dôn fiche d'radich', de vèrjûs et d'toumate;
Pour nous, chein tchi nos' faoût, ch'est la chiéze patate!

Chiéz' petite patate, ah! tch'est qu'n'ou f'sait sans té?
Bouoyie ou fricachî, tu t'grée à toute saoûce:
Dans la soupe ou l'grêvin, tu peux tréjous t'gouôté.
Si tu-es bein apprêtèe, tu n'sas janmais faoûsse.
Eh bein! fiche d'radich', de vèrjûs et d'toumate;
Pour de mé, chein tchi m'faoût, ch'est ma chiéze patate!

Ichin y-en a fouaîzon, de tout' les qualitès;
De chînquant' sortes d'noms – la piate et pîs la ronde.
Ch'est à l'Expôzicion qu'n'ou peut veis ses biaoûtès;
Ch'est là qué n'on l'admize – et v'chin le cri d'tout l'monde:
Fiche d'la radiche, du vérjûs, d'la toumate;
Pour nous, chein tchi nos faoût, ch'est la chiéze patate.

En Jêrri, d'pîs longtemps, ch'est l'or piain le d'vânté.
Es vendeur' de guênno, patate est diz' fortunne.
A pûs d'iun d'nous, férmièr', oul' a bâti l'châté,
Chés supèrbes z-êtablle', où-é l'bestiâs n'ou z-arunne.
Dôn fiche d'la radich', du vèrjûs, d'la toumate;
Pour nous, chein tchi nos faoût, ch'est la chiéze patate!

Mais, dam! ouïyiz-mé bein – pas d'bouffle de gniolin:
Si j'voulon' des hèrpîns, – ou savéz? pas d'bêtîze –
I' faoût touânné l'fiellet, et bigre! l'temps à v'nin
Bailli de tchi pûs bon, de millieu' marchândîze.
Et pîs, fiche d'radich', de vèrjûs et d'toumate;
Pour nous, ch'est la patate – hourâs pour la patate!

The Potato, *1889*

Oh, if in Guernsey they grow
radishes, grapes and fine tomatoes galore,
we in Jersey have lots
of something more nourishing – the great potato!
I don't care a jot for the radish, the grape or the tomato;
for me, what I need, is my dear potato!

Where could you go, tell me, to find anything healthier?
Eat up the potato, and soon your belly
will become very round, you'll build up your kidneys,
your blood, your flesh, your nerves – your body will be stocked up.
I don't care a jot for the radish, the grape or the tomato;
for me, what I need, is my dear potato!

Do you want to treat yourself and have a slap-up meal?
With pork, with beef, the potato has its place.
(You should choose in future Mr Vigot's:
you barely need to boil it, and it mashes just like that)
So that's why I don't care a jot for the radish, the grape or the tomato;
for us, what we need, is our dear potato!

Dear little potato, ah! what would we do without you?
Boiled or fried, you are fit for every sauce:
in soup or gravy, you can always be tasted.
If you're well prepared, you'll never play us false
Well, I don't care a jot for the radish, the grape or the tomato;
for me, what I need, is my dear potato!

Here they are plentiful, of all qualities;
there are fifty varieties – flat and round.
It's at the Show that you can see its beauties,
that's where it's admired – and this is what everyone cries:
We don't care a jot for the radish, the grape or the tomato;
for us, what we need, is our dear potato!

In Jersey for a long time it's meant apronfuls of gold.
To fertiliser merchants, the potato means a fortune.
It's built the castle of more than one of us farmers,
the superb cowsheds where the cattle are billetted.
So we don't care a jot for the radish, the grape or the tomato;
for us, what we need, is our dear potato!
But listen to me well now – no nonsense:
if we want cash – you know, no fooling –
we have to turn the page, and in the future
offer something better, better merchandise.
And so we won't care a jot for the radish, the grape or the tomato;
it's the potato for us – hurray for the potato!

Sir Arthur de la Mare retired to his native Trinity after a lifelong career in the British Foreign Office. In the stories he wrote for the newspaper, he combined the rural conservatism of his boyhood in a humble Jersey farming family with the cosmopolitan outlook of the scholarship student who rose to became an ambassador. But it is sometimes surprising, for a retired ambassador, how undiplomatic his stories could be.

Sir Arthur de la Mare ('Le vièr Trin'tais')

Les patates et la politique, *c.1992* (Jèrriais)

'Djatre sait'; s'fit l'Ph'lip Desclios qui r'venait d'tchérier eune chèrge éd patates au 'dump', mais tchi triste saisoun ch't'année! Jé n'mé rappelle pas d'en aver veu ieune si mauvaise qué chétchein'.

'Tu n'as pas la mémouaithe bein lounge, dounc,' j'li rêpounnis, car dans la tchulbutte dé prix après la dgèrre dé quatorze i'n valait souvent pas la peine dé porter ses patates au 'bridge'.

Mais au mains nou'n'les tchériet pas au dump, nou'les dounnait à mangi ès couochouns. Malheureusement, au jour d'aniet les fèrmiers né gardent pas d'couochouns, et d'même les patates né valent rein du tout. Et pis, dans l'vièr temps, i'n' couâtait pas tant à faithe des patates tchi fait qu' si la saisoun 'tait mauvaise nou'n' perdait pas tant d'sou qu'nou' perd achteu.'

'Ma fé', s'fit l'Ph'lip, 't'as bein raisoun là. Achteu, reinqu' pour dêfoui, i'faut des macheinnes qui couâtent des milliers dé louis, tandi'qu'dans l'bouan vièr temps tout ch'tchi fallait ch'tait eune frouque à foui, eun couply éd pannièrs, tchiques bathies d'quat' cabots, et nous avait tout ch'qui fallait pur chèrgi la vainne et s'mett'en route pour le 'bridge'.'

'En effet', j'lis dis, 'au jour d'aniet si nou'n' dépense pas des sou à tort et à travers les siens disent qué nous est countre él progrès. Et ch'en est d'même pas seulement dans la fèrmerie mais dans tout tchi s'passe en Jèrri dé non jours. Quandtchi qu'les gens apprendrount qué l'souo-disant progrès ch'n'est qu'eune illusioun? Ergarde él tourisme: dans l'vièr temps nou'n'avait qu'tchiques visiteurs, et nou' 'tait countents d'les vaie car ch'tait d'buoannes gens qui savaient s'coumporter. Mais achteu les siens tchi fount l'tripot du tourisme i'veulent lé progrès, ch'est à dithe qué la gourmandise s'est emparée d'ieux. I veulent attirer acquo pus d'touristes et d'même i' faut acquo pus d'hotels et pus d'attractiouns vuldgaithes pour les faithe v'ner.'

'J'tais l'aut'mardi à écouter sus l'radio les débâs dans l's'Etats. I 'taient à distchuter l'tourisme et y'avait là eun pèrrot – je crai qu'il est senateu – que palit tant d'bêtises et d'balivèrnes que v'là tchi m'rapp'lit mon temps au Foreign Office quand j'avais à aller à la Chambre des C'meunnes, m'assiéthe dans l'banc en drièthe dé mon Ministre – eun banc tchi, s'loun les règlyes d'la Chambre n'existe pas mais qu'en pratique est là pour le souastchein des Ministres, pour lus soufflier dans l'ouarthelle coumment rêpoundre à eune tchestioun minse par l'Oppositioun. Ah, mon garçoun, à tch niollin qué j'avais à êcouter et tchi niollin qué j'avais à soufflier au Ministre pour y rêpoundre! Même au jour d'aniet, d'y penser v'là tchi m'fait rouogi d'hounte.'

'Mais, sâbre dé bôuais', s'fit l'Ph'lip, 'tu n'est pas en train dé m'dithe qué les membres éd nos Etâts sount aussi bégauds qu'les membres d'la Chambre des C'meunnes?'

'Bah, bah', j'li dis, y'en a tchiqueseuns dans l's'Etats coumme chu sénateu dé tchi qué j'vainne de t'pâler, qui sount des pus achocres de tchi qu'j'aie jamais entendu. Mais, les prenant en gros, pour l'imbécilité j'ai n'crai pas qué y'ait grand' chose entre l's'Etats et la Chambre éd C'meunnes. La pus grand'bétise qué Jèrri fit après la dgèrre, ch'tait d'érformer' les Etâs. Nou'n'éthait jamais deu mett' les juges et les récteurs à la porte: i' valaient autrement mus qu'chutte niais'rie d'senateurs. Mais enfin, mon Ph'lip, j'éspèthe qué la saisoun tchi veint s'ra mijeuthe qué chétchein pour les fermiers, car la fermerie ch'est la cheintâthe de sauvetage du vrai Jèrri.

Mais j'voudrais étout qué non férmièrs erveint à la vieille mode dé fèrmer. La Royale est acquo la miyeuthe patate du mounde, mais achteu qué pour engrais nou's'sert dé chémiques et qu'nou' la couvre avec chutte salop'rie d'plastique oulle a perdu bein d'chu goût spécial qu'oulle avait quand nou' graissait avec du bouân fumi d'fèrme et du vraic. Nos experts nos disent qu'i' faut mett' pus d'soign à présenter et à paqu'ser nos patates, et il'ount assez raisoun, mais chein qu'y'a d'pus important ch'est l'goût d'la patate. I' nos est dit dans l's'Ecrituthes qué si l'sé a perdu sa saveu' i'n vaut pus rien. Il en est d'même dé la Royale.'

Potatoes and politics, c.1992

"Damn," said Phil Desclios on his return from carting a load of potatoes to the dump, "but what a miserable season we're having this year! I can't recall having seen one as bad as this one."

"You can't have a very long memory, then," I replied, "for in the price slump after the Great War, it often wasn't worth taking one's potatoes to the Weigh-bridge."

"But at least we didn't cart them to the dump; we gave them to the pigs to eat. Unfortunately, nowadays famers don't keep pigs, and so the potatoes are worthless. And then, in the old days, it didn't cost so much to grow potatoes, so that if the sea-son was bad one didn't lose so much money as one loses nowadays."

"My goodness," said Phil, "you're quite right there. Now, just for digging, you need machines which cost thousands of pounds, while in the good old days all you needed was a digging fork, a couple of baskets, some four-cabot barrels, and you had all you needed to load up the van and set off for the Weighbridge."

"Actually," I told him," nowadays if you don't spend money left, right and cen-tre, they say that you're against progress. And that's the case not only in farming, but in everything that goes on in Jersey nowadays. When will people learn that so-called progress is only an illusion? Look at tourism: in the old days we only had a few visitors and we were happy to see them, because they were good folks who knew how to behave. But now those who do all the tourism business want progress, which means that greed has overtaken them. They want to attract more tourists, and so we need even more hotels and more vulgar attractions to get them to come."

"The other Tuesday, I was listening to the States debates on the radio. They were discussing tourism, and there was one bloke – I think he's a Senator – who spoke such stuff and nonsense that it quite reminded me of my time in the Foreign Office when I had to go to the House of Commons and sit on the bench behind my Minister – a bench that doesn't exist according to the rules of the House but which is there in practice to provide back-up for Ministers, in order to whisper in his ear how to respond to a question put by the Opposition. Ah, my lad, what non-sense I had to listen to and what nonsense I had to whisper to my Minister in reply! Even thinking of it today is enough to make me blush with shame."

"But, strewth," said Phil, "you're not telling me that our States Members are as halfwitted as Members of the House of Commons?"

"Pah!" I said to him, "there are some in the States, like that Senator who I was just telling you about, who are among the biggest nitwits I've ever heard tell of. But all in all, for stupidity I don't think there's all that much in it between the States and the House of Commons. The biggest mistake Jersey made after the war was to reform the States. They should never have thrown out the Jurats and Rectors: they were much more valuable than all this Senators rubbish. But in conclusion, Phil, I hope that next season will be better than this one for farmers, because farming is the true Jersey's lifebelt.

But I'd also like our farmers to get back to the old way of farming. The Jersey Royal is still the best potato in the world, but now they use chemical fertilisers and cover it with that awful plastic, it's lost a lot of that special flavour it had when it was fertilised with farm manure and vraic. Our experts tell us that we should take more trouble in presenting and packing our potatoes, and they're right enough, but the most imporant thing is the taste of the potato. We're told in the Scriptures that if the salt has lost its savour, it is worthless. And that goes for the Jersey Royal too."

Louisa Lane Clarke, a cousin of the son of the last Hereditary Governor of Alderney, wrote a tourist guide to Alderney. This guidebook is a useful record of folklore and invaluable for the scraps of the now-extinct Auregnais contained in it.

Louisa Lane Clarke

From The Island of Alderney ... being a companion and guide for the traveller, *1851*

Quaipeaux

To the thoughtful traveller there will be a peculiar interest in this little island town with its confusion of farm-houses and cottages side by side – the manure heap in corners of the street – the straw-yard and piggery beside the small shop or dwelling house. On solid granite walls, thatched roofs, and on cottage walls, the old custom of drying the quaipeaux in the sun still prevails. What are *quaipeaux*? They are cakes of the dung of the good Alderney cow smeared thickly on the walls, and, when dry, chopped off for fuel. *Quaipeaux* are also dried in the field, and used in Guernsey for the same purpose; but the Alderney method is peculiar to itself. These cakes make a bright fire, and are valuable to an island where wood is scarce.

[The *couêpé* (dried cowpat – plural *couêpieaux* (Jèrriais), *couêpiaoûx* (Guernesiais) is also well-known in Guernsey, Jersey and Sark.]

From Guernsey Magazine, *1891*

During the long winter evenings, when the storm blasts swept over the Blaies, and shook each individual hut of the Bourgage hamlet, then it was that the old folk-lore displayed its riches. Here we find humanity, that "maketh all the world kin," ever the same. Recreation of mind, as well as of body, is a human need, and, as to-day, in Alderney, it finds its outlet in Huret concerts, or Victoria Room choir meetings; so, in medieval times, the Bourgage ingle nook *badl'goulaine* had its chosen hour. On the *âtre* glowed the red hot embers of the dried *varech*, or *quêpiaux* (Alderney-coal) fire, which sent its lighting glare into every corner of the Aurignean house. Farming implements, of primitive make and texture, leaned against the walls, on which hung *les mailles de filet* that thus betokened the almost amphibious nature of the occupant's life. From the mantel swung the primitive flickering *crasset*, whose dim light helped the vigorous *ouvreuses* to steadily ply their stocking needles on the insular hose and *corsets d'oeuvres* already world renowned. On the sanded floor sat the farm hands and the fisher lads, gathered in for the *veillée*, even then an all-important factor in Channel Island domestic economy. Through an open doorway, or from behind an improvised curtain, a distinct low, or the steady chewing of the cud, or that aromatic odour peculiar to stabled kine, would attest to the near contiguity of all living stock that formed the household. And in the *âtre* corner, in central position, *en place d'honneur*, would sit the aged sire, whose one chief function was to keep interest alive, by the narration of ancestral folk-lore, and immemorial tradition.

It is to these *veillées*, that one must assign the reason of the continuance of the old-time superstition in our rural neighbourhood. Belief in sorcery, in witches, in the baleful influence of the evil eye is still as much rampant in the Bourgage and Rue des Vâches households of to-day, as it is in the remote hamlets of our Guernsey rural parishes.

Pork was a traditional food for Islanders. Guernsey bean jar and Jersey bean crock are the Islanders' equivalent of cassoulet, made with trotters and whatever bits of pork were spare. Christmas dinner was traditionally most often pork, until the fashion for goose and later turkey grew up in the later nineteenth century. Denys Corbet's 'L'Touar de Guernesy' includes a scene of slaughter, and we also have an extract from a comparable tale by E. J. Luce. Luce's poem was reprinted during the Occupation years in a newspaper that also carried in the same issue official announcements on the compulsory registration of piglets – since little original writing was permitted for publication under the régime of German military censorship, historic texts were one way of allowing the satirical gaze to continue without blinking. Later on, as we consider the German Occupation during the Second World War, Michael Vautier will remind us of the importance of illicit pork production under those circumstances.

Denys Corbet ('Bad'lagoule')

From L'Touar de Guernsey, *1884* (Guernesiais)

La Tuerie

> La mênagière, ichin, hors d'halaïne à sen touar,
> Et raufignie adret, s'en r'tourni dans sen fouar
> De cuisìne, où qu'la fllàmbe et la fumâïe étou
> Airaient engômaï l'guiâtre, ou fait d'l'aut' bord de fou,
> Là, dame, à c'menche, à pouaent, à ragottaïr sen monde,
> A passaïr tout en r'veue, en ordre, et à la ronde;
> A chaupoutraïr la bêsse, à bougounnaïr l'valet;
> Enippànt les crâgnons d'châcun leus hobodet;
> Codpiant l'cat et pîs l'tchen, ch't-inchìn dans sen bingot,
> Et l'autre frànc par l'u, sàns mìme un p'tit mingot.

Ah! dame, à quànd l'bouachier vit tout s'n-allaïr au guiâtre
I' craeut qu'il'tait grànd temps d'am'naïr la trie au quiâtre
Et dans p'tit d'temps, ma fînge, a' couinait bel et bien,
Tant qu'des crâgnons bientôt non n'vit brâment pus rien:
Les pus p'tits, morts de peux, et prom'tànt d'êter bouans,
S'en vont brâment s'fourraïr dans tous les p'tits racouans
Caêr la mère a promis – respet d'la compengnie –
Qu'les mauvais s'raient fourraïs dans l'ventre à la viêill' trie.
Quànt ès grànds, la pupart, s'couillottent l'rond du parc,
Et de d'là Guiu sait où – la fllèche en sortànt d'l'arc
N'va pouit grànd'ment pus vite – et rien qu'pour évitaïr
D'aïguer à la tûrie, ou d'ouir l'aver couinaïr.
Tous, exceptaï l'pus grànd, l'hériquier principa',
Que l'Maît' Sam, d'sen couain d'ieil, a veû, coumme i s'en va,
Et qu'il a fait r'viraïr pour li bailler l'bouquet
Dans qui saïgner la bête, et, squiter coumme orvet,
Qu'i' happe au couain d'l'oreille, et meune à l'établli,
Et li fait t'nir la coue – Ah! d'màndous s'ill' a ri?
Et si l'mâdraï d'bouachier, tout en saïgnànt sa bête,
A du maufait d'crâgnon la grànd' termeur à fête!
Si ritoche et si cllinte, en d'muchon et sous câpe,
Au pouasshìn quànd la coue, adret graissie, écâppe?
Et quand i la raguìne, à but d'deigts, pinch'-belingue
Pour la r'lâquer r'drissaïr entre aeux coumme un' verlingue?

Mais tout' chose à sa fin: sus l'drain la trie est morte:
Châcun dit s'n-opinion s'alle est faillie ou forte,
Grasse ou maigre; et pîs, d'vànt la plaïchier, r'faut la djougue.
Les crâgnons yun à yun r'dévâle' avau la hougue,
Leus peux évaubarâïe, un caoup l'meurte accoumplli;
Et châcun vient s'rangier tout autouar d'l'établli,
Pour s'enter davouêgner à saver qu'est qu'aira
La rate et la vessie, et l'quaï qui rôtira
La prumière; et l'quaï d'aeux qu'a la fâmeuse halaïne,
Ou la forche d'poumons, pour bien soufftllaïr la draïne.

Slaughter

And here the housewife, out of breath in her turn,
and quite flustered returned to her oven
in the kitchen where the flames and the smoke as well
were enough to have choked the devil, or sent him raving mad,
and there you have it, she begins giving her personnel a right belabouring,

checking everything over, in order, and all round;
scolding the maid-servant , and swearing at the manservant;
dishing out a box on the ears to each of the children;
kicking the cat and then the dog, the latter in its basket,
and the other right out through the door, with nothing at all.
Ah! goodness gracious, when the butcher saw everything going to the devil
he thought it was high time to bring the sow to the pig bench
and in no time, my goodness, it was squealing away like anything,
so much so that the kids disappeared from view like a shot:
off go the smallest ones, frightened to death, and promising to be good,
to burrow themselves away in small corners;
for their mother promised – excuse the language –
that the naughty ones would be stuffed into the belly of the old sow.
As for the adults, the majority, slink off around the sty,
and God knows where – the arrow leaving the bow
couldn't go much faster than that – and all simply in order to avoid
helping with the slaughter, or to hear the porker squealing.
All, except the eldest, the main heir,
who Mr. Sam, out of the corner of his eye, saw leaving,
and who he brought back to give him the bucket
in which to bleed the beast, and, wily as a slow worm,
taking him by the ear and leading to the bench,
and making him hold the tail – Ah, imagine how he laughed!
And how the sly butcher, whilst bleeding the beast,
made great sport of the unlucky kid's trembling!
How he sniggers and winks, behind his back, while laughing up his sleeve,
at the little chick when the very greasy tail slips out of his hand,
and when he picks it up again, with his finger tips, like a clothes peg
only to let it slip through them again like a cowry.

But all things come to an end: at last the sow is dead:
everyone gives their opinion as to whether she was weak or strong,
fatty or lean; and then, before dividing her up, the pitcher is needed again.
The kids one-by-one come back down the hill,
their fears evaporated, once the murder done;
and everyone arranges themselves all around the bench,
to sort out amongst themselves who will get
the spleen and the bladder, and which one will roast
the former; and which one of them that has the puff needed,
or the strongest lungs, to blow the latter up like a ballon.

E. J. Luce ('Elie')

From **Nécrologie Porcine, *1909* (Jèrriais)**

Il est bein mort! La corde au nez
J'l'avons traînè de d'dans sa cotte,
Y'un hallait; mais ch'tait pon assez
Il a fallu l'pousser d'ma botte!

Mort! Vaithe i' l'est! Mais, j'en réponds,
I' nos a dounnè d'la minzèthe!
I' marchait d'travers, à r'tchulons,
Et s'assiéyait sus san driéthe!

Oui, mort, enfin! Mais ah! l'quétot!
V'là qu'est têtu! Ch'est incriyabl'ye!
J'avons failli nos rompre l'co
En nos êtrav'lant l'long d'l'êtabl'ye!

Mort! Oui, bein mort! Mais malgrè li!
D'un grand coup d'couté dans la gorge!
Et n'na-t-i' heurlè!! Tout san bri
Empêchait d'ouï l'combat d'la forge!

J'l'y'avons dounnè san prumié bain! –
Dans un grand tchué plien d'ieau bouoillante.
Mais il 'tait mort; i' n'a dit rein!
Sa couenne ach't'euthe est êcliatante!

J'l'avons pendu à notr' gambi
Les pids en haut; et, souos sa tête,
Y'a l'grand bouchet. Alentou d'li
Sont cats et tchans attendant fête!

Tout grand ouvert de haut en bas,
L'bâton l'fait garder sa postuthe!
Nou vait-i coumme il est bein gras:
Ch'est les panais et la pétuthe!

Un linge a 'tè mins par dessus
Pour le préserver d'la poussiéthe;
Car je faisons tréjous d'notr' mus
Pour les précautions sanitaithes!

Ch'est fini pour té, vièr couochon!
Tu n'crains pus les r'vers de fortune!
N'ya pas d'dangi d'la salaison
Tu'es bein mort au montant d'la lune!

Tu'es mort, vièr quetto! J'sens d'ichin
La bouanne odeur dans la tchuisine.
J'allons-t-i' n'n'aver un festin!
A nos en litchi les babbines!

Ma missis est à fricachi
Faie et couothèe ov des châlottes;
V'là qui s'sa bon, un coup dréchi
Ov du grévin et des carottes!

From A Pig's Obituary, 1909

He's quite dead! We dragged him
from his sty with a rope through his nose,
One of us pulled him, but that wasn't enough
I had to push him with my boot!

Dead! Indeed he is! But, I say in reply,
he gave us trouble!
He walked sideways, backwards,
and sat down on his backside!

Yes, dead at last! But what a porker!
Unbelievably stubborn!
We nearly broke our necks
sprawling the length of the stable!

Dead! Yes, quite dead! But he put up a fight!
Stabbed in the throat with a knife!
And how he squealed! The noise he made
drowned out the noise from the smithy!

We gave him his first bath!
In a large vat full of boiling water.
But he was dead and said nothing at all!
And now his hide is sparkling clean!

We hung him feet first from our gambrel,
and beneath his head
there's the big bucket. Round about him
are expectant cats and dogs!

Wide open from top to bottom,
the stake keeps him in position!
Just look how fat he is:
That's from the parsnips and mixed grain!

A cloth has been placed over him
to keep the dust off him;
because we always do our best
to observe food safety measures!

It's all over for you, old pig!
No more worries for you!
You're not in danger of salting,
you died on a rising moon!

You're dead, old porker! I can smell from here
the lovely smell from the kitchen.
What a feast we're going to have!
Really lipsmacking!

My wife is frying
liver and lights with spring onions;
that'll be good, once served up
with gravy and carrots!

After all the hard work, whether in the fields or at home, there is nothing like having a good cup of tea and putting your feet up. Tam Lenfestey reminiscences about how family life centred around the big fireplace. Alice de Faye is one of the Jersey female writers who reminds us that housework also has its place in literature.

Tam Lenfestey

Aut'fais, *1873* (Guernesiais)

Ah! vaïsin Jean, quant té et mé,
Etêmes garçons dans not janne temps
Dans nos grandes âtres à toubaquié,
Et à pâlaï du bouan vier temps,

En r'pernant s'halaine nou chaquié,
Ah! mon Dou, avêmes ju du sens.

Nos belles grandes âtres ils ont briqui,
Où nou pouvait mette la véture,
Y'a paine du run pour un terpi,
Ah! s'i à bavaï, nou s'y aventure,
J'en ais quâsi perdi l'esprit,
Ah! que pour mé, l'affaire est dure.

Les paures genouais n'ou n'peut cauffaï,
Ni d'nos garçons, ni de nos filles,
N'y'a l'run d'dormi, ni l'run d'hautaï,
Ni l'run de s'qué, ses poures guenilles,
Aurun d'conforts, c'hés d'la biautaï,
I voudraient imitaï les villes.

N'i'a d'run pour se, ni pour ses d'chens,
Ils y f'raient tous une poure figure
Si par hâsard qui qu'un d'nos gens,
A v'nir nou vée i s'y aventure,
Pour bien en dire, i g'nia poui d'sens
Ah! que pour mé, l'affaire est dure.

Et sous nos pids, ch'n'est q'des q'carpets,
I s'mettent à en couvrir notre aire,
Ils en ont par tous nos endrets,
Pour mé, j'n'en ai quâsi q'd'en brair
Ah! si j'avais tous mes souhaits,
J'les sabionn'rais, si m'laissaient l'faire.

Nos biaux bachins si éclairants,
Valaient bien muc q'la laie picture,
Et la côniére atou des jants,
La vieille aumare atou s'en beurre,
Valaient bien mue pour nos effants.
Ah! que pour mé, l'affaire est dure.

Et parmi tout leux biaux boucâs,
Ils ont l'sofa, aurun d'liét d'fouaille,
J'nen f'rai jamais un bien grand cas,
Pour y dormi ch'nest rien qui vaille,

Et pis, v'la qu'est terjous trop bas,
Pour un vier lassaï qui travaille.

Devant d'avé d'si biaux parleux,
J'avion du lard dessus nos lattes,
A persent nou s'en à grand peux,
I faut du boeu, s'nous s'en acate,
Et n'ou s'en assoum'rai des boeux
De tout leux trains, n'ou s-en est mattes.

Quand j'sis lassaï de m'en travas,
Not femme, qui fus terjous si propre,
Dit, si t'es paraï de t'n'embarras,
Halle tes saulai, n'seit poui malpropre,
Tout est r'paraï, et jusqu'au ch'nas,
N'seit poui terjous un vier a'chocre.

Ah! vaîsin Jean, quant té et mé,
Eteimes garçons dans not janne temps
Dans nos grandes âtres à toubaquié,
A faire des contes du bouan vier temps,
En r'pernant s'n'halaine nou chaquié,
Tout est changi, j'apprends du sens.

Time past, *1873*

Ah, neighbour John, when you and I
were boys in our youth
smoking away in our big hearths,
and talking about the good old days,
when we caught our breath we shook,
Ah! my goodness, how much sense we had.

Our fine big hearths have been bricked up,
the ones that were big enough to get a carriage in,
there's hardly room for a trivet,
Ah! if you venture in to have a chat,
I've almost lost the will,
Ah! how hard things are for me.

You can't warm your poor knees,
nor can our boys or girls,
there's no room to sleep, no room to doze,

no room to dry your poor clothes,
instead of comfort, it's beauty,
they're trying to copy the town ways.

There's no room for yourself, no room for your offspring,
they'd all cut a poor figure in there
if it should happen than one of our folks
should come to see us and venture in there,
really and truly, there'd be no point.
Ah! how hard things are for me.

And underfoot, it's all carpets.
They lay them to cover our floor,
they've got them all over the place,
really, I could shout about it.
Ah! if I had my way
I'd put down sand floors, if they'd let me.

Our beautiful gleaming bachins
were of more use than that ugly picture,
and the inglenook with its furze,
the old cupboard with its butter,
were much better for our children.
Ah! how hard things are for me.

And among all their fine furniture,
they've got a sofa instead of the green-bed,
I'll never care much for it,
it's no good for sleeping on,
and anyway, it's always too low
for a tired old working man.

Before we had such fine parlours,
we had pork on the kitchen bacon rack,
nowadays people are afraid of it,
and must have beef, if you can buy it,
and they butcher bulls for it.
You get really fed up with all their fuss.

When I'm tired from working,
my wife, who was always so proper,
says, if you've cleared up your clutter,
take off your shoes, don't be messy,

everything's been cleaned as far as the hayloft,
don't always be a clumsy old fool.

Ah, neighbour John, when you and I
were boys in our youth
smoking away in our big hearths,
and telling tales of the good old days,
when we caught our breath we shook,
Everything's changed, I'm learning some sense.

Alice de Faye ('Livonia')

Le Pot à Thée, *1912* (Jèrriais)

Ches là l'ammein de toutes les lav'resses,
Quand ils l'vais sus la jô du grés y sont à lus aise;
S'ou voulais qui faiche lus d'vé d'vant la traie,
Donnais lu d'vaut qu'menchi eune bouanne tasse de thée.

Et à onze heuthes quand ils ont bein travaillyi,
Et que ou lus donnais eunne bouochie a mangi,
Donnais lu le frico qu'on voulais, mais –
Donnais lu étout eunne bouanne tasse de thée.

Si au dîné ou les avais par malheur oubliais,
Ou f'thont rein pour toute l'arlevais;
Et à la piéche de yieunne y lus en faout treis,
Quand veindra le temps pour baithe le thée.

Mais si dans l'mitan de l'arlevais,
Ou lus en donnais eunne tasse bein chucraie;
Pas du randuinait, mais fait tout frais,
Y travailllont avec couothage jusqu'au thée.

Et quand y sont finies et qu'on les paithais,
Donnais lus-en occouo eunne raide bouanne tassais,
Es ou verrais qui r'veindront vos r'vais,
Car ès lav'resses y lus faout du thée.

Mais ch'nest pas seulement ès femmes qui vont lavé,
Mais acheteu, ches toute la mode dans l'gentry;
Souvent quand ou zentrais à vais des amis,
Y vos donne tout d'un coup eun afternoon tea.

L'aoutre jour en me promenant je rencontrais
Daeux anciennes dames qui lus entre tchitais;
Yieunne dis good-bye ma Julie, vein don me vais,
Et j'éthons ensemble eunne bouanne tasse de thée.

Nou dit que pour connaître l'humeur des gens,
Ch'nest pas seulement de les vais en passant;
Mais nou peut les connaître dans eunne fais,
Si nou za ensemble eunne bouanne tasse de thée

Eunne tasse de thés est bein rafraîchissante
Et en même temps étout bein dailassante
Mais autant comme il est sain et bon,
Y faout tout de même en usé à discrétion,
Et ne pas baithe trop de thée.

Car yia le trop et le trop p'tit.

The Teapot, *1912*

It's every washerwoman's friend,
when they can see it on the ledge of the grate they feel at ease;
if you want them to do their duty at the washing trough,
give them a good cup of tea before they start.

And at eleven o'clock when they've been working hard
and when you offer them a snack,
give them whatever food you want, but
give them a good cup of tea too.

If you've unfortunately forgotten them at lunchtime,
they won't do anything all afternoon long;
and instead of one, they'll need three,
when it comes to teatime.

But if in the middle of the afternoon
you give them a well-sweetened cuppa,
not of stewed tea, but freshly brewed,
they'll work heartily until teatime.

And when they're finished and you pay them,
give them another really good cuppa,

and you'll see that they'll come back to see you,
because washerwomen really need their tea.

But it's not only for women who go and do washing,
but now it's all the fashion among the gentry;
often when you go in and see friends,
they offer you straightaway an afternoon tea.

The other day while out walking I met
two elderly ladies who were saying goodbye to each other;
one said "Goodbye, Julie, come and visit me,
and we'll have a good cup of tea together."

They say that it's not just by seeing people in passing
that you can find out what they're like;
but you can get to know them in a trice
if you have a good cup of tea together.

A cup of tea is very refreshing
and at the same time very relaxing.
But healthy and good as it is,
all the same you have to use it with discretion,
and not drink too much tea.

Because you can have too much of a good thing.

Trade and Technology

Belonging neither to the Kingdom of England nor to the Kingdom of France, for centuries the Channel Islands made use of their neutral status between the two frequently-warring kingdoms to trade with both sides. This neutrality was finally abolished by the Privy Council under William III.

We have seen how the development of the agricultural trade and the trans-Atlantic cod fisheries was reflected in literature. Trade was not all export of produce and labour, though: Islanders also imported the latest fashions and technological advances changed lifestyles and, through new media, widened horizons, even to the uttermost ends of the universe.

George William de Carteret ('Caouain', 'G.W. de C.')

Ma Motor-Bike, *1931* (Jèrriais)

> Tch'est qui, dans djaix-neu chents vingt-iune,
> Me couôti une petite fortune,
> Et qu'a causé tant d'amiertume?
> Ma motor-bike.
>
> Tch'est qui m'avait mins an défi
> De r'pather de la maîtrîsi
> Et qui m'êlindgi dans vivyi?
> Ma motor-bike.
>
> Tch'est qui, quand je r'vimmes bouans amins
> Et d'la manier j'avais apprins
> M'encouothagi à couorre les c'mins?
> Ma motor-bike.

Tch'est qui, à la héche des chapelles
Va s'stationner comme sentinelle
Et qu'êblouît toutes les hardelles?
Ma motor-bike.

Tch'est qu'a un couossin en drièthe,
Pour inviter à v'nin s'y assièthe,
Tchique jeune et jolie passagièthe?
Ma motor-bike.

Tch'est qu'avec ses fanfaronnades
Troublye le r'pos d'touos les malades.
Dépis Gouôrey à St. Brelade?
Ma motor-bike.

Tch'est qui, un jour à St. Cliément
Brûlait la route follâtrement,
Et fut la cause d'un accident?
Ma motor-bike.

Tch'est qu'ch'est qui m'lannedi d'vant la Cour
Et m'fit attraper vingt-huit jours
Pour l'affaithe de la Prumié Tour?
Ma motor-bike.

Tch'est qu'ch'est qui happi l'mors-ès-dents
Touos les piétons êparpillant
Et m'fliantchi contre un char-à-banc?
Ma motor-bike.

Tch'est qu'est siez Hunt le marchand d'chiques
Et qui n'mé jouôtha pas d'aut'es triques
Tch'est qu'ch'est qu'j'ai envié siez l'Vier Nique?
Ma motor-bike.

My motorbike, *1931*

What was it, in nineteen twenty one,
that cost me a small fortune,
and that caused such anguish?
My motorbike.

What was it that had challenged me
to succeed in mastering it
and that flung me in the pond?

What was it, when we became good friends again
and I'd learnt to handle it,
that encouraged me to go gallivanting around the lanes?
My motorbike.

What was it, at the gate of the chapels,
that took up a post as sentinel
and that amazed all the girls?
My motorbike.

What is that has a cushion behind,
so that some young and pretty female passenger can be invited
to come and sit?
My motorbike.

What is it that, with its boasting,
disturbs the rest of veryone who's ill,
from Gorey to Saint Brelade?
My motorbike.

What was it, one day in Saint Clement,
that burned up the road madly
and was the cause of an accident?
My motorbike.

What was it that landed me before the Court
and got me twenty-eight days
for the affair of First Tower?
My motorbike.

What was it that got the the bit between its teeth,
scattering all pedestrians,
and that threw me against a charabanc?
My motorbike.

What is it that's at Hunt's the rag merchant
And that won't play me any more tricks?
What is it that I've sent to the Devil?
My motorbike.

T. A. Grut ('T.A.G.')

St. Peter-in-the-Wood calling! Good Afternoon, everyone!, 1927, (Guernesiais)

Our Topical Talk today will be given by Sophie Pallot, the celebrated St. Pierraise, who is to give us her experience of the "wireless."

MISS PALLOT:–

La Compagnie du A.B.C. m'a d'màndeï si j'leux f'rais l'houneur de douneï la "Tropical Talk" su un' sujet qu'est bien près d'men cueur, ch'est la "wireless."

J'vous dounerai quiques paroles d'introduction, je sies la persône à qui Madâme Galiâne lassi toutes ses hârdes, de d'sus et de d'sous, tous ses chapiaux caûches et saulers, et toute la pêque, et y'en a asseï pour le restànt d'ma vie, car j'errai septànte àns le perchain mais, et j'errai la pension pour la viellesse.

Durànt ma longue vie, j'ai sauveï vingt livres sterling, pour vivre dessus quànd j'errai septànte àns; mais atou la pension de huit chelins la semaïne, j'decidi d'aver la "wireless" atou les vingt livres sterling, eh donc, j'alli sies Mess Laker, au Bordage, et j'acati le pus biaux "set" qu'il avait dans la shoppe et l'affaire est fixaïe justement bien; un but du "aerial" est amarreï à ma chimnaïe, et l'autre but est amarreï à la coue du coq de L'Egllise de Tortevà, eh donc la réception est si bouânne, qu'au ser quànd tout est trànquille, et l'temps cllaïre, j'peux ouïr les ànges chànteï dans l'ciel. Les gens disent que l'coq n'bouge poui d'autre, et reste auve le bec pointu au nord'est, eh donc, j'erron terjous bel. J'ai daeux cages pour mettre sur la tète pour écouteï; la daeuxième j'loue à sixpennis par heure es vaïsins, et si l'coumerce continue, j'acaterai acouâre des câges, pour faire pus d'sou, et j'pourron être chinq ou six autouor d'la tablle dans la cuisaine.

J'ai daeux "incubator," pour être seur qu'la musique ne mànquerà pâs par la làmpe s'éteindre.

Ch'est au Dêmânche au ser que j'me pllais l'mûe, caer le service c'menche à huit heures; j'ai men livre de perières et men càntique, et j'prends part dans tout l'service et quànd vient la collecte j'mêts men penni dans l'box pour les pauvres. Les siens qui viennent baïlle tous à ma collecte, et si jamais j'me trouve dans l'besoin, j'errai bouen dérouet d'pinchier les sous.

Dans l'hivar quànd i' piouvrà, et tormenterà, j's'rai donc bien à coteï du faeu, à ouïr les sermons au Dêmânche au ser, et gardeï men bouen chapé et mes pids sec.

Le Prince du Gâles pâle justement bien, et si cllaïre; mais pour Mester Churchill, nous a mal à l'estoumâ à l'écouteï, i'n peut peut poui s'en dépiôquier; enfin, ch'n'est pâs tous qu'ont la langue bien pendue. J'pâlais l'autre jour à Messe Taudevin qu'a l'wireless, mais i' veur s'en défaire, caer il est au but d'ses sens.

Au ser quànd il est quoishi, les effàns mettent le "loudspeaker," et les v'là tous, et vallet et les baisses, à dànseï au touor d'la cuisaine, jusqu'à daeux haeures au matin; et pis, à chinq haeures quànd i' deverais être l'vaï pour soigner es bêtes, et traire, i' sont tous à ronflleï comme des cochons, et Messe Taudevin ne peut poui les évillier.

D'vier neuf haeures i'c'menche à prendre vie et s'en vont pour traire, mais les poures bêtes sont en détresse, caer le piécho n'a qu'd'en querveï.

Vous veyie que y'a du pour et du contre partout.

Un sam'di au ser un manière de prêtre nous dît que Londres était à faeu partout, et les membres du Parlément étaient pendus ès làmpes par les rues; j'en eu quâsi l'sang tourneï, caer nous creyie que la fin du monde était v'nue; mais ch'tait toutes des men'tries, et l'mâbé fut quâsi envyeï es travaux forchis pour aver dit d'itaï que.

Y'a autre chose contre le wireless, ch'est qu'les gens sont à écouteï, quànd i'devrais être à faire leux travâs, ou bian au lliet; mais pour les gens d'bouen sens, qui saïvent s'en servir comme i'faut, ch'est un' bénédiction.

J'sies un' paeure fâmme, mais j'veur être enterraïe hounètement, eh donc, j'ai fait men testament, et j'ai mis Mess Chen des Chens comme executeur. J'désire qu'men "wireless" seit vendu au pus offrànt dès que j's'rai morte et atou les l'argent, Mess Chen c'màndrâ un biaux coffre de quesne et un' belle pierre pour mettre su ma fosse, atou l'inscription "à la memouaire de Sophie Pallot, du Crocq, St. Pierre. Sa perte à la Pâresse est incalculabille." Le "Denouncer" vient justement de m'dire, Miss Pallot, time up; et donc me v'lo paraïe pour chu caoup.

Au revoir, Sophie.

St. Peter-in-the-Wood calling! Good Afternoon, everyone!, 1927

Our Topical Talk today will be given by Sophie Pallot, the celebrated St. Peter's Lady, who is to give us her experience of the "wireless."

MISS PALLOT:–

The ABC Company has asked me if I would do them the honour of giving a "Tropical Talk" on a subject that is close to my heart, the "Wireless".

I will give you a few words of introduction, I'm the person to whom Mrs Gallienne left all of her clothes and underclothes, all of her hats, socks and shoes, and everything else, and there is enough for the rest of my life, as I will be seventy years old next month and will have the old age pension.

During my long life, I have saved twenty pounds sterling to live off when I'm seventy years old; but with a pension of eight shillings a week I decided to have the "Wireless" with the twenty pounds sterling, and so, I went to Laker's in Le Bordage, and I bought the finest "set" that he had in the shop and it is properly installed; one end of the "aerial" is tied to my chimney, and the other is tied to the tail of the weather cock on Torteval church, and the reception is so good that in the evening, when all is quiet, and the weather clear, I can hear angels singing in the heavens. People say that the weather cock no longer moves, and stays with its beak pointing north east, in that case, we'll always have good weather. I have two "cages" which you wear on your head to listen; the second I hire out at sixpence an hour to neighbours, and if business carries on, I'll buy more "cages", in order to make more money, and we'll be five or six around the table in the kitchen.

I have two "incubators" to ensure that the music does not stop if the lamp should go out.

I enjoy Sunday evenings the most, as the service starts at eight o'clock; I have my prayer book and hymn book and I take part in all of the service, and when comes time for the collection I put my penny in the poor box. Those that come to listen give also to my collection, and if ever I find myself in need, I will have every right to dip into the funds.

In the winter, when it rains and is stormy, I will be alright beside the fire, listening to the sermons on Sunday evening , and keeping my good hat and my feet dry.

The Prince of Wales speaks just so, and so clearly; but as for Mr. Churchill, listening to him is enough to give you indigestion, he can't get his words out; never mind, not everyone has the gift of the gab. The other day I spoke to Mr. Tostevin who has the "wireless", but he wants to get rid of it, because he is at his wit's end.

In the evening when he is asleep, the children put the "loudspeaker" on, and there they all are, the farmhand and the maids, dancing around the kitchen, until two o'clock in the morning; and then, at five o'clock when they ought to be up in order to go and attend to the animals, and to milk, they are all snoring like swine, and Mr. Tostevin can't wake them up.

At around nine o'clock, they start to come to life and off they go to milk, but the poor cattle are distressed, because their udders are full to bursting.

You see that there's always an upside and a downside.

One Saturday evening, a kind of priest told us that everywhere in London was on fire, and that Members of Parliament were strung up from street lamps; my blood ran cold, as we thought that the end of the world had arrived; but it was all lies, and the scoundrel was nearly sentenced to forced labour for having said such things.

There's another downside to the wireless, and that's that people are listening to it, when they should be doing their work, or else in bed; but for sensible people, that know how to use it properly, it is a blessing.

I'm a poor lady, but I want to be buried decently, so, I have written my will, and I have put Mr. Jehan from the Jehans as executor. I wish my "wireless" to be sold to the highest bidder as soon as I'm dead, and with the money, Mr. Jehan is to order a fine oak coffin, and a beautiful grave stone to put on my grave with the inscription "in memory of Sophie Pallot, of Le Crocq, St. Peter. Her loss to the parish is incalculable." The "Denouncer" has just told me, Miss Pallot, time is up; so, there I'm finished for this time.

Au revoir, Sophie.

Abraham de Gruchy and his wife, Marie Le Brocq, had been running a general store in Saint Peter, Jersey, since 1810 when they opened new premises in the centre of Saint Helier in 1825. De Gruchy's store expanded over the years and became a department store, adding a shopping arcade in 1883. Mathilde de Faye, who wrote as Georgie, found it impressive enough in 1897 to advise readers of *La Chronique de Jersey* on their Christmas shopping. De Gruchy's department store continues to attract shoppers in the twenty-first century.

Mathilde de Faye ('Georgie')

Hélas! Hélas!! Ah! 'My Good', *1897* (Jèrriais)

> *J'pensais que j'tais dans eun aoutre monde,*
> *N'yia pas pus bé, à Paris ou à Londres.*

J'ai tet vaies chute Belle Grande Boutique;
Et, mon doux!!! qué tout est magnifique,
Chest bein vrai chein qu'la Gâzette dîzet,
Nou peut avai de tout là à san grèt.

Ma vaiezeinne y vint avec mé,
Ou trouvit tout diversément bé,
Ou fut si êtonnaie que tout tet à si bas prix;
Qu'oul acatti eun fat, pour touos ses p'tits.

Ouprès qu'ou fut rentraie siez yi,
Ou diz à san buoun homme, sitôt qu'oul vit:
J'ten prie acatte tes habits siez d'Gruchy,
Si tu saveais comme y vendent à bouan marchi.

Chest vrai; ils ont des braies et câzaques toutes faites,
Des vèstes, corsets, chapieaux et castchiettes,
Des qu'mînzes, kauches, guélesses et collets,
Et touos lus habits sont extrêmement bein faits.

Ils ont yieu des médalles à l'Exhébition,
La marchandise, le travâs, tout fut trouvet bon;
Y font des robes pour les membres des Etats,
Pour le Bailli, les Juges, Ministres et Avocats.

Y font des uniformes pour toutes les grades,
"(Vâ-là man Nicqlesse acatté tes hardes)."

Pour Officiers, Captaines, Maître d'Port et aoutres,
Y peuvent avai tout là, sans lus en troubyié d'aoutre.

Y font des robes pour les dames qui vont à chva;
Pour les siennes qui vont sus rouelles, ils en font en drap;
Y gardent eun assortiment d'habits tuous faits,
A la dernièthe mode, et y sont tous bein fraîs.

Yia notre Johnny qu'a grand besoin d'habits,
Y faut l'emné en ville, yieun d'chest Samedis,
Y dit qu'touos ses ammins vont siez d'Gruchy;
Et qu'sils alleais ailleurs, y paîthaies bein pus chi.

Yia notre Mary Jane qui s'en va s'mathié,
Hélas!! combein qui s'en va nos en couôté;
Il est grand temps d'acatté san trousseau,
Car j'comprends qui s'en vont en finit au pus tôt.

Il y ra Jane Hélène qu'à bésoin d'un fro,
Il est vrai chest êfants là sortent bieaucoup trop;
Ou'l a à r'cité eunne pièche à l'examen,
Et lus sermons chest Dimanche t'chi-vein.

Enfin man Nicqlesse y'n faut pas san gêinné,
J'cuourait en ville demain au matein;
Les êfants m'ont dit qu'ils en ont veu à bouan marchi,
Etalées dans les f'nêtres siez les Messieux d'Gruchy.

Ah!! combein qui m'teurmentent et qui m'vange la vie,
Y savent bein qui vendent lus marchandises à bas prix;
Ils ont des boas et des "muffs", quâzi à donné:
Craît tu qu'jen acatteais yieun pour notre p'tite Néné?

Y n'faut pas lâissi d'côtet, notre Nathanaël,
Il est engagi à eunne bein belle hardelle;
Aussi bein yiavé eun portmanteau siez d'Gruchy,
Car quand y s'ont mathiéz, y sen vont viagi.

Y faut bein lus donné t'chique chose pour lus Noué,
Y yia Mary Ann, il y faut eun chappé;
Pour Rébecca et Sara, j'lus acatté des robes,
Et touos les p'tits, ont grand bésoin d'calobres.

Nicqlesse se lève du matein, et prépathe le dêjeuné,
Car y fallet bein vite, en ville nos en allé;
Y mint jusqu'à sa "Frock Coat" et san "Tappeur,"
Y voulet être habillyi comme eun vraie Seigneur.

Y n'tet jamais v'nu avec mé boutitchyi,
Il tet pus qu'content, il en étet tout fi;
Mais chu panfaique là ergardet t'y les filles;
Y faut l'pardonné, chnest pas souvent qui va en ville.

Tchi belle boutique à vaisselle qu'ils ont là,
J'navons qu'à acatté des tasses et un pia,
Y nos faut étout des assiettes et des bolles,
Y'n faut pas oublié eunne pêsle, et eunne castrolle.

J'avons assées bésoin de dueux-streis breinges,
J'prendraîesmes bein avai d'zeaipîlles à leinges,
J'éthons t'y eunne lampe pour le p'tit parlueux?
Les êfants voudraient eunne lanterne, la nyiet ils ont peuex.

Tandis que j'sai à faithe chest êmpiettes là,
Acatte eunne couvertuthe pour la vaque et le chva;
Chest chein qui yia d'bon siez d'Gruchy;
Nou peut yiavé de tout, et nou n'en paie pas chi.

Et pis n'yia pas bésoin d'emporté ses ballots,
Ils envient tout siez vous, les p'tits comme les gros;
Y vont toutes les s'maines partout Jerri,
Et y n'vos cherge pas eun sou pus chi.

Nicqlesse êmni le pus p'tit d'nos garçons à vaies l'Arcade,
Chest êtonnant comme des êfants prenne d'avis et qui r'garde;
De pis chu jour là, y n'a fait que de m'tempêté,
Y dit qui veux être habillyi comme un p'tit frégatein.

Sans doute qui vit d'chest Sailors' Suits dans lus f'nêtres;
Tchesque y sait: p'têtre que l'pèthe l'y meint chonna dans la tête;
J'sai bein qu'ils en ont tréjous un bouan assortiment;
Chest aussi bein d'en avai pour les deuex, Tomesse et Jean.

Mais man Nicqlesse il est temps d'nos en allé,
Si j'restons ichein, j'nos z'nallons nos ruiné;

Enfin, j'tai dithait, n'yia pas pus près qu'sais êfants,
Nou n'veux pas qui scais pièthe que les siens à d'aoutres gens.

Nicqlesse fut si enchantet d'la boutiques,
Qu'il avet ergret d'san allé si vite;
Y m'dîs chest vrai chein q'tu m'as souvent dit:
Nou va dans chute boutique là avec piêzi.

Ah! dame chest qui n'voudrait pas allé ailleurs,
Y n'aime pas d'aoutre marchandises que la leurs;
Pour dithe vrai, chest eun homme qu'aime l'honnêtetet,
Y sait bein si va là qui n'sa jamais trompet.

Y puoret aiêlvé chute boutique l'à jusqu'est nuéez;
Y n'est pas l'seul, ou'l a eunne bouanne ernoméez.
J'ai tréjous entendu "qu'chest vrai chein q'tout l'monde dit,"
Y disent: Alleais siez d'Gruchy pour du bon et bouan marchi.

Ou n'pouveais pas faithe mus, que d'yiallé l'Samedi d'Noué
Pour veais lus Bézaar, Oh! Mais que tout est bé;
Gennes hommes, qui vouleais donné à votre fille eun cadeau:
Acatteais lé siez d'Gruchy, pour n'en payi pas trop.

J'vos souette à tous eun bouan Noué, et bouanne Annéez.

Alas, alas, oh my goodness!, *1897*

I thought I was in another world,
there's nothing finer in Paris or London.

I've been to see that beautiful department store;
and gracious me, how splendid everything is.
It's true what the newspaper said,
you can get everything you want there.

My neighbour came with me,
she found everything quite lovely,
she was so astonished that everything was so cheap,
that she bought suits for all her little ones.

When she got home,
she said to her husband as soon as she saw him:

I beg you to buy your clothes from de Gruchy's,
if only you knew how cheap their prices are.

It's true, they've got trousers and jackets off the peg,
waistcoats, jumpers, hats and caps,
shirts, stockings, braces and collars,
and all their clothes are extremely well made.

They've had medals at the Exhibition,
there they found all the goods and workmanship good;
they make robes for States Members,
for the Bailiff, Jurats, Rectors and Advocates.

They make uniforms for every rank,
(off you go, Nicholas, and buy your clothes there).
For Officers, Captains, Harbourmaster and others,
they can get everything there without having to go to any further
effort.

They make dresses for ladies who go riding;
for those who go skating, they make them in wool;
they stock a range of off-the-peg clothes
in the latest fashion, and they're all very fresh.

There's our Johnny who really needs clothes,
we'll have to take him into town one of these Saturdays,
he says that all his friends go to de Gruchy's
and if they went anywhere else they'd pay much more.

There's our Mary Jane who's getting married,
alas! how much it's going to cost us;
it's high time to buy her trousseau,
because I believe they'll see to it as soon as possible.

And then there's Jane Helen who needs a dress,
It's true those children go out too much;
she recited a piece at the church reading day
and their sermons are next Sunday.

Finally Nicholas, you mustn't worry,
I'll run into town tomorrow morning;
the children have told me that they've seen cheap goods
on display in Messrs de Gruchy's windows.

Ah! how they torment me and make my life a misery,
they know quite well that they sell their goods at low prices;
They've got boas and muffs, practically giving them away:
Do you think I ought to buy one for our little Nancy?

And we mustn't forget about our Nathanael,
he's engaged to a very pretty girl;
we really should get a trunk from de Gruchy's,
for when they're married, they're going travelling.

We ought to get them something for Christmas,
there's Mary Ann, she needs a hat;
For Rebecca and Sarah, I'll buy them dresses,
and all the little ones really need pinafores.

Nicholas gets up in the morning and gets breakfast ready,
because we've got to be off quickly into town;
he went so far as to put on his frock coat and his top hat,
he wanted to be dressed like a real Seigneur.

He'd never come shopping with me,
he was over the moon, he was pleased as Punch;
but how the old scoundrel ogled the girls!
But you have to forgive him – he doesn't often come into town.

What a beautiful china shop they've got,
we only need to buy cups and a plate,
we also need plates and bowls,
we mustn't forget a cooking pot and a frying pan.

We rather need a couple of brooms,
it would be a good idea to have some clothes pegs,
how about a lamp for the small parlour?
The children would like a nightlight, they get frightened at night.

While I'm running all those errands,
buy a coat for the cow and the horse;
that's what's good about de Gruchy's;
you can get everything there, and without costing a lot.

And then you don't need to carry your parcels home,
they deliver everything to your door, both small and big parcels;

every week they go round Jersey,
and they don't charge you a ha'penny extra.

Nicholas took our youngest boy to see the Arcade,
it's amazing what children see and take notice of;
since that day, all he's done is pester me,
he says he wants to dress like a little sailor.

He must have seen some of those sailor suits in their windows,
who knows, perhaps his father put the idea into his head;
I know that they've always got a fine assortment of them;
it would be best to get some for both Thomas and John.

But, Nicholas, it's time to be off,
if we stay here we'll bankrupt ourselves;
And I tell you, there's nothing as dear as one's children,
you don't want them to be worse off than other people's.

Nicholas was so delighted by the store
that he was reluctant to leave so soon;
he told me, "It's true what you've often told me:
you visit this store with pleasure."

Well, sure enough he didn't want to go anywhere else,
he doesn't like anyone's goods but theirs;
to tell the truth, he's a man who likes honesty,
he knows that if he goes there he won't be cheated.

He could praise that store to the high heavens;
he's not the only one, it's got a good reputation.
I've always heard "that it's true what everyone says,"
they say: go to de Gruchy's for what's good and cheap,

You can't do better than to go on Saturday before Christmas
to see their bazaar. Oh, but how pretty everything is;
young men, if you want to give your girl a present,
buy it at de Gruchy's so you don't pay too much for it.

I wish everyone a merry Christmas and a happy New Year.

This piece won first prize at the Guernsey Eisteddfod in 1925. Henry W. Le Ray's
description of how life might be in 1974 may have been far from accurate in its pre-

dictions (and the ubiquity of mobile phones took a bit longer to come to pass), but it is certainly a picture of how trade and technology brought new words from English into the vernacular of Guernsey folk. Both 'Georgie' and Henry W. Le Ray show us how important clothing was for status, propriety and practicality. We will see later how the way tourists dressed affected writers, and the emancipation of women from their corsets and crinolines will be reflected elsewhere.

Henry W. Le Ray

Guernesey ill'a chinquànte ans, Guernesey aniet, et Guernesey dans chinquànte ans, 1925 (Guernesiais)

Comparaïr Guernesey d'ill'y-a chinquànte àns à Guernesey d'ach't-heure, v'là qu'est tout bian pour chaeux qui furent naïs dans les sésànte, mais pour chaeux qui furent naïs ll'y-a un' trentaîne d'annaïes ou moins, ch'est ossi difficile pour iaeux que pour chaeux d'ach't-heure de dire qu'est qu'Guernesey s'ra à chinquànte àns d'ichin.

En mil huit chent septànte-quatre le coumerce de Guernesey, n'faisait, s'nou veur dire, que c'menchier. Nou-n'véyait rian quiqu' "greenhouse" par les cànts et ch'tait des "lean-to" bâties esprès pour d'la grappe, et nou n-véyait quâsi pas pâlaïr d'tommates. Il est vrai que les "steam" allaient et v'naient tous les jours d'ichin en Anglléterre et vive-versa; mais ch'tait des "steam" bian pus p'tits qu'les cians d'ach't-heure et qu'allaient bian pus douchement. En chu tems là n'y-avait pas chu qu'nou s'appeule du "perishable stuff," ch'tait pus des patates qu'étaient shippaïes, et si r'targeaient d'un jour ou daeux, n'y-avait pas d'embarras.

A'ch't-heure l'île est quàsiment couverte de verre ou coum nou dit de "span," et ch'est à chents touniaux d'tommates qui sortent de Guernesey tous l's'àns.

Les "steam" d'àch't-heure sont bian pus grànds et vont bian pus vite et dans l'cueur d'la saison i-n'en faut daeux quàsi tous les jours et souvent ll'y-a accore une route de viâges d'"out-shippaïes." Si l'coumerce continue d'ichin à chinquànte àns Guernesey s'ra si rempli de "span" qu'n'y-éra pas d'run d'y-en bâti yun d'autre.

Ill'y-a chinquànte àns n'y-avait pas d'"greenhouse" à cauffaïr. Nou n'véyait pas d'àntrécaïte, mais ch'est un bouan jab qu'y-en a qui caûffe à ch't-heure caër la foule des tommates n'viè. t pas toute d'un caoup, ou s'alle faisait, che s'rait d'qué bian triste. S'les choses continuent, en mil neuf chent septànte quatre i'n'faudra pas de "steam" en tout. Tout viendra et ira dans l'air. J'n'cré pouit qui faudra même de querbon, caër les "span" s'ront tous caûffaïs par l'électricitaï, et j'cré même qu'ill'y-éra des stations partout l'île pour collectaïr les tommates, et, qui saït, i s'en iront p't'être drette d'chés stations-là pour les marchis d'Anglleterre.

La ville étou a bian chàngi. Les rues ichin d'vànt étaient bian pus p'tites et étraites. Les choppes n'étaient pas si gràndes ni si à la mode. Nou n'véyait pas de "bus" ni d'motor-cars qu'allaient et v'naient continuellement coum à ch't-heure, mais les gens du païe allaient à la ville à pid ou en quériot et les cians qu'en avaient, atou leus caravanes à daeux ou quatre reux.

N'y-avait pas d'van; i c'menchait justement a ll'avait des "spring-carts" et tout l'quéré s'faisait atou des quériots. A'ch't-heure ch'est "vans," "lorries," "motor-cars," "bicycles," "motor bikes," "chaises à tyres," et les gens peuvent pas marchier daeux perques ou i s'raient hors d'état. Dans chinquànte àns tout chunna n's'ra pouit. Quiqu'grànd savànt era inventaï quiqu'sorte de manivelle que vou mettraï autour de vou, vou pousseraï un bouton et dans quiqu'minutes vou s'raïz d'Pllainmont à la ville ou vice-versa.

Ill'à chinquànte àns nou véyait des courtillies d'bllaï de toutes les sortes, et les femmes allaient atou leus dards aïgué à l'battre. A'ch't-heure ch'est des "bulbs" et des tommates, et vou n'véyie quàsi jamais une femme dans un courtil ou moins qu'j'n'sait une frànçaise.

Ll'avait d'grànd-quérues à dix ou douze bêtes, où nou-s'en faisait un festin. Nou's-avait d'bouannes doraïes d'burre et d'la mouarue à mié-matin, d'la gâche à si à mie-r'lévaïe, et au ser à soupaïr, d'bouan jambon et d'la houichepote à frit et du cidre à gogo, et pis d'la dànse et d'bouannes vieilles chànsons jusqu'au jeur au matin.

A'ch't-heure nou quérue atou daeux ch'vaux ou atou l'tracteur, n'y-a pas une goutte à ll'avait et à bian des taques faut queriaïr sen bisa. A chinquànte àns d'ichin, les choses éront chàngis. I n's'ra qu'faire de ch'vaux ni d'tracteur. Vou s'éra une sorte de machîne que vou piqu'raï à n'un but et tout chu qu'y'era à faire s'ra être un houmme à chaque but pour r'viraï la machîne et a f'ra s'n-affaire à sen tout saeu.

Ichin d'vànt étou ll'avait d'grànds gardins poummes à muche et à cidre. Ill'avait des prinsaeux partout pour pillaïr les pommes et en faire du cidre et n'y-avait pas quàsi une ferme qui n'eûsse sa barrique de cidre. En chu tems là nou s'avait d'bouaune gâche mêlaïe et entr'daeux crôtes et pis des poummes douces à la r'traite au four qui rendaient un amas d'siro qu'nou aîmait à la follie. Nou s'avait étou des panais à la graisse, parfais un fricot d'trippe à la craque au fricasshies, parmi d's'ougnons, d'l'étuvaïe et du maq'ré salaï, A'ch't-heure tout est chàngi. Ch'est du boeu rôti et toute sorte de qué au range, des "jellies," du "custard" et toute sorte de boucas stewaï. En mil neuf chent septànte-quatre, n'y-éra rien d'chunna. Quiqu'autre grànd savànt éra inventaï la manière de condensaïr toute nourriture. Nou s'en prendra un morcé dans sa paute de corset de d'sous et nou s'en mangera daeux ou treis brins daeux ou treis caoups par jour et v'là tout. I n's'ra qu'faire de couquer ni d'sali d'vessiaux ni rian d'itaï qué.

Ill'a chinquànte àns n'y-avait pas d'téléphones ni d'"wireless." Tout chu qu'il-l'avait ch'tait des "telegram" qui v'naient à la ville et s'y-en avait yun pour la campagne nou-s'allait l'portaïr à ch'va. A ch't-heure tous s'enter parlent de sie iaeux atou l'téléphone; et l'"wireless" d'sen côtaï fait d'grànd progrés. Mais à chinquànte àns d'ichin tous éront l'"wireless" dans leus pautes et tous pourront s'entre palaïr ou communiquer l's-uns dauve le's-autres, même jusqu'en Anglléterre.

Et pis les modes d'y-a chinquànte àns ont bian changis. En chu tems là les bouannes vieilles femmes et les jannes étou, allaient à la ville atou leus scoup. I m'taient d'gros châles de laïne et d'gros cotillons d'flané. Ciz iaeux i m'taient des fros d'coton ou d'linsi et gros saulers. Au dimmanche, i m'taient leus gaìnnes de souée, leus froc d'mérino et leus bottes à lastique. Ch'était l'tems des "hoops" et y'en avait d'si gràndes qui leus fallait à peu près tout l'marchepid à leus tout saeu.

L's-hoummes avaient d'longs bllu fros d'coton et des brées d'futâine, d'rond chapiaux ou bian des câlottes à saluette, qu'nou s'appelait des "cheesecutters." Au dimmanche i m'taient leus longues cottes à pannaïe ou d'gros corsiaux blu drap, et des hauts box.

Ach-t-heure les dames vont écourtaïes, émanchies, décolletaïes et sàns chapé, et si n'vont pouit sàns cauches, i sont si tenvres qu'nou vait leus paumets l'travers. I leus faut des saulers, à strappes et haut talons, ou bian des bottes à boutonnaïr quasi au genouaï. Pas d'cotillons, ni d'châles, ch'est des "combinations," des "jumpers," des "mackintosh," et nou n'ot palaïr qu'd'georgette, d'crêpe de chîne, d'moccasin, et j'n'sait qui. L's'hoummes n'en rabattent pas grànment. I vont étou decolletaïs, d'courtes brées, dauve des "cuffs" ès pids. Ch'est des "Jersey hats," des "panamas," des "golf caps," et des "suits" de toutes les couleurs.

Qu'est qu'en s'ra d'ichin à chinquànte àns, j'n-peux pouit dire; mais s'les choses continuent j'cré bian qu'les tems d'Adam et d'Eve s'ront r'venus.

En terminànt ma p'tite lure j'finirai par dire qu'les chose n'ont pouit amendaï, et n'amendent pouit. L'Education à fait d'grands progrès mais l'monde n'a pouit amendaï. Les bouannes vieilles femmes d'ichin d'vànt allaient à la veille ou vîllaient ciz iaeux, où qu'ils ouvraient des corsiaux d'laine ou des cauches et tâchaient d'gagner d'penni. A'ch't-heure, ch'est ès pictures ou quiqu' autre sortie, et bian j'sis d'avis qui faut de la récréation, j'cré que l'monde en fait un dérègle. Qu'est que s'ra en mil neuf chent septànte-quatre j'n-peux pouit m'l'imaginaïr; mais donc j'n'm'en gêne pouit, caër y'éra longtems que j'n's'rait pouit d'chu monde.

Guernsey fifty years ago, Guernsey today and Guernsey fifty years from now, *1925*

Comparing Guernsey from fifty years ago with Guernsey today is all well and good for those people born in the 1860s, but for those that were born thirty years ago or less, it is as difficult for them as for those people now to say what Guernsey will be like in fifty years time.

In eighteen hundred and seventy four business in Guernsey was just, one could say, beginning. We used to only see a few greenhouses around and about and there were lean-tos, built specifically for grapes and there was almost no talk of tomatoes. It is true that steamships came and went everyday from here to England and vice-versa; but the steamships were much smaller than the ones now and they went much more slowly. At that time there wasn't what is called "perishable stuff", rather it was potatoes that were shipped, and if they were delayed a day or two, there wasn't a problem.

Now the island is almost covered with glass, or as we say with "span," and there are hundreds of tons of tomatoes that leave Guernsey every year.

The steamships nowadays are much bigger and much faster, in the height of the season two are needed everyday and often a lot of loads are "out-shipped". If the trade continues, in fifty years' time Guernsey will be so full of "span" that there won't be any room to build another one.

Fifty years ago there were no heated greenhouses. You didn't see anthracite, but it's a good thing that there are heated ones now as the bulk of tomatoes doesn't come all at once; if it did, it would be very unfortunate. If things continue, in nineteen seventy four we won't need steamships at all. Everything will come and go by air. I don't think there will even be a need for coal as the "spans" will all be heated by electricity, and I even think that there will be stations all over the island to collect the tomatoes, and who knows, they may go straight from these stations to the markets in England.

Town has also changed a lot. In the past the streets were much smaller and narrower. The shops were not as big, nor so fashionable. You didn't see buses or motorcars continually coming and going like now, but country folk went to town by foot or in a box cart and those that had one, in their two or four-wheeled hooded wagonette.

There were no vans; they were just starting to have "spring-carts" and all transporting was done with box carts. Now there are vans, lorries, motorcars, bicycles, motorbikes, carriages with tyres, and people cannot walk two perches without it being too much for them. In fifty years time all of that will be no more. Some great scientist will have invented some kind of device that you will put around yourself, you will press a button and in a few minutes you will go from Torteval to town and vice-versa.

Fifty years ago you could see fields of all kinds of cereal, and women with their sickles helping to cut it. Now there are bulbs and tomatoes, and you almost never see a woman in a field unless she is French.

The "deep ploughs", the ones requiring ten or twelve animals pulling them, were great events and an occasion to hold a party. We had good sandwiches of butter and cod mid-morning and suet cake mid-afternoon, and in the evening for supper, good ham and fruit pudding and cider galore, and then dancing and good old songs until morning light.

Now we plough with two horses or with a tractor, there's not a drop to have and at a lot of places you must carry your packed lunch. In fifty years' time things will have changed. You won't have to bother with horses and tractors. You will have a kind of machine with which you'll start the furrow at one end and all that there will be to do is to have a man at each end to turn the machine around and it will do its thing on its own.

In the past there were big orchards full of apples to store and for cider. There were cider presses everywhere for crushing the apples and making cider and there was hardly a single farm that didn't have its barrel of cider. At that time we had good gâche mêlaïe and apple or rhubarb pies and sweet apples baked in the oven as it cooled after the bread had been taken out that gave out a lot of caramelised syrup that we went mad for. We also had basted roast parsnips, sometimes a feast of tripe, fried till crisp, with onions, stew and salted mackerel. Nowadays everything has changed. There is roast beef and all kinds of things cooked on the range, jellies, custard and all sorts of stewed things. In nineteen seventy four there will be none of that. Another great scientist will have invented the way to condense all foods. You will put a piece in the pocket of your waistcoat and you will eat two or three bits two or three times a day and that's all. There will be no need to cook nor dirty dishes or any such thing.

Fifty years ago there were no telephones nor wirelesses. All that there was were telegrams that arrived in town and if there was one for the country it was delivered on horse back. Now everyone talks to everyone else from their homes by telephone; and as for the wireless, it is making great progress. But in fifty years' time everyone will have a wireless in their pocket and everyone will be able to speak to each other or communicate with everyone else, even as far as England.

And then fashions of fifty years ago have changed a lot. At that time the good old ladies and the young as well went to town with their bonnets. They wore big woollen shawls and big flannel petticoats. At home they wore cotton or linsey-woolsey dresses and heavy shoes. On Sundays, they wore silk gowns, their merino dresses and their elastic-sided boots. It was the age of "hoops" and there were some that were so big that they took up nearly all of the pavement on their own.

Men had long blue cotton smocks and fustian trousers, round hats or else peaked caps, that were called "cheesecutters". On Sundays they would wear their long frock coats or big navy tops, and top hats.

Now ladies go out in short skirts up to here, with shirtsleeves up to here, plunging necklines down to there and without hats, and if they don't go out without stockings, they are so thin that you can see their calves through them. They must have shoes with straps and high heels, or else boots that button up almost to the knee. No petticoats, nor shawls, Now it is all combinations, jumpers, mackintoshes and all you hear about is georgette, crêpe de chine, moccasins, and I don't know what else. The men don't stint themselves much either. They also go around open-necked, in short trousers, with turn ups on their trousers. It's all Jersey hats, panamas, golf caps, and suits in every colour you can think of.

What will it be like in fifty years' time, I cannot say; but if things carry on I think that we will be back in the times of Adam and Eve.

In ending my short tale I will finish by saying that things haven't improved a bit, and are not getting better. Education has made great progress, but people are no better than they were. The good old ladies in the past used to go to evening get-togethers or spent the evenings at home, where they knitted woollen sweaters or stockings and strived to earn a penny or two. Nowadays it's to the pictures or some other outing, and although I'm of the view that you need entertainment, I think that everyone goes a little too far. What will it be like in nineteen seventy four, I cannot imagine; but after all I don't worry about it, as I'll have been long gone by the time that comes around.

The importance of auction sales for changes in farm ownership, social interaction and the vernacular has been reflected in literature. Philippe Le Sueur Mourant wrote a tale about Bram Bilo's misadventures at an auction which became a classic of Jèrriais literature. T. A. Grut later translated adventures of Bram Bilo into Guernesiais. This may have inspired him to compose this depiction of a tussle between auctioneer and bidder, which is less well known, but deserves an outing.

T. A. Grut

From La vente au pus offrànt!, *1931* (Guernesiais)

Oy'ous, mess Editeur, av'ous jamais ataï à un' vente dans les hautes Pâresses? Si qu'non, allaï donc à quique détouor, et vous y erraï du pllaisi.

Nico Berhaut des Marchez mouorri draïnement sàns l'sier fâmme ou effàns, et l's hériquiers criaient tous pour leus shâre, et furent trachier l'Encànteur pour vendre tout, et leus baïllier l'argent.

J'n'étais poui pour acataï, mais comme j'aïme à fourraï l'naïz partout, je n'mànque poui un' chànce d'allaï vée chu qu'y'a à vée.

Ch'tait un' vieille maison, d's établles, dix vergies d'terre, des parcs à cochons, fourques et bêques, selles à bûrre, et tout l'boucâs d'un' ferme. J'alli du partên, mais y avait déjà un' guène de gens de toutes les sortes. Y en avait comme mé, chu qu'nous appelle des "nosey parker," d'côte les siens qu'étaient pour accataï.

Quànd l'Encànteur s'trouvi, i' c'menchi sa lure par dire que l'pus offrènt s'rait l'acheteur, et que si daeux avaient l'malheur de baïller le caoup d'tête au même moment, qu'ils erraient à s'battre, et l'vaïnquieur s'rait l'acheteur.

Si ch'tait daeux fâmmes, qu'ils erraient à s'battre justément comme les hômmes. Si ch'tait un' hômme et un' fêmme, les conditions s'raient chàngies; la fâmme s'rait permise de capuchier l'hômme; et quànd a' s'rait hors d'étât et évanie, l'hômme, si àcore en vie, s'rait contaï l'acheteur.

L'encànteur c'menchi ses élogies d'la maison par dire, qu'al' avait daeux chents àns, et si biean bâtie, qu'a' durerait acore un autre daeux chents, et qu'au but du temps, a' voudrait pusse qu'un' toute neuve bâtie ochetaeure. Quànd nous vint ès établles ch'tait la même lure, et pour les parcs à cochons, s'ti, av'ous jamais veue un parc dérocqui? un parc à cochon durera jusqu'à la fin du monde et un an ou daeux après. Y'avait trais vacques, vieilles et secques et maigres, mais l'Encànteur nous dit que la sécheresse s'pâsserait si nous les m'tait au courtil quànd i' piouvrà.

Y avait étout un' douzaîne de vieilles poules qui n'avaient poui pounu pour bien d's àns, mais i' nous dit qu'il avait l'idée qu'i' c'menchaient à rouogir, et qu'i' poun'raient à quique détouor.

La selle pour le ribot était toute ouverte et cracquie, mais il avisi de mettre du potin ou d'la târe dans les cracques.

D'vier onze heures, l'Encànteur c'menchi par dire: faites mé un offre pour chu bel héritâge, maisons, terres, et toute la pêque; mille livres sterling, neuf chents, huit chents, chinq chents; pas d'offre. Eche pour vous moquier d'mé qu'ous êtes tous v'nu ichin? J'la prendrai pour les chinq chents, et si vous n'êtes poui vite, j'la prendrai pour men fils qui s'en va s'mariaï à la saint Jean; je n'prendrai pâs "d'bid" moins de vingt chinq livres sterling, et dépêch'ous, caer je n'resterai poui ichin jusqu'à la niet.

Ma fâmme est à m'préparaï un fricot d'ormers, et si j'targe trop, la famille grierà l'plliât.

Après chenna l'affaire marchi un p'tit pus vite, et l'bargain fut "knocked-down" à Pierre Berhaut des Marchez, ieun des hériquiers. Quand vint pour payer les dix pour chent sus l'bargain, Pierre "qu'avait ieue trop à bère" et voulait faire montaï l'prix, vouli s'en dépiauquier par dire que chu qu'l'Encànteur avait print pour un caoup d'tête, etait un "d'jerk" caûsaï par un' puche qui l'mordait au derrière d'sen co.

L'Encànteur en fit bien mâri, caer quâsi tout l'monde était parti, et n'y avait poui moyen de r'quemanchier la vente. L'Encànteur vouli forchier Pierro de payer le dix pour chent, mais comme il 'tait sàns le moindre d'argent, 'n'y avait qu'à l'mettre en prison. Ils allirent trachier l'connêtablle, et Pierro douni s'n expllicâtion; étànt ieun d's hériquiers, il avait fait des "bids" pour faire montaï l'prix, mais, que par malheur, il en avait baïlli ieun de trop, et pour s'en déhallaï qu'il avait mis la blliâme sus la puche.

L'Encànteur s'n'alli pour la maison pour sen fricot d'ormers, et r'mit l'ânnonce dans la Gâzette pour la s'maïne en r'vénànt.

Pierro fut libéraï, en promettànt de s'gardaï hors d'la vée des ventes durânt sa vie naturelle, et un an après.

From **Sold to the highest bidder!**, *1931*

Well, Mr Editor, have you ever been to an auction in the higher Parishes? If not, go there some time and you'll enjoy it.

Nick Bréhaut of Les Marchez died recently without leaving any wife or children, and the heirs were all calling for their share, and sent for the auctioneer to sell the lot and give them the proceeds.

I didn't go to buy, but since I like to poke my nose in everwhere, I didn't pass up the opportunity to go and see what there was to see.

It was an old house, stables, ten vergées of land, pigsties, forks and spades, butter churns, and all the clobber of a farm. I went early but there was already a crowd of all sorts of people. There were some like me, what they call nosey parkers, besides those who were there to buy.

When the auctioneer was in position, he started off his spiel by saying that the highest bidder would be the purchaser, and that if two should be so unlucky as give the nod at the same time, they'd have to fight each other for it, and the winner would be the purchaser.

If it was two women, they'd have to fight each other for it just like the men. If it was a man and a woman, the rules would be different: the woman would be allowed to hit the man, and when she was incapable of going on and flat out, the man, if he was still alive, would be judged the purchaser.

The auctioneer started off praising the house to high heaven, saying that it was two hundred years old, and so well constructed that it'd last another two hundred, and then it would be worth more than a brand new building constructed now. When we got to the stables it was the same story, and as for the pigsties, he said, have you ever seen a tumbledown pigsty? A pigsty will last until doomsday and a couple of years after that. There were three cows, old, dry and skinny, but the auctioneer told us that the dryness would go away if one put them out in the field when it rained.

There were also a dozen old hens that hadn't laid in many a long year, but he told us that he thought they were starting to get broody and that they'd be laying one of these days.

The butter churn was open and cracked, but he advised filling in the cracks with some putty or tar.

Around eleven o'clock the auctioneer started off by saying: make me an offer for this fine property, buildings, land, and the whole kaboodle; a thousand pounds sterling, nine hundred, eight hundred, five hundred; no bid. Have you all just come here to make me look a fool? I'll take five hundred, and if you're not quick about it, I'll take it for my son who's getting married at midsummer; I'm not taking any bid under twenty five pounds sterling, and get a move on, because I'm not staying here until dark.

My wife's cooking me up a slap-up meal of ormers, and if I'm too late, the family will have wolfed the lot.

After that things went a bit more quickly, and the bargain was knocked down to Peter Bréhaut of Les Marchez, one of the heirs. When it came to paying the ten per cent down, Peter who'd "had a drop too much" and had tried to push the price up, tried to wriggle out of it, saying that what the auctioneer had supposed to be a nod was a twitch caused by a flea that had bitten the back of his neck.

This got the auctioneer very angry, because almost everyone had left, and there was no way of starting the auction over. The auctioneer wanted to force Pete to pay the ten per cent, but as he didn't have any money at all, the only thing to do was to have him imprisoned for debt. They fetched the constable, and Pete gave his explanation; as one of the heirs, he'd made bids to push the price up, but unfortunately he'd made one bid too many, and to try to get out of it he'd put the blame on the flea.

The auctioneer went off home for his ormer slap-up, and put the advert in the Gazette again for the following week.

Pete was released, having promised to stay away from auctions for the rest of his natural life, and for a year after that.

Edward Le Brocq's long-running series of tales of Ph'lip and Merrienne, an old Jersey married couple from Saint Ouen, started in the *Jersey Critic* before the Second World War. After the Liberation, the English language newspaper the *Morning News* re-opened under Edward Le Brocq's editorship and with a weekly installment of domestic banter and bickering and social and political commentary from Ph'lip and Merrienne. The *Morning News* folded in 1949, but Ph'lip and Merrienne re-appeared in *Les Chroniques de Jersey* the following year, carrying on like the old married couple they were until *Les Chroniques de Jersey* closed in 1959. They transferred to the *Evening Post* where they kept up regular appearances until the author's death in 1964. This article appeared in February 1962, when the American astronaut, John Glenn, was in the news.

Edward Le Brocq ('Ph'lip')

Ph'lip va à la lune, Et en vait de pus d'une sorte, *1962* (Jèrriais)

À Portinfé
Saint Ou

Moussieu l'Editeu

J'ai yeu yunne des pûs drôles d'expéthiences d'ma vie chutte semaine, mais d'vant qu'menchi à vos la raconter j'voudrais vos rapporter la conversation que j'eûmes, la Merrienne et mé, en dêjeunant hièr matin.

Ou qu'menchi par mé dithe qu'oulle 'té lâssée d'entendre de chu Colonel Glenn sûs l'radio. "Après tout," ou s'fit, "tchèsqu'il a fait de si merveilleux qu'les Russes n'avaient pas fait d'vant li?"

"Il a fait l'tour du monde trais fais dans sa machine," j'li dis, "sans aver arrêté une seule fais et il est r'venu sain et sauf."

"Epis?" ou d'mandit. "Par chein qu'les gâzettes en ont dit il avait 'té trais ans à s'prépather et sa fichue machine étout. Mais chein que j'voudrais saver ch'est tchi bein qu'il a fait en circhulant, auve l'aide de ses instruments trais fais?"

"Ch'n'est qu'un qu'menchment", j'li dis, "car les Améthitchains ont idée d'aver deux hommes dans la machine la préchaine fais, et i'sont prèsque seux qu'à quatre ans d'ichin i' pouôrront arriver jusqu'à la lune."

"Ouèsque i' n'y a autchune vie et ouèsque rein n'peut craitre," ou dit "Bieau prospect, ma fe! Mais d'vant aller pûs lyien, Ph'lip je n'crais pas pour un moment que j'vivons sûs un globe, car si ch'tait vrai et qu'nou pâssait à travers l'air à une pathelle velocité nou n'pouôrrait jamais sé t'nin d'but. Nouffé quant à mé, j'si de l'opinion du moussieu tchi pâslit sûs l'radio hièr au sé, disant que la têrre était pli-atte. Il ajouôtit que y'avait une mâsse dé monde qu'en 'tait aussi seux comme li, et si j'pouvais l'vaie j'li dithais bein vite que j'en si yunne. Mais apart de chonna, estche-tchi n'y a pas assez à nos otchuper sûs la têrre d'nos jours sans nos badrer de chein tchi y'a sûs la lune? Sans doute le Colonel Glenn a fait chein tch'i' d'vait faithe mais chonna s'en ya-t'i' réconciller nos fermiers et les marchands, ou empêchi l's Etats d'continuer à faithe des bêtises?"

"Nennîn, bein seux, Merrienne," j'li dis, "mais après tout, i' n'faut pas oublier que y'a un côté d'la lune que j'n'avons jamais veu et sûs chu point-là, j'm'en vais te raconter le réve que j'ai yeu la niet pâssée."

"Tchiquechose d'intérêssant sans doute," ou s'fit, "par la manièthe que tu'as gig-oté pour une bouonne heuthe ne m'permettant pas une minute de r'pos. Si j'n'avais pas creu que tu 'tais sûs l'point d'aver une attaque d'apoplexie, j'éthais bétôt prînt des m'suthes pour te garder trantchille, mais enfin tchèsque-en est d'chu rêve?"

"J'rêvis," j'li dis, "que j'avais 'te transporté, je n'sais pas comment, au côté qué j'n'avons jamais veu et crais-lé s'tu veur, ch'tait un vrai paradis. Y'avait d'l'herbe si riche qu'une vaque jêrriaise éthait enflié d'sûs et crevé dans une démi'euthe et des bouais des chents pids d'haut. Y'avait des belles petites rivièthes et i' faisait tréjous jour, car lé sole lisait tout-l'temps mais la chaleu tait tempéthante, et nou n'enhan-nait pas, car hommes et femmes 'taient touos nûs."

"Et te?" ou d'mandit "tu'avais ocquo tes habits, sans doute?"

"Nouffé, Merrienne," j'li dis, "car j'avais yeu à me deshabillyi pour être comme lé restant. Chein tchi 'tait l'pûs drôle de tout j'avais rajeuni de pûs d'chinquante ans. I' n'y avait pas de vielles gens, et i' n'y avait pas d'mathiage, car tout était libre. Nou pouvait se mathier aussi souvent comme nou voulait, et i' n'y avait ni églyises, ni chapelles, ni ministres pour vos dithe comment qu'nou dév'thait s'comporter. Et, bein seux, i' n'y avait pas d'divorce car quand un homme et sa femme décidaient de se s'pather, i' l'faisaient sans autchune rantchune. En un mot, comme je t'lai dit, ch'tait un vrai paradis et quand j'me si rêvillyit et trouvé que ch'n'tait, après tout, qu'un rêve, j'éthais peut plieuthé."

"Si tu'avais 'té un homme respectablye," ou s'fit, "tu'éthais deu plieuthé d'honte à l'âge que tu'as. Tu n'm'as pas dit, pour une chose, si les femmes 'taient comme les bouais, des chents pids d'haut."

"Nennîn," j'li dis "I' 'taient comme les femmes d'ichin sinon bein pûs belles. Oh vèthe, y'avait du chouaix!"

"Une autre chose qu'tu n'm'as pas dit," ou s'fit, "et ch'est combein d'fais que tu t'mathyit."

"Eh bein, Merrienne," j'li dis "de chonna j'n'ai autchune mémouaithe."

"J'pensais bein," ou dit, "Eh bein, man Ph'lip, tout ch'que j'te donne en avis ch'est d'oublier chu gniolin-là, épis ne r'quémenche pas, car la préchaine fais j'pouôrrais m'marri. A ch'teu, r'venons à notre bouon-sens et n'pâslons pas d'un paradis mais de chein tchi s'arrive ichin dans notre p'tite Ile dé Jêrri. Tchèsque en est de nos patates?"

"Eh bein, ma chièthe," j'li dis, "la seule difféthence que j'peux en vaie ch'est que l'fermyi peut exporter san produit de six ou sept difféthentes manièthes, mais tréjous il étha à péyi les frais du transport et la commission à tchique marchand. J'peux m'tromper mais i' m'semblye que si par malchance la saison est tardive, les pouôrres fermiers du nord et d'autres parties d'l'Ile n'éthont pas grand profit à montrer quand veindra les dernières s'maines, mais si n'veint pas de r'but, lé prospect est assez bé."

"Et tchèsque tu pense de l'idée au Douar' Lé Feuvre?"

"Pas grand'chose," j'li dis, "et je n'crais pas que hardi d'fermiers lé support-éthont. Quant à mé, j'n'y vais pas grand avantage, et je doute que nous en r'ouïtha pâsler fort. Le Douar' est comme sans pèthe, tch'avait tréjous d's idées mais i' n'taient pas tréjous bouonnes."

"I' nos reste lé tourisme," ou dit, "tchi gouverne tout. Y'a toute appathence dé pûs d'visiteurs que jamais, et les hôtels en sont si seux tch'i' sont à dêpenser un tas d'sous pour êlargi lûs prémisses."

"J't'ai dit pûs d'une fais, Merrienne, tchèsque qu'j'en crais du tourisme, et je n'ai rein à ajouôter agniet. Chein tchi m'intérrêsse ch'est la djobbe d'Avocat-Général, tchi n'est pas ocquo remplie; par conséquent, nou n'peut pas dithe pour seux que y'étha une vacance pour Sénateur et une êléction contestée."

"R'vénant à tan réve pour une minute," ou dit. "A-t'i' fait du bein à tan dos car il est temps de t'mettre à froutchi ta bordeuse?"

"Man dos," j'li dis, "n'a pas amendé et je n'pouôrrais pas entreprendre pathelle djobbe, mais si l'Bram n'veint pas la faithe au pûs tôt, je n'vais pas pourtchi, qu'en pâssant l'temps tu n'pouôrrais pas t'y mettre car j'ai tréjous oui que n'y a rein milleu qu'un mio d'travas sûs la têrre pous les cors. Si fait bé dans un couplye d'jours tu pouôrrais faithe pièthe."

"Et mûs étout, vièr pièrcheux!" ou dit. "Si tu arrête à m'vaie dans ta bordeuse, tu'as ocquo longtemps à vivre. J'm'en vais au liet!"

Philip goes to the moon and gets more than he bargained for, 1962

in Portinfer
Saint Ouen

Dear Mr Editor,

I've had one of the strangest experiences of my life this week, but before I start to tell you about it I'd like to tell you about the conversation we had, Mary Ann and me, over breakfast yesterday morning.

She started by telling me that she was fed up hearing about that Colonel Glenn on the radio, "After all," she said, "what's he done that's so wonderful that the Russians hadn't done before he did?"

"He went round the world three times in his vehicle," I told her, "without having to stop once and he came back safe and sound."

"So?" she asked. "According to what the papers have said, he'd been three years getting ready along with his wretched vehicle. But what I'd like to know is what what good has he done going round in a circle like that three times with the help of his instruments?"

"It's only a start," I told her, "for the Americans intend having two men in the vehicle next time, and they're almost sure that four years from now they'll be able to get to the moon."

"Where there's no life at all and where nothing can grow," she said. "A fine prospect, indeed! But before going any further, Philip, I don't believe for a moment that we live on a globe, for if that was true and we were passing through the air at such a speed we'd never be able to stand upright. No way. As for me, I think the same as the gentleman who spoke on the radio yesterday evening, saying that the earth was flat. He added that there were a whole lot of people who were as convinced as him, and if I could see him I'd tell him straightaway that I was one of them. But that aside, haven't we got enough to occupy us on earth nowadays without bothering ourselves about what's on the moon? Colonel Glenn has doubtless done what he had to do but is that going to bring our farmers and merchants together, or stop the States from continuing to act stupidly?"

"No, of course not, Mary Ann," I told her, "but after all, we mustn't forget that there's a side of the moon that we've never seen and on that topic, I'm going to tell you the dream I had last night."

"Something interesting no doubt," she said, "by the way you wiggled for a good hour and prevented me getting a minute's rest. If I hadn't believed that you were about to have an attack of apoplexy, I'd have soon taken steps to keep you quiet, but, come on, what about this dream?"

"I dreamed," I told her, "that I'd been transported, how I don't know, to the side we've never seen and believe it or not, it was a real paradise. There was grass so rich that a Jersey cow would have swollen up on it and died within half an hour, and trees hundreds of feet tall. There were lovely little rivers and it was always daylight, because the sun shone all the time but the temperature was mild, and no one suffered because men and women were all naked."

"And what about you?" she asked, "you still had your clothes on, I suppose?"

"Not at all, Mary Ann," I told her, "because I'd had to get undressed to be like the others. The strangest thing was I grown fifty years younger. There weren't any old folk, and there wasn't any marriage because everything was free. You could get married as often as you liked, and there weren't any churches, or chapels, or priests to tell you how you should behave, And of course there wasn't any divorce because when a husband and his wife decided to separate, there did it without any bitterness. In a word, as I told you, it was a real paradise and when I woke up and found that after all it was only a dream, I could have wept."

"If you'd been a respectable man," she said, "you should have wept with shame at your age. And another thing, you haven't told me if the women were like the trees, hundreds of feet tall."

"No," I told her. "They were like women here, only prettier, Oh yes indeed, there was a good selection!"

"And something else you haven't told me," she said, "and that's how many times you got married."

"Well, Mary Ann," I told her, "I have no memory of that at all."

"I thought as much," she said. "Well, Philip, all I can advise you is to forget that nonsense, and don't start again or else the next time I'll get angry. Now, let's get back to common sense and instead of talking about a paradise, let's talk about what's happening here in our little Island of Jersey. What about our potatoes?"

"Well, my love," I told her, "the only difference that I can see is that the farmer has six or seven different ways of exporting his produce but he still has to pay transport costs and commission to some merchant. I might be wrong but it seems to me that if through bad luck the season is late, the poor farmers in the north and other parts of the Island won't have great profit to show in the final weeks, but if it doesn't turn out badly, the prospects are fairly good."

"And what do you think about Edward Le Feuvre's idea?"

"Not much," I told her, "and I don't think that many farmers will support it. As for me, I don't see any great advantage in it, and I doubt we'll hear much more about it. Edward's like his father, who was full of ideas, but not always good ones."

"We're left with tourism," she said, "which rules everything. There's every sign of more visitors than ever, and the hotels are so sure of it that they're spending lots of money enlarging their premises."

"I've told you more than once, Mary Ann, what I think of tourism, and I've got nothing to add today. What interests me is the post of Solicitor-General which hasn't been filled yet; consequently, we can't say for sure if there'll be a vacancy for Senator and a contested election."

"Getting back to your dream for a minute," she said. "Has it done your back any good because it's time for you to go and fork over your vegetable patch?"

"My back," I told her, "hasn't got better and I couldn't undertake any such job, but if Abraham doesn't come to do it soon, I can't see why, to pass the time, you couldn't get down to it yourself because I've always heard that there's nothing better for corns than a spot of work on the ground. If it's fine in a couple of days you could do worse."

"And better, too, you old lazybones!" she said. "If you expect to see me in your vegetable patch, you'll have a long time to wait. I'm off to bed!"

The 1969 moon landing inspired Amelia Perchard with more optimistic thoughts about peace and progress than those of Ph'lip and Merrienne a few years earlier. But the modernity of the theme is balanced by an appreciation of traditional beliefs.

Amelia Perchard ('A.L.P.')

Eune Supposition, *1969* (Jèrriais)

> Les êtres humains n'împorte iou
> En tout âge et généthâtion,

Ont admithé la Leune au liain –
Dépis lé temps d'la Créâtion,
D'Adam jusqu'à chu jour ichîn,
Sa lumiéthe les a êcliaithis
Sus la tèrre et la mé, sans r'lâche –
Avau l's années sus l'c'mîn d'la Vie.

Les poètes, auv' lus don spécial,
Ont louangi sans cêsse sa bieauté
Atout des vèrsets à s'n égard,
L'app'lant souvent "Reine dé la niet";
Reine oulle est étout ès auteurs,
Qu'ont raconté dans tant d'lus chants
Lé mystéthe qui l'a entourée –
Suspendue là pour des mille ans.

Toutes les crianches entouorre la Leune
Qui nos sont v'nus dé péthe en fis,
Ont couomme l'histouaithe dé san pouver
Lus originne dans l'temps jadis.
Dé vaie l'craissant l'travèrs d'eune f'nêtre
Amène la mauvaise chance, nou dit.
Coumme fait étout sa réfléction
Dans l'ieau dé canné ou vivyi.

Il est counnu qué cèrtaines gens
A la plieine leune ont dêrangi,
Étout qué l'pouver des chorchièrs
A chu temps-là est renforchi.
Mais mauvaise chance et chorchell'lie,
Sont bein liain d'être dans les pensées
Des amouotheurs tchi lus promènent
Au cliai d's rayons argentés.

Mais les crianches au temps à v'nin
Né s'sont pon counnues par les gens,
A cause des êvénements d'ch't' année,
Quand d's hoummes d'un esprit tchestchionnant
Eûtent lé couothage d'aller pour vaie
S'oulle 'tait vraiement faite dé fromage,
Ou s'i' trouv'thaient l'hoummme dans la Leune
A l's attendre à la fin d'lus viage!

Ches deux-s-trais jours-là en juillet –
Toutes les nâtions 'taient à l'attente
Dé chu moment-là historique,
Quand lus machinne f'thait la descente,
Et qu'l'houmme pour la toute preunmié fais
Sus chut autre monde mettrait san pid,
S'exposant pour l'amour d'la scienche
A i' n'savait dgéthe tchi dangi.

Mais les millions d'gens qu'attendaient
La nouvelle dé lus aventuthes,
Pensant qu'i' trouv'thaient singne dé vie,
Ou p'têtre tchique genre dé créatuthe –
Fûtent-t'i' déchus d'saver qu'la Leune
N'tait rein d'pus qu'un énorme d'sèrt,
Et qu's'i' y'a vie à part d'ichin
Qu'ou s'trouve ailleurs dans l'Unnivèrs?

Tch'est qu'ch'est qu'il' espéthaient trouver
Là dans les Cieux si liain dé nous,
Qu'éthait changi la vie qu'nou mène,
Ôté l'fardé' qu'nou porte tous?
Car i' y'a bein raison à craithe,
Qu'au jour d'aniet un tas d'gens pensent
Qu' i' n'reste rein dans chu Monde-chîn
Pour justifier lus existence!

Et, tch'est qui sait? S'peut qu' y'ait tchique bord
Dans l'înmensité d'l'Unnivèrs,
P't-être eune aut' civilisâtion
Auve la rêponse qué tout l'monde chèrchent;
Et, l'ayant trouvée, ou pouôrrait
Être la cause d'unni les nâtions,
Pour qué paix et bouanne volanté
Es'saient auve nou Ichîn tréjous!

A Supposition, *1969*

Human beings everywhere
in every age and generation,
have admired the moon from afar –
since the time of Creation,
from Adam until this day,

its light has shone on them
on land and sea, constantly –
down the years along the path of Life.

Poets with their special gift
have praised her beauty without ceasing
with verses addressed to her,
often calling her "Queen of the night";
She's also the Queen for authors,
who've described in so many of their tales
the mystery which has surrounded her –
hanging up there for thousands of years.

All the superstitions about the Moon
which have been handed down from father to son,
have like the story of its power
their origin in olden times.
Seeing the new moon through a window
brings bad luck, so they say.
As does its reflexion
in the water of a stream or pond.

It's well known that at a full moon
certain people go out of their mind,
and also that the power of witches
is strengthened at that time.
But bad luck and witchcraft
are far from the thoughts
of lovers who go for walks
in the light of its silvery beams.

But superstitions in the future
will be unknown to people,
because of this year's events,
when men of an inquiring mind
had the courage to go and see
if it was really made of cheese
or if they'd find the Man in the Moon
waiting for them at the end of their journey!

Those couple of days in July –
all the nations were anticipating
that historic moment

when their vehicle would make its descent
and when man for the very first time
would set foot on that other world,
exposing himself for the love of science
to who knew what danger.

But the millions of people who were waiting
for news of their adventures,
thinking that they'd find signs of life,
or perhaps some kind of creature –
were they disappointed to find out that the Moon
was nothing more than an enormous desert,
and that if there's life apart from here
it's to be found elsewhere in the Universe?

What did they expect to find
up there in the Heavens so far from us,
which would have changed the life we lead,
relieved us of the burden that all must carry?
For there's reason to believe
that nowadays a lot of people think
that there's nothing left in this World
to justify ther existence!

And, who knows? It may be that somewhere
in the the immensity of the Universe
there's another civilisation perhaps
with the answer that everyone's looking for,
and once we've found it, it could be
the cause to unite the nations,
so that peace and goodwill
might be with us here forever!

Language

The linguistic situation in the Islands has inspired comment from many visitors. The vernacular languages, spoken in the home and workplace, found themselves sometimes squeezed between French, language of law and the Church and the only official language until the twentieth century, and English, language of commerce and increasing numbers of settlers throughout the nineteenth and twentieth centuries. Breton seasonal workers, political refugees and other immigrants all added to the linguistic mix. Some passing observers were confused by the multiplicity of languages, sometimes unable or unwilling to distinguish between French and the indigenous languages. Other observers had cultural prejudices to parade. Patriotic writers who wanted to champion their languages could, however, find some supportive commentators.

Philippe Falle, Rector of Saint Saviour, Jersey
From An Account of the Island of Jersey, *1694*

The Language is *French*. Divine Service and Preaching, Pleadings in Court, Public Acts, Conversation among the more genteel and well-bred, all these are in good *French*; but what the Vulgar do speak, is confessedly not so. Yet even That is not so properly a corrupt, as an obsolete and antiquated *French*. For, excepting the viciousness of Pronunciation, it seems to be the very same that obtained in *France* in the Reigns of *Francis I* and *Henry II*; as appears from the Books and Writings of that Age, wherein one finds abundance of Words, retained to this day by our People, which a polite modern *Frenchman* would not use, perhaps does not understand. All Languages are subject to change, but none has undergone more or greater alterations than the French, whether for better or worse is not agreed among their own Writers; some of whom complain that their Language has been impoverished by too much refining it, and casting off Words of great usefulness and significancy.

After all, there are spoken in many Provinces of that Kingdom various *Jargons*, not a whit better than the worst amongst us; and what is said by them of themselves, *que les gens de Qualite, et les gens de Lettres, parlent bien par tout,* i. e. that People of Fashion, and Men of Learning, speak well every where, is (I trust) no less applicable to others. It ought not therefore to deter *English* Parents from sending their Children hither to learn *French*, though at the hazard of carrying back a few less modish and less elegant turns of Speech, which Books and good Company will easily correct afterwards. Here, they will be out of the way of Men who who *lye in wait to deceive*, and their Religion and Morals will be safe, which cannot be said of the Places they go to. Add to this, a saving and lessening of Expence. Albeit *French* be our ordinary Language, there are few Gentlemen, Merchants, or considerable Inhabitants, but speak *English* tolerably. The better to attain it, they are sent young into *England*. And among the inferior sort, who have not the like means of going abroad, many make a shift to get a good smattering of it in the Island itself. More especially in the Town of St. *Helier*, what with this, what with the confluence of the Officers and Soldiers of the Garrison, one hears well-nigh as much *English* spoken as *French*. And accordingly the weekly Prayers in the Town-Church, are one Day in *French*, and another in *English*.

Joan Tapley's characterisation of the language through the shapes of the letters makes a rare emotional connection with the writing system. With the pressures of standardisation pushing writers to adopt either French or English spelling conventions, the look of the vernaculars has never been as close to people's hearts as the sounds.

Joan Tapley

Lé Jèrriais, *1996* (Jèrriais)

L   Un haut homme mâté èrgardant vèrs l'av'nîn,
é   Eune femme accliutchie, ses pensées vèrs démain,

J   Un bâton touônné sus sa tête, janmais sèrvi i' né s'sa,
è   Not' langage comme eune balle, codpîsée 'chîn et là,
r   Eune femme baîssie à assemblier des lettres et des affaithes,
r   San janne homme baîssi étout à chèrchi des mémouaithes,
i   Un p'tit garçon, pour ouï not' vielle langue il arrête,
a   Un ballot d'vièrs livres pitchis oubliés dans eune boête,
i   La p'tite mousse qu'apprendrait vite, car oulle est bein sage,
s   Les gens agenouoillis, suppliant dé sauver not' vièr langage!

Jèrriais, *1996*

L   A tall man standing looking towards the future,
é   A crouching woman, her thoughts turned towards tomorrow,

J   A walking stick turned on its head, never to be used,
è   Our language like a ball, kicked hither and thither,
r   A woman stooping to gather up letters and stuff,
r   Her boyfriend, also stooping to look for memories,
i   A little boy stops to hear our old language,
a   A bundle of old books thrown into a box and forgotten,
i   The little girl who'd learn quickly, because she's very good,
s   People kneeling, praying to save our old language!

George Métivier

Not' Guernesiais, *1867* (Guernesiais)

Not' guernesiais, ô ma coummère!
Il est, chu qu'tu'es, l'éfànt d'sa mère,
Vif, espritu, malin, joli,
Hounnête et bouan, s'i n'est poli.
Quànd j't'o, m'n oreille en est ravie,
L's Angllais m'font pus d'piti qu'd'envie,
Suffliant d'laids mots, les tristes gens,
Du but d'la lichouette et des dents.

Pour mé, je m'fais ouir, dès que j'chante;
D'mànde à Mnémosyné, que j'hànte!
A men travsain, la belle, amors,
Vient m'écàntaïr, si tôt qu'j'm'endors.
Les vers, i s'font, sàns qu'nou-s y pense;
Et n'faut-i pas en marmounnaïr,
En attendànt sen déjunaïr?

Sus not' vier fest d'gllie, l'hirondelle
Dit bon jour à la draïne ételle,
et là, dans sen creux, guilleri,
Fier et godin, s'niche à l'abri.
L'mêlot, sus l'meis d'Mai, fait la vie,
I n'veurt pas qu'a' targe, s'amie,
Et tout-au-ras, sous un motté,
L'alouette écharde l'aoûté.

Que d'brit, mon secours, dans nos belles!
Les mâlards font bel à leus belles;
Et que d'galànts, à longs ergots,
M'élourdent d'leus coquedicots!
Sus l'nouaisier i plleut des souciques;
Raïne ou roué, y'en a-t'i des triques?
Et véyous l'ribé, l'malin piànt,
L'verdeleu, l'moigne et l'vert-bruànt!

L'matin d'St. Philippe et d'St. Jaque,
A l'asinànt, l'éfànt désaque,
Mouissette et mouisson, herbe en flleur,
Bras-d'ssus, bras d'ssous, la jouaie au coeur.
Je l's o qui rient, parlafrandine,
Sous la laurière et sous l'épine;
L'amour, i volte sous leus pas,
La gnet d'chu matin-là, n'dort pas.

Quànd la rousâie, à la Pènt'coûte,
Quéyait sus l'frie, et, goutte-à-goutte,
Faisait étinch'laïr, je n'sai c'ment,
L'pourpre et l'âzur, l'or et l'argent,
Je m'cllùngeais au fin-fond d'la maïre,
et j'avalais la sauce amaïre,
Pillvaudànt, coumme un viau, l's ieillets,
L'gllajeur, le coq, et les cllaquets.

Our Guernesiais, *1867*

Our Guernesiais, oh my godmother!
It is, what you are, the child of its mother,
lively, witty, clever, handsome,
honest and good, if not necessarily polite.
When I hear you, my ear is taken with you,
I pity the English rather than envy them,
whistling ugly words, the sad folk,
from the tips of their tongues and teeth.

As for me, I make myself heard as soon as I sing;
ask of Mnemosyne, with whom I keep company!
That beauty regularly comes to my pillow,
to entertain me as soon as I fall asleep.
Verses write themselves, without having to think about it;

and don't you just have to murmur them,
whilst awaiting breakfast?

On our old roof thatch ridge, the swallow
says good day to the last star,
and there, in its hollow, twittering,
happy and joyous, nestles in the shelter.
The fledgling blackbird, in the month of May, lives fast,
he doesn't want her to delay, his female friend,
and right down at the foot of a mound
the skylark teases the male skylark.

What a noise, my goodness, in our courtyards!
The drakes are courting their beauties;
and how many long-spurred suitors,
importune with their cock-a-doodle-doos!
On the nut tree it is raining gold-crested wrens;
queen or king, aren't there a lot of tricks?
And can you see the wren, the clever chap,
the hedge sparrow, the chaffinch and the greenfinch!

The morn of the feast of St. Philip and St. James,
at dawn, the youngster comes running out.
Lovebirds together, pasture in bloom,
arm in arm, with joyful hearts.
I hear them laughing, by Jove,
under the shrubbery and under the hawthorn;
love, fluttering in their footsteps
in that morning's twilight, does not sleep.

When the dew, at Whitsun,
was falling on the wet meadow, and, drop-by-drop,
making, I know not how,
the purple, the azur, the gold and the silver sparkle,
I would dive down into the depths of the sea,
and I would swallow the bitter saltwater,
trampling, like a calf, the thrift,
the flag iris, the costmary, and the foxgloves.

Thomas Lyte

From A Sketch of the History and Present State of the Island of Jersey, *1808*

The language of this Island is French: that in general use, is the old French of Normandy, and is the only language used by the lower class of people: the higher ranks understand good French, but unfortunately they descend to the language of the lower class, in their general conversation with them, instead of making use of good classical language, which might, in time, improve the jargon at present spoken. The English language is understood and spoken by the higher class of inhabitants. It is usual for every family who can afford it, to send some of their children to England, to be educated, by which means they acquire the English language grammatically; and, from the great intercourse with England, and the number of troops quartered in the Island, they have abundance of opportunities to practice it.

W. Plees

From An Account of the Island of Jersey, *1817*

The vernacular language is French. Divine service, and preaching, the pleadings at court, and the public acts, are all in good French; though, in legal documents some obsolete forensic terms are still retained. The upper ranks understand and occasionally speak it; but, in compliance with custom, and to avoid the appearance of an affected superiority, over the lower classes, they, *too frequently*, converse in the provincial tongue, or, as it is called, *Jersey French*. This is a heterogeneous compound of antiquated French, intermixed with modern expressions and gallicised English words, so that it may be termed a kind of *lingua franca*, and it is pronounced, especially in the country districts, with a most abominable *patois*. The different parishes even vary in these respects, so that there are more dialects in the language of *Jersey* than in the ancient Greek. This medley is really disgraceful to the island, and it is extraordinary that no efforts have yet been made to remedy the defect. English is, however, becoming daily more and more prevalent; the necessity of comprehending the soldiery has made it understood, even by the market women: it would indeed be soon equally spoken throughout the island, as the present jargon, were it particularly encouraged. Political considerations seem to render this highly desirable.

E. J. Luce makes an appeal for the dignity of Jèrriais against the competing claims of English and French. This poem was written some time before 1918, probably for performance at a concert or the Jersey Eisteddfod. It was published in *Les*

Chroniques de Jersey in 1943, as a piece of morale-boosting patriotism, under the noses of the German military censors.

E. J. Luce ('Elie')
"Vive lé Jèrriais", *c.1918* (Jèrriais)

> Lé monde à ch't heu pour faithe un complyîment
> Ne s'craient polis qu'en oubliant l'Jèrriais;
> Et chatchun s'sert à tout moment
> Et tant bein qu'mal, d'Angliais ou bein d'Français.
>
> Mais pour dé mé, j'aime acouo man canton;
> J'n'ai pas besoin, pour mé montrer civil,
> D'autchun langage autre que notr' vièr jèrgon –
> Et auprès tout, criy'ous qu'i' s'sait si vil?
>
> Les êtrangièrs, qui n'font que d'atterrer
> Sont limités à chein qu' i 'pâlaient d'vant;
> Mais les Jèrriais dev'thaient dithe en Jèrri
> Ès Jèrriais, en Jèrriais, lus sentiments.
>
> Certains ont honte – ou peux d'paler l'Jèrriais;
> I' bargouaich'chont du Français mal apprins,
> Ou d'l'Angliais d'France – ah! si janmais s'ouïaient!
> Et chein qu'est drôle – i'craient qu' i' sont malins!

Long live Jèrriais!, *c. 1918*

> To be courteous, people nowadays
> think they're being polite only if they forget Jèrriais;
> and anyone can use at any moment,
> whether well or badly, English or French.
>
> But as for me, I still love my stomping ground;
> I don't need, to show my civility,
> any other language than our old lingo –
> and, after all, do you think it's so base?
>
> Foreigners who've only just landed
> are limited to what they spoke already;
> but Jersey people ought to express their feelings in Jersey
> to Jersey people in Jèrriais.

Some people are ashamed, or afraid, of speaking Jèrriais;
they'll gabble some badly-learnt French,
or some English à la française – ah, if only they could listen to themselves!
And the funniest thing is – they think they're being clever!

Thomas Quayle

From General View of the Agriculture and Present State of the Islands on the coast of Normandy, subject to the Crown of Great Britain, *1815*

A Jersey gentleman mentions, that when a prisoner, he happened, when speaking of an under garment, to use the term of his own country, *braies*, instead of *culottes*: the previous suspicions of his captors, were then declared, that he was in truth a native of Normandy, where the same word is still applied to the same article of dress...

The property in the insular tithes and advowsons, which was vested in foreign religious houses, must also have helped to draw these ties more closely; and as there existed an identity of laws and of manners, so probably there was of dialect, with that of Normandy. Many terms not adopted in the politer dialects are still in common use with both, and the tone and accent with which each is spoken, retain a resemblance discernible even to an Englishman.

Since the loss of this valuable truce, and the separation of their churches, various causes, besides commercial intercourse in peace, have tended to keep up the communication between the Continent and the islands; and consequently, to bring back their dialect to the standard from which their closer connexion with England must lead to its constantly swerving. During the long warfare in France between Catholics and Huguenots, the latter, when unfortunate, deserved and received, in these islands a constant asylum.

There, several of the French ministers exercised their sacred functions; and the young islanders destined for holy orders, were sent to receive instruction at the protestant seminaries in France; particularly, at that of Saumur. The pulpit necessarily influences language: but many young men besides those designed for the church, were habitually sent for education to Normandy, even till recently: indeed, at the present day, this practice, however little to be commended, has not come to a total termination in Jersey.

During the rabid period of the French Revolution, whilst the angel of extermination was abroad, the objects of persecution here sought refuge, by thousands, from their assassins. Their residence continued for some time; their nobles conversed with the gentry; their priests instructed the youth: this had some effect on their language; and the lessons of various kinds received at that time, are not yet forgotten.

Still, England, and every thing English, is dear to them: thence are derived their habits of life; thither the majority of their youth resort for education, and for preferment: our books are their study: our notions they have thoroughly imbibed; and English hearts beat in their bosoms.

Terms of art are derived from the language of those who are their instructors in the art itself; and not only the terms, but the English idiom appears frequently introduced into their own dialect. Whilst it adopts new phrases and terms, that of the French capital itself, it should be observed, undergoes as great mutations. In many instances, it is evident, that the words in use in these islands are less dissimilar from the parent Latin, and from the least corrupted of the jargons derived from it, the Italian, than is the modern French. *Vaque, querbon, quemin, pesson, bere*, for instance, bear a stronger resemblance to the same terms in Latin and in Italian, than the French *vache*; *charbon*; *chemin*; *poisson*; *boire*. At this day, all intercourse of the islands with that ill-fated nation is completely cut off: former friendships and connexions have passed away; the residence of numerous English among the islanders, and their own general adoption of English habits and manners, must be rapidly corrupting their dialect; and would lead, if a little aided, to its extinction altogether. In Guernsey, in particular, it is at present neither French nor English. In other provinces of the British empire, languages were once spoken which are now passed, or passing into oblivion, and of which the use is at this day more strictly confined to the humbler classes, than that of French is, in these islands; of these languages, the speaker had no need to be ashamed: they were not, as is that of Jersey, the tongue of an enemy; a branch of a dialect, of a jargon; only comprehended, within the area of a few square miles; but branches of an ancient and expressive language, of which the origin is lost in the night of time. These they wisely agree to forego. In order to identify themselves more perfectly with their fellow-subjects, they prefer the tongue of their metropolis.

And why should not these islands? The gentry shew the example. Their ordinary table-conversation, with very few exceptions, is English. It is spoken, not merely fluently and correctly, but with great precision; marked by some Gallicisms in accent, and a few idioms; but in many individuals, not the least. The conversation of the parlour being then in English, it might be thought in this instance, not difficult to introduce "high life below stairs:" but in order to effect this, the first and most important step is yet to be taken; that is, in the general education of females. Our first tongue, as it is received from our mothers and nurses, is properly termed our *maternal* tongue. In this island, it signifies little that the husband and father has received an education in England, and has acquired a competent knowledge of its language; his wife and female servants carrying on their ordinary conversation in the insular dialect, teach it to his children. In the next generation, the process is to recommence, and the English is to be taught as a foreign language. Had a small annual sum been devoted half a century ago, to the support of a decent English matron, to reside near each of the churches, and instruct female children, at a moderate charge, in English, the struggle between the two tongues would now have been over.

A. A. Le Gros also reacts to the denigration of the vernacular and stakes his literary claim on the reputation of Wace.

A. A. Le Gros ('A.A.L.G.')
Notre Vier Lingo, *1874* (Jèrriais)

> Vrais Jêrriais nès, et Normands d'race,
> Oublliérait-nou la langue d'Wace,
> Le vier lingo, tuos les buons d'vis,
> Que nou-s-aimait au temps jadis.
>
> Au coin de s'n-âtre et d'sa cônière,
> Nou n'cherche pon dutout à nière;
> Et qu'est qu'i puorrait enhanner
> D'nos ouir chanter et badiner.
>
> Si nou peut séquir une lerme,
> A quique peine mettre un terme,
> J'ter des suôrits par chin par là,
> Par ses chansons – y-a-t-i grand ma?
>
> La ruogeur quique feis m'en monte,
> Quand j'vei des Jerriais aveir honte
> De leux jergon, et d'leux pays;
> Quand j'vei d'itè, j'en sis payi.
>
> Jêrry! Jêrry! bénin coin d'terre,
> Dans men biau p'tit vallon d'St.-Pierre,
> Ten vier lingo je chanterai,
> Tant que j'puorrai, tant que j'vivrai.

Our old lingo, *1874*

> True-born Jersey people, and Normans by race,
> shall we ever forget the language of Wace?
> The old lingo, all the old expressions
> that were loved time past.
>
> By the fireside and in the inglenook,
> we don't try to do any harm;
> and who could be any worse off
> from hearing us sing and chatter?

If we want to dry a tear,
put an end to some sorrow,
cast smiles here and there,
through our songs – is there any harm in that?

I sometimes get worked up
when I see Jersey people be ashamed
of their lingo, and of their country;
when I see that, I'm fed up.

Jersey! Jersey! blessed patch of earth,
in my beautiful little valley in Saint Peter,
I will sing your old lingo,
as long as I can, as long as I live.

George Métivier makes loftier claims for the literary status of his language. The language unites Apollo and the muses with the poet and the ploughman, and infuses the Island's landscape and nature. In notes to this 1856 poem he acknowledges having taken borrowed some imagery ('a line too charming not to have been stolen') from the Occitan poet Jacques Jasmin, who had been awarded a pension by the Académie Française in 1852.

George Métivier

Au Nico des Nicos, *1856* (Guernesiais)

Que d'grammairiens, ma fé j'en jure,
N'sont qu'des verveux, vier des Moulins!
I n'ont jamais veu la Nature;
Jusqu'au couté guerre ès malins!
Apollon les excoumunie,
Dansànt, chantànt sus les côtis
Auve Euterpe et Polyhymnie:–
A bas, à mort les sots mouftis!

Revlà l'ouaisé qui mord l'aigrette
D'nos cardons giànts, Golias d'Icard!
L'temps va, vient, cueurt, sàns que j'le r'grette,
L'soleil me jette ùn si doux r'gard.
L'grànd Milton, dès que v'nait l'Autoune,
Riait, harpe en maïn, d'sessànte hivers.
Vé-tu la maïre? A' joue, a' toune,
Ma jouaie est folle, i plieut des vers.

Même au meis des morts, l'éfànt cuille
Des flieurs sàns nombre au Moulin-Huet,
Les flieurs qui charmaient l'rimeux d'l'île
Sus roc et hure, hougue et houmet.
Des suchets pure était l'halaïne,
En Avoût, dans les Saint-Germâïns,
Et Flore au Mont-Durànd est Raïne,
A' règne à Jerbourg, à Fermâïns.

Où l'hublot dort, il y a des fieilles
Dans l'creux d'la falaise illo-bas;
Là, terjous vertes, jamais vieilles,
Linné m'la dit, i n'mourront pas. –
Mourront-i, malgré l'insolence
Qui rit du jargon des Normànds –
Houni, houni qui mal y pense! –
Les mots chéris des seuls vrais grànds?

Le peuple est mort, i n'a pus d'mère,
L'ingrat! – i n'est rien, désormais! –
En r'cordànt nos chànsons naguère,
Dans ùn russé d'mieil je m'bagnais!
L'coeur me disait: "l'prêtre qui prie,
L'maître, l'valet, l'villais, l'terrien,
L'faucheux d'nos fàïns, l'quereux d'nos fries,
N'ont tous qu'ùn langage et ch'est l'mien!"

To the Nick of Nicks, *1856*

How many scholars, I swear,
are nothing but chatterboxes, my old friend from Les Moulins!
They've never seen Nature;
let's stick it to these people who are too clever by half!
Apollo excommunicates them,
dancing, singing on the côtils
with Euterpe and Polyhymnia:–
down with the foolish muftis, death to them!

Here comes again the bird who pecks the flowers
of our giant thistles, the Goliath of Icart!
The time goes, comes, runs, without me regretting it,
the sun casts such a tender look on me.
The great Milton, as soon as Autumn came,

would mock, with harp in hand, sixty winters.
Do you see the sea? It plays, it turns,
I'm mad with joy, it's raining down verses.

Even in the month of the dead, the child picks
innumerable flowers at Moulin-Huet,
the flowers which charmed the island poet
on rock and mound, tumulus and peninsula.
The breath of the honeysuckle was pure,
in August, at Saint Germain,
and Flora is Queen at Mont Durand,
she reigns at Jerbourg, at Fermain.

Where the black-backed gull sleeps, there are leaves
in the cave of the cliff down there;
There, evergreen and unaging,
Linnaeus told me so, they'll never die. –
Can they die, despite the insolence
that mocks the speech of Normans –
let him be spurned, spurned, whoever thinks evil of it! –
the cherished words of the only true great ones?

The people is dead, it no longer has a mother,
the ingrate! – it is nothing any more! –
While recalling our songs recently,
I bathed in a stream of honey!
My heart told me: "the priest who prays,
the master, the farmhand, the town dweller, the farmer,
the mower of our hay, the ploughman of our pastures,
have only one language, all of them, and it's mine!"

Henry D. Inglis

From The Channel Islands, *1835*

The unsettled state of language in Jersey, must be admitted to be a great obstacle to the refinements of civilization. The use of a pure language as, one universal medium of communication, offers to the moral and intellectual condition of a people, as great a facility for improvement, as rail roads, and steam, offer to commerce. But this medium, Jersey has not yet the advantage of. The universal language is still a barbarous dialect. French, though the language of the court proceedings, and of the legislature, is not in common use even among the upper ranks: nay, the use of it, is even looked upon as affectation; and although the English language be sufficiently comprehended for the purposes of intercourse, and is most usually spoken in the best mixed society, it is certainly not understood by many, in its purity. The constant use of a dialect, necessarily induces a distaste for any other purer tongues. Their beauties are not, and cannot be appreciated; and thus, an effectual barrier is opposed to that refinement, which is the sure result of the knowledge and appreciation of the productions which belong to every perfected language.

(....)

The dialect of Guernsey differs considerably from that of Jersey. But it is of course difficult, if not impossible, to explain the difference. The dialect is even different, in different parishes: for the nearer these lie to the towns, the less pure is the dialect, spoken. The word "pure" may be thought by some, to be inappropriately used; but in fact, the *patois* of both islands, as it is spoken in the interior parishes, is nearly the pure French of some centuries ago; and while the French has changed, the language of these Norman islands remains nearly as when Wace, the Jersey poet, composed his "Roman du Rou," in the year 1160. Indeed, the inhabitants of the Channel Islands, in those parishes where their families have constantly intermarried, are purer Normans, than are now to be found elsewhere. The people of Normandy are French.

(...)

More and better English alliances have been formed in Guernsey, than in Jersey. The greater attractions of Guernsey society, and the less temptation which the higher prices of Guernsey have held out to residents, have brought to that island a somewhat superior class of strangers; and I would add, that the residence of Lord De Saumarez on his patrimonial ground, has also had its influence in raising the tone of society.

If I am asked, where are the proofs of superior civilization, – I may answer, that none are required; since it is impossible, that the different circumstances in which Guernsey and Jersey are placed, could fail to produce a difference in their respective states of society. But this superiority is seen in a thousand things. It is observable, in more varied topics of conversation; in more extended, and more liberal views; in more amenity of manner; in greater respect for talent and acquirements; above all, in a more perfect understanding of the English language, which not only facilitates an acquaintance with those models which cannot be studied without corresponding effects; but excludes the use of a dialect which is as unsuited to civilized life, as are the habits of the people among whom it was employed two centuries ago.

Jean Sullivan managed to coax a testimonial out of Victor Hugo in 1864. Naturally enough, being the shameless self-publicist that he was, Sullivan promptly had it published in the press.

Victor Hugo

Testimonial, *1864*

Hauteville-House, 19 Mai, 1864.

Monsieur, – Je sors d'un travail long et absorbant, ceci vous explique le retard de ma réponse; je n'ai pas lu vos vers avant d'avoir l'esprit libre; la poésie veut l'homme tout entier. Aujourd'hui, à tête reposée je vous ai lu, et je suis charmé de ce que j'ai lu. Vos vieilles rimes jersiaises m'ont enchanté. Votre antique idiome, est un de nos grands pères; il y a du sang Normand en vous comme en nous; vous êtes, Monsieur, dans cette précieuse langue locale, un vrai Poëte. Je suis heureux de vous le dire.

Recevez l'assurance de mes sentiments très distingués.

Victor Hugo

À Monsieur John Sullivan,
Brunswick House,
Victoria Road, Jersey

Sullivan's own translation:

Sir, – I have just finished a long and absorbing work, this will explain why I have not written to you sooner. I have not read your Poems before my mind was absolutely free. Poetry requires man's entire attention. To-day, at full leisure, I have read them, I am charmed by what I have read; your old Jersey rhymes have enchanted me; your antique idiom is one of our Grand-Fathers; there is in you as in us Norman blood; you are, Sir, in that precious local language a true Poet, I am happy to tell you so.

Receive the assurance of my most distinguished sentiments.

(Signed) *Victor Hugo*

A letter to La Gazette de Guernesey, *1867* (Guernesiais)

Moussieu, – J'vou asseure donc qu'j'étais fier de vée, Sam'di drain, sus vot' charmant papier d'nouvelles, une longue libelle écrite dan notre bouanne vieille langue. Che n'tait pouit tant l'sujet qui m'frappait, bien qu'i l'tait bouan assaï – coum ch'tait la langue. I'me r'semblliait, ma finge, que j'étais r'venu à men bouan janne temps, quand j'patuflliais d'pis l'matin jusqu'au ser chu bouan vier djergon là, et que j'n'en oyais pouit d'autre.

Tout l'temps passaï, moussieu, j'créyais qu'vou étaites yun d'la cllique qui voudrait n'ouïr en Guernesi que d'l'anglliaictin, ou p't-être une miette de bouan français, et qui tournent leux naïs quand il' ôent une p'tit' parole d'la langue d'leux anchêtres, mais, dame, je sies bien fier d'vée que j'me trompais, et qu' vou n'êtes même pas trop orguilliaeux pour la pubilliaïr sus not' noblle Gazette. Ch'est donc chu qui m'a déterminaï à vou adeurchier daeux-o-trais mots dans not langue maïse, car bien que j'peux me r'paraïr bien assaïz du français, j'préfère bieaucaoup not' balivernin.

Moussieu, v'chin chu que j'voulais vou dire; ch'est qu'i ll'ya une tapâie d'gens par ichin qui trouvent à r'dire parce que nous laisse les éfans pâlais la langue de Guernesi dans l'zécoles du pâie. I' faudrait, suivant yaeux, s'bornaïr à l'anglliaictin, ou au bouan français à quand nou leux pâle, et moussieu, ch'est chu qu'nou n'peut pouit terjous faire, du moins, pouit mé; et d'même, aurun que d'pâlaïr daeux langues, l'zéfans d'not' école en pâlent trais, chu qui vaut accouare mûx; mais, coum je dis, nou'z est bllîâmai, sans r'preuche.

A letter to La Gazette de Guernesey, *1867*

Sir, – I can tell you that I was very pleased to see, last Saturday, in your charming newspaper, a long yarn written in our good old language. It wasn't so much the topic that struck me, although that was interesting enough – as it was the language. My goodness, I fancied myself back in the good old days of my youth, when I'd natter away from morning till evening in that good old lingo, and I never heard anything else.

And all this time, Sir, there I was thinking that you were among that gang that would prefer to hear nothing in Guernsey but Englishry, or perhaps a smattering of Parisian French, and who turn their noses up when they hear the slightest word of the tongue of their forefathers, but, well, I'm very pleased to see that I was wrong, and that you're not above publishing it in your fine Gazette. So that's what has prompted me to address you with a couple of words in our mother tongue, for though I can get by in French not too badly, I much prefer our patter.

Sir, this is what I'd like to tell you; there's a lot of people roundabouts who find fault because children are allowed to speak the Guernsey language in the country's schools. One ought, according to their way of thinking, to restrict oneself to Englishry, or to Parisian French, when one speaks to them, and, Sir, that's what one can't always do, at least, not me; and in that way, instead of speaking two languages, the children in our school speak three, which is more useful; but, as I say, we get the blame, and undeservedly.

Philippe Langlois' tour round the dialects of nineteenth-century Jèrriais is invaluable as a record of how the linguistic differences were seen at the time. It is also an enjoyable text for recitation as the speaker has to change accent, and exaggerate for effect, throughout the reading of the poem. The poem also contains yet another reminder of the rivalry between the Toad and Donkey: note the Jersey expression 'la dgèrnésiaise' (in modern spelling) for diarrhoea. Guernesiais speakers have got their own back with one of the euphemisms for going to the toilet – *tiraïr aen Jèrriais* (shooting a Jerseyman).

Philippe Langlois ('St.–Louorenchais')

Le Jerriais, *1873* (Jèrriais)

> J'avons entendu des Anglliais
> Se moquir du bouan vier Jerriais;
> De trouver à r'dire est lus mode,
> De cmander partout est lus code;
> S'i' n'se trouvent pon bein ov nous,
> Faut lus dire allouoz-en siez vous.
> Mais empliy'ons mus notre pllume,
> Et frappons sus une autre enclume.
>
> Les Jerriais sont tous d'un bâté,
> Et devraient aimer lus râté;
> Car il est vraiment respectabllé,
> Fort ancien et fort vénérablle;
> Sans aver le même paler,
> Je pouvons fort bein deviser
> Entre nous sus aucune affaire,
> Et d'une faichon assez cllaire.
>
> Les gens de l'Est ont un accent
> Du chein du Vouest bein différent;
> Dans le Vouest nous frume la bouoche
> Et la voix sembllé être pus douoche;
> Dans l'Est i'montrent pus les dents,
> Et autrement sont différents;
> Ch'est au point que j'avons ouï dire,
> Mais j'pensons que ch'tait pour rire,
> Qu'un marchi n'pouvait s'faire aut'fais
> D'St. Ouennais a St. Martinais;
> S'il êtait question de mariage,
> Fille et garçons s'entendraient j'gagé;
> Es cheins qui voudraient en douter,
> Je lus requemande d'êprouver.
>
> A St. Martin i'dizent *veze*.
> Faisant d'l' *r* un *z* comme en *peze*,
> Nouz y leve les pids en *haaut*,
> Et nous y bet daut'chose que d'll'*iaaue*;

Les autres paraisses vaisines
De chu pàler là sont couosines;
l' vont à la pêque eu *batquaaux*,
Et à terre cachent des *chvaaux*;
Mais ous puorrez mus le comprendre
En allant sus les llieux l'entendre.

Les St. Ouennais vont au *Puléc*
Ramasser des trainées de *vréc*,
Et aussi bein à Ste Marie
Nouz en fait autant je parie.

L'St. Breladais pâle d'la *Touo*,
Atou du geon cauffe le *fouo*,
Appele les vlicots des *coques*
Est tout environné de roques.

A *St. Louthains* et à *St. Pierre*
Nou prend d'temps en temps un ptit *vèrre*
Nouz y pale le jerriais pliat
Et nou dit Coin *Vathin*, *vethe-guia*
L'*r* entre voyelles se change
En *th*, est che pon étrange?
D'autre côté a St. Martin
Ch'est un z que nou l'fait devnin
Nouz y touanne à la grande *quethue*
Nouz y fait servir tour et cue,
Dans qui nou met le cidre doux,
Dont nous peut bere sans ête souls,
Mais nou n'en est pas pus à s'n aise,
Car i' donne la guernesiaise,
Je n'cherche pas à faire affront,
J'espere que tous le creront.

Che n'est pas là toute l'histouaire
Du Jerriais, comme ou pouvez craire;
Je n'ai que touchi le sujet,
Qui sans doute sera l'objet
D'une etude de main de maître,
Et n'tergera pas à paraitre.

Lé Jerriais, *1873*

We have heard the English
making fun of good old Jèrriais:
They're always finding fault;
and make it their business to order everyone around.
If they don't like it here with us,
we should tell them to go back home;
but let's make better use of our pen,
and hammer on about something else.

Jersey people are all in the same boat,
And ought to value their heritage;
because it is really respectable,
very ancient and very venerable:
even if we don't have the same dialect,
we can quite easily talk
to each other on any subject,
and in quite a clear way.

The folk in the East have a accent
different from those in the West:
in the West they close their mouths,
and their voice seems softer;
in the East they show their teeth more,
and are different in other ways;
in fact we've heard it said,
although we think it may have been in jest,
that in times gone by a transaction couldn't be made,
between someone from Saint Ouen and Saint Martin:
if it were a question of marriage,
I bet that a girl and a boy would understand each other:
to those who care to doubt it,
I advise them to try it.

In Saint Martin, when they say "yes" they say véze (instead of *vére*),
making the r into a z like péze (instead of *pére*).
There they lift their feet up hi-i-gh,
and drink something besides wa-a-ter:
the other parishes neighbouring that dialect
are of the same family;
they go fishing, in bo-a-ts ,
and drive ho-o-rses on the land;

but you can understand it better
by going to listen to it on the spot.

People in Saint Ouen go to Le Pulec (with an open *e*)
to collect sled-fuls of vraic (with an open *e*),
and I bet in Saint Mary
they do the same thing.

In Saint Brelade they speak of the Tower (with a round *o*),
and heat the oven, roundly, with gorse,
they call winkles, whelks,
and are completely surrounded by rocks (with a *ck*).

In Saint Lawrence and Saint Peter
they like to have a gla-a-ass now and then;
they speak broad Jèrriais,
and say Coin Vathîn (not *Varîn*), "véthe-dgia" (not *vére-dgia*);
between vowels, "r" turns into
"th", isn't that odd?
On the other hand, in Saint Martin
they turn it into a "z":
they plough with the big plough they call "tchézue" (not *tchéthue*),
and the apple crusher is a "tour" with an "r" (the cider vat is a *tchue*),
into which the unfermented cider goes,
that you can drink without getting drunk:
although you're no better off,
because it gives you diarrhoea;
I'm not trying to offend anyone,
I hope that everyone will believe me.

That's not the whole story
about Jèrriais, as you might think;
I've only touched on the subject,
which will undoubtedly be the object
of a study by some expert,
and will not take too long in coming.

Jean Louis Armand de Quatrefages de Bréau

From Rambles among the Channel Islands, *1857*

The language spoken in the Channel Islands is a species of Norman French. In the
towns tolerable English is spoken, though often with a French accent; but in the

country districts, although English is very commonly partially understood, the patois in question is generally used. The original stock from which this patois has been derived, appears to have been the old Norman French, but in progress of time it has received numerous additions and concretions from other tongues, and more particularly from the English language. Many of the words in common use are in fact English, with the addition of a French termination; the result is consequently occasionally very ludicrous. In all probability, as education advances among the poor, the English language will supplant this patois, and this process appears in fact to be now gradually being accomplished.

Although the particular English accents of the Islands are not as distinctive among the young, brought up on television, radio and popular music, the indigenous languages of the Islands have left traces in the speech even of some of those whose ancestors never spoke them. The accent of Channel Islands English is sometimes described as a sort of South African twang, and some words of Norman origin are so engrained in the language of English speakers that many of them do not realise that they are using Jèrriais or Guernesiais words.

Transcriptions of dialect for comic effect are common enough, as we have seen in Jan d'la Maze's 1890 story of the unveiling of the statue of Queen Victoria. Here is a fairy story by David Jones, written down in a transcription of Jersey English and published in the *Island Topic* magazine in 1967. David Jones was a journalist from Wales who settled in Jersey and was struck, as an outsider, by the particularities of English as spoken in Jersey. The editor-in-chief of the magazine, a Jerseyman, was doubtful about running Jones's stories in the magazine as he thought that it would be seen as disrespectful mockery of the Jersey readership. Jones convinced him, though, and the stories were a success – so much so, that the editor found that reading extracts from them made for much-appreciated after-dinner entertainment. The preoccupations of the 1960s can be seen in the references to miniskirts and drugs.

David Jones

Redrardinood, *1967*

Ahwelleh, it srainin and you cornt go out to play, arwoojew lark to yer a storyeh? You would? Good, well sicomfortably becorse Ah'm gonna tell you all abart Redrardinood.

Redrardinood wassa narse littel gerl who lived wither mother somewhere in the country – Sanepeters Ah think itwaseh. Well, one day er mother calder an said "Now, little Redrardinood. Ah wunchew to take this beancrock to your Grannie. Sheas not been very welleh an the vitimins will doer good."

The sweet lettel gerl, who was loved bah everyone, unwraptastickagum, poptittin er mouth, an said she would go. She larked seein Grannie becorse the old lady wasso easily shocked eh. Redrardinood remembered the first tarm er Grannie ad seen er inner miniskirt eh ... farvinchis above the knee itwas, bychri ... an she nearly fainted. Crarky! "Bottomziz personal things," she muttered. "Young people today are so cheeky."

"Be careful owyou go now, eh," warned Redrardinood's mother. "Stay clear of the main road becorse there are toomeny irecors abart an the visitors dowtreally know ow to drarve overyer. Keep to the path an dodge the vayickles."

Grannie lived qwartsomewayaway – passed the churchan Misterlemarquand's shop turn rart bah the farm andstrayton eh. The sweet lettel gerl settof but before she ad gone very far a bloody wolf mettereh.

"Comment sa va, littel gerl?" he said. "Wosyor name?" Littel Redrardinood spatowter gum ... Ah tolledyew she ad the makins of a lady. That's manners that is, spittinowt yer gum before you replar.

"Whar, wozzit to you, hairy?" she asked. Whatta cleva retort eh? Brains ranniner family – all that runsin ourziz noses.

"An ow older you, mah dear?" asked the wolf, thinkin wotta tasty mouthful she would be.

"Ah'm gonna be thirteen," replard the littel gerl, andinanser to the wolf's questions, tolldim where she was going, and whar she was takin the beancrock to er Grannie.

The wolf ... e adjus come over for the season, an spent most of is tarm drinkin byer in a pub darn bah the pyer ... decided to eattup both Grannie an Redrardinood. E it on a plan. "See, Redrardinood," e said, all crafty lark, "ow pritty the flowers are about yer. Whar donchew pick some for your Grannie?" After the littel gerl ad setabart pickinip bunches of flowers which was wrapped in cellophane-paper, the wolf leptinto is borrowed car an racetoff to Grannie's cottage. E knocked on the door.

"Who is there eh?"

"Littel Redrardinood bringin you a beancrock," called the bloody wolf in a squeeky voice.

"Liftup the latch eh," shouted Grannie inner very deep voice. "Mah screwziz killinme an Ah cannot getowt of bed."

The wolf laughed, "Ahhhar, a rumblin, recumbent rheumatic wreck," he alliterated. What? What does alliterate mean? Well, it means ... er ... well, thatchew can read an are not illigitimut Ah suppose. Illigitimut? Well that means being able to read the werds on the imsheet achore parunts weddin eh.

But anyway, thassal besard the point. The wolf liftidup the latch, rushtinto the room an devoured Grannie. Then, after goin to the kitchinan avin a swigasauce to washer darn, he pouttoner clothesan nartcapan got into bed.

In the meantarm Little Redrardinood ad been stopped from pickinup the bunches of flowers orf the graves bah the Recter an she maderway to Grannie's cottage. She liftidup the latchan saw the wolf larnin bed.

"Oh Granmother," she said, "what big yers you ave eh?"

"The betta to yer you with, mahluv."

"But Grannie, what big eyes you ave."

"Too much mainlarnin mah dear," replard the wolf ... an itwas true eh. E was ooked tarter than that conger Misterlucasseldestboyflip caught larsweek.

"Oh, but Grannie," exclaimed littel Redrardinood, "what big teeth you ave got... is that through avin fluorard in the water where you come from? Wedownt avityer..."

The wolf was staggered. E was gettin ready to say somethin lark "All the bettato eatchew with, mahluv" an to leap outta bed an start the gastronomic action – withorwithart Tourism's permission. "Fluorard," he yelled, "is thata new karnda kick?"

Wottabloodynoisy made eh. Shoutinanravin. Well, at that very moment who should appen the be parsinbah but a centinyer. This onnerypleesofficer strode into the room, cleardis throatan said "Ah'm a centinyer an Ah've been sentinyer to see what all the trouble is abart."

Wunnell of a struggle followed eh, but eventually the wolf was taken away to the parishorl ... an everyone lived appily everafta eh.

There, now it as stopped rainin you cannall go out to play. what do you mean, that wasunta propa endin. Of course it was. What appened to the ol crock? Whar, they ate it acourse. Oh, Ah see, you mean the other ol croc... er, dear sweet Grannie!

Ahwelleh, you've eard of a wolf in sheepsclothin, well in this case itwazza more modern version, whatchermartcall a she clothed in wolf eh? Shuttup, shuttup. If ah say that ow it ended thats ow it ended. Ah dontwanteny arguements from you childrun. Runnalong an play wharl the sun is sharnin, it will soon be bedtarm.

Walter Cooper Dendy

From The Islets of the Channel, *1858*

In the afternoon the market is a sort of fashion; but the grouping of the buyers and the loungers is not picturesque, the costume being chiefly the formal cut of England, or the sombre colours of Normandy. The colloquial language is a mingling of French and English: the children are taught both, but, whether in truth or in courtesy, several assured us that they preferred the English.

Edward T. Gastineau

From A Hobble through the Channel Islands in 1858; or, the Seeings, Doings and Musings of one Tom Hobbler, during a four months' residence in those parts, *1860*

The language spoken in Jersey is now generally English, though the working classes talk a kind of patois, called Norman French, which is a terrible jargon, and quite unintelligible to either English or Frenchmen. The upper classes speak both English and French as well as the Jersey patois.

Camille Vallaux

From The Channel Islands, *1913* (translated from French)

The speech of Sark has often been represented as a language apart among the Norman dialects of the Channel Islands; a peasant fisherman from La Vauroque, used to ferrying foreigners and "puffing up" his island, affirmed the same thing to me. It seemed to me, having heard the language of Sark spoken by adults and above all by schoolboys and schoolgirls alike, that the Sarkese language only really differs from the Norman language of Jersey in its intonation. This intonation, in Sark, is drawling and even modulated. Vowels are drawn out. It is a gentle and melodic language similar to that of certain old areas of the French countryside (...) One would believe oneself far removed from an English country or an Anglicised one when one hears schoolgirls saying to each other *Nenni* (no), and repeating in response to everything the expression *et tout* or *itou* (also) that the old wives of the French provinces are so addicted to. But suddenly an English word or expression framed by this peasant French alters the conclusion. One freely mixes *mistake* for French *méprise*, *entrance* for *entrée*.

(...)

One would have only a very incomplete impression of the living reality if one were content simply to study the language of Guernsey in the books of esteemed experts, some of the most brilliant literary quality, who have been trying for a century to set it down and give it a literature. (...) One mustn't read Guernesiais; one must hear it. In the narrow roads of Saint-Pierre-du-Bois and Torteval, on the arching shores of Vazon and Cobo, and even in Forest, Saint Andrew and Castel, occasion to speak to the people of the country, in French or Norman French, easily presents itself. Some speak what can be called pure Guernesiais: particularly the women. Others speak a Guernesiais diluted with ordinary French and fairly numerous English words.

It is not always easy for a French person to follow the conversation of someone speaking pure Guernesiais, especially when they speak quickly. One can imagine that English people, even those most conversant with the French language, cannot understand anything.

From Encyclopaedia Britannica, *1876*

The language spoken in ordinary life by the inhabitants of the islands is in great measure the same as the Old Norman French, though modern French is used in the law courts, and English is taught in all the parochial schools, and is familiar to a gradually increasing proportion of the population, especially in Jersey and

Alderney. The several islands have each its own dialect, differing from that of the others at once in vocabulary and idiom; and a very marked difference is observable between the pronunciation in the north and the south of Guernsey. It has even been asserted that every parish in that island has some recognizable peculiarity of speech; but if this is the case, it is probably only in the same way in which it could be asserted of neighbouring parishes throughout the country. None of the dialects have received much literary cultivation, though Jersey is proud of being the birth-place of one of the principal Norman poets, R. Wace, and has given a number of writers to English literature. The Guernsey patois is rendered pretty well known to the philologist by the *Rimes Guernesiaises* of George Metivier, who has since pub-lished a *Dictionnaire Franco-Normand, ou Recueil des mots particuliers au dialecte de Guernesey*, 1870; and a fair idea of that of Jersey is obtainable from the *Rimes et Poesies Jersiaises de divers auteurs*, by A. Mourant, 1865.

Blanche B. Elliott

From Jersey: An Isle of Romance, *1923*

The question is often asked whether the inhabitants of Jersey are English or French, and the answer is "Neither; they are Jersey." And the dialect is neither English nor French, but a survival and corruption of the old Norman-French mixed with some English words.

It has been stated that the Jersey patois can be understood by the Welsh and the Celts, but this, I gather, has yet to be proved. The Jerseyman can with an effort speak intelligible modern French, but, like his English, it is strongly accented, and does not please a cultured ear.

The *Deutsche Inselzeitung*, in Jersey, and the *Deutsche Guernsey-Zeitung*, were propa-ganda newspapers produced for their troops by the occupying Germans 1940-1945. They may have been confident that they were occupying British territories, but the German authorities still had to cope with populations that were capable of bamboozling the occupiers, when occasion demanded, with their own little-known vernaculars, as well as French and English.

Deutsche Inselzeitung, *1943* (translated from German)

The Islanders

Of all the ancient traditions of the Jerseyman, the language still undeniably lives on: – Jersey French. In a town, in which naturally one hardly hears anything but pure French and, especially after the First World War, English which repressed the former administrative language of the island. A typical case of the confusion in the national character can be illustrated by the following: I spoke English to an old woman and she replied in French. So I continued the conversation in French, and she spoke horrible English back, however, until we came to an agreement to speak in sentences, half in English and half in French.

Deutsche Inselzeitung 11 September 1943

From The Crapaud, June *1835*

Forty-Eight Hours in Jersey

Though not a general market day, much bustle and animation prevailed under the neat piazzas which were densely crowded with english men and french women – the latter rendered peculiarly conspicuous by the altitude of the *coiffure*, and the clatter of their tongues and *sabots*. One side the square is appropriated exclusively to the sellers of butter, viz., the wives and daughters of the Island peasantry – whose bonnets, so like inverted coal shoots – brown calico spencers – black petticoats, and red striped aprons, seemed but ill-calculated to enhance the effect of personal beauty. The attention of these rustics appeared to be wholly engrossed by their well stored baskets and knitting needles. The meat shambles occupy the centre in two double rows of stalls. Here the important business of buying and selling is carried on in the most uncouth jargon that ever grated upon ears polite. "*Allons*, bear a hand John, *happe ton* chopper *et cope chutte* leg *là*," said a butcher, in my hearing, to his apprentice. "My goodness," exclaimed a good woman, "*douze sous les* mutton chops – *combien les* beef steaks," and so forth. The friendly salute of recognition too, of the natives, amused me much. "Ho-d'e-do, *commeut va*, good bye, *à la prechaine*, odd rot it, *mon garçon, ven nos vés*, you're welcome to come."

George Métivier had published his *Dictionnaire Franco-Normand* for Guernesiais in 1870, and Philippe Langlois, A. A. Le Gros and Thomas Gaudin had compiled glossaries in Jersey. Inspired by the 1924 *Glossaire du Patois Jersiais*, Frank Le Maistre started correcting errors and omissions and collecting variants and specialised vocabulary. This led to the publication of his encyclopaedic and voluminous *Dictionnaire Jersiais-Français* in 1966, supported by the States of Jersey as part of the celebrations of the 900th anniversary of the Norman Conquest of England, which was the culmination of a century's development of Jèrriais lexicography. None of which dissuaded an anonymous Jersey joker from scouring the dictionary for words borrowed from English to put together the following skit, dated 1971.

Anonymous

Dictouionnaîthe, *1971*

> Now come along, my young Fraînque,
> and help your Auntie at the sink.
> I'm terribly beheinedaine.

Wash me that heavy sâsse-paine.
Tchèrli can scour the smaller one
if he knows how, sénévéganne;
and you can pour away the slops
while I prepare some fresh tournopse.
We'll cook them in the new tinne-pot,
so see the fire is very hot,
riddle it out with the pôqueur
bequeathed me by ta mère, ma soeur.
Your fire is dead. Bring wood, you dunce,
paper and tondre-bosc at once.
Don't look for it upon the floor;
it's in my dressine-têbl'ye drawer,
or, half a minute, dans ma poche.
Then hurry with the scrobine-broche
and clean that mess around the stove;
and then some bliatchin, my love.
Tomorrow will be laundry-day,
when tout le monde va ouâchinner.
We're out of marguérinne, by Damn!
I'd better have my evening dranme,
And then a pépèr'mène, (you see
the Curé might drop in for tea);
and then I think I'll take a stroll
to pick a bunch of plieunm'tholle,
unless some tourist leunatique
has snatched them all on his pique-nique.
Some here and there he may have spared,
though not for others, the blégèrde,
but as he munched his last sannouiche
he missed a few, sénévébitche.
I'd better wear my old jèrtchîn;
and if it rains while I'm away,
make sure you spread the tèrpalîn
over the stack of drying hay.

(Other poets may take over the burden of this refrain, weaving in Ouêmue, Porche'mue, pîn'tchébècque, Côletèrre, lîngot, sno, stînme; and those of nautical bent might work in tâp-sèle, and bouête-hook).

François-Victor Hugo, son of Victor Hugo, issued a rallying cry in his 1857 book on the Channel Islands *La Normandie inconnue*. In its way, it laid down a marker for the Pan-Norman cultural movement that developed towards the end of the nine-teenth century, as well as issuing a typically Romantic challenge for the renewal of literature in the French language by seeking 'authenticity' in the literature of the distant past and the far-flung fringes. And once again, it is to Wace that appeal is made.

François-Victor Hugo

From Unknown Normandy, *1857* (translated from French)

Latterly I was walking in the parish of Saint Ouen, the wildest and the most Norman of the twelve parishes of Jersey, the one in which the local language has been preserved in its purest form and where ghosts still condescend to speak to the living. On the road, sitting on a little stone bench at the doorway of a cottage that had thatch on its roof and lace at its window, an old woman was singing. I approached. It was neither English nor French that she was singing in, it was a strange language that fascinated me and which was not at all, however, new to me. There were words I understood, others that I did not understand. From time to time, I caught a phrase; from time to time, it eluded me. What I was hearing was for me at once as clear as day, and as clouded as night. This darkness was the shadow the Middle Ages made as they passed me by.

(...)

Thus, in the fields of Jersey and Guernsey, peasants still sing the old language of the trouvères, in the same way as, in the fields of the south of France, they still repeat the refrains of the troubadours. However, alive as it may still be in the coun-tryside, the Oïl language has died away in the towns. In Saint Helier, as in Saint Peter Port, the local language has been forgotten, not in order to learn French, but to learn a foreign language.

All of you! brave Normans of the Channel Islands, who blush to speak as your forefathers spoke, and who have your sons taught in English, you who remove old French names from your streets in order to give them British names, you who transform so zealously your ancestors' cottage into a Saxon bungalow, know this: your local language is a venerable one, your local language is a sacred one; for it is from your local language, just as a flower sprouts from its root, that the French lan-guage came forth that was thereafter to become the language of Europe.

Your local language: your forefathers from Normandy died to take it across to England, to Sicily, to Judaea, to London, to Naples and even unto the tomb of Christ. For they knew that to lose one's language is to lose one's nationality, and that by carrying with them their speech, they brought with them their homeland.

Yes, your local language is a venerable one, for the first poet who spoke it was the first of French poets.

I say and will say that I am
Wace from the island of Jersey.

It was in Jersey, in your little Island "that lies out to sea to the West", that this great French poetry was born. It was before the mysterious monuments that the druids set up on your soil, it was under the long arches of your lanes, it was on the peaks of those rocks lashed by the Ocean and its highest tides, it was in the shade of your macabre caves, it was on the flowers with which you bestrew your granite-paved floors, it was in the heart of that nature so full of contrasts, by turns so charming and so threatening, between rays of sunshine and the lightning flash of storms, that French poetry took its first step and uttered its first cry. That new-born poetry was rocked gently in this sublime cradle by the boundless sea as God had commanded!

Visits and Exchanges

The literatures of the Islands have not developed in isolation. Writers have been influenced from outside. As he tells us, Wace was taken to Caen when young, and may well never have written a single word in Jersey. Matthew Le Geyt is credited with being the first Jèrriais poet to be published in the literary renaissance that followed the introduction of printing at the end of the eighteenth century, and he may have been influenced by the 'Purin' literature of eastern Normandy. The influence of Burns and other regional writers of the Romantic period on Métivier, Langlois and others is evident. Translations were made, circulated and admired; and voices of the diaspora called back to the Islands.

No complete Bible has ever been published in any variety of Norman, although Thomas Martin's manuscript translation into Guernesiais, along with his versions of the complete plays of Shakespeare and others, may be the largest body of literary production extant in the whole of Norman literature.

The growth of tourism, enabled for the well-to-do in the nineteenth century by steamships and railways, became a mass phenomenon in the twentieth century. An ambivalence about the arrival of tourists and the impact of hotels and entertainments has been felt by Islanders; we have already seen this reflected in the writings of Sir Arthur de la Mare and Edward Le Brocq.

Writers from outside the Islands too have travelled and found inspiration. And scholars have travelled to study the Islands' indigenous tongues. In the nineteenth century French writers and journalists sought exile in the Islands from revolution and political persecution – chief among these was Victor Hugo. Frederick Tennyson, Alfred Tennyson's brother, lived in Jersey for 36 years, met Robert Browning in the Island, and met his brother there for the last time before the Laureate's death. Among other British literary visitors and residents in the nineteenth century were Algernon Swinburne, George Eliot and her partner George Henry Lewes (who had been briefly educated in Jersey), Walter Savage Landor, Alice Meynell, Samuel Lover, Philip James Bailey, and Mary Elizabeth Braddon.

Compton Mackenzie was Tenant of Herm in the 1920s. Most of these left little impact on the vernacular literatures of the Islands, except perhaps in reinforcing the vernacular writers' sense of the status of writing.

The phenomenally popular nineteenth century writer, Martin Farquhar Tupper, was through his father part of a long established Guernsey family. Métivier translated his trans-Atlantic bestseller *Proverbial Philosophy* into French, and Tupper himself translated some of Jean Sullivan's poetry into English. Literary visits did not always result in harmony – Tupper recounts how, as a result of a falling out between his family in Guernsey and Victor Hugo, the French author refused to receive him when Tupper called at his home in Saint Peter Port.

Wace

From **Roman de Rou,** *12th century* **(Old Norman)**

> Se l'on demande qui ço dist,
> qui ceste estoire en romanz fist,
> jo di e dirai que jo sui
> Wace de l'isle de Gersui,
> qui est en mer vers occident,
> al fieu de Normendie apent.
> En l'isle de Gersui fui nez,
> a Chaem fui petiz portez,
> illoques fui a letres mis,
> pois fui longues en France apris;
> quant jo de France repairai
> a Chaem longues conversai,
> de romanz faire m'entremis,
> mult en escris et mult en fis.
> Par Deu aïe e par le rei
> – altre fors Deu servir ne dei –
> m'en fu donee, Deus li rende,
> a Baieues une provende.
> rei Henri segont vos di,
> nevo Henri, pere Henri

From **The Story of Rollo,** *12th century*

> If anyone asks who says this,
> who wrote this story in Romance language.
> I say and will say that I am
> Wace from the island of Jersey
> that lies out to sea to the West,

and appertains to the fief of Normandy.
I was born in the Island of Jersey,
and was taken to Caen when little,
there I was set to learning writing,
and then studied for a long time in France.
When I came back from France,
I stayed a long time in Caen
and set to writing in the Romance language:
I produced and wrote a lot.
Through God's help and with the help of the king –
I must not serve anyone but the king –
and God reward him for it, I was given
a prebend in Bayeux.
I tell you it was King Henry II,
grandson of Henry and father of Henry.

In 1862, Prince Louis-Lucien Bonaparte, a cousin of Napoleon III and a distinguished philologist, visited the Islands. While in Guernsey he met George Métivier with whom he had already corresponded, and besides his day-trip to Sark, he also collected a version of the Parable of the Sower in Alderney. As a result of this encounter, the Prince published Métiver's translation of Saint Matthew's Gospel in 1863. Stephen Martin kept the version of the Parable, copied down into his pocket-book by the Prince in Sark, until his death. A copy was provided to J. Linwood Pitts who published it in a volume along with Métivier's version of the Sermon on the Mount.

The Prince also consulted Sir Robert Pipon Marett. According to one source, Sir Robert also provided a Gospel translation in Jèrriais, but no copy of this has been found.

Nouvelle Chronique de Jersey, *1862* (translated from French)

The Prince, wishing to hear the language of the Sarkees spoken, went to Sark last Monday, accompanied by Mr. Stephen Martin, H. M. Sheriff. His Highness made the crossing from Guernsey to Sark aboard the steamer Queen of the Isles, along with 120 other daytrippers. On disembarking the Prince was received by the Seigneur of Sark, who invited him to get into his carriage to be driven to the Seigneurie. He accepted, but before leaving he gathered together a certain number of islanders and asked them to translate for him the Parable of the Sower into the island dialect. The islanders did so most willingly, and the Prince gave them a sovereign as he left them. Those poor people were left in astonishment at such munificence. After having taken refreshment at the Seigneurie, the Prince toured the island and visited the places of greatest curiosity that it contains; then, returning to the Seigneurie, he stopped at the Icart hotel, under the management of Mrs Vaudin, and wished to ascertain if the translation of the Parable was correct. To this effect he entered into conversation with the landlady and her daughter, who indicated several omissions which were corrected. In the evening of the same day, His Highness returned to Guernsey with the other daytrippers.

Parable of the Sower (Sercquiais version, from Saint Matthew)

S. Makyu. Chap. XIII.
L'chen qui sème s'n allit s'mai;
4 Et tàndis qu' i s'maitt une partie d'la s'menche quitt le long du ch'mìnn et l's oesiaux du ciel vìndrint et i la màndgirent.
5 Une aûtre quitt dans d's endréts roquieurs, où alle n'avait pas fort de terre; et ou l'vist ossivite, parçe que la terre où al' 'tait n'était pas ben avant.
6 Mais l'solé se l'vitt et ou fut brulaie; et coumme ou n'avait pas d'rachinnes, ou s'quitt.
7 Une aûtre quitt dans d's épinnes, et l's épinnes vìndrent à craitre, et l'etoupidrent.
8 Une aûtre enfin quitt dans d'bouanne terre, et ou portit du fritt; quiq' grâins rèndirent chent pour un, d'aûtres sessànte, et d'aûtres trente.
9 L'chen qu'a d's oureilles pour ouit qu' il ouêt.

Parable of the Sower (Guernesiais version, from Saint Matthew)

St Maku
Chapitre 13

s'ti vla un s'meux qua sorti pour s'mai
Et quand i s'mait une partie dla s'menche kiei dans la rue et laie mouissons vinre et la maghire toute
Et un aut partie kiei parmi du rokats ou'aie qui ny'avoit pouin grand terre et alheuré a l'vi car a n'etoit pouin biaen avant dans la terre
Et quand l'Soleil fut l'vai a fut gerdie et par n'avé pouin d'rachine a ski
Et un aut partie kiei parmi ds' epines et ls' epines montire et la tuire
Et l'aut partie kiei dans d'bouanne terre et apporti du frit un graien shent l'aut sessante et l'aut trente
que l'siaen qua ds' oraeilles pour oué qu'il os

Parable of the Sower (Jèrriais version, from Saint Matthew)

La Pathabole du S'meux
St. Matchi, Chapitre XIII, vèrsets 3 à 9
Un s'meux s'n allit pouor s'mer;

Et comme i' s'mait, eune partie d'la s'menche tchit l'long du c'mîn; et l'ouaîselîn vînt et mangit tout.

Eune aut' partie tchit sus du grupé, ioù tch'i' n'y'avait pon grand' tèrre, et ou l'vit tout d'un co, pa'ce qué la tèrre n'était pon bein avant.

Mais l'solé sé l'vit et ou fut haûdrie; et comme ou n'avait pon d'réchinnes ou s'tchit.

Eune aut' partie tchit parmi d's épingnes, et l's êpîngnes vindrent à craitre et l'ê-touffîdrent.

Mais acouothe eune aut' partie tchit dans d'bouonne tèrre, et ou portit frit; eune graine en donnit chent, eune aut' souaixante, et eune aut' trente.

Lé chein tch'a d's ouotheil'yes pouor ouï, tch'i' ouaie.

Translation

Behold, a sower went forth to sow;

And when he sowed, some seeds fell by the way side, and the fowls came and devoured them up:

Some fell upon stony places, where they had not much earth: and forthwith they sprung up, because they had no deepness of earth:

And when the sun was up, they were scorched; and because they had no root, they withered away.

And some fell among thorns; and the thorns sprung up, and choked them:

But other fell into good ground, and brought forth fruit, some an hundredfold, some sixtyfold, some thirtyfold.

Who hath ears to hear, let him hear.

Parable of the Sower (Auregnais version, from Saint Luke)

Ein s'maeux sortit pouor s'maeu soun graïn et quaound il s'mait, eine partie du graïn quiyit daouns lé qu'meïn et i fut piliaeu d'sus; et les mossouns en mangi-drent.

Et eine aôt' partie quiyit sus l'galot et quaound i c'meinchit à craït', l'graïn séquit, maounque d'iaô.

Eine aôt' partie quyit daouns l's épeïnes et les épeïnes creüdrent et en maïme teimps il l'eïtoufidrent.

Eine aôt' quyit daouns d'la bouounne taïrre, et lé graïn ayaount creü raportit du bououn frit, chont pouor chont.

Translation

A sower went out to sow his seed: and as he sowed, some fell by the way side; and it was trodden down, and the fowls of the air devoured it.

And some fell upon a rock; and as soon as it was sprung up, it withered away, because it lacked moisture.

And some fell among thorns; and the thorns sprang up with it, and choked it.

And other fell on good ground, and sprang up, and bare fruit an hundredfold.

Thomas Martin translated the Bible and a hundred plays from the work of Shakespeare, Molière and Voltaire, and Pierre and Thomas Corneille, into Guernesiais. He was far from the only vernacular writer in the Channel Islands to be influenced by Shakespeare, although nobody else went so far as to translate the entire theatrical canon.

Thomas Martin

From L'Songe d'une gniet d'Etai, *late 19th/early 20th century* (Guernesiais)

> J'counai un coeti ou'aie qu'la thyme sauvage souflle
> Que lz'iers de beu et la violette qui pend craie
> Enkairemain couvert auve du biau suchet
> Auve daie douces roses muskies et auve de vertes arbres
> Titanie dort la de quik temps dla gniet
> Berchie dans sh'aie fyieurs la auve dans'ries et pyaiezi
> Et la l'serpent elaieze sa pel picottaie
> Large assai pour envloppai une faie d'dans
> Et auve le jun d'shunshin j'en frottrait su sez iers
> Et j'la f'rait pyaiene de horriblles idées
> Prend naen et trache a travers cht allaie ichin
> Une belle dame d'Athenes aie en amour
> Auve un jan homme qui n'la vou pouin met naen su sez iers
> Mais fait le pour que la perchaiene chose qui verra
> Seit la dame Tu counietras l'homme
> Par laie hardes Atheniaennes qu'il a su li

From A Midsummer Night's Dream

> I know a bank whereon the wild thyme blows,
> Where ox-lips and the nodding violet grows;
> Quite over-canopied with luscious woodbine,
> With sweet musk-roses, and with eglantine:
> There sleeps Titania sometime of the night,
> Lulled in these flowers with dances and delight;
> And there the snake throws her enamell'd skin,
> Weed wide enough to wrap a fairy in:
> And with the juice of this I'll streak her eyes,

And make her full of hateful fantasies.
Take thou some of it, and seek through this grove:
A sweet Athenian lady is in love
With a disdainful youth: anoint his eyes;
But do it when the next thing he espies
May be the lady: thou shalt know the man
By the Athenian garments he hath on.

A. A. Le Gros ('A.A.L.G.')

En mémouère de Shakspeare, Tribut d'un rhymoeux Jerriais, *1864* (Jèrriais)

A Shakspeares, à l'âme si pure,
Tchi viyait tant d'sermons divers
Dans chutte belle et fraich' nature,
A li ches vers.

A ch't-i'-là tchi de sen esprit
Pour touos temps des leçons nos sert,
Shakspear' not' maitre et notre ami,
A li ches vers.

O Jerriais! tch'il est bé le livre,
Tchi contetient ses noblles pensaies;
I' nos y montre comment vivre,
Et j'y somm's tous traçaies.

Le bouon-homm' Lear, abandonnai,
Cachi de sa propre maison
Par ses filles, et tant maltraitai
Tchi perd raison.

Antonio tch'offre sa vie
Pour cautionner san jeune ami;
Le Juis tchi, remplyi de furie,
Rest' sans pitchi.

Les p'tits faitchieaux et les schorchiais
Dansant au biau clié de la lune,
Et les r'venants tchi veinn'nt nos r'vais
Quant veint la brune.

O notre maitre et notre ami,
Tchi nos fais bein rire et plieuré,
Jamais nou ne r'verra d'esprit,
O grand Shakspear' comme té.

In memory of Shakespeare, Tribute of a Jersey poet, *1864*

To Shakespeare, to the soul so pure,
who saw so many varied sermons
in this beautiful and fresh nature,
to him these verses.

To the one whose mind
has furnished us with lessons for all time,
Shakespeare our master and our friend,
to him these verses.

Oh Jersey people! how lovely is the book
that contains his noble thoughts;
It shows us how to live,
and we are all depicted therein.

Old Lear, abandoned,
driven from his own house
by his daughters, and so abused
that he loses his reason.

Antonio who offers up his life
to underwrite his young friend;
the Jew who, full of fury,
remains pitiless.

The fairy folk and the witches
dancing in the beautiful moonlight,
and the ghosts who come to see us again
when twilight comes.

O our master and our friend,
who makes us cry and laugh so well,
we will never see a mind,
oh great Shakespeare, like you.

English author William Arthur Dunkerley wrote, as John Oxenham, a number of popular novels set in Sark. *Carette of Sark*, *A Maid of the Silver Sea* and *Pearl of Pearl Island* contain occasional words of Sercquiais for local colour. Here the author gives an impression of arriving in Sark.

William Arthur Dunkerley (John Oxenham)
From Carette of Sark, *1907*

Sercq, in the distance, looks like a great whale basking on the surface of the sea and nuzzling its young. That is a feature very common to our islands; for time, and the weather, and the ever-restless sea wear through the softer veins, which run through all our island rocks, just as unexpected streaks of tenderness may be found in the rough natures of our Island men. And so, from every outstanding point, great pieces become detached and form separate islets, between which and the parent bles the currents run like mill-races and take toll of the unwary and the stranger. So, Sercq nuzzles Le Tas, and Jethou Crevichon, and Guernsey Lihou and the Hanois, and even Brecqhou has its whelp in La Givaude. Herm alone, with its long, white spear of sand and shells, is like a sword-fish among the nursing whales.

In the distance the long ridge of Sercq looks as bare and uninteresting as would the actual back of a basking whale. It is only when you come to a more intimate acquaintance that all her charms become visible. Just as I have seen high-born women, in our great capital city of London, turn cold, unmoved faces to the crowd, but smile sweetly and graciously on their friends and acquaintances.

As you draw in to the coast, across the blue-ribbed sea, which for three parts of the year is all alive with dancing sun-flakes, the smooth, bold ridge resolves itself into deep rents and chasms. The great granite cliffs stand out like the frowning heads of giants, seamed and furrowed with ages of conflict. The rocks are wrought into a thousand fantastic shapes. The whole coast is honeycombed with caves and bays, with chapelles and arches and flying buttresses, among which are wonders such as you will find nowhere else in the world. And the rocks are coloured most wondrously by that which is in them and upon them, and perhaps the last are the most beautiful, for their lichen robes are woven of silver, and gold, and gray, and green, and orange. When the evening sun shines full upon the Autelets, and sets them all aflame with golden fire, they become veritable altars and lift one's soul to worship. He would be a bold man who would say he knew a nobler sight, and I should doubt his word at that, until I had seen it with my own eyes.

The great seamed rocks of the headlands are black and white and red and pink and purple and yellow; while up above, the short, green herbage is soft and smooth as velvet, and the waving bracken is like a dark green robe of coarser stuff lined delicately with russet gold.

Now I have told you all this because I have met people whose only idea of Sercq was of a storm-beaten rock standing grim and stark among the thousand other rocks that bite up through the sea thereabouts. Whereas, in reality, our island is a little paradise, gay with flowers all the year round. For the gorse at all events is always aflame, even in the winter – and then in truth most of all, both inside the houses and out; for, inside, the dried bushes flame merrily in the wide hearth-places, while, outside, the prickly points still gleam like gold against the wintry grey. And the land is fruitful too, in trees and shrubs, though, in the more exposed places, it is true, the trees suffer somewhat from the lichen, which blows in from the sea, and clings to their windward sides, and slowly eats their lives away.

Holinshed, in his account of 1577, is mistaken to suppose that the Île du Raz has anything to do with rats, misled by the Alderney pronunciation of 'raz' (tidal race) which has preserved the final consonant longer than in any of the other Islands (he could have compared the Norman word for 'son' in its old pronunciation as preserved in Anglo-Norman names such as FitzGerald or FitzRoy).

Raphael Holinshed

From Holinshed's Chronicles, *1577*

I cast about to Gersey and Gernsey which Isles with their appurtenaunces appertayned in tymes past to the Dukes of Normandye, but now they remayne to our Queene as percell of Hamshyre and belonging to hir Crowne, by means of a Composition made between King John of England & the King of Fraunce when the dominions of the said Prince began so fast to decrease as Thomas Sulmo sayth.

Of these two Gersey is the greatest, as an Island having 30 miles in Compas as most men doo conjecture. There are likewise in the same twelve Parish churches, with a Colledge, which hath a Deane and Prebendes. It is distant from Gernsey full 21 myles or there abutes.

In this latter also there have been in times past five religious houses and nyne Castelles, howbeit in these days there is but one Parish Church left standing in the same. There are also certayne other small islands, which Henry II in his donations called "Insuletas," (besides very many rocks) whereof one called S. Helieries (wherein sometyme was a Monastery) is fast upon Gersey, another is named ye Cornet, which hath a Castll not passing an arrow shoot from Ger[n]sey.

The Serke also is betweene both, which is five myles about, and hath another annexed to it by an isthmus or Strictlande, wherein was a religious house, and therewith all great store of conyes.

There is also the Brehoc, the Gytho, and The Herme, which latter is four myles in compasse, and therein was sometime a Canonry that afterwarde was converted into an House of Franciscanes. There are two other likewyse neere unto that of S. Helerie of whose names I have no notice.

There is also the rockye isle of Burhou, but nowe the isle of Rattes (so called of the huge plentie of Rattes that are found there) though otherwise it be replenished with infinite store of Conyes, between whome and the Rattes as I conjecture those we calle Turkie Conies are oftentimes produced among those few houses that are to be seen in thys island.

Besides this there is moreover the isle of Alderney, a very pretie plot, about seven miles in Compasse, wherein a Priest not long since did find a Coffin of Stone in which lay ye body of and huge gyaunt, whose for teeth were so bygge as a man's fist, as Leland doth report.

Certes that is to me no marueile at al, sith I have read of greater, and mencioned them already in the beginning of this booke. Such a one also have they in Spayne, where unto they go in pilgrimage as unto S. Christopher's tooth (...) But to returne agayne unto the Isle of Alderney from whence I have digressed. Herein also is a pretie Towne with a Parish Church, great plentie of Corne, Cattell, Conyes and Wildefoule, whereby the inhabitauntes doe reape much gayne and commoditie, onelye woode is theyr want, which they otherwise supply. The language also of such as dwel in these isles, is Frenche, but the attire of those that lived in Gernesey and Gersey, until the time of King Henry the eyght was al after the Irish gyse. The Isle of Gernsey also was sore spoyled by the French 1371, and left so desolate that only one Castel remained therein untouched.

The Jersey author Sir Robert Pipon Marett was proud of a letter written to him by Swinburne which stated: "You have turned your local dialect into a classic tongue."

Algernon Swinburne

In Sark, *1883*

Abreast and ahead of the sea is a crag's front cloven asunder
With strong sea-breach and with wasting of winds whence terror is shed
As a shadow of death from the wings of the darkness on waters that thunder
Abreast and ahead.

At its edge is a sepulchre hollowed and hewn for a lone man's bed,
Propped open with rock and agape on the sky and the sea thereunder,
But roofed and walled in well from the wrath of them slept its dead.

Here might not a man drink rapture of rest, or delight above wonder,
Beholding, a soul disembodied, the days and the nights that fled,
With splendour and sound of the tempest around and above him and under,
Abreast and ahead?

Up to the Reformation the Channel Islands were still, despite attempts to transfer episcopal control to England, under the bishop of Coutances. At the Reformation, the Islands turned predominantly Calvinist under the influence of French language Protestant literature from Geneva and elsewhere. Anglicanism was eventually imposed in the seventeenth century, but the nonconformist streak re-emerged with an enthusiasm among the peoples for the Methodist religious revival. John Wesley visited the Islands in August 1787, preaching at times through interpreters. He recorded his impressions in his *Journal*.

John Wesley

From Journal, *1787*

Soon after we set sail and, after a very pleasant passage through little islands on either hand, we came to the venerable castle, standing on a rock about a quarter of a mile from Guernsey. The isle itself makes a beautiful appearance, spreading as a crescent to the right and left; about seven miles long and five broad; part high land, and part low. The town itself is boldly situated, rising higher and higher from the water. The first thing I observed in it was very narrow streets and exceedingly high houses. But we quickly went on to Mr. De Jersey's, hardly a mile from the town. Here I found a most cordial welcome, both from the master of the house and all his family. I preached at seven, in a large room, to as deeply serious a congregation as I ever saw.

Thursday, 16th. – I had a very serious congregation at five, in a large room of Mr. De Jersey's house. His gardens and orchards are of a vast extent and wonderfully pleasant; and I know no nobleman in Great Britain that has such variety of the most excellent fruit; this he is every year increasing, either from France or other parts of the Continent. What a quantity of fruit he has you may conjecture from one sort only: this summer he gathered fifty pounds of strawberries daily, for six weeks together.

In the evening I preached at the other end of the town, in our own preaching-house. So many people squeezed in (though not near all who came), that it was as hot as a stove. But this none seemed to regard; for the Word of God was sharper than a two-edged sword.

Wesley visited Jersey, and remarked on the ancient grammar school of Saint Mannelier (1477–1863) and La Hougue Bie, the prehistoric burial mound that has been such a landmark of the Jersey landscape.

Tuesday, 21st. – We took a walk to one of our friends in the country. Near his house stood what they call the college. It is a free school, designed to train up children for the university, exceedingly finely situated in a quiet recess surrounded by tall woods. Not far from it stands, on the top of a high hill (I suppose a Roman mount), an old chapel, believed to be the first Christian church which was built in the island. From hence we had a view of the whole island, the pleasantest I ever saw; as far superior to the Isle of Wight as that is to the Isle of Man. The little hills, almost covered with large trees, are inexpressibly beautiful; it seems they are to be equaled in the Isle of Guernsey. In the evening I was obliged to preach abroad on "Now is the day of salvation" [II Cor. 6:2]. I think a blessing seldom fails to attend that subject.

Thursday, 23rd. – I rode to St Mary's, five or six miles from St Helier, through shady pleasant lanes. None at the house could speak English, but I had interpreters enough.

Jean (John) Sullivan (Oméga)

Sonnet à Monsieur Georges Métivier 28 Juin *1865* (Jèrriais & Guernesiais)

Salut, jouie et santai, noble et cliever rimmoeux,
J'géris dans ton cottage ov pliaisir ovec jouaie,
Chest un austel pour mé, chest un temple enchantoeux,
J'y z-ouait des dieux les chants dans l'son de ta douoche vouaie.

Jé vait sus tan biaux front un reflet pur, divin,
Qu'esperluz com' l'escliaït de ton coeur et de t'nasme,
Oh! men Gui qu'est que j'sens? ... respond grand escrivain...
A t'n aspect, man chier Georg', je tréfis, je me pasme...

\# Palfrancordingue, os tu, Jean vier rimmoeux gériais;
Prend d'man fortificat, chest un corguial, un balme,
Meilleur que l'vin bruslaï du vier Nico Pérais.

★ ★ ★ ★

Ouait-tu, Georg', les biaux chants?... oh! v'lo v'nier les neuf soeurs,
Pour couronner ton front, pour te baillier la palme,
Qu'Appollon a quilly pour té, roy des rimmoeurs.

\# Ces trois lignes sont en lingo guernesiais.

Sonnet to Mr George Métivier, 28 June 1865

Hail, joy and health, noble and ingenious poet,
I have made my appearance in your cottage with pleasure and with joy,
It is an altar for me, it is an enchanting temple,
here I hear the songs of the gods in the sound of your sweet voice.

I see on your handsome brow a pure and divine glow,
which dazzles like the light from your heart and from your soul,
Oh, my God, what is it that I feel?... reply, great writer...
at the sight of you, dear George, I tremble, I swoon...

Good gracious, do you hear, Jean, old Jersey poet;
have some of my liquor, it's a cordial, a balm,
better than Nick Perrée's mulled wine.

★ ★ ★ ★

Do you hear, George, the fine songs?... oh! here come the nine sisters
to crown your brow, to give you the palm
that Apollo has plucked for you, king of the poets.

These three lines are in the Guernsey lingo.

George Métivier and Robert Pipon Marett ('Laelius') engaged in a public exchange
of compliments in 1850. Métivier sent a tribute in verse congratulating him on the
poem 'Le Vier Garçon' (The Bachelor), which was published in November 1849
in the newspaper *La Patrie* and of which an extract can be read elsewhere in this collection. Métivier's poem was published in *La Patrie* at the beginning of January
1850, to be followed by Laelius's response in the columns of the newspaper at the
end of that month.

George Métivier ('Un Câtelain')

L'Rimeux du Câté au Rimeux d'Saint Heliér, *1850* (Guernesiais)

S'fait George l'rimeux à Lélius:
S'tu viens cîs-nou, fier coum Cyrus,
Men vier garçon, j't'ouvrirai l'us,
L'u d'ma caumine,
Et tu'y verras, rangis sur m'n ais,
Des livres qu'exercent mes dets,
Parlafrandine!

Alignis contre ma paret,
J'n n'ai ni Rousseau, ni même Arouet;
Men la Fontaïne est sous l' tarouet,
Et l'grand Boccace,
Trop curiaeux pour être banni,

Là, dans l'gros livre de Manni,
Quiq'feis m' délasse.

Il y'a des jours où j'monte au cieil:
Seul auprès de m'n ombre, au soleil,
J'écoute Alighiéri, l'bouan vieil,
Et, que j'n'en mente,
Quand j'n'ai ni forche ni vertu,
Pour me r'levaïr l' coeur abattu,
I' n'y'a que l'Dante.

Que d'feis, gav'laï sus l'mélilot,
Ou sus l'châté d'Albecq, illo,
J'ai ouï la cahouette et l'hublot
Pâlaïr ès vagues!
J'y riais, où l'crax était nichi.
Des propos d'l'ôsaï Tassoni,
L'roué des pernagues.

Si jamais j'vé flleurir l'meis d'Mai,
J'prendrai, j'en jure, un nouvé plié:
V'là déjà Burns, vis-à-vis d'mé,
Sus m'n ais d'chim'nâïe,
D'poussiér viliannaï, l'chèr ami,
Et dame Iragne en fait sen ni'
La d'vergondâïe!

Quant à l'Arioste, mis au couaïn,
En pénitence il est maisouaïn;
Quand l'houme est vieil, a-t-il besouaïn
D'itaïs compères?
Jusqu'au menton dans les Rabbins,
J'pratiq'rai tout chu q' j'y'ai apprins,
Du moins, j'lespère.

Mais les chansons, mais les chansons,
Anacréon des "Viers Garçons"!
Ch'est té qui les f'ras j'en réponds,
Et d'vant qu'i' meure.
L'rimeux loyal des Guernesiais,
Dans tes vers, apprendra l'Jériais,
S'il en vét l'heure!

The Poet from the Castel to the Poet of Saint Helier, *1850*

Says George the poet to Laelius:
If you come to our land, happy as Cyrus,
my old friend, I'll open to you the door,
the door of my cottage,
and there you'll see, lined up on my shelf,
books which exercise my fingers,
on my oath!

Lined up against the partition wall,
I have neither Rousseau, nor even Voltaire;
my La Fontaine is locked away,
and the great Boccaccio,
too intriguing to be banished
there in the big book of Mani,
sometimes whiles away my time.

There are some days that I rise to the heavens:
alone beside my shadow, in the sun,
I listen to good old Alighieri
and, no word of a lie,
when I have neither strength nor courage,
to lift up my downcast heart,
there is nothing like Dante.

How often, stretched out on the common melilot,
or there on the Albecq castle,
have I heard the chough and the black-backed gull
speaking to the waves!
There I laughed, where the stonechat was nestled,
at what daring Tassoni put forward,
the king of antics.

If I ever see the may tree blossom,
I swear I'll turn over a new leaf:
already there's Burns, facing me,
on my mantlepiece,
disfigured by dust, the dear friend,
and dame Arachne makes her nest there,
the hussy!

As for Ariosto, he is, for the time being,
placed in the corner to teach him a lesson;
when a man is old, does he need
such cronies?
Up to the eyeballs in Rabbis,
I'll practise all that I've learnt there.
At least, I hope so.

But as for songs, but as for songs,
Anacreon of "Bachelors"!
It's you that will make them, believe me,
and before he dies
the loyal poet of Guernsey folk,
in your verses, will learn Jèrriais,
if he lives to see the day!

Sir Robert Pipon Marett ('Laelius')

From Laelius au Rimeux du Câté, *1850* (Jèrriais)

Amin Rimeux 'ous avez p'têtre
Creu tout chu temps que je d'vais être
Un sorte d'corps ben mal èlevé,
De n'avé pon ocquo env'yé
Un mot d'rèponse à votre èpitre,
Où-est qu'ou m'donnez, pardingue, un titre,
Et m'comblez d'un tas d'complimens,
Qui m' fraient pus orguillieux qu' les paons,
Si je n' me doutais que j'les dai,
Ben mains au mérite que j'ai
Qu'à votre générosité,
Qui vos engage à m'dire dité. –

(...)

J'n'ai pus d'excus' pour différer
De vos répondre, et vos r'mercier,
De la manière si fliatteuse
Et à la fais si généreuse,
Dont votre adress' fait allusion
A quiqu's chansons de ma faichon
Qui ont, signées d'un nom latin,
Paru dans les gazett's d'ichin.
J'l'ai déjà dit, je dai chenna

A vot' bonté, je l'sais; ch'est chla
Ben pus qu'la bonté de mes vers,
(Rimés trop souvent tout d'travers),
Qui fait qu' 'ous en pâlez si ben;
Mais ov tout chla i' n'en est ren,
J'admettrai franch'ment sans biaisi,
Que votre èpitr' m'a fait pliaisi.
N'y a pon d'rimeux qui n'aim' l'enchens,
Et tout pèr' chérit ses èfants,
Or entre l's autr's rimeux et mai
I' n'y a pon l'èpaisseur d'un daigt,
Et faut dir' pour n'en menti pas,
Je r'ssemble assez ès autr's papas. –
Quand donc j'apprins qu'mes chansonnettes,
Que j'craignais n'êtr' que des sornettes,
Etaient pourtant assez d'vot' goût,
J'en fus fort content je l'avoue.
Chla les r'hauchi dans m'n opinion,
Je m'dis, i' faut qu'il y ait du bon
Parmi l'mauvais, car comment craire
Qu'ils airaient, autrement, peu pliaire
A un' personn' de qui l' esprit
Est cultivé, et ben nouorri
De tout ch'que chaque fameux auteur,
Connu pour sa joyeuse humeur,
A laissi pour èguayer l' monde:
Et douée lié-mêm' d'un' vein' féconde. –
Un' tell' personn' ne s'mèprend pon,
Dans mes chansons il y a du bon!

(...)

Quaiqu' j'aie trop allouogni chutt' lettre.
Je n'peux et ne veux pas omettre,
Avant d'fini, de vos r'mercier
D'être si poli que d'm'inviter
D'aller vos vais à Guernézi,
Si par hasard j'y mets le pi'.
Permettez-mai, de man côté,
D'ajouter que je s'rai charmé
S'ou visitez jamais Jèri,
De vos r'chever et de bargouaichi
Ov vous sus toutes sortes d'sujets,

Sans oublier nos viers patouais.
Au pliaisi donc, Amin Rimeux,
En attendant séyiz heureux.

From Laelius to the Poet of Castel, *1850*

Friend poet, you have perhaps
believed all this time that I must be
some sort of badly brought-up person,
for not yet having sent
a word of reply to your epistle,
where you give me, good heavens, a title,
and overwhelm me with a lot of compliments
which would make me more full of pride than peacocks
if I did not feel that I owed them
much less to any merit of my own
than to your generosity
which prompts you to say this to me.

(...)

I no longer have any excuse to put off
replying to you, and thanking you,
for the manner, at once so flattering
and so generous,
in which your address alludes
to some songs of my making
which, signed with a Latin name,
have appeared in local newspapers.
I have said it already, I owe that
to your goodness, I know; it is that,
rather than the quality of my verses
(too often composed in a disorderly fashion)
that causes you to speak so highly of them.
But that is by the by,
I will freely admit with no equivocation
that your epistle pleased me.
There is no poet who does not like incense,
and every father cherishes his offspring,
and between other poets and myself
there is not so much as the thickness of a finger,
and I have to say, so as not to tell a lie,
I resemble other fathers quite a lot. –

So when I learned that my little songs,
that I had feared no more than nursery rhymes,
were nevertheless rather to your taste,
I must admit that I was very contented.
That raised them up in my opinion,
I said to myself, it must be that there is some good
among the bad, for how could I believe
that they could otherwise please
a person whose mind is cultivated, and well nourished
on all that every famous author,
known for his joyful mood,
has left to distract people:
and being himself gifted with a rich seam. –
Such a person cannot be mistaken,
there is something good in my songs!

(...)

Although I have stretched out this letter for too long,
I cannot and do not want to omit
before finishing, to thank you
for being so courteous as to invite me to go and see you in Guernsey.
If by chance I should set foot there,
permit me for my part,
to add that I should be charmed
were you to ever visit Jersey
to welcome you and natter
with you on matters of all sorts,
not forgetting our old local languages.
I look forward to seeing you, Friend Poet,
and in the meantime be happy.

The Norman literary renaissance in the Cotentin Peninsula of mainland Normandy was strongly influenced by the activities of the writers of the Islands. One of the most important of these Cotentin writers was the chansonnier Alfred Rossel, of Cherbourg. Between the 1870s and the early twentieth century he produced many popular songs and monologues, including 'Su la mé' (On the Sea) – the anthemic song of the peninsula which is also sung in the Islands. Followers of Rossel consciously attempted to raise the ambitions of Norman literature, and with the foundation of the literary magazine *Le Bouais-Jan* in 1897, mainland authors such as Louis Beuve, François Enault and Jean Tolvast emulated the writers of the

Islands. Here is a text by Alfred Rossel which gives a flavour of how the Islands and mainland had come to be countries 'separated by a common language'.

Alfred Rossel

À Guernésey, *published 1913* (Norman, from the Cotentin)

Ch'est en alaunt à Guernésey
Qu'en pllein étaè, j'ai failli fair' nâofrage;
Ah! qui viage! A bord, no s'disait:
Fâot-i péri avaunt d'vei Guernésey?

A Guernésey, no vit pus yais' qu'en Fraunce,
Où d'trop d'impôts lé peuplle est acrasaè;
Nous percepteus, d'eunn' si rare exigence,
Sount incouneus, lo-bas, à Guernésey.

Pllaingniz l'ouésé qui n' sort paè d'sen bôcage,
Qui fait sen nind tréjous ou même endreit;
Dé ses veisins, il ignore l'ramage.
Ah! qu'no dévrait pus sorti qu' no n' lé fait!

Sâof lé dinmaunch', no-z-y fait ses empllettes,
Cigar's et p'tun, tout y est à bouon marchi;
N'y a qu'eun malheû, ch'est qu'les jolies fillettes
S'fich'nt du Fraunçais qui veut trop byin prêchi.

Chu p'tit payis a pouor nous l'avauntage
Qu'ses habitaunts sount pus Nourmaunds qu'Aungllais,
Et qu'en patoués, counservaè coum' laungage,
No pueut enco s'fait' coumprendre à peu prés.

Si vo-z-alaez à Guernésey,
N'partaez janmais du port par temps d'orage;
Vo séryiz en route esposaè,
Malade ou noun, à veî l'pcount arrousaê.

In Guernsey, *1913*

It was while going to Guernsey
that I was nearly shipwrecked in the height of Summer.
Oh, what a journey! On board, we wondered:
Are we to perish before seeing Guernsey?

In Guernsey, life's more comfortable than in France,
where excessive taxation grinds the people down;
our exceptionally demanding tax collectors
are unknown over there in Guernsey.

Pity the bird that never strays from its hedgerows,
that always makes its nest in the same place;
he has no idea of how his neighbours sing.
Oh, how we ought to get out more often than we do!

Apart from on Sundays, we do our shopping there,
cigars and tobacco, everything is cheap;
there's only one drawback, and that's the pretty girls
who don't care for a Frenchman who tries to talk too proper.

This little country has the advantage for us
that its inhabitants are more Norman than English,
and that it's in the lingo, that's been kept as a language,
that we can still just about make ourselves understood.

If you go to Guernsey,
never leave port in stormy weather;
you'll get a battering on the way,
and whether you're sick or not, you'll see the deck sluiced.

Sibyl Hathaway, the Dame of Sark, tells us in her autobiography that 'then, as now, I could speak the island patois'. Although Sark is an autonomous part of the Bailiwick of Guernsey, the language of Sark is a descendant of the Jèrriais spoken in the sixteenth century by the families brought by Helier de Carteret, the Seigneur of Saint Ouen, from Jersey to colonise the then deserted Island. Helier de Carteret had received the lordship of Sark from Elizabeth I in return for preventing pirates using the Island as a base. It is this feudal relationship that still governs Sark's relationship with the Crown.

As Crown Dependencies, the constitutional relationship of the Channel Islands is with the Crown, and centuries of comparatively benign neglect have permitted an affection for the monarchy to flourish. The toad and the donkey still, however, occasionally tussle over the extent of their respective loyalty, since during the Wars of the Kingdoms in the seventeenth century Guernsey declared for the Parliamentary forces, while Jersey held out for the King, and sheltered the Prince of Wales, later Charles II.

Sybil Hathaway

From Dame of Sark, *1961*

It was he [Cachemaille] too who wrote an account of Grandfather's influence on the island at the time he took over, in the course of which he noted that hitherto no member of the royal family had ever put foot on Sark. But as several personages near the Queen had visited the island and described its beauty to her, it seemed likely that Her Majesty would visit Sark in passing through the Channel.

Hopes of the visit ran high when the Admiralty sent the royal yacht Osborne to look for a safe anchorage at a convenient place, but lamentable weather intervened; rough seas indicated all too clearly that it would be both difficult and uncomfortable for the Queen to land and the great expectations came to nothing.

However, when she visited Jersey in 1859 she passed close to Sark and coasted all along the east side. The islanders supposed that she intended to disembark, but no. Her ship continued to steam away en route to Jersey. My grandfather ordered a salute to be fired in her honour, which no doubt she heard distinctly. All this time, still hoping for a visit, the whole family was down at the harbour. The old arched rocky tunnel leading up from the harbour was decorated with flowers, flags were flying, my grandfather was at the head of his militia in full regalia, standing on the red carpet which had been laid down on the temporary landing-stage, and a banquet worthy to be set before a queen had been spread out in the dining-room of the Seigneurie. But meanwhile an unforeseen disaster occurred. Peacocks had entered the dining-room through the french windows and ravaged the table. They scattered the flower decorations with their many-eyed tails (which are supposed to bring bad luck), broke irreplaceable glasses and plates, then strutted screeching among the havoc they had wrought. It was just as well that the Queen did not land.

When Queen Victoria visited the Islands in 1846, she was accompanied in Jersey by royal aide-de-camp Sir John Le Couteur. The Jerseyman recorded some of his conversation with the royal visitor in his journal: '...the old Norman, it is NOT French. A Frenchman of rank once said to a market-woman that he did not understand English, when she had spoken Jersey to him ... to which the Queen replied, "well I respect those old attachments to language. There is something pleasing to see the Welsh for instance retaining their ancient tongue. Those national habits and manners are always interesting, and I should not like to see a people deprived of them. I noticed that the police spoke in Jersey French to each other, though they spoke to me in English!" "They always converse in the vernacular tongue, Your Majesty, but can all speak in English, so does everyone in the Town. In the country they do not, but there are English schools in every parish. The Court and States speak French."'

Jean (John) Sullivan ('Oméga')

From La Visite de la Reine en Gesry, lé 2 d'Stembre 1846 (Jèrriais)

JEANTON

Et chest nos Magistrats, Gieu les sauve et les garde.
Et n'erconnai-tu l'on l'couësin Fransais Erthu,
Qui queur comme un cherf pour faire san salut
Maia oué-tu, v'là l'canon, chest signe que v'la la Reine,
Ou s'ra bétot ichin, v'la le *skeam bouet* qui l'ameine.
Ah le v'la z'arrivai, vait tu chest biaux batiaux,
La Reine est dans chtichin et ses grands généraux;
Viyous la v'là au d'gré parmi les Demouëselles
Qui l'y donnent la main tandi qu'les p'tites hardelles
Chantent de biaux versets et la couvrent de flieurs,
En marchant sus l'tapis, sus de belles couleurs.
Viyiez où va monter dans sa belle véture,
Avec le PRINCE ALBERT. Oh qui noble picture:
Restons ichin au coin arrangis dans l'hernais,
Et j'les verrons passer, n'manquons pas à les vais.
Moman, Papa, Merguitte – ah les v'chin là tout près,
Criais – Vive la Reine! où nos paslla zoprès.

(La Reine passe et ergarde avec bontai chest pouers viers et les salue gracieusement; et la hernachie ne pousse qu'un cri: "LA REINE GIEU SAUVE ET GARDE!" VIVE LA REINE!)

(Me. Phlip, et sa bouenne femme s'ergardent en lermant.)

MANON

Ah man Phlip, j'nen peux pus, man bonheur est complet
As tu veu chu doux regard, et la fête qu'ou m'a fait;
Jen l'oublierai jamais, j'en sis toute ra-vie,
Mes jours en s'ront pus doux – et j'fini-rai ma vie
En pensant … au bonheur d'avé veu ses biaux yeux,
Et je prierai qu' oul ait un règne glorieux.

(Pouere Manon est si en joie qu'ou n'peut dire un p'tit mot; Me. Phlip, Jeanton et Merguitte sont toues esmues.)

JEANTON

La joie à bain d'leffet, pronons toues bouan conrage,
Et allons nos prom'ner et vais tout chu resmuage.

J'men vais vos m'ner à vais chu biaux p'tit pavillon
Ouest qu'oul à tai s'assez ovec la procession;
Là, prend man bras Moman – Papa, crochte Merguitte
Et j'verrons chu biaux quai; pis j'ervaindront bain vite
Pour la vais erpasser, pour aller s'emberqui
Dans chest biaux p'tits batiaux que v'lo zoprès l'roqui.
Nos v'chin an Pavillon, v'lo le Prince et la Reine
Plaichis des deux costés, chest juste comme ieux même,
R'gardais bain les couleurs chest chain qui ya d'pus fin
Faites exprès pour angniet, chain qu'a dit Jean Voisin.
Mais entrais par dedans, ou verrais bain des choses,
Viyiez chu biau tapis oquo tout couert de roses,
Et chu biau grand fauteuil ouest qu'ou s'est minse dedans
Touchis y tous achteu, car j'en pasllons long tems;
Mais ne v'lo la musique estche qu'oul est desjà v'nue,
Allons vite au hernais devant quou sait d'scendue,
J'marchons comme à quinze ans, et je jouissons de tout,
J'avons veu les biautais qui sont pliantais partout,
Ah nos v'chin au quériot, montons y tout de suite
Et j'la verrons oquo passer ovec sa suite.
Mais les v'lo v'nin Papa, allons d'la fermeté
Et saluons la Reine admirons sa bonté.

(La Reine et sa suite erpassent, en saluant la quériotaie des patriotes, qui l'y lanchent forche de complimens, de bouans souhaits, de bénédictions et de houras.)

ME. PHLIP
Et bain mes pouer zesfans, ou nos à erconnues,
Ou r'gardait pour nos vais, j'en sommes esperdues
Oul a souri si blanc en faisant ses agieux,
Et m'a dit en passant: "Vieillard soyez heureux."
S'oul avait arrestai j'lyairais dit bain des choses
Et j'lyairais bain offert un biau bouquet de roses;
Mais ourvaindra nos vais dans le Stembre qui vain,
Et j'maprestrai bain d'seux pour que je chasquions d'main,
Ah on n'merfusera pon, ou n'est pon orguilleuse
Bévons à sa santai, piesse talle être heureuse.

JEANTON
Ah sa faut nos naller, j'avons un but d'qu'min;
Merguitte prend tan bridot, la gniet s'en va r'venin
Ya zillumination assessé dans la ville,

Mais ov de vielles gens n'on n'peut rester ma fille
Man Papa et Moman sont lassais de lus jeu,
Faut nos rader siez nous et mettre l'geon à feu;
Et j'pasllons à VICTORIA quand je s'rons sus la veille
A grisli des paids ronds et viégui la bouteille.
Ah sa montons ichin – nos y v'la bain juindais;
Fait trotter tan Bidet j'iron es Quenvais,
Lus dire tout chu qué bé que j'avons veu en ville,
Et que tout s'y est passai si bain et si tranquille;
Janmais nou n'avait yeu rain d'si bé zen Gesri,
Tout de Roses était couert et chergi de Louri,
Et toutes les maisons paraissaient animées
Ov lus grandes couleurs, jusque sus les chimnées...

From **The Visit of the Queen to Jersey, 2nd September 1846**

JOAN
And there are our judges, God keep them and preserve them.
And don't you recognise cousin Francis Arthur,
running like a deer to make his greeting.
But listen, that's the cannon, it's a sign that the Queen is there.
She'll soon be here, there's the steamboat bringing her.
Ah, there, it's arrived. Can you see those fine boats,
The Queen is in that one with her great generals;
Do you see her there on the step among the ladies
assisting her while little girls
sing fine verses and cover her with flowers,
while walking on the carpet, on pretty flags.
Do you see her getting into her fine carriage,
with Prince Albert. Oh what a noble picture:
let's stay here on the corner settled in the cart,
and we'll see them go past, let's not miss seeing them.
Mum, Dad, Margaret – ah, here they are, very nearby,
Shout – Long live the Queen! She'll speak to us close by.

(The Queen passes and looks kindly on those poor old people and greets them graciously, and the passengers in the cart shout only one thing: "God keep and preserve the Queen! Long live the Queen!")

(Master Philip and his wife look at each other with tears in their eyes.)

MARY
Ah, Philip, that's as much as I can take, my happiness is complete.

Did you see that kind look, and the honour she did me;
I'll never forget it, I am quite overcome,
my life will be sweeter from now on, and I'll end my life
thinking... of the the joy of having seen her beautiful eyes,
and I'll pray for her to have a glorious reign.

(Poor Mary is so filled with joy that she cannot say any more; Master Philip,
Joan and Margaret are very much moved.)

JOAN
We're overcome by joy, let's pull ourselves together,
and go for a walk and see all the bustle.
I'll take you to see that lovely little pavilion
where she sat with her entourage;
There you go, take my arm, Mum – Dad, grab hold of Margaret
and we'll see that fine quayside; then we'll come back quickly
to see her pass by again when she gets back on board
those lovely little boats out there by the rock.
Here we are at the pavilion, there are the Prince and the Queen
placed either side, it's just like them,
look at those flags, those are the finest things
especially made for today according to John Voisin.
But go inside, you'll see lots of things,
look at that fine carpet still covered with roses,
And that fine big chair in which she sat.
Touch it now, all of you, because we'll be talking about this for a long time;
But there's the band. Has she come back already?
Quickly, let's go to the cart before she comes back down.
We're walking as though we're fifteen again, and what a splendid time we're
                                                          having,
we've seen the beautiful things which have been set up everywhere.
Ah, here we are at the cart, let's climb in straightaway
and we'll see her go past again with her train.
But there they are coming, Dad, let's go boldly
and greet the Queen, let's admire her goodness.

(The Queen and her train pass by again, greeting the cartload of patriots, who
shower her with compliments, good wishes, blessings and cheers.)

MASTER PHILIP
Well, my poor children, she recognised us,
she looked out for us, we're flustered.
She gave such a broad smile as she made her farewells,

and said to me as she passed: "Be happy, old man."
If she had stopped I would have said loads of things to her
and I'd have offered her a fine bouquet of roses;
but she'll come back to see us next Autumn,
and I'll do my best to ensure we shake hands,
Ah, she won't refuse me, she is not proud.
Let's drink to her health, may she be happy.

JOAN

Well, we must be off, we've got a long way to go;
Margaret take the reins, night will be on us.
There are illuminations this evening in town,
but, my girl, we can't hang around, what with the old folk:
Dad and Mum are tired out,
we've got to get home and light the gorse;
and we'll speak about Victoria when we're making an evening of it,
cooking peas and drinking.
Well, up we get – here we are up top;
set your horse trotting, we're going to Les Quennevais
to tell them all the fine things we've seen in town,
and that everything went off so well and so quietly;
There's never been anything so fine in Jersey,
everything was covered in Roses and decked with Laurels,
and all the houses seemed lively
with their large flags, right up to the chimneys...

Thomas Henry Mahy was the author of verse tales that were published regularly from 1916 in *La Gazette Officielle de Guernesey*. The style is homespun and down to earth, varying between domestic farce to moralising tales. T. H. Mahy's ambition was a simple one: to amuse and divert the readers of the newspaper, and his writing never strives for the erudition or polished literary forms of Corbet or Métivier. A collection of pieces was published in 1922 under the title *Les Dires et Pensées du Courtil Poussin*. This is an extract from an account of the visit of George V in 1921. The King also visited Jersey during the Royal Visit to the Channel Islands, and was greeted as Duke of Normandy. He was also ceremonially challenged in Jèrriais on a visit to Mont Orgueil as this translated extract from the newspaper *Les Chroniques de Jersey* describes: 'At the moment that the procession presented itself at the gate, the sergeant halbardier lowered his halberd to a defensive position and cried out: Tchi va là! (Who goes there!) Whereupon the Bailiff replied: Le Roy (the King), and the sergeant halberdier cried out: Passez (Pass).'

Thomas Henry Mahy

From En Mémeoire de la Visite du Roué George, d'la Reine Mery et d'la Princesse Mery, *1922* (Guernesiais)

L'Deaimanche au ser, entre cinq et six,
Prumier qu'nou vé qui dépique,
Deaux navires de guère et deaux yachts,
Qui sont justement bien gardaï, guia!
Nous n'vé pas souvent d'itaï qué;
Faut pensai qu'ch'est la propriétaï du Roué!...

Mais caï houneur pour Guernesey,
Qui n'est qu'un bien p'tit pays!
Mais, dans! l'Ille, y en a qui sont gros,
Large d'épeaule et joliment haut:
En même temps, i l'ont du chervé
Assaï pour entertenir le Roué.

Coum' ch'est l'deaimeanche qu'il arrive,
I' reste tout'la niet dans leurs navires,
Qui sont sus la rade, à l'eancre.
Là pourteant, i'n'paraisse pas greand:
Mais, à vée leux appareance, nous vé,
Et protectaï comme i' sont, que ch'est au Roué!...

La Reaine et la Princesse y sont étout,
Y'a d'la c'moditaï, et l'run qui faut;
Et j'creis bien qui sont entertinse coume i'faut,
Leux morcieaux d'vieande, ch'n'est pas tout os:
J'n'ai pas étai y vée, mais j'le creis,
Parce que ch'est les navires du Roué.

Ch'n'est pas tous qui sont admis à bord;
Selment quiqu's-uns qui sont d'un haut reang
Et couneux par la Fomille Royalle;
D'autres, i'faut que j'seis, d'un bu qui r'garde;
N'faut pas éprouvaï à en appercier;
Ch'est la propriétaï du Roué.

Mais l'lundi matin, caï émeute!
Ch'nest pas l'navire que les gens veille:
Mais tout l'monde a bouanne attente
De vée la Fomille qu'est d'dans,

Cronieant bien de n'les vée pas débarquer:
La Reaine, la Princesse, et le Roué.

Oprès avait bien r'gardaï, nous vé,
Du meutin le long du côtaï du baté;
Et, dans p'tit temps, caï émotion!...
La pus magnifique embarcation;
Qui, dans p'tit temps, vient s'reangier
Le long d'la Cauchie atout le Roué.

Ch'est-là qu'y en a, des hourras d'enviaïs!...
Jomais, j'pense, n'y en avait yeut d'itaï;
Les ch'veaux en r'deurchait sus la tête!...
Pour un p'tit d'temps, nous n'savait qui en craire.
Mais, tout d'un caeu, ch'est un calme qui s'fait,
Les gens ont l's iers fixaï sus le Roué.

Il est parmi ses soudarts, et j'creis bien,
Que sen souhait, ch'est leux bien;
J'sai qui s'sont dévouaï pour li,
Et bien d'ch'es-là qui sont affigi:
Vous font pensaï tout's sortes de qué,
Et en font pensaï étout au Roué.

Et la Reaine, qui qu'a' pense?
Y'en a d'pus d'une sorte, j'pense;
Sinon les soudarts, éouck qu'a' serait,
Ossi bien coum' nous, au jour d'oniet?
I l'ont chena sus l'idée pu qu'nous n'creit,
Y'elle, la Reaine, ossi bien coum' le Roué.

Pour la Princesse, a' parait bien sensible,
Et bieaux qu'à n'fait d'c'mochier sa vie,
Nous vé qu'a' prend d'l'idée à chu qu'a' vé;
A'parait une bouaun' personne tout-à-fait;
Ch'nest qu' par ses monière que nou vé
Que ch'est la Princesse, la Fille du Roué.

From In memory of the visit of King George, Queen Mary and Princess Mary, 1922

Sunday evening, between five and six,
at first we see coming into view,

two warships and two yachts,
which are really well guarded!
It's not often that you see the like;
after all, this is the property of the King!...

But what an honour for Guernsey,
that's only a tiny country!
But, in the Island, there are those that are big,
broad-shouldered and very tall;
at the same time, they've brains
enough to entertain the King.

As it's Sunday when he arrives,
they stay all night on board their ships,
that are in the roads, at anchor.
Yet out there, they don't look big:
but, seeing how they look, you can see,
and protected as they are, that they belong to the King!...

The Queen and the Princess are there as well,
there are all the provisions and the space they need;
and I believe that they are entertained correctly,
their cut of meat, it's not all bone:
I haven't been to see, but I think that's the way things are,
because these are the King's ships.

Not everyone is allowed on board;
only those that are high ranking
and known to the Royal family;
others, including me, let it be said, have to look on from a distance;
you mustn't try to approach;
this is the property of the King

But on the Monday morning, what a riot!
It's not the ship that people are watching: for,
but everyone is expectant
to see the Family that's within,
fearful of not seeing them disembark:
the Queen, the Princess, and the King.

After having had a good look, we can see
activity along the side of the boat;
and, in no time, what emotion!...

The finest landing party;
that, in no time, is drawn up
along the pier with the King.

It is then that cries of hurrah go up!...
Never, I think, has there been the like;
hair stood up on the back of your neck!...
For a little while, we didn't know what to think.
But, suddenly it is calm,
people have there eyes fixed on the King

He is amongst his soldiers, and I think,
that his wish, is their wellbeing;
I know that they are devoted to him,
and many of those that are afflicted
make you think all sorts of things,
and make the King think as well.

And the Queen, what does she think?
There is more than one sort, I think;
without the soldiers, where would she be,
and us as well, nowadays?
They have this in mind more than we think,
her, the Queen, as well as the King.

As for the Princess, she looks rather sensible,
and whilst she is only beginning her life,
you can see that she takes in what she sees;
she looks like a thoroughly good person;
it is not only by her manner that you can see
that she is the Princess, Daughter of the King.

Marjorie Ozanne

From **Le Jour d'la Praincesse – et d'la Grënmaire,** *1949* (Guernesiais)

Et bien me v'la derchier dans le bouan p'tit Guernesi, et auprais avait travlaï comme j'ai fait droïnemënt est bian fiar de s'trouvaï à la maison.

Et shais que j'print grën sain de v'ni en temps pour etre ichain quën la Praincesse vianraï. J'me r'souvians de la viaille roïne Victoria (i parais qu'al 'tait enamas strict). J'ensai quiqu'a dirais à r'venaï auchetaure.

J'pense qu'a s'en irait au pus vite de waique a s'rait v'nue surtout quën a viraï les gens quasi tous-fins-frai-nu par les bënques – et parfeis par les rues. I'm'disent que y'a des moiniaires de colonies ou i n'mettent pas rian du tout. Oh là là, et secours d'la vie. Mais v'la qui n'me fait pas de rian.

Et pie, j'm'r'souvians du rouai Edouard. En famaux piën – et d'sa faume, dauve tous ses cauyais et li dauve sa scarf en byu par sus ses epaules. Et la baille biënche barbe qu'il avait étou.

Enne auprais y'avait le rouai George, et la roïne Mairy. J'es vit quën i vinrent en 1921, dauve leux fille – Nous les vit justemënt bien sus Cambridge Park quëns i furent vaie les efëns des écoles d'la ville. Et pie j'feumes dans ën bataï autouor du yacht. Mais j'fut malade comme ën tchen et j'n'en vit pas grën choses, et pour courounaï tout, j'perdit mes fausses dents par dessus le bord du bataï. Sh'tait en bouan job que j'en avais enne autre sat à la maison.

Et pie quën le Praince de Galles vint pour ouvri le Val de Tairres, j'le vit étou, mais paraissait-i eniaï. J'pense que vla qui pensait deja à s'n-amourause.

Et pie donc quën notre rouai vint dauve la roïne à l'haüre auprais que j'feumes liberais, j'les vit étou. Nous fut s'assiais su la muraille à Cobo pour les vais passaï, et quiqu'uns dirent, "Les v'lo."

J'stretchi mën co, et dounnit enne coutes à Marguerite pour attraire s'n-atten-tion, et pis, les v'la passais. J'die, "Et bien, ma fai, nous en a veux qu'la poussiaire; allons Marguerite pour Cëndie ou pu vite. I faut que j'les vais mue qu'shenna."

J'aumes ën 'lift' dans le lorry du vaisain Toumas et nous trouvit à Cendie et par 'good luck' j'aumes enne bouanne pieche. Quën la roïne me passit (et sh'tait d'prais étou), j'l'y die, "and How do m'am moussieu" et j'fit enne itaï biaux salut que j'faiyisit a m'assiais. Et craiyais mai ou poui, à me r'gardit et souryit et le rouai étou.

J'aumais je n'le rombirais. Derriaire mai y avait la Mrs. Le Tau du Haut Pas, et a certifiyi que sh'tait à yaille qu'ils avaient souri. Mais j'savais mue, et j'aurent du camas hot and tight, comme i disent, et craiyie mai ou poui, mais jaumais n'ma pala d'en pie shu jour là.

Mais en maime temps j'saï qu'sh'tait à mai qui souryitent, et pas fichumënt à yaille.

From The Day of the Princess – and of Granny, *1949*

Well here I am back in good old little Guernsey, and after travelling like I've been doing recently it's lovely to be back home.

And I really did take great care to be here in time for the Princess coming. I remember the old queen Victoria (it seems she was very strict). I don't know what she'd say if she came back now.

I think she'd head straight back where she came from especially when she saw people almost starkers on the beaches – and sometimes in the street. I'm told that there are colonies where they don't wear anything at all. Oh, goodness gracious me. But that doesn't bother me.

And then I remember King Edward. A great big man – and his wife, with all her necklaces and her with her blue scarf round her shoulders. And he had a lovely white beard too.

After that came King George, and Queen Mary. I saw them when they came in 1921, with their daughter. You got a good view of them in Cambridge Park when they went to see the town schoolchildren. And then we had a boat trip round the yacht. but I was as sick as a dog and I didn't see much at all, and the crowning glory was that I lost my false teeth overboard from the boat. It was a good thing I had another set at home.

And then when the Prince of Wales came to open Le Val des Terres, I saw him too, but how bored he seemed. I think his mind was already on his mistress.

And then there was the occasion when our king came with the queen just after we were liberated, I saw them then too. We were sat on the wall at Cobo to see them go by, and somebody said, "There they are."

I stretched my neck, and gave Margaret a nudge to get her attention, and then they went past just like that. I said, "Well, my goodness, all we got to see was dust; Margaret, let's head for Candie as quickly as possible. I've got to see them better than that."

We got a lift in neighbour Tom's lorry and got to Candie and by good luck we got a good place. When the queen passed me by (and she was close up too), I said to her, "And how do, ma'am, sir," and I made such a nice curtsey that I all but ended up in a heap. And you can believe me or not, she looked at me and smiled and the king as well.

I'll never forget it. Behind me there was Mrs Le Tocq from the high parishes, and she insisted that it was at her that they'd smiled. But I knew better, and we had an argument, hot and tight, as they say, and you can believe me or not, but she's never spoken to me from that day since.

But all the same, I know it was me they smiled at, and I'm damned if it was her.

Royal visitors have been very much in the minority compared to ordinary tourists. Holidaying for the comfortably-off started in the nineteenth century. Steamboats and railways made getting to the Islands easier, and the development of hotels around the bays and picturesque parts of the Islands made staying more pleasant – and more profitable for the populations. The arrival of mass tourism and the era of the bucket-and-spade beach holiday gave added impetus to social change.

George W. de Carteret ('Caouain', 'G. W. de C.')

Lé Caouain et la touriste, *1932* (Jèrriais)

Il est dit que nou dev'thait traiter son prochain comme nous aimethait qu'il vos trait'tait vous-même et l'Caouain a tréjous êprouvé à agi d'auprès chu maxime-là.

Que ch'fusse en donnant un coup-d'main à tchique pouore malheutheux qu'en avait besoin ou bain en tâchant d'alligi les souffrances de tchique malade et ainsi d'suite.

Mais souvent en suivant ches principes-là i' faut procéder avec la plus grande précaution, parce qu'i' y'a tréjous des gens qui sont assez mèchants pous vos atchuser d'aver tchique motif mercenaithe ou autrement, et votre action, qu'ou sait tant innocente que nou voudra est r'gardée avec soupçon par des gens de chu calibre-là.

Je m'en vais vos en donner un exemplye, un cas qui m'est arrivé à mé pas pus tard que la s'maine passée.

Une arlevée qui je n'étions pas trop embarrassés à la boutique, je m'décidi d'aller m'promener et prendre l'air pour une heuthe ou deux.

Je prin la direction de West Park et comme à ches dernyi i' s'est arrivé des exemplyes que les piétons ne sont pas en seutheté d'lus vie sus les routes publiques, pour êviter tout dangi je d'valli dans la grève.

Opprès aver marchi à peu près deux chents verges, je passi l'long d'une jeune fille qui m'avait la mine d'une visiteuse et qu'était assise sus une pierre au pid d'la grand muthaille. Ou m'pathu être en souffrance de tchique sorte car oulle 'tait à ma grande stupéfaction je m'aperchu qu'oulle 'tait à plieuther.

Avec le tchoeu tendre comme j'ai, un spectacl'ye comme chenna me causi la pus vive êmotion et je m'en fus m'assiéthe à coté d'lyi et m'exprimant en anglais du mus qu'j'pus, je li d'mandi bain sympathiquement:

"Tch'est qu'tu as don, ma p'tite?"

"Oh, je n'sais pas," qu'ou m'raîponni," mais le dos m'pique affreusement, je crai qu' j'ai 'té mordue par des moustiques, est-che qu'i' y en a en Jêrri?"

"Je n'crai pas qu'i' y en a d'si dangereuses comme chenna," je li dis, "mais ch'tait p't-être un vêpre. T'en est-i' d'rain que je r'garde?"

"Pas du tout," qu'ou' s'fit. Et en m'disant ch'la ou m'touâni iune des pus belles pathes d'êpaules que j'ai jamais veu d'ma vie.

Mais tchi dêfidguthation!

"Ma chiéthe éfant!" je m'êcriyi, "ouest don qu'tu as 'té? Tu as l'dos comme du lard, et tu es à la maintchi p'lèe!

"Oh" ne m'faites pas d'peux!" ou s'êcriyi. Et ou se r'mins à plieuther comme de pus bé.

Ah ça, tch'est qu'je d'vais faithe, mé?

Ou pouvez en craithe ch'qu'ou voudrez, mais je la r'consoli d'une manièthe tout-à-fait paternelle et je li dis qu'i' n'fallait pas s'faithe de mauvais sang, que che n'tait pas rain d'bain sérieux mais qu'oulle 'tait raique brulée du solé.

Je li explitchi que toute la vieille pé s'en allait tchaie et que dans deuxtrais jours ou s'en allait touâner d'un superbe brun comme nous en viyait tant d'autres.

Pour li faithe vaie j'en pinchi un p'tit morcé qu'était souôlevé et en hallant d'sus bain douochement il en vint une cliu grand comme une pièche d'êtcheu.

"Là!" j'li dis ou s'en va toute tchaie comme chenna. Je n'vos ai pas fait d'ma, aije?"

"Oh nan, mais v'là tchi catouolle un mio."

"J'peux-ti en haller oquo?" j'li d'mandi.

"Oui s'ou voulez."

Et avec le pus grand soin j'en peli un couplye d'lizèthes que j'mins dans man portefeuille.

"Tch'est qu'ous allez faithe de chenna?" ou me d'mandi.

"J'm'en vais les garder comme un p'tit souvenir"

Devant la tchitter je fis un appointement avec lyi de la r'trouver à la même pli-aiche dans quatre jours afin de vaie comment que l'brunissage progrèssait et je r'prins le c'min pour le bureau.

Quand j'arrivi à la boutique Marie Hibou était là à pâler à Mess Simon et i' faut que j'admette que j'fis preuve d'un grand manque de jugement.

Sans m'otchuper d'autchunes conséquences qui pouorraient s'en suivre je dêhalli man portefeuille et je pôsi bain soigneusement sus l'conteux mes deux pré-cieux p'tits morciaux.

"Là!" j'lus dis je gage qu'ou n'pouvez pas d'viner tch'est qu'ch'est qu'chenna!"

Marie Hibou ne vouli pas s'donner la peine de r'garder.

Mais Mess Simon li dit comme chenna, "Autchun imbécile peut vaie tch'est qu'ch'est! Ch'est du papi à cigarettes."

"Eh bain, d'vines oquo in aut'e feis, man vi," j'li dis, "tu n'y est pas!"

Mais i' n'pouvait pas arriver à dêcouvri tch'est que ch'pouvait être et à la fin i' me d'mandi de li nommer la marchandise.

"Eh bain ch'est la piau d'une touriste!"

La dessus Marie Hibou bondi de dans sa tchaithe et c'manchi à faithe du tinta-marre et vouli une explication.

Je li raconti tout ch'qui s'était passé, comptant qu'ou f'thait preuve d'un mio d'sympathie.

Mais au contraithe ou s'mins à m'insulter avec des patholes mal-sonnantes et ou m'en chantit de toutes les sortes.

"Comment!" qu'ou m'dit, "quand j't'ai tchiquefais d'mandé d'êcréder un vra ou une brême que j'avais acaté au marchi, tu as tréjous r'fusé en disant que des djabes comme ch'la te faisais horreur, et pis tu vais passer tan temps à gratter l's êpaules à des créatuthes que tu rencontre sur l'plian!

Et ou m'en a voulu tout l'temps d'pis.

Chein qui prouve ch'que j'vos ai dit au c'menchement de m'n articlye, que y a des gens qui sont tréjous prêts à donner une fausse interprétation à la pus inno-cente des actions.

The Owl and the Tourist, *1932*

It is said that one should treat one's neighbour as one would like him to treat you too and the Owl has always tried to act in accordance with that particular principle.

Whether by lending a helping hand to some poor unfortunate in need of aid or else by attempting to relieve the suffering of someone who's ill, and so on.

But often one must proceed with the greatest circumspection when following these principles because there are always people who are so evil minded as to accuse you of having some mercenary motivation or other motive, and your action, no matter how innocently intended, is regarded with suspicion by that class of folk.

I'm going to give you an example; a case which happened to me as recently as last week.

One afternoon when we weren't too busy in the office, I decided to go for a walk and take the air for an hour or two.

I headed in the direction of West Park and as there have recently been cases whereby pedestrians have been at risk of their lives on the public highways, in order to avoid all danger I went down onto the beach.

Having walked about two hundred yards, I passed by a young girl who looked to me like a tourist and who was sitting on a stone at the foot of the seawall. She seemed to me to be suffering from something or other because to my great astonishment I noticed that she was crying.

Seeing as how I'm as soft-hearted as I am, a sight of that sort evoked deep emotion in me and I went and sat down next to her and spoke in English as best I could and asked her in a most sympathetic manner:

"What's the matter with you then, my dear?"

"Oh, I don't know," she replied, "but my back stings terribly, I think I've been bitten by mosquitoes. Are there any in Jersey?"

"I don't think there's anything as dangerous as that," I told her, "but it might perhaps have been a wasp. Would you mind if I had a look?"

"Not at all," she said. And as she spoke, she turned and presented me with one of the prettiest pairs of shoulders that I've ever seen in my life.

But what a disfiguration!

"My dear girl!" I cried, "Where have you been? Your back looks like roast pork, and you're half peeled!"

"Oh, stop scaring me so!" she exclaimed. And that set her off again, crying her eyes out.

Well, what was I to do?

You can believe what you want to, but I consoled her in a way that was purely paternal and I told her that she oughtn't to get upset, that it wasn't anything really serious and all it was, was that she had got sunburn.

I explained to her that all her old skin was going to fall off and that in a couple of days she was going to turn a splendid brown just like you could see so many others do.

In order to make her see, I took hold of a little piece, that was coming away, and pulled at it very slowly until a patch of skin about the size of a half-crown came off.

"There!" I told her, "It'll all come off like that. I didn't hurt you, did I?"

"Oh, no, but it did tickle a bit."

"Can I pull some more off?" I asked her.

"Yes, if you like."

And with the greatest of care I peeled off a couple of strips that I put in my wallet.

"What are you going to do with that?" she asked me.

"I'm going to keep them as a little souvenir."

Before leaving her I made a date with her to meet her again in the same place in four days' time so as to see how the tanning was getting on and I headed back to the office.

When I arrived in the office Mary Owl was there talking to Mr Simon and I must admit that I happened to make a great error of judgment.

Without worrying about any consequences that might follow I got out my wallet and I very carefully set down on the counter my two precious little fragments.

"There!" I said to them. "I bet you can't guess what that is!"

Mary Owl didn't care to take the trouble to look.

But this was what Mr Simon said to her, "Any fool can see what that is! It's cigarette paper."

"Well, guess again, old chum," I told him, "you haven't got it yet!"

But he couldn't manage to work out what it could be and finally he asked me to name the goods.

"Well, it's tourist's skin!"

Whereupon Mary Owl jumped up from her chair and started making a hullabaloo and wanted an explanation.

I told her everything that had happened, expecting her to show a bit of sympathy.

But on the contrary she began to insult me using improper words and called me every name under the sun.

"What!" she said, "When I've asked you from time to time to clean the scales from a wrasse or bream that I've bought at the market, you've always refused, saying that jobs like that made you shudder and then you go and spend your time scratching the backs of creatures you meet on the beach!"

She's been angry at me ever since.

And that proves what I told you at the beginning of my article, that there are people who are always prepared to put a false interpretation on the most innocent of actions.

False interpretations also feature in an account by E. J. Luce of a trip made to Sark in 1910 by members of the municipality of the parish of Saint Ouen in Jersey. Originally published in *La Nouvelle Chronique de Jersey*, it was quickly republished as a booklet. Here, the party arrive in Sark. Later on in the course of their visit to Sark, the party is regaled with stories of the wonders of the Sark gasworks, the Sark marathon, the Sark theatre, the Sark markets, the Sark railway and so on, until they realise they have been having their legs pulled by a wily Sarkee. The English language Jersey newspaper, *The Morning News*, reviewed this story in these terms: 'Interesting as is this language, passed from pre-Conquest times through the generations of Jerseymen even to the present day, one must be to the manner born to understand its queer pronunciation and grasp its idioms, but a bi-lingual cum patois friend has made a rough translation into English, which, though doubtless losing some of the "snap" of the original, enables me to write this slight appreciation of a bit of native humour. (...) I have rarely read a more vivid or realistic description of the horrors of sea-sickness.'

E. J. Luce ('Elie')

From En Sercq, *1910* (Jèrriais)

Compte-rendu d'la Visite des St.-Ouennais, le Lundi 22 Août 1910

Quand not' Courier arrêti le long d'l'autre Courier, à une petite distance de la tête de l'unique cauchie, il arrivi alentou' du "steamer" une racachie de p'tits batcheaux sercquais. Châtchun 'tait monté par un homme en dark-blues braies, corset d'oeuvre et castchette à saluette.

Lus mains sont brunes et i' vos man'yient les avithons aussi aisîment coumme je ramas'saîmes une frouque à fain.

Pour plusieurs de nous, ch'tait la prumié fais que j'ouïaîmes du sercquais. Mais coumme i' ne d'visaient pas fort, nou-s-éthait peu craithe que ch'tait du jerriais que nou z'entendait, sinon pour lus drôle de maniéthe d'app'yer longuement sus la dernièthe partie d'lus mots et d'lus phrases: par exempl'ye: "J'peuc en prendre acco trâââis," s'faisant y'un qu'avait san baté bétôt plien, tandis qu'nou d'sendait d'dans.

J'avais espéthé qu'en d'vallant du courier, dans ches p'tits batcheaux, j'éthions yeu le pliaisi d'vaie tchic incident qu'éthait valu la peine de noter bas dan man p'tit livre, mais rien!

Ch'éthait 'té si drôle de vaie, disons un membre du Comité d'Taxation, sauté a maintchi en d'dans et à maintchi en d'hors du baté; se tremper jusqu'à la cheintuthe et être obl'yigi d'emprunter des braies d'dun'grie à un mat'lo pour pouver v'nin à terre ov un mio d'confort. Mais pas l'mains du monde. J'avais man livre tout dêhallé et fallit le r'serrer! Si ch'tait pas fichant!!

Et né v'la les batcheaux touos pliens d'Jerriais et d'touristes angliais qui filent l'un souentre l'autre en d'dans d'la cauchie.

Oul' est tchuthieuse, lus cauchie; et d'pis que j'sis en allant, autant vaut donner une petite description de chein qu'nou vit – pour le bénéfice des siens qu'étaient restès en Jerry.

En appréchant du havre (qu'ils appellent le Creux) nou vé de p'tits îlots à droète et à gauche, ov des p'tites tacques d'herbe et des grand' mauves dessus.

Pas d'maisons en veue: des hautes falaises couvertes d'grapue, ov la bruyèthe en fieur qui les couleuthe d'un bieau pourpre.

Le hâvre n'est pas grand comme Bouanne Niet; bein s'en faut, et le d'vant en est tout mastchi par la haute cauchie, sauf l'entrée, qu'est sus la gauche. En effet, lus cauchie fait un grand coute et s'en va coumme pour rencontrer la falaise de l'autre bord, mais s'arrête justement d'vant qu'd'y v'n'in, et laisse du run pour un p'tit "steamer" à passer quand la mé s'adounne. Ch'tait à cause de l'êtat d'la mathée que j'dêbèrtchîmes en p'tits batcheaux. En passant l'long d'la cauchie, d'vant dêtouanner en d'dans, j'fumes si près des hardelles qu'étaient assises sus l'haut que si lus soulier avait êcappé d'lus pi'd il êtait peu nos tchaie sus la tête! Mais n'y'êtait pon yeu grand ma car les Jerriais ont la tête duthe et pis ches hardelles là ont d'si p'tits pi'ds! Ch'êtait 'té un pliaisi pustôt qu'un accident ... Ch'est un Expert qui nos l'dis.

Une fais dans la cauchie nou z'est coumme dans un p'tit lac et ma fé, y'a de tchi qui vaut la peine de r'garder aillieurs qu'en Jerry. Y'a un p'tit mio d'grève au haut d'la baie, grand coumme un mouochet d'pouchette. Tout campagnards que j'étions, nou n'pouvait s'empêchi d'admither la scène. Les falaises, flieuthies en pourpre parmi le vert des herbes, d'vennent de pus en pus grises en d'vallant; tout au bas, nou vé l'gravi rouogeâtre de tchi qui sont en partie faites. Deux-treis tunnels ont 'té copés souos la falaise pour aller d'un bord et d'l'autre.

Tandis que j'dêbertchions, 'Douar Le Feuvre, des Landes, t'nait les batcheaux le long d'la montée; i' finit même par s'y tremper, bottes, cauches et braies jusqu'au d'sus d'la g'ville du pi'd. Mais i' n'est pas l'garçon pour s'en faithe de mauvais sang.

Et nos v'la ramontant la cauchie, tandis que deux ou trais traînards 'taient à châtchi d'main ov des Sercquais d'lus counnaissance.

Sus la cauchie, y'avait quatre ou chin' cabs – toutes à un gh'va – et des touristes angliais, sustout des d'moêselles. Ah! i' n'se gênent pon en Sercq, les dames touristes, pas pus qu'en Jerry. J'avons d'nos Jerriaises qui n'ithaient pas à la boutique sans d'vanté mais j'en vîmes-t-i de difféthentes sortes là bas. Des slippeurs à s'melle de corde ou "d'guttapercha," pas d'cauches, les dghéthets nus jusqu'au poummé d'la gambe et touos brunis par le solé, comme les bras d'un dêfoueux. De p'tits courts cottillons d'fro, qui n'vont pas fort pus bas qu'lé g'nou dans bein des cas; un blianc corset d'oeuvre, qui lus colle au corps quâsi coumme un costume de bain. Y'en a qu'ont de petits bounnets ouvrés; d'autres ont des chapiaux d'paille; hardi, coumme la sienne de d'sus la haut d'la cauchie, laissent lus gh'veux voler au vent. Touos les St.-Ouennais, n'ayant pon lus femmes avec yeux, n'mantchaient pon d'trouver ches modes là charmantes ... J'en vi même qui se r'touannaient pus que d'raison à r'garder driéthe yeux. Seulement, le solèt finit par lus bruni la fache, les bras et les gambes à ches filles et nous les prendrait pour des Espagnoles!

La cauchie nos mène dré dans une tounnelle de plusieurs perques d'long, copèe dans l'rotchi et large coumme une grand' route. La d'sous, le long d'la banque à l'abri d'la pl'yie et du solèt, y'a des tas de cliavieaux et des batcheaux.

Coumme ou viyiz, pas de douanes, pas d'impôts, pas d'policemen. Nou peu entrer ov des pautes pliennes de p'tun; nou peu avec d'l'ieau d'vie ou d'l'ieau d'Cologne – s'lon qu'nou z'est houmme ou femme – et n'y corps d'âme pour vos embêter. Heutheux pays!

From In Sark, *1910*

An account of the visit of the party from Saint Ouen, Monday 22nd August 1910

When our mailboat pulled up alongside the other mailboat, a short distance away from the only quay, a whole load of little Sark boats came up round the steamer. Each of them was handled by a man in dark blue trousers, sweater and peaked cap.

Their hands were brown and they handled their oars as easily as we'd pick up a pitchfork.

For many of us, it was the first time we'd heard Sercquiais. But as they didn't speak much, you could have thought it was Jèrriais you were hearing, except for their strange way of drawling the ends of their words and phrases: for example: "I can take 'nother threeeeee," as one said whose boat was almost full up, while we were getting into it.

I'd hoped that in getting down off the mailboat into these little boats, we'd have had the pleasure of seeing some incident that would be worth noting down in my notebook, but not a thing!

It would have been so funny to see, let's say, a member of the Assessment Committee jumping half in and half out of the boat; getting soaked up to his middle and being obliged to borrow a sailor's dungarees in order to come ashore in some comfort. But nothing like that at all. I had my notebook out and had to put it way! How annoying that was!

And there went the boats full of Jersey people and English tourists filing one after another into the harbour.

Their harbour is strange; and while I'm at it I might as well give you a little description of what we saw – for the benefit of those who stayed in Jersey.

Approaching the harbour (which they call Le Creux – the hole) you can see small islets to right and left, with little patches of grass and large seagulls on them.

No houses to be seen: high cliffs covered in furze, with the heather in bloom colouring them a lovely purple colour.

The harbour isn't as big as Bonne Nuit, far from it, and the front of it is quite masked by the high pier, except for the entrance which is on the left. In effect, their quay makes a large dog-leg almost meeting up with the cliff-face on the other side but stopping just before making contact and allowing room for a small steamboat to pass through when the sea permits. It was due to the state of the tide that we disembarked into the little boats. Passing along the quay before turning to enter, we were so close to the girls sitting along the top that if one of their shoes had happened to slip off one of their feet it could have fallen on our heads! But there wouldn't have been any harm in that because Jersey people are hardheaded and anyway those girls had such small feet! It would have been more of a pleasure than an accident... One of the assessors told us so.

Once inside the harbour it's like being on a small lake and, my goodness, there are things worth seeing outside Jersey. There's a little piece of beach at the top of the bay, the size of a pocket handkerchief. Although we were all country folk, we couldn't help but admire the scene. The cliffs, blooming in purple among the green of the grasses, get greyer and greyer further down; right at the bottom, you can see the reddish gravel they are partly made of. A couple of tunnels have been cut into the cliff to get to either side.

While we were disembarking, Edward Le Feuvre, from Les Landes, held the boats alongside the slip; he ended up getting his boots, socks and trousers soaked to just above the ankle. But he's not a lad that takes something like that badly.

And so we climbed up the quayside, while a few laggards were shaking hands with some Sarkese they knew.

On the quayside, there were four or five cabs – all one-horse cabs – and some English tourists. especially some young ladies. Ah! these lady tourists are very easy-going when in Sark, just like when in Jersey. We've got some of our Jerseywomen who wouldn't dream of going to the shop without their aprons on, but what a different class of woman we saw there. Slippers with rope soles or guttapercha ones, no stockings, legs bare to the calves and all tanned, like a potato-digger's arms. Little short-skirted dresses, which in many cases barely descend below the knees; a white sweater, which clings to the body almost like a bathing costume. Some had little knitted bonnets; others had straw hats; many of them, like the one at the top of quayside, let their hair blow in the wind. All the men from Saint Ouen, not having their wives with them, had no trouble being charmed by these fashions... I even saw some of them taking more backward glances than was reasonable. The only thing is that the sun ends up tanning the faces, arms and legs of these girls until you could mistake them for Spanish women!

The quay takes us straight into a tunnel several perch long, cut into the rock and as wide as a main road. Under there, along the roadside and sheltered from rain and sun, there are lots of lobster pots and boats.

As you can see, no customs, no excise duties, no policemen. You can arrive with pockets filled with tobacco; you can come in with brandy or perfume – depending on whether you're a man or a woman – and there's not a soul to bother you. What a lucky country!

Denys Corbet was also among those writers who have taken the opportunity to remark on how foreign a place Sark has sometimes seemed to other Channel Islanders. In this extract from an 1886 story, we see again a scene of arrival at Le Creux harbour. The steep cliffs of the coasts of Sark do not offer any convenient landing place. The harbour of Le Creux was started in the sixteenth century with the first tunnel dating from 1588 – the harbour really is a hole in the cliff. The physical challenge of disembarking in Sark and the particular palatalised 'k' sound in the Sark words for 'who', 'fall' and 'quay' have made the question quoted in this extract almost a proverbial tongue twister.

Denys Corbet ('Bad'lagoule')

From Bad'lagoule en Serk, *1886* (Guernesiais)

Grâce ès baquiaux, et acouare pus à nos chìnq pennis par tête, j'nos trouvìmes bientôt sus la causshie du Creux. Quaï nom pour un hâvre! biaû qu'les Serquais
l'appeulent pus souvent les quas, ou putôt les quaïs, coum i disent dans leus langage, qui n'est pouit mal curiaeux. J'vou-s-en baïdrai un p'tit exàmplle. Parmi tout
l'broûs d'l'attêrrage j'ouis quiq-un keriaïr: "N'en v'là yun bas!" Là d'sus un
Serquais d'màndi: "Qui-aït qu'aït quaï?" et un aût répounni: "Tchaït-un Serquaïs
qu'aït quaï sus laïs quaïs." Je n'paeut m'empêchier d'ricaner – à ma honte de l'dire
– à quànd j'ouis chunna. Et pourtànt j'avais tors, caêr men langage n'est sàns doute
guère pus poli à leus oreille que n'métait l'laeur.

From Chatterbox in Sark, *1886*

Thanks to the boats, and still more to our fivepence a head, we soon arrived on the
jetty of Le Creux ("the hole"). What a name for a harbour! Although the Sarkees
most often call it the quays, or rather the "k-yaay" as they say in their language,
which is really rather bizarre. I'll give you a little example. Amid all the fuss of the
landing I heard someone call out, "Someone's down!" Whereupon a Sarkee asked,
"Who is it who's fallen?" and another replied, "It's a Sarkee who's fallen down on
the quays". I couldn't keep from sniggering, I'm ashamed to admit, when I heard
that. And, you know, it was wrong of me, because my language really can't sound
much classier to their ears than theirs does to mine.

The *Exposition universelle* held in Paris in 1889 marked the centenary of the French
Revolution and was the wonder of the age. The centerpiece of the exhibition was
the Eiffel Tower, and among visitors who came to marvel at the displays and entertainments were Channel Islanders. Philippe Le Sueur Mourant wrote a series of
letters which were published in the newspaper, *La Nouvelle Chronique de Jersey*.
These impressions of the Paris exhibition were a runaway success, being immediately reprinted in booklet form. The character of Bram Bilo, an innocent abroad,
had further adventures, and was influential with other writers, including the mainland Norman vernacular author Octave Maillot (1861-1949) who wrote in an
Orne dialect. The stories were also successful in Guernsey. T. A. Grut was amongst
those writers influenced and his Guernesiais translations of the Bram Bilo stories
were published in Guernsey in the 1920s.

Philippe Le Sueur Mourant ('Bram Bilo', 'Piteur Pain' etc)

Bram Bilo's visit to the Paris Exhibition, *1929* (translation of 1889 Jèrriais original into Guernesiais by T. A. Grut)

A Paris
Chu 8 S'tembre

Moussieu, – Nous y v'chin dans chu Paris, d'pis hier au ser.

J'nous embarquêmes avan'-hier dans l'baté d'Granville; men cousin Lise et ma belle-mère étaient v'nus nous condire dans l'van, atou not' câsse. J'eumes un' fière peux justement quand l'baté quittait la cauchie, caer, ma belle-mère qu'étéait v'nue dans l'steam pour vée la machaine, s'écrilli sus la plianche en allant à terre, et quai dans la cauchie, les pids en haut. Le Cap'taine n'arrêti poui pour la r'pêquier, mais y criyi "Go a-head," sans pus s'en gênaï; heureusement, qu'un matelot dans un baté la r'pêqui par sen cotillon. J'n'cré pâs qu'al' en mourra acouare chu caoup.

Y'avait un moussieu français dans l'traïn, tout à fait charmant – j'lis dis que j'nous en allions pour Paris; que j'étais Chant'nyi à Saint-Ouen, et y m'dit là-d'sus que les Chant'niers et autres gens distingués étaient hardi r'cherchi à Paris. Ma poure Nancy qui n'avait ataï qu'daeux fais dans l'traïn de St. Aubin, avait grànd peux; a trouvait que l'traïn allait trop vite, et a criait qu'la machaine s'était écappaïe. Le moussieu français la rasseuri là-d'sus, mais a n'tait poui en tout trànquille, et quànd j'nous arrêtèmes à un' stâtion, a s'n'alli pâlaï à "l'engineer," et li dit que ch'n'était pas prudent d'allaï si vite, et y offrit six pennis pour alaï pus douoche-ment.

J'avaimes emportaï des sauchisses et un' miette de moirue dans un' pouque, et j'acati un' bouteille de bière.

Enfin, j'arrivaimes! quaï broue! quaï combât à chute stâtion! Nancy me t'nait "tight" par l'brâs, de crainte de s'éguerraï, et, ma fé, al' avait raison. Y'en avait du monde et du brit!! J'n'savais poui à quaï Hotel allaï, et tandis que j'regardais autouor de mé, un hômme s'en vint m'dire: "Mylord cherche quelque chose?" "Vèreguia," j'lis dis, "Pourrait 'ous m'indiquier un Hotel respectablle et poui trop chier?" Y r'pouni qu'oui, et là-d'sus nous v'lo allaï. Y voulait portaï ma câsse, mais "not for Joe," "N'lis laisse pâs," s'fit Nancy, "ch'est p't-être un 'pickpocket!' "

Y nous condisi à un grand Hotel, mais l'propriétaire nous dit qu'i' n'prénait pâs des gens de not' espèce. "Quéman," j'lis dit, "sav'ous bien que j'sis Chant'nyi à Saint-Ouen?" V'là qui l'radouci, et nous v'la dans s'n Hotel, au seizième étâge; mais i'n'y a pâs d'dégreïs à montaï: nous entre dans un' manière de d'sous d'degraï, et y vous hïste ahaut dans un cllïn d'iel; chenâ s'appelle un encenseur.

Tandis que j'étaimes dans not' chàmbr, mé à m'râsaï, et Nancy à coûtre un' amâre à sen chapé, v'là un garçon qu'arrive àtou un livre ouesqu'i fallait écrie nos noms; j'écrivis brav'ment:
Chant'nyi BILOT est sa fâmme,
propriétaires à Saint-Ouen, JERRI.

In Paris
This 8th of September

Sir, – Here we are, here in Paris, since yesterday evening.

We boarded the boat to Granville the day before yesterday; my cousin Lise and my mother-in-law had come to take us and our case in the van. We had quite a fright just when the boat was leaving the quay as my mother-in-law, who had come aboard the steamship to have a look at the vessel, slipped whilst on the gangway when returning ashore and fell head first into the harbour. The Captain didn't stop in order to fish her out, but he called out "Go a-head", without another care; luckily a sailor in a boat fished her up by her petticoat. I don't think that's enough to finish her off, this time.

There was a French gentleman on the train, altogether charming – I said to him that we were going to Paris; that I was a Centenier in Saint Ouen, and on saying this he said that Centeniers and other distinguished people were very sought after in Paris. My poor Nancy, who had only been twice in the train from St. Aubin, was very frightened; she felt that the train was going too fast, and she thought that the engine was out of control. The French gentleman reassured her, but she clearly wasn't at all calm about it, and when we stopped at a station she went to speak to the "engineer", and told him that it wasn't sensible to go so fast, and she offered him sixpence to go more slowly.

We had brought some sausages and a piece of cod in a bag, and I bought a bottle of beer.

Finally, we arrived! what a commotion! what a mob at that station! Nancy held me "tight" by the arm, fearing that she would get lost, and, my goodness she was right. Weren't there a lot of people and noise! I had no idea which hotel to go to, and whilst I looked around me a man came up and said to me: "Milord is looking for something?" "Quite right" I said to him, "Could you point out a respectable hotel, and not too expensive?" He replied that he could, and on that we set off. He wanted to carry my case, but "not for Joe", "Don't let him," said Nancy, "Perhaps he is a pickpocket!"

He led us to a big Hotel, but the owner said that he didn't take our sort of people. "How's that", I said to him, "don't you realise that I am a Centenier in St. Ouen?" That softened him up, and there we are in his Hotel on the sixth floor; but there are no stairs to climb: you go into a kind of understairs cupboard, and it hoists you up in the blinking of an eye; it is called a heaven-later. Whilst we were in our room, me shaving and Nancy sewing a strap onto her hat, a boy showed up with a book in which we had to write our names; I boldly wrote:

Centenier BILLOT and his wife,

Property owners in St. Ouen, JERSEY.

In 1927 *La Gazette Officielle de Guernesey* published a letter from Jean Bonamy Fallaize, a nephew of Denys Corbet, who had settled in the United States about 40 years previously and ran a business as J. B. Fallaize and Co., 'The Linen House', in Atlanta, Georgia. He adapts slightly the opening line of the 'Dedication to the Guernseypeople of Guernsey' of his uncle's 'Les Chànts du Draïn Rimeux' to make it applicable to the friend back home the letter was originally sent to. The description of the lifts can be compared to that in Philippe Le Sueur Mourant's classic description of Bram Bilo's visit to Paris in 1889.

Jean Bonamy Fallaize

Lettre d'un Guernesiais en Amérique, *1926* (Guernesiais)

Le 20 Novembre 1926,
Atlanta, dans la Georgie,
Etats-Unis.

"Acoure un caoup, cher Guernesias."
Première ligne du Drain Rimeux
(Denys Corbet.)

Au Vaïsin George, d'St. Martin.

Eh bien, mv'chin lien du p'tit Guernesi, mes acoure vous en jure un vrai Guernesias.

I' y a des moments quand j'm'trouve à pensaï du bouan vier temps, et j'sais bien qu'vous m'en crérez quand j'vous dis que j'm'trouve à P'tit Bôt ou l'Moulin Huet. Ch'est là des pièches que ja'ime à la folie.

Mais pour te dire un p'tit d'not' Grand Pays, d'not' belle ville Atlanta, ch'est, j'vous asseure, un bel endré; tout est grand et moderne. Ch'n'est pas d'la p'tite bire. Y'a des bâtiments qui vont presque au ciel. I' y en a de vingt et jusqu'à vingt-quatre étage. On les appelle des "Office Buildings." I' y a de chinq à six chens personnes qui travaillenet dans un seul bâtiment, et des "Elevators" qui vont "zip zip" et vous envient dans un instant jusqu'au "tip top." Et pis en retournat, vous v'là "zouap" dans l'fin fonds. Mais ch'n'est là rien quand vous y'ietes accoutumaï. Pour continuer, not' ville a pu d'tres chens mille de gens! y'en a des biaux et des laids, des riches et des pauvres, comme en Guernesi. Et pis y'a des nègres a peu près querante par chen. J'vous en jure qu'j'avons des jolies rues. Not' Grande Rue est nommaïe "Peachtree Street," qui est seize milles de longueur. Y'a des trams et des bos, et pour les automobiles, j'en avons pus d'trente mille. I' y' en a de toutes les sortes, d'pis les engins de Mess Ford jusqu'aux "Rolls Royce." Et i' sont niet et jour comme le vents, et ch'est sauve qu peut. Y' a des accidents dix ou douze feis par jour. Mais ch'n'est là rien, i' s'en vont comme le vier gris.

Tout est si grand et si biau, que j'vou d'mande que n'faut pas nou bllamaïr si y'a des temps qu'not' tête est pus grande que not' bounet.

Mais, cher Vaïsin, j'pourrais t'en dire de toutes sortes, et j'espère que men bal-livernise te douneras un p'tit l'pllaisi. De toute not' population not' famille est la seule ichin qui est Guernesiaise. Aux Savannah, qui est tres chens milles d'ichin, i' y' a une famille de St. Martin: Peter Rabey et Stephen Rabey, peut-être bien qu'tu les counais.

Pour en fini, Vaïsin George, j'veux bien te dire que la santaï d'n't' famille est bouanne, et pour mé, j'me porte bravement assaï. J'vis terjous en esperance d'veni à Guernesi l'annaïe perchaine.

Et pour en fini, j'veux t'dire d'une vielle fàmme qui v'nait vée ma mère quand j'd'murrons à la Ville au Roi. Quand a s'en allait, a disait: "S'l'y en cas (if in case) j'viens, vou' m'verrez, mais s'l'y en cas j'en viens pas, vou' n'verrez pas!"

J'espère que ma lure vou trouv'ra dans la pu grànde santaï. Et pour chut' fais, j'vou dirai à la perchaine.

Vot' vier ami,
Jean Bouain-Ami Fallaize

Letter from a Guernseyman in America, *1926*

20 November 1926
Atlanta, Georgia
United States

"Once again, dear Guernseyman"
First line of the Last Poet
(Denys Corbet.)

To neighbour George from St. Martin.

So, here I am far from little Guernsey, but I still swear to you that I'm a true Guernseyman.

There are times when I find myself thinking of the good old days, and I know well that you will believe me when I tell you that I find myself at Petit Bôt or Moulin Huet. These are places that I love madly.

But to tell a little of our Great Country, our beautiful town of Atlanta, it is, I assure you, a fine place; all is big and modern. It's no small beer. There are build-ings that almost reach to the sky. There are some with twenty and even up to twenty four floors. They are called "Office Buildings". There are five or six hun-dred people who work in a single building, and "elevators" that go "zip zip" and send you in an instant up to the "tip top". And then returning you "zouap" right down to the ground, but this is nothing when you are accustomed to it. To con-tinue, our town has more that three hundred thousand people! There are the good and ugly, the rich and poor, like in Guernsey. And then there are the black people, about forty percent.

I swear to you that we have pretty streets. Our High Street is named "Peachtree Street", and is sixteen miles long. There are trams and buses, and as for automobiles, we have more than thirty thousand. They are of all kinds, from Mr. Ford's motor cars to "Rolls Royce". And they are there day and night, breezing along, and it's every man for himself. There are accidents ten or twelve times a day. But this is nothing, they go like the devil.

All is so big and beautiful, that I ask you not to blame us if sometimes we get a little bigheaded.

But, dear neighbour, I would like to tell you all sorts of things, and I hope that you will enjoy my chatter. Of all of our population, our family is the only Guernsey one here. In Savannah, that is three hundred miles from here, there is a family from St. Martin: Peter Rabey and Stephen Rabey, you might well know them.

In finishing, neighbour George, I want to say that our family is in good health, and as for me, I'm well enough. I live always in the hope of coming to Guernsey next year.

To finish, I want to tell you of an old lady that used to come to see my mother when we lived at the Ville au Roi. When she was leaving, she would say: "If it so happens that I come, you'll see me, but if it happens that I don't come, you won't see me!"

I hope that my tale will find you in the best of health. And for this time, I will say to you until next time.

Your old friend,
Jean Bonamy Fallaize.

T. A. Grut's regular articles in *La Gazette Officielle de Guernesey* employed a cast of characters. Here, the tradition of the innocents abroad, following the example of Bram Bilo, is continued in this extract which combines reportage on the exotic with light social comedy.

T. A. Grut

From La Pourmenàde de George Tourtel et d'sa vieille fàmme à l'etrangier, *1926* (Guernesiais)

Nous avait arrangi pour startaï au premier d'juin, et biaux que l'temps était justement bel, j'pernèmes des "pills" contre le mal de maïr, caer j'ai ouï les gens dire que les "stewards" n'aïment poui à viégueir les bassins, mais seul'ment à faire la collecte quànd nous est près d'allaï à terre. La Mary-Ann dît que d'pis que j'n'avions poui ataï malâde, que nous n'doun'rai rien ès "stewards," qui sont bien peyi par la Compagnie et par les siens qui leux ont douneï du travâs. Ch'tait notre prumière fais à quittaï Guernesi, et 'y'avait assaï d'qué vée pour nous faire gardaï l's iers bien ouvart, et la goule bien frumaïe, mais quànd j'arrivaimes à l'hotel à Londres, et qu'j'étion dans notre chàmbre, nos langues furent déliaïes, et j'pâlaimes jusqu'à miniet; et l'lend'maïn matin après un bouen déjunaï d'païson et d'eux fricachis, nous alli à la Stâtion pour joindre la compagnie.

Le conducteur était sur la platte-forme et paru nous r'counitre tout d'suite, et vînt en d'vier de nou, et dît, "Monsieur et Madame Tourtel de Guernesey," et après, en angllais, "I am pleased to meet you, and will be your guide and guardian during the entire Tour."

Quaï soülâgement qu'sen p'tit "speech" nous douni! eh donc, nous n'tait poui d'autre miette gênai, et nous l'sirent ès soins du Moussieu en parfaite securitaï. Mais que l'monde est bel; de notre départ de Londres à notre arrivaïe à Lucerne, ch'n'tait qu'jouaix et raviss'ment.

La ville de Lucerne est magnifique, et l'entouorâge de montagnes est superbe, et pour le lac, ch'est quâsi comme unn' maïre. Les "steam" vous prânent partout, et les côtes du lac sont manifiques, mais ch'est quànd nous sort du "steam" pour s'mettre dans un "box" derrière un engin qui và quâsi tout drette en amont, qu'nou perd s'n halaïne; et pour le mont Pilate nous en frémit, tant qu'ch'est rède en amont. La Mary-Ann en tremblliat, et d'mandi au moussieu qui cachait l'engin; "ouéque nous irai si l'affaire mànquet"; mais sa réponse la dédjougli acouare pus, caer i' dît; "Ça dépend, madame, comment vous avez vècu." Quànd nous s'trouve au haut, nous est parmi la née et la glliache.

La Mary-Ann à rajanni terribllement, et m'fait allaï au ser ès pictures ou au théâtre, et j'en trembile quand j'y pense, à chu'qu'sen conducteur de clâsse dirà quànd i'viendrà à en ouïr.

Si les gens qu'ont l'moyen, savaient donc comme le monde est bel, il' iraient faire comme nou, caer not' conducteur est hardi faisànt, et nous arrange toutes les excursions, justement, comme s'nous était d's effànts aux soins d'leux père et mère. Après avec montaï toutes les montâgnes dans l'entouorâge de Lucerne, nous alli à Milan, pour vée, parmi autr'choses la Catedrâle. Après daeux jours à Milan, j'quittaimes pour V'nise ouéque j'restaimes pour huit jours, mais ch'est unn drôle de plliieche, nous n'saï poui quâsi s'nous est à terre ou à iaue; 'y' à des canals, et des p'tites rues partout qui sont si étraites que 'n'y à ni chaise ni quériot, seul'ment des p'tits quériots à t'chen.

L'Egllise de Saint-Marc est superbe, et l'Palais des Doges est étout bel. Le grànd canal est magnifique, atou les Palais qui paraissent être batis dans l'iaue; mais les p'tits canals en V'nise, ch'est donc d'qué qui pù quànd i'fait caüd, et j'étaimes contents quànd l'conducteur nous c'màndi d'paquer nos bagâges pour allaï à Florence, pour vée les gal'ries à pictures, qui sont contaïes d'être les pus belles du monde; mais pour vous dire la veritaï, unn picture est unn' picture, qu'a seit painturaïe par un artiste Italien, ou par men cousin Nico Tardif; j'n'vé poui d'différence.

Après huit jours en Florence (ch'est ochetaeure Firenze) nous alli à Rome. Ch'est donc unn' belle pllièche; l'Egllise de Saint-Pierre est la plus grande du monde, nous 'y est perdu; et pour la cour en d'vant d'l'Egllise, nous y parait comme des mouques. Le Colosseum est en ruènes, mais est bien intéressànt tout d'même, caer il est si grànd, et quànd nous pense qu'les gens y allaient par milles pour vée des poures misérablles être mangi par des bêtes.

George Tourtel and his old lady go for a trip abroad, *1926*

We'd arranged to start out on the first of June, and whilst the weather was fine, we took some "pills" for seasickness, as we'd heard people say that the "stewards" don't like emptying the basins, as the only tipping they're interested in is receiving gratuities on disembarcation. Mary-Ann said that as we'd not been at all sick, that we wouldn't give anything to the "stewards", who are well paid by the company and by those that have given them work. It was our first time away from Guernsey and there was so much to see that we kept our eyes wide open, and our mouths tightly shut, but when we arrived at the hotel in London, and were in our room, our tongues were untied and we talked until midnight; and the following morning after a good breakfast of fish and fried eggs we went to the station to join the group.

The guide was on the platform and seemed to recognise us straight away, and came towards us and said, "Monsieur et Madame Tourtel de Guernesey," and then afterwards in English, "I am pleased to meet you, and will be your guide and guardian during the entire Tour".

What a relief his short "speech" was to us! And so, we were no longer worried at all, and we left everything in the hands of the gentleman in perfect security. But isn't the world beautiful; from leaving London to our arrival in Lucerne, it was a joy and a delight.

The town of Lucerne is magnificent, and the surrounding mountains are stunning, and as for the lake, it's almost like a sea. The "steamboats" take you everywhere, and the lake's coastline is wonderful, but it is when you leave the "steamboats" and place yourself in a "box" behind an engine that goes virtually straight up, that your breath is taken away; and as for Mount Pilatus, it gives you the shivers, as it is so steep going up. Mary-Ann was all of a tremble, and asked the gentleman who was driving the engine; "Where we would go if something went wrong"; but his reply unsettled her even more, because he said: "that depends, madam, how you have lived." When you're at the top, you're amongst snow and ice.

Mary-Ann's started behaving terribly like a young girl, and she's been making me go to the pictures or to the theatre in the evenings, and I dread to think what her [Sunday school] team leader will say about it when he hears about it.

If people who have the means knew how beautiful the world is, they'd do like us, as our guide is very accommodating, and arranges all of the excursions for us, just as though we were children in the care of their mother and father. After having gone up all of the mountains around Lucerne, we went to Milan to see, amongst other things, the Cathedral. After two days in Milan, we left for Venice where we stayed for eight days, but it's a strange place, you can hardly tell whether you're on land or water; there are canals, and little roads everywhere that are so narrow that there are neither carriages nor box-carts, only small dog-carts.

St. Mark's Basilica is stunning, and the Doge's palace is beautiful as well. The Grand Canal is magnificent, with its palaces that appear to have been built on the water; but the small canals in Venice don't half smell when when it's hot, and we were pleased when the guide told us to pack our bags to go to Florence to see the art galleries that are considered to be the most beautiful in the world; but to tell the truth, one picture's like another, whether it's by an Italian artist, or by my cousin Nick Tardif; I can't tell the difference.

After eight days in Florence (now Firenze) we went to Rome. That's a nice place; St. Peter's Basilica is the largest church in the world, you can get lost in it; and as for the square in front of the church, you're like ants. The Colosseum is in ruins, but all the same, it's interesting as it's so big, and when you think that people went there in their thousands to see poor wretches being eaten by beasts.

Writing for a readership composed largely of farmers and people with an interest in agriculture, an author such as 'Le Campagnard' (the countryman), not very surprisingly, found something to write about on a horticultural theme even when describing a trip North of the Arctic Circle – as in this extract. The mixture of Guernesiais, English and Norwegian gives a particular flavour to this piece. In the face of pressures on minority languages from other languages, writers adopt different attitudes. Some strive for purism, rejecting where possible outside influences and borrowings; others, like 'Le Campagnard', seem not to have been bothered in the slightest.

'Le Campagnard'

From Là, i n'y a pas d'gniet, *1967*

Au dehors de la ville, sus une tairre sabllonneuse sont les greenhouses de Hr. Tessem. Quànd j'l'ai trouvaï, i'vendait des pot plants aux coutumiers (i' vend etou des graines, et les outis de gardin) et i' m'a mourtaï sen nursery. Les spans sont des types Aeroplane et Dutch light dauve iun en plastique qu'est erigiaï en avril et demontaï en octobre. Dauve le cauffage á l'huile, des blackouts en plastique ner, et des lampes electriques, i' peut produire tout qu' nou produit en Guernesi. Y'a des bedding plants, des pot plants, de la fern (asparagus), et des cactus. I' pllànte des chrysanths en féverier pour flleurir en octobre-novembre. Enne partie de ches chrysanths furent produits des cuttings acataïs du LOG á Oslø qui les a produits des cuttings obtenus d'un groweur à Guernesi! Dauve des coutumiers qui veullent pllantaïr leux gardins dans le court étai arctique, et qui veullent des house plants dans le long hivaer, et des choppes flleuristes de la ville, ch'est enn commerce qu'-nou peux envier.

Jusqu'à chutte sièclle i'n'y'avait pouint de routes, au vouest de Norvége, et, mesme ach't'heure nou vyage en baté le long d'la caöte. Le billferge (car ferry)

Gildeskål est prêt a dêmarraïr quànd j'vais au Fergekai traversaïr le 'ramp', passaïr des lorries et des vans, et grimpaïr les dégrais au grànd pont et le pont restaurant.

Chut baté, du Saltens Dampskibsselskab, navigue enter Bodø, Horsdal et Sund en faisant la traversaîe de Saltfjorden. Ch'est enn baté à diesel, longue de 52 metres, bian large et bian haut. Le pont à guet est en d'sus du pont restaurant. La chim'naïe est enn 'dummy', l'exhaust passànt par des pippes jumets qui sont des derrickposts.

J'dêmarrons, et, de la maïr, Bodø, atouartillaï des montaïgnes, parait bian. Coum i'fait frêt sus lé pont, j'm'assiéds à côtaï d'enne des gràndes f'nêtes du restaurant vère la panorame de la caôte.

Y a bian de passagiers et enn bouan lot rentrent ciz-ieux dauve leux pâniers apres le choppingue à Bodø. I' fait caud, dans le restaurant, ou la fille du cafeteria vends tout plloin du cafi, de la bire, et du smørrebrod.

Saltfjorden traversaï, nou vait d'près les hautes montaïgnes de l'arctique. I' sont couvertes de la gllache et de la neis, la neis parfeis jusqu'au pid. Ichin et là, au pid d'enne montaïgne ner, enn étret courti, pie des grises pierres, et le galet gris; étou enne p'tite d'meure en bouais, des 'frames' dauve du païsson sec.

Ach't'heure le baté a fini de sen roulment, car j'soumes à l'abri des îles coum Sørarnøy et Sanbbornøya. J'passons daeux batés à païsson, chacun dauve enne pile de boscs sus le pont, et appeurchions l'amas de Märnes. A Horsdal, machine en arrière, j'ammarraïons à la cauchie faire atérraïr des vans, des lorries et des passagiers, car d'ichin enn ch'min meunne dans les montaïgnes. Des mauves et d'auters mouissons de maïr criaïrent.

From There, there is no night, *1967*

Outside of the town on a sandy soil there are Hr. Tessem's greenhouses. When I found him he was selling pot plants to customers (he also sells seeds and garden tools) and he showed me his nursery. The glasshouses are Aeroplane and Dutch light types with one in plastic that is erected in April and taken down in October. With oil-fired heating, black plastic blackouts and electric lights, he's able to produce all that we produce in Guernsey. There are bedding plants, pot plants, asparagus. He plants some chrysanths in February so that they flower in October-November. Part of the chrysanths were produced from cuttings purchased from LOG in Oslø who produced them from cuttings obtained from a Guernsey grower! With customers who want to plant out their gardens in the short Arctic summer, and who want house plants in the long winters, and town florists, it's an enviable business.

Up until this century there were no roads in the west of Norway, and even now you travel by boat along the coast. The billferge (car ferry) Gildeskål is ready to set off when I go to Fergekai crossing over the ramp, passing lorries and vans, and climbing the stairs of the main and restaurant decks.

This Saltens Dampskibsselskab boat sails between Bodø, Horsdal and Sund doing the crossing from Saltfjorden. It's a diesel boat, 52 metre long, very wide and tall. The bridge is above the restaurant deck and the chimney's a 'dummy', the exhaust passing through twin pipes that are derrick posts.

We cast off and, from the sea, Bodø, surrounded by mountains, looks nice. As it's cold on deck I sit down beside one of the large restaurant windows to see the coastal panorama.

There are a lot of passengers and many of them are going home with their baskets after doing shopping in Bodø. It's warm in the restaurant where the girl in the cafeteria is selling plenty of coffee, beer and smørrebrod.

Having crossed Saltfjorden, we can see the high Arctic mountains close up. They're covered in ice and snow, sometimes snow down to the base. Here and there, at the foot of a black mountain, a narrow field, then grey stones, and grey shingle. Also a small wooden dwelling, some frames with dried fish.

The boat's finished rolling now as we're sheltered by islands such as Sørarnoy and Sanbornøya. We pass two fishing boats, each with a pile of boxes on the deck, and we approach the landmass of Märnes. In Horsdal, the boat reverses, we tie up to the jetty to discharge vans, lorries and passengers, as from here a roadway leads up into the mountains. Gulls and other sea birds cry out.

P. W. Luce was the brother of E. J. Luce. He took his pen-name of 'Ph'lippe d'la Golarde' from the road where he was born, Rue de la Golarde, in Saint Lawrence. Another writer of the diaspora, he left Jersey at the beginning of the twentieth century, and only came back to visit twice – once in 1909 and again in 1920 after the death of his brother.

P. W. Luce ('Ph'lippe d'la Golarde')

Nou-s-est oquo mus d'être siez sé, *1904*

Bein yain d'siez mé, je m'trouve à ch't heu,
Bein des milles de terrain j'ai veu,
J'ai visité et j'ai viagi:
Je m'sis prom'né, j'ai travailli
Et veu d'bieau grain, 'té dans des minnes,
J'ai veu des ours me faithe d'laies grinnes:
Malgré tout ch'la, pour dithe le vrai,
J'aimthais oquo mus être siez mé.

D'pis que j'sortis, dans l'mais d'avri,
J'ai tout l'temps veu la scène changi:
D'abord fallait crouaîsi la mé,
Pis le Canada traverser:
De l'Est au Ouest, du Sud au Nord,
De long en large, j'vais d'touos les bords:

Mais malgré ch'la, pour dithe le vrai,
J'aimthais oquo mus être siez mé.

Y'a des chents villes où'est qu'j'ai passé
Et des douzaines qu' j'ai visité,
De Prince Albert à Regina,
De d'pis Moose Jaw jusqu'à Panser:
J'vais d'Winnipeg pour vaie Souris
Et souvent j'passe par Balgomie:
Mais après tout, pour dithe le vrai,
J'aimthais oquo mus être siez mé.

N'faut pas qu'j'oublie de mentionner
Que l'oncl'ye Sam j'vais visiter,
Car de Portal tandis qu'je sis
J'vais jusque dans l's Êtats Unis:
Mais s'i' m'fallait les nommer toutes,
Qu' j'en finithais j'ai bein des doutes:
En d'pit d'lus nombre, pour dithe le vrai,
J'aim'thais oquo mus être siez mé.

Pourtant ch'est bé que de viagi,
D'vaie les bieautés d'un autre pays,
Lacs et riviéthes, des grands hauts monts,
Crouaîsi les prairies, les vallons,
Et sus des bieaux hauts ponts passer
Et vaie tout chein qu'i' y'a d'pus bé:
Tout d'même, m's amins, j'dis chein qu'est vrai:
Où'est qu' nou s'trouve le mus, ch'est d'étre siez sé.

You're much better off at home, *1904*

I find myself now very far from home.
Many miles of terrain I've seen.
I've visited and I've travelled
and I've seen fine corn, been down mines,
I've seen bears pulling faces at me:
Despite all that, to tell you the truth
I'd much rather be at home.
Since I left in the month of April,
I've seen the scenery change all the time:
first I had to cross the sea,
then cross Canada:

from East to West, from South to North,
from far and wide, I travel all over the place:
Despite all that, to tell you the truth
I'd much rather be at home.

There are hundreds of towns I've passed
and dozens I've visited,
from Prince Albert to Regina,
from Moose Jaw as far as Pense:
I go from from Winnipeg to see Souris
and I often pass through Balgonie:
But after all, to tell you the truth
I'd much rather be at home.

I mustn't forget to mention
that I go and visit Uncle Sam,
for while I'm in Portal
from there I go into the United States:
but if I had to name them all
I really doubt I'd be able to finish:
despite their number, to tell you the truth
I'd much rather be at home.

However it's a fine thing to travel,
to see the beauties of another country,
lakes and rivers, large tall mountains,
cross prairies, valleys,
and pass over fine high bridges
and see all the most beautiful things:
all the same, my friends, what I say is true:
the place you're best off, is at home.

Devils, Witchcraft and Things that go Bump

The closeness of the communities of the Islands was emperilled by the belief in witches. Did you suspect your neighbour of casting the evil eye on your cows? Or shape-shifting? Or taking part in Friday night witches' sabbats? Victor Hugo recounts some of the history of the persecution of suspected witches, and native writers have too turned their attention to witchcraft – although the educated and enlightened writers of the nineteenth century were more likely to turn their satirical gaze on the beliefs of simpler folk. The traditional meeting place for les gens du Vendrédi (the Friday people) in Jersey was the outcrop of rock on the coast of Saint Clement called Rocqueberg (in Jèrriais Rocque Bèr) or, in English, the Witches' Rock. In Guernsey, covens met at the dolmen of Catioroc. Dolmens were also associated with *les p'tits faîtchieaux* (in Jèrriais) or *les faiquiaoux* (in Guernesiais) – the little people, the fairies – who were often dangerous, sometimes malevolent.

The traditional animal nicknames of the Islanders are perhaps not without some basis in the beliefs of the Islanders in how the boundaries between the human world and the animal world could be transgressed – those who knew how could, so people believed, transform themselves into animal forms, and supernatural animals prowled the paths, valleys and cliffs.

Charles Picot wrote a series of spooky tales for the annual almanacs. Although his native parish of Trinity, in Jersey, is best known for the great black Dog of Bouley (lé Tchian d'Bouôlé), here is the climax of a tale of a witches' sabbat which takes place, not at Rocqueberg, but in a more feline corner of Trinity.

Charles Picot

From **Le Sabat des Chorchièr', 1891 (Jèrriais)**

Il tait si foncè dans ses pensèes, tch'il en allait la tête toute baîssie en bas, et d'maîmme quand i' vînt à un cèrtain cârrefour, tch'est qui fît ... i' prîns l'maoûvais k'min, et s'en fut, dans l'savé, s'fouôrré dans des ruettes et des garamiézes où-est qui n'avait que de s'drotchi à chaque pas tchi faîzait; mais i' filait tout l'temps bouân traîn. Enfin, i' vînt à un aoûtre cârrefour, et ch'fut là qui se r'connut. Le pouôre mînzézablle, véze! i r'connut bein où-est qu'il avait tè s'fouôrré. Il ézait bâilli bein d'tchi pour en être hor'! car i' savait bein – du meins, i l'avait ouï bein des feîs dize à sa moman, et à d'aoûtres èttou, tchi s'pâssait d'tèrriblles sçainnes là dans des temps, et pîs i' s'ramémouaizi tout d'un cou' que ch'tait Vendrédi la nièt!!! – Ch'est là qu'la paeûx l'prîns; et est-che ètonnant? Nannin, ma fingre! I' prîns la paque; mais dia! i' fut bein gardè d'allé liain; car i' n'avait pas sélement dêbroussè d'unne pèrque que tchique chose lî crouaîzait les gambes, et clliaque! le v'la allé tout sân long dans le k'min, à maîntchi êbaoûbi!

Mais, diâtre! i' n'y fut pas longtemps, bas; car, quand i' rouvrit l's-yièr' i' vit tch'il tait atourtillyi d'un mouoché d'bêtes tchi dansicotaient à l'entou d'li, et tch'êprouvaient à grîmpé partout sûs li. J'vos l'di occouo unne feîs, i' fut bétôt sûs ses pîds, mais inutile de chèrchi à s'saoûvé, les boustres de bêtes – ch'tait un tâs d'bitches de câts – ne voulaient pas l'laîssi pâssé. I' n'y-avait qu'unne toute petite ouvèrtuze d'un bor' par où est tchi pouvait allé, et il avânchit par là pour s'êcapé; mais l's'aoûtres avânchaient èttou, et d'vant que l'pouôre Douar' le sûsse, i' s'trouvit pitchi sûs un treîs-cârres à la main dêtre du cârrefour, dans l'mitan d'un rond, li tout seu', et un tâs d'baloques de câts assis tout-à-l'êntou, à le r'gardé attou d's'yièr' êffriyablles, tchi r'lîzaient comme des chandelles. Il êprouvit bein occouo à s'saoûvé; mais sitôt tchi bouogeait, mêssieux les câts étaient prêts à lî volé sûs l'co. I' fut dôn bein oblligi d'resté là où-il tait; et où-est chi trembllait m'nu comme la fielle, et suait comme un anneton – i' n'en avait pas un fi d'sèt sûs l'co!

Je n'sézais, vos dize mes bouannes gens, combein d'temps tchi fut dans ch'êtat-là; mais au but d'unne volée, Douar' ouï tout à l'entou d'li le pûs horiblle miaoû tch'il eûsse janmais d'sa vie entendu, et dans un cllin-d'yi touôs les câts étaient d'but, draits comme des pitchets. Notre janne homme, tout êffritè qu'il tait, vit bein comme unne ombre tch'était en d'sûs d'li, en l'air. I' lève la tête en haoût, et ... d'mandèz si l'pouôre cor' deut avait paeûx – i' vit, véze! i' vit un objèt tchi d'cendait comme des nûes, à ch'va sûs l'manche d'un ênorme g'nêts à nêtché l'aize, et dans meins d'unne ségonde, l'objèt, tchi n'tait rein aoûtre chôse qu'un grand-affraeûx cat, treîs feîs pûs grand que l's'aoûtres, s'en vînt bidéranne t'cheis d'but, comme un êtend-pèrque à côtè du malheûzaeûx Douar' tchi n'eut qu'd'en mouozi.

Touôs l's'aoûtres saluizent.

Ch'tait lûs K'mandant!

I' n'perdit pon ennetou d'temps; car à painne était-i' bas, tchi fit unne motion atou sân g'nêts, et aussitôt la djaîngue se mîns à dansé d'un pid sûs l'aoûtre, et à touânné tout à l'entou, et à s'teurtre, et à caoûvi l's'ouozèlles, et à faize toutes sortes d'morgaches. Pîs bétôt unne musique charmante, comme ou' n'avèz janmais d'votte vie occouo ouï: i' y-avait des vouaîs d'piplo et d'fliûtes, et pîs d's'èltons, et des téneur! et des bâsses, et occouo d'aoûtres tchi rempllissaient entre, pour faize la musique occouo pûs belle; et pîs d'temps en temps des miaoûs supèrbes sûs touôs les tons. Enfin, pour en pazé pûs cour, le tintamârre tchi fizent pour bein un cou-plle d'heuzes, ne sézait s'imaginé par les siens tchi n'l'ont veu ni ouï, et il' taîent bein une tchézântainne.

Douar' était là dans l'mitan sans poué s'êcapé. I'y-eu jusqu'à chînq ou sièz des pûs affrontès tchi lî grîmpizent sûs l'dos, et lî trillizent sa bouanne câsaque de tout fin nièr dra' tchi mèttait pour la quatrième feîs sélement. Le pûs impèrtînan de tous lî grimit maîmme le co et la fache, et lî mordit l'gras de l'ouozèlle dêtre!

Douar' se d'fandait tant qui pouait; mais, hélâ! tch'est qui gangnait?

Pour fini tout, quand la musique et les danses, et les miaoûnenies, et les heurles fuzent finis, daeûx des pûs biaoûx mêssieux d'câts, tchi faîzaient la cârre à la maîmme démouêzelle, mîndrent les griffes en l'air, et k'menchizent à s'grimé et à s'mordre en veur-tu? mé j'en veur, et dans daeûx s'gôndes, le pé volait d'touôs bor', et pîs i' s'ente-prîndrent à la gorge attou lûs grîns, et pîs ch'tait êcopîs, et miaoûne et râclle, et pîs mor'. Et la p'tite vilainne tch'était la caoûse de tout l'brit, se t'nait là à r'gardé ses daeûx galânts s'ente-dêchizé. Oul' avait pûtôt l'air toute fiéze; car quândi tchi s'battaient, ou' continuait à faize sa touélètte et à filé à tize-larigo! Che n'fut que quand les daeûx fuzent êtendus sûs l'dos les quatre fièr en haoût, qu'la batâle cêssit. Il 'taient touôs les daeûx bein médjaîchis, allez! I' r'fuzent bétôt d'but et prêts à r'kémanchi; mais dans l'temps tchi k'manchaient â rêcopi, i' lûs tchit à touôs les daeûx unne raidde tappe le travèr de la hézèque du dos, que l'maître lûs baîllit, tant et si bein tchi n'en r'voulizent pon d'aoûtres, et chutte feîs ichîn la batâle fut bein finie.

En maîmme temps le k'mândant s'mînt à miaoûné d'unne vouaîs comme un ôrage treîs coups.

I' s'rângizent daeûx à daeûx et k'manchizent à battre la marche, et miaoûnizent tous occouo unne feîs; mais boustre! il' tait tro tar', l'heuze était arrivée, i' n'y-avait pûs de r'mièdde –

LE SABAT ÉTAIT FINI!

Car à la pièche de s'en r-allé comme il' taient v'nus, souôs la forme d'autant d'câts et d'cattes, à sân grand êffrait, Douar' ne vit pûs qu'un fiotchèt d'hommes de d'fammes à l'êntou d'li, touôs paînneur', tchi dêcampizent touôs patte-à-coue, sans lî dize un mot; mais, dia! tchi r'gard' tchi lî lânchizent en lûs z-n-allant! – le Chef le m'nichit maîmme attou sân mânche de g'nêts!

Et Douar' fur laîssi là tout seu'.

I' crut bein en r'connaître pûs d'iun et pûs d'iunne; mais i' n'voulit janmais dize tch'est que ch'tait. Et j'vos assaeûze tchi fît bein; car si l'avait fait, il 'tait saeûx d'sân cou' – i' n'ézait pon temps en vie. I' s'contentit d'avé veu

L'SABAT DES CHORCHIÈR'

AU

BÉTCHÈT-ÈS-CÂTS.

Le pouôre Douar' n'a janmais seu comme-est tchi r'gângnit sièz li; mais il en r'pazit à la fin, et s'pitchit bein vite au lièt tout d'puzant d'sueu.

From The Witches' Sabbat, *1891*

He was so lost in his thoughts that he kept his head down as he walked on, and so it was that when he came to a certain crossroads, what did he do?... he took the wrong road and went off, without realising, to wander into lanes and steep stony paths where he all but stumbled at every step he took; but he kept on going at a fast pace. Finally he came to another crossroads and it was there that it came to him. The poor wretch, yes! he recognised the place he had wandered to. He would have given anythng to be out of there! because he knew well – at least, he had heard many times from his grandmother and from others too, that terrible scenes occurred there from time to time, and then he remembered suddenly that this was Friday night! And it was then that he was seized by fear; and is there any surprise in that? Not in the slightest! He took off; but he was prevented from getting very far at all, for he had barely managed to scarper a perch when something tripped him up, and splat! down he went headlong in the road, half-stunned! But he wasn't down a devil of a time; for when he opened his eyes again he saw that he was tangled up in a heap of animals dancing round him and trying to clamber all over him. I'll tell you again, he was up on his feet pretty quickly, but he had no way to escape, the damn animals – it was a load of wretched cats – wouldn't let him pass. There was only one little opening on one side that he could get through, and he went that way to make his escape, but the others went with him and before poor Eddie knew he found himself thrown onto a triangle to the right of the crossroads in the middle of a circle, all alone, with a lot of perishing cats sat all around looking at him with terrifying eyes which shone like candles. He continued to make great efforts to get away, but as soon as he made a move, the cats were ready to jump him. He was therefore forced to stay where he was, trembling like a leaf and sweating buckets until he didn't have a dry stitch on him!

I couldn't tell you, dear readers, how long he spent in that state, but after a time, Eddie heard all around him the most horrible miaowing he had ever heard in his life, and in the blink of an eye all the cats were standing bolt upright. Our young man, as frightened as he was, saw something like a shadow in the air above him. He raised his head up and... you can imagine how frightened the poor devil must have been – he saw, yes! he saw something descending out of thin air, astride the handle of an enormous broom of the sort you use for sweeping the floor, and in less than a second, the object which was none other than a scarily big cat, three times bigger than the others, came down, stark upright, slap bang next to the unhappy Eddie who almost died of fright.

All the others greeted him.

It was their Leader!

He didn't waste any time either, for as soon as he was down, he gestured with his broom, and straightaway the mob began to dance from one foot to the other, and turning in a circle, and twisting themselves, and cocking their ears and making all sorts of faces. And then there came a charming music like you've never heard before in your life: there were the voices of fifes and flutes, and altos and tenors! and basses, and others filling in between, to make the music more beautiful still; and then from time to time there were splendid miaows in all keys. Then, to cut a long story short, the hullabaloo they made for a couple of hours could only be imagined by those those who have seen or heard it, and there must have been about forty of them.

Eddie was in the middle of them with no way of escaping. Five or six of the boldest of them climbed on his back and ripped his fine black woollen jacket that he'd only worn three times previously. The most impertinent one of all scratched his neck and his face and bit his right earlobe!

Eddie defended himself as well as he could, but alas! to what avail?

In the end, when the music and the dances and the miaowing and the howls were over, two of the handsomest cats, who were wooing the same young lady, put their claws up and began scratching and biting seven bells out of each each other, and in two seconds fur was flying everywhere and then they had their claws at each other's throat, and spat and mewled and hawked and bit. And the little minx who was the cause of the fight stood there watching her two suitors tearing each other apart. She seemed very pleased with herself, because as she watched she preened herself and purred like mad! It was only when the two of them were stretched out flat on their backs that the fight was over. They were both pretty well mangled! They were soon back on their feet and ready to start again, but as they were beginning to spit again, they both received a wallop across the back from their master which was so hefty a blow that they didn't want another one, and that time the battle was definitely over.

At the same time the leader began to mew in a voice like thunder, three times. They lined up in twos and began to beat a march, and all miaowed once more; but damnation! it was too late, the time had come, there was no help for it – the sabbat was finished!

For instead of going as they had come, in the shape of so many cats, Eddie saw with fear only a crowd of men and women around him, all sheepish, who went off in single file, without saying a word to him; but, gracious! what looks they gave him as they left! – the Chief even threatened him with his broom handle!

And Eddie was left there all alone.

He thought he recognised more than one of the men and women, but he never wanted to say who. And I can assure you that it was just as well, for if he had done, he was absolutely sure not to be long for this world. He contented himself with having seen the Witches' Sabbat at Lé Betchet ès Cats (the cats' corner).

Poor Eddie never knew how he got back home; but he turned up eventually and threw himself into bed, dripping with sweat.

Gilbert Parker

From The Battle of the Strong, *1898*

The Isle of Jersey, like a scout upon the borders of a foeman's country, looked out over St. Michael's Basin to those provinces where the war of the Vendee was soon to strike France from within, while England, and presently all Europe, should strike her from without.

War, or the apprehension of war, was in the air. The people of the little isle, living always within the influence of natural wonder and the power of the elements, were deeply superstitious; and as news of dark deeds done in Paris crept across from Carteret or St. Malo, as men-of-war anchored in the tide-way, and English troops, against the hour of trouble, came, transport after transport, into the harbour of St. Heliers, they began to see visions and dream dreams. One peasant heard the witches singing a chorus of carnage at Rocbert; another saw, towards the Minquiers, a great army like a mirage upon the sea; others declared that certain French refugees in the island had the evil eye and bewitched their cattle; and a woman, wild with grief because her child had died of a sudden sickness, meeting a little Frenchman, the Chevalier du Champsavoys, in the Rue des Tres Pigeons, thrust at his face with her knitting-needle, and then, Protestant though she was, made the sacred sign, as though to defeat the evil eye.

This superstition and fanaticism so strong in the populace now and then burst forth in untamable fury and riot. So that when, on the sixteenth of December 1792, the gay morning was suddenly overcast, and a black curtain was drawn over the bright sun, the people of Jersey, working in the fields, vraicking among the rocks, or knitting in their doorways, stood aghast, and knew not what was upon them.

Some began to say the Lord's Prayer, some in superstitious terror ran to the secret hole in the wall, to the chimney, or to the bedstead, or dug up the earthen floor, to find the stocking full of notes and gold, which might, perchance, come with them safe through any cataclysm, or start them again in business in another world. Some began fearfully to sing hymns, and a few to swear freely. These latter were chiefly carters, whose salutations to each other were mainly oaths, because of the extreme narrowness of the island roads, and sailors to whom profanity was as daily bread.

In St. Heliers, after the first stupefaction, people poured into the streets. They gathered most where met the Rue d'Driere and the Rue d'Egypte. Here stood the old prison, and the spot was called the Place du Vier Prison.

Men and women with breakfast still in their mouths mumbled their terror to each other. A lobster-woman shrieking that the Day of Judgment was come, instinctively straightened her cap, smoothed out her dress of molleton, and put on her sabots. A carpenter, hearing her terrified exclamations, put on his sabots also, stooped whimpering to the stream running from the Rue d'Egypte, and began to wash his face. A dozen of his neighbours did the same. Some of the women, however, went on knitting hard, as they gabbled prayers and looked at the fast-blackening sun. Knitting was to Jersey women, like breathing or tale-bearing, life itself. With their eyes closing upon earth they would have gone on knitting and dropped no stitches.

La Gazette de Césarée

Au chen qui mint des versets sus Les Chorchiers, *1812* (Jèrriais)

> Mousieu qu'avaits aicrit des vers
> Sus la gazette de Césarais,
> Dam, ou vouos fzais r'gardé d'travers
> Par qui qu'un d'nos Saintaubinais.
> Ou dite que yiun a yeu ses ch'vos
> Et ses volailles enchorchellêts,
> Oh, quouz en faites un bieau nigos,
> Et l'y mettais une brid sus l'nêts.
> Ola mousieu, sunn cryaits pon
> A chez chorchiers ni quézos.
> Pour me quand jétais p'tit garson
> J'les cryais tréjous sus men dos:
> Et ben, quan jy crezais encouéze
> Jeun sezais pas tout seu; et ben,
> Avous pon oui chutt vielle histoize
> Quiss dit ... quiss dit ... de ... de ... ain ... ain?
> Oh vrain ment jenn men rappel pon
> Mais d'mandêts ly quant ou voudrêts,
> Y vouos diza que sen couchon
> Et sen ch'va sont enchorchellêts:
> Et quan y fut vais chutt hardelle,
> Y dit quour chu un co d'couté,
> Que chen fut pas drièze louozeille
> Mais a quiq' bord lien du muzé.
> Enfin, tandi qui ly t'nai l'bras
> La pouore hardelle étoit pinchie
> Par des chorchièrs quin viyait pas,
> Qui faisaient chenna par magie.
> Me qui sie pouore Saintaubinais,
> Quai tréjous yeu lesprit pezant,
> Je vouos asseuze que jy cryais
> D'vant davé llieu vouos vers charmants,
> Mais vraiment, y mont converti

Ach teu jenn crai pus és chorchiers
Et jen sie tout a fait guézi
Dépis que j'ai llieu vouos bieaux vers.
Mais comm iss pouozai rencontrai
Que quiq qun med'manddai pour vous
Dite oueq'nou pouozai vouos trouvai?
Les r'miaides qu'ouz offzaits sont si dous,
Que je me fais ceux et certain
Que pus dunn hardell' des demain
Couoza partout d'mandé pour vous.

To the person who published the poem about the Witches, 1812

Dear sir, who wrote the verses
in La Gazette de Césarée:
Well, you've made some people of Saint Aubin
look at you askance.
You say that someone has had his horses
and his poultry bewitched,
Oh, you've made a fool of him
and led him by the nose.
Well sir, if you don't believe
in those witches and warlocks.
As for me, when I was a little boy
I believed they were always after me:
well, if I still did believe in them
I wouldn't be alone in that; and well,
have you heard that old story
told by ... told by ... um ... er ...
Oh really I can't remember
but you can ask him if you want,
he'll tell you that his pig
and his horse have been bewitched:
and when he went to see that girl,
he says she was stabbed with a knife,
that it wasn't behind the ear
but somewhere far from the face.
Finally, when he was holding her arm
the poor girl was pinched
by witches that he couldn't see,
who were doing it by magic.
I'm only a poor man from Saint Aubin

and have always had a serious mind,
I assure you that I believed it all
until I read your charming verses,
but really, they have converted me
and now I no longer believe in witches
and I'm completely cured
since I read your fine verses.
But as it may turn out
that someone inquires after you,
tell me where you can be found.
The remedies you offer are so gentle,
that I'm as sure as anything
that from tomorrow more than one girl
will run about asking for you.

George Métivier ('Un Câtelain')

La Vieille Marie; ou La Maison Ensorchellaie, *before 1831* (Guernesiais)

Un ser, j'étais dans ma cahutte,
Assis au couain d'une belle fouaie d'vrec,
De bouan fort cidre dans ma jutte,
Et le ptit but d'pipe à man bec:
L'vent qui hurlait dans ma guerbiere
Faisait que l'crâsset brûlait bliu,
Ma femme ouvrait su la jonquiere –
S'talle, nous abat l'u du grant u!

Jem'déroqui su la vieille bingue,
Et j'dîs, k'est-k'est là, malvarin;
Tu tape en sergeant, palfrandingue!
Est-che que mn uss est un tabouarin?
Ah mon dou! vla l'terpi qui danse,
S'fait nott Madlaine, tout en tersaut,
Les chinq brocs font l'pott à daeux anses,
Et la catte a les grins en haut!

Mais, sais-tu k'est k'est vnu, maufaite?
Fis-ju; de mes daeux iers, Madlon,
J'ai veue les cônes, vere, et la couette,
Ma chair en terfit, du démon:
J'ai veue su san gnêt, éperquie

Derriere le ner tout en travers,
Tu sai bien qui ... all est partie
Au Cakiau Ro ou ... en enfer.

Et s'all yest, mordi, k'all y reste –
(Le bon Gu m'pardonne de jurair,)
K'all y sait graillie – la vieille peste
Est vnue pour nous ensorchellair!
Hier au matin tu lvi tan burre
Vert coum la plize, et dame, i puait,
Et tout l'cidre, ma fé, j'en jure,
Est coum de l'aigre dans l'émet.

Nicolas, stalle, fais ta perière:
Mais, nennin, tu n't'en scie de rien,
Ch'est té qui nou porte bouzière,
Qui nou ruinras, mauvais chrékien:
Si tu allais brament à l'Egllise,
Aurun d'sipottair au Mont-d-Va,
Tu n'érais pas veue la vieille grise,
Ni l'vier querouin – mon dou, les vla!

En effet, la daunaie laie trie
Avait passai coum un écliair
A travers hecq, uss et ussrie,
Clianque et serraeure et taroué d'fer!
J'la vime, auve ses longues dents grinchies,
Accliuquie su le ptit bignon,
Et (j'nen mens miette) à sa brachie,
A tnait un catt et un genon.

A ritounnait, la vieille indigne,
Et, l'crérioûs bien? un vollié d'cats
Travssant l'porta et la cuisine,
Désaqui l'long d'l'étchelle au chnas:
L'fonzé d'Madlon en faisait d'belles,
Le roué à san tout saeu tournait,
L'villiain pernaguait dvant la seille,
Et la chifournie chifourniait.

Quand nou nouz envyi une bouffaie
D'vent ... un rabat jamais itai
De chendre et d'sie, par la chimnaie ...

J'en fûme, nos daeux ner émittais:
Rats, mulots, souaris, coum guerzille,
Orviaux, raines, pêle-mêle gabouaret,
Sous l'guenillon d'la vieille sorille,
Il en plliuvait, il en couarait.

S'fît Madlon, prie Gu, vier sans cure,
Llié tes sounnets, malécatant,
Vé-tu tous les orviaux des Hûres,
Tous les ranntiaux du malétant?
Mussieu Babau, l'chier petit houme,
Jamais n'en griera la maison –
La vla, coum un beu k'nouz assoume,
Ah! pataflias, en pamouaîson.

Me qui n'crâins rien, j'happe ma bayounne,
Pendue es rouaies à san croquet,
J'accroque, en jurant, la guénounne,
J'leve le bras pour l'épistoqué:
Mais, dès qu'a sent l'fer, vere et vite,
A prend san vol, et l'guiable étou,
Auve une paîne de lard, la maudite,
Heurlant, kè-hou-hou! kè-hou-hou!

J'érouzi la fache à Madlaine,
Et l'iaude frède la ravigotti;
Et pie j'men fu, tout hors d'halaine,
Ramplli ma jutte, à l'appanti:
La kerbounnaie bûlliait dans l'être,
Nott tchien Turc rouânait sous l'étrain –
La vieille s'en vient derrière san maître,
Me baille une jaffe, et crie man drain!

Grand merci, fis-ju, l'émittaie!
L'cidre est bouan, veur-tu en goûtair?
J'en suppi une demie crâsstaie –
Et j'dîs, cônu, à ta santai;
Tout démon qu'il est (ll'yen a d'pieres)
I fut étounnai d'ma vertu,
Et par dessu l'hecq, auve sa chère,
I s'en fut, riant coum un perdu.

Coum je rentrais, dans nott cuisine
J'vi une caouette, un engoulvent,
Un guenon, atout sa houissine,
Eperqui su l'dos d'un cahouan:
La caouette faisait vie de guiable,
L'guenon criait, "toure-la," et "jaue,"
Le cahouan voltait su la table,
Eboudinant rats et mulots.

Ha, ha, fis-ju, ma vieille mouissette,
Coum est k'tuès vnue? L'uss était cllios,
Et vchin la clliai dans ma poukette –
"Couâs, couâs," si-t-alle, "va-t-en la haut."
Osaie, viens-tu dans ma caumine,
Cmandair l'maître de la maison;
– J'attrappe une fourque, et, palfrandine,
Jla lli pique a travers l'aileton.

Et aussitôt, Messiûs, Mesdames,
Et Mesdmoîselles qui m'écoutaiz,
Raines, mulots, caouette, cahouan, dame,
Nous vit tout chunna déroutair:
Je lz oyais (en baisant ma jutte)
Criair, " Allon! allon! allon!"
Et i n'resti dans nott cahutte
Que mé, la catte, et nott Madlon.

Old Mary; or The Bewitched House, *before 1831*

One evening, I was in my cottage
sitting in the corner by a fine vraic fire,
good strong cider in my tankard
and the bit of my pipe in my bill;
the wind howling through my gable loft-door
making the cresset lamp burn blue,
my wife was knitting on the green-bed –
says she, "Someone's knocking down the front door!"

I stumbled over the old skep
and said, "Damn you, who's there;
you're beating like a military tattoo, for heaven's sake!
What do you take my door for? A drum?"
"Good God! the trivet is dancing,"

says Madeleine, with a start,
"The five crocks are dancing akimbo,
And the cat has her claws out and raised!"

"But, do you know who's dropped by, God help us?"
said I; "with my own two eyes, Madlon,
I saw the very horns and little tail,
it makes my flesh creep, of a demon:
I saw astride her broom,
behind Old Nick, the old so-and-so,
you know very well who ... and off she went
to Le Catioroc ... or to hell."

"And if she is there, for God's sake, let her remain there –
(the Good Lord forgive me for swearing,)
let her be roasted there – the old witch
came to cast a spell on us!
Yesterday morning you churned your butter
green as sea grass, and my goodness how it stank,
and all of the cider, my goodness, I swear it,
has turned to vinegar in the trough."

"Nicholas", says she, "say your prayers;
but, no, you care about nothing,
it is you who brings evil on us,
who will bring ruin on us, you poor excuse for a Christian:
if you went to Church as is right and proper
instead of drinking it up at Le Mont de Val,
you would not have seen the old witch,
nor the old rascal – my goodness, there they are!"

And so it was, the damned ugly cow
had passed like a flash of lightning
through the half-door, the door and the doorway,
latch and lock and iron bolt!
I saw her with long gnashing teeth
crouched on the little cushion,
and (without the word of a lie) in her arms,
she held a cat and a monkey.

She was sniggering, the old hag,
and, you have to believe me a volley of cats,
crossing the hall and the kitchen,

appeared all along the loft ladder:
Madlon's thread-clew pranced,
the spinning-wheel turned by itself,
the cresset stand capered in front of the churn
and the hurdy-gurdy whined and quavered.

When she sent a gust
of wind … a downdraft like never felt before,
of ash and soot, down the chimney …
we were both black with soot:
rats, voles, mice, like hail,
slow worms, frogs higgledy piggledy and confused,
from under the rags of the old witch
they poured out and they ran out.

Said Madlon, "Pray to God, you old layabout,
say your prayers, you ne'er-do-well,
see all of the slow worms from Les Hures,
all of the froglets from the stinking swamp.
Mr. Babault, the dear little man,
never will clear the house of them –"
And down she goes like a stunned ox,
with a crash, fainted dead away.

Me, I'm afraid of nothing, so I take my bayonet
hanging from the beams on its hook,
I take on, swearing, the old hag,
I raise my arm to slay her:
but, as soon as she feels the iron, and no hanging about,
she takes flight, and the devil too,
with a bacon flitch, the damned old hag,
howling, "Kè-hou-hou! kè-hou-hou!"

I sprinkled Madlon's face,
and the cold water revived her;
and then I went, quite out of breath,
to fill my jug in the shed.
The brindled cow was lowing in the stall,
Our dog Turk was growling under the straw –
The old hag came behind her master,
gave me a slap, and cried: "And that's one for luck!"

"Mercy me!" said I, "here's the filthy hag!
The cider is good, would you like to try some?"
I myself drank half a bumper –
and I said: "Horny, to your health!"
As much of a demon as he is – there are some worse –
he was astonished at my coolness,
and over the half-door, with his doxy,
he disappeared, laughing like one possessed.

As I came back into our kitchen,
I saw a chough, a night-hawk,
a monkey, with his switch,
astride an owl's back.
The chough was making the devil's own row,
the monkey was shrieking: "Turn there, gee-up!"
The owl darted on to the table,
disembowelling the rats and voles.

"Haha," said I, "my old bird,
How did you come here? The front door was shut,
and here's the key in my pocket." –
"Caw, caw", said she, "get up there!"
"How dare you come into my cottage
and order the master of the house?"
I caught up a fork and, by George,
I stuck it through her wing.

And instantly – Gentlemen, Ladies,
And young Misses, who are listening to me –
– frogs, voles, chough, owl, yes,
we saw the whole lot skedaddle!
I could hear them – as I fondly put my tankard to my lips –
cry: "Away! away! away!"
And there remained in our cottage
only myself, the cat, and our Madlon!

Victor Hugo uses the word 'belle' – a courtyard – one of the words of Norse origin surving in the Norman languages of the Islands.

Victor Hugo

From Toilers of the Sea, *1866* (translated from the French)

Gilliat lived in the parish of Saint Sampson. He was not liked in the neighbourhood. There were reasons for that.

To begin with, his home was a "haunted" house. Sometimes in Jersey and Guernsey in the countryside, even in town, going through some isolated spot or in a street with many inhabitants, you will happen to come upon a house, the entrance to which is completely boarded up. Holly obstructs the doorway, hideous boards are nailed over the ground floor windows; while the casements of the upper storeys are neither closed nor open, for all the window-frames are bolted shut, but the panes are broken. If there is a courtyard, grass grows there, and its perimeter wall is crumbling away. If there is a garden, it is choked with nettles, brambles, and hemlock, and strange insects abound in it. The chimneys are cracked, the roof is falling in; so much as can be seen of the inside of the rooms is dilapidated in appearance. The woodwork is rotten, the stonework mildewed. The wallpaper has peeled away, so you can study old fashions in interior decoration – the scrawling patterns of the Empire Style, the crescent-shaped draperies of the Directory, the banisters and balustrading of Louis XVI. The thick draperies of cobwebs full of flies indicate the undisturbed peace enjoyed by the spiders. You may sometimes notice a broken pot on a shelf. Such is a haunted house. Where the devil visits by night.

Houses can become corpses like human beings. A superstitious belief is all that is needed to cause their death. Then they become terrifying. These deathly houses are common in the Channel Islands.

Rural and maritime populations do not rest easily in the presence of evil. The people of the Channel, of the English Islands, and of the French coast, have definite beliefs on this subject. The devil has his representatives all over the earth. It is certain that Belphegor is hell's ambassador in France, Hutgin in Italy, Belial in Turkey, Thamuz in Spain, Martinet in Switzerland, and Mammon in England. Satan is an emperor like any other. Satan Caesar. His court is well organised. Dagon is grand almoner; Succor Benoth, chief of the eunuchs; Asmodeus, banker at the gaming-table; Kobal, manager of the theatre; and Verdelet, grandmaster of ceremonies. Nybbas is the court jester. Wiérus, a learned man, a fine expert in the occult, and a man well versed in demonology, calls Nybbas the great parodist.

The Norman fishermen of the Channel have to take many precautions at sea, by reason of the illusions cast by the devil. It has long been believed that Saint Malo inhabited Ortac, the great square rock in the sea between Alderney and the Casquets; and many old-time sailors used to swear that they had often seen him there from afar, seated and reading a book. So sailors, as they passed, were in the habit of kneeling many times before the Ortac rock, until the day when the fable was dispelled, and replaced by the truth. It has been discovered, and is well known today, that the inhabitant of the rock of Ortac is not a saint, but a devil. This devil, whose name is Jochmus, had the cunning to pass himself off for several centuries as Saint Malo. Even the Church itself fell into this error. The demons Ragubel, Oribel, and Tobiel were saints until the year 745, when Pope Zachary, having flushed them out, removed them. For these sorts of purges, which are certainly very useful, one needs to be extremely knowledgeable about devils.

The old folk of the country tell – though all this refers to time past – that the Catholic population of the Norman archipelago was once, though quite involuntarily, even more intimate with demons than the Huguenot population. Why? We do not know. What is certain is that this minority were formerly very bothered by the devil. He had taken a fancy to the Catholics, and sought out their company a good deal – which led to the belief that the devil is Catholic rather than Protestant. One of his most insufferable liberties consisted in paying night-time visits to married Catholics in bed, just when the husband had fallen fast asleep and the wife was half-asleep. And that is how things went awry. Patouillet was of opinion that this was what led to the birth of Voltaire. Not improbable in the circumstances. The whole matter is clearly laid out and described in the formulas of exorcism, as set down in the rubric "About nocturnal delusions and the seed of the devil". The situation was particularly acute in Saint Helier towards the end of the last century, probably as a punishment for the crimes of the Revolution. The consequences of revolutionary excess are incalculable. However this may have been, the possibility of a visit from the demon at night, when it is impossible to see clearly, when one is asleep, troubled many observant wives. Giving birth to a Voltaire was not a pleasant notion. One of these women, in some anxiety, consulted her confessor on how to fend off the fraud in time. The confessor replied, "To make sure if you are dealing with the devil or your husband, feel his forehead. If you find horns, you will know..." "Know what?" asked the woman.

Gilliatt's house had been haunted, but no longer was. That made it only the more suspicious. Everybody knows that when a wizard moves into a haunted dwelling, the devil considers the house sufficiently tenanted, and does the wizard the courtesy of no longer coming round, unless called for, like the doctor.

This house was known as the End of the Road. It was situated at the extremity of a promontory of land, or rather of rock, which formed a small separate anchorage in the creek of Houmet Paradis. At this spot the water is deep. This house stood on its own on the promontory, almost cut off from the island, with just enough ground around it for a small garden. High tides sometimes covered the garden. Between the harbour of Saint Sampson and the creek of Houmet Paradis there is a large hill, surmounted by the block of towers and ivy known as Vale Castle, or the Château de l'Archange; so that, from Saint Sampson, the End of the Road could not be seen.

Nothing is commoner than wizards in Guernsey. They exercise their profession in certain parishes, untrammelled by the nineteenth century. Some of their practices are truly criminal. They set gold to boil. They gather herbs at midnight. They cast the evil eye upon people's cattle. When people consult them, they have bottles containing the "water samples of the sick" brought to them and they are heard to mutter, "the water looks sad." One day in March 1856 one of them found seven devils in a patient's sample. They are feared and fearsome. One of them recently bewitched a baker "along with his oven". Another is so wicked as to seal and deliver, with the greatest of care, envelopes "with nothing inside." Another goes so far as to have in his house three bottles on a shelf labelled "B". These monstrous deeds have been observed. Some wizards are obliging and, for two or three guineas, will take your illness on themselves. Then they roll around on their beds, uttering cries. While they are racked thus, you'll say, "There! There's nothing wrong with me now." Others can cure illnesses of all kinds simply by tying a handkerchief round the body of a sufferer. This is a remedy so simple that it is astonishing that no one had thought of it before. In the last century the Royal Court of Guernsey used to put them on a pile of faggots, and burn them alive. Nowadays it sentences them to eight weeks in prison, four weeks on bread and water, and four weeks in solitary confinement, alternately. Chains love change.

The last witch-burning in Guernsey took place in 1747. The town used one of its open spaces its squares, the Bordage crossroads. Between 1565 and 1700 eleven witches and wizards were burned at the Bordage crossroads. Generally, the guilty confessed. They were helped to confess by means of torture. The Bordage crossroads has also rendered other services to society and religion. It was here that heretics were burned. Under Mary Tudor, a mother and two daughters, among other Huguenots, were burnt here. The mother was called Perrotine Massy. One of the daughters was pregnant. She gave birth at the stake in the midst of the flames. As the chronicle says, "Her belly burst open." From that belly came a living child; the new-born infant rolled out of the inferno. A man named House picked it up; but the baillif, Helier Gosselin, like the good Catholic he was, had the child thrown back into the fire.

Frank Le Maistre

Rigodon d'Chorchel'lie, *1953* (Jèrriais)

> Né v'chin l'alibêle
> Des gens du grand sang,
> Chorchièrs et tchéthauds
> Et tou lus pouver!

> *Erfrain*
> *Dé La Fontaine ès Mittes*
> *Jusqu'à Rocque Bèr*

Et La Hougue Bie,
Touos les vendrédis!
J'faisons nouot' rigodon!

I' y'a l'blianc chorchyi,
Et pis la néthe méthe,
A tout nièr onguent
Dé verjus au dgiâbl'ye –

Sans pâler des cheins
Tchi vouos laîssent bein couorre,
Eune raide achie d'pouèrs,
Véthe, à vouos vengi.
L'ourteu et l'tchi-cô,
Et l'tchian du Bouôlay,
Atout ses chaînes traînantes
A êpouvanter!

Quant ès p'tits faîtchieaux –
N'en ayiz pon d'peux,
Mêfi'ous des r'vénants
Et du bélengi!

Erfrain
Dé La Fontaine ès Mittes
Jusqu'à Rocque Bèr
Et La Hougue Bie,
Touos les vendrédis!
J'faisons nouot' rigodon!

Et lé gros nièr cat
Du Carrefour à Chendres –
La vielle cauminne hantée
D'La Craque au Ouéthou!

La Ruette à la Vioge,
La Valette au Meurtre
Et Lé Betchet ès Cats –
J'hantons tout chenna!

Witchcraft rigadoon, *1953*

Here's the rigmarole
of the witch clan,
wizards and warlocks
and all their power!

Chorus
From La Couochette ès Nonnes
to Les Trais Rocques
and to Le Pulec
we dance our rigadoon
every Friday!

There's the white wizard,
and the leader of the coven,
with black ointment
made from deadly nightshade.

Not to mention those
who plague you
with a great infestation of lice,
indeed, to torment you.

The ourteu and the black Dog of Death,
and the Dog of Bouley
with his dragging chains
to scare you!

As for the fairy folk
don't be afraid of them,
beware ghosts
and the will o' the wisp!

Chorus
From La Fontaine ès Mittes
to the Witches' Rock
and La Hougue Bie,
every Friday
we dance our rigadoon!

And the great black cat
of Le Carrefour ès Chendres –

the old haunted cottage
of La Craque au Ouéthou!

La Ruette à la Vioge,
La Valette au Meurtre
and Le Betchet ès Cats –
we frequent all those!

Le Bailliage, *1888*

Alderney

Who has not heard of the haunted house near the Longis Nunnery? The belated picnickers would often relate how, in passing La Mare du Rô, strange noises, marvellous sighing, clanking of chains, and horrible groans peculiar to ghostly stories were heard, causing *la Belle Suky* to cling all the closer to hardy Med' Jean as he spurred his affrighted steed through the Mannez Plain. For our merry, pleasure-seeking grandsires were superstitious enough to believe in ghosts. Of course, we, their intelligent sons and daughters have out-grown this. Ghosts, and witches, and the evil eye, are things of the past, and fit only for Bourgaze cronies. To our grand-dames, however, these were realities. The headless ghost of the Longis Canteen was the thrilling event of those Whitsuntide festivities. Old Pierre O., was wont to relate, how, when lighting his old fashioned crasset as it stood attached to the wall, he had seen three headless antique-looking men, deliberately enter, and seat themselves by the Canteen fire. And thus was Alderney possessed of its genuine ghost story.

To-day we have become more prosaic. We have hardly faith enough to believe the white goat yarn of Essex Farm. Its author, chief of twelve, states, how, when out rabbit hunting, one moonlit night, near la Roque Pendante, there would sometimes start before him a swift-footed goat all in white. It always kept at the same distance from him. When he ran, it ran; when he walked, it walked; when he stopped, it stopped. Once it came near the closed gate of Essex Park. "*Cette fé, je m'en vais t'avé,*" said he! *car la hêche est frumaï.*" But the good doyen reckoned, this time, without the power of ghosts. The mysterious goat, like all spirits, stopped at no obstacle, but passed through wall, gate, and furzebrake without let or hindrance. Needless to say, that, on such a night, no rabbit would our hunter get. The white goat had constituted itself the warren's defender.

La Gazette de Guernesey

Collas Roussé, Une histouaire du bouan vier temps, *1867*

Un bouan houme et sa femme avaient autefais une p'tite ferme és environs du Vazon: Collas Roussé et sa femme, Nency Guille, etaient des gens trànquilles, qui faisaient d'leux mûs pour elvaï leu famille, mais i' l'taîts r'nomaï pour changié leux forme a volontaï.

Une belle serâïe d'Etaï nou vit un biau lievre dans l'gardin du Probytère qui dansait autouar d'une vaque qu'etait la fiquie.

La vaque se mins a r'gardair le lievre qui toute suite se buti su ses daeux pattes dé deriere faisànt des pernagues coum si voulait invitaï la vaque a dansaï d'auve li. Les gens n'savaient pas qui en craire ou qu'est que q'ela qui voulait dire. Ls' uns disaient que ch'tait Collas Roussé ou sa femme, d'autres pensaient q'nou f'rait mûs de l'tiraï, d'autres enfin disaient que l'lait d'la vaque s'rait gataï et q'la vaque jamais n'vaudrait sa tuache.

Le lecteur, Pierre Simon, qui s'trouvait la par ecanche, s'en fut tout doucement pres du lievre, l'attrapi et s'mis a l'frottaï a r'brousse pé, les uns li criaient d'li teurtre le cô, l's'autres d'li rompre les gambes, et pis nou verait bien vite si ch'en 'tait poui Collas Roussé ou sa femme. Ls uns disaient qu'il avaient vaeus le lievre v'nir dret du Vazon, mais qu'il avait ieux la malice, de prendre un ch'min detournaï, d'autres vaïsins etaient d'avis de prendre le prumier lait d'la vaque et de l'mettre a bouidre su une bouane fouaie d'vrec et q'nou verrait bientôt Collas Roussé et sa vielle v'nir d'mandaï une goutte de lait bouilli; ch'tait là la vraie maniere d'les decouvrir. Pierre Simon fut bien bllamaï de toute la contraie pour avé laissi la bête ecapaï, mais i disait pour raison qu'les lievres etaient sujets a des maux d'tetes coum d'autres personnes et que ch'tait pour chunna qui l'avait frottaï. Il aimait la soupe de lievre coum d'autres, mais que ch'n erait pas etaï bien d'sa part de prendre avantage d'la paure bête.

Le bouan vier Mêsier en palant d'l'affaire disait: "Je n' voudrais pas dire du ma d'personne, sait keriature ou cheva, mais j'ai mes pensaies au sujet de Collas Roussé et sa femme; l'annaie passaie coum j'allais r'muaï nos bêtes de bouan matin qu'est que j'vis sinon daeux biaux lievres a roguer ma raie-grasse. J'fis du bruit, et i s'en furent couarant d'vier le Vazon, et un matin j'm'ecryi 'Tu devrais en aver honte Collas.' "

Eh bien, chu jour là i s'en furent derriere le prinseux, trav'sirent le belle, et, j'n' ments poui, j'cré qui passirent par d'sous l'u. Mais terjous, que j'aie tort ou raison, ni Collas ni sa femme n'ont peux me r'gardair en fache d'pis chu jour-là.

Jamais n'ou ne me fra craire que g'nia pouit bien de chose que nous n'serait expliqué. J'en ai oui d'bien des sortes d'pis m'en jane temps. J'ai souvent oui la raeue du prinseux tournaï a mignet que g'niavait fi d'ame par dehors; j'ai vaeux not' cat aquand i' ventait gros assis l'dos tournaï au faeu, guettànt l'us et la f'netre coum si s'attendait a veer quiq'un entraï, et parfais i poussait de droles de cris, j'vous en reponds, et not t'chen s'muchai derriere ma caire quand j'disais mes perieres, parfais i' braq'tait dans s'en dormir coum s'il 'tait a s'battre d'auve d'autres t'chens; ch'est m'n avis que des cats et des t'chens vée l's affaires d'une autre maniere que nous, et j'cre que ch'est grand piti que tous cheux qui s'dementent de changier de forme n'aient affaire a yeux."

Collas Roussé, a story from the good old days, *1867*

A husband and his wife in bygone days had a small farm around Vazon; Collas Roussé and his wife, Nancy Guille, kept themselves to themselves, and were people that did their best to raise their family, but they were well known for changing shape at will.

One fine summer's evening people saw a handsome hare in the Rectory garden that was dancing around a cow tethered there.

The cow began looking at the hare which stood up straight away on its hind legs and began capering around as if he wanted to invite the cow to dance with him. The people didn't know what to make of it or what it meant. Some said that it was Collas Roussé or his wife, others thought that it would be best to shoot it, finally others said that the cow's milk would be ruined and that the cow would never be worth its slaughter.

The clerk from the parish church, Pierre Simon, who turned up by chance, gently went up close to the hare, caught it and began to rub it up the wrong way, some called out to him to twist its neck, others to break its legs and then they'd soon see if it wasn't Collas Roussé or his wife. Some said that they had seen the hare come straight from Vazon, but that out of malice it had taken a roundabout route, other neighbours were of the view that they should take the beestings from the cow and set it to boil it on a good vraic fire and that you would be sure to see Collas Roussé and his old lady come and ask for a drop of the boiled milk; that this was the true way to expose them. Pierre Simon was blamed by the whole neighbourhood for having let the creature escape, but he explained it away by saying that hares were subject to headaches like other people and that was why he had given it a rub. He loved hare soup like everyone else, but it would not have been good, on his part, to take advantage of the poor creature.

The good old cowherd speaking of the event said: "I would not want to speak ill of anyone, be it beast or horse, but I have my thoughts about Collas Roussé and his wife; last year when I went to move our cattle early one morning, what did I see if it wasn't two hares nibbling away on my rye grass. I made some noise, and they left running towards Vazon, and one morning I called out, 'You should be ashamed of yourself, Collas.'"

So, that day they went behind the cider press building, across the yard and without the word of a lie, I think that they slipped underneath the door. However, whether I'm wrong or right, neither Collas nor his wife have been able to look me in the eye since that day.

You will never make me believe that there aren't many things that cannot be explained. I have heard all kinds of things since my young days. I have often heard the wheel of the cider press turning at midnight when there wasn't a soul outside; I have seen our old cat when it was very windy, sitting his back to the fire, fixed on the door and window as if he expected to see someone come in, and sometimes he would let out strange cries, believe me, and our dog would hide behind my chair when I was saying my prayers, sometimes he would bark in his sleep as if he was fighting with other dogs; I think that cats and dogs see things in a different way from us, and I believe that it is a great shame that all those who go in for shapeshifting don't have to deal with them.

Denys Corbet gives a picture of the relationship a community can have with its neighbourhood practitioner of the magic arts. In the days before accessible medical care or other social services, the witch or wizard was valued for what it was hoped they could accomplish. But they were equally feared for the spells they could cast. These extracts, supposedly recounting the memories of an elderly and distant relative told to the young Corbet, have as their background a civil suit brought against the witch for the death of an allegedly cursed dog.

Denys Corbet

From L'Histouaire du pârain d'l'onclle d'ma grànd'mère, *1886*

... Pour copaïr l'conte au court, i résulti du témouagnage que Lizabo Sansk'vaeux était un' vieille veuve qui d'meurait prumièr'ment au *Grippé*, à St. Martin, et pus tard toute seule dans un vieille cahutte à Pllainmont, justement là oùest qu'est la maison hàntàïe, de qui m'n-ami Victor Hugo – à Guiu seit-i – a fait mention dans ses "Travailleux d'la Maïr."

La vieille Lizabo était un' sorchière coum i n'y-en avait pouit à païne une autre itaïlle en tout Guernesey.

A' n'creyait pouit seul'ment ès sorchiers, mais à s'comptait la prumière désor-chel'resse de l'île, et en effet i s'peut qu'al' avait raison, pour chu que j'm'en s'cie. Al' tait consultàïe par jànnes et viers, et tout l'monde avalait chu qu'à' leus chàntait coum autànt d'évàngile. Al' tait âgie de près d'nonànte àns. A' n'avait pouit un seul k'vaeu restàï sus la tête, ni un seul chicot d'dent dans la goule; et quand a' marchait ch'tait quâsiment les daeux buts en yun, coum un fllais d'grànge; mais pour tout chunna al' tait vive coume un' vieille belette et squître coum une hitre. Quànd les villais, ou, fuche, les jêrriais v'naient la consultàïr – caêr il en v'nait des quat' couains d'l'île, sàns pâlaïr du milli, ossi bien que d'Serk et d'Aur'ny – i dépendait enquièr'ment d'l'humeur qu'al' tait d'dans; caêr s'a' n'tait pouit d'goût a'vou les saccageait d'auv' un ragot de g'nêt, et l'cïen qui s'y frottait un daeuxième caoup était cueuru, j'vou-s-en asseûre. Mais pour tous cheux qu'a' counnîssait n'y-avait pouit d'dàngier. Vou-s-étête-oûs blessaï; ou brûlaï, ou vou-s-étête-oûs rompu ou débouaîti bras ou gàmbe, ou l'co' – l'bouan Guiu sait pour nou – ch'tait à ielle qu'i fallait allaïr; la vieille vou guérissait sus l'chàmp. Ah! dame, ch'tait d'partout qu'hoummes, femmes et éfànts v'naient vê la vieille indine pour êter guéris, et ll'apportaient l's-uns un' caboche, l's-auters des patates ou d's-oeus; ou si, par caoup d'écànche, nou-s-avait tuaï trie ou pouché – respet d'la compengnie – nou ll'apportait un morcé d'grasse-joe. Dans l'cas mìme ou nou-s-airait étaï affligi, ch'est-à-dire difforme, ou aveuglle, ou qu'nou-s-airait ouï dûr, i n'y-avait qu'à consultaï la vieille Lizabo...

A' vou r'gardait dans l'bllànc d's-iers; a' touarnit, a' s'teurtait en dànsotànt tout autouar d'vou; a' soufflaìt sus vot' ma' et marmounnait du patufllìn qu'chair-d'âme ne compernait et la seule chose qu'a' d'màndaìt du malade, ch'tait la fouai, ou la créyànce qu'il allait êter guéri. Vère, et ch'est qu'al' en guérissait à chents; et n'y-a miette à s'en étounnaïr; caêr al' tait si guiâterment laie que rien qu'a' r'gardaïr dans un cannâîe d'lait était assaïz pour que dans un cllin i tournisse. Et coum vou pouvaïz bìen l'creire, les vaïsìns avaient bouan soin de s'gardaïr dans ses bouans livres; caêr ch'tait malheur au cien de quì l'nom était kerouaï-si d'auv' un' kerouâx seit dans la chim'nâïe, seit derrière li; pour un itaï il airait valu mûx qu'i' n'aeusse étaï jamais naï...

Un jour i fut quesquion d'un grànd navire chergi d'or, qu'avait étaï perdu durànt la niet sus les Hanouais, et la vieille fît travâîller tous les pêqueux d's-environs pour quâsi daeux meis à trachier chu fâmaeux tersor; et quànd a' vit qu'tout' la fouill'rie ne v'nait à rien, a' s'ékeryi qu'yun d'aeux avait un' vaque qu'avait du sàng dans les cônes. I' m'faudrait longtemps pour vou contaïr la trache qu'aeut llu, et combien d'vaques écônâïes nou véyait sus les deunes. Malheuraeusement qu'la Sociétaï Protectrice de-s-Animaux n'existait pouit au temps de qui j'pâle. Au reste, i n'pouvait êter quesquion d'cruautaï endviers un' vaque à qui nou-s-a copaï un' cône, à quànd la Cour faisait margainchier l's-oreilles à d'jolies femmes et mìme à d's-éfànts. Pour ak'vaïr, l'tersor n'se trouvi pouit; et coum la vielle éberquedent disait:– "Enterchié qu'ou' la trouvaïz et qu'ou' la tuaïz, et qu'ou' versaïz l'sàng d'ses cônes sus la terre, durànt l'prumier quartier d'la leune, ch'est païne en vain d'trachier pour chu tersor."

Si un ch'va était volaï ou adiraï, et qu'i s'agissait d'attrapier l'voleux et le ch'va, al' ordounnait qu'nou prìnses treis crìns d'la coue d'l'anima; qu'nou les copisses en m'sures égales, et qu'nou-s-en fisse un naeud; et pîs, à soleil couachi, nou les mettait sus un' palette, ou pêlle, et nou mettait l'faeu à châcun des buts, et pîs, suivànt l'côtaï qu'les crìns tournaient, le ch'va était parti. En après, i fallait enfouir au ras d'l'établle chu qui restait, et v'là qui forchait l'voleux à r'venir. Tout chu que l'propriétaïre avait à faire était d'faire guet pour attrapaïr le ch'va à quànd i r'venait.

S'la vieille voulait asquier l'piss d'un vaïsìn, a' brûlait d'la flleur de seux, et mettait d'la chendre dans la goule d'un' raïne, qu'a' lâquait quê dans l'piss. S'a' voulait faire les vaques de quiq-s-un bailler du sàng aurun d'lait, a' les faisait marchier sus des raïnes. A' faisait les vaques sèques r'bailler du lait. Qui d'pus est, all' arrêtait l's-écllairs et l'tounnerre, et faisait poussaïre les récoltes. A' faisait avortaïr les bêtes, et faisait la pus belle fille dev'nir la laie des laies. A' vou-s-empêchait d'creître; mettait les millaeux mênages en camas, et r'apaisait les familles en camas. Pour bien dire, a' faisait tout; et, coum nou peut bien l'creire, ch'tait un' sorchière, chette-là; un' terriblle et r'doutabllc sorchière...

Pour ak'vaïr, après que l's-avocats aeurent baragouinaï l'pour et l'contre pour je n'saï combien longtemps, la vieille avoui aver ensorchelaï l'tchen, et la Cour la condâmni à peyer les six grànds doublles en doummages et intérêts. Et l'bailiff lî dit qu'si jamais a' r'comparaissait d'vànt li, qu'i la mettrai à la cage dans l'milli du marchi, et lî f'rait perchier l'oreille gauche. La paure vieille en aeut tànt d'peux qu'en r'venànt cîz-elle a' s'gav'li sus sen liet d'fouaille, où nou la trouvi quiq' jours après raide morte coum un mànche de g'nêt torti.

From My grandmother's uncle's godfather's tale, *1886*

... so to cut a long story short, it came out in the testimony that Lizzie Baldpate was an old widow who lived first at Le Grippé in St Martin, and then later on by herself in an old hut at Pleinmont, just where the haunted house is, the one my friend Victor Hugo (God rest him) mentioned in his "Toilers of the Sea".

Old Lizzie was a witch the like of whom you could scarcely find anywhere in Guernsey.

She didn't just believe in witchcraft, but was considered the finest remover of spells in the Island, and that might very well be true for all I care. She was consulted by young and old, and everyone swallowed whatever rigmarole she gave them as though it was gospel. She was about ninety years old. She didn't have a single hair left on her head, and not even the stump of tooth left in her mouth, and she walked almost doubled up, like a threshing flail; but for all that she was as lively as an old stoat and as wily as an oyster. When townsfolk, or perhaps Jersey people, came to consult her – for they came from the four corners of the Island, not to mention the middle, as well as from Sark and Alderney – it all depended on what sort of mood she was in; for if she didn't feel like it she'd belabour you with a broom stem, and it was a brave person who dared rub her up the wrong way twice, I can tell you. But for all those she knew personally there wasn't any danger. If you'd injured yourself, or burned yourself, or broken or dislocated an arm or a leg, or your neck – God help us – it would be her you'd have to go to; the old woman would heal you on the spot. Well, men, women and children came from all over to see the old devil to be healed, and some would bring a cabbage, others, potatoes or eggs, or if, by a stroke of chance, they'd slaughtered a sow or piglet – begging your pardon – they'd bring her a piece of cheek. And even in cases of physical difformity or blindness or deafness, all you had to do was consult old Lizzie...

She'd look you straight in the eye; she'd turn round, striking poses while dancing round you; she'd blow on the site of the pain or illness and would murmur some gobbledygook that nobody could understand and the only thing she asked from the patient was faith, or the belief that he'd be healed. Indeed, she healed hundreds that way; and one shouldn't be the least surprised because she was so infernally ugly that just looking into a can of milk was enough to turn it just like that. And as you might well believe, the neighbours took great care to keep in her good books; for woe on whoever had their name marked with a cross either in the chimney or behind them; for anyone like that it would have been better if they'd never been born...

Once there was the question of a big ship laden with gold which had been wrecked in the night on the Hanois, and the old woman had all the fishermen thereabouts looking for that famous treasure for almost two months; and when she saw that all the searching was coming to nothing, she cried out that one of them had a cow with blood in its horns. It would take me a long time to tell you of the search that took place, and how many dehorned cows that could be seen on the dunes. Unfortunately the Society for the Prevention of Cruelty to Animals didn't exist at the time I'm talking about. Besides, there couldn't be any question of cruelty towards a cow that's had a horn cut off, when the Court was having the ears of pretty women and even children hacked off. As it turned out, the treasure wasn't found; and as the old gap-tooth said:– "Until you find it and kill it, and you pour out the blood from its horns on the ground, in the first quarter of the moon, it's a waste of effort to look for that treasure."

If a horse was stolen or went astray, and it was a matter of catching the thief and the horse, she ordered that three hairs from the animal's tail be taken; that they be cut into equal lengths, and that they be tied in a knot; then, at sunset, they were to be put on a peel or shovel and set alight at each end, and then, according to which way the hairs turned, that's the way the horse had gone. After that, what remained had to be buried near the stable, and that forced the thief to return. All the owner had to do was to stand watch to catch the horse when it came back.

If the old woman wanted to dry up a neighbour's well, she'd burn elderflower, and put the ash in a frog's mouth, which she'd drop down the well. If she wanted to make somebody's cows give blood instead of milk, she made them walk on frogs. She'd make dry cows give milk again. And on top of that, she'd stop lightning and thunder, and would make crops grow. She'd cause cattle to miscarry, and would make the most beautiful of girls become the plainest of the plain. She'd stop you growing; would set the best households in an uproar, and would calm uproarious families down again. Putting it plainly, she'd do the lot; and, as you might well believe, she was a witch; a terrible and redoubtable witch...

In conclusion, after the advocates had blethered for and against for I don't know how long, the old woman admitted having cast a spell on the dog, and the Court sentenced her to pay the six grands doubles in damages and interest. And the bailiff told her that if she ever came up before him again, he'd put her in the cage in the middle of the marketplace, and would have her left ear pierced. The poor old woman got such a fright that when she got back home she collapsed on her greenbed, where they found her a few days later, dead as a twisted broom handle.

Politics and Parishes

Centuries of self-government and the origins of the administrations in Norman law have left their mark on the titles and offices held by Islanders. Many of the writers, as people active in their communities, also held political office of one sort or another. Denys Corbet, and A. A. Le Gros were among those who served as Constable; Robert Pipon Marett was elected Constable of Saint Helier, and later became Bailiff of Jersey; Philippe Langlois was among those elected Jurat. Such grassroots democracy and the controversies and pretensions of officeholders have provided fruitful source material. It is hardly surprising that Deputies, Vingteniers, Douzeniers, Centeniers and other notables should appear in many texts – often the butt of satire.

The directness of democracy and the variety of different systems across the Islands can seem odd to outsiders. The attachment to the parish is strong: in Jersey the parishes are administered by an elected Constable, or Connétable, with other elected officials such as Procureurs du Bien Public, Centeniers, Vingteniers and Constable's Officers fulfilling various functions, including responsibilities in the vingtaines, subdivisions of the parishes; in Guernsey the parishes are administered by elected councils called Douzaines with two Constables elected in each parish. In Jersey, the Constables also represent their Parish in the legislature; in Guernsey, the Constables lost their membership of the legislature in 1844.

The legislatures of Jersey, Guernsey and Alderney are called the States, or in French, Les États – meaning the estates. Originally the three estates of the Crown, the Church and the people were summoned together. The Jurats, the elected judges, were removed from their historic legislative rôle in post-Occupation constitutional reforms, as were the clergy, leaving democratically elected political representatives comprising the legislatures of Jersey and Guernsey under the presiding leadership of Crown-appointed officials (since 1948 the States of Alderney has an elected President). Sark's historic feudal legislature, the Chief Pleas, has in recent years been reformed with elected Conseillers making up the legislators.

The traditional consensus-based system of committee government, as mentioned in Florence Hacquoil's 'Nout' Libèrté', was replaced in Jersey in the early twenty-first century by a system of ministerial government with a Chief Minister. In Guernsey a consensus system remains, although Presidents of departments became Ministers and the office of Chief Minister was created in 2004. Government remains a subject for comment and satire.

Florence Mary Hacquoil ('F.M.H.')

Nout' Libèrté, *1967*

Nout' pépée voudrait saver
Ouècque est don nout' libèrté?
Quand un houmme au jour d'agnièt
Dé bâti n'a pon lé drouèt.

Ch'avait 'té san întention,
Dé bâti eune belle maison,
Ouècque i' pouorrait s'èrtither
Et un gardin tchultiver.

I' n'avait pon rêalisé,
Qu'ch'est ès Comités dé décider,
S'il étha la permission
De faithe autchune construction.

D'Biautés Naturelles, le Conmité
Vint la pliaiche examiner.
I' trouvites qu'la maison gât'tai,
D'la Vingtaine, toute la biauté.

Ch'n'est pon là l'seul conmité
Tch'a lé drouèt dé vos r'fuser;
Y'a accouo, les Travaux Publics –
Sans pâler d'la Santé Publique.

Même s'i' vos permettent dé bâti,
La maison nou' n'peut couvri
En tuiles, s'ils ont décidé
Qu'les ardouaises f'thaient sa biauté.

Nos anchêtres au temps passé,
Dans lus caves au bord d'la mé,

N'avaient pon de Conmités
Dé la sorte à les c'mander.

S'ou voulez chonna changi,
Et les contrôles aboli;
Chouaissis coum' Député
Un houmme qu'aime nout' libèrté.

Our Freedom, *1967*

Our dad would like to know
where has our freedom gone?
When a man nowadays
doesn't have the right to build.

It had been his intention
to build a lovely house,
where he could retire to
and tend a garden.

He hadn't realised
that it's for Committees to decide
if he could have permission
to undertake any construction.

The Committee of Natural Beauties
came to inspect the site.
They found that the house would spoil
the beauty of the whole Vingtaine.

That's not the only committee
that has the right to turn you down;
there's also Public Works,
not to mention Public Health.

Even if you are given permission to build,
you can't roof the house
with tiles if they've decided
that slates would be more attractive.

Our ancestors time past
in the seaside caves

didn't have any Committees
of that sort to tell them what to do.

If you want to change that,
and get rid of controls;
choose as your Deputy
a man who loves our freedom.

Philippe Asplet ('L'Anmin FLIPPE')

Election de La Trin'tait, *c.1864* (Jèrriais)

Enfin, garçons, chès pour Mardi,
Soignis de n'pas vos apierchi,
Et trouvous en temps à l'Ugnion,
Car chest bain seux qu'il y f'sa bon.
Je fésons cuize une tapais d'qué,
Pour cheux qui voudront lus stoffé;
Yéza du baize et du mangi
Pour goudalé et pour mâqui:
Y yen aiza pour tous les goûts,
Yeza du su, yeza du doux
Pour les uns yeza du paîvret,
Et pour les autres du salet;
Enfin tout y sça comme y faut.
Il est vrai quî gnièza rain d'caud,
Tout sça frait. Mais y sça bain cui,
Chez John de Caen qui va l'couqui;
J'nos allons avé les jambons,
Respé d'vous, de deux p'tits couochons
Qu'étaient justement bouans à prendre.
Je sis seux que ché sça d'qué tendre,
Et pis un tas de beu rôti;
Y yen aiza et tout d'bouilli,
Et pis du cidre et du pain frais,
Des pommes de terre et des pannais;
Et si quiqu'un est haîniqueux,
Yéza du podin sus l'drécheux,
Y yen aiza pour tout le monde.
Ou pouais v'nin d'un mille à la ronde,
Et mangi tous à tigue de cor
Comme sous étiez à la "Pomme d'Or."

Enfin, pour en bâfré vot' lot,
Votais pour le Chant'gni Cabot,
Et nommais le vot' député.

J'vos en prie venais du Huzé
Du Ban'lais, de la Taûpin'nie,
Du Clos Duzé, d'la Carros'sie,
D'la Huzette, d'la Mauve, et des Hayes,
Du Haut-de-l'Orme, et de Cambrais,
Du Tas-de-Jan, du Vert-Pignon,
De la Fosse et du Houguillon,
Du Pont, de la Hocquardézie,
D'la Ville-ès-Normans, des Côtis,
Du Moulin d'Haut, du Moulin d'Bas,
Du Carrefour, du Becquet-ès-Cats,
De l'Epine, et d'la Maze d'Angot,
D'la Quesnêe et d'Lamont Billot,
De Diélament et des Câtiaux,
Des Bouillons, des Hèches, et des Vaux,
D'la Parfonde-rue, d'la Pièche-Maugi,
Du Câté, du Pot-du-Roqui,
Et de l'Egypte et des Jannièzes,
Des Forges, et du Haut-des-Queizezes,
Des Hautes-Crouais, du Clos-Bisson.
De Sous-les-Bouais, d'la Grande-Maison,
D'la Maison d'Haut, du Haut-Pavet,
Dz'Augrès, du Gardin-d'Olivet,
D'la Houle-ès-Chians et du Creux-Bouonne;
J'entends si yavait quiqu' personne
Qui sçait là d'dans, déhalais-lé,
Et le faites v'nin déjeuné.

An election in Trinity, c.1864

At last, lads, it's on for Tuesday,
take care not to be late,
and be on time at the Union inn,
for it's certain there'll be a good time there.
We'll have a whole load of food cooked up
for those who want to stuff themselves;
there'll be drink and food
to guzzle and chew:
there'll be enough for all tastes,

there'll be savoury, there'll be sweet,
peppery for some
and salty for others;
in a word, everything will be as it should.
It's true that there won't be anything hot,
it'll all be cold. But it'll be well cooked,
it's John de Caen who'll be doing the cooking;
we'll have hams
from two little pigs (begging your pardon)
of just the right age.
I'm sure that it'll be nice and tender,
and then a lot of roast beef;
and there'll be porridge as well,
and cider and fresh bread,
potatoes and parsnips,
and if anyone's picky,
there'll be pudding on the dresser,
there'll be something for everyone.
You can come from a mile around,
and all eat with all your might
as though you were at the "Pomme d'Or" hotel.
Finally, so you can gobble your share,
vote for Centenier Cabot
and put him in as your Deputy.

I beg you to come from Le Hurel,
from Le Bannelais, from La Taupinerie,
from Le Clos Durel, from La Carrosserie,
from La Hurette, from La Mauve, and from Les Hayes,
from Le Haut de l'Orme, and from Cambrais,
from Le Tas de Geon, from Le Vert Pignon,
from La Fosse and from Le Houguillon,
from Le Pont, from La Hocquarderie,
from La Ville ès Normans, from Les Côtils,
from Le Moulin de Haut, from Le Moulin de Bas,
from Le Carrefour, from Le Bétchet ès Cats,
from L'Épine, and from La Mare d'Angot,
from La Quesnée and from L'Amont Billot,
from Diélament and from Les Câtieaux,
from Les Bouillons, from Les Hèches, and from Les Vaux,
from La Profonde Rue. from La Pièce Mauger,
from Le Câtel, from Le Pot du Rocher,
from Egypt and from Les Geonnières,

from Les Forges and from Le Haut des Carrières,
from Les Hautes Croix, from Le Clos Bisson,
from Sous les Bois, from La Grande Maison,
from La Maison de Haut, from Le Haut Pavé,
from Les Augrès, from Le Jardin d'Olivet,
from La Houle ès Chiens and from Le Creux Bouonne;
I mean, that if there was anyone
in these places, drag them out
and get them to come and eat.

La Gazette de l'Île de Jersey

Eune lettre dé 1788 (Jèrriais)

Mousieu l'Éditeu,

Je sis un habitant de la paraise de S. Ouen. Un ergot de Cour est venu chute semaine me demander ma voix pour pliachir M. De la Perrelle connétable. Je lis dis que toues étais pour M. Ricard; qu'il étoit un brave homme; qu'il avoit diversement ben agi; qu'il n'avoit pas levait d'argent sur la paraise; qu'au contraire il avoit opposet cheux qui vouloient en lever; qu'il avoit souetenu nos droits contre les seigneurs de S. Ouen, & que d'ailleurs je ne donnez pon ma voix a un touanne casaque, car j'étois trop vié pour touanner la menne. Je lis dis de plus que je viez ben qui cherchoit à divisé noute paraise come chelle de S. Marie, afin d'avé un moyen de nous plumer. Je lis fis un calcul de che que chez bouane gens avois depenset en bille d'ajontion & procès dans le couzant de ch'année, qui samonte à pus de 60 louis dor, & que duzant tout le temps que M. Ricard avé était connétable, je n'avion eu presque aucun procès; que j'aimion mus nous en remettre à li que d'aller sieze les ergots come li en Cour perdre noute temps & bailli nous sous que javions tant de penne à gagni. Je vis ben, par la mine de noutre homme, que j'avois justement devinet ses raisons pour qui y hampchionoit dans noute paraise à demandé des voix, car y sen fut comme un chian à qui jezais rompu une gambe.

A letter from 1788

Dear Mr Editor,

I am an inhabitant of the parish of Saint Ouen. A court official came this week to ask for my vote to elect Mr De La Perrelle as constable. I told him that everyone was for Mr. Ricard; that he was a fine man; that he had acted extremely well; that he had not raised parish rates; that on the contrary he had opposed those who wanted to raise them; that he had stood up for our rights against the seigneurs of Saint Ouen, and that besides I would not give my vote to a turncoat, because I was too old to turn my own coat. I told him furthermore that I could see very well that he was trying to split our parish like the parish of Saint Mary, so as to be able to fleece us. I did a sum for him of what that lot had spent on bills of transfer and court cases in the course of this year, which adds up to more than 60 louis d'or, and that during the whole time that Mr. Ricard had been constable, we have had hardly any court cases; that we would much rather place our confidence in him again than go off to court after legal officials like him and waste our time and hand over our money that we have had so much trouble earning. I could see very well, by the expression on our man's face, that I had rightly guessed the reasons why he came limping into our parish asking for votes, for off he went like a dog whose leg I had broken.

Denys Corbet ('Bad'lagoule')

Les Cliiques, *1901* (Guernesiais)

Ichîn d'vànt, Gatdérabotin!
Quànd nou rencontrait quiq accouain,
Cîz-sei, par l'marchi, l'long du ch'min,
Nou c'menchait par s'ent'châquer l'poin.
Et pîs donc ll'avait des "hôdi,"
Des compllîments jamais itaïs:
Des "ch'est-vou!" des "d'charme-tainqui,"
Des "c'm'est donc qu'vont tout'les sàntaïs?"

A persent, ch'n'est pus d'mème en tout;
Fichu tout l'bouan vier amîti;
Qu'nou s'en âïlle i' n'y-a compte éyou,
Partout nou-s-est d'charme éplluqui.
L'accouain vou r'gardera d'travers:
"Et pîs, tei," s'ti, "d'quaï cllique es-tu?"
En vou-s-épiànt frànc dans bllanc d's-iers,
"D'la nôtre, ou d'l'autre au perchain u?"

"Es-tu d'la cllique à not "papier,"
Ou d'la cienne au maufait d'Aur'gnais?"
Est-che au "patouais" qu'tu veur aïguer,
Ou bien à ch't-infernal d'Angllais?
Es-tu tout pour l'éducation,
Pour l'avànch'ment et l'vrai progrès?
Ou s'rait-ce enquièr'ment la r'ligion
Qui f'rait d'tes efforts tous les frais?

"Mei, j'sis d'la cllique à taïl et taï,
S'tu-en ès, v'là qu'est bien, j'f'ron baté;
Mais à quiq auter s'tu t-ès vouaï,
J'nairai pus rien à faire à tei.
Tu f'ras d'ten bord, et j'f'rai du mien,
Ronbllie étou qu'tu m'as counneû;
Men pus grànd d'sir est, qu'pour ten bien,
Tu cache au pus vite au malheû."

Je n'dirai pouit qu'en autànt d'mots
Nos accouains sufflent tout chunna;
Mais ch'est les faits pus qu'les propos
Qu'ont ieû d'tous temps l'pus grànd flleflla.
Et v'là chu qu'i' disent, j'creis-mei,
Tous les jours que l'bouan Guiu fait v'ni;
Où d'pus en pus partout nou vei
L'intérêt torchier l'amîti.

Factions, *1901*

It used to be, I swear to God!
that when you met some acquaintance,
at home, by the market, in the road,
you'd start off by shaking hands.
Then there'd be the "how are you"s
and suchlike pleasantries,
like "there you are!" and "fine, thankee"
and "so how are the family keeping?"

Nowadays, it's not like that at all;
the good old friendliness is out the window;
it doesn't matter where you might go,
everywhere you're given a right going-over:
"So, you," he says, "what's your faction?"
And looking you straight in the whites of the eyes,
"Ours, or that lot down there?"

"Are you in our newspaper's faction,
or that wretched Alderneyman's one?
Are you in favour of helping our lingo,
or else that damnable English?
Are you all for education,
for advancement and real progress?

Or is it strictly for religion
that all your best efforts are intended?"

"Me, I'm in so-and-so's faction,
And if you are, that's good, we'll get along nicely;
but if you're siding with someone else,
I won't have any more to do with you.
You go about your business, and I'll go about mine,
forget that you've even known me either;
what I really want is, for your own good,
for you to go to the devil as quickly as possible."

I'm not saying that our acquaintances
rattle all that out in so many words;
but it's deeds rather than words
that have always been most convincing.
And that's what they say, and what I think,
every day that God sends;
when everywhere more and more you see
interest betraying friendship.

George William de Carteret ('G. W de C.')

Les Députâtions, *1913* (Jèrriais)

Jêrri, not'e pays, touos les treis z-ans.
En Dézembre,
Chouaîsis touos ses représentants,
Aux Etats.
N'v'là qu'est v'nu l'grand moment,
Cèrtainement,
Des députâtions, touos l's'embarras,
Qui plieuve ou qui vente,
Au Parish Hall nou s'rend,
Formé députâtion,
Pour passé l'compyîment
Au vièr représentant.
Enfin, nou s'met en route,
Et nou peut les vaie patte-à-coue:

Le Connaîtablle et le Recteur,
Les Surveillants, les Collecteurs,
Les Principaux, les p'tits ouasseurs,

Les Chentenièrs, les Vingtenièrs,
L'enregistraeux, les Apprécieurs,
Les Inspecteurs, les Officièrs,
Les Procureurs du Bein Public!
Ah! que ch'est bé et magnifique!

Siez-li, pllien d'ordji, l'Député,
Enervè,
Prépathe san bieau speech, destinè,
Comme d'amor,
A dithe qui pensait d's'ertithé,
Dans l'privé,
Tandi qui veur la poste occouo!
Madame pendant chu temps,
Ermèrque à la sèrvante:
As-tu bein êpoussetè
Toute la malpropretè:
Souogne que tout sait rangi,
I' faout vite en fini,
D'pit que bétôt i' s'en vont v'nir.

Le Connaîtablle et le Recteur,
Les Surveillants, les Collecteurs,
Les Principaux, les p'tits ouasseurs,
Les Chentenièrs, les Vingtenièrs,
L'enregistraeux, les Apprécieurs,
Les Inspecteurs, les Officièrs,
Les Procureurs du Bein Public!
Ah! que ch'est bé et magnifique!

Les v'là arrivés près le d'vant,
D'la maison,
Achteu i' faout pathaître content,
Ch'est le moment,
Même quand nou souhaitte qui dise Non
En raîponse.
I' faout l'i faithe chu compyîment,
Nou z-entre dans l'parlaeux,
Nou s'assièd comme nou peut.
L'sien qu'est le porte-vouaix
S'avanche dans l'mitan du bel appartément,
Et tch'est qu'est bein content
De vaie parmi les cheins présents:

Le Connaîtablle et le Recteur,
Les Surveillants, les Collecteurs,
Les Principaux, les p'tits ouasseurs,
Les Chentenièrs, les Vingtenièrs,
L'enregistraeux, les Apprécieurs,
Les Inspecteurs, les Officièrs,
Les Procureurs du Bein Public!
Ah! que ch'est bé et magnifique!

Achteu, si d'visé ès Etats,
I n'fit pas,
Sans doute du bouan bor' i' vota,
Sans tracas.
Es Coumitis i' prins part
Au travâs,
Qui y-est fait sans embarrâs.
Ne v'là chein qu'nou raconte,
Tréjous l'même p'tit conte,
Qui fait hardi d'pliaisi.
Pis de whiskey verre rempyi,
Touos les verres bein nettis,
Pour bèthe à la santè
Du Député, des gros bonnets,

Le Connaîtablle et le Recteur,
Les Surveillants, les Collecteurs,
Les Principaux, les p'tits ouasseurs,
Les Chentenièrs, les Vingtenièrs,
L'enregistraeux, les Apprécieurs,
Les Inspecteurs, les Officièrs,
Les Procureurs du Bein Public!
Ah! que ch'est bé et magnifique!

Ne v'là le moment du départ,
Dêjà tard,
Allons, garçons, vite daeux p'tits d'gouts,
Unne cigâre,
Devant de vos remèttre en route.
Prennez garde
D'avé fraid et de l'influenza.
Oprès la châquethie d'main
Avec touos ses vièrs z-anmins,
Freumme l'hûs pour s'erpôsé,

Rentre vite dans sa chambre,
Et quand il est couochi,
Qui ronflye, i' faout l'entendre,
Ch'est qu'i' vait alentou d'san lièt:

Le Connaîtablle et le Recteur,
Les Surveillants, les Collecteurs,
Les Principaux, les p'tits ouasseurs,
Les Chentenièrs, les Vingtenièrs,
L'enregistraeux, les Apprécieurs,
Les Inspecteurs, les Officièrs,
Les Procureurs du Bein Public!
Ah! que ch'est bé et magnifique!

Deputations, *1913*

Jersey, our country, every three years
in December,
chooses all its representatives
for the States.
So the big moment has come
for sure,
deputations, all the activity,
come rain or wind,
they go to the Parish Hall
to form a deputation,
to present their compliments
to the old representative.
At last, they set out,
and you can see them in single file:

The Constable and the Rector,
Churchwardens, Sidesmen,
Principals, little yappers,
Centeniers, Vingteniers,
the Registrar, Assessors,
Roads Inspectors, Constable's Officers,
the Procureurs du Bien Public!
Ah, how fine and splendid it all is!

At home, the Deputy is pleased with himself
but nervous,
and prepares his fine speech, intended

as usual
to tell how he had been thinking of stepping down
and returning to private life,
but all the time he still wants the post!
The Deputy's wife in the meantime
speaks to the maid:
Have you dusted properly
all the dirt:
check that everything is tidied up,
you must finish quickly
because they'll soon be here.

The Constable and the Rector,
Churchwardens, Sidesmen,
Principals, little yappers,
Centeniers, Vingteniers,
the Registrar, Assessors,
Roads Inspectors, Constable's Officers,
the Procureurs du Bien Public!
Ah, how fine and splendid it all is!

Here they come approaching the front
of the house,
now they must appear happy,
it's the time for it,
even if they're wishing that he'd say No
in reply.
They have to pay him this courtesy.
They go into the drawing room,
they sit down as best they can.
The one who is spokesman
steps forward into the middle of the fine room,
and he's very pleased
to see among those present:

The Constable and the Rector,
Churchwardens, Sidesmen,
Principals, little yappers,
Centeniers, Vingteniers,
the Registrar, Assessors,
Roads Inspectors, Constable's Officers,
the Procureurs du Bien Public!
Ah, how fine and splendid it all is!

Now, he could have spoken in the States,
but he didn't.
But he'll vote the right way, no doubt,
without any fuss.
He took part in
Committee work,
and made no trouble at all.
That's what they speak about,
always the same little story,
which makes people very happy.
Then glasses are filled with whiskey,
all the glasses are emptied
to drink the health
of the Deputy, the top brass,

The Constable and the Rector,
Churchwardens, Sidesmen,
Principals, little yappers,
Centeniers, Vingteniers,
the Registrar, Assessors,
Roads Inspectors, Constable's Officers,
the Procureurs du Bien Public!
Ah, how fine and splendid it all is!

Now it's time to leave,
it's already late,
Come on, lads, another quick drink,
a cigar,
before setting off.
We don't want you
catching cold or flu.
After shaking hands
with all his old friends.
he closes the door to get some rest,
goes back quickly to his bedroom,
and when he's asleep,
how he snores, you should hear him!
What he's dreaming of is, all around his bed:

The Constable and the Rector,
Churchwardens, Sidesmen,
Principals, little yappers,
Centeniers, Vingteniers,

the Registrar, Assessors,
Roads Inspectors, Constable's Officers,
the Procureurs du Bien Public!
Ah, how fine and splendid it all is!

Nico Robilliard

La visite d'Nico Robilliard de Torteva, â l'Assembllaïe d's Étâts, *1925* (Guernesiais)

J'vous dirai en c'menchânt, que j'sies valet à Moussieu Lenfestaï, qu'a la pus belle ferme dans la Pâresse, et est situaïe au Val Tortu, et j'm'avisi un jour (ch'tait un mardi) de lie d'mândaï pour le jour en suivânt pour allaï à l'Assembllàie d's Étâts.

Y'avait déjâ d's âns qu'j'y' pensais, et l'aute jour je m'die, "Nico, tu vieillis, n'targe poui, caer quand tu s'râs mort, i's rà trop tard de lie d'màndaï, et t'errâs perdu ta chânce." Men maître me r'pouni qu'oui, mais de n' poui trop targier au ser caer le touarré est mauvais comme le guiable et i'n'y a qu'mé qui peut en appeurchier; j'le r'mercyi, et donc le mêceurdi matin, quand j'eux soigni ès bêtes, j'me lavi et m'démêli comme pour le Dêmanche, et mie mes bouânes hardes, et me vlô tout prêt pour la bosse qui va pour la Ville.

En arrivânt, j'alli tout drette pour la Cour, j'monti les degreïs, et m'mie dans un biaux bânc qu'était quâsi comme les bâncs d'l'Egllise; après un p'tite achie, i s'trouvi un' manière de policeman qui m'déhalli d'ma pllieche, et m'fit allaï pu en derière ou'est qu'les bâncs étaient trop étrêts pour m'n assiette; j'eux à m'y contentiaï. Un p'tit d'vànt dix haeures et d'mie les Mêssieûs c'menchirent à v'nir: les premiers étaient les r'persentânts des douzaines et les deputaïs, et pis l'Procureux et l'Contrôle, le Greffier, l'Peurvôt et l'Sergeànt du Roué, et draïnement les Recteurs et les Magistrâts; tout d'un caoup, le mânière de policeman me fit tersautaï en criânt tout chu qui pouvait haut "Le Président," et d'vant que j'peûsse prendre m'n' halaïne, l'autre manière de policeman auve une vouaix d'tounère nous c'mandi "Stand up, please!" Nous vlo donc tous d'but.

A quand le Baillif fut à sa pllieche, i d'mândi au Peurvôt (qu'était dans la galrie atou une magnifique chaïne en or autouor d'sen co) si Son Excellence assisterait à la séance, et i' r'pouni, "Pas aujourd'hui, Monsieur le President!"

Le Greffier fit la périere (mais gâche à penne va t'i rède; nous vé bien par sa manière qu'i la fait tous les jours sies li pour s'gardaï au couorânt).

Après chennâ, i' crie tous les noms pour vée s'y' en à qui mânquent, et pis l'coumerce c'menche.

La principale question était su l'changement proposaï au Hâvre, et j'vous assaeure qu'nouz y' avait du pllaisi à les ouî. Les tous pu grands mêssieûs qui s'craient savé tout, v'naient enragi quand aucuen autre membre avait l'couârâge et l'affront de n'être poui d'leux avis; j'pensais même qui s'en allaient s'battre, comme j'ai ouï dire qui font à Paris, et même à Londres, mais j'pense qu'ils ont peux du

President et se r'quiâne un p'tit.

Quând i' c'menche y'avé trop d'brit. Le Sergent, qu'est assis à un' tâblle atou sa ganne, tappe comme un maître d'école su' sen dexe pour les gardaï en ordre. Après un' achie y'en à qui sortent trânquillement, p't-être pour avé un p'tit d'rafraïchisse-ment ou d'fortificât.

Y'en a quiques-uns qui sont d'bouâns orateurs mais la pupart ne sont qu' moyens, y'en â qui pâlent trop vite, d'autres trop bas, et quiques-un qui paraissent avé la goule, pllaïne de bouaillie; mais i'm'est avis qu'les pus sâges gârdent la bouche frumaïe. D'viers un' haeure, nous vé que les membres c'menchent avé l'cueur failli, et veulent trachier leux dênaï, caer i' sont terjous à r'gardaï à l'ôlorge. Après un' achie l'Président dit à l'assemblaïe: "Allou z'en jusqu'à daeux heures et d'mie." L'zeuns s'en vont pour la maison et d'autres ès hôtels et restaurants, et p't'être ès "couke shoppes," mais pour mé, j'alli au débarcadère pour un' couppâïe d'caffi et des dorrâïes.

A daeux haeures et d'mie nou r'vélô tous en plleiche, sinon daeux ou treis des pus faillis qui sont partis pour la maison. Après un' p'tite achie y' en avait qui s'en-dormirent, et pis quând vint le temps pour votaï, i'n' savaient poui qui dire, "pour ou contre." Y' en a étou qui n'ô poui grand'ment et qui disent "pour" quând ils éraient dit "contre" s'ils avaient peux ouir.

A treis haeures et d'mie, j'me trouvi lâssaï, et j'voulais attrappaï ma bosse, qui partait à quatre haeures.

A m'n arrivaïe à la maison, je m'changi vite pour allaï soigner ès bêtes, caer si j'avais appeurchi du touarré comme j'étais grâïe en r'venânt d'la ville, i' m'errait tuaï pour bien saeur.

Au ser, quând men travâs fut fini, et d'vànt que d'm'n'allaï à men galtâs, j'entri la grand' cuisaïne, pour bien remerciaï men maître, Messe Lenfêtaï, et lie dire qu' j'avais pâssaï le pus grând jour d'ma vie.

Quànd vint le samedi au ser, men maître me peyi ma semaïne de quinze chelins, sans aucuen rabàt, et daeux chelins six d'côte pour peyer men dênaï et ma bosse.

Votre humblle serviteur,
Nico Robilliard

Nick Robilliard from Torteval's trip to a States' sitting, *1925*

To begin I would say that I'm farmhand for Mr. Lenfestey, who has the finest farm in the parish, and is situated in the Val Tortu, and one day (it was a Tuesday) I decided to ask him for the following day off to go to a States' sitting.

I had thought about going some years ago, and the other day I said to myself, "Nico, you are growing older, don't delay, as when you are dead, it will be too late to ask him, and you will have missed your chance." My boss said yes, but that I shouldn't be too late back in the evening as the bull is as bad as the devil and I'm the only one who can go near him; I thanked him, and then Wednesday morning, when I had seen to the animals, I washed and combed my hair as if it were Sunday, and put on my good clothes, and there I was all ready for the bus that goes to town.

Having arrived, I went straight to the Court building, I climbed the steps, and sat down in a fine bench that was almost like the pews in church; after a short while, a kind of policeman turned up who made me get up out of my place and go more towards the back where the benches were too narrow for me to sit down; I had to be settle for that. A little before half past ten the gentlemen began arriving; the first to arrive were the douzaine representatives and the deputies, and then the Procureur and the Comptroller, the Greffier, the Sheriff and HM Sergeant, and lastly the Rectors and Jurats; suddenly, that policeman-type fellow made me jump up by calling out at the top of his voice, "The President", and before I could get my breathe back, the other 'kind of policeman' with a thundering voice ordered us to "Stand up, please!" So there we are, all standing.

When the Bailiff was in his place, he asked the Sheriff (who was in the gallery with a magnificent gold chain around his neck) if His Excellency would be present for this sitting, and he replied, "Not today, Mr. President!"

The Greffier said the prayer (but my goodness doesn't he say it quickly; you can tell by his manner that he says it everyday at home to keep up his fluency).

After that, he called out all of the names to see if there were some missing, and then business begins.

The main question concerned changes at the harbour, and I can assure you that it was fun to hear them. The most important gentlemen who believe that they know best, became enraged when any other member had the courage and nerve to disagree with their view; I even thought that they were going to fight, like I have heard said that they do in Paris, and even in London, but I think that they are afraid of the President and settle back down a little.

When it becomes too noisy, the Sergeant, who is sitting at a table in his gown, taps like a school master on his desk to keep them in order. After a while some leave quietly, perhaps for a refreshment or pick-me-up.

There are some that are good orators, but the majority are average, there are those who speak for too quickly, others too quietly, and some that seem to have mouths full of broth; but in my view the wisest keep their mouths closed. Towards one o'clock it is clear to see that the members are beginning to lose heart, and want to go for their lunch as they're always looking at the clock. After a while the President says to the Assembly, "Off you go until half past two." Some of them go home and others to hotels and restaurants, and perhaps to "cook shops", but as for me I went to the landing stage for a cup of coffee and some sandwiches.

At half past two we all are once again all in our places, except for two or three of the most lacking in stamina who have gone home. After a little while some had fallen asleep, and when came the time to vote, they didn't know whether to say, "aye or no". There are also some who are a bit hard of hearing and who say "aye" when they would have said "no" if they had been able to hear.

At half past three, I started feeling tired, and wanted to catch my bus, which left at four o'clock.

Arriving home, I changed quickly in order to tend to the animals, as if I had gone up to the bull dressed as I was coming back from town he would have surely killed me.

In the evening when my work was done, and before going to my garret, I went in to the main kitchen, to thank my boss, Mr. Lenfestey, and to tell him that I had had the grandest day of my life.

When Saturday evening arrived, my boss paid me my fifteen shillings for my week, without any deductions, and two and six besides to pay for my lunch and bus fare.

Your humble servant,
Nick Robilliard

The Alderney language became extinct in the twentieth century, but was already under considerable pressure from English in the nineteenth century. The influx of workers involved in the construction of fortifications and the abortive naval harbour project threatened to overwhelm the indigenous population. The size of the British military garrison in proportion to the civilian population also had a great influence on language shift. Here are two rare letters from Alderney published in *La Gazette de Guernesey* in 1867, which are among the few written records of informal vernacular writing in Auregnais.

Two Letters from La Gazette to Guernesey (Auregnais), *1867*

A Moussieu le R'dacteur de la Gazette

Moussieu, – Il i'a lent-ems que les aurenais gronde de payaï une taxe pour un policeman, ils disent qu'in en ès' pas besoin, mais v'la tout! toutes les fais que les cunnétaibles vont tranchaï chette taxe; ils sont grounu casiment à toutes les maisons.

Ils n'ian a qu'in veulle pas payaï, mais quand ils o' qu'ils sent vont aitre amnaï d'vant la Cour, ils quaire vite sie le cunnétaible portaï l'eux argent, pars'qu'ils ont paït d'aite servi coum' le gros Bot qui r'fusi de payaï, ait qui fût obligi de payaï une gross' amende, ou' ben aite min à prïson pour j'ne-saï-pas comben d'tems.

Chu que j'voudraï savaï moussieu, c'hest chunchin, on-ti tort de gronde ou on-ti raison: j'allon vaï. Prumièrement moussieu, quand les policemen fûde etabei, il i'a environ die ans, il i'avait dans l'isle une population d'environ chin-milles abitants, il i'avait des irlandais et des courniches qui fésais du camas tous les sers dans la ville, n'ou n'tait pas à seurtaï d'sa vie; mais quand les travaux sont v'nu à moli, tous ches étrangers s'en s'ont allaï d'iou qu'ils tais v'nu; ait à present moussieu, j'pense pas qu'il i'a pu de quinse-chents personnes dans l'isle. Il n'ès pas d'on difficile à comprende que j'navon pas besoin de policeman à nou' protégaï, ils f'raient b'en meus de li allai la côte de d'su l'dôt, et envaï à gagnaï sa vie hunnêtement.

Si l'ia des manques dans chunchin, j'espaire moussieu que vou pas'raï par dessu' coum chés la prumiaire fais que je d'mente d'écrire not' patouais, en espérant que vou l'trouveraï assaï important pour qu'il mérite un p'tit coin dans vot biau papier.

Je d'meure v'ot humble serviteur,

J.H.

Dear Mr Editor

Sir, – The people of Alderney have been moaning for a long time about paying a tax for a policeman. They say there's no need for him, but so much for that! Every time the Constables go to collect this tax, they are moaned at at almost every house.

There are those who don't want to pay, but when they hear that they'll be brought before the Court, they run quickly to the Constables carrying their money, because they're afraid of being treated like big Bott who refused to pay and who was forced to pay a large fine, or else be put in prison for I don't know how long. What I'd like to know, sir, is this: are they wrong to moan or are they right: we'll see. Firstly sir, when the policemen were set up about ten years ago, there was a population of about five thousand inhabitants. There were Irishmen and Cornishmen kicking up a racket every evening in town – you were taking your life in your hands; but when the pace of construction slowed, all those foreigners went back where they'd come from; and now, sir, I don't think there are above fifteen hundred people in the island. It's therefore not hard to understand that we don't need policemen to protect us. They'd do much better to turn their back on him and go and earn an honest living.

If there are faults in this, I hope, sir, that you will overlook them as this is the first time that I've tried to write our local language, in the hope that you will find it important enough to merit a small spot in your fine paper.

I remain your humble servant,

J.H.

Moussieu, – Daprie q'vou navaï fait l'piëtzi de mettre la lettre que j'vou z-avais ecrit, atuèrt le policemen, dans la Gazette nou no qu'chuna partout, qu'nou vaille y'ou qu'nou voudra, l'policemen est l'sujet de toutes les conversàtions. I n'y'en a qui disent: "Si fait sen devoir nonn'en dirait rain." Mé j'dit qui na pas devoir à faire: et j'men vais vou z'en donnaï la preuve.

La prumiére chose qui fait au matin, ch'est d'allaï l'vaï l'zallachons qu'il a tendu oùn saï su l'têrrain des gens; chunna fait, I va tràire ses biches; ch'est une chose qui faut qui sait faite matin et saï; et pie l'restànt du temps il l'passe à la sache'; et oùn saï coum tout autre, i s'pourmaine par la ville pour passaï l'temps.

Mais, moussieu, ch'n'est pas que j'veur biâmaï l'policemen pour accraitre ses beins; ben ou contraire, j'ladmire de dissipaï des esprits; car, après tout, peut-i' restaï tout l'long d'ses jours dans s'en coin d'âtre à fumaï sa pipe? i faut qu'j'le dise moussieu, le policemen est un ômme sobre,★ intelligent, et l'pu capàible dans l'île pour rempii chute pièche là.

Mai, moussieu, d'vànt finìn, i faut que j'vou dise le réponse que m'douni un Douzenier qu'ànt j'li d'màndi à qu'èque les policemen servaie. (I m'traitra p'tètre de conte-pait). "Un pays est ben pauvre si n'peut pas fournìn un policemen." Belle raison moussieu, si un pays est riche qui faut atchupaï s'n'argent avaux les rues.

Dans l'espérance que vou trouv'raï un p'tit coin dans vot biau et repàndu papier pour y séraï l'triste sort des aur'nieés.

Je d'meure moussie
Vot devouaï serviteur
J.H.

★Titre que ben d'z'Aurniais n'peuvent pas recliamaï.

Dear Mr Editor

Sir, – Since you made me happy by putting the letter that I'd written to you, about the policemen, in the Gazette, that's all you hear about all over the place, wherever you might go, the policeman is the topic of all conversations. Some say: "If he performs his duties, we've got nothing to say about it." As for me, I say he's got no duties to perform: and I'm going to prove it to you.

The first thing he does in the morning, is to go and take up the snares that he set in the evening on people's land; having done that, he goes to milk his goats; that's something that needs to be done morning and evening; and then the rest of the time he spends hunting; and in the evening like everybody else, he walks around town to pass the time.

But, sir, it isn't that I want to blame the policeman for trying to increase his assets; far from it, I admire him for keeping himself occupied; for, after all, how could he stay all day long by his fireside smoking his pipe? And I must say, sir, the policeman is a man who is sober,★ intelligent, and the most capable in the island of filling that post.

But, sir, before I finish, I have to tell you the reply I was given by a douzenier when I asked him what good the policemen were for. (He'll probably call me a tell-tale). "It's a very poor country that can't afford a policeman." A pretty justification, sir, that if a country is rich it should throw its money underfoot.

Here's hoping that you'll be able to find a small spot in your fine and widely-read paper in which to insert the sad fate of the people of Alderney.

I remain, Sir,
Your devoted servant
J.H.

★A title that few Alderney people can lay claim to.

Marie De Garis was born in Guernsey in 1910 and died a few weeks after celebrating her centenary in 2010. Her *Dictiounnaire Angllais-Guernesiais* was published in 1967, the first dictionary of Guernesiais since Métivier's. Among her other writings are plays. Here is an extract from a play in which some neighbours are so scandalised by political proposals to permit gambling that they decide to put up a candidate for election. This unpublished script may have been written in a style to help actors learn their lines, therefore the spelling does not necessarily always follow the principles of the dictionary.

Marie De Garis

From A Pouognie Mess Allès, *n.d.* (Guernesiais)

ALBERT: Hum, vere, vere. Et bian la prumiere affaire ch'est comme tchi qu'nou peut arretai chéna.

LOUISE: Travaers les Etats

HENRI: Souognier d'elire des députais qui saont caontre a la perchoine électiaon.

LOUISE: Faire enne pétitiaon.

HENRI (*scornfully*): Et tchi qu'enne pétitiaon vaux. I n'en prendre ni caont ni taile dé chena es Etats.

LOUISE (*hopefully*): Il f'raient p'tete dé chet-chin.

HENRI: La pétitiaon pren'rait lé mesme ch'min dé tous les aoutes qu'y'a iaeux. Lé ch'min qui meunent au faeu, Albert, i faut qu'nou garde nos iaers fixai sus la perchoine electiaon, faire nos pllàns pour chena.

ALBERT: Tchique nous fra?

LOUISE: Ah, j'sait mé. I faudra qu'tu compose aen manifesto.

HENRI: Aen tchi?

LOUISE: Aen manifesto.

HENRI: Tchi qu'est chena.

LOUISE: Enne addresse, aen moniere dé p'tit sermaon, enne laette adeurchie es électeurs dé la paraesse.

ALBERT: Aen, aen program,

LOUISE: Oui.

HENRI (*enthusiastic*): Ah vraiement vere (*To* ALBERT) ouecque tu mettras tous tes pouoins en d'vant. (*To* LOUISE) mais tu rembilles qué yen a raide qui saont en faveur dé tout chutte gag'rie la.

LOUISE: Ah vere, mais Albert peut composair lé manifesto dé tant mogniere qué caontre peut ete prins quasi comme pour.

ALBERT: Ch'n'est pas p'tete justement hounnette chena.

HENRI: Men garcon, il l'faont tous, pas riocque en Guernesi, mais en Jerri, et en Anglleterre etou.

ALBERT: I saont tous pret de bailler la leune dévant l'electiaon, i faudra qui seit écrit dauve du souogn dja, pour qué pour parrait pour, et caontre parrait pour.

HENRI: Et caontre parrait caontre, et – pour parrait caontre.

ALBERT (*desperately*): Nous mé meslai, pour qué pour parrait pour ou caontre et pour parrait caontre.

HENRI: Oui, v'la l'affaire.

ALBERT: Mais comme tchi qué j'peux faire ditai tché?

LOUISE: T'est bouan écollier, tu gogni aen "Scholarship" a L'Ecole.

HENRI: Nou-s-était dans la mesme classe, nos treis, et t'etais terrous lé prumier d'la classe Albert.

LOUISE: Et té lé droin Henri.

HENRI: J'admets chéna, et mé v'la auch't'haeure riche assaiz pour vous accatai vos daeux quasi dauve lé poussier d'ma paoute.

LOUISE (*sourly*): Ch'est les impudents qui vivent.

(*Tempers seem about to rise again. Albert hurriedly nips trouble in the bud*)

ALBERT: J'pense qué j'pourais fabricher tchique chaose si j'avais d'laigue. (*gets up to sideboard and gets out large sheet of paper*) La v'chin du papier et aen pinceau, faut sie maette, comme tchi c'menchier.

HENRI: Ecrit ton naon en grands laettres pour l'entetement.

ALBERT: Bian (*writes*) J'ai fait chena, et tchi auch't'haeure?

LOUISE: Ah j'sai, quand j'etais en visite ciz ma coussaene a Laondre y'a aen p'tit temps, y'avait enne électiaon en allant, y'avait de toute les sortes dé gens qui vinre a la maisaon, des Conservatives, et des socialists, et des communists et d'aoutes, éprouvair a faire ma coussaenne votai pour laeux, et i baillais des tas dé paprasses. Arretaiz, j'en ait iun ou daeux dans ma bourse. (*She fumbles in her handbag while the others look on. She puts various things on the table much to their interest.*)

LOUISE: Ah en v'chin iun. (*She brings out a crumpled small poster, the others scan it*)

HENRI: Vere vraiement, tu pourrais traduire chenchin, Albert, t'ecrivras tché en bas caont la gagrie, et v'la ten manifesto fait. V'la qui f'ra magnifique.

LOUISE: T'eras ten pouteret la haout comme ch'tes'chin.

HENRI: Suévu par ten naon en grands laettre comme j'disais.

LOUISE: Suevu par lé manifesto.

ALBERT (*writing Albert Alles in big bold letters and shewing it to the others*): Et tchi auch't'haeure?

LOUISE (*consulting the poster and translating*): J'men vais t'lé lliere et traduire, "Tchi qu'est Albert Alles" (*ecrit chena*) (*Albert writes*)

LOUISE: Pourtchi qui faut qué vous votaiz pour li? v'chin la raisaon. I y'est jone et vigouraux, nou-s-a-besouyn de gens comme li dans le Parlement, nen-nin dans les Etats.

ALBERT: Creiyous qué j'devrais maette chena. J'n sis pas daoute jone opres tout.

HENRI (*heartily*): Certainment, tu sais tchi qui disent, la pus grande la mentrie, le pus qué les gens la creissent.

ALBERT: I'n n'faut pas sé faire motcher –

LOUISE: Et bian, met enn haomme venerablle aurun.

HENRI: I r'semblle qué ch'est aen viaer sans qu'vaeux chena.

ALBERT: J'men vais maette enn haomme respectablle. (*Writes*)

From **Hand over fist, Mr Allès,** *n.d.*

ALBERT: Um, yes, yes. Well the first thing is how it can be stopped.

LOUISE: Through the States.

HENRI: Make sure to elect Deputies who are against it at the next election.

LOUISE: Get up a petition.

HENRI (*scornfully*): What use is a petition! They don't pay any attention to that in the States.

LOUISE (*hopefully*): They might to this one.

HENRI: The petition would follow the same route as all the others there've been. The route onto the fire. Albert, we've got to keep our eyes fixed on the next election, make our plans for that.

ALBERT: What shall we do?

LOUISE: Oh, I know. You ought to draw up a manifesto.

HENRI: A what?

LOUISE: A manifesto.

HENRI: What's that?

LOUISE: An address, a sort of little sermon, a letter addressed to the electors of the parish.

ALBERT: A, a programme.

LOUISE: Yes.

HENRI (*enthusiastic*): Oh yes indeed, (*To* ALBERT) in which you can put forward all your points. (*To* LOUISE) but you're forgetting that there are a lot of people who are in favour of all this gambling.

LOUISE: Oh yes, but Albert can draw up his manifesto in such a way that "against" can just about be mistaken for "in favour".

ALBERT: That's not really very honest, that is.

HENRI: My old chap, they all do it, not just in Guernsey, but in Jersey and in England too.

ALBERT: They'll all promise the moon before the election. It'll have to be really carefully written, so that in favour looks like in favour, and against looks like in favour.

HENRI: And against looks like against, and – in favour looks like against.

ALBERT (*desperately*): I'm getting muddled: so that in favour looks like in favour or against and in favour looks like against.

HENRI: Yes, that's the job.

ALBERT: But how can I do that?

LOUISE: You're good at writing – you won a scholarship to the School.

HENRI: We were in the same class, us three, and you were always top of the class, Albert.

LOUISE: And you were bottom, Henri.

HENRI: I admit it, and now here I am rich enough to buy you both up practically with the dust in my pocket.

LOUISE (*sourly*): Where there's muck, there's brass.

(*Tempers seem about to rise again. Albert hurriedly nips trouble in the bud*)

ALBERT: I think I could put something together if I had help. (*gets up to sideboard and gets out large sheet of paper*) Here's paper and a pencil. Must get down to it. How should I begin?

HENRI: Write your name in capitals for the heading.

ALBERT: Right you are. (*writes*) I've done that; what now?

LOUISE: Oh, I know. When I was visiting my cousin in London a while ago, there was an election going on, and all sorts of people came to the house, Conservatives, and socialists and communists and others, trying to make my cousin vote for them, and they gave out loads of bumf. Hold on, I've got one or two of the leaflets in my handbag. (*She fumbles in her handbag while the others look on. She puts various things on the table much to their interest.*)

LOUISE: Ah, here's one. (*She brings out a crumpled small poster, the others scan it*)

HENRI: Yes indeed, you could translate this, Albert, you'll write something down against betting, and that'll be your manifesto done. That'll do wonderfully.

LOUISE: You'll have your picture at the top like this one.

HENRI: Followed by your name in capitals like I was saying.

LOUISE: Followed by the manifesto.

ALBERT (*writing Albert Alles in big bold letters and shewing it to the others*): And what now?

LOUISE (consulting the poster and translating): I'll read it to you and translate. "Who is Albert Alles" (*write that*) (*Albert writes*)

LOUISE: Why should you vote for him? Here's why. He's young and thrusting, we need people like him in Parliament, no, in the States.

ALBERT: Do you really think I ought to put that down? I'm not young any more, after all.

HENRI (*heartily*): Certainly, you know what they say, the bigger the lie, the more people will believe it.

ALBERT: I don't want people to laugh at me –

LOUISE: Well then, put down "a wise old man" instead..

HENRI: That makes him sound as though he's bald and on his last legs, that does.

ALBERT: I'll put down "a well-respected figure". (*Writes*)

Nature

The satirical gaze of Channel Island writers sometimes softens and takes in the charms of the natural world. But you can easily get the feeling that a farmed landscape is more highly valued than a wild one – not so surprising, given that the small scale of the Islands and the density of population mean that wilderness is in short supply.

Pierre Le Lacheur

La Biautaïe d'Haerme, *c.1996* (Guernesiais)

Il y as enamma d'visiteur qui vang en Haerme
au r'nouvé et l'etai
à s'pouremai sur les cotils
pour veis la vrais biautaïe

Les vaque s'countot a mangier l'herbe
qu'il baille le biau jaune lait
il n'y as pas grand chause milleux a bere
supareillement quan t'es plaï d'sec

Mais qu'les berbis parais belle
il sang boaune dauve à p'tit d'mente
s'tu vere les vais a p'tit plus d'pres
il t' fauras tes hautes bottes

Nous vè souvent des paissounniers
ils dees qu'y as d'la pêque par la

si t'as d'la chànce tu peut attrapaïr
du macré, du lu, ou a vra

Dans l'hivaer quand nous va a la sache
il y as pus q'enne chentôine d'lapins
les pigeaons sang pus difficile a tiraïr
pasque il's'muche dans les sappins

Dans l'caberet au but du jour
il y as pas érain milleaux
dauve enne verai d'bire à la moin
assise en d'vant du faeu

Il y en à q'écànche d'meuraïr en Haerme
il r'semblle qu'il ang tout lot
arret! nous à tout chenna à Guernési
il y as pas qu'faire d'allaïr si llian

The Beauty of Herm, *c.1996*

There are a lot of visitors that go to Herm
in spring and in summer
to go walking on the cliffs
to see real beauty.

The cows are content eating the grass
which produces the lovely yellow milk.
There are not many things better to drink
especially when you're thirsty.

My! The sheep look good.
They're good with a little mint.
But if you want to see them a little closer
you'll need your Wellington boots.

We often see fishermen.
It's said that there are good catches around there.
If you're lucky you can catch
a mackerel, a whiting or a wrasse.

In winter when we go hunting
there are more than a hundred rabbits.

The pigeons are more difficult to shoot
because they hide in the pine trees.

In the pub at the end of the day
there's nothing better
with a glass of beer in your hand
sitting in front of the fire.

There are some lucky enough to live in Herm.
It seems they have everything.
Wait! We've got all that in Guernsey.
There's no need to go so far.

Published in 1934, this piece describes a côtil in Egypt, Trinity, belonging to the Howard Davis Farm, the agricultural experimental farm of the States of Jersey. Frank Le Maistre started working at the States Farm in 1931 and followed a 25 year career there, dealing amongst other things with controlling harvests during the Occupation and outbreaks of Colorado beetle. As part of his work, he visited farms all over the Island and collected words from all dialects for inclusion in his dictionary. Although the subject of this poem is located in the North East of Jersey, Doctor Frank, as he was known later in life, commented that he uses, in his Saint Ouen dialect, words for birds and plants that differ from those known in the East.

Frank Le Maistre

Ma p'tite bouaîs'sie, *1934* (Jèrriais)

Ch'est eune bouaîs'sie qué j'connais bein,
Tch'est l'sujet d'ma chanson,
Un p'tit côti à La Trinneté,
Un paradis au pid d'siez mé.

Lé calme y règne, dans man côti,
Tout seu nou-s'y'est tréjous à s'n aise,
Ouaithe qu' isolé n'y'a dgéthe d'ennion
Dans ma bouaîs'sie tout à banon.

Avaû un drédillet à gauche
Ou à drouaite, comme i' vouos pliaitha,
Pâssez par-'chîn, né faites pon d'brit,
Pouor vaie la bieauté d'man côti.

En pliein êté remplyi d'vèrduthe,
Et à la tchête un tapis d'fielles,
Dé toutes les sortes dé belles p'tites flieurs
Et l'chant d's ouaîthieaux touos bein heûtheurs.

Bieaux grands hauts bouais tout à l'entou
Et un fieillage dé toutes couleurs,
La musique du canné dans l'fond
Tchi russelle douochement tout du long.

Des peupliers, pus hauts qu' touos l's aut's,
Des tchênes en mâsse et des tchênelles,
Deux'trais chât'gnièrs, des ormes, et pis
Un bieau grand fau – rouai d'la bouaîs'sie.

Tchiques pétits frênes, deux'trais êpîngnes,
Des ronches tout pliein et du dgèrrue,
D'la mousse 'chîn et là souos les pids,
Feûgiéthe et geon à tête flieuthie.

Mais au r'nouvé quand y'a l'pus d'chouaix –
Les g'zettes, les bliuets, les pipots,
Quand l'bliu coucou est dêhalé
Et les mèrgots – ch'est ch'la tch'est bé!

Et pis pus tard du rouoge coucou
(Chein qu' nou-s-appelle des vièrs garçons),
Du potithon, pis du chuchet
Tout teurt sus l'mort-bouais endgèrrué.

Des p'tites feûgu'tholes et du frêgon,
Du paîvre à j'vaux – y'en a tréjous,
Quand veint lé s'tembre la vèrge d'or,
Jalousie, menthe – tchi bel êffort!

Y'a du cresson et d'la sûthe-ieaux,
D'la chue, du han et du gliajeu,
D'l'ôsyi, du saulx et du jontchet
À la braichie avaû l'canné.

Dans ma bouaîs'sie j'sis bein èrchu,
Ch'est si pliaîthant d'ouï la musique –

Tout l'ouaîthelîn chante à forte vouaix
A londgeu d'jours parmi les bouais.

Lé cri d'la pie m'est familyi,
La teurtérelle, tchiquefais l'coucou,
Les geais étout à bieau plieunmage,
Et d'autres ouaîthieaux tchi sont en viage.

J'connais l'bouvtheu et la rouoge-gorge,
Et touos les mêles m'sûffl'yent beinv'nue,
La grive, lé vèrdreu et l'mouosson.
Et l'rossîngno (tch'est un pînchon),

Tchiques bieaux jaûnouais et des souciques,
Et pis l'tui-tui dans l'mais d'avri,
L'êtournieau, l'craquelîn et l'gliaineux,
Des d'mouaîselles et des p'tits mêssieux.

I' y'a étout lé rouoge linnot,
Lé pique-en-bouais et l'vèrmîngnon,
Lé p'tit raîté – eune vraie dgilouette –
Et la mîngnonne dé cardrinnette.

N'oublions pon les papillotes,
Atout lus ailes si couleuthées –
N'y'éthait d'bieauté dans man côti
Sans papillotes à voltilyi.

Par haut, par bas, n'împorte iou
(Y'a bein des c'mîns dans ma bouaîs'sie),
En toutes saisons, d'amont, d'ava,
La paix, l'èrpos sont tréjous là.

La bieauté qué j'aimons touos nous,
Trajet d'chutte vie bénin et doux,
Mèrveil'yes dé la Natuthe et pis –
Mais, v'n-ouos-en tous vaie ma bouaîs'sie!

My Little Wood, *1934*

It's a wood that I know well
that is the subject of my song,

a little côtil in Trinity,
a paradise just by my home.

Calm reigns there in my côtil,
one is at one's ease alone there,
although isolated there's no boredom
wandering in my wood.

Down a winding path to the left
or to the right, according to your fancy,
pass this way, do not make any noise,
to see the beauty of my côtil.

In high Summer full of greenery,
and in the Fall a carpet of leaves,
beautiful little flowers of all kinds
and the happy singing of all the birds.

Beautiful big tall trees all around
with leaves of all different colours,
the music of the stream down below
which slowly trickles along.

Poplars, taller that the rest,
a mass of oaks and acorns,
a couple of chestnut trees, elms and
a beautiful large beech tree – king of the wood.

A few little ash trees, a couple of hawthorns,
plenty of brambles and some ivy,
moss here and there underfoot,
bracken and gorse with tops in bloom.

But in spring when there's most to choose from –
daffodils, bluebells, buttercups,
when the dog violet is out,
and the daisies – that's what's beautiful!

And then later the red campion
(what we call bachelors' buttons),
foxglove, and honeysuckle
entangling the dead-wood overgrown with ivy.

There's always small bracken and butcher's-broom,
and redshank,
when Autumn comes there's goldenrod,
hemp agrimony and mint – a fine showing!

There's cress and lesser marshwort,
hemlock water-dropwort, galingale and yellow iris,
osier, willow and rushes
by the armful along the stream.

I'm made welcome in my wood,
it's so pleasant to hear the music –
all the birds sing loudly
all day long among the trees.

I'm familiar with the call of the magpie,
the turtledove, sometimes the cuckoo,
the jays too with their beautiful plumage,
and other migratory birds.

I know the bullfinch and the robin,
and all the blackbirds whistle me a welcome,
the thrush, the hedge warbler and the sparrow,
and the chaffinch.

Some beautiful yellowhammers and long-tailed tits,
and then the wryneck in the month of April,
the starling, the blackcap and the wagtail,
great tits and bluetits.

There's also the linnet,
the green woodpecker and the greenfinch,
the little wren – always changeable –
and the goldfinch.

Let's not forget the butterflies,
with their wings so brightly coloured –
there wouldn't be anything beautiful about my côtil
without butterflies fluttering about.

High and low, no matter where I go
(there are many paths in my wood),

in all seasons, up and down,
peace and rest can always be found there.

The beauty that we all of us love,
the blessed and sweet journey through this life,
wonders of Nature, and –
but, why don't all of you come and see my wood!

George Métivier

Octobre, *1857* (Guernesiais)

A ma f'nêtre tapotànt,
S'font les suchets, tu dors tànt,
Ten mouisson, l'faeu sus la gorge,
A biau criaïr, ch'est mé, George!
Vier Octobre! vier Huitembre!
Du temps passaï tu m'ramembre;
Te vlà v'nu pour élouaisiér
Fieille après fieille au nouaisiér,
Pliumaïr nos ormes coquènes,
Halaïr les qu'vaeux ès durs quênes,
Niaïr nos gens, coum, autànt d'rats,
Les cliùngeànt dans leux treis-mâts,
Quànd tu gronds, la vague émue
Rouâne et vole et fend la nue,
A' dànse au son des galots;–
Jouaïz, cormarans, ners salops!
Gôlias fieillu! tes castaïnes,
J'en ai rôgui des chentaïnes,
Dorlotaï dans tes longs bras!
Dis-mé qu'tu t'en souviendras,
Giànt chéri, m'n abri, ma d'meure,
Men lliét, men ber, et qu'j'y meure!
J'm'en irai, coum je sis v'nu,
Fier d'ùn bien p'tit (GRÀND) r'venu,
Car ma rachine était forte! –
En attendant qu'a' seit morte,
Nouon, nouon, pus llien qu'Ouessànt!
Sauton par dessus l'croissànt!

October, *1857*

Tapping at my window,
the honeysuckles say, you sleep too much,
your bird with the fiery throat
has called in vain, it's me, George!
Old October! Old October!
you remind me of time past;
and now you've come to shake loose
leaf after leaf from the nut tree,
pluck our scarlet elms,
pull the hair from the hard oaks,
drown our folks like so many rats,
plunging them in their three-masters,
when you rumble, the wave is moved
and wracks and flies and cleaves the sky,
it dances to the sound of the shingle;–
Play, cormorants, foul black birds!
Leafy Goliath! your chestnuts,
I've munched hundreds of them,
cradled in your long arms!
Tell me you'll remember it,
dear giant, my shelter, my dwelling,
my bed, my cot, and let me die there!
I'll go as I came,
proud of a very small (BIG) returnee,
because my root was strong! –
And while we're waiting for it to die,
let's swim, let's swim, further than Ushant!
Let's jump over the crescent moon!

Esther Le Hardy ('Le Bourdon')

Les Airangnis, *1853* (Jèrriais)

Les airangnis ch'nez pas d'qui rare,
Nou zen trouve à toutes les carres,
Niers, blianches, pilais, vlousais,
Mondoux partout l'yen a assais,
Long, court, p'tits, gros
Les môques nont pas d'erpos,
Y chuche le sang d'tout,
Bourdons, vêpres, môques à mi,

Toutes à lus goût,
Tout lancheon, macré;
Ah! mes pouors fréres de môques, ah! prennais m'navis,
Et n'allais pas hanté parmi les airangnis.

Chez de lais saloppris,
Que chez bêtes d'Airangniz;
Et les bêtes de chutte sorte
Une fais dans dans vot porte
Mène la vie la pus belle
Ove leus chiquette de telle,
Quil entasse en gros clius
Q'nou peut frumer l'hue,
Et une fais dans vos creux
Y crais tout à lieux
Ah! mes pouors fréres de môques, ah! prennais m'navis,
Et n'allais pas hanté parmi les airangnis.

Y casse
Y ramasse
Ils entasse
Et font un tiné,
En vos fliattant la pé,
Tandis que tout l'temps,
Y s'abreuvent de vot sang,
Si ou zête à lus gous
Damme chest fini pour vous
Car y dise q'la qués fait,
En pure charitai
Pour empêchi vot graisse
De v'nin trop épaisse
Ah! mes pouors fréres de môques, ah! prennais m'navis,
Et n'allais pas hanté parmi les airangnis.

Quand Satan se fait moine
Y paque ses mitaines
Ov les griffes minse en d'dans
D'une belle pare de gants,
Et fait le grand saint
Pour vos prendre en ses mains,
Et pis y s'erpaque
Dans sa vlousaie câsaque
Qués faites m'est avis

De telles d'Airangnis,
Car ou sent hardi l'sens
De chez pouors innocens
Ah! mes chiers frères de môques et prennais m'navis,
Et n'allais pas hanté parmi les airangnis.

Spiders, *1853*

Spiders are not scarce,
they can be found in every corner,
black ones, white ones, bald ones, hairy ones,
my goodness, there are lots of them everywhere,
long, short, small, big,
flies never have any peace,
they suck the blood of everything:
bumblebees, wasps, honeybees,
all to their taste,
sand eels and mackerel;
Ah, my poor brother flies, ah, take my advice,
and do not hang around with spiders.

They are awful dirty beasts,
those spiders;
and creatures of that sort
Once inside your door
lead the easiest of lives
with their rags of webs
which they build up in large patches
You can close the door
and once in your nooks
they think everything belongs to them
Ah, my poor brother flies, ah, take my advice,
and do not hang around with spiders.

They break
they gather
they build up
and make a to-do
while stroking your skin
but all the time
slaking themselves on your blood
If they find you to their taste,
well then, it is all over with you,

for they say it is done
out of pure charity
to stop you getting fat
and becoming too big
Ah, my poor brother flies, ah, take my advice,
and do not hang around with spiders.

A wolf in sheep's clothing
puts on mittens
to cover up the claws inside
with a beautiful pair of gloves
and pretends to be a great innocent
in order to get you in his clutches
and then off he goes again
in his hairy coat
which I think is made
of cobwebs
because it smells strongly of the blood
of those poor innocents
Ah, my poor brother flies, ah, take my advice,
and do not hang around with spiders.

George Métivier

Les flleurs de nos fries, *1867* (Guernesiais)

Nou les oyait chantaïr, en trayant leûs vaquottes,
D'vànt l'asinànt du jeur, l'naïz au vent, j'en réponds:
Mais, l'long des ch'mìns flleuris, nou n'les ot pus, les sottes –
Et les flleurs de nos fries, oh ma chère! où'est'qu'i'sont?

Nou n'vet pus les gaillards les échardaïr et rire,
Nàn, les fièffaïs cahouans, la pipe est leux écant;
A sen tout-seul, hélas! la fillette, a' soupire,
Prend sa canne, et s'en va, l'coeur pènsif et dolent!

Quand j'faison notre avoût, les terriens, muets et pâles,
Ont l'visage enquilli, mort, défait, jaune et long;
Dame, au vrec, à la fère, i'n'font pus leux trigalles –
Et les flleurs de nos fries, oh ma chère! où'est'qu'i'sont?

Entre l'jeur et la gnèt, i'n'jouent pus, nos fidèles,
Autouar de nos tas d'orge, à tuntìn, les mignons!

J'verson lerme sus lerme, en r'gardant les ételles –
Et les flleurs de nos fries, oh ma chère! où'est'qu'i'sont?

The flowers of our pastures, *1867*

You used to hear them singing, while milking their little cows,
before dawn, into the wind, I tell you:
but along the flowery lanes, you no longer hear them, the silly girls –
and as for the flowers of our pastures, my darling, where are they now?

You no longer see the lads teasing them and laughing,
no, the blighters, the pipe is their amusement;
all alone, alas! the girl sighs,
takes her milking can, and off she goes, with a thoughtful and heavy heart!

When we harvest, the farmers are silent and pale,
their faces wrinkled, dead, undone, yellow and long;
indeed, out vraicking, at the cattle market, they're no longer up to tricks –
and as for the flowers of our pastures, my darling, where are they now?

In the twilight, our faithful ones no longer play
around our barley stacks, the little ones playing blind man's buff!
We shed tear after tear, gazing at the stars –
and as for the flowers of our pastures, my darling, where are they now?

This round-up of the weather, nature and seasonal activities in 1969 was written by 'Le Campagnard', a pseudonym which has hidden the identity of what, judging by his language, was one of the last speakers of his Saint Martinnais dialect. This countryman's almanac was published in booklet form in 1970-1971, and gives an accurate account of the weather conditions on the days described. Although the style is unsophisticated, the selection of observations is well judged to give a tapestry of a year's passage, picked out with details which contrast the timeless and the fashionable.

'Le Campagnard'

Enne annaïe à la campagne, *1969-1970* (Guernesiais)

Janvier Le meis d'janvier, et des heures passàïes au d'vant d'enn faeu de bouais; enn p'tit de travas au gardin en sercllant, et en mettant des pots à flleurs au d'sus de la rhuborbe, pour la faire craitre. La prumiere s'moine, j'ai trouvaï enn snowdrop, et quillaï le prumier soleil d'or de l'annaïe. La fin du meis i plleut avers.

Feverier J'quille des chrysanths dans le span; pie j'fais des tranchies pour les tamates; au gardin j'ai quillaï des violattes. A la fin du 2 féverier i neigit enn p'tit, mais la neis s'en va le loang d'maoin.

Mars I'y'avait de la pllie, et i faisait frêt, mais la fin de la prumiere s'moine était coum enn r'nouvé, et j'ai quillaï du palm (pussy willow) à Petit Bôt pour la maison. En mi-meis j'envie mes pouorreons au marchi, pie j'ai butai des patates.
Ach't'heure ch'est le Spring Flower Shaux, et le prumier jeur du r'nové. Partout y'a des pissenllets aux fossaïs; enn de ches fossaïs dans le val de Petit Bôt, est enn amas des paq'rolles. Le 28. le lorry viant dauve mes whalehide pots et du Chasmore pour les tamates, et j'sis plloin d'travas.

Avril Ch'est le prumier des treis milleux meis de l'annaïe. A Pâques j'quille des pouorreons et de la rhuborbe, etou j'ai r'pllàntaï des chives; i fait soleil et, le 11, commence á pllantaïr mes tamates. Le perchain jeur a c'menchie deul, mais par mi-jeur i faisait biau soleil; en d'valànt à cheva le val de Petit Bôt, j'veis que les arbres sont en différents couleurs de vèr, et qu'ya enn bouan lot des paqu'rolles et des pouorreons. Enn lapin court dedans la petite fouoret pour jouaïr. Les ch'vaux quittent le ch'min, traversent le douit, et pis ch'est enn biau galop en amont á travers les arbres.
    Le 19 avril, et les fossaïs sont pu vèrs, dauve enn amas paqu'roles. J'pllàntes des faïves. En la droine s'moine j'veis que la nère épaene flleurit partout; ach't'heure ch'est la pllànterie des patates, des nouvelles pllàntes de frâses et des Brussels sprouts. Le 27 avril nou s'entend le coucou qu'est á travers du val près de not'-gardin.

Mai Le deuxième jeur, et les faïves poussent; acore treis jeurs, et j'quille d'la rhuborde dans la pllie. J'amarraï mes tamates. Ch'est la deuxième s'moine, et les paqu'rolles sont prèsque disparues, mais des coneilles flleurissent, et les hiraöundelles arrrivent. En la treisième s'moine j'veis de l'épaene á Petit Bôt. I plleut seulement treis ou quatre feis durànt les droines quinjours du meis.

Juin Le meis d'juin, et nou ne s'en souvient d'enn pus magnifique tems. Qu'iques jeurs de pllie, mais auterment i faisait reid bel. Dans la campagne, l'herbe et les fossaïs d'viennent fânaïs. Y a bian des visiteurs. Ch'est la s'moine du haut d'l'étai, et nou paque les tamates; bian que les pus grandes s'moines sont passaïes, la récolte est acore grande.
    Dans le shed nou prépare pour le travas, pie la prumiere quertaïe arrive des spans, et j'semmes vraiment dans l'embarras. Mé, j'b'saï des casses viedes, enviaïs le long des rollers par enne jâne bretonne. All tip étou des tamates sus la machaene et papeur les casses. La frànçaise à l'auter but du shed b'saï les tamates paquaïs. All est bian graïe dans des braies de nere tixette, et des bottes faites pour marchier, enne crâne en miniature pende des boutonnières d'enne large belt de cuir. Les treis paquraesses guernesiaises á la machaene (les travas qu'est importànt) sont des

expaerts, à l'iel et la main vite, faisant allaïr vite le travas. Y'a le camas d'la machaene, les rollers font clliquetaïr, et les casses vièdes vont á mé pour ête b'santaïs, étampaïs, et mit en tas. En attandànt, les tas de casses paquaïs augmentent au but du shed, prêts pour le lorry qui les prend au dépôt.

Y'avait enn matin de pllie, le jeur avant le Saint Jean, pie c'menche des s'moines et acore des s'moines de caud.

Juillet I fait bian caud acore, et, le ser, nou' trouve pllaisir en allant á L'Erée ou nou' pâque le car, d'vise dauve des accoints et vère les gens sus le galet et autouour du café. Partout par la campagne nou veit des suchets, mais l'herbe est fânaï.

J'aime bian le traditionel thée de daimanche de crabe, mais j'trouve qu'i faut bian de travas pour préparaïre enn pincllos.

Le 6 juillet y'avait pus de pllie que nou's'a jamais ramembraï: 2,3 pouces enter 1030 et 1630 heures, et enn fort grànd vent q'a rompu des arbres. Pie i d'vint acore trop caud. Les fermiers ont quâsi finis de quertaïe le föin, et quànd j'vais à cheva dans les Blanche Pierre lanes, j'veis enn arbre en arche à travers d'la ruette toute couverte des suchets. Dans la propagation house i fait caud – á cuire! dit enne des frànçaises.

Le droin daimanehe du meis y'avait enne épaisse breunne d'la maïr.

Aout Les sers sont pus courts. A neuf heures à l'Erée, ou la maïr est argent – grise – bllue, y'a des écllairs du Hanois, et nou veit les lueurs des maisons sus Plleinmont. Biantôt i fait nere de gniet, et les floodlights du café Sunset Strip r'llèrent sus les motos et des gens allànt et v'nànt.

Dans la propagation house daeux students de l'Université de Rennes poussent des picotaïs dans du compost. Enne des filles (graïe à la mode frànçaise en étraits gris cord shorts jusqu'au genouais) pâle l'angllais mux que nous-auters (dit le fore-man). All érrousse l'établlie à picotaïs dauve enn haose. L'auter fille ne pâle pas angllais, ch'est enne p'tite souriànte Saïgonnaise dauve des longues neres q'vaeux. Les daeux filles font des p'tits pertus dans le compost dauve enn outi, prendent des picotaïs des pouques plastiques, mettent les pids des picotais dans du poudre à l'hormone, pie les poussent dans le compost. La frànçaise dit qu'all s'est allai à ch'va le daimenche; étou que daeux guernesiais l'a dit chutte s'moine qu'il' n'oiment pas les angllais.

En arlevaïe les galets sont tout plloïn des gens, mais y'a pus de breune les sers, et i d'vint pus frais. A la fin d'la s'moine, le 24 et 25, au Horse of the Year chaux aux Vauxbelets, i fait bel assi au soleil, vère la saut'rie, et d'visaï dauve des auters qu'oi-ment les ch'vaux.

A l'Erée enne plloïne leune r'leure derrière la haute lande, la maïr sounne sus le galet, et y'a les lueurs des maisons et du lighthouse. Les sers, quànd j'arrivons çix nou, i fait nere et j'ouie des criquet qui chantent prés de men garage; le cat nous fait le bian v'nu, en trottant jusqu'à l'hus pour que nou le patouille.

Depis le mi-meis j'fais des défriquages de la fin de saison au gardin.

Septembre Le meis c'menche dauve enn holiday, et i fait soleil. Tout le longue d'la côte, de l'Ancresse par Portinfer et Albecq y'a bian de gens, mais nou n'en veit grànment dans les ruettes. L'arlevaïe, j'allons à Plleinmont, jusqu'aux radio masts. La qualitaï de mes tamates est bouanne, mais j'n'oime pas les prix.

Enn matin j'ai dounaï enn cô d'main à men ami qu'est v'nu au cold store dauve enne des filles pour paquer des chrysanth cuttings (ch'est pour les exportaïr). Nou fait des tas de casses pour qu'ils s'ront taquetaïs, chacun pour enn coutumier, pie nou's'emplliet d'auters boscs, et mette les tiquets sus les vièdes casses prêt à les empllier.

J'sis en holiday, et y'a des heures haeurraeux en s'en allant en moto par les ruettes enter les arbres et les fossais en soleil. Etou allaïr à ch'va les matins, parfeis sus enne bllanche jument qu'est grande et forte. I faut la tenir bouan, mais j'sis bian à men aise la, en allànt le longue des ruettes de Saen Martin, trottànt de temps en temps, pie galoppànt à travers enn courti, la grande jument halànt fort à la groumette.

I ne fait pas terjou grànd soleil, y'a des temps nerchis et des scoualles; des hiraoundelles volent tout près du ch'min en d'vant du moto. 'I font des préparatifs pour s'en allaï'. Des gens étou: quànd j'acate enn cafi dans enn restaurant de la vouest côte, la fille au cash desk, grasse en était ner miniskirt, me dit qu'ail va çiz-all en Yorkshire la s'moine qui vian, pasqué (all dit) 'j'n'oime pas ête ichin. Guernesi est vraiment mediéval, et les gens étou!'

Chutte s'moine je ne fais pas de travas, sinon de quiller mes tamates. Tèrjou j'mangêmes not'desnair dans enn café à Saen Martin, ou nou veit des accoints. Ch'na nous fait pllaisir.

J'ai quillaï les droines figues de not' figuier (le sécret du succès: dounnaï enn amas d'yaux aux figuiers). Allànt à ch'va, le 11 septembre, i plleut, et y'a treis gens qui sont bien trempaïs! La dernière s'moine du meis, les hiraoundelles sont partis, mais nou veit des cauve-souoris les sers (et ches sers sont courts). Dans le chip shop à l'Erée, le 26 du meis, daeux empilleis d'hôtel me disent que leux saisaön est fini.

Daimanche le 28: l'Assembllaïe tient le service d'la moissaon à Sion (Saen Pierre). Ch'est magnifique d'ête dans la chapelle, decoraïe dauve des l'geumes, des fruits et des flleurs, ouïr le service en not' langue et de chàntaïr des càntiques frànçais, coum 'Nous labourons la terre' et d'auters qui sont bian oimaïs. Pie en le car, par la gniet, çiz-mé.

Et l'étai est fini et ch'est l'automne.

Octobre J'allons çiz enn ami qu'est fermier, acataïr daeux sacs de patates et d'visaïr dauve li et sa faume et sa fille. J'ai quillaï not' bouanne récolte de paömmes, le Laxton Superbe dounànt mux que l'auter variétai. J'ai enviaï la droine casse de tamates le 8 octobre. Toute la s'moine i fait raid caud, pus que 20 degrés. Chut octobre fut le pus caud d'pis le 18 ème sièclle et y'avait moins d'la pllie enn feis seulement en 100 annaïes.

Novembre J'ai abbataï les tamates dans le span, aiguaï par enne Saen Martinnaise r'v'nue d'anglleterre. I plleut avers le 6 et y'a enn grànd vent la gniet, pis enne s'moine de pllie. Le 25 i fait frêt et y'a d'la neis. Nou-s oime nos visites çiz not' Co-op les venderdis sers. Ach't'heure – ch'est novembre nou c'menche à faire le chop-pingue de Noué.

J'ai tailli la Albertine rose sus le mur d'la maison, et sercllaï le muguet.

Décembre J'allons à la ville le 9 faire le choppingue de Noué, et nou-s est bian fiaire quand nou-s acate des persents (y'a bian de chouaix) dans des choppes toutes decoraïes pour la saisaön. Et tous les gens des choppes sont prêts à nous aïguer, tous fiaires; tout est gaï.

Pie à Saen Martin faire acore du choppingue, et j'allons à Petit Bôt, ou y'a des gens sus le galet qui défouirent d'la bette. Dans enne grànde choppe à Saen Pierre des gens decorirent acore des murs (dauve du houisse, des ételles, et du tinsel), et enne souriànte assistaente laisse amarraïr sa paper chain pour nous servir.

I faisit frêt et le temps fut mouâlli, le 13, mais nou-s avait enne bouanne pour-ménade à cheva, autouar de Saen Martin.

La Serveille, et tout le maound est à la ville, ou le band de l'Armaïe du Salut joue des càntiques de Noué à côtaï de l'arbre de Noué.

Et pie ch'est le Noué dauve des cartes et des càntiques, des faeux de bouais, des bouans souhaits, des persents et des gràndes visites enter fâmilles et amis.

Le dauxième jeur de Noué, nou veit les bluebirds dauve leur coconut tandis que nou mangit not' déjeunaïr. Pie j'allons en moto atouar de Saen Martin et avau le val de P'tit Bôt. Le temps s'nerchi et y'a d'la bllâse.

Alors viant la fin d'l'annaïe.

A year in the country, *1969-1970*

January The month of January and hours spent in front of a wood fire; a little work in the garden weeding, and placing flower pots on top of the rhubarb to make it grow. The first week I found a snowdrop, and picked the first soleil d'or narcis-sus of the year. At the end of the month it rains heavily.

February I pick chrysanths in the greenhouse; then I make the trenches for the tomatoes; in the garden I picked some violets. At the end of the 2nd of February it snows a little, but the snow goes away the following day.

March There was rain and it was cold, but the end of the first week was like spring, and I picked some pussy willow at Petit Bôt for the house. In the middle of the month I send my daffodils to market, then stood my potatoes.

Now it's the Spring Flower Show and the first day of spring. Everywhere there are celandines on the hedgerows; one of these hedgerows in Petit Bôt valley is full of primroses. On the 28th the lorry arrives with my whalehide pots and some

Chasmore fertiliser for the tomatoes and I have plenty of work.

April It's first of the three best months of the year. At Easter I pick daffodils and rhubarb, also I replant my chives; it's sunny and on the 11th I begin planting my tomatoes. The next day starts out dull, but by midday it was fine and sunny; going down Petit Bôt valley by horse I can see that the trees are different shades of green and that there a lot of primroses and daffodils. A rabbit runs into the little wood, playing. The horses leave the path, cross the stream, and then gallop well up hill amongst the trees.

The 19th of April and the hedgerows are greener with a lot of primroses. I plant my broad beans. During the last week I notice that the blackthorn is in blossom everywhere. Now's the time for planting potatoes, new strawberry plants and Brussels sprouts. On April the 27th we hear the cuckoo across the valley near our garden.

May The second day and the broad beans are growing; another three days and I pick some rhubarb in the rain. I tied up my tomatoes. It's the second week and the primroses have almost disappeared, but bluebells are flowering and swallows are arriving. During the third week I notice the hawthorn at Petit Bôt. It rains only three or four times during the last fortnight of the month.

June The month of June, and one can't remember more glorious weather. A few days of rain, but otherwise it was very fine. In the countryside the grass and the hedgerows start turning to hay. There are a lot of tourists. It's midsummer week and we are packing tomatoes; although the most important weeks have passed the crop is still good.

In the shed we're preparing for the work, then the first cartload from the greenhouses arrives and we're really busy. Me, I weigh some empty boxes sent along the rollers by a young girl from Brittany. She also tips tomatoes onto the machine and lines the boxes. The French girl at the other end weighs the packed tomatoes. She's well dressed in black corduroy trousers and walking boots, a miniature skull hangs from the holes of a wide leather belt. The three female Guernsey packers working at the machine (the important work) are experts, with rapid eye and hand work, making the work go quickly. There's the machine noise, the rollers go click clack, and the empty boxes go to me to be weighed, stamped and stacked. Whilst waiting the stack of packed boxes at the end of the shed grows, ready for the lorry that takes them to the dépôt.

There was one morning of rain, the day before Midsummer's day, then weeks and more weeks of hot weather begin.

July It's still very warm and in the evenings we enjoy going to L'Érée where we park the car, speak to people that we know and see the people on the beach and around the café. All about the countryside there's honeysuckle, but the grass is dry.

Sundays I like to have the traditional crab tea, but find that preparing spider crabs involves a lot of work.

On the 6th of July there was more rain than we can ever remember: 2,3 inches between 1030 and 1630 hours, and a very strong wind which brought tree branches down. Then it became too warm again. The farmers have almost finished carting the hay and when I go horse riding in the Blanche Pierre Lanes, I see a branch arched across the lane all covered in honeysuckle. In the propagation house it's hot enough to cook, says one of the French girls.

The last Sunday of the month there was a thick sea fog.

August The evenings are shorter. At nine o'clock at L'Érée the sea is silver – grey – blue, there are flashes from Les Hanois lighthouse, and we can see the light from houses on the top of Pleinmont. Soon the night is very dark, and the floodlights at the Sunset Strip café shine on the cars and the people that are coming and going.

In the propagation house two students from Rennes University plant seedlings in compost. One of the girls (dressed in the French style, in close-fitting grey cord shorts down to her knees) speaks English better than us others (says the foreman). She waters the seedling staging with a hose. The other girl doesn't speak English, she's a small, smiling, Saigonese girl with long black hair. The two girls make holes in the compost with a tool, take the seedlings from plastic bags, place the base of the seedlings in hormone powder, then plant them in the compost. The French girl says that she went horse riding on Sunday; also two Guernsey men told her this week that they don't like the English.

In the afternoons the pebble beach is full of people, but there's more fog in the evenings, and it has become fresher.

At the end of the week, the 24th and 25th, at the Horse of the Year Show at Les Vauxbelets it's nice sitting in the sun seeing the jumping and speaking to other people who like horses.

At L'Érée a full moon shines behind the raised heath, the sea can be heard on the shingle, and there's light from houses and the lighthouse. In the evenings, when we arrive home, it's dark and I can hear the crickets singing near to my garage; the cat welcomes us, trotting up to the door so that we stroke him.

Since the middle of the month I've been doing end of season clearing in the garden.

September The month begins with a holiday, and it's sunny. All along the coast, from L'Ancresse through to Portinfer and Albecq there are a lot of people, but we don't see many in the lanes. During the afternoon we go to Pleinmont, as far as the radio masts.

My tomatoes are of a good quality, but I don't like the prices.

One morning I helped my friend who came to the cold store with one of the girls to pack chrysanth cuttings (they're for export). We stack the boxes so that they can be marked up, each one for a customer, then we fill up the other boxes, and put labels on the empty boxes ready to fill them.

I'm on holiday and there are contented hours spent going by car through the lanes between the trees and the hedgerows in the sun. Also going horse riding in the mornings, sometimes on a big, strong white mare. I need to hold on well, but I'm comfortable there, going along the lanes of St. Martin's, sometimes trotting, then galloping through a field, the big mare pulling hard on the curb chain.

It's not always so sunny, there are times when the weather's dark and there are showers; the swallows fly very close to the lane in front of the car. they're preparing to leave. People as well: when I buy a coffee in a restaurant on the west coast, the girl on the cash desk, dressed in a skinny black miniskirt, tells me that she's going home to Yorkshire next week, because (she says) 'I don't like being here. Guernsey is truly mediaeval, and the people as well!'.

This week I don't do any work, except picking my tomatoes. We always eat our midday meal in a café in St. Martin's, where we see people that we know. This we enjoy.

I picked the last figs from our fig tree (the secret of success: water fig trees a lot). Whilst horse riding on the 11th it rains and there are three very soaked people! The last week of the month the swallows have gone, but we see bats in the evenings (and these evenings are short). In the chip shop at l'Érée, the 26th of the month, two hotel employees tell me that their season is finished.

Sunday the 28th; L'Assembllaïe holds the harvest service at Sion (St. Peter's). It's wonderful to be in the chapel, decorated with vegetables, fruit and flowers, to hear the service in our language and to sing French hymns like, 'Nous labourons la terre' and other favourites. Then in the car, by night, home.

And summer is past and it is autumn.

October We go to a farmer friend's home to buy two sacks of potatoes and to speak to him and his wife and his daughter. I picked our good harvest of apples, Laxton's Superb cropping better than the other variety. I've sent the last box of tomatoes on the 8th of October. All week it's very warm, more than 20 degrees. This October was the warmest since the 18th century and there was less rain only once in the last 100 years.

November I have taken down the tomatoes in the greenhouse, helped by a girl from St. Martin's returned from England. It rains heavily on the 6th and there's a strong wind in the night, then a week of rain. On the 25th it is cold and there's snow. We like our visits to our Co-op Friday evenings. Now that it is November we begin doing Christmas shopping.

I pruned the Albertine rose on the wall of the house, and weeded the lily of the valley.

December We go to town on the 9th to do the Christmas shopping, and we are happy when we're buying presents (there's a good choice) in the shops that are all decorated for the season. And all the people in the shops are ready to help us, all happy; all is jolly.

Then to St. Martin's to do more shopping and then we go to Petit Bôt where there are people on the beach digging bait. In a big shop in St. Peter's people are still decorating the walls (with holly, stars and tinsel), and a smiling assistant leaves tying up her paper chain to serve us.

It was cold and the weather was wet on the 13th, but we had a good horse ride around St. Martin's.

Christmas Eve and everyone's in town where the Salvation Army band plays Christmas carols beside the Christmas tree.

And then it's Christmas with cards and carols, wood fires, good wishes, presents and visits amongst family and friends.

Boxing Day we see bluebirds with their coconut whilst we are eating our breakfast. Then we go in the car around St. Martin's and down Petit Bôt valley. The weather becomes dark and it starts to drizzle.

Then the end of the year arrives.

Tam Lenfestey's 1877 description of an August stroll starts with a reference to the proverbial early-rising hero of the fourteenth century attack by Owen of Wales. There is not much else that is heroic in this simple tale of an early morning walk, except possibly the touch of social comedy of the narrator's return to his wife.

Tam Lenfestey

La Matinaie, *1877* (Guernesiais)

> Une journaïe j'fis coume Jean Letocq,
> En me l'vant d'vant l'accoutumaïe,
> Et m'traînant comme un écarbot,
> J'voulais jouir de la belle matinaïe.
>
> Et en me l'vant d'si bouan partems,
> J'laisis not' femme bien endormie,
> Car veyant qui faisait biau temps
> J'voulaie un p'tit jouir de la vie.
>
> Marchant l'long des fossaïs et duis,
> J'oyais là les chants des mêlesses,
> Tandis qu'les melles étaient assis,
> Leu réponnant leus politesses.

L'ribé dans l'us de sen p'tit nic,
En m'saluant m'faisait quasi rire,
L'grobé était assis sus l'gllic,
Tandis qu'sa belle couvait, j'l'admire.

Les courtils étaient remplis d'flieurs,
Des bianches, des rouages, des jaunes,
Qu'éraient réjoui bien des coeurs,
Auv' les pacrolles et l's'animones.

J'véyais nos vaques à se r'posaï,
En ruminant tout long couochiés,
Nos gens s'en v'naient les faire levaï,
Pour avé l'lait pour les bouillies.

J'vis l'vier Nico à r'muaï ses viaux,
La Rocho à traire des vaques,
Et j'oyais l'camas des pourchiaux,
Qui n'avaient d'ouvri l's'us des parques.

J'véyais l'baté des paissonniers,
De biaux garçons atou leux barbes;
Pour qu'nous puissions tous en mangier
I' ramassaient macré et crabes.

J'véyais les tas par les courtis,
Et les gardins couverts de pommes,
Je n'trouvait personnes évillis,
I' dormaient tous de si bouans sommes.

J'vis la lune qui s'en fut s'couchié,
L'soleil se l'vai la matinaïe,
Et ma maison j'men fu r'trachié
Pour vé si ma femme était l'vaïe.

Et j'lis conti tout m'en tragé,
Tandis qu'all 'tait bien endormie,
J'avais travailli, vuc bien d'qué,
Et j'avais joui un p'tit d'la vie.

Se fit, ma femme, t'as vu bien d'qué,
Mais a'n'peut pas me faire la vie,

J'étais men maître, et sans braguié,
J'pouvais faire une pu grande' folie.

The Morning, *1877*

One day I did like John Le Tocq
and got up before my usual time,
and dawdling like a beetle,
I fancied enjoying the fine morning.

In getting up so early
I left my wife fast asleep,
because since the weather was so fine
I fancied enjoying life a little.

Walking along the hedgerows and streams,
I heard the female blackbirds singing there,
while the male blackbirds were sitting
and replying to their courtesies.

The wren at the door of his little nest
almost made me laugh when he greeted me,
the sparrow was sitting on the thatch,
which his sweetheart was sitting on the eggs – and that I admire.

The fields were full of flowers,
white, red, yellow,
which would have cheered many hearts,
with the primroses and the anemones.

I saw our cows at rest,
chewing the cud and all laid out,
our folks were just coming to get them up
so as to have milk for the porridge.

I saw old Nick moving his calves,
and Rachel milking the cows,
and I heard the row the pigs made
who wanted the doors of the pigsties open.

I saw the fishermen's boats;
they're fine lads with their beards;

so we can all get to eat some,
they gather in mackerel and crabs.

I saw the haystacks round the fields,
and the orchards covered in apples,
I didn't find anyone up and about,
they were all sleeping like logs.

I saw the moon set
and the sun rise in the morning,
and back I went to my house
to see if my wife was up.

And I told her all about my journey,
while she'd been sound asleep,
I'd worked, seen a lot,
and I'd enjoyed life a little.

My wife said, "So, you've seen a lot."
But she can't scold me.

I was my own master, and not to boast,
I could do worse things.

Helier Le Cheminant

Le Viar Tchene, *c.1971* (Guernesiais)

Ya enn arbre dans la vallaï, j'lai counnaise toute ma vie,
Enn demeure pour tout mouisson – du grosbec a la pie;
Les pigeons vont y juquer, y sie carchule bian saeur
Dans le tchene dans la vallaï au cotaï d'labeurvair.

Ch'tai enn abri dans l'hivar quand le vent était grand
Ou s'la neis avait t'chais et que tout était blianc.
Les aut'e arbres étais nue dauve leu fieilles toutes quiergies
Mais les branques du viar t'chaine en 'tais acore chergies.

Dans bian des squalles d'orage nous a trouvai d'l'abri,
Et d'es chaleur d'l'étaï tus nous a protegi.
Man viar granpere sie couochait le Daimanche a dormi
Comme sans pere l'avait fait pour des annaïes d'vant li.

Nous ramasser tes tchainaux, nous l's'avait a ponraïe,
Et les pourchiaux d'man granpere l'sont mangit pour d's'annaïe;
Nous y pendit enn shaullatte – nous y'a rit, nous y'a jouaï;
Nous y'a chantaï et plleuraï, sous le tchaine dans le praï.

Viar tchaine, dauve tes branques étendues tout en rond,
Nous tai grimper souvent quand nous était garçons;
Tu nous muchais d'es filles quand nous n'les voulait pas,
Ou nous d'jetais les baissier ou les t'ni dans nos bras.

Les grosses tampete d'hivar ont souvent éprouvaï
Dauve tout changement de vent a te t'chulbutaï;
Mais de tous leux efforts tu peut bian te moquer
Car tes rachines sont fonsaïe dans le choeur du rocher.

Tout autour, y'a des changements et l'passage des annaïes
Transforme t'n'environement, ches la ta destinaïe;
Mais dans t'n'orgueul immense, et dans t'n'independance
T'ignore toutes les saisons, et les temps et les change.

The Old Oak Tree, *c.1971*

There's a tree in the valley, I've known it all of my life,
a dwelling place for all kinds of birds – from sparrows to magpies;
pigeons go and perch there, they feel completely safe
in the oak tree in the valley alongside the watering trough.

It was a shelter during the winter when the wind was strong
or if the snow had fallen and all was white.
The other trees were bare with the removal of all their leaves
but the branches of the old oak tree were still weighed down with them.

During many thundery showers we found shelter there,
and from the heat of the summer you protected us.
My old Grandfather would lie down and sleep there on Sundays
like his father had done for years before him.

We gathered your acorns, by the basketful,
and my Grandfather's pigs ate them for years;
we hung a swing from it – we laughed, we played;
we sang and cried, there under the the oak tree in the meadow.

Old oak tree with your branches stretching out all around,
we often used to climb up you when we were boys;
you used to hide us from girls when we didn't want them,
or you used to watch us when we kissed them and held them in our arms.

The big winter storms have often tried,
no matter in which direction the wind was blowing, to uproot you;
but you can mock all their efforts
because your roots are deep in the heart of the rock.

All around there's change and the passing years
transform your environment – that's your destiny;
but with your great pride, and independence
you ignore all the seasons and times and changes.

Folks and Families

Relationships and families are universal themes. Whatever language or dialect, writers find inspiration in love and marriage, in the battles of the sexes, in conflicts between the generations, and in growing up and growing old.

We have seen that Métivier dubbed Robert Pipon Marett the 'Anacreon of Bachelors', a reference to this poem. For a deeply politically engaged reformer, few of Sir Robert's poems are political. This is one reason why they became so popular in mainland Normandy – without requiring any knowledge of Jersey's politics, government and institutions, the psychological portraits of domestic relationships could be understood as universal. His particular skill was in the handling of long poetic monologues which nevertheless manage to suggest the personalities and reactions of the non-speaking supporting cast. By the end of the poem from which this extract comes, the bachelor has shifted his position considerably on the question of marriage, and the reader can realise that the bachelor had been fooling himself at the beginning of the poem.

Sir Robert Pipon Marett ('Laelius')

From **Le Vier Garçon,** *1849* **(Jèrriais)**

> Qu'i' sont heureux, les viers garçons.
> I n'ont ni èfants ni maisons,
> Ni femm's à leux badrer la tête.
> Je dis pour mai, qu'i' faut êt' bête,
> Quand nou-z est libre et sans souci,
> De prendre une femm' pour vos plaigui.
> Je ne l'f'rai pon! – nennin! – nennin!
> Quand nou-z est ben, i' faut s'y tenin!

Non non! non non! je ne l'frai pon!
Je resterai bouan vier garçon:

Quand nou-z est comm' je sis à-ch'teu,
Assis à s'n aise auprès du feu,
Fumant sa pipe à san tout-seu':
Dites-mai! n'y fait y pon millieu',
Que d'avé matée endrait sai,
Une femme, ufutche à vos gronner!
Et d's èfants, par dessu' l'marchi.
A vos assommer de leux brit!

Oh! oui, oui, oui: qu'ou n'm'en pâl' pon,
Je sis et serai vier garçon!

Ch'n'est pas, quand quiqu'fais nou s'ennyie.
Un' femm' vos tiendrait compagnie;
Et si l'ma' vent vos empoigni,
I' n'y a qu'les femm's pour vos soigni.
Et qui sairait ioù en trouver
Un' belle et bouonn', qui vos aim'rait,
Nou-z y pens'rait quiqu' petit: – mais,
Nou peut ben s'y brûler les daigts!

Le mus ch'est de n's'en mêler pon!
Et d'rester tranquill vier garçon!

Car ben des femm's sont comm' not' catte! –
Tout s'pass' de charm' tant qu'nou la flatte,
Ou vent se frotter contre vous,
En miaunant, et fait patt' de v'lous,
Que tout d'abord en viyant ch'la,
Nou dirait qu'ou n'peut faire de ma',
Mais qu'non la prenne à la r'bours pé,
Ou sort ses griff's pour vos grimer.

Le pus seû', ch'est de n's'y fier pon!
Pour mai je reste vier garçon!

(...)

Si n'fallait qu'prendre un' femme au mains!
Mais ch'est l's aviers! V'là chen que j'crains!

J'vais siez not' frère de temps en temps.
Ch'est là que j'vai chen qu'ch'est qu'd'èfants!
Il en a une raccachie!
Quand i' sont touos ennemble, i crient
Et font leux sabbat que de vrai,
Nou n'en a que d'en raffoler!

Quand j'vai ditai, je m'dis bon! bon!
Ah! que j'sis ben d'êt' vier garçon!

Ocquo s'i' restaient tréjous p'tits!
Nou-z aime assez à ouir leur d'vis,
Et ch'est fort amusant que d'vais
Les drols de tricks qu'i' font parfais,
Mais dès qu'un co' ils ont grandi,
Nou' n'peut pus, dam! s'en arrangi;
Ils us'eraient jusqu'au fé des reues,
Et faut êt' tréjous souotre ieux.

I vaut ben mus n'en avé pon!
Et vivre en paix comme vier garçon!

From **The Bachelor,** *1849*

How happy are bachelors.
They have neither children nor houses,
nor wives to do their heads in.
What I think is you'd have to be daft,
when you're free and without care,
to take a wife to plague you.
I won't do it! No! No!
When you're happy as you are, you should stay that way!

No, no! No, no! I won't do it!
I'll stay a good bachelor:

When you're like I am now,
sitting comfortably by the fire,
smoking your pipe all on your own:
tell me, isn't that better
than having a wife
standing opposite you, perhaps nagging you!

Or children into the bargain
overwhelming you with their noise!

Oh! yes, yes, yes: don't speak to me about it,
I am and will remain a bachelor!

Although, should you get fed up from time to time,
a wife would keep you company;
and were you to fall ill,
there's nothing like women for looking after you.
And if anyone knew where you might find
a good and beautiful one, who would love you,
you might well consider it – but
you can get your fingers burned that way!

The best thing is not to get mixed up with them!
And to remain a peaceful bachelor!

For many women are like our cat!
Everything goes well as long as you're stroking her,
she comes and rubs herself up against you,
miaowing and with velvet paws.
And seeing that to begin with,
you'd say that she couldn't do any harm.
But rub her up the wrong way,
and she gets her claws out to scratch you.

The safest thing is not to trust her!
I'm going to stay a bachelor!

(...)

At least if you could simply take a wife!
But there's the children! That's what I'm afraid of!
I visit my brother from time to time.
And that's where I see what children are like!
He's got a whole pack of them!
When they're together, they shout
and make such a din that really
it's enough to drive you mad!

When I see something like that, I say to myself: well!
Ah! how much better off I am as a bachelor!

And at least if they would just stay as babies!
It's nice enough listening to them babble,
and it's very amusing watching
the funny tricks they sometimes do,
but as soon as they've grown up a bit,
you can no longer keep them under control;
they'd wear you to the bone,
and you have to keep running after them.

You're much better off not having any!
And live in peace as a bachelor!

Tam Lenfestey ('T. L. des F.')

L'Amiti, *1883* (Guernesiais)

J'avais juraï d'restaï garçon,
A'l avait juraï d'restaï fille,
D'pensaï à s'mariaï j'en pouvion,
Et l'idée était dificile,
J'voulais d'é'vnit un grand esprit,
A voulait v'ni une antiquaire,
et j'cré que c'h'tai par amiti,
La fille était terjous à m'sière.

J'voulêment terjous restaï amis,
Mé, coumme David, et i'êtes utile,
L'bouan Jonathan, à surpassi,
Surpassant l'amiti d'la fille.
Atout la joie, a tout l'chagrin,
J'mêlêment terjous notr' amiti,
Et si j'étaiment à quique festin,
Si j'la r'gardais, v'nait un souri.

Nous s'pourmenait par sus les monts,
Et c'h'tai terjous par amiti,
Nous s'pourmenait par les valons,
Et c'h'tai terjous pour du plaisi,
J't'trachais des flleurs, des papillons,
Pour v'ni auteur, et faire un livre,
Et sa veillait de vieilles maisons
Un antiquaire à voulait suivre.

Jamais d'amour à n'me pâlaï,
A'l'tai pourtànt une jolie fille,
J'n'avais pas l'coeur de l'i faire lai
A m'était terjous si docile.
Mais i fallit bientôt s'quittaï,
Pour sa maison, mé, pour la ville,
J'navais quâzi que d'en pleuraï,
A i'elle les plleurs étaient facile.

J'devais bientôt passai la mair
Et m'en allaï à une autre île,
Et si j'avais le coeur amaïr,
J'avais du r'grèt d'quittaï la fille.
Et c'h'tai terjous par amiti,
et à quique'uns, v'la qu'ès utile,
A quànd nou' a un p'ti d'esprit
Nou s'en aime un par dessus mille.

I faut don s'talle s'en't'dire adi,
Et les regrès s'ront inutiles,
Tu t'en vas pour un aute pays,
T'y verras sans doute des filles.
Ses 'iers rencontrirent les miens,
I s'trouvirent bientôt coumme l'huile,
C'h'tai pour men coeur des aliments,
Pour ne jamais quittaï la fille.

Et j'fis chut que j'n'avais fait d'vànt,
I faut vou' l'dire, là, j'la baisi,
Et j'n'étais pas malecantànt,
Dans bien p'ti d'temps j'fus sen mari.
N'vou vantaï pas d'restaï garçon;
N'vou vantaï pas de restaï fille;
A' i restaï tous n'ont pas l'don,
Et à s'mariaï nou' s'rend utile.

Friendship, *1883*

I had sworn that I would remain a bachelor,
she had sworn to remain a spinster,
we couldn't think of getting married
and the very idea was difficult,
I wanted to become a great thinker,

she wanted to become an antiquarian
and I think that it was through friendship,
the girl always followed me.

We wanted to always remain friends,
I, like David, to be useful to her,
surpassing the good Jonathan,
surpassing the friendship of the girl.
With joy, with sorrow,
we always mixed our friendship,
and if we were at some party,
if I looked at her, a smile came to my lips.

We walked together over the hills,
and it was always in friendship,
we walked through the valleys,
and it was always for pleasure,
I looked for flowers, butterflies,
to become an author, and write a book,
and she looked out for old houses;
an antiquarian she wanted to be.

She never spoke to me of love,
and yet she was a pretty girl,
I didn't have the heart to take advantage of her,
she was always so gentle with me.
but soon we had to go our separate ways,
for her house, and me, for town,
I almost felt like crying,
tears came easily to her.

I was soon to go overseas
and to go to another isle,
and if I had an embittered heart,
I was sorry to leave the girl.
And it was always through friendship,
and for some, that is good enough,
when you have some intelligence
you love one above a thousand.

We must, said she, say farewell,
and regrets will be of no use,
you are going to another country,

there you will probably see girls.
Her eyes met mine,
they soon melted into tranquility,
which fuelled my heart's desire
to never leave the girl.

I did what I had never done before,
I must tell you, there, I kissed her,
and I did it without any sinister intent,
in a short time I was her husband.
Don't brag about remaining a bachelor;
don't brag about remaining a spinster;
not everyone has the gift to stay that way,
and by marrying we find a purpose in life.

Louisa Lane Clarke

From The Island of Alderney... being a companion and guide for the traveller, *1851*

A True Love Tale

I was not able, when in Alderney, to coax a single fairy-tale or ghost-story out of the old women there; but I did hear one simple tale of true love, and I saw the lovers, after twenty years of married life, still happy, – and what I heard I will tell, only changing their names.

"Pierre Nomis was an only son. The house wherein he was born was his heritage – the farm he tilled for a widowed mother was her own; they were well to do in the world, and he was considered the best match in Alderney. Pierre was a handsome boy, too, and steady enough, excepting a flirting propensity which threatened his mother with a daughter-in-law from every family in town, which had a pretty sisterhood.

"Sunday after Sunday Pierre was in the old Church-porch, choosing the damsel he would that day make happy by his company, and every Sunday he changed his love as he changed the flower at his button-hole. Pierre was a decided flirt. Yet Pierre has a heart, and the heart was not as free as the light laugh and the rattling tongue might choose to tell.

"There was another widow in the good town of Alderney, poorer than Mrs. Nomis, but as happy in the possession of a good child – an only daughter, who lived with her and worked for her. She was a bright, merry-hearted girl – not beautiful, and yet very beautiful; for the smile of a sweet temper and the clear light of truthfulness lit up her countenance, and made it a refreshing and a winning face.

"Not with her did Pierre ever walk from the Church-porch. Betsy had been taught at the Mouriaux School, that the House of God was a holy place, and the Lord's Day a holy day, and that good words were meant to be remembered, and the teaching of her Church to be practised: so Betsy walked home at her mother's side, and had not much talk with any one. He would be a poor husbandman who, after sowing a field with good seed, took no pains to scare the wild and hungry birds from picking it all away; and little better than a madman he, who, futhermore, turned in his own barn-door fowls to undo the work of his own hands. Yet this is the Sunday work of those who, gossiping and chattering in the stream of church-goers, soon pick away all good from their own and their bearers' hearts.

"Pierre did not venture to walk home with Betsy; but they knew each other well, and many a time by the full-moon's light had Pierre filled Betsy's basket on the Braye Sands *à la pêque du lançon*, or gathered a dish of *'fllies' à basse eau* for Widow Houguez. A quiet chat over the pig-sty when Betsy had given the evening meal – a gossip in the winter nights when the *quaipeaux* fire was bright, and the mother and daughter knitted under the 'crasset'. This Pierre had done for many a month, and told his real love many a time before his mother heard that, flirt as he might with others, her son meant to give her Betsy Houguez for a daughter.

This poem was originally published in the columns of Robert Pipon Marett's newspaper *La Patrie* in 1849. Having been quoted by François-Victor Hugo in his *La Normandie inconnue*, this became the most widely admired of Robert Pipon Marett's poems.

Robert Pipon Marett ('Laelius')

From La Fille Malade, *1849* (Jèrriais)

Vos vlà, vaisine, à vos prom'ner,
Ch'est miracle' qué d'vos rencontrer!
Nou n'vos trouv' jamais par les rues,
Comme est qu'i s'fait qu' non n'vos vait pus?
– Ah! chest qu' dépis qué ma Nancy
Est si pouôr'ment, j'n'ai peu sorti:
Quand ou m'aidiait ch'tait ben ocquo,
Mais à ch't'eu, tout mé cheait sus l'co!
Mon dou'! mon doue! ah! la! la! la!
Et qu'est donc qu'ou mé contez-là!

Et qu'est qu'oulle a, chut' fill? – Hélah!
Pour dire lé vrai jé né l'sais pas.
Les docteurs ne peuv'nt l'expliqui,
I'li ont donné un tas dé qui,
Et boutillie sus boutillie,

Pourtant ou' n'en chang' pon un' mie!
Mais pustôt ou n'fait qu'empiéri,
Qué j'en ai un divers souci.
Oh! ché n' s'ra ren! bah! bah! bah! bah!
Les jeun's fill's ne meur'nt pas comm' chla!

Ou savez combain oull' 'tait guaie,
Ou d'visait tant, qu'la dernié fais
Qu'ou vintes, et qu'ou la vîtes siez nous,
Ou dites en riant, vos en rapp'l'-ous'?
"Chett'-là, ben seû' n'a pas l' filet!"
Chu coup ou n'diriez pus ditait;
Tout l'long du temps, ou n'ouvre pon
La bouoch', qué pour dire oui ou non!
– Ah! qu'est qu'ou dites! – Oh la! la! la!
I faut qu'oulle ait changi pour chla!

Aut'fais ch'tait un' bouonn gross' hardelle,
Fraîch' comme un' rose et aussi belle!
Ach't'eu ch' n'est pus qu'un' pouôr' pâl' fache,
Faillie, et maigre comme un' hache.
Ma fé, ch'est pitié qué d'la vais!
Jé n'sais pon qui miracle ch'est!
Nou dirait qu'ou n'a pus d'idée!
Jé crai qu'oulle est enchorchelée!
– Ah! qui dommage! Ah! lai! lai! lai!
Et qu'érait jamais creu d'itai!

(...)

Ou dans d'aut' temps, oulle ira p'têtre,
Sé mâter d'but dévant la f'nêtre,
R'gardant la mé, pour pus d'un' heure.
Et pis ch'est récommanche et plieure!
Ov ch'la ou n'fait pour dire, espèce
De chose, – mais enfin, jé la laisse,
Car s'ou travaill' ch'est pière ocquo,
Oulle est bain seue dé faire quiqu' dro!
Est-i pôssible! et la! la! la!
Qui drôle de maladie qué chla!
Au sé, dès qu'i né fait pus jeu'
Ou va s'pliaichi tout près du feu,
Et là, accliouquie dans un coin,

San menton app'yé sus sa main,
Ou reste ofut-che tout l'long du sé,
A r'garder les tisons brûler,
Sans pâler, ou sans bouogi pus,
Qué si ou'll' 'tait un imâ'nue.
– Ah qu'il état! – man père bénin!
Qué tout chenna m'fait du chagrin!

(...)

– Et qu' est-che qué ch'est? – Ècoutez-mé;
Quand John s'ra r'venu dé la mé
Qu'i li accate un' bell' bague en or,
(I' l' f'ra, ch'est un' bouon sorte d'corps!)
Pis qu'un biau matin à l'église,
Bras d'ssus bras d'ssous, i la condise,
Et là, i n'a qu'à l'y couler,
Dévant l'Ministr' chut' bague au daigt!
– Hô! ho! ho! ho! – Hah! ha! ha! ha!
Ou verrais qu'chla la r'guérira.

A Girlish malady, *1849*

"There you are, neighbour, out for a walk,
what luck bumping into you!
We never meet you in the streets,
how is it that we no longer see you?"
"Ah? That'll be since my Nancy
has been so poorly, I haven't been able to go out:
When she was helping me, everything was still fine,
but now, everything falls to me"
"My goodness! my goodness, ah! la! la!
What sort of story is that?"

"And what's the matter with that girl?" – "Alas!
To tell you the truth, I don't know.
The doctors can't explain it,
They've given her loads of stuff,
bottle after bottle of it.
But it doesn't produce the slightest change in her!
Except she seems to get worse,
so much so that I'm very worried."

"Oh, it's nothing! Pah!
Young girls don't die just like that!"

"You know how cheerful she used to be,
how she used to chatter so much, that the last time
you came and saw her at our home,
you said laughingly, do you remember?
"She's got the gift of the gab, that one!"
But you wouldn't say that now;
all day long, she'll only open
her mouth to say yes or no!"
"Ah! You don't say! – Oh, dear!
She must really have changed!"

"She used to be a lovely buxom girl,
fresh as a daisy and as lovely!
Now her poor face is pale,
and miserable and thin.
Goodness, it's pitiful to look at her!
I simply have now idea what the matter can be!
Anyone would say that she's out of her mind!
I think she's been bewitched!"
"Ah, what a pity. Ah, me!
I'd never have believed it possible!"

(...)

"Or sometimes she might go
and stand at the window,
looking at the sea for more than an hour.
And then she starts up again crying.
You can't get her to do anything to speak of –
I leave her to it.
Because if she's working away it's even worse,
she's sure to have some mishap!"
"Really? Dearie me!
What a strange illness she's got!"

"In the evening, as soon as the sun goes down,
she settles down by the fire,
and there, huddled in a corner
with her chin resting on her hand,
she may spend the whole evening

watching the embers burn,
without speaking, and without moving,
as though she were an apparition."
"Oh, what a state she's in! Oh dear!
I'm very sorry to hear all this!"

(...)

"And so, what is it?" – "Listen to me;
when John gets back from the sea,
get him to buy her a beautiful gold ring
(he'll do that, he's a good lad!)
Then one fine morning,
let him lead her, arm in arm, to Church,
and there, all he'll have to do is slip
the ring on her finger in front of the priest!
Ho ho! Ha ha!
You'll see that that will cure her!"

George Métivier

Content dans l'condan, *1867* (Guernesiais)

Vì-t-en, joli coeur, et vite!
L'mien bat fort, dès que j'te vé;
N'appèrhende rien, ma p'tite,
Et met ta maïn où tu sai!

Que t'n habit seit d'v'louss ou d'laïne,
Si tu m'pllais, ah! ch'est tout ùn;
Jeur et nhiet, tu s'ras ma Raïne,
Au coin de m'n âtre et sus l'dùn.

Si ch'est d'même, ill'y'a d'qué bouidre,
Sus l'terpid, matìn et ser,
S'i' n'h'y'a pas d'vìn, ll'y'a du cidre,
S'nou n'gagne rien, qui'est' qu'nou perd?

Not' paradis s'ra la terre,
Sàns faire un p'tit pas, j'y s'ron,
Et jour aprés jour, ma chère,
S'envol'ra coumme un mouisson.

D'bel et d'laid, où nou gabarre,
Matìn et ser, ill y'en a,
Mais s'nou-s est daeux, l'mal se chare,
Et coumme i vient, i s'en va.

Quànd viendra Noué, r'viendra Paque,
Belle, en airon-ju du sguìn?
L'tronquet, j'lo, m'est avis, craque,
J'o les glou-glou-glous du vìn.

Contentment in the cottage, *1867*

Come here, my sweet, and quick!
My heart starts to pound, when I catch sight of you;
Don't be scared at all, little one,
and put your hand you know where!

Whether you're dressed in velvet or wool,
if I fancy you, ah! it's all the same to me;
day and night, you'll be my Queen,
in the corner of my hearth and on the eiderdown.

If that's the way it is, there'll be something on the boil,
on the trivet, morning and evening,
if there's no wine, there'll be cider,
if there's nothing to gain, what can you lose?

Our heaven will be the earth,
no need to take the smallest step, and there we'll be,
and day after day, my darling,
will fly like a bird.

There's good and ill, wherever you trudge,
morning and evening, there it is,
but if we're both together, trouble is shared,
and as it comes, so it goes.

When Christmas comes, and Easter comes round again,
my beauty, how much fun shall we have?
I think I can hear the log crackling,
I can hear the glug-glug-glug of the wine.

The growth of tourism in the nineteenth century and the presence of radical political exiles meant that the inhabitants of the Islands came into greater contact with advanced social ideas and daring fashions than in many conservative rural environments elsewhere. We have seen how Elie described the easygoing way of dressing young English female tourists had in Sark. Women's emancipation has been among the social themes covered by writers from the Islands – a theme that could take some coverage, given the complicated and incremental nature of the reforms of the franchises.

Single Jerseywomen over 20 got the right to vote in parochial elections in 1919, the same year that Jerseywomen over the age of 30 and wives of rate-paying husbands got the right to vote in public elections. Jerseywomen were given the right to stand for election to the States in 1924 – it was not, however, until 1948 that Ivy Forster (née Le Druillenec) became the first woman to win election to the legislature. She was honoured as a British Hero of the Holocaust in 2010 for her resistance efforts during the German Occupation. Voting age in Jersey was equalised for men and women in 1945.

In Guernsey in 1891, unmarried women, widows, and women separated from their husbands, gained the right to vote, if ratepayers, in assemblies of heads of households. This meant, as they elected Douzeniers, they participated in indirect elections for members of the States of Guernsey. When directly-elected People's Deputies were added to the legislature in 1899, the same categories of women formed part of the electorate. In 1920, all Guernseywomen over the age of 30 were added to the electorate. The first woman, Marie Randall, won election to the States as a Deputy in 1924. Voting age was equalised at 20 in 1938, with the law coming into effect in 1939, just before war and occupation suspended normal politics.

The political advance of Guernsey's womenfolk over their Jersey counterparts in the late nineteenth century seemed an inevitable marker for future progress, as this extract from a letter published in *La Nouvelle Chronique de Jersey* in November 1891 shows. Naturally enough, progressive sentiment does not preclude a traditional dig at those from the other Island. The pseudonymous correspondent 'Couosine Rachel' is apparently a Jerseywoman writing from Guernsey.

'Couosine Rachel'
From Le Vote des Femmes, *1891* (Jèrriais)

J'fus agriabliément surprinse l'aute jour, en liaisant une gazette dé Guernsi, d'vais que la Cour avé ne loi par lachelle les fammes de chu païs là d'vais avé voië dé votai dans les assembliaies, et "d'y bailli d'lus becque," comme nou dit, ah, mais! chesque les affaithes s'en vont marchi!! j'té promès bein, y pouorront p'tête avé du gaz ashteu pour éclairith lus ville; et gardan lus écoles ouertes, à sel fin que touos les pouores p'tits mousses ne saient pon à couorre les rues, et les pouorres maîtres et maitrîsses à cherchi lus pain! S'en va yavé d'la r'forme sans aucune doute, et

Guernsi, chi, comme nou dit, est chent ans en arrièthe de Jerri, s'en va brilli comme une planette parmi les autres îlots d'Manche, car quant toutes chais femmes s'mettront à d'visé dans les assembliaies, chachunne à sans tou, car fâut qu'tout sai fait en raigle; forche essai ès hommes de cédai, jamais lus pouorront y résistai, car comme tu sai, par expérience, les fammes ont tréjours raison et d'même y sont tréjous dans la majorité.

From The Women's Vote, *1891*

I was pleasantly surprised the other day while reading a Guernsey newspaper, to see that the Court had passed a law by which the women of that country were to be able to vote in assemblies, and to "wag their tongues" there, as they say. Well, that'll get things moving! I tell you, they might soon have gaslight now in town, and keep their schools open so the poor little children won't be running round the streets, and the poor schoolmasters and schoolmistresses can earn a crust! There's no doubt reform will come, and Guernsey, which is, so it's said, a hundred years behind Jersey, will shine like a planet among the other Channel Islands, for when all those women get to talking in the assemblies, each in her turn, because everything will have to be done according to the rules: the men will be forced to give way, and they'll never be able to resist, for as you know from experience women are always in the right and what's more they're always in the majority.

Sark's feudal system meant that women had always been able to wield political influence through property rights. The position of Dame of Sark could be acquired either by inheritance or by purchase. Unmarried women and widows had never been excluded from taking their seats in Chief Pleas, although until 1974 a married woman was represented by her husband. When elected People's Deputies were added to Chief Pleas in 1922, women got the vote along with the menfolk.

In Alderney, since elections for Jurats were based on property qualifications, single women and widows could historically vote, as ratepayers, from the age of 21. When People's Deputies were added to the States of Alderney in 1923, Alderneywomen over the age of 21 got the vote along with men over the age of 20. Voting age was equalised at 20 in 1948.

This poem by Jean Picot, written at the beginning of the twentieth century, foresees a century of progress in women's lives. The intention is good-natured satire, but the predictions turned out to be not so exaggerated as readers at the time might have believed. However, househusbands are not, so far at least, the oppressed victims portrayed.

Jean Picot ('J. P.')

La femme du temps à v'nin (New Woman), *1903* (Jèrriais)

La femme du temps à v'nin? jé crait qu'oull'est desja v'nue,
Y'm semble dé l'aver veue sé proumm'ner dans la rue,
En casaque, rond chapé, haute djènne, et jutchie en braies,
Et dé bein courtes étout, pour montrer ses mollets;
Un bâton à la main et fumant sa cigarette,
Faisant les piétons filer dévant sa bicyclette,
Sé fichant bein des hoummes, car ou compte qu'acht'eu
L'houmme a y'ieu san temps – chest Madame qu'est Moussieu!

La femme du temps à v'nin – ou touôn'ra tout à l'envers,
Ché s'ra au pouôre medjiant d'houmme à soigni des avers:
Madame s'en ira à san Club, on bein à s'en' office –
Ou s'ra Avocat, Docteu', Captainne dans la Milice!
Et n'ou la verra peut-être occuo siègi dans l's Etats!
Des soins du maînage l'houmme êtha l'embarras –
Madame sé proummén'ra – l'y les manches ertroussèes.
S'ra à nierpionner lé grais – ou a scrobber l's allées!...

La femme du temps à v'nin – ou né s'ra pus la servante
Ni l'escliave dé l'houmme – et dèsjà ou sé vante
Qu'ou lé laiss'ra ... netti les chambres et faire les lyits,
Coûtchi toute la vitaille – faire dé la pâtissh'rie –
Vaire maîme soigni du baby – dé l'y dounner lé chuchot,
Et s'y'l a la coqueluche dé l'stoffer dé syrop –
Et pis occuo ov tout san tripot dé tchuisinne
Ou l'y laiss'ra ses bottes, pour qu'y l's y biâtchinne!

La femme du temps à v'nin – coumm'est qu'ou f'ra l'amour?
Bein seûre coumme tout aut'chose, ché s'ra à l'arbours
Si oull' a idée sus tchiq' houmme, ou né perdra pon san temps
A lé catliner ou à lé fêter – pas dé longs engagements:
Tchiq' biau matin y's'verra empoigni par lé collet
Entraînè à l'Eglyise et bein vite mariè –
Et dévant qu'y piesse crier: "Au sécours! aidjis-mé!"
Oull' rammen'ra dé là ov baggue au daigt! –

La femme du temps à v'nin – ou né f'ra pas dé teurs ni dé cris
Quand ou verra couôrre sus lé plianchais unn' pétite souôris:
Ché s'ra l'houmme, tchi, tout peûreux, minsèrable
Sé grimp'ra sus unn' tchaise ou bein sus la table! –

Ou copp'ra ses guéveux touôs courts, qui saient niers, rouôges, ou bruns
Et – quoiqu' j'ai d'la peinne à l'craithe – j'ai ouï dire – à tchiqs'-uns
Qu'ou s'frottra dé l'onguent lé long des joes et souôs lé nèz
Pour tâchi d'y faire craître – dé chin qu'ou savèz! –

La femme du temps à v'nin – ou soign'ra dès Elections –
L'houmme s'ra à rempiéter les caûches, à couôtre des boutons –
Era t'y seulement droit dé voter? ma fingre, jé n'lé sais pas –
Car les femmes s'ront tout: eslecteurs, candidats;
Et y dischut'ront dans les Gâzettes, et sus la piatteforme,
Pas modes ni faishons, mais lé Progrès, lé Réforme!
Et ché s'ra tout fait en Angliais – car ov' changement pareil
L'Angliais s'ra, bein seûre, not' langue officielle!...

La femme du temps à v'nin – coumment faire san pourtrait?
Pour l'houmme, chose certaine, ou n'éra pus d'attrait –
Mais jé n'en dirait pas pus long – y'l'est temps qué j'en finisse,
J'aime mûs la femme d'acht'eu ov tout sen caprice:
Et y faût y'ien allouer tchiq' mio – mais tout en raison:
Si ou veurt gâgni tchiq' sous qué ché sait pour la maison,
Pour lé comfort et lé bein-être du sexe maschulin,
Qu'étha assez dé minséthe, allez, ov la femme du temps à v'nin!

The woman of the future (New Woman), *1903*

The woman of the future? I think she's already here.
I think I've seen her walking down the street,
in a jacket, a round hat, high collar, and haughty in trousers,
very short ones at that, to show off her calves;
a cane in her hand and smoking her cigarette,
making pedestrians flee before her bicycle,
not caring about men, because it is considered today
that man has had his day – it's Madam who's the gentleman!

The woman of the future – she'll turn everything upside-down,
it'll be for the poor fool of a man to look after the children:
Madam will go off to her club, or to her office –
she'll be an advocate, a doctor, a captain in the Militia!
And we might even yet see her sitting in the States!
The man will have the trouble of housework –
Madam will stroll about – he'll have his sleeves rolled up,
blackleading the grate – or scrubbing the hallways!

The woman of the future – she'll no longer be the maid
or the slave of her husband – and she's already boasting
that she'll leave him... to clean the bedrooms and make the beds,
cook all the food, make pastry,
even look after the baby, indeed, – give him his dummy,
and, if he has whooping-cough, stuff syrup down him –
and then with all the to-do in the kitchen he has,
she'll leave him her boots, so he can polish them!

The woman of the future – how will she make love?
Naturally enough, like everything else, it'll all be backwards.
If she takes a fancy to some man, she won't waste time
babying him or making a fuss of him – no long engagements:
some fine morning he'll find himself grabbed by the collar
and dragged to church and very quickly married –
and before he can cry out: "Help! Help me!"
She'll bring him back with a ring on his finger!

The woman of the future – she won't put on a performance or scream
when she sees a little mouse run across the floor:
it'll be the man, who, trembling with fear and misery,
will climb up on a chair or even onto the table!
She'll cut her hair short, whether it's black, red or brunette,
and, although I have trouble believing it, I've heard, so some say,
that she'll rub ointment on her cheeks and on her top lip
so as to try and grow – you know what!

The woman of the future – she'll take care of elections –
the man will be darning socks, sewing on buttons –
will he even have the vote? Gracious, I don't know –
because it'll be all women: voters, candidates;
and they'll be discussing in the newspapers and on the platforms,
not fashion, but Progress and Reform!
And it'll all be done in English – because with such a change
English will surely become our official language!

The woman of the future – how can one draw a picture of her?
But I won't go on – it's time for me to finish.
I prefer the woman of the present day with all her whims,
and you've got to allow her that, a bit – but within reason:
if she wants to earn some money, let it be for the household,
for the comfort and wellbeing of the masculine sex,
who'll have enough on their plate with the woman of the future!

George F. Le Feuvre ('George d'La Forge')
La femme en gângne!, *1984* (Jèrriais)

San Antonio, Texas, USA
Lé 28 dé janvyi, 1984.

Moussieu l'Rédacteu,

J'm'èrsouveins qué quand eune femme fut êlue comme Député ès États pour la preunmié fais (ch'tait-i' pon Madanme Ivy Forster, eune St Ouënnaise, née Le Druillenec?), ma lettre au Rédacteu d'chu temps-là faîsait à saver mes doutes au sujet d'la sagesse d'aver des femmes dans la Chambre Législative. Sans doute, ieune toute seule né pouvait pon faithe grand' difféthence, mais nombreuses es'sait aut' affaithe. I' m'sembliait les vaie s'entreèrgarder d'un yi d'travèrs et compathaître habits et chapieaux et oublier pourtchi tch'il' 'taient là. Un tas dg'ieau a pâssé par La Corbiéthe dépis qu' j'avais d's idées d'même, et si j'm'en r'souveins, Madanme Forster fut sieue par Député Mdlle. Enid Le Feuvre (M.B.E. à ch't heu), tchi s'fît respecter comme championne des pauvres et înforteunés. V'là tchi m'faîsait penser tch'il 'tait temps pour mé dé m'rêvilyi et rêaliser qu'les temps avaient changi et tch'i' fallait s'y'accouôteunmer.

Sans doute, un vyi comme mé n'peut pon oublier l'vièr temps et les vièrs ditons. Par exempl'ye, y'en a iun tchi nouos dit qué "Femme tchi caqu'te et poule tchi pond, font du brit dans les maîsons." Un aut' nouos dit qué "Ch'est tréjous par les femmes qué l'brit veint." Et sachant tch'i' y'a tréjous d'la caqu'téthie dans L's États, j'avais l'impression qué ch'tait mal à propos d'y ajouôter des femmes!

Mais j'avais tort, et j'l'adveins bein. Ma m'mèe et ma manman vivaient à l'êpoque qu'eune femme 'tait ordgilleuse d'êt' femme dé mênage et maitrêsse d'la maîson, l'souôtchein dé s'n homme et l'adouothée d'ses êfants. Lé pâssage du temps n'a pon changi m'n idée qué v'là tch'est l'idéal, et heutheusement tch'i' y'en a acouo d'même en Jèrri et tchiques-eunes ichîn en Améthique. J'en ai veu la preuve, à man profit, en Jèrri.

Ichîn, quâsi toutes les femmes travâlent comme les hommes, dans l's offices et dans l'mêtchi. Lé rêsultat en est qué l's êfants, touos seurs quand i' r'veinnent dé l'êcole, né savent pon tchi faithe dé lus pieaux et v'là tchi mène au mêché. Et si ch'-tait pas d'même et les femmes restaient à souangni d'lus mênages comme dans l'temps pâssé, i' n'y êthait pon tant d'hommes sans travas par les c'mîns.

J'viyais dans la gâzette du 5 dé janvyi tch'i' y'avait eune femme tchi voulait êt' Offici d'Connêtabl'ye dans ieune des pâraisses, et dans la cheinne du 12 dé janvyi, qué j'veins d'èrchéver, y'en a ieune tch'aspithe à êt' Connêtabl'ye dé sa pâraisse. Et j'en avons ieune sus l'Banc d'Justice dans la Cour Rouôyale. V'là tchi c'menche à m'dithe qué dans l'temps à v'nîn, en Jèrri comme en Améthique, les femmes éthont prîns du pid et l's hommes es'sont sans travas!

Ch'est la même turlute au Cannada. Eune lettre èrchue dé man n'veu Sydney d'Ottawa m'dit tch'i' pathaît y'aver l'intention d'nommer Jeanne Sauvé (actuellement "Speaker" d'la Chambre Cannadgienne des Communes) Gouvèrneur-Général du Cannada. Et i' n'faut pon oublier qu' j'avons eune illustre deuxième Lîsabé sus l'trône dé l'Angliétèrre, eune danme tch'est Preunmié Minnistre, et eune aut' tch'est "Lord Mayor" d'Londres, toutes en même temps, et qué ch'est ches danmes méthitouaithes tchi sont à aîdgi à r'mett' l'Angliétèrre, longtemps ravagie par des gouvèrnéments vîsionnaithes mais încapabl'yes, sus ses pids. Ch'est en tchi ch'est p't-êt tout pour lé mus et tch'i' faut s'attendre à un av'nîn adouochi par l'înfluence féminine. Et i' n'faut pon oublier étout l'histouaithe illustre et l'êcraîssance dé l'Angliétèrre souos l'règne dé la preunmié Lîsabé, et la grandeu d'l'Empire Britannique souos l'règne dé Victoria.

Mais j'mé d'mande tchi pliaîsi qu'eune femme peut trouver comme Offici d'Connêtabl'ye dans la Police Honorifique ches jours tch'i' y'a tant d'travas qué mêmes les Vîngt'nièrs et Officièrs d'Connêtabl'ye sont appelés à toute heuthe au bésoin, et ch'n'est pon tout roses pour la police. Ch'tait difféthent l'temps pâssé. Y'avait si p'tit d'mauvaîtchi et d'crînme par les c'mîns qué ch'tait rare qu'un Chent'nyi eûsse bésoin d'aîgue.

I' m'sembl'ye m'érsouv'nîn qué ch'tait l'fanmeux Euripide, illustre poète Grec (480–405 avant J.C.), tchi nouos dît qué la pus précieuse possession d'l'homme est eune femme sŷmpathique. Et j'sis du même avis.

Enfîn, nou sait bein qu'les changements sont en ordre, et i' faut qu' les vièrs comme mé tchittent à gémi et rêver du temps pâssé et profiter du laîsi et abondances du temps actuel.

Women gain ground!, *1984*

San Antonio, Texas, USA
28th January 1984

Dear Mr. Editor,
I recall that when a women was elected to the States as a Deputy for the first time (wasn't it Mrs. Ivy Forster, a woman from Saint Ouen, née Le Druillenec?), my letter to the Editor at that time made known my doubts about the wisdom of having women in the Legislative Chamber. No doubt, one woman on her own could not make much difference, but if there were many of them, that would be another matter. I imagined seeing them looking askance at each other to compare clothes and hats and forgetting why they were there. There's been a lot of water under the bridge since I had such ideas, and if I remember, Mrs Forster was followed by Deputy Enid Le Feuvre (now an M.B.E.), who earned a reputation for championing the poor and those down on their luck. That is what made me think that it was time for me to wake up and realise that times had changed and that one had to get used to it.

Doubtless, an old man like me cannot forget the old days and the old sayings. For example, there is one that tells us that "A chattering woman and a laying hen make hubbub about the houses". Another tells us that "It is always women who are behind any trouble". And knowing that there is always chatter in the States, I had the impression that it would not be fitting to add women!

But I was wrong, and I have no problem admitting it. My mum and my grandma lived at a time when a woman was proud of being a housewife and mistress of her house, the helpmeet of her husband and the object of the affection of her children. The passage of time has not changed my opinion that that is the ideal, and luckily there are still some like that in Jersey and a few here in America. I've seen proof of it in Jersey, to my benefit.

Here, almost all women work like men do, in offices and in trades. The result is that the children, all on their own when they get back from school, are at a loose end and that leads to trouble. And if it was not like that and women stayed to look after their homes as in time past, there would not be so many unemployed men around the place.

I saw in the newspaper of 5th January that there was a woman who wanted to be a Constable's Officer in one of the parishes, and in the 12th January edition that I have just received, there is one who aspires to become Constable of her parish. And we have one on the Bench in the Royal Court. That is what sets me thinking that in the future, in Jersey as in America, women will have the upper hand and men will be out of a job!

It is the same old story in Canada. A letter I received from my nephew Sydney in Ottawa tells me that there seems to be the intention to appoint Jeanne Sauvé (currently Speaker of the Canadian House of Commons) as Governor-General of Canada. And one must not forget that we have an illustrious second Elizabeth on the throne of England, a lady who is Prime Minister, and another who is Lord Mayor of London, all at the same time, and it is these worthy ladies who are helping to put England, for so long ravaged by idealistic but incompetent governments, back on its feet. And one must not forget either the illustrious history and growth of England under the reign of the first Elizabeth, and the grandeur of the British Empire under the reign of Victoria.

But I wonder what enjoyment a woman can get out of being Constable's Officer in the Honorary Police nowadays when there is so much work that even Vingteniers and Constable's Officers are called out on duty at all hours, and it is no piece of cake for the police. It was different time past. There was so little misbehaviour and crime around that it was rare for a Centenier to require any assistance.

I seem to recall that it was the famous Euripides, the illustrious Greek poet (480–405 BC), who told us that a man's most precious possession is a sympathetic wife. And I agree with that.

In the end, one is aware that change must come, and old folk like me must leave off groaning and dreaming of time past and make the most of modern times and the leisure and plenty that come with them.

Although most of Philippe Le Sueur Mourant's stories about the Pain family were narrated in the character of Piteur Pain, his strait-laced wife Laizé and gormless daughter Lonore occasionally stepped forward to put their side of the story. The *Morning News*, as an English language newspaper, included coverage of events and politics in the United Kingdom; the French language newspapers tended also to include coverage of events and politics in France. At the date of this article, readers of the *Morning News* were reading about the Suffragette movement and the Prisoners (Temporary Discharge for Ill Health) Act 1913 passed in the UK (known as the Cat and Mouse Act). Lonore Pain, a young woman of extraordinary naïvety, has the situation explained to her by Samuel (another of Le Sueur Mourant's alter egos under whose name he wrote in French and Jèrriais in *La Chronique de Jersey*).

Philippe Le Sueur Mourant ('Bram Bilo', 'Piteur Pain' etc)

Lonore's little ways with Suffragettes, *1913* (Jèrriais)

Moussieu Samuel et mé, j'passîmes la séthée ensembye, l'aut' sé. Pépée 'tait hort a eunne reunion pour Ne pas Taxé la Biethe, et mémée a eunne Reunion pour Empèchi les Servantes d'avé des galants; et Moussieu Samuel avait promins a mémée d'resté m'aidji a dèsvié du vigonia pour faithe des cotillons ès négresses des pays cauds.

"May I smoke?" qué m'dit Moussieu Samuel. Et quand j'y'eut dit qu'j'aimais hardi l'odeu de p'tun, i' dèshalli un grand long cigare Amethitchin qu'avait couoté, qui m'dit, trente sous, et l'mint dans la carre de sa bouoche, la pointe en haut, coumme Moussieu Journeaux quand il est a jugi les bêtes a Moussieu Pérrée, et qu'les autres juges ne sont pon de s'n'avis.

Je d'visimes d'choses et d'autres: d'la Taxe sus l'Tée: du prix du beurre: du dernié sermon sus la condite des filles dans la rue d'drièthe: et d'eunne nouvelle race de poules qui pounnent des oeus carrées. Et pis j'nos minmes a pâslé des Suffragettes. Moussieu Samuel s'y counnait la d'sus. I' liét un tas d'gazettes; et i' counnait toutes les morgaches de chès femmes la coumme s'i' l's'avait veues.

Quand i' vint a m'dithe qu'y'en a qui d'pichent des ozennes de boutique, qui flianquent d'la booe sus des messieux, qui versent de l'encre dans les bouetes-a-let-tres, et qui brulent des maisons: j'n'en r'venais pas! Et pourtchi qu'chès souépinnes la font ditét Moussieu Samuel? que j'lis dis. 'Pas'-qué nou n'veurt pon les laissi voté dans l's'Assembliées d'Paraisse,' qui m'rèspounni.

J'n'en r'venais pas! de tout ch'que Moussieu Samuel me dit sus les Suffragettes. Des femmes qui passent lus temps a buchi tout, a marchi 'up-an-down' dans les rues en hurlant, a envié des pierres a travers les f'nètres et a faithe les chent coups partout!

Et pourtchi que l'Gouvernement n'les met pon en prison, chès dèsvergondées la? que j'dit: pourtchi q'nou n'les punit pon pour être a galvaudé les qu'mins, a la plieche d'être siez yeux a èspousté lus meubye? – ou a dèsvié du fi ov un naice jeunne houmme? que j'dit, en rappréchant ma tchaise de Moussieu Samuel.

"Toutes chès femmes là, ch'est des têtes cratchies, Miss Lonore, que s'fit Moussieu Samuel; et l'Gouvernement n'sait pon coumment s'y prendre pour les faithe porté r'pos! Ou pâslez d'les mettre en prison! Mais nou l's y met! Mais sitot enfreummées, les bitches r'fusent de mangi! Nous a bieau les mettre du fricot d'vant yeux: d'la soupe, d'la steak, du maq'thé, d'la caboche, du podin-d'riz! les hardelles n'touchent a rin, et s'laissent enhanné la faim putot que d'manji! L'Gouvernement a èsprouvé a lus engardjichounné d'la bouollie eunne illiéte, mais les suffragettes freumment lus bouoches, coud'pisent les docteurs, et donnent des talmouzes ès gardjiennes et èscopissent dans la fache de tout l'monde – n'y'a pas moyen d'lus faithe prendre de neurtuthe. Pour ne pas les vaie mouothi en prison, l'gouvernement les laisse couore au bu de quat' ou chinq jours – et i' se r'mettent a buchi tout coumme devant.

J'pâlimes oquo tchique temps la d'sus, et Moussieu Samuel (i' s'était rappréchi oquo pus près d'mé, pour dithe cheunna) me dit que l'Gouvernement 'tait si ennié d'lus farces, qui s'n'allait yavé un prix d'offert a tchi trouvthait moyen d'lus faithe porté r'pos. Samuel (il avait mins san bras autou d'mé pour êtr' pus près) me dit tchès qu'en criais, mé qu'étais fille de bouan sens, quand a les puni, ches "hunger strikers" la, qui s'motchaient des messieurs d'la Cour d'Angliéterre. J'lis promins d'y r'pensé en m'couochant (i' s'était mins a joué avec mes deigts) et que j'lis dithais pus tard.

J'y'ai r'pensé! Et ne v'chîn coumment j'm'y prendrais avec chés hardelles la! J'lus dithais coumme cheunchin. Ou r'fusez d'mangi! et quand nou vos entounne d'la pétuthe, ou vos plégnies ès gazettes que nou vos a grimmé la langue! Eh bin! J'nos n'allons èsprouvé aut'chose! J'nos n'allons continué a mettre tout plien d'tchi bon a mangi sus vot' tabye, persounne ne vos forchétha a en prendre; et si ou r'fusez d'manji, nou vos laisra couore au bu d'chinq jours!Ou pouorez vos n'allé tout drét hort de prison. Véthe! que j'lus dithais: ch'est d'même. Allouos en hort d'ichin! Mais, d'vant vos n'allé! et justement pour vos faithe r'souv'né d'nous, j'nos n'allons vos copé les ch'veux a ras d'la tète – et pis après j'la ras'ons! Ou sortithez d'prison sans avé 'té forchis d'manji, mais ov la tête nue coumme un jambon! Mais je n'vos f'thons pas eunne mie d'ma!

Ch'est d'même que j'vos les djéthithais, ches d'mouèzelles suffragettes. Et j'ai dans l'idée – j'sis d'mouèzelle me mème – qu'a ben près toutes aimthaient mus manji quat' r'pas par jour que d'se vaie eunne tète coumme un navet.
Miss Lonore Pain

Ellie's little ways with Suffragettes, *1913*

Mr Samuel and me, we spent the evening together the other evening. Dad was out at a meeting Against Putting Tax on Beer, and Mum at a meeting to Prevent Maids having boyfriends; and Mr Samuel had promised Mum to stay and help me wind some alpaca wool into skeins to make petticoats for negresses in hot countries.

"May I smoke?" Mr Samuel asked me. When I said that I really liked the smell of tobacco, he pulled out a great long American cigar that cost, so he told me, one-and-three, and he stuck it in the corner of his mouth, pointing upwards, like Mr Journeaux does when he's judging Mr Perrée's cattle, and the other judges don't agree with him.

We spoke about various things, the Tea Tax, the price of butter, the latest sermon on the way girls behave in King Street, and a new breed of hens that lay square eggs. And then we got to talking about Suffragettes. Mr Samuel knows something about all that. He reads a load of newspapers, and he knows all about what those women get up to as though he'd seen it himself.

When he got round to telling me that some of them smash shop windows, throw mud at gentlemen, pour ink into letter boxes, and burn down houses, I couldn't get over it! And why are those trollops doing that sort of thing, Mr Samuel? I asked him. "Because they don't want to let them vote in Parish Assemblies," he replied.

I couldn't get over everything that Mr Samuel told me about Suffragettes! Women who spend their time breaking everything, marching up and down the streets, shouting, and throwing stones through windows and causing trouble all over the place!

And why don't the Government put those hussies into prison? I asked: why aren't they punished for being out roaming the streets instead of being at home dusting their furniture? or winding skeins with a nice young man? I said, pulling my chair up closer to Mr Samuel.

"Those women are all loony, Miss Ellie," said Mr Samuel, "and the Government doesn't have a clue how to get them to shut up! It's all very well for you to say, put them in prison! But they do put them in prison! But as soon as they're locked up, the silly buggers refuse to eat! No matter what grub is placed before them: soup, steak, mackerel, cabbage, rice pudding! those girls won't touch a thing, and would rather suffer from hunger pangs than eat anything! The Government has tried a funnel to force-feed them porridge, but the suffragettes close their mouths, kick the doctors, slap the prison matrons round the chops and spit in everyone's face – they just can't get them to eat. So that they won't die in prison, the government lets them go after four or five days, and they set to smashing everything up again like before.

We spoke a bit longer about all that, and Mr Samuel (who budged up a bit closer to me, to tell me this) told me that the Government was so fed up with their tricks that there was going to be a prize offered to anyone who could find a way to get them to shut up. Samuel (he'd put his arm round me to get closer) asked me what I thought, me being a sensible girl, about how to punish these hunger strikers who mocked the legal officers of England. I promised him that I'd have a think about it when I went to bed (he'd started playing with my fingers) and I'd tell him later.

And I did have a think! And this is how I'd deal with those girls. I'd tell them this. So you refuse to eat! And when we stuff you with mixed grain, you complain to the newspapers that your tongues have been scratched! Well! Let's try something else then! We'll carry on setting all sorts of scrummy food on your table – nobody will force you to eat it, and if you refuse to eat it, we'll let you go after five days! You'll be able to go straight out of prison! That's right! I'd tell them: just like that. Get out of here! But before you go! And just so's you won't forget us, we're going to cut your hair right off – and then after that we'll shave your heads! You'll leave prison without having been forced to eat, but as bald as a ham! But we won't hurt you any!

That's how I'd cure those little miss suffragettes for you. And I think, as a young lady myself, that just about all of them would rather eat four meals a day than go around with a head looking like a turnip.

Miss Lonore Pain

Lillie Langtry (née Le Breton, later Lady de Bathe), mistress of the Prince of Wales (later Edward VII), society beauty and actress, was a Jèrriais speaker and is known to have performed in Jèrriais at the opening of the Opera House in Jersey in 1900, as well as in Canada during the First World War to raise funds from members of the patriotic Channel Island diaspora.

Lillie Langtry

From The Days I Knew, *1925*

Living the life of my brothers transformed me into an incorrigible tomboy. I could climb trees and vault fences with the best of them, and I entered with infinite relish into their practical jokes. I have a lively recollection of my youngest brother and myself patrolling the old tree-shaded churchyard at midnight (when we were supposed to be in bed) mounted on stilts and draped in sheets, disquieting late passers-by very effectually. This prank continued until someone wrote to the Jersey papers, promising the ghosts at St. Saviour's graveyard a dose of cold lead if they appeared again. We had a veritable passion for annexing door-knockers, and scarcely a door in the parish was allowed to retain one. We braved threats, dogs, enraged house-holders, even shot guns to obtain these trophies.

One of our chief targets was an old man named Wilkins, a retired tradesman, who lived, with his two spinster daughters, at the head of the Deanery Lane. He was patient and long-suffering, but occasionally we exasperated him beyond endurance, and he would reluctantly descend on my father with a formal complaint. Having relieved him of his door-knocker one evening, we tied a long, strong cord to his bell, making the other end fast to a stone, which we threw over a wall opposite, with the result that everyone who passed by, either afoot or on horseback, struck the cord, causing the old man's bell to ring furiously. At each fresh clanging, Wilkins emerged with the promptitude of a cuckoo clock striking the hour, and hurled the most violent language at the innocent wayfarers. Finally, our audible chuckles behind the wall located the real culprits, and Wilkins preceded us to the deanery, where, after an interview with my father, fitting chastisement was inflicted on us.

About the last escapade which I remember was one in which my sex prevented me from taking an active part. A time-honoured statue of an anonymous personage, wearing a wreath of laurels and a medley of garments, was salved by the Jerseyites from a Spanish ship wrecked on our shores during the reign of George II. As it seemed a pity to waste it, the Islanders labelled it "George Rex," after the Hanoverian king, and erected it in the Royal Square of St. Heliers, where it had stood unmolested ever since, until my brothers conceived the appalling idea of tarring and feathering this royal and stony individual. I shall never forget the tremendous and wrathful outburst which ensued when the townspeople discovered the outrage. It is an ill wind, however, which does not blow profit to some quarter, and an enterprising photographer coined money by snapping his spurious Majesty for souvenir purposes before scourers and painters had made him presentable again. Not infrequently, through our reputation for all manner of pranks, my brothers and I got the name without the game, everything mischievous that was done being attributed off-hand to the "dean's family."

While the tomboy element was conspicuous in me, I had my serious side as well, and would read for hours; longer sometimes than my parents thought good for me. I never went to school, and for that reason had few girl friends. A French governess laboured faithfully to impart knowledge to me, but I am afraid I was rather a handful. My brothers were all educated at Victoria College (the Jersey public school), and the only real work I did was with their tutor when he came each evening to overlook the preparation of their work for following day. He gave me a fairly good education in the classics and mathematics, which was supplemented by lessons from German, French, music and drawing masters. My father, being a remarkably clever and progressive man, believed firmly in the higher education of women.

At the age of thirteen I developed, with two girl friends, a taste for spiritualism and table-turning, and gradually, through our interesting experiences, became engrossed in it. One particular table which we used in our seances displayed such extraordinary agility, cut so many capers, and answered some of our questions so intelligently, that I began to regard myself as a medium, and to feel that I really was, as the spirits we evoked assured me, the cause of these manifestations. Even to this day table-turning fascinates and mystifies me. Some years subsequent to my youthful experiments I discussed the subject with Victorien Sardou, the famous French dramatist, himself an ardent spiritualist, and asked him why the spirits never really enlightened me, although they were quite ready to rap out answers after I had sat for a few moments at the table. He replied that I had not pursued the matter far enough, and that I was as yet in touch only with the cuisiniers (by which I presume, he meant the underlings of the occult world). He made an assertion which I did not and do not credit, that spooks may reveal themselves by showering flowers about the room and performing other seemingly impossible acts, and wound up with the sweeping statement that only fools did not believe in the super-natural.

George F. Le Feuvre ('George d'la Forge')
Lé Texas – et la belle 'Jersey Lily', *1969* (Jèrriais)

San Antonio, Texas,
U.S.A.
Lé 15 dé févri, 1969

Moussieu l'Rédacteu,

Lé Texas est un êtat întérêssant. Dévant qué l'Alaska d'vînsse iun des chînquante États d'L'Améthique du Nord y'a deux-s'trais ans, ch'tait l'Texas tch'était l'pus grand des États-Unis. Dévant 1846, année dé s'n annexion par l'Améthique, lé Texas apparténait au Mexique, et des batâles assez acharnées entre les Mexitchains et l's Améthitchains d'la contrée 'taient l'ordre du jour jusqu'à 1836, quand les Mexitchains assiégîdrent l'Alamo – un bâtisse tch'était en êffet églyise et mission Catholique Romaine tch'avait 'té fondée en 1718 sus l'empliaichement tch'est actuellement la ville de San Antonio. Dans lus êfforts pour qué l'Texas gângnîsse sén îndépendance du Mexique, les soudards Améthitchains lus r'nardîdrent dans la mission, 150 dé ieux. Il' y fûdrent machacrés par les deux-s'trais mille soudards Mexitchains contre ieux auprès aver rêsisté l'siége pour douze jours. Les Mexitchains pèrdîdrent 1,800 soudards dans la batâle. Lé bâtisse dé l'Alamo a 'té restauré et présèrvé comme monûment historique, et est vîsité par eune foule dé touristes touos l's ans.

Y'a bein des choses întérêssantes entouor lé Texas, et d'vant aller pus liain i' n'faut pon oublyiyer la ville dé Langtry dans l'ouêst d'l'État. Viyant qu'la fanmeuse Jèrriaise Lillie Langtry (née Le Breton) allit vîsiter chutte pétite ville-là dans san vivant, il est supposé par un tas d'gens qué ch'tait lyi tchi fut la cause qu'ou fut nommée d'même, mais i' pathaît qu'la vraie raison est qu'ou' fut nommée Langtry d'après l'înginnieux tchi seurvilyit la construction des rails du "train" tchi travèrse la contrée!

Mais qué ch'fûsse pour eune raison ou l'autre qu'ou' fut nommée d'même, la ville est r'nommée pour sa connexion auve Lady de Bathe viyant qué l'Juge Roy Bean, ouaithe tch'i' n'l'avait janmais veue, 'tait emmouothachi d'Lillie Langtry – sans doute par les portraits tch'il avait veu d'lyi.

Un drôle d'ouaîsé, chu Roy Bean-là. Pèrsonne né sait par tch'il autorité tch'i' s'était êtablyi comme juge, mais i' s'appelait "La louai ouêst dé La Pecos!" La Pecos est eune riviéthe tch'est par-là. Chose assez tchuthieuse pour un Jèrriais à com-prendre, il 'tait juge absolu dans la contrée à l'ouêst dé la riviéthe, et quand i' condamnait un homme à mort il 'tait pendu sans aver l'drouait d'appel contre eune si tèrribl'ye condamnâtion!

Lé Juge Bean avait eune pétite bijuque oùest tch'i' faisait valer un p'tit conmèrce dé vente au d'bit. Parmi l's annonces en d'ssus d'sa porte, y'en avait ieune tchi disait "The Jersey Lily". Quand i' fallait siégi comme juge, i' m'ttait eune tchaîse à côté d'un bathi touanné l'fond en haut tchi li faisait sèrvi d'tabl'ye, et il annonçait san jugement en donnant un coup d'maillot sus l'fond du bathi. I' s'adonnait qu'la grand' partie des causes tch'il avait à jugi 'tait l'vol dé j'vaux. Dans chu temps-là, lé j'va 'tait à bein près lé seul transport dé l'homme dans ches parages-là, et i' s'trouvait si épithoté s'i' pèrdait san j'va – p't êt' des milles et des milles dé sa destinnâtion – qué l'vol d'un j'va 'tait considéthé crînminnel.

Un bouan jour, né v'la-t-i' pon un îndividu présenté d'vant l'Juge pour aver volé un j'va – et i' savait bein à tchi s'attendre, mais i' n'avait autcheune envie d'êt' pendu! Comme il 'tait d'la contrée, et savait qué l'juge 'tait emmouothachi d'Lillie Langtry, i' lî vînt eune idée dans la tête tch'il espéthait pouver p't êt' lî sauver la vie. I' dit au juge tch'il avait eune corle des j'veux à la belle et charmante "Jersey Lily" et tch'il 'tait prêt à lî faithe un présent d'la corle en êchange pour sa vie! Lé juge 'tait si content d'pouver mett' la main sus un mio des j'veux à la danme tchi lî pâssait si près du tchoeu tch'i' s'y accordit, et i' dêchèrgit l'atchûsé!

I' pathaît qu'la supposée corle dé j'veux 'tait en rêalité du crîn d'la coue d'un j'va tch'était d'la couleu des j'veux à Madanme Langtry, mais comme ch'est bein connu qu'l'amour est aveug'ye, lé juge né s'en appèrchut pon!

Ouaithe tch'i' y'a longtemps qué l'Juge Roy Bean n'est pus, sa r'nommée et s'n amour pour Lillie Langtry sont restés dans la mémouaithe des gens du Texas, et sa bijuque est acouo d'but à Langtry dans l'ouêst d'l'État. Oulle est gardée en bouan ordre, et est un objet d'întéthêt pour les vîsiteurs et touristes tchi pâssent par-là, et l'annonce "The Jersey Lily" est acouo sus l'haut d'la porte. Ou' pouvez en vaie un portrait, bouannes gens, dans L'Musée d'La Société Jersiaise en ville. Ou' l'trouvethez pendu sus la muthâle dans l'coin tch'est rêsèrvé pour montrer l's êffets tch'apparténait à la fanmeuse et belle "Jersey Lily"!

Texas – and the beautiful Jersey Lily, *1969*

San Antonio, Texas.
U.S.A.
15th February 1969

Dear Mr. Editor,

Texas is an interesting state. Before Alaska became one of the fifty States of North America a couple of years ago it was the largest of the United States. Until 1846, the year of its annexation by America, Texas belonged to Mexico, and there were regular ferocious battles between the Mexicans and the Americans of the region until 1836, when the Mexicans laid siege to the Alamo – a building that was actually a Roman Catholic mission and church which had been founded in 1718 on the site of what is now the city of San Antonio. In their efforts to gain Texas's independence from Mexico, American soldiers had holed up in the mission, 150 of them. They were slaughtered by the couple of thousand Mexican soldiers opposing them after having resisted the siege for twelve days. The Mexicans lost 1800 soldiers in the battle. The building of the Alamo has been restored and conserved as a historic monument, and is visited by crowds of tourists every year.

There are a lot of interesting things about Texas, and before going any further one must not forget the town of Langtry in the west of the State. Because the famous Jerseywoman Lillie Langtry (née Le Breton) went and visited that little town during her lifetime, many people assume that she was the reason it got its name, but it turns out that the real explanation is that it was called Langtry after the engineer who supervised the construction of the railroad that crosses the region!

But whatever the reason it got that name, the town is famous for its connexion with Lady de Bathe because Judge Roy Bean, although he had never set eyes on her, was enamoured of Lillie Langtry – no doubt from pictures he had seen of her.

A strange fellow, that Roy Bean. Nobody knows by what authority he set himself up as judge, but he called himself "The law west of the Pecos!" The Pecos is a nearby river. It is a strange thing for a Jerseyman to understand, but he was an absolute judge in the region west of the river, and when he sentenced a man to death, he was hanged without having the right of appeal against such a terrible sentence!

Judge Bean had a little shack in which he ran a small retail business. Among the advertisements over the door, there was one which said "The Jersey Lily". When he had to sit in judgment, he put a chair alongside a barrel turned upside-down which he used as a table. As it turned out the majority of cases which came before him were of horse-theft. At that time, the horse was fairly much the only transport for a man thereabouts, and if a man lost his horse, he would find himself so marooned, sometimes miles and miles from his destination, that the theft of a horse was considered a crime.

One fine day, who should be brought before the Judge but a man accused of stealing a horse, who knew perfectly well what to expect, but who had absolutely no wish to be hanged! Since he was local, and knew that the judge was enamoured of Lillie Langtry, he hit upon an idea that he hoped might save his life. He told the judge that he had a lock of the lovely and charming Lillie Langtry's hair and that he was prepared to give him the lock of hair as a present in exchange for his life! The judge was so happy to be able to get his hands on some of the hair of the lady he was so fond of that he agreed and let the defendant off!

It seems that the supposed lock of hair was really a hank of horse's tail which was the colour of Mrs Langtry's hair, but as everyone knows that love is blind, the judge didn't realise!

Although Judge Roy Bean has not been with us for a long time, his fame and his love for Lillie Langtry have stuck in the memory of Texans, and his shack still stands in Langtry in the west of the State. It is kept in good repair, and is one of the sights for passing visitors and tourists, and the advertisement saying "The Jersey Lily" is still over the door. You can see a picture of it, folks, in the Société Jersiaise museum in town. You will find it hanging on the wall in the corner dedicated to a display of personal objects that belonged to the famous and beautiful "Jersey Lily"!

A folk rhyme from Guernsey introduces us, like Denys Corbet's tour round the parish nicknames, to the girls from each parish in turn. As usual the Saint Andriaises are left behind and left out – after all, they are the *crainchons*.

Anonymous

Les Demoiselles des Parreisses, *n.d.* (Guernesiais)

> Ch'est les filles d'la Ville,
> Ch'en est des jolies belles.
> Ch'est les filles de St. Samsaön,
> Qui saönt bouannes pour le lanchaön.
> Ch'est les filles du Valle,
> Terjous prêtes à faire du ma.
> Ch'est les filles du Casté,
> Terjous prêtes pour la djaitai.
> Ch'est les filles de St. Sauveux,
> Qui saönt toutes de bouanne humeur.
> Ch'est les filles de St. Pierre,
> Ah, qui saönt terjous a braire.
> Ch'est les filles de Torteva,
> Qu'aont braiment des pids de ch'fa.
> Ch'est les filles de la Fouoret,
> Daume, qui saönt laids.
> Ch'est les filles de St. Martin,
> Qui saönt gnais coum' des lapins.
> Ch'est les filles de St. Andri,
> I' s'raönt tous les delaissies!

The Girls from the parishes, *n.d.*

> There are the girls from Town,
> they're really pretty.
> There are the girls of Saint Sampson
> who are fun to go sand-eeling with.
> There are the girls from the Vale

always ready for mischief.
There are the girls from Castel
always ready for a good time.
There are the girls of Saint Saviour
who are always in a good mood.
There are the girls of Saint Peter
who are always shouting.
There are the girls of Torteval
who really have horse's hooves.
There are the girls of Forest,
well, they're ugly.
There are the girls of Saint Martin
who are as silly as rabbits.
There are the girls of Saint Andrew
who will be left out!

Rimes et poësies jersiaises, the first anthology of Jèrriais poetry published in 1865, included a poem 'Les piaintes d'une vielle tante a mai' attributed to a poet described by the compiler as 'Le jeune Le Touzel' (the young Le Touzel). Many have wondered who this otherwise unknown poet might be, and why no other work attributed to this author survived. It has become clear that the Le Touzel in question was James Charles Le Touzel who emigrated from Jersey to the Americas, and disappeared almost entirely from the literary scene in Jersey. He continued to write occasional poetry though, and sent back a poem in 1873 on the birth of his son, Harry St. George Le Touzel. This poem was published not only in Jersey, but also in *La Gazette de Guernesey*. It references Le Touzel's previously anthologised piece and characters described in it.

Here we see a more positive equivalent of the sort of rough music we have seen described by Denys Corbet. The bachîn, a large round brass preserving pan, had many uses. Now seen in homes generally as an ornament, the bachîn would be used for making black butter, preserves, pickling, washing and even music. It could be struck, or a strange moaning harmonic can be coaxed from it by stroking reeds across the rim in the custom called "faithe braithe les peîles", done to celebrate midsummer and scare away evil spirits. When not in use, it was polished to a gleaming golden yellow and hung high on the wall or on a shelf in order, in the days before efficient lighting, to reflect light to where women would be spending the evening knitting or mending, while one of the men of the household would read aloud pieces from the newspaper, perhaps vernacular stories and poems like this one, to the family.

James Charles Le Touzel ('Le jeune Le Touzel')
Shu Nouviau Garçon, *1873* (Jèrriais)

Naissance. – Le Vendredi 30 du mais d'Mai derni', dans la ville de Goderich, sur le bord du Lac Huron, (Améthique), l'êpouse de Mess' James Charles Le Touzel, d'un biau garçon.

> Sonnais les tikles et les bashins
> Les poêles, les pots et les castrolles,
> Et dêliezment siez les vaisins
> Portaiz-lu vit'ment les nouvelles,
> Du Nord au Sud, – de haut et d'bas
> De lien et d'près tuônez vos pas,
> Et dites ès gens, par chin, par là,
> Qu'chest un garçon, chutt' buonn' fais là.

> A tig de corps, criyis des brais,
> Et vos poumons un miot forchis;
> D'un but à l'autr' partout cuorrais,
> Et dites la nouvell' que j'envie.
> Dans vot' cherriot, à pi à ch'va,
> Allaiz ben vit' sans perdr' de temps;
> Et dites ès gens, par chin, par là,
> Qu'chest un garçon, chutt' buonn' fais là.

> Ne mangie pas un' seul' buochie!
> Ne restaiz pas à prendr' hallaine!
> Dêpêchous-vit' je vos en prie
> Et n'siyis pons fids de vot peine.
> Que la nouvelle sait rêpandue,
> Et qu'ou sait par le monde connue;
> Et dites ès gens, par chin, par là,
> Qu'chest un garçon, chutt' buonn' fais là.

> Par les grands k'mins, au coin des rues,
> Dites-le à tous et faites d'vot mûs;
> Et s'ou viyis chique fill' chi pieurre,
> Pour un galant qu'ou peut avait,
> Dites-li ben vit y'ou qu'je demeure,
> Car oull l'éra, s'oull prend ach'teurre.
> Mais dites ès gens, par chin, par là,
> Qu'chest un garçon, chutt' buonn' fais là.

S'ou rencontrais chiq' vier garçon
Chi n'a ocquo peut faith s'sen choies,
Rasseûrrais-le de chutt' faishon: –
Qu'unn bell' hardell' la préchaine fais
Sa seurr' des v'nin, et qu'il l'étha,
Si veut la prendre dès qu'ou vaindra.
Mais dites ès gens, par chin, par là,
Qu'chest un garçon, chutt' buonn' fais là.

Chutt' brav' et buonn' "vieill' tante à mai,"
Chi ouvr' sa cauche près d'la jonchièthe;
N'là manchis pas! dites-li que j'ai
Voulu qu'oull' suss' y'un des premièthes;
Et à M'ait' Jean – li chi cliopenn'
Et march' à l'aid' de s'en bâton,
Dites-li duoch'ment! – d'peux qu'irr' chopenne
A la nouvel' de chu garçon.
Mais dites ès gens, par chin, par là,
Qu'chest un garçon, chutt' buonn' fais là.

This new-born boy, *1873*

Birth: – on Friday 30th of May last, in the town of Goderich, on the banks of Lake Huron (America), to the spouse of Mr James Charles Le Touzel, of a fine boy.

Sound the kettles and ring the bachîns,
the large pans, the pots and the frying pans,
and without delay carry the news quickly
round the neighbours,
from North and South, from high and low,
from far and near, make your way
and tell people here and there
that this time, it's a boy!

With all your might, shout it out,
and use your lungs to their limit;
from one end to the other, run everywhere
and tell the news I've sent.
In your cart, on foot and on horseback,
go quickly and don't waste any time;
and tell people here and there
that this time, it's a boy!

Don't stop to have a snack!
Don't stop to draw breath!
Hurry quickly I beg you
and don't spare your efforts.
Let the news be spread,
and let it be known to everyone;
and tell people here and there
that this time, it's a boy!

Along the main roads, at street corners,
tell everyone about it and do your best;
and if you see some girl crying
for lack of a boyfriend.
tell her quickly where I live,
because she can have him if she claims him now.
But tell people here and there
that this time, it's a boy!

If you come across some bachelor
who hasn't yet settled on his chosen one,
reassure him thus: –
that next time it's sure to be
a beautiful girl and that he can have her
if he wants to claim her as soon as she arrives.
But tell people here and there
that this time, it's a boy!

As for that good "old aunt of mine"
knitting her stockings by the sofa;
don't miss her out! Tell her that
I wanted her to be one of the first to know;
and Master John – the one who limps
and walks with the aid of his walking stick,
tell him gently! – lest he stumble again
at the news of this boy.
But tell people here and there
that this time, it's a boy!

Augustus Asplet Le Gros returned repeatedly to the theme of women. Although not best known as a humorous writer, A.A.L.G.'s genre scenes can invoke a certain wry amusement – as in the case of this portrait of an exasperated but loving mother.

Augustus Asplet Le Gros ('A.A.L.G.')

Ch't Avé, *1865* (Jèrriais)

Et r'garde don, ma pouor' Nenné,
Ne vait-tu pon que chut avé
Renversera sa bollaïe d'soupe!
Ah! mon doux. Oupe!
La v'là, ma fé, bein estrueillaie. –
Ah! chu malprope:
Chu p'tit salope!
I mérit'rai un' bouonn' fouotaïe.

V'là don un bieau net doublii;
Et son calobre est tout graissi;
Nous n'gagne rein de li en mettre un autre,
Chu sale apôtre;
Mêm' son p'tit fro en est tout mucre. –
Essuie ses yeux,
Il a ieu peux:
Donn' li, ma fille, un lopyn d'schucre.

Las! las! mon doux, mon doux, Nenné,
Ne v'lo-t-i' pon ov' un couté?
Assaïz pour se fair' ma es daits:
I n'y a pon d'paix,
Devrai, ov' ieux. Le v'là tchi brait.
Tchi cris piteurs!
Tchi lermes et plieurs!
I sembl' qu'nou l'tue, chu p'tit portraït.

Le v'là-t-i pon auprès du feu?
Ah! combein d'fais tchi m'faït trimeu.
Ov' li i n'y a ni but, ni fyn.
Vein-t'en ichyn;
Assieds-te là comme un bouon p'tit,
(Chu p'tit chéri!)
Là, restez-y:
Maman t'fouett'ra s'ou t'vait bouogi.

Un moment d'paix tréjous achteu,
Et nou l'prends bein ... Mon doux, chu feu!
R'garde d'sus, ma pouor' Nenné. –
J'crai tch'il a sai:

S'tu li donnais une goutte à bethe,
Il en s'ra d'mus. –
Ecout', j'ouai l'hus;
Ch'est p't-estr' Mollé, ou bein son pethe.

Chutt' bouonn' fais là, je n'en veux pus. –
Mollé, beurge-nous bein vit' l'hus;
I veint les sept vents sus mon co. –
Ov' chu marmot
I n'y a d'r'pos ni niet, ni jeu.
Ah! ou n'sait guethe,
Tchi n'est pon methe.
Nou s'rait bein mus à son tout seu.

Et ou-est donc tu'es, ma pouor' Nenné?
Veint vit', j't'en prie, pour le happé,
Car pour de mai je n'peux bouogi,
Et va l'couochi:
Ov' li nou n'fait goutt' de bouon sang. –
Ah, pour une fais,
Me v'là en paix!
Et j'voth enshaille, il en est temps.

That child, *1865*

Look, my poor Nancy,
can't you see that that child
is going to tip over his bowl of soup!
Oh my goodness. Hup!
There it goes, all over the blessed place.
Ah, what a dirty beast!
What a mucky pup!
He deserves a good spanking.

There goes a nice clean tablecloth,
and his pinafore is all greasy;
it's not worth changing him into another,
the dirty little devil;
even his little frock is all damp now.
Dry his eyes,
he's had a fright:
give him a sugar lump, my girl.

Oh! Oh! Good heavens, Nancy,
isn't that a knife he's got hold of?
He could hurt his fingers with it;
there's really no peace
around them. Now he's wailing.
What pitiful cries!
What tears and crying!
You'd think we were trying to kill him, the little devil.

Now what's he doing by the fire?
Ah! how often he gives me a scare.
He never lets up.
Come here,
sit there like a good little boy
(you little darling!)
Now stay there:
Mummy will smack you if you move.

At last, a moment of peace now
and a chance to enjoy it ... Gracious, look at the fire!
Take care of it, my poor Nancy.
I think he's thirsty:
it would be best
if you gave him a drop to drink.
Listen, I can hear the door;
it might be Molly, or perhaps his father.

That's it, I can't take any more.
Molly, close that door quickly;
I'm feeling a terrible draught here.
With this brat
there's no rest by night or day.
Ah! Only a mother
can truly understand.
One would be much better off on one's own.

Where have you got to, my poor Nancy?
Come here quickly, please, and pick him up,
because I can't move,
and put him to bed.
With him there's nothing but worry.
Ah! for once

I've got some peace!
And it's high time too, I can tell you.

It is of course not just parents that can be exasperated. A child's outlook on life has
been expressed by the writers of the Islands – whether in terms of wistful reminiscence, or through poems written for children. Although the vernacular languages
were discouraged in schools, and in some cases excluded, the annual Eisteddfod
competitions have provided both an outlet for children reciting vernacular poetry
and for poets writing for children. Among the stalwarts of the Jersey Eisteddfod for
many years was Amelia Perchard.

Amelia Perchard ('A.L.P'.)

From Les Garçons, *1964* (Jèrriais)

Les garçons, danme n'm'en palez pon.
J'n'ai janmais veu patheils!
I' n' ont ni manniéthes, ni principe –
I' n'lavent pas lus ouothelles!
Les av'ous veus s'n'aller s'traînant,
Lus salles mains dans lus pautes
Et coumme s'i' sont tellement lâssés
Qu'i' n'peuvent pas marchi d'autre?

Nou dithait qu'ch'est tout lus pliaîsi
D'etre coumme des êpeûthas.
Et janmais dé lus dêrangi –
Vraîment, j'les comprend pas!
Ou n'verrez pas des filles d'lus age
Janmais sorti d'siez ieux
Sans être propre et bein habillies
Et aver grée lus g'veux!

Les garçons pouorraient faithe bein piéthe
Que d'prendre patron sus nous
Pour apprendre à lus comporter
Et aver un mio d'goût!
Faudra qu'i' changent devant d'être grands
Car, bieau qu'iun d'ieux m'voudrait
Ch's'ra pas me qui m'abaissitha
À m' mathier à d'ité!

From Boys, *1964*

Boys! Don't talk to me about boys.
I've never seen anything like them!
They haven't got any manners, or principles –
they don't wash their ears!
Have you seen them straggling along
with their dirty hands in their pockets
as though they were so tired out
that they couldn't walk any more?

Anyone would say that all they care about
is looking like scarecrows.
And they never look after themselves –
really, I can't understand them!
You'll never see girls of their age
leave their homes
without being clean and well-dressed
and doing their hair!

Boys could do much worse
than taking us as a model
to learn how to behave
and have some good taste!
They'll have to change before they grow up
because, even if one of them wanted to have me,
I personally wouldn't stoop
to marrying one of that lot!

In this poem Frank Le Maistre records and celebrates baby talk.

Frank Le Maistre

En mémouaithe dé mes p'tits jours, *1976* (Jèrriais)

Jé m'rappelle bein, quand j'tais tout p'tit,
Dé chu dgèrgon si fanmilyi,
Des preunmièrs sons qué nou-s-entend
D'la bouoche d'la méthe tchi vouos apprend.

Des touos p'tits mots, et si aisis,
Châtchun connait bein chu p'tit d'vis;

A peine hors du bèr nou les sait
Tous par tchoeu d'vant pouver pâler.

Les touos preunmièrs tchi m'veinnent à l'ouïe
"Pé-pèe", "Mé-mèe", bein seux, et pis
"Pa-pa", "Man-man", un p'tit pus tard,
Pouor mé dêjà les deux vieillards.

Quand j'avais faim, quat' fais par jour,
Ch'tait du "naine-naine" qué j'piaillais pour,
Et nou m'donnait bein vite man lait,
Du papa caud ou du grué.

Respé vouot' honneu – tout poli,
Pouor ses bésoins ch'tait faithe "pi-pi",
Véthe, étout, quand ch'tait pouor aller
Ch'tait faithe "ca-ca" qué nou dîthait.

Tchiquefais j'tais bèrchi par man p'pèe,
Mais j'ouïyais des lèvres d'ma m'mèe –
Là, fai "lô-lô, tu'as grand sommé,
Man chièr pétchiot, là, endors-té!"

Et quand par chance jé m'trébutchais,
Ch'tait du "ma-ma" qué jé m'faithais,
Quand j'avais tchée ou fait tchique dro
Fallait "plieuser", "çu" pouôrre pétchiot.

Mais quand jé m'promenais auve nouos gens
Dans ma cârrosse par un bieau temps,
Lé mot dé tous qu' j'aimais bein ouï
Aller à "dè-dée" ... tchi pliaîthi!

Aller à "jo-jo" (ou à j'va),
Ch'tait pus souvent sus l'genou d'man p'pa;
Combein d'chucrîns qu' j'ai ieu d'donnés
Ah, des "dou-doux" par la pap'sée!

Pis dans les livres dé bieaux "bi-bis"
J'tais tout à ièrs, mouôn Doue d'la vie!
J'faithais "cou-cou" – un bein bouôn ji –
A man tout seu pouor mé muchi.

Y'en a acouo, qu' ma mémouiathe tcheint,
Qué jé m'rappelle tout à fait bein –
Un oeu des glinnes 'tait un "co-co",
Et nouot' nièr tchian lé gros "ouo-ouo".

I' n'faut pon craithe qu' ch'est du bêtîn,
Qué chu dgèrgon est du niolîn;
Dans toutes les langues nou trouve chu d'vis
Tout prînmitif du temps jadis.

In memory of when I was little, *1976*

I remember very well, when I was very little,
all that familiar baby talk,
the first sounds you hear
from your mother's mouth as she teaches you.

Really small words, and such simple ones,
everyone knows that small talk;
you know them all by heart
when you're barely out of your cradle, before you can talk.

The first ones of all to reach my ears –
"Da-da", "Ma-ma", of course, and then
"Gran-pa", "Gran-ma", a bit later,
who were already a couple of old folks to me.

When I was hungry, four times a day,
it was "yum-yum" that I wailed for,
and I was quickly given my milk,
warm pap or gruel.

Begging your pardon – for politeness,
when you had to go, it was going "pee-pee",
Yes, and then for number twos,   —
you'd say, go "poo-poo".

Sometimes I was rocked by my daddy,
but I heard from mummy's lips,
"Go beddy-byes, you're very sleepy,
my darling boy, off you go to sleep!"

And if I should happen to stumble.
it was "nasty hurts" that I had,
when I fell or had an accident,
little "boysie" had to "grizzle".

But when I was out for a walk with the family
in my pram in fine weather,
the word I most liked to hear
was to go "walkies"... what fun!

Playing "horsey" (or horseback),
that was often enough on grandad's knee;
How many sweets I had given to me.
Ah, paper-bagfuls of "sweeties".

Then, pretty "piccies" in my books.
My goodness, I couldn't take my eyes off them!
I played "peep-oh" – a lovely game –
hiding all on my own.

And there are others that I remember,
still in my memory –
a hen's egg was an "eggy-weg",
and our black dog the big "bow-wow".

You mustn't think that this is foolishness,
or that this baby talk is nonsense;
This way of talking can be found in every language,
the primitive way of talking from time past.

Almost as the flipside to his 'Le Vier Garçon', Robert Pipon Marett offers a mother's view of children. It is interesting to compare this poem with A.A.L.G.'s 'Ch't Avé' which we have already seen. Sir Robert manages to add a little twist, in the final lines of the poem, to the mother's exasperation.

Robert Pipon Marett ('Laelius')

Les Avièrs, *1851* (Jèrriais)

Lo-lô, lô-lô ne crie pon tant
Ne fais pon tant d'sabbat j't'en prie!
Qu'est donc qu'il a l'bénit efant? –
Là, veurs tu prendre d'la bouillie?

Ach' t'eu est-i' ben barbouilli!
Reste donc tranquille ov' ta main, –
Bon, est-tu content, p'tit vilain!
Man bedgown en est tout touoilli!

Et, ch't'avé, qu'est donc qu'i'ly enhanne!
Qu'est qui l'possèd'? Crie donc, p'tit bête! –
J'appréhend' ben qu'i'n' se vilanne,
Ch'est assez pour en perdr' la tête! –
Après ch'la que nou m' pâl' d'èfants, –
I' vaudrait mue n'avé – chent fais –
Qu'un r'pas par jeu' et vivre en paix!
Ah benheureux cheux qui sont sans!

I' faut qu'i' saient ben à d'laisi,
Les gens qui désir'nt d'en avé! –
S'i craient qu' nou-z y trouv' du pliaisi,
Je peux leux dir' qu'i s' tromp'nt, ma fé
Quand nou-z-a d's'aviers, ch'est paré!
Ni niet ni jeu, dans aucun temps,
Non n'peut êtr' seû pour deux moments
De paix ni de tranquillité! –

Car ch'est tréjous pleurer ou rire,
Piailli' ou bouder sans raison,
Dèpich', trébuque, ou ben dèchire!
Ou galopp' par tout' la maison!
S'i' sont tranquill's, ch'est pière ocquo!
Cess'nt' i' un minut' de bouogi,
Alors ou pouvez ben gagi
Qu'i' pass'nt leux temps à faire quiqu' dro!

Quand i'n' peuv'nt mue i' s'rouoll'nt dans l'aire!
Il' us'raient jusqu'au fé des reues!
Je défie qui qu'ché sait de faire
Un' goutt' de bouon sang avec ieux!
Car j'ai r'marqui que ch'est assez
Qu'il y'ait de quiqu' bord du dangi,
Pour, comme exprès pour vos vengi.
Qu'il' aill'nt ben vite y pôqui l'nez!

Pour en parer, ch'est d'la minsère! –
– Et j'avons, nous, tout à souffri!

Car ch'est comm' rein d'en êtr' le père! –
Ah! si j'avais à r'commenchi!
Mais ch't'èfant-chin est un satan! –
– Ah! v'là qu'i c'mmenche à s'apaisi! –
– La! là! sais bouon, man p'tit chéri!
– Allons, fais *ma* à ta maman!

Children, *1851*

There, there, don't cry so.
Don't make such a din, please!
What's the matter with the blessed child?
There, do you want some pap?
And now you've got it all over you!
Keep your hand still –
Right, are you happy now, you little imp!
My bedgown is covered in it!

What's the matter with the child?
What's up with him? Go ahead and cry, little devil!
It's not as though he's going to do himself a mischief.
It's enough to drive you out of your mind!
From now on, don't mention children to me,
it'd be a hundred times better to have
only one meal a day and live in peace!
How lucky they are who don't have any!

People who want children
must be very well off!
If they think that you can get any pleasure out of them,
I can tell them that they're wrong.
When you have children, it's over!
At no time, at night or during the day,
can you be sure of getting a couple of moments
of peace and quiet!

Because there's always crying or laughing,
wailing or sulking without reason;
breaking, stumbling, or even tripping!
Or gallopping all over the house!
And if they're quiet, that's even worse!
If they stop moving about for a minute,

then you can bet
that they're spending their time up to mischief!

When they've nothing better to do, they roll on the floor!
They'll wear you out completely!
I challenge anyone
not to get worked up over them!
For I've noticed that it's enough
for there to be something dangerous somewhere
for them to go, as if on purpose to torment you,
and poke their noses into it!

To round things off, it's terrible!
And we've all of us got to suffer!
But being the father is nothing by comparison!
Ah, if I had my time again!
What a devil this child is!
Ah! now he's starting to calm down!
There, there! be a good boy, darling!
Now, how about a little kissy for mummy!

Henry Luce Manuel stands out among Jèrriais poets of the nineteenth century for his elegiac tone. His dramatic and metaphysical poems can be stirring, thoughtful or even lighthearted, in the voice of an enraptured music-lover, a thirsty drunkard or, as here, a bereaved father. His poems, though, never stray into bombast or pomposity.

Henry Luce Manuel

Leignes à M'n Efant qui vein d'muori', *1859* (Jèrriais)

Tout est fini. La vallée de la mort
Là v'là passée. Le souffrant ach'teur' dort.
Pus d'cris, ni r'gards, ni termes d'agonie!
N'ya pas à souffri' iou n' yia pus la vie.
O, Gieu merci!
Tout est fini.

Tout est fini. Les rêv's que l'amour eut
Sont touos détruits. Mais, qui? ... Chès rêv's euss'nt pu
Condire à ma' ... Pein' pour nous et pour li!
Or, tout c'qui est, est bein, le Sage a dit.
Donc, Gieu merci!
Tout est fini.

Tout est fini. A li sont épaignis
Les grands combats, les minsèr's de chutt' vie.
Et, ô surtout! la quiession: "Mus valu
"N'eut i' pas que je n'euss' jamais vécu?"
Aquôr', – Merci!
Tout est fini.

Tout est fini? – Mais, non! – Chôs' qu'est créée
N'périt jamais. Ou' peut êtr' transformée –
Mais cessi d'êtr'? Jamais! – Mort, donc tu vis!–
O men éfant, – Tu n'nos as qu'dévanchis!
Mon Gieu! – Merci!
Rein n'est fini.

O mill' fais nan: – Rein n'est fini! L'tombé
N'est que le c'min, grand Gieu, qui mène à Té!
S'menchis je somm's ichin, – v'la tout. – Che n'est
Que quand nou' meurt qu'à vie réell' nou' naît!
Seigneur, Seigneur – Merci!
Je vé: TOUT VA Q'MENCHI!

Lines to my child who has just died, *1859*

Everything is over. The valley of death
has been passed through. The one who was suffering is now
sleeping.
No more cries, nor looks, nor death throes!
Where life has departed, there is no longer any suffering.
Oh, thank God!
Everything is over.

Everything is over. The dreams that love had
have all been destroyed. But what of it?... Those dreams might
have led to evil... Trouble for us and for him!
But, all that is, is good, as the wise man said.
So, thank God!
Everything is over.

Everything is over. He has been spared
the great battles, and the miseries of this life.
And above all! the question: "Would it have been better
if I had never been born?"

Again, thank you!
Everything is over.

Is everything over? – No! – Something that has been created
never perishes. It may be transformed –
but cease to be? Never! – Dead, so you are alive! –
Oh my child, – you have only gone on before us!
My God! Thank you!
Nothing is over.

A thousand times no: – nothing is over! The tomb
is only the pathway, great Lord, which leads to You!
We are sown here, – that is all. – It is only
when we die that we are born to real life!
Lord, Lord – Thank you!
I can see: everything will begin!

Tragedy can strike the most ordinary family – but there is nothing ordinary about
the Pain family. When, through ludicrous mishap, Piteur injures his wife's leg, it
seems for a while that surgery may be necessary. But Piteur is far from being the
most selfless husband.

Alice de Faye also suggests that men may not always treat their wives as they
should.

Philippe Le Sueur Mourant ('Bram Bilo', 'Piteur Pain', etc)

Funeral postponed – Leg comes off, *1913* (Jèrriais)

Tout bin cartchullé, j'soummes d'avis, ma femme et mé, qu'il en couota mains d'lis
coppé la gambe souos le g'nou, que ... mais n'paslons pas d'cheunna, a ch't'eu
qu'j'avons décidé pour l'opéthation. Et pis! m'viyous tout seu, ichin d'dans, sans
femme a m'coutchi mes r'pas, a me t'nin mes habits en r'pathe, et a villyi sus not'
fille! M'viyous tout seu ov la responsabilité d'eunne grande, forte, piessante hardelle, qu'est tréjous a s'met' dans tchiq' "scrape" quand nous a l'dos touoné! Chose
seuthe que, la maintchi du temps, quand j'rentréthais siez nous, l'ouézé s'ait
èscappé du nid! Lonore s'ait horte a galvaudé nou n'sait iou!

Ch'est-tan-tchi, quand j'en eumes r'pâslé ensembye, Laizé et mé, et qu'l'affaithe
fut enfin décidée d'chu bord là, je n'fis ni ieunne ni deux, j'prins man chapé, et
j'm'en fut en sifflant siez l'docteu – l'sien qui vint drénnement d'accaté eunne scie a
la dernié faîchon – lis dithe qui pouait v'nin a sa c'modité, et d'apporté ses ôtis en
même temps.

Ch'est pour après d'main – après man dèsjeunné. J'tais d'avis d'faithe l'amputation ichin, sus la tabye d'la tchuisinne, ov de la moulée d'scie êstendue sus l'aithe

pour ne pon faithe de mess; mais les docteurs – y'en etha deux! Rin n'mé couote, quand ch'est pour faithe pliaisi a ma femme – les docteurs ont pretendu qu'la tabye craulait des pids, et que v'la tchi pouorait dèsrangi l'couté si ofuche Laizé tressautait la moindrement.

Sans doute, d'la tchethié a l'Hopita s'en va m'occasionné des frais! mais, tchès qu'ou voulez! Eunne fais n'est pas couotume! J'avais pensé d'mandé a Samuel de m'aidji a la porté jusqu'a l'hopita, entre niet et jour, mais les docteurs n'ont pon voulu. Y'etha don eunne cab a payi. Nou m'a prév'nu que l'Coumiti d'l'hopita pouorait bin m'envié un compte pus tard. Es ch'qu'is en ethaient la chose? J'sis bouan Jerriais, j'paie rât; et j'ai tréjous voté du bord que l'Counêtabye m'a dit!

Tout chu tintamarre ichin n'est pas bon pour man fille, nintou! Quand j'sis a bas, otchupé ès affaithes de la gazette, n'y'a persounne a villyi d'sus. Quand j'ramonte pour mes r'pas, n'y'a rin d'fricachi l'pus bé du temps – ou n'pense qu'a sa méthe. J'sis souvent oblyiji d'm'en allé a man tout seu manji siez tchiq restaurant; et chaque fais ch'est au mains trente-siex ou quarante sous!

Enfin! Coumme j'disais a Laizé hier au sé justement d'vant que d'sorti pour allé passé la séthée a joué ès dominos – faut avé patienche! S'tout va bin m'a dit l'docteu, Laizé r'sétha sus pid – sus un pid – dans un couplye d'mais. Nou lis f'tha faithe une solide gambe de bouais en frêne – j'ai justement, tchiq bord souos les d'gré un morcé d'avithon d'baté, qué j'pouorai rabotté mé même tchiq séthée – et, cache ma Laizé! Te r'véla d'bu ma femme!

Ou pens'ez en nous, j'vos en prie, après d'main! Et si par chance l'affaithe touonait mal ... mais je n'veurt pon pensé a cheunna! Mais si en tout cas l'affaithe touonait ... nou n'sait jommais ... mais si en tout cas ... si par chance ... enfin! faut s'prépathé a tout ... counaitréthious tchiq jeunne veuve qui séthait coutchi?

Funeral postponed – Leg comes off, *1913*

Once we've added it all up, me and my wife think that it'll cost less to amputate her leg below the knee, than ... but let's not discuss that, now that we're going for the operation. Well! Can you honestly see me here on my own, with no wife to cook my meals, mending my clothes for me, and looking after our daughter! Can you see me all on my own with responsibility for a great big hefty girl who's always getting herself into some scrape or other as soon as our back is turned! You can be sure that half the time, when we get home, the bird will have flown the nest! Ellie will be out roaming heaven knows where!

So, once we'd had another talk about it, Liza and me, and we'd come down on that side of the question, I didn't shilly-shally, I took my hat and off I went, whistling, to see the doctor – the one who's just bought one of those newfangled saws – to ask him if he could pop round when he had a moment, and bring his instruments with him while he was at it.

It's set for the day after tomorrow – after I've had my breakfast. I thought of doing the amputation here, on the kitchen table, with some sawdust spread on the floor so as not to make a mess; but the doctors – there'll be two of them! Expense is no object when it comes to keeping my wife happy – the doctors claimed that the table was wobbly, and that might cause the knife to slip if Liza were to make any sudden movement.

Doubtless, having her carted off to the Hospital is going to cost me a packet! but there you go! It's something you don't do every day! I had thought of asking Samuel to help me carry her to the hospital, at daybreak, but the doctors were against it. So I'll have to pay for a cab. I've been warned that the Hospital Board might send me a bill later. What are the blighters thinking of? I'm a good Jerseyman. I pay my rates. And I've always voted exactly as the Constable has told me to!

All this hullabaloo is not good for my daughter either! When I'm downstairs, busy working for the newspaper, there's nobody to look after her. When I go back upstairs for my meals, there's nothing fried up most of the time – all she thinks about is her mother. I'm often obliged to go off alone and eat at some restaurant; and that costs me each time at least one-and-six or one-and-ten!

Well! As I was saying to Liza yesterday evening just before I went out to spend the evening playing dominos – we have to have patience! If everything goes well, so the doctor said, Liza will be back on her feet – on her foot – in a couple of months. They're going to make a good quality wooden leg for her, out of ashwood – it so happens that somewhere under the stairs I've got a piece of an oar off a boat that I could plane down myself one evening – and then, up you get, Liza! You'll be up and running again, my dear!

So please spare a thought for us the day after tomorrow! And if, by any chance, it should turn out badly .... but I don't want to think about that! But, in any case, if it turned out ... you never know ... but if it should ... by any chance ... well, you've always got to brace yourself ... you wouldn't happen to know of any young widow who can cook?

Alice de Faye ('Livonia')

Les Promesses d'Homme Mathiet, *1919* (Jèrriais)

>Les promesses d'un homme Mathiet,
>Sont comme la crôate d'un bouan Patait,
>Quest bein faites pour être bein dépichie,
>Chèst chonna quarivi eun jour avec Joe et Melie.
>
>Comme la saison des patates avé bein péyi
>Joe dis eun jour a Mélie comme t'uas bein travaillyi
>Je m'en vais te faithe eun biaux gros présent,
>Tchique chose de valeur d'or ou d'argent.

Ou, voudrais tu avé; eun "nice" grand Piano,
N'vla qui nos divertirait au sé eun mio,
Je pouorais joié et chanté pour te diverti,
Tandi que tu ergrais mes habits et soigne le p'tit
Then the music would Play.

Nannin ou dis je'n veux pas d'autre ornements,
J'en av'ons dèja bein assez dans touos les apartements
Chaque je voudrais sait eun "Motor" pour me porté
Et que je pouorais souvent sorti sans te badré.

Joe ne dis pas grand chose mais y pensi
Eun " Motor" mais chenna couote bein trop chi
Et pis ou sait trejous a s'proumné et se diverti
Et me restait a r'grais mes hardes et soigni le p'tit.

Si j'acate eun "Motor" ne v'la qui me ruinetha
Et ma piante de tomate tchez qui me la paitha
Je voudrais en faithe l'Anaie tchi vein,
Car dans mes terres, ils y viendrais bein.

Y s'en alli en ville chu mème jour la
Pour faithe comme y dis s'en magnifique achat,
Y s'en alli tout drait, vais "Miss A" sies d'Gruchy
Pour vais si par chance y'avait chique chose de reduit.

Et quand y r'vins siès li avec s'en p'tit patchet
Y dansait et chantait coumme eun critchet.
Là, y dis à Melie, n'en v'la pour tout l'hivé
Ne v'la tout le présent que je peu te donné
Tchet eun motor "veil"
Then the music did play.

Santait de vier homme,
Biaux temps d'hivé.
Prommesses de gentilhomme
Sont trais choses qui ne faut pas se fié.

The Promises of a married man, *1919*

The promises of a married man
are like the crust of a good pie,

made well to be well broken.
That's what happened one day to Joe and Amelia.

Since the potato season had been lucrative,
Joe said one day to Amelia, "Since you've worked hard,
I'm going to give you a lovely big present,
something valuable in gold or silver.

Or would you like a nice big piano,
that would be something to entertain ourselves with a bit in the evening,
I could play and sing for your enjoyment,
while you mend my clothes and look after the little one.
Then the music would play."

"No," she said, "I don't want any more ornaments.
We've already got quite enough in all our rooms.
What I'd like is a motor car to carry me about
and that I could take out often without bothering you."

Joe didn't say much, but he thought,
"A motor car! But that costs far too much,
and then she'll always be going for a drive and enjoying herself,
and I'll be left behind to mend my clothes and look after the little one.

If I buy a motor car, it'll ruin me.
And how will I be able to afford my tomato seed?
I wanted to try that out next year,
because they'll come up well on my land."

He went into town that very day
to make his magnificent purchase, as he'd said.
He went straight off to see Miss A. at de Gruchy's
to see if by any chance there was anything reduced.

And when he got back home with his little parcel,
he was dancing and singing like a cricket.
"There you go," he said to Amelia, "that'll see you through the winter.
That's all the present I can give you."
It was a motoring veil.
Then the music did play.

An old man's health,
fine weather in winter,

and a gentleman's promises
are three things you should never rely on.

This poem in Auregnais by Nicholas Bott is one of the few literary texts from
Alderney in the vernacular.

Nicholas Bott

Chanson en pliat Auregniéz, Coume dit les Anglais (founded on fact), *c.1866* (Auregnais)

En Auregny il y avoit deux fraïres
Qui s'entre aimoient coume p'tits moutons
Chèst ma-fé vrai sou voulaït m'craïre
C-h-toit tandis quils etoient p'tits garçons
Quand y furent grand Pierot dit Craimé
R'chard faut qu-chacun ait sen tchi sé
Tient tai tchi té, et mé tchi mé
Laffaire en ira mue ma-fé
Tient tai tchi té, et mé tchi mé
Laffaire en ira mue ma-fé

Pierrot vint riche Dieu sait coument
A forche de faire le p'tit bàri
A fraudaï y gagni d'largent
Vint gros et gras et l'coeu durchi
Quand il-tait buttaï à sen haizait★
Si R'chard venoit y lie criait
Tient tai tchi té, et mé tchi mé
Laffaire en ira mue ma-fé
Tient tai tchi té, et mé tchi mé
Laffaire en ira mue ma-fé

Un vier oncle vint à mouori
Laissant ses herpins à pou-our Dick
Dan ausitot que Pierrot l'oui
Y sen fut trouvaï R'chard ben vite
Mais R-chard le r-garde et dit hé hé
Tu ten vens m-vée parce que j'ai d'qué
Tient tai tchi té, et mé tchi mé
Laffaire en ira mue ma-fé
Tient tai tchi té, et mé tchi mé
Laffaire en ira mue ma-fé

Mais s-fit Pierrot ch'toit m-n'oncle itout
Im vént quic-chose j'devrais craïre
Alons R-chard tan garde pas tout
Car y faut agir en bouan fraïre
Ah ah s-fit R-chard quand jetaois paure
Comme tu disois je l'dit accoére
Tient tai tchi té, et mé tchi mé
Laffaire en ira mue ma-fé
Tient tai tchi té, et mé tchi mé
Laffaire en ira mue ma-fé

Mais si tout l'monde en faisoit d'mème
Che s-rait d'qué tristre en veritaïs
Si nou suivait un-taï sistème
Y-n y-éroit pus de sociétaï
Quand à mai jaime allaï vous vée
Et que vous r-venaï me r-vée quic fée
Jirai tchi tai tu vendras tchi mé
L'affaire en ira mue ma fé
Jirai tchi tai tu vendras tchi mé
L'affaire en ira mue ma fé

* haizait en Auregniez est héchot en Jersiais & héchet en Guernesiais petite heche de clios ou de bel (cour) de maison

les deux freres étoient Pierre et Richard Gauvain, et l'Oncle qui mourut étoit Monsr. Robinson. J'étois à son enterrement et j'entendis Richard dire à Pierre Quand jetois paure tu n'venais pas m'vée he ben apresent tient tai tchi té Ce qui me donna l'idée plus tard d'ecrire cette chanson

Song in broad Aur'gnais, As the English say: founded on fact, *c.1866*

In Alderney there were two brothers
who loved each other like lambs.
My goodness, it's true, if you want to believe me;
it was while they were little boys.
When they grew up, Pete said, "Believe me,
Richard, it'll be better if we each have our own home.
You stay in your home, and I'll stay in my home.
Gracious me, things will be better that way.
You stay in your home, and I'll stay in my home.
Gracious me, things will be better that way."

Pete got rich, God knows how.
By means of smuggling liquor
he earned money,
became big and fat and hard-hearted.
When he stood at his gate⋆,
if Richard came by, he shouted to him:
"You stay in your home, and I'll stay in my home.
Gracious me, things will be better that way.
You stay in your home, and I'll stay in my home.
Gracious me, things will be better that way."

An old uncle happened to die
leaving his money to poor Dick.
As soon as Pete heard
he very quickly went off to find Richard.
But Richard looked at him and said: "Ha ha!
You've come to see me because I've got something.
You stay in your home, and I'll stay in my home.
Gracious me, things will be better that way.
You stay in your home, and I'll stay in my home.
Gracious me, things will be better that way."

"But," said Pete, "he was my uncle too.
I think I'm due to come into something.
Come on, Richard, don't keep the lot;
behave like a good brother."
"Ah ah!" said Richard. "When I was poor,
this is what you used to say to me, so I'll say it again:
You stay in your home, and I'll stay in my home.
Gracious me, things will be better that way.
You stay in your home, and I'll stay in my home.
Gracious me, things will be better that way.

But if everybody behaved like that,
it would be a sad thing indeed.
If one followed such a system,
there wouldn't be any society any longer.
As for me, I like going to see you,
and you can come to see me sometimes.
I'll go to your home, and you'll come to my home.
Gracious me, things will be better that way.
I'll go to your home, and you'll come to my home.
Gracious me, things will be better that way."

*a small gate of a field or courtyard is "haizait" in Auregnais, "héchot" in Jèrriais and "héchet" in Guernesiais.

The two brothers were Peter and Richard Gauvain, and the uncle who died was Mr. Robinson. I was at his funeral and I heard Richard say to Peter, "When I was poor you didn't come to see me. Well, from now on you can stay home." That gave the idea later to write this song.

This poem was originally published in 1874, and later a version of it was incorporated by Denys Corbet into his epic 'L'Touar de Guernesy' where its wayward picaresque quality fits well (although Corbet toned down the dig about Darwinism). With thwarted love, madness, inter-racial marriage, and the trans-Atlantic connection, the poem manages to cover a lot of terrain – as many Channel Island families have done, down the years and around the world.

Denys Corbet

M'n-onclle. Histouaire véritablle, *1874* (Guernesiais, with footnote in French)

J'l'ai d'vànt l's-iers, m'n-onclle, taï qu'je l'vis,
D'vànt qu'en Terr'neuve i' s'en allisse;
Pour qu trouvaïr yun pair à li,
D'bouan matin fallait qu'nou se l'visse:
Un grànd mâbet d'chinq pîds dix d'haut,
Des daeux pus fort que not' cavale;
Mainti terrien, mainti tchen d'ieau;
V'là, chiers bénis, l'piant de qui j'pâle.

Que d'seirs, après l'solail gav'laï,
L'trouvaient au ras du Pont-Allaire;
Sus l'coupé d'la hêche appaouaï,
A chàntaïr d'charme à sa mennière
Quiq' chânson faite au déguerni,
Quèr', d'pis les pids jusqu'à la téte;
Biau qu' jamais n'fît daeux mots d'écrit,
M'n-onclle avait, dame, étai naï pouète.

Che n'tait pouit sel'ment ses chânsons
Qui forgeait, mais ch'tait sa musique;
Et dès qu'arroutaï, j'en réponds,
Des passânts, dame, i' n' s'en s'ciait chique;
Mais, s'nou li d'màndait de r'lataïr

Quiq' chànson qu'airait ieû bouann' mine,
J'craet-mei qu'il airait peû volaïr,
Pus accaoup qu'd'en r'trouvaïr un' line,

Pourtànt l'garçon n'tait brin gênaï,
Quèr' sa tète n'tait jamais viède;
Et sàns y-aver miette âgnounnaï
Dans un cllin i trouvait sen r'miède;
"Ah!" s't-i', "chett'-là, je n'la saïs pus;
Mais n'en v'chin, dame, un' bien pus belle";
Et i' s'mettait, coumme un perdu,
A vou-s-en chântaïr quiq' nouvelle,

Ch' n'est pouit, ma fei, là tout: l'gaillard
Fut yun d'nos tous prumiers sachaires;
Et pour pliumaïr oie et canard,
Coumm' li, ma fei, n'y-en avait guères;
Dame, à chu bouan temps là, l'gibier
Juquait brâment dans nos cllôtures,
Biau qu'a persent pour un pllouvier
En vain non trav'serait les hures.

Accouare i' me r'semblle qu' je l'veit,
Atou s'n-arme coumme une ormette,
Et d'six longs pids d'bari, ma fei,
Qu'i' maniait coumme une allamette;
Che n'tait pouit coumme les canons d'seux
D'nos bourjlotins qui font "bedoue,"
Souventre alouette' et verdeleux,
Qui leux tournent brâment la coue.

D'côt' chunna, m'n-onclle, parcordi!
Etait tout-fin-pllain d'touars et d'farces;
Vrai pllâgue en publlic et cîz li,
Et pour faire étrivaùr les garces,
Fallait l'vêir en long cotillon,
Au soir, gindaï sus sès ékaches,
Ou sous les tas à ventrillon,
Pour nou-s-épeurir d'ses grimaches.

Pourtànt, m's-amis, dans tout chunna,
Biau qu'nou se r'binfrait contre, à ch't-heure,
Nou n'y véyait, dame, aucun ma',

A chu temps là, j'vou-s-en asseure;
Quèr', biau qu'nou-s-creit bein pus rassis,
Et qu'nou s'seit défait d'pus d'un' dâgue,
Au fond nou-s-a bien empiéri,
Et nou n'est pus d'la vieille érague.

Mais j'pâlais de m'n-onclle, et, j'me r'mêts
Qu'il aeut, ma finge, une amouareuse;
Biau qu'auve elle i' n'paeut jamais s'grêi';
Al' tait si rouaître et si guicheuse;
A'l'rassâsi si bien d'grounards,
Qu'i' d'vint pus raufigni que l'guiâtre;
Si bien, ma fei, qu'un freid meis d'Mars,
I' la lâqui dans sen couain d'âtre.

Nou craeut qui fut mal consilli,
Ou bien qu'jamais n'l'airait quittâie;
Ch'est pus d'à chents caoups qu'nou m'l'a dit,
Vère et je l'creit, ma fei jurâie.
Quànd à ielle, i parait qu'ses gens
Ll'avient sufflaï d'si bell' flleurailles,
Qu'a' lî fit, dâme, un fichu traen,
D'vànt que d'lî r'bailler ses fiànchailles.

Dès qu'auve elle i' fut débourgui,
I' fît brâmant ses paquotilles;
Et oprès li-même i' s'paqui,
Pour jamais ne r'v'ni 'vêi' nos îles.
A quând la garce l'vit s'nallaïr,
Al' aeut, dame, une itaille assuâie,
Qu'a' n'paeut jamais la surmontaïr,
Et mouarit au cachot ... troubllaie!

Pour quânt â l'onclle, i' s'en alli
Coumme j'vou l'ai dit, pour Terr'neuve,
Où j'ouis, par après, qu'i' s'marii –
Et v'chin, parcordi, chu qui m'greuve:
A un' négresse! – l'créirait-n-on?
Qui fît, l'tout en travers, not' tante!
Mais vaut mûx chunna qu'un guénon,
Pour d'ses gens – coumm'll'a qui s'en vante.★

Pour li, jamais ne r'fît biau saut;
I' s'était mariaï par guervànce,
Et il aeut terjoûs l'cueur tro' gros
Pour sa falle, et n'r'aeut jamais d'chànce.
D'couain et d'autre i' fut d'canvachi,
Et, sus l'drain, dans la flleur de s'n-âge,
L'paure infortunaï décampi
Pour sen drain, sen tout pus long viage!

I' s'alli d'l'âge à tous l's-empllâtres.
Et lâqui brâment sa négresse,
Et sen troupé de p'tits molâtres
A vivre, d'leus mûx, sus leus graisse!
Qu'est qu'en est dev'nu j'n'en saïs rien;
Nou n'en a jamais oui vent n'vagues;
Pourtânt je n'leus veur que tout bien,
Quând j'pense à m'n-onclle et ses pernâgues.

Ah! v'là par tro' souvent coumm' ch'est,
A quànd les viers sont trop tout-s-mêles,
Et, respet d'nos avers, qui creient
Qu' jamais n'ont étaï d'jannes r'belles.
A père et mère auve un crâgnon,
Qui s'grie en cotillon ou brée,
J'dis: fillaïz-li la corde un mion,
Et qui s'amouarache à s'n-idée.

Pourtànt guia, n'faut pouit s'y trompaïr,
Ch'n'est pouit que j'veur que nou les lâque,
Par rue et v'nelle à couanvardaïr,
Sâns d'bouans avis, ou fu-che, un cllaque.
Mais quànd sen d'veir est un caoup fait,
Qu' cheux qui n'en veulent rien s'en passent;
I' s'couach'ront coumme i' f'ront leus liet,
Et che s'ra leus soins si n' s'acllasent.

Bouann' gens, vou m'creiraïz si vou pllaît,
Je n'viens pouit vou contaïr d'menties;
Vère, et, parcordi, j'en mettrais
Ma main dans la fllàmbe ou l's-orties.
J'l'ai veû d'mes daeux iers chu qu' j'ai dit,
Et ouï, ma fei, d'mes daeux oreilles;

J'sîs fier s'ou-s-'n-agriaïz l'récit,
Biau qu' n'y-a miraclles ni méreilles.

* Plus d'un savant à prétendu gravement prouver que le genre humain est descendu des singes

My Uncle. A true story, *1874*

There he is before my eyes, my uncle, as I saw him,
before he went off to Newfoundland;
to find his equal,
you'd have to get up early:
a big fellow of five foot ten,
twice as strong as our nag;
half landlubber, half sea dog;
there, my dears, that's the bloke I'm talking about.

How many evenings, after sundown,
found him down at Pont Allaire
lounging on top of the gate
singing away in his own manner
some improvised song,
because, from tip to toe,
although he couldn't put two words together in writing,
my uncle had really been born a poet.

It wasn't just his songs
he made up, but it was his music,
and once he got going, I tell you,
he really couldn't care less about passers-by;
but if you asked him to repeat
some song that was worth it,
I think he'd just as soon have flown
as be able to recover a line of it.

But the lad wasn't a bit bothered,
for his head was never empty,
and without hesitating a moment
in a blink he'd find the answer;
"Ah!" he'd say, "that one I've forgotten,
but here's one that's really a lot nicer,"
and he'd start off madly
singing you a new one.

And, goodness me, that's not all: the lad
was one of our finest hunters;
for plucking goose and duck,
I tell you there was scarcely anyone like him;
in those days, you know, the game
perched right in our enclosed fields,
while nowadays you'd traipse up and down
in vain for a plover.

I seem to see him still,
with his gun like a young elm,
and its six foot long barrel, indeed,
that he handled like it was a matchstick;
it wasn't like the pop-guns
of our young swells which go "bang",
in pursuit of larks and hedge sparrows
that promptly turn their tails at them.

Besides that, goodness! my uncle
was brimful of practical jokes and tricks,
a real menace in public and at home,
and in order to give the girls a scare,
you should have seen him in a long nightdress,
of an evening, tottering about on stilts,
or flat on his belly under the haystacks
pulling faces to frighten us.

However, my friends, in all that,
although we'd object to it now,
then we didn't see any harm
in it at all, I assure you;
for, although we think ourselves much more refined,
and we'd be put out by all sorts of actions,
deep down we're no longer what we were,
and we're no longer of the old stock.

But I was speaking about my uncle, and I'll get back to saying
that he had, you know, a sweetheart;
although he could fix things up with her;
she was so short-tempered and difficult to get along with;
he'd had so much of her grumbling
that he became as ruffled as the devil;

so much so, indeed, that one cold March
off he went and left her by her hearth.

We thought he'd been badly advised
or else he'd never have left her,
I've been told that more than a hundred times, indeed,
and I believe it, I swear.
As for her, it seems her family
had told her such fancy tales
that she really gave him a hard time
before returning his engagement ring.

As soon as he'd got rid of her,
he straightaway packed his bags,
and then he packed himself off,
never to return and see our islands again.
And when the girl saw him go off,
that really shook her up so much
that she never got over it,
and died ... in a padded cell!

As for uncle, off he went
as I told you, to Newfoundland,
where, I heard later, he got married –
and this is what gets me:
to a negress! – would you believe it?
Which made the blessed woman our aunt!
But better that than an ape
in the family tree – as some people boast of.★

But things never went right for him after that;
he'd got married out of pique,
and he was always rather down
in the mouth, and his luck failed him.
He was chased from pillar to post,
and at the last, in the prime of life,
the poor unfortunate set out
for his final and longest journey!

He passed away at the age of all jokers.
And promptly left his negress,
and his pack of little mulattoes
to live as best they could with what they had!

What happened to them I don't know;
we've never heard a whisper from them;
but I wish them nothing but well,
when I think of my uncle and all his pranks.

Ah, that's all too often the way it goes,
when the old folks meddle too much,
and, no offence to our children, think
that they were never young and foolish themselves, once.
To a father and mother with a child,
whether dressed up in petticoat or trousers,
I say: cut them a bit of slack
and let them fall in love as they want to.

But make no mistake,
it's not that I want them to be left
to run wild in street and lane,
with no helpful advice nor perhaps a slap.
But when one's duty is done,
let those who are not involved leave well alone;
as they make their bed, they'll lie in it,
and it'll be their problem if they can't get to sleep.

Friends, you can believe me if you please,
I haven't just been telling you a pack of lies;
So help me, I'll put
my hand in the flame or in nettles.
I've seen with my own two eyes what I've told you,
and heard, indeed, with my own two ears;
I'm happy if you approve of this tale
even though it contains neither miracles nor wonders.

*More than one scientist has seriously claimed to have proved that humankind is descended from apes

---

The rise of the rebellious teenager in the 1960s and the craze for pop music did not go unremarked, as this extract, from a comic playlet performed at the annual Eisteddfod, shows. The Beatles had performed in Jersey and Guernsey in August 1963, and this play manages to involve The Beatles, drug-taking among the young, the changing expectations of young women, and the generation gap before contriving a happy ending. The text of this unpublished play is taken from one of the original scripts for the cast: it was intended to enable the actors to learn their lines, rather than be printed, which goes to explain the lack of consistent spelling and punctuation.

Stan Le Ruez ('S. P. Le Ruez')

From Les Temps Changent, *c.1965* (Jèrriais)

La clioche sonne

JANE *respond et dit*: Chez un télegram de la Suisse.

(*Oulle donne a* LOUISE)

LOUISE: Ouvre et l'ai John, ches p'têtre de mauvaises nouvelles, j'en tremblye.

JOHN *l'ouvre et s'ecrie*: Chez Marguerite ou s'en vin agniet – avec un ami.

LOUISE: Chez p't'etre son jeune homme, mais ch'est p't'etre unne jeune fille mais ch'la fait d'rein. Oh' t'chi joie?

LOUISE *va au telephone et dit*: Mamam vin t'en tout d'un coup oh' fiche du coq.

JOHN: Jane. Va t'en lavé, et grais tes ch'veux et change ta robe. Si ta soeur te vait d'meme oulle e'tha honte, et sus toutes choses ne l'y pasle pas tes sucrins. Entends tu?

JANE *dé côté*: Y sont vont avait un chocque.

La clioche sonne.

LOUISE: Va vite John. Chez yeux bein seux.

JOHN *va à la porte et l'ouvre et vait deux betes nicks, et lus dit*: Nonnin Mercis j'navons pas besouin des gens comme vous.

(*Freumne la porte, et a* LOUISE)

Ch'est deux betes nicks, ch'est desgoûtant, sait pas même si ch'est des garçons ou filles.

JANE *rentre pas changie.*

John *a Jane*: J't'avais dit d'aller laver.

JANE: J'ai bein oui me, ch'est des betes nicks, pathait aussi bein qu'eux.

LOUISE: Pour me faithe plaisi ma p'tite va t'approprie.

La porte ouvre et les deux betes nicks entrent.

JOHN: Ou s'en avez d'l'affront. J'vos ai dit d'fichi l'cant, allons en route.

MARGUERITE: Tu m'erconnais pas don, chez ta Marguerite, la sienne qu'ai t'adoraient.

LOUISE *met la tete dans les mains et s'ecrie.*

Ch'n'est pas possble.

JOHN: Mais absolument ch'est un rêve, tu n'est pas not chiethe Marguerite.

JOHN (*dé côté*): J'vos avez bein dit d'vos prepathé pour un chocque.

JOHN (*téléphone a maman*): Mamam' ne t'en vin pas, tout est changi abetôt.

MARGUERITE: J'ai grand r'gret de m'presenté d'même, mais chez tout a fait necessaithe. A not College y en a de toutes les sortes, de toutes classes, jusqu'a des naithes, des filles adoptées, mais sommes toutes considethées d'être de la meme classe. Quant j'arrivi au College y m'appelaient eune poupette, eune carree, et bein d'autres choses qu'ai j'peux pas vos dithe, et les premiers trais mais j'eu eune vie quasiment insupportable, j'nai pas honte de dithe qu'ai plieuthi bein des fais.

A LOUISE. Memes, ne prend pas trop a t'choeu ma vielle car...

JOHN: N'en v'la assez, et t'ch'est est chu perrot la avec tai.

MARGUERITE: Ch'est un grecque. Son nom est Pietro Soudisanto.

JOHN: Il a bein l'air d'eune bolée d'graisse.

MARGUERITE: Ne sait pas insultant s'y plait, j'vai bein sommes pas les beinvenues, et comme chenna j'n'avons qu'une chose a faithe, et ch'est de nos s'nallé.

(*Prend* JIM *par le bras et sont vont a la porte*)

LOUISE (*en plieuthant*): Margeurite' Marguerite' ne t'en va pas, ne t'en va pas.

JOHN: Laisse les allé.

MARGUERITE (*a la porte*): Mon pourre v'y'i, tu crait tes bein sage, mais helas tu'as un tas t'chi apprendre.

(MARGUERITE *et* JIM *s'en vont*).

JOHN (*la tete dans les mains*): Et bein, Louise, ma vielle, ne v'la résultat de ton sacrifice, no dévotion, de nos ambitions, n'ou ethait jamais penser. Rappelle tait qu'a matin j'paslâimes de not châté en l'air, et bein le v'la bein t'chulbuté.

LOUISE: Et j'me d'mande, pourt'chi, j'avons tout ch'la t'chi nos faut autrement, est'y possiblye qu'ai j'avons tait trop ambitieux et sans l'voulé tu'as tait un mio trop du.

JANE: La' ou viyiez bein acheteu, ou s'avaient mins touous vos sou pour faithe eune d'moiselle de Marguerite. Mai, j'tais rein et bein n'en v'la l'resultat ou n'voulez pas accepté les temps d'acheteu mais ou savez bein les temps changent.

(*continue*)

Et veulle ou n'veulle pas y faut l'accepté et si oulle n'voulez pas, ausse bein tappé vot tête contre eune muthaille.

La clioche sonne.

LOUISE: Jane, va respondre, j'ai n'somme pas en etat de l'faithe.

JANE *va a la porte et l'ouvre toute grande, et* MARGUERITE *et* JIM *entrent dans lus habits ordinaithes.*

MARGUERITE *s'en va tout drait a sa methe et l'embrache.* JOHN *veurs faithe la meme chose, mais* MARGUERITE *l'arrête.*

JOHN: Ch'tait eune farce.

MARGUERITE: Ch'tait pas eune vraie farce, mais eune espreuve, et s'y plait faut tu m'escoute. Jane m'a escrit a m'dithe comment tu n'as tréjous contre y'i.

JOHN: Mais tu sait bein...

MARGUERITE: Ch'est a mai la patholle.

(*dit a* JIM) Va t'assiethe s'y plait.

J'vos asseuthe qu'ai d'vant faithe chunne'chin y'ait donné un tas d'pensée. J'en ai pliethé même, mais ayant yeu l'opportunité d'aller au College, j'ai apprins bein d't'chi. Tu n'as pas accou realise qu'ai sommes eune nouvelle génération, mais tu sait bein n'ch'est pas viyant q'nou vait sus la Poste touous les siers qu'un tas jeunes gens sont en embarras, qu'ai j'devthaime êtes tous tathées avec la meme bringe. J'aime ma soeur telle qu'oulle est. J'ai y'eut un grand avantage sus yi Tu sait bein pépes faut tu l'encouthage. As tu realisé qu'oulle est a sacrificié sa vie pour vos soigni. Est t'alle appreciée. Nonnin. La j'en ai dit assez. Mais y s'en va fallait tu decide. Est tu prêt a accepté Jane tel qu'oulle est. Ou adoptites Jane pour ma compagnie et ou tetes viers assez pour realisé ch'la qu'ou faisaites. La Loi d'adoption d'mande qu'ai vos esfants adoptées ou pas ont droit es memes privileges. Et tais Mémès, tu'est bein tranchille, mais j'veurs pas d'faithe de peine, tu m'as tait trop bouanne. Avec vot permission j'allons couochi ichin asessé, v'la t'chi vos donna eune chance de vos decider, mais realisée bein qu'ai si ou n'êtes pas prêt a accepter ma soeur telle qu'oulle est, j'vos dit bein séthieusement ou s'en pas s'en v'nit avec mai. Je sis prête a sacrifié ma vie pour y'i.

LOUISE: Le jeune garcon, et t'y'i ton jeune homme.

MARGUERITE: Ah' mais nonnin, je n'avions pas seulement pensé. Il est estudiant étout. J'nos entre aidgions, chez tout.

JIM (*se leve et dit*): J'peux vos dithe qu'ai vot fille est la pus populaithe du College. Tous l'admithe et quant a mai ou m'a tait eune diverse aide, mais la t'chestion de sa soeut l'y fait un tas d'peine. J'voudrais plaid'gi avec vous et ou vos en er'grettez pas.

From **The Times they are a-changing,** *c.1965*

The bell rings.

JANE *answers it and says*: It's a telegram from Switzerland

(*She gives it to* LOUISE)

LOUISE: Open it, John, it might be bad news. I'm nervous.

JOHN *opens it and exclaims*: It's from Margaret. She's arriving today – with a friend.

LOUISE: That might be her boyfriend, or perhaps it's a young girl, but that doesn't matter. How happy I am!

LOUISE *goes to the telephone and says*: Granny, come round straightaway. Oh, never mind about the cockerel.

JOHN: Jane. Go and wash, and do your hair and change your dress. If your sister sees you like that she'll be ashamed, and above all don't mention those sweets. Do you understand?

JANE (*aside*): They're going to get a shock.

The bell rings.

LOUISE: Go and get it John, quickly. That must be them.

JOHN *goes to the door, opens it and sees two silly devils* (beatniks), *and tells them*: No thank you, we don't need your sort.

(*Shuts the door, and says to* LOUISE)

It's a pair of silly devils (beatniks), it's revolting, you can't tell whether they're boys or girls.

JANE *comes back without having changed.*

JOHN, *to* JANE: *I told you to go and wash.*

JANE: I heard. Those beatniks, if they can be like that, so can I.

LOUISE: Just to please me, darling, go and get ready.

The door opens and the two beatniks enter.

JOHN: You've got some nerve. I told you to buzz off, off you go.

MARGARET:So you don't recognise your own Margaret, your loved one?

LOUISE *puts her head in her hands and exclaims*: It's not possible!

JOHN: But it must be a dream, you can't be our dear Margaret.

JANE (*aside*): I told you you'd be in for a shock.

JOHN (*phones up Granny*): Granny, don't come round. It's all changed. Goodbye.

MARGARET: I'm really sorry to turn up like this, but I really have to. At our college there's all sorts of people, of all classes, even black girls and adopted daughters, but we're all considered to be the same class of person. When I arrived in college they called me a dolly, a square, and lots of other things I can't tell you, and for the first three months my life was almost unbearable, and I'm not ashamed to say that I spent a lot of time crying.

To LOUISE

Mum, dear, don't take it too much to heart because...

JOHN: That's enough, and who's this bloke with you?

MARGARET: He's Greek. His name is Pietro Supposedo.

JOHN: He looks like a bowl of grease.

MARGARET: Don't be rude, please, I can see that we're not wanted, and if things are like that, there's only one thing to do, and that's leave.

(*takes* JIM *by the arm and they go to the door*)

LOUISE (*crying*): Margaret! Margaret! Don't go, don't go!

JOHN: Let them go.

MARGARET (*at the door*): My poor old man, you think you know it all, but alas, you've got a lot to learn.

(MARGARET *and* JIM *exit*)

John (*his head in his hands*): Well, Louise, old girl, that's what's become of your sacrifice, our devotion, our ambitions. You'd never have believed it. Do you remember that this morning we were talking about our castle in the air, well it's come crashing down to earth now.

LOUISE: And I'm asking myself why. We've got everything we need, otherwise. Is it possible that we've been too ambitious and, without meaning to, you've been a bit too hard?

JANE: There, you can see it now. You'd spent all your money on making Margaret into a young lady. Me, I was nothing, and so you can see what you're left with. You don't want to accept the way things are now, but you know that the times they are a-changin'.

(*carries on*)

And whether you like it or not, you have to accept it, and if you don't want to, you might as well knock your head against a wall.

The bell rings.

LOUISE: Jane, go and answer it. I'm in no fit state.

JANE *goes to the door and pulls it wide open, and* MARGARET *and* JIM *enter in their ordinary clothes.*

MARGARET goes straight up to her mother and hugs her. John wants to do the same, but Margaret stops him.

JOHN: It was a joke.

MARGARET: It wasn't really a joke, but a test, and you must listen to me, please. Jane wrote to me to tell me how you've always been against her.

JOHN: But, you know...

MARGARET: It's my turn to speak.

I assure you that before going ahead with this I gave it a lot of thought. I even cried over it, but having had the opportunity to go to College, I've learned a lot. You haven't realised yet that we are a new generation, but you know it's not because every evening you see in the Evening Post about a lot of young people in trouble, that we should all be tarred with the same brush. I love my sister just the way she is, I've had a great advantage over her. You know, Dad, you ought to encourage her. Have you realised that she's sacrificed her life to look after you? Is she appreciated? No. There, I've said enough. But you're going to have to decide. Are you prepared to accept Jane just the way she is? You adopted Jane to keep me company, and you were old enough to know what you were doing. The Adoption law requires that your children, whether adopted or not, have the right to the same privileges. And you, Mum, you're very quiet, but I don't want to trouble you, you've been too good to me. With your permission, I'll spend the night here, and that'll give you a chance to make your minds up. But you've got to realise that if you aren't prepared to accept my sister just the way she is, I tell you seriously, she's coming with me. I'm ready to sacrifice my life for her.

LOUISE: The young lad, is he your boyfriend?

MARGARET: Oh no! There's nothing like that between us. He's a student too. We're helping each other out, that's all.

JIM (*gets up and says*): I can tell you that your daughter is the most popular girl in the College. Everyone admires her, and as for me, she's been a great help to me, but the question of her sister has been bothering her greatly. I'd like to plead with you, and you won't regret it.

War and Peace

The Islands bear the traces of the fortifications of thousands of years – from prehistoric earthworks now settled into the curves of the landscape to the massive blocks and towers of German concrete intervening sharply in the cliffs and coasts. We have seen tales of Vandal raids, Owen of Wales's attack of 1372, the Norman Conquest of England in 1066, and piracy. The great breakwaters of Alderney and Saint Catherine in Jersey are the remnants of grand projects for military harbours. The coasts are ringed by defensive towers of the Napoleonic period, some now domesticated to other uses. Mediaeval castles rise and later fortresses sprawl. In the face of external threat, service in the militias was a civic duty and a social rite for generations of Guernseymen and Jerseymen, and sometimes described by the writers within their ranks – and their smart parades were observed by the wives, mothers and girlfriends among Jerseywomen and Guernseywomen, and also sometimes described by the writers within those female ranks.

Sir Gilbert Parker's *The Battle of the Strong* (1898), is a novel based loosely on the life of Jerseyman Philippe d'Auvergne who became Prince of Bouillon and was a spymaster during the Napoleonic Wars, only to see the small European principality he inherited swept away in the reorganisation of continental territories by the Congress of Vienna. The novel is larded with phrases in Jèrriais to provide local colour. The New York Times reviewed the novel in 1898 and said, "There is perhaps too much of dialect, but at this moment it is too much to expect any novelist to court the aspersion of being unable to write in more than one language, and Jersey dialect is a reflection of the Jersey mind and conscience, a constant fluctuation from French to English and English to French, a key to the speaker's thought and feeling."

Sir Gilbert Parker

From **The Battle of the Strong,** *1898*

On a map the Isle of Jersey has the shape and form of a tiger on the prowl.

The fore-claws of this tiger are the lacerating pinnacles of the Corbiere and the impaling rocks of Portelet Bay and Noirmont; the hind-claws are the devastating diorite reefs of La Motte and the Banc des Violets. The head and neck, terrible and beautiful, are stretched out towards the west, as it were to scan the wild waste and jungle of the Atlantic seas. The nose is L'Etacq, the forehead Grosnez, the ear Plemont, the mouth the dark cavern by L'Etacq, and the teeth are the serried ledges of the Foret de la Brequette. At a discreet distance from the head and the tail hover the jackals of La Manche: the Paternosters, the Dirouilles, and the Ecrehos, themselves destroying where they may, or filching the remains of the tiger's feast of shipwreck and ruin. In truth, the sleek beast, with its feet planted in fearsome rocks and tides, and its ravening head set to defy the onslaught of the main, might, but for its ensnaring beauty, seem some monstrous foot-pad of the deep.

To this day the tiger's head is the lonely part of Jersey; a hundred years ago it was as distant from the Vier Marchi as is Penzance from Covent Garden. It would almost seem as if the people of Jersey, like the hangers-on of the king of the jungle, care not to approach too near the devourer's head. Even now there is but a dwelling here and there upon the lofty plateau, and none at all near the dark and menacing headland. But as if the ancient Royal Court was determined to prove its sovereignty even over the tiger's head, it stretched out its arms from the Vier Marchi to the bare neck of the beast, putting upon it a belt of defensive war; at the nape, a martello tower and barracks; underneath, two other martello towers like the teeth of a buckle.

The rest of the island was bristling with armament. Tall platforms were erected at almost speaking distance from each other, where sentinels kept watch for French frigates or privateers. Redoubts and towers were within musket-shot of each other, with watch-houses between, and at intervals every able-bodied man in the country was obliged to leave his trade to act as sentinel, or go into camp or barracks with the militia for months at a time. British cruisers sailed the Channel: now a squadron under Barrington, again under Bridport, hovered upon the coast, hoping that a French fleet might venture near.

But little of this was to be seen in the western limits of the parish of St. Ouen's. Plemont, Grosnez, L'Etacq, all that giant headland could well take care of itself – the precipitous cliffs were their own defence. A watch-house here and there sufficed. No one lived at L'Etacq, no one at Grosnez; they were too bleak, too distant and solitary. There were no houses, no huts.

Edward Gavey's historical novel *In Peirson's Days* (1902) contains fragments of both Jèrriais and Jersey-English, as well as French, and gives a romanticised picture of the Island at the time of the Battle of Jersey in 1781. On 6 January 1781 a small contingent of French troops landed in Jersey and took the Lieutenant Governor, Moses Corbet, by surprise and before he could know the true numbers of the invading force. Acting in ignorance of the real situation, Corbet surrendered. The senior ranking British officer in the Island at that moment was a young major from Yorkshire, Francis Peirson, as the more experienced British officers had returned to Great Britain for Christmas leave. The Island was unprepared for the invasion, especially as Islanders were still generally celebrating Christmas according to the old Julian calendar at that time. Major Peirson defied the command to surrender and led troops against the French into the Royal Square ('le Vièr Marchi' – the old market place) in Saint Helier. He was shot and killed on entering the Square; the commander of the French forces, Baron de Rullecourt was shot during the short battle and died after a few hours in the doctor's house in the corner of the Square. The doctor's house later became a pub, The Peirson, which we have already seen mentioned in Jean Sullivan's poem about the races.

Edward Gavey

From In Peirson's Days, *1902* (English & Jèrriais)

After the service, most of the congregation repaired to their beloved "Vier Marchi," and here the battle was fought over again. Listen to one stout militiaman who, with head erect and the air of a conqueror, is relating to "la buonne femme," and an admiring crowd, what he did on that memorable day. "Sthe ichen que je tua l'Français. Il vint a mé avec sa bajonétte pour me tué, mais devans ch'il eu fait chunnà j'li bailli une cliamuse a la goule avec le gran' but d'man fusi, en disans: Prenéz chunnà, man garçon. Apres ch'la, j'li donnit une tappe a la tête, et dans une minute il etait mort." His recital is received with cries of "Brav' Mait'e Jo; r'gardez ta buoune femme, ou'lle est bain fiere d'vous. Le Gouverneur té f'ra sergeant pour ch'la."

A little further off a group is gathered round a smart young fellow, who, in Jersey-English, is endeavouring to describe the battle in which he took part. In fact, his story may be called: "How I won the battle of Jersey." "Well, my byes, it was like to this. I was 'long with Captain Lumsden, to the Highlanders. We marched down 'La Grande Rue,' an' who should come up at us? Why old Corbé. My good! you should have heerd our men grind their teeth at 'im. He puts up 'is 'ands an' tals us not to shoot, but at onst we gave 'im som bullats that sent 'im about 'is bizness. Then we pass at the double into Lib'ry Place, but som' of us got 'it by the big gun; "Mais, ma fé," we run quick an' soon knock over the gunners. "Ah bain!" we got into the "Vier Marchi," an' then, my byes, that was a time. You know Tom Le Gresley. Well, pore bye, he was kill'd just 'longside to me, an' I had three shots to my 'at. After that, just then, the French cry out "Victoree," an' we ask, what for? The cry comes down the "Marchi": "Peirson is killed." " Man dou d'la vie," that made us mad, an' I sez to Ph'lip Muorant, "Look heere, Ph'lip, I'm goin' to shew to them who's got to the victoree. You shoot that 'rein chi valle' De Rullecour on the steps theere." I fired first an' 'it 'im in the jaw, an' Ph'lip 'it 'im in the body. That settled 'im. Now I sez, byes, 'Shoot at Corbé,' for we all looked at 'im as a French enemy; but nobody could kill 'im that day – all he got was two shots to 'is vat as he made to carry De Rullecour into "La Cohue." After that we all got jammed up like a lot of conger in Uncle Jean's boat. It was push heere, an' 'it theere, but we could-n't load our "vier fusis." Ah! it was a time, an' no mistake. The French they kick to us like mad, an' we gave 'em som' good "patawarres" with our fists. Never in all my life have I heerd such a "train" as the French made; but we kept shouting to one another – "Remember Peirson," an' each time that cry was made we went for 'em like to the 'ammer an' tongs. Well, my byes, they fighted well, an' no mistake; but we were too many for 'em, an' we had 'em like rats in a trap. Well then, at 2 o'clock they cried out: "Sauve qui peut," an' ran like a lot of rats into the houses an' shops. Then we make 'em all prisoners, an' the Captain sez to me, "Well done, Tom Vautie'. I'll mantion you to the Governor as the man that killed De Rullecour, an' won the battle of Jersey," an' that's what is it.

Translation

After the service, most of the congregation repaired to their beloved Royal Square and here the battle was fought over again. Listen to one stout militiaman who, with head erect and the air of a conqueror, is relating to his wife and an admiring crowd, what he did on that memorable day. "It was here that I killed the Frenchman. He came at me with his bayonet to kill me, but before he could do it I clouted him in the face with the big end of my gun, and said "Take that, my lad", After that I hit him on the head, and in a minute he was dead." His recital is received with cries of "Well done, Master Jo; look at your wife, she's very proud of you. The Governor will make you sergeant for that."

A little further off a group is gathered round a smart young fellow, who, in Jersey-English, is endeavouring to describe the battle in which he took part. In fact, his story may be called: "How I won the battle of Jersey." "Well, my boys, it was like this. I was accompanying Captain Lumsden, of the Highlanders. We marched down Broad Street and who should come up to us? Why old Corbet. My god! you should have heard our men grind their teeth at him. He puts up his hands and tells us not to shoot, but at once we gave him some bullets that sent him about his busi-ness. Then we pass at the double into Library Place, but some of us got hit by the big gun; "But, my goodness," we run quick and soon knock over the gunners. "Ah well!" "we got into the Royal Square and then, my boys, that was a time. You know Tom Le Gresley. Well, poor boy, he was killed just next to me, and I had three shots to my hat. After that, just then, the French cry out "Victoree," and we ask, what for? The cry comes down the Square: "Peirson is killed." "Goodness gracious me," that made us mad, and I says to Ph'lip Mourant, "Look here, Ph'lip, I'm goin' to show them who's got to the victoree. You shoot that no-good De Rullecour on the steps

Keith James

performs

The Songs of
LEONARD COHEN

Each Song stripped back. Desolate Naked and Sensual

'Some of the most atmospheric and emotive music you will ever hear' The Independent

'Musicians brave enough to make the music they really believe in. Keith James is one of these' Bob Harris BBC Radio

'Passing it on through the generations. Genuinely inspirational" BBC Radio Manchester

'Keith James has become a pillar of trust. A sublimely intimate and engaging voice' Sunday Times

Also included are Poems by Federico Garcia Lorca and Leonard Cohen that Keith has set to music.

Falmouth Poly, TR11 3TG
Thursday March 6th   8pm   £12.00
Box office 01326 319461 or online www.thepoly.org
www.keith-james.com

there." I fired first and hit him in the jaw, and Ph'lip hit him in the body. That settled him. Now I says, boys, 'Shoot at Corbé,' for we all looked at him as a French
enemy; but nobody could kill him that day – all he got was two shots to his hat as
he made to carry De Rullecour into the Royal Court building. After that we all got
jammed up like a lot of conger in Uncle Jean's boat. It was push here, and hit there,
but we couldn't load our old guns. Ah! it was a time, and no mistake. The French
they kick at us like mad, and we gave them some good wallops with our fists. Never
in all my life have I heard such a fuss as the French made; but we kept shouting to
one another – "Remember Peirson," and each time that cry was made we went for
them like hammer and tongs. Well, my boys, they fought well, and no mistake; but
we were too many for them, and we had them like rats in a trap. Well then, at 2
o'clock they cried out: "Run for it," and ran like a lot of rats into the houses an'
shops. Then we make 'em all prisoners, an' the Captain says to me, "Well done,
Tom Vautier. I'll mention you to the Governor as the man that killed De Rullecour,
and won the battle of Jersey," an' that's how it was.

The Guernsey militia, like that of Jersey, was a mediaeval creation. It became the
Royal Guernsey Militia in 1831 (the Royal Jersey Militia also received the title of
royal favour – the occasion being the fiftieth anniversary of the Battle of Jersey in
which the men of the Militia served with distinction), but lost military, if not social,
significance as the nineteenth century wore on. Vernacular literature reflects concern about status and rank, military reforms, changes in uniform, and much else
about such a feature of Island life. Many of the writers we have met were proud of
their militia service – among them, George W. de Carteret served as Military
Vingtenier for the West of Jersey, Jean Sullivan was a Captain, Philippe Langlois
was a Major and Medical Officer. During the First World War the Royal Guernsey
Militia was suspended and the Royal Guernsey Light Infantry became a part of the
British Army. The Royal Guernsey Militia was reformed, in a much reduced form,
during the inter-war years and was mobilised in 1939. But it was suspended in 1940
before the Occupation. The Royal Jersey Militia's last duty was manning Fort
Regent in Saint Helier, before marching to the harbour in 1940 to embark for serv-
ice in the British Army – the name survives in Jersey's Territorial Army unit, the
Jersey Field Squadron (Royal Militia of the Island of Jersey). The Guernsey
Militia's motto was Diex Aïx (God's help) – the war cry of the Normans at the
Battle of Hastings as described by Wace in the Roman de Rou.

Of course, not all was honour and nobility, as military order could sometimes be
reduced to farce, as Denys Corbet reminds us.

Published in 1884, Corbet's story recalls life in the Guernsey Militia under
Major-General Sir William Napier, Lieutenant-Governor of Guernsey 1842–1848.
At that time, Corbet was in his late teens and early twenties, and Napier was a con-
troversial figure. Napier engaged in a power struggle with the civilian government
and court, and in an attempt to intimidate the Guernsey authorities landed a 600-

strong British military force. George Métivier launched a satirical barb at Napier in November 1847 in anticipation of Napier's removal from office.

George Métivier ('Un Câtelain')

From Moussieu Napier, *1847*

...Si ch'tait là tout, les Guernesiais, mes garçons, v'là qu'est seur,
N'airaient pus rien à dire ès siens qui leux font mal au coeur;
Mais les soudards à côtillons, ah! goule enferouagnie!
Malheur, malheur à Guernesi, si jamais nou l's oublie!

[If that was all, the Guernsey people, that's certain, my lads,
wouldn't have anything else to say to those who've made them sick at heart;
but the Highlanders, ah! what an ugly-looking crew!
Woe, woe to Guernsey, if ever they're forgotten!]

The passage of time, however, had softened the memory of the Lieutenant-Governor's arrogance, and in Denys Corbet's reminiscence, the Major-General's foibles are more a target of fun. It is also fair to say that by the end of the nineteenth century, the functions of the Lieutenant-Governors of Guernsey and those of Jersey were changing, and becoming more like the functions which their modern successors fulfil at the present time.

Denys Corbet ('Bad'lagoule')

Ch'est pour la Raïne, gatdérabotin, *1884* (Guernesiais)

Ha! mes bénites bouannes gens, ouê qu'j'en étion? Es grànd's mourtes du Regiment Bllu. Eh bien, j'en avon oui assaïz sus chu chapîter là, et l'sujet d'not' balivernin d'aniet s'ra, "Un Jour de naissànce d'la Raïne, au temps du béni vìer Gen'ral Napier – à Guiu seit-i." Ch'tait sus l'*Play-Field*, coum les soudards du pâïe s'entrinaient à l'app'laïr, et l'appeulent accouare, exceptaï quiq-s-uns qui disaient *Pray Field*; et j'cré-mé qu'chès-chin avaient l'pus raison; caër ill'aeut pus *periaï* que *jouaï* chu jour là, et accouare pus juraï, en bas, du moins. L's-uns periaient qu'i n'pllusse pouit d'autre; l's-auters qu'i pllusse dûr assaïz pour gardaïr l'Gén'ral cïz lî, et l's-env'yaïr cîz aeux; tànt que l's-autres juraient leus p'tits leus grànds qu'nou n'les y rattrap'rait pus d'itaï temps pour aucune Raïne ou aucun Gén'ral du monde.

    Ch'tait sus la citadelle qu'nou-s-allait à chu temps là, coum nou le r'fait à ch't-heure. L'bouan vìer Gén'ral était tro grànd guêrrier pour allaïr ès soudards âïlleurs. L'Hyvreuse était tro p'tite, et la neuve cauchie n'existait pouit. I' n'y-avait qu'la citadelle, Làncresse ou l'Vazon, et ch'tait à yun d'chès treis endrets là qu'nou-s-allait touar à touar; ch'est-à-dire sus la citadelle à quànd ch'tait pour la Raïne, et à l'Ancresse ou au Vazon à quand ch'tait pour des *shamfights*, mot qui veur dire faire mìne de s'enter battre. Eh bien, l'caoup de qui j'vou pâle ch'tait sus la citadelle et pour la Raïne.

I' pllouvait à fìne décllaque au matin à quànd nou se l'vi. Tou dépurait. Tous crèyaient qu'i' n'y-airait pouit d'mourtes d'itaï temps; mais, dame, il' avaient contaï sàns leus Gén'ral, ma fìnge. Nou n'aeut que d'perdre ses iers à r'gardaïr les moulins à vent dans châcune des pâresses; créyànt y vê haïstaïr les couleurs pour dire qu'i' n'y-airait pouit d'mourtes chu jour là. J'vo-s-en fiche. Les couleurs restirent paquies dans leus haleux. I' n'y-aeut qu'les ciennes des régiments qu'nou dépaqui; et ch'tait pour se mettre en marche. S'nou créyait que l'Gén'ral était effràïe de quiq bouq'tâïe d'iaû freide, pus qu'i n'tait d'faeu, nou s'trompait, ma fìnge. En âgnounànt et grounànt châcun s'gueriit donc dans les bllànches brées d'teile que nou mettait à chu temps là, et la rouage cotte, et nou-s-n-alli pendànt l's-oreilles à travers la pllie coum autànt d'tchens fouittaïs. L's-uns avaient prìns leus parapllies et d'auters leus gros corsiaux pour allaïr jusque là ouê qu'nou-s-assembllait – caêr nou n'avait pouit d'grand's cottes de mourtes à chu temps là. Bien d'vànt qu'de v'nir à la citadelle nou-s-était dèpurànt coum des ann'tons. Pouit de r'mìède; fallait duraïr. La draïne lueur d'espérànce était que l'Gén'ral trouv'rait tro mauvais temps et n'viendrait pouit. Fioûs-y. Nou n'fut pouit pus tôt sus la citadelle qu'nou l'vìt v'nir les fins-faeux d'âllés, siévu de toute sa suite, atou leus grànds chapìaux coquus, et leus pllumaches volànt au vent. Nou-s-airait dit autànt d'Inguiens sauvages. Après nou-s-aver fait faire mille menoeuvres, i nou fit allîgner un p'tit d'vànt l'caoup d'douze, pour tiraïr l'faeu de juée; sel'ment ch'fut un faeu d'deul chu caoup là. Ch'tait pus aîsi d'keriaïr "fire" que de l'faire. L's-armes étaient accouare à la vieille mode à chu temps la; ch'est-à-dire, à sacries, et atou des roques à faeu et des fisis. A quànd nou vint à débandaïr n'y-en aeut qu'daeux-treis par compengnie qui prinrent; mais coum nou n'pouvait pouit saver lesquâïlles qu'avaient fait "Bedoûe," nou chergeait terjoûs, si bien qu'à quànd j'fus fìni j'trouvi qu'j'avais treis cartages dans men vier bari-d'arme, l's-uns sus l's-autres. S'il avait écànchi d'prender faeu la trêsiéme feis, il airait brâment volaï en mille berdelles, et m'airait gav'laï sus l'dos raide mort coum un magot. Par bounheur pour mé qu'l'arme n'prìnt pouit. Après chaque caoup qu'nou tirait, ou qu'nou-s-y-éprouvait, la musique faisait mìne de jouaïr; mais les fifres et les cornes etaient pllains d'iaû, et avaient la rhime. Nou n'pouvait ouir les tabourìns, tànt l'parchemìn des buts était fllac et pllifraeux. Une tâîlle musìque n'nou réjouissait guère. Après l'faeu – qu'i n'y-aeut pouit – nou nou fit r'formaïr en compengnies pour passaïr par devànt l'Gouverneux et sa suite; mais à quànd nou vìnt pour marchier, après aver étaï d'but si long temps, nos brées d'teile trempâïes s'cllappaient conter nos guèrets – respet d'votre hounneur, si bien qu'nou n'pouvait quâsi mettre un pid l'un d'vànt l'autre, et nou faisait *right wheel* et *left wheel* à peu près ossi en ligne coum un troupé d'berbis. L'vier Gouverneur enguiâbllait – l'bouan Guiu seit pour nou – et tànt pus i rouâbllait, tànt pus la pllie quéyait.

Après la r'veue; ch'est-à-dire, après aver passaï daeux caoups par devànt s'n-

Excellence, j'créyion à tous moments qu'i s'n-allait nou libéraïr. Boûe! trachîz pour! j n'avion pouit c'menchi! L'gouverneux était décidaï d'vé quâîlle sorte de soudards que j'étion; si j'étion faits d'shucre ou pouit, ou si j'pouvion "stennaïr" l'iaû ossi bien coum le faeu. Coum j'disais à l'heure, la r'veue finie, i falli aver un p'tit *shamfight*, s'i vou pllait. Ch'en était un *shamfight*, en effet. A quànd nou v'nait pour tiraïr l's-uns sus l's autres, aurun d'faire "Bedoûe," nou n'oyait rien qu' "Cllic, cllic, cllic." Etion-ju biaux dans par chu temps! En copion-ju d'belles figures! Nos "slingues" avaient étaï bllènchies au matin, et la pllie avait lavai hors tout l'pllâtre, et l'avait douâbaï sus nos rouages cottes. Nou-s-airait dit qu'nos bllànches brées avaient étaï painturâïes d'auv du ver-de-gris, par nou-s-aver fait nou-s-agenouaïller dans l'herbe et la brìnche quâsi haute coum nou. A tous les pas que j'faision l'iaû faisait clloup-clloup dans nos saulers – ch'tait des saulers qu'nou mettait à chu temps là et des "guêteurs" de teile par dessus. Pouit d'bottes. Les saulers étaient à-peu-près d'la façon d'ouêsiaûx à morquier, et quâsi ossi p'sànts. Il' 'taient tous tro grànds et sabottaient à tous les pas qu'nou faisait, éyànt étaï faits coum les ciens à l'irlândais, ch'est-à-dire, "ossi grànds qu'possible pour le prix."

D'viers mié-r'levâïe l'mennière de *shamfight* finisit. Nou nou r'formi, et, après nou-s-aver fait faire un autre guiâtre-et-d'mi d'menoeuvres, nou s'prépari d'nou faire marchier hors de d'sus l'courti. Etion-ju fiers! J'pension qu'nou s'-n-allait-nou libéraïr à quànd j'vienderion au carr'four d'la citadelle. Bah! j'n'y counnîssìon rien.

A quànd j'vìnmes là, i falli continuaïr sa route, musique en tête, taille qu'alle 'tait, tout avau Hauteville, la rue des Cônets, la Grànd-rue, la rue des Forges, et jusque vis-à-vis l'office du Gouverneux. J'me r'met qu'en d'valànt et amontànt chès rues là, toutes les f'nêtres étaient ouvertes et toutes-fines-pllaïnes de cllichards et d'cllichardes – respet d'votre hounneur – à nou r'gardaïr. L's-uns avaient assaïz d'sens pour nou pllaindre; l's-auters se moquaient d'non, en nou d'màndànt si je v'nìnmes du vraix, ou si j'avion ieû hardi d's-ormers à basse-iaû. Quànd à mé, si j'm'étais creû, j'en airais braït d'guervànce.

V'nus oprès l'office du Gouverneux, nou nou fit faire "halte." Là tant qu'la plli déversait, nou nou fit une longue hérangue que j'creyais que n'finirait jamais. Nou-z-airait fichi l'càmp s'nou-s-avait peû, mais l's-officiers avaient tous l's-iers sus nou, coum des câts sus des souaris, nou n'osait mouvir. Un ou daeux éprou-virent à s'couillottaïr hors des rangs et furent rapp'laïs à leus pllèches. J'n'entendimes pouit un seul mot d'la hérangue, du moins, pouit mé, je n'l'écouti mime pouit. J'n'avion rien qu'l'idée d'fichier l'camp cîz nou. Sus l'drain, après qu'j'avion perdu toute espérànce d'en jamais r'sortir, nou nou dìt tout d'un caoup d'nou s'n-allaïr. Dame, i n'fut pouit besouain d'nou r'lataïr, j'vou-s-en asseure. D'màndous si j'nou minmes à houraïller! L'bouan-vìer Gén'ral craeut, sàns doute, que ch'tait pour le saluaïr, mais, j'cré mé que rien n'était pus lien d'not' pensâïe à chu moment là. Nou n's'en fut, fichter, pouit s'pourjolaïr et beire par la ville coum nou-s-a coûteume au jour de naissànce d'la Raïne. Nou-s-en avait ieû pour ses doublles, et nous-était si bièn trempaïs en d'hors, qu'nou n'aeut pouit besouain d'l'être en d'dans, pou un p'tit miraclle. Quaï bel écan pour un jour de bête!!!

It's for the Queen, by gum, *1884*

Ah! my good old friends, where were we? At the grand militia review of the Blue Regiment. So then, we have heard enough about that topic, and the subject of today's little natter will be, "One Queen's Birthday, in the days of old General Napier – God rest his soul." It was on the Play-Field, as the soldiers from the country insisted on calling it, and call it still, except some who used to say Pray Field; and I for one believe that they were closer to the truth, as they had prayed more than played on that day, and still more swore under their breath, at least. Some were praying that it would stop raining; others that it would rain heavily enough to make the General stay at home, and also send them home; while others swore on their grannies' lives that they would never be caught dead in such weather again, not for any Queen or any General in the world.

It was to the citadel that we went in those days, as we do again now. The good old General was too great a warrior to play soldiers anywhere else. L'Hyvreuse was too small, and the new docks didn't exist yet. There was only the citadel, L'Ancresse or Vazon, and it was one of those three places that we went to in turn; that is, to the citadel when it was for the Queen's Birthday, and to L'Ancresse or Vazon when it was for the shamfights, a word for military exercises which means to pretend to fight each other. So then, the time I'm telling you about was in the citadel and for the Queen's Birthday.

It was absolutely tipping it down when we got up in the morning. Water running everywhere. Everyone was thinking that there would definitely be no parading in such weather; but, blow me down, they had not counted on their General, by Jove. We almost wore our eyes out staring at the windmills in each of the parishes; thinking to see the flags being raised there to say that there would be no parading that day. Well, I ask you. The flags remained folded in their drawers. There were only those of the regiments that were out; and that was to get us on the move. If you thought that the General was afraid of being under a few buckets of cold water, any more than of being under fire, you'd be dead wrong. So shilly-shallying and grumbling, everyone got themselves rigged out in the white twill trousers that we wore in those days, and in the red jackets, and off we went, very hangdog, through the rain like a pack of whipped mongrels. Some had taken their umbrellas and others their thick sweaters to go as far as where we were to assemble – as we certainly didn't have any parade greatcoats back in those days. Well before arriving at the citadel we were dripping like cockchafers. No getting out of it; we had to see it through. The last glimmer of hope was that the General would find the weather too bad and that he wouldn't come at all. You could bet your life he would. No sooner were we at the citadel, when we saw him coming along full of enthusiasm, followed en masse by his entourage, with their big cocked hats, and their plumes blowing in the wind. You'd have said that they looked like a bunch of wild Indians.

After we'd been made to do a thousand manoeuvres, he made us line up, a little before the stroke of twelve, in order to fire the gun salute; only it was more like a dead-and-gone salute that time. It was easier to shout "fire", than to fire. The guns were still of the old-fashioned type in those days; that is the flintlock kind, with flints and paper cartridges. When it came time to pull the trigger there were two or three per company that went off; but as there was no way of knowing which ones had gone "bang", we carried on loading, to the point that when I had finished I found that I had three cartridges in my old gun barrel, one on top of the other.

If it had happened to fire the third time, it would surely have exploded into smithereens, and I would be flat on my back, stone dead as a maggot.

Luckily for me, the gun didn't go off. After each round that we fired, or that we tried to fire, the band got set to play; but the fifes and the horns were full of water, and sounded like they had a cold. We couldn't hear the drums, as the drumskins were so floppy and had lost their tension. A band like that could scarcely keep any-one's spirits up. After the salute had been carried out – which it hadn't – we were made to form up again in companies in order to march past the Governor and his entourage; but when we came to march off, after having been standing around for so long, our twill trousers were so soaked through that they were clinging to our thighs (pardon my language) so tightly that we could only just about put one foot in front of the other, and we did 'right wheel' and 'left wheel' with about as much military precision as a herd of sheep. The old Governor stormed and raged – Lord help us – and the more he fumed, the more the rain fell.

After the review; that is, after having paraded twice in front of his Excellency, we thought that at any moment he was going to let us go. Fat chance! We'd scarcely started! The Governor was set on seeing what kind of soldiers we were; to see if we were chocolate soldiers or not, or if we could stand firm under water as well as under fire. Like I was just saying, once the review was done with, there was to be a little shamfight, if you please. And it really was a shamfight. When it came to fire at each other, instead of there being a "Bang", all you could hear was 'Click, click, click". And by that time, didn't we look a pretty picture! Didn't we cut fine figures! Our belts had been whitened in the morning, and the rain had washed out all of the blanco, which had smeared all over our red coats. You would have said that our white trousers had been painted with bluey green from us having been made to kneel on the grass with the blades almost as tall as us. Every step that we took, the water went slip slop in our shoes – we wore shoes back then with cloth leggings over them. Certainly not boots. The shoes were boxy, like mortar hods, and almost as heavy. They were all too big and clumped about at every step we took, having been made like the ones that the Irish wore, that is, "as big as possible for the price".

Towards mid-afternoon the sort of shamfight ended. We formed up again, and after they'd made us do more damn silly manoeuvres, we got ready to march out of the field. Weren't we pleased! We thought that we were going to be dismissed, when we got to the junction of the citadel. Bah! That shows you how much we knew.

When we got there, we had to carry on going, the band, such as it was, out in front, right the way down Hauteville, Cornet Street, the High Street, Smith Street, and as far as opposite the Governor's office. I recall that, going down and up those roads, all the windows were open and crammed full of "spurters" (pardon my language), both male and female townies looking at us. Some had enough sense to commiserate with us; others made fun of us, asking us if we'd just got back from vraicking, or if we'd got many ormers while low-tide fishing.

As for me, if I'd have had the confidence, I'd have given vent to my anger. Arriving alongside the Governor's office, we were brought to a halt. There, while the rain came pouring down, we had inflicted on us a hectoring lecture that I thought would never end. We would have cleared off if we could have, but the officers had their eyes on us like cats on mice, we dared not move. One or two tried to skulk out of the ranks and were called back into line. We simply couldn't hear a word of the lecture, at least, I couldn't, I wasn't even listening. All we could think of was clearing off and going home. At last, after having given up all hope of ever getting out of there, all at once we were told to go.

Well, we didn't need telling twice, I can assure you. Just imagine how we began to cheer! The good old General probably thought that this was in his honour, but, for me, I think that nothing was further from our thoughts at that time. We didn't even bloomin' well go off on a pub crawl around town like we normally did on the Queen's birthday. We were fed up to the back teeth, and had been so soused on the outside that we certainly didn't need to be soused on the inside, strange as it may seem. What a turn-up for a grand day's rout!

Founded in the sixteenth century on the tidal islet in the bay off Saint Helier where the monastery of Saint Helier had been and next to the rock where the saint himself had lived, Elizabeth Castle had outlived its military usefulness to the British Crown by the early years of the twentieth century. The Castle, in a dilapidated state, was handed over to the people of Jersey in 1922. The States of Jersey set about restoration, but the castle was refortified for military purposes by the Germans barely twenty years later. Although it is now a museum and heritage site, as foreseen by Livonia, the problems of access at high tide continue to provoke debate and controversy. Livonia's proposal of a high-decked travelling platform as in the Breton resort of Saint-Servan (which we have already met in Geoffrey of Monmouth's tale of Cadwalla) was among many proposals that never came to anything.

Alice de Faye ('Livonia')

Lé Chaté Lizabeth, *1923* (Jèrriais)

> Achteu ches à nous, ches à nous qu'il appartient,
> Ches à nous étout d'en prendre eun divert soin,
> Quand la bouanne Reine le donni à Jerri,
> Comme ou'l savais bouanne gens tchet pour nos protégi,

Tchet pas pour en faithe eun cafè chantant
Comme y yiavait tait t'chestion yià tchique temps,
Je crait qui yian a assais ditait pour les jeune gens.
Y faut donné eune chance est pouorre vielle gens.

J'eume eune belle fête le jour qui nos fut donnait,
Des soudard de toute sorte rouoge, brun, tout tet dehalait,
V'là qui faisait paiesi d'er vais les rouoge casaque,
Les breune sont belle mais y n'ons pas le même attraque,
Nou peut les vais marchi d'un mille à la ronde,
Nou peut être contents de nos hommes et n'en avé pas d'honte.

Le vaisin Tom nethait pas voulu y mantchi
Et il l'dit eun jour à sa bouan vielle Betsy,
Y faut yialé et nos habiyi comme le passait,
Chapé, casaque, bottes et gants rein n'y manchait,
Betsy mins sa robe de soie que sa grand-mèthe yiavait donnais.
Quand ou s'mathi à Tom yia déjà bein d'annais
Ou'l avait eun tout tchet coumme eun gros Bathi
Et n'ou l'entendait v'nir d'un mille sans menti,
Tchet la yieune des belle fête que nou'n'pas oublié,
Ches à nous bouanne gens de bein en profité.

Pourtchi n'en faithe pas eun p'tit, mais biaux Musée,
De toute les tchuriozitais que nou pouorais vais
Et eunne tcheuisine Jerriesse tchique ou yen dite,
Mé je crai que s'rait tchique chose de magnifique
Avec tout chaque qui yiavait le temps passait,
Depis le trépi, le bachin, la chaudiethe et le craset,
Et la coniethe pour mettre le boïe de dans,
Et les banchets pour s'asiethe au sé à se chaufé,
Et la chandelle et l'changli pour pouvé allumé.

Acheteu y faut pensé au frigot,
Car quand n'ou yest si près de la mé nou mange trop,
Y nos faut tchique chose du temps passait,
De la gâche à corinthe et du bouan patait,
De la mouothue et du bouan pain de biet,
Des bourdelos et du bouan lait épeuthait.
Criyious que n'ou n'peut pas se grès de chonna,
Pour de mé y m'semble que je sis dejà la
Avec doeux ou trés dame habiyie à la vielle mode,
Etre avnante charmante et kmode.

Y faudrait avé eun pont roulant comme à St. Servan.
Quîthat et viendrai eun mio souvent,
Y faus espethait que yietha tchique chose de fait
Et prendre bouan soin' du Chaté Lizabeth.

Elizabeth Castle, 1923

Now it's ours, it belongs to us,
It's also our responsibility to take great care of it.
When the good Queen gave it to Jersey,
as you know, folks, it was to protect us.
It wasn't to turn it into a dance hall
like there was talk about some time ago.
I think there's enough of that for the young people
you should give a chance to the old folks.

We had a lovely celebration the day it was handed over to us,
Soldiers of all sorts, in red and brown, all came out,
What a pleasure it was to see the red jackets again,
the brown ones are nice but aren't as attractive.
You can see them from a mile off,
you can be proud of our men and not be ashamed of them.

Neighbour Tom wouldn't have missed it,
and he said to his old Betsy one day:
"We should go and we'll get dressed up like in the old days,
hat, coat, boots and gloves, without leaving anything out."
Betsy put on her silk dress that her grandmother had given her
when she got married to Tom many years ago now.
it had a bustle which was like a great barrel
and you could hear it coming a mile off, no word of a lie.
It was one of those lovely celebrations like we can still put on,
so, folks, it's up to us to make the most of it.

Why not turn it into a small, but nice, museum
for all the curios, for us to see,
with a Jersey kitchen, what do you say to that?
I think that would be a magnificent idea
with everything there used to be in it time past,
from the trivet, the bachîn, the boiler and the cresset lamp,
and the inglenook for the wood,
and the seats to sit on in the evening to keep yourself warm,
and the candle and the candlestick for lighting.

Now we should think of food,
because, when you're so close to the sea, you eat too much,
we need something from time past,
currant cake and some nice pie,
cod and good bread,
apple dumplings and good strained milk.
Don't you think we could we could manage that?
I can already see myself there
With a couple of ladies dressed in old fashions,
being helpful, and charming and practical.

We ought to have a marine railway like at Saint Servan
which would come and go fairly frequently,
We have to hope that something will be done
and that good care will be taken of Elizabeth Castle.

The First World War had a less dramatic impact on the lives of Islanders than the experience of Occupation in the Second World War. But, from Jersey, almost 6,300 served in the British armed forces and over 2,300 in the French armed forces. Shortages of newsprint and economic problems forced the merger in 1917 of Jersey's two French language newspapers, both of which published Jèrriais literature. *La Chronique de Jersey* (founded 1814) and *La Nouvelle Chronique de Jersey* (founded 1863) merged to form *Les Chroniques de Jersey* (closed in 1959). The editor of the new merged newspaper was E. J. Luce.

War poetry in the Islands had no voices from the Western Front. There is vernacular testimony in surviving letters home, but the newspapers and almanacs provided a literary commentary of the years 1914–1918. From jingoism to grief, from war news to light-hearted musings on the tribulations of daily life on the home front, writers in the Islands reflected the concerns and interests of their readers. In Jersey, George W. de Carteret provided a stream of comment, and Philippe Le Sueur Mourant recounted the often farcical reactions of the Pain family to war work and domestic privations until shortly before his death in 1918. From 1916 a series of poems by T. H. Mahy appeared in La Gazette de Guernesey including war themes. Popular culture from elsewhere influenced the writers too: E. J. Luce produced a Jèrriais version of 'It's a Long Way to Tipperary', a song which had become popular with British troops, and Jean Picot translated some of the war poems by Canadian author Robert W. Service from his 1916 collection Rhymes of a Red Cross Man. One writer who might have provided valuable insight into a Jerseyman's life at the front was George F. Le Feuvre, who saw action in the battles of the Somme, Vimy Ridge, Messines Ridge and Cambrai: however, despite covering the widest variety of topics in his hundreds of articles and leaving detailed reminiscences of his service in the Royal Jersey Militia before 1914, he barely mentions his war experiences in his literary output. Perhaps, as Annette Torode has suggested, 'it may well be that he found the whole experience so horrible that he either did not want to remember or felt that his readers would not wish to be reminded of it.'

The great influenza pandemic at the end of the Great War also had consequences in the Islands – among its victims was E. J. Luce, whose early death was a tragedy for the Jersey language and its literature – and George F. Le Feuvre's wife, whose death prompted him to emigrate to North America.

Many lawyers in Jersey have moved into gleaming new offices as they have taken on new business connected with international finance. As a result, Hill Street in Saint Helier is no longer the concentration of lawyers' offices clustered alongside the Royal Court building as it was when E. J. Luce wrote this poem. Nevertheless, lawyers still have to deal with the legacy of ancient property dues, calculated in the equivalents of cabots and sixtonniers of wheat, predating the property law reform pushed through by another poet, Sir Robert Pipon Marett.

E. J. Luce ('Elie')

En route pour Berlin (Dédié respectueusement à O.M.), *1917* (Jèrriais)

> I' n'y'a rein d'nouvé souos l'solei'
> J'savons tous l'vièr dicton;
> Et pus d'une fais nous a prouvè
> Qu'il en est d'même en véthitè.
>
> J'n'aithais jamais pensè, pourtant,
> À chein que j'vis, Sam'di,
> Dans "Hill Street" (app'lèe dans l'vièr temps,
> La Rue ès Trais Pigeons, j'comprends).
>
> Un soudard en kharki s'en v'nait
> Amont la rue bouan rond
> Et, 'slindgi sus san dos, portait
> San sa' tout plien, comme nou l'viyait.
>
> Aupi d'la pompe il arrêti
> Pour pâler à tchiqu'un;
> I' print san sa', le dêblioutchi,
> Et sav'ous tch'est qu'il en halli?
>
> D'vinèz ... d'vinèz ... errêprouvèz ...
> Nannin dja, ou' n'y'êtes pas ...
> D'vinèz autant coumme ou' voulèz,
> J'gag'geais qu'jamais ou' n'y pens'sèz!

Tchi don' qu'un soudard sus san dos,
Dans un sa' peut porter?
D'l'ammunition? tchullièrs? coutcheaux?
Des blankets pour se garder caud?

Noufait! N'y'a qu'dans l's'Iles de la Manche
Que nou' peu vaie d'itèt.
J'm'en vais l'dithe vite car l'heuthe avanche;
I' m'passi un livre d'tchittanches!!

Mais tandis qu'l'armèe en plien c'min,
Pense ès cabots et siextonn'yièrs
Inscrits dans l'livre en parchemin,
Je n'soummes pas sûs être à Berlin!

On the way to Berlin (respectfully dedicated to O.M.), *1917*

There's nothing new under the sun.
We're all familiar with that old saying;
and it has proved more than once
to be true in real life.

I'd never thought, however,
to see what I saw on Saturday
in Hill Street (or as it was called in the old days,
the Street of the Three Pigeons, as I understand).

A soldier in khaki came
up the street at a lick
and, slung on his back, he was carrying
his kitbag, which you could see was full.

He stopped by the pump
to speak to someone.
He took his kitbag, untied it,
and do you know what he pulled out of it?

Guess ... guess ... try again ...
No, you're way off...
You can guess as much as you like,
but I bet you'll never get it!

So what could a soldier
be carrying on his back in a kitbag?
Ammunition? Spoons? Knives?
Blankets to keep warm?

Not at all! Only in the Channel Islands
could you see the like.
I'll tell you what it was because the time is getting on;
he handed me a receipt book!

As long as the army as it marches along
is thinking of the cabots and sixtonniers
noted down in a parchment book,
it's not certain we'll get as far as Berlin!

Much of Channel Island vernacular literature has an immediacy and a closeness to its readers. Since most literary output appeared in newspapers, it is generally framed in a context of news, comment, letters to the editor, and births, marriages and deaths. T. H. Mahy's poem on the end of 1917 and another year of war first appeared in *La Gazette Officielle de Guernesey* at the beginning of January 1918 – a newspaper that contained news from the front and information about Guernsey men – fathers, sons, husbands, brothers, neighbours, sweethearts – away fighting.

Thomas Henry Mahy

Une Onnaïe d'Guerre Finie.... (Mil neuf cent dix-sept), *1918* (Guernesiais)

Mais si alle est finie, a' n'est pas roubiyaïe!
Alle en a mis beaucoup deàns l'mâ et l'embarras!
Combien qu' y en a, sis nous, qu'ont étaï mis deàns l' deul
Par en aver perdu quiqu'un des leux?
D'autres ont veû les leux r'v'ni délabraïs
Qu' nou vée aver étaï, sus quiqu' monièr', blessaïs.
Et d'autres sont restaïs des onnaïes seâns nouvelles
Ou i's sont bien gèanaïs, ou mêm' bien en affaire.
D'autres en ont quiqu's-uns d'malad's ès hôpitaux
Et voudraient bien l's aver d'auve yeaux au tout plustôt.
Et combien qu'i' y en a qu'ont les leux prisounniaïrs!
Ch'n'est miette en tout d's'ravi s'i's voudraient les raver.
A tous chen-chins, j'envie ma sincère sympathie
En leur souhaitant bouanheûr pour l'onnaïe c'mochée!
Pour bien des gens, ch't'onnaïe en feût yun' de misère;

Faut pensaïr qu'alle érait pu être acaur' pus pière!
En Guernesey, j'avons étaï plutôt treànquilles;
J'avons yeû chu qu'était néchessaire à la vie,
Du peàn atout d' la vieande, acaure un p'tit peu d' beûrre!
Des patat's en des temps, et d' par ichin, du chucre!
Nou n'est pas, Deiu merci, envêraï par l's air-raids
Coume i's l' sont si souvent, oniet, par l'Englleterre.
Ichin, nou-s-est terjous treànquill', l' jour et la niet,
Ossi bien au travâs coum' je seimes en nos yets.
Vraiment, sinon qu'nou vée, tous les jours, quiqu's nouveilles
Sus les papiers, nou n'creirait pas qu'i' y a la guerre!...
Les Guernesiais, brament, sont des favorisaïs,
Faut êtr' recounisseant, et n' jomais murmuraïr...
Sustout qu' nou v'là osteur' sur l'bouan bord, le geânieànt!
Coum' l'enn'mi est cachi, oniet, n'y a pas greànd cheànce.
Faut donc, tous un chacun, brament reprendr' courage;
Ch'est la Victoir' pour nou, et j'l'espèr, chutte onnaïe.
I' n' faut pas s'adoulaïr s'i' y a de p'tit's renverses:
Y en a yeû, y en éra, et che s'ra terjous d'même.
Si dix-neuf cent dix-sept' peut pas êtr' roubiyaïe,
Faut espèrer qu'la neuve, a' nous s'ra profitable.
Pour tout le mond', pour tout' la terre,
Aurun de s'vée en guerre, que pour tous la Paix règne,
Mais d'empie qu'la nouveille onnaïe est arrivaïe,
J'aïm'rais brament à tous souhaitaïr
Es Lecteurs d' la *Gazette*, ès petits coume aux greànds,
Aux tout plus ignoreànts coume aux tout pus saveànts,
A l' Editeur, à tous les siens qu'sont à son aïgue,
Une onnaïe coum' jomais nou n'en a veû d'itaille
Ou la paix, et parfait', nou sera accordaïe.
Oh! quaï bouanheur, quaïll' bouanne onnaïe!
L'Bouan Deiu veuille à tous nou l'accordaïr
Deàns sen amour, et deàns sa greànd' bontai.

A year of war over (Nineteen-seventeen), *1918*

Although it's over, it is not forgotten!
It's caused pain and difficulties for many people!
How many are there, back home, who are grieving
for having lost one of their nearest and dearest?
Others have seen family members return in a broken-down state
that, we can see, have been, in some way, wounded.
And others who've been for years without news

or who live in worry, or even have great concerns.
Others have dear ones ill in hospitals
and would really like to have them back with them as soon as possible.
And how many are there whose loved ones are prisoners of war!
It's not at all surprising that they would like to have them back.
To all of these, I send my sincere sympathy
wishing them happiness for the year that's beginning!
For many people, this year was a wretched one;
but you have to think that it could have been much worse!
In Guernsey, things have been fairly quiet;
we've had the necessities for life,
bread with meat, and still a little bit of butter!
Potatoes sometimes, and from around and about, sugar!
We aren't, thank God, bothered by air-raids
like they are so often, today, in England.
Here things are always quiet, night and day,
just as much at work as when we're in bed.
Truly, if it wasn't that we see, every day, some news
in the papers, we wouldn't believe that there's a war on!...
The Guernsey folk have been, without question, favoured.
Let's give thanks, and never mutter...
Especially as we're now on the right side, the winning side!
As the enemy's being driven back, today, they haven't got much of a chance.
Each and all must therefore, henceforward, pluck up courage;
it's Victory for us, and so I hope, this year.
Let's not grow mournful if there are little setbacks:
there have been some, there will be some, and that will always be the case.
If nineteen seventeen cannot be forgotten,
let's hope that the new one will be profitable for us,
for everyone, for the whole Earth,
rather than seeing ourselves at war, let peace reign for everyone,
but now that the new year has arrived,
I would like, straight off, to wish all
readers of the 'Gazette', the small as well as the great,
all the most ignorant as well as the most learned,
the Editor, and all of those who help him,
a year such as we've never seen the like
where peace, perfect peace, will be granted us.
Oh! what happiness, what a good year!
May the Good Lord see fit so to grant it to all of us
in his love, and in his great goodness.

The Channel Islands were occupied by the Germans 1940–1945. Although those who stayed were able to use their native tongues to keep secrets among themselves under conditions of military Occupation, many children had been evacuated to the United Kingdom before the arrival of German troops. With much of that generation spending formative years in a purely English speaking environment, the years following Liberation saw further weakening of the position of the vernacular languages, and of French, in favour of English. The almost total evacuation of Alderney and the devastation of the Island during the years of Occupation sealed the fate of Alderney's own language.

In an interview in 1960 for the *Evening Post*, Edmond Delaquaine, editor of *Les Chroniques de Jersey*, recalled the reaction of the German military censors: "The Germans could not understand the language so they decided that it must be a secret code of some sort. I was summoned before the Gestapo, at College House, and informed that I was a spy. Eventually the articles were sent to be studied by experts in Paris, who decided that they were quite harmless. After that quite a few Germans became interested in learning the vernacular."

Some brightness showed during the dark years, though. Frank Le Maistre continued to write, as Marie la Pie, articles in Jèrriais for *Les Chroniques de Jersey*, which also kept up a stream of Jèrriais classics reprinted weekly, although the German censor forbade the use of the little illustration of the magpie that had until then headed the Marie la Pie articles. Frank Le Maistre also used the curfew hours to work on his dictionary and to produce what, apart from his dictionary, he considered his finest literary work, his Jèrriais translation of Edward FitzGerald's version of the Rubaiyat of Omar Khayyam.

In August 1940, under the noses of the Germans and shortly before his death, George W. de Carteret published this call to linguistic resistance in the newspaper *Les Chroniques de Jersey*:

Si ch'est que vous voulez m'en craithe, acheteu l'pus nous pasle en vièrr patois l'mus ch'est pouor dithe chein qu'nou veur pon qui sait oui par d'autres que les vièrrs jerriais.

(*If you want to take it from me, now the more people speak the old lingo, the better it is to say what you want said without having it overheard by anyone other than old Jersey folk.*)

The Germans, having commandeered the printing presses of the local newspapers, churned out propaganda in the *Deutsche Inselzeitung*, in Jersey, and the *Deutsche Guernsey-Zeitung*, that they produced for their troops. In 1943, the third anniversary of the start of the Occupation brought forth a spasm of triumphalism – but the following year, the occupiers and the occupied were both isolated by the destructive Liberation of mainland Normandy after D-Day.

E. Hohl

From Deutsche Inselzeitung, *1943* (translated from German)

Jersey in German hands for 3 years
Outpost of Fortress Europe
From war correspondent E. Hohl

Jersey, 1st July.

In the wake of the dramatic final phase of the Western campaign, German reconnaissance fliers landed in the former British Channel Islands and in a short handover brought this jewel of the British crown into German hands. The European continent has, through the power of the German sword, brought about a correction of its strategic security cordon, which revealed the complete nonsense of the historical political situation in the peripheral waters of the Channel. Nevertheless, as shown by the history of centuries of hostility on the part of the British Isles to the continent, England had understood the strategic and economic value of holding onto the Norman islands and of consolidating and constructing from a historical oddity a permanent condition, at which even the French, as a result of their policy over the last hundred years of being in thrall to England, had taken no offence.

The sharpness of the German sword has wiped this deviation of state politics from the map of Europe. German soldiers have since 1 July 1940 held watch on the rocky coasts of the island. From the towers, those fixed towers, built by England along the beaches out of the fear of Napoleonic attack, German posts peek over the Channel, facing the enemy.

The face of the island has changed.

In three years the inhabitants have watched in amazement from close-up the miracle of German organization, the planned utilization of all natural features, boldly overcoming all technical and geographical difficulties to bring about a structural transformation of the islands, whose importance will be demonstrated to the Englishman if he wanted to try to impress his fellow countrymen by means of any sort of operations. Then the fiery mouths of the batteries would open up, green curtains would fall and thousands of rounds of ammunition be unleashed from bunkers and bases, and against the enemy would be concentrated the fire of coastal defence, of which he just got a slight foretaste in his Dieppe adventure.

From a playground for pleasure-seeking Englishmen and an open-air retirement home for shrivelled-up sterling millionaires, the Norman islands have today been incorporated into the huge system of the Atlantic Wall, protecting Europe against the ambition of the sea-bandits of the British Isles. They are outposts of Fortress Europe, ready to attack when their time comes.

The genius which has transformed the coast of France into a cordon of steel and concrete, an invisible network of bunkers, bases, machine gun emplacements, artillery posts, transformed B-posts, erected heavy tank walls at likely landing places and strung the beaches with minefields and wire entanglements – this same genius has also been at work in the Norman islands. Day and night, hammers pounded, construction machinery stamped, machines steamed and hissed. In this manner, islands renowned for tomatoes and early potatoes have become floating outposts of the European continent, and where, in previous years, the atmosphere of a more or less sophisticated culture of sun and sea clouded the mind, today beats the strong rhythm of determination, of alertness to duty, and the application of the will.

Behind the wall of iron and concrete, the German soldier stands in the calm certainty of his power. Countless hours of preparation for hardship and discipline, and training in ruthlessness, has turned him into a fighter, and he awaits his hour. Then he will show that steel and concrete lives to win through the heart of fighting men.

The German soldier in the Norman Channel Islands is aware of his task. While his comrades in the vastness of the Russian steppe are in a life and death struggle with Bolshevism, he, on a lonely outpost in the Channel, guards the coasts of Europe from enemy attack. No matter how much the agitating Jews across the Channel may whip into a frenzy the fanfares of invasion and attempt to sweep under the carpet the shameful memory of Dieppe, his weapons will bring their frenzy crashing down.

Michael Vautier

M'n Otchupâtion, *1998* (Jèrriais)

L'année trente-quatre, Octobre 'tait l'mais,
Né à La Fontaine à Millais.
Jé n'tais qu'un mousse en courtes braies
Quand not' p'tite Île fut otchupée.
Sans doute ch'tait un temps bein gênant
Pour gens dé l'âge dé nos pathents.
Pour nous, les p'tchiots, eune autre affaithe,
J'n'en r'tcheins seulement dé bouonnes mémouaithes.

Des milles gens sortîtent par baté
Pour tâchi d'la dgèrre s'êcapper
Les gens d'la campagne fûtent les sages!
I' restîtent souongni lus bèrnage.
Les villais dîsent, ch'tait lus êfforts
Tchi lus gardit la vie au corps!
I' n' y' a pas d'doute qué sans l'fèrmyi
N'y' éthait pas ieu grand' chose mangi.

Dans l'temps, si nou voulait un porc
I' fallait bein l'muchi tchique bord,

P'pèe avait êl'vé des quétots,
Parmi un tas dé vièrs fagots.
Mais pour les tuer, et les d'biter
Nou faîsait ch'na dès tchi v'nait l'sé.
Lé bouôn parleux, la bouochel'lie!
Par eune chandelle 'tait êcliaithie.

Ma M'mèe t'nait l'lard, man P'pèe l'couté;
Mé, j't'nais la chandelle, tch'tait man d'ver.
Boudîns et sang, jé n'aime pas vaie
J'tais mâté là, les ièrs freunmés.
Ma M'mèe crie "John, j'sens d'tchi brûler"
J'avais mîns l'feu dans san d'vanté;
Oulle eut les tchiêsses presque brûlées,
Et mé j'eus l's ouothelles êcaûffées!

Touos les samedis, dans l'arlévée
Not' p'tite jument dans l'querre 'tait liée,
Et mes pathents s'n allaient en Ville
Auve nouôrrituthe pour lus fanmil'ye,
Chutte bordée, muchi souos lus banc,
Un gigot d'lard, en lîncheu blianc,
Du beurre et d's oeufs, d'autre choses acouo,
Pour les villais, un vrai fricot.

En Ville les v'là presqu' arrivés,
Mais à West Park, la route bârrée,
Les Boches 'taient là, bein înstallés
Et touos les pâssants i' fouoillaient.
P'pêe, vite sa junment touônnit d'bord
Et pour la maison il 'tait hors.
Oulle allait comme un êpart dé feu,
I' pensit "p't-être tch'i' n'm'ont pas veu"!

Mais dès lé lendemain au matin
Né v'là les Boches qui d'valent lé c'mîn.
"Pourtchi t'sauver dé not' barriéthe"?
"Mais j'avais toutes mes vaques à traithe."
I' prîndrent sa junment et ses graies!
Ah, ch'est-i' tristre d'être dênoncés!
Lé j'va câssé tchi l'a rempliaichi
Man péthe nommit tout d'suite "Gerry".

Y'avait ieune d'mes tantes étout
Qui fût presque happée à san tou.
Dévant tch'i' vîntent pour la fouoilli,
Lé beurre muchi dans san pangni,
Ou fouôrrit bein vite dans ses braies.
Et don la v'là pus rasseûthée.
L' Allemand èrgarde dans san pangni,
Et heûtheusement, rein n'y trouvit.

Montant vite sus sa 'bike' après,
Si contente d' n'être pas happée.
Mais, mes bouonnes gens, et né v'chîn l'noeud,
Lé beurre fond vite à la chaleu!
Sa selle dé tchui fût bein huilée
Oulle en avait même dans ses souliers!
Dé d'pis, en portant beurre ou lait,
Ou n'portait pas d'drâses en flianné!

Un jour en m'en r'vénant d' l'êcole
Un soudard m'adréchit la pathole.
Y'avait li et san bouon amîn
Tch'avaient envie dé saver l'c'mîn.
Poussant un tchéthiot remplyi d'soupe,
Nouôrrituthe prîncipale des troupes,
Aller à Sorel ch'tait lus d'si,
Au fond du Mouothi j'les envyis.

Dans l'temps qué nos deux mousses 'taient p'tits,
Quand j'étions à tabl'ye assis
Il' êcoutaient auve întêthêt
Les scènes dé ches temps racontées!
Et pis à ch't heu qu'not' fis est péthe,
J'espéthe la même chose i' va faithe.
Pour qué nou-s-apprêcyie la paix
Faut pas qu'ches temps es'saient oubliés!

My Occupation, *1998*

It was in '34, the month was October,
when I was born at La Fontaine in Millais.
I was only a boy in short trousers
when our little Island was occupied.
Doubtless it was a very difficult time

for people of our parents' age.
For us children, it was different,
I only have good memories of it.

Thousands of people left by boat
to try to escape the war.
The country folk were the wise ones!
They stayed to look after their goods and chattels.
The townsfolk said that it was their efforts
that kept body and soul together!
There's no question that without the farmer
there wouldn't have been much to eat.

At that time, if you wanted a pig
you had to hide it somewhere,
Dad had raised porkers
among a pile of old faggots.
But to kill them, and carve them up
we had to do that after dark.
The drawing room was the slaughterhouse!
It was lit by candlelight.

My Mum held the pig, my Dad – the knife;
Me, I held the candle, that was my task.
I don't like seeing intestines and blood.
I stood there with eyes closed.
Mum cried out "John, I can smell something burning"
I'd set her apron alight;
She had her thighs nearly scorched,
while I got a roasting!

Every Saturday afternoon,
our little mare was harnessed in the cart,
and my parents went off to Town
with food for their family.
On this occasion, hidden under their seat,
was a leg of pork wrapped up in a white cloth,
some butter and eggs, and other things as well,
a real feast for the townsfolk.

And so they'd almost arrived in Town,
but at West Park there was a roadblock.
The Boche were settled in there,

checking all those passing through.
Dad quickly turned the mare round
and off he headed home.
She went like lightning,
and he thought "perhaps they didn't see me"!

But first thing the next morning
there were the Boche coming down the road.
"Why did you flee from our barrier?"
"But I had all my cows to milk."
They took his mare and harness!
Ah, how sad it is to be informed on!
The broken-winded horse that replaced
was immediately called "Gerry" by my father.

There was an aunt of mine too
who was almost caught in her turn.
Before they came to search her,
she quickly stuffed the butter she'd had hidden
in her basket, down her pants.
And that made her more confident.
The German looked in her basket,
and luckily, didn't find anything.

Getting quickly back on her bike afterwards,
so pleased at not being caught.
But, folks, here's the rub,
butter melts quickly when it's warm!
Her leather saddle was well lubricated,
she even got some in her shoes!
After that, if she was carrying butter or milk,
she never wore flannel knickers!

One day coming back from school
a soldier spoke to me.
He and his comrade
wanted to know the way.
They were pushing a cartload of soup,
which was the main sustenance of the troops,
and wanted to go to Sorel.
I sent them down the bottom of Mourier Valley.

When our two children were little,
and were were sitting round the table,
they used to listen with interest
to tales of those days!
And now our son is a father himself,
I hope he'll do the same.
In order to appreciate peace,
we must never let those times be forgotten!

John James Le Marquand, known to everyone as "J. J." was a farmer from Saint Ouen. He wrote playlets and other pieces in Jèrriais during the Occupation to keep up morale, and to cock a snook at the Germans. But J. J. is not primarily known as a writer. The optimistic vision in this poem of a prosperous future for everyone, once Liberation came, points to his progressive politics. He was elected Deputy of Saint Ouen in the post-war election of 1948 under the reformed constitution, and was elected Senator in 1951. He left politics to qualify as a lawyer, so as to better represent ordinary people and help solve their problems. He returned to the Senatorial benches in the elections of 1966.

J. J. Le Marquand

Vivons en espéthance, *c.1944, published 1946* (Jèrriais)

Le ciel est nier, les nouages épais,
La fraid est duthe, la glaie nos pique,
Le soleil n'brille presque jamais,
La niet est longue, nôt vie est triste.

Notr' corps est maigre, nôt fache hallée,
Nos pids sont nus, nos habits viers,
Notr' mangi pauvre, notr' biethe passée,
Et j'avons tous d'la peine dans l'yiers.

Nos femmes pélent trejous lus patates,
Pour tuos nos r'pas, ov nôtr' puorre pain,
Et le ptit mio d'beurre que d'sus nou gratte
Esche ravissent q'javons trejous faim.

J'navons pas d'cherbon a faithe de feu,
Le lait q'javons n'a pas grand crème,
Notr' fromage marche trejous tout seu',
La minsethe néthe, est dans son reigne.

Enfin buonnes gens, faut vivre en espethance,
Le ciel ov ses gros nuages, se cliairgitha;
Le soleil se r'montretha ov une brilliance,
Qui la niet r'accourchitha et nos peines abolitha.

Je r'mangeont tous du buan bianc pain,
Sans imiter l'systeme des vaques,
En mangeant tous des brins d'êttrain,
Des gâches ettout, et a notr' faim.

Nos mousses réthont des gâches shucrées,
Tout plein d'chucrins, et d'biaux ribans,
De belles neuve bottes, et d'biaux souliers,
Du chocolat, et d'bouonnes beurrais.

Nos femmes réthont lus cauches de souaie,
D'belles casaques, et d'biaux chapiaux,
De biaux souliers sans s'melles de bouais,
Et tout d'chi neu, et comme y faut.

Les hommes réthont lus cigarettes;
Puorrons r'craitre lus fameuses tomates;
Réthont d'la petrole, pour les tracteurs,
Et du guano pour lus patates.

J'nos r'promenons dans nos motos,
Vaie les course à Pliemont;
J'r'prendront tous des biaux photos,
Ouithont musique su pousse boutons.

A vous? A vous? viers St. Ouennais,
A vous? quils menent trejous partout;
Riez tous d'buon chouex, et tous chantez,
La paix appréche, et vite ettout.

Let's live in hope, *c.1944, published 1946*

The sky is black, the clouds thick,
a bitter cold, the frost nips us,
the sun hardly ever shines,
the night is long, our life is sorrowful.

Our bodies are thin, our faces drawn,
our feet are bare, our clothes old,
our food poor, our beer flat,
and we all have trouble in our expressions.

Our wives keep peeling potatoes,
for all our meals, with our poor bread,
and the little bit of butter that we scrape on it:
is it any wonder we're always hungry?

We haven't got any coal to make a fire,
the milk we've got isn't very creamy,
our cheese can walk about on its own,
black misery reigns over us.

Well, folks, we have to live in hope.
The sky with its large clouds will clear;
the sun will come out again, shining brightly enough
to shorten the night again and do away with our troubles.

Once more we'll all eat good white bread,
without doing as cows do,
and eating wisps of straw,
and we'll have cakes too, enough to fill us up.

Our children will have fancy cakes again,
lots of sweets, and pretty ribbons,
lovely new boots, and fine shoes,
chocolate, and good sandwiches.

Our wives will have their silk stockings again,
pretty jackets, and nice hats,
pretty shoes without wooden soles,
and everything brand new and just right.

Men will have their cigarettes again,
they'll be able to grow their famous tomatoes again;
they'll have petrol again, for the tractors,
and fertiliser for their potatoes.

We'll go out for drives again in our cars,
see the racing at Plémont;

we'll all take lovely snapshots again,
and hear music on the radio.

You! You! People of Saint Ouen!
You! Take this with wherever you go;
laugh heartily, all of you, and everybody sing,
peace is coming, and even so, comes quickly.

Into the New Millennium

T he vision of a better life described by J. J. Le Marquand and a return to
prosperity after Liberation in 1945 was borne out. The Islands rebuilt and
developed their economies, attracting new workers and new industries.
The voices of the toad and the donkey have not yet been drowned out by the voices
of finance, tourism and international media. Can the donkey and the toad continue
to be heard in the centuries to come?

Radio and communications technology helps the languages of the Channel Islands
to be heard in their own communities and across the world. La Lettre Jèrriaise, a
weekly talk in Jèrriais, has become an institution. At the end of 1999 Brian Vibert,
former headmaster and lay preacher, invited his audience to look forward to the
new millennium and back to eternal truths.

Brian Vibert

From La Lettre Jèrriaise, donnée lé vîngt-six dé Dézembre 1999

Véthe, v'là Noué d'pâssé et dans siex jours jé s'sons tous à célébrer eune nouvelle
année, lé c'menchement d'un nouvieau siècl'ye et l'opporteunité d'écrithe la date
2000 pour la preunmié fais. Les siens tch'ont dêja célébré le chentième annivèr-
saithe dé lus naîssance pouôrront dithe tch'il' ont vêtchu dans trais difféthents siècl'yes et, man doux, tchi changements tch'il' ont veu! Nou dit souvent qué si nos
anchêtres, tchi n'sont pus, èrvén'thaient i' s'en r'îthaient bein vite car i' s'saient
tellement surprîns dé vaie comment qué la vie a changi.

Ma grand'méthe Amîn m'avait dit qu'un jour, quand oulle 'tait p'tite mousse i'
y'a chent ans, san grand'péthe à lyi l'avait am'née déhors dans l'bel et li' avait dit
"Ergarde là haut, ma p'tchiotte, un jour i' y'étha des machinnes tchi vol'thont dans

l'ciel." Dans chu temps-là les anciens criyaient tous qué si j'dév'thêmes voler qué Dgieu nos éthait donné des ailes. Mais au jour d'aniet nou monte à bord un avion pour viagi, qué s'sait en Améthique ou en Australie, aussi aîsiement comme à prendre eune beusse pour aller à Gouôrray. Et i' n'faut pon oublier qué l's humains ont viagi à la leune – tchi qu'éthait pensé qu'un homme éthait marchi sus la leune et qué j'éthêmes peu l'vaie sans sorti de not' parleux. Télévision, machinnes fax, ordinateurs, l'"internet" – ou l'îthangnie comme j'ai ouï dithe – sont tous parties dé not' vie et toutes des înventions des années 1900. La grande dé mes fil'yes veint d'pâsser Noué en Australie – ou pousse tchiques boutons, lé téléphone sonne siez nous et j'nos entré-pâlons comme si j'têmes ensembl'ye dans la maîson. Oulle êcrit eune lettre, pousse tchiques autres boutons et la lettre appathaît tchiques s'gondes après sus la tabl'ye siez nous. Les progrès technologiques dé chu siècl'ye sont încriyabl'yes. Et pis, tchi qu'en est des progrès scientifiques et dans la méd'cinne? La puspart des maladies tchi 'taient sans dgéthîson peuvent être dgéthies aniet; les docteurs peuvent rempliaichi eune hanque ou un g'nou et nou peut èrchéver même un nouvieau tchoeu. Les scientistes ont inventé lé pouver nucléaithe tchi peut nos béni et nos dêtruithe étout. Les înventions amènent des problèmes – l'hôrreu d'la bombe atomique et dé hardi des armes dé dgèrre et des drogues tchi cliâment tant dé nos jannes gens comme victimes.

Progrès ... progrès ... progrès ... j'sommes tous èrconnaîssants qué ma généthâtion a joui des progrès dé chu siècl'ye. Quand i' fait fraid j'sis bein content qué la p'tite maîson n'existe pus au bas du gardîn et j'sommes tous heutheux qu'i' n'y a pon bésoin d'alleunmer l'"copper" et dé scrober lé linge lé jour du lavage. Mais j'habitons acouo un monde où'est qu'i' y'a tristesse et mauvaîtchi – i' y'a acouo dgèrre et fanminne, pauvrété, haine et jalousie, violence, friponn'thie et mensonges.

J'sommes tout d'scendants d'Âdam et sa femme et j'avons héthité la capacité dé péchi. Lé jour dé Noué nos ramémouaithe qué Dgieu env'yit san Fis pour nos sauver dé nos péchés et, grâce à san Saint Esprit, pour nos aîdgi à vivre la vie qué Jésu-Christ vêtchut. Auve li j'pouvons connaître la jouaie, la paix, la véthité, l'amiêtchi et toutes les bouonnes choses qu'i' nos offre. Ch'est san d'si qué jé s'sêmes tous ses discipl'yes afin dé l'suivre. Ch'est li seul tchi peut nos m'ner en seûtheté et en bonheu. Eune nouvelle année nos donne l'opporteunité dé considéther l'avnîn et dé décider si j'voulons aller auve Jésû-Christ ou sans Li.

From The Jèrriais Letter, given on 26th December *1999*

So that's Christmas over and in six days we'll all be celebrating a new year, the start of a new century and the chance to write the date 2000 for the first time. Those who've already celebrated their hundredth birthday will be able to say that they've lived in three different centuries and, goodness, what changes they've seen! People often say that if our ancestors, dead and gone, came back they'd be off back where they came from pretty quickly as they'd be so surprised to see how life has changed.

My grandmother Amy told me one day, when she was a little girl a hundred years ago, her grandfather had taken her outside into the yard and told her "Look up there, my little one, one day there'll be machines that'll fly in the sky." In those days the old folk all believed that if we were meant to fly, God would have given us wings. But nowadays people get on board a plane to travel, whether to America or Australia, as easily as taking a bus to Gorey. And we mustn't forget that humans have travelled to the moon – who'd have thought that a man would have walked on the moon and that we'd have been able to see it without leaving our living room. Television, fax machines, computers, the Internet – or the Web as I've heard it called – are all part of our lives and all inventions of the 1900s. My eldest daughter has just spent Christmas in Australia – she presses a few buttons, the telephone rings at our home and we speak to each other as though we were in the house together. She writes a letter, presses some other buttons and the letter appears a few seconds later on our table at home. This century's technological advances are incredible. And then what about advances in science and medicine?

Most diseases that were incurable can be cured today; doctors can replace a hip or a knee and you can even receive a new heart. Scientists have invented nuclear power which can bless us and destroy us too. Inventions bring problems – the horror of the atomic bomb and of many weapons and of drugs which claim so many of our young folk as victims.

Progress ... progress ... progress ... we're all grateful that my generation has enjoyed this century's progress. When it's cold I'm very happy that the outside toilet no longer exists at the bottom of the garden and we're all pleased that there's no need to light the copper and scrub the laundry on washdays. But we still live in a world where there's sadness and evildoing – there's still war and famine, poverty, hate and jealousy, violence, cheating and lies.

We're all descendants of Adam and his wife and we've inherited the capacity to sin. Christmas Day reminds us that God sent his Son to save us from our sins and, thanks to his Holy Spirit, to help us to live the life that Jesus Christ lived. With him we can know joy, peace, truth, friendship and all the good things he offers us. His desire is that we all be his disciples in order to follow him. He alone can lead us in safety and happiness. A new year gives us the chance to consider the future and to decide if we want to be with Jesus Christ or without him.

This is the opening of a short story by Geraint Jennings that, in 2008, won a competition for storywriting in varieties of the Norman language held in conjunction with La Fête des Rouaisouns, the annual festival that brings together Norman speakers from across Normandy. The story is partly an exercise in style, attempting to balance elements of the fantastic, the erotic, the farcical and the tragic within a compact form, and using parallelism and cross-cutting to approach a cinematic pace that leads to the dénouement.

Geraint Jennings

From **Feu et feunmée,** *2008* **(Jèrriais)**

Coumme les preunmié barres du jour dêlachaient les liefs d'la ville, l'ouaîthé ouvrit ses ailes dorées dé laîze. I' s'craînchit, et s'mâtit là sus san nid d'papi, d'tés et d'brantchettes souongneusement avieillotté sus l'faît du bâtisse. L'ouaîthé espéthait les rayons ravigoteurs et, coumme lé solé s'mouontrait à la sîl'ye des maîsons, l'dun dé s'n estonma c'menchit à soûssinner. Les buts d'ses plieunmettes – rouoges, oranges, jaunes – lus nièrchissaient. Ses grîns êtînch'laient dans l'nid d'papi. Des touothâles dé feunmée montaient d'ses pids en vithevardant. Des fliambes cratchaient souos l's ailes dé l'ouaîthé et avaû san corps lé brûlîn faîthait lithe les longues plieunmes coumme des lândgets d'fliambe.

Êcliaithi dans l'solé du matîn, l'ouaîthé l'vit san bé d'or et piaillit d'jouaie coumme lé radgîn rôtissait ses gambes et san corps. Ses ailes ouvèrtes atchilyaient la lueu du solé et les louêmes dé caleu. Trans'mé, l'ouaîthé freunmit ses ièrs dé topaze en s'solilyant dans sa brûl'lie bénite à li. Des fliaûmêques dansicottaient l'tou du nid d'feu, lus dans'sie entouortilyie par les cos d'fliambe et d'air mais qu'i' fûtent lâtchies et fliottîtent ava dans la ruette.

À bas dans la ruette, Mess Corbet dêbârrit l'us dé s'n apotiqu'sie et sortit, eune brînge à la main, à seule fîn d'netti l'avant à la boutique d'vant l'èrc'menchement d'eune journée d'affaithes. I' dgettit sa mouontre. Pâssé siêx heuthes un quart. Il avait l'temps même pouor scrober les sîles d'vant dêjeuner. Lé temps s'tait fait, à chein tch'i' pathaîssait, et i' n'y'éthait pon d'plyie. Véthe, i' pouôrrait scrober quandi qu'lé solé lithait. Autrément, qu'i' s'dit, i' pouôrrait rarreuner sa d'vantuthe. Car il avait justément r'stotchi atout des boutillies d'sitho d'colînmachon, et les nouvieaux patchets d'boulets d'cône dé chèr moulue 'taient hardi bieaux et attrio-qu'thaient sans doute d'la pratique. L'apotitchi restit eune pause affroutchi sus sa brînge: scrober ou rarreuner? rarreuner ou scrober? Ou bein dêjeuner d'vant c'menchi lé travas? Car i' sentait du brûlîn. Y'avait un vaîthîn tch'avait brûlé san pain rôti. Ou ch'tait-i' du lard feunmé? Nânnîn, ch'tait pus à co du poulet, du poulet brûlé. Mess Corbet fit eune morgache et roublyit san dêjeuner. Assa, i' faudrait scrober, car il avait justément r'mèrtchi des nièrmitons sus sa d'vantuthe. I' r'prînt sa brînge dans les deux mains pouor clièrgi chutte fichue salop'thie mais d'un co eune jaune plieunme fliambante voltilyit ava l'avant à ses ièrs êcalés. Mess Corbet r'gardit à haut et tréfit.

"Au feu, au feu!" qué l'apotitchi briyit. "Au feu! Y'a un phénix! Au feu!" I' laîssit tchaie sa brînge sus l'pavé et s'moustrit quédaine avaû la rue pouor sonner l'alarme. "Un phénix! Un phénix sus l'lief! Au feu!"

* * *

Siêx heuthes dgix. Les barres du jour rîlyaient l'liet l'travèrs des vénitiennes. Un ouothilyi dans l'aithe. L'êdrédon à la frouque. Les draps chuchotés. Des chuchots achéthinnés.

Coumme ou s'èrposait sa tête souos san moton, i' fliattait sa hanque. Ou s'èrposait sus san caud corps, les chîn dés anichis dans l'pé corlé dé s'n estonma. Les gambes entouortilyies, les tchoeurs enrontchis. Ou dêviait san pé entre ses fîns dés, trachant des formes, des fidguthes, des mots qu'ou n'ôsait pon lî chuchoter même dans chu nid. Sa pé brûlait, qu'ou pensit, coumme sa main drissait douochement sus san bouton. I' squouîzit sa tchiêsse. "V'là tch'est l'heuthe," qu'i' dit et s'dêgourdit en s'êbâillant.

"Tcheins-mé acouo chîn minnutes," ou lî murmuthit.

I' s'craînchit. "Nou-fait, ma douoche," qu'i' dit en lyi baillant la joue. "Ch'est l'heuthe. Ch'est man quart." I' l'embraichit d'vant sé l'ver. "J'dais m'n aller en travas. Et tch'est qu'i' y'éthait si l'bouonhoumme rentrit?"

"Rhabil'ye-té don et j'té graiethai l'dêjeuner," qu'ou dit en s'êtalant l'travèrs du liet coumme i' r'gardait ses seins nus et r'lithants.

"P'tite garciéthe, né m'tente d'aut'! J'gaff'thai eune sannouiche sus lé c'mîn." I' mînt ses braies et s'zipit. "Et tch'est qu'i' dithait don, tan bouonhoumme, s'il arrivait auprès eune niétchie d'travas pouor trouver sa bouonnefemme înnouothante à laver deux mogues et deux assiettes à sinne dé jeu?"

"I' m'extchûth'thait, l'vièr, car i' sait hardi bein qu'j'ai... un grand appétit." Ou souôrit et s'èrtouônnit sus l'liet. I' n'avait pon acouo mîns sa c'mînse. Ou l'gaffit et halit sus la boucl'ye dé sa cheintuthe. Douochement ou c'menchit à l'èrdêziper.

★ ★ ★

Lé phénix brûlait. I' brûlait d'mârrisson et piaillait coumme dé pus bé. San nid 'tait raîque d'la chendril'ye. Et des nouages dé chendre lus l'vaient à l'entou d'l'ouaîthé coumme il éprouvait dé s'protégi contre les galots fliantchis d'en bas dans la rue par eune dgaîngue dé villais. Châque fais qu'un galot l'tapit, i' pèrdit eune plieunme fliambante et fut êbézoui en eune achie d'êtînchelles et d'fliaûmêques. Lé phénix piétinnait dans san nid d'chendril'ye, châtchant sa tête fliambante, et dgettait d'un yi d'feu et d'un aut' la dgaîngue veng'rêsse là-bas.

Des mousses lî jouôtaient des pièrres sans cêsse. Des fil'yes couothaient en r'lais auve des d'vant'lées d'galots et d'gravyi. Un moussetchot avait s'n êlîngue. I' mithit, et lanchit un bliotchet au phénix. Lé bliotchet tapit l'aile dêtre d'l'ouaîthé atout eune forche pouor en dêteindre la maîntchi des plieunmes. Lé phénix vioûlit d'ma coumme ses tîthons d'plieunmes fûtent êtrav'lés à l'entou d'li pouor traler l'lief.

Et les clioches d'alarme sonnaient acouo.

★ ★ ★

Ou brûlait. Ou brûlait d'pâssion, et piaillait. San liet 'tait raîque des chiques, et des nouages dé musc lus l'vaient à l'entou d's amouotheurs. Châque fais qu'i' l'embraichit, ou fut êbézouie en eune achie d'fliaûmêques et d'êtînchelles. Coumme ou piétinnait, ses gambes lus drédilyant, ou châtchait sa tête fliambante. Coumme i' pompait, i' la dgettait d'ses ièrs dé feu. Sans cêsse, i' lyi jouôtait quandi qu'ou vioûlait d'pliaîsi. Ses habits 'taient êtrav'lés à l'entou d'ieux sus l'liet tralé.

Épis i' ouït eune sonn'nie. Siêx heuthes vîngt.

From Fire and smoke, *2008*

As the roofs of the town emerged in the light of dawn like rocks being uncovered by the retreating tide, the bird opened its gilded wings wide. It shook itself down, and stood up straight on its nest of paper, rubbish and twigs, all carefully piled up on the ridge of the roof of the building. The bird awaited the enlivening rays and, as the sun appeared at the roofline of the houses, the down on its chest started to singe. The ends of its smaller feathers – red ones, orange ones, yellow ones – blackened. Its talons gave off sparks in the paper nest. Spirals of smoke rose erratically from its feet. Flames crackled under the bird's wings and down its body the burning made the long feathers glow like little tongues of flame.

Illuminated in the morning sun, the bird raised its golden beak and screeched with joy as the blaze roasted its legs and its body. Its open wings welcomed the sunshine and the waves of heat. Struck with enchantment, the bird closed its topaz eyes and bathed in its own glorious pyre. Smuts skipped around the fire-nest, their dance woven by blasts of flame and air until they were released and floated down into the lane.

And down in the lane, Mr Corbet unlocked the door of his chemist's and came out carrying a broom, to clean up in front of the shop before once again starting a business day. He looked at his watch. Gone a quarter past six. He even had time to scrub the sills before breakfast. The weather was set fair, it seemed, and it wouldn't rain. Yes, he could scrub while the sun shone. Alternatively, he said to himself, he could re-jig his window display. Because he had just stocked up on bottles of snail syrup, and the new packs of ground deer horn were really attractive and would certainly bring in some customers. The chemist spent a moment propped up on his broom: scrub or re-jig? re-jig or scrub? Or else have breakfast before starting work? For he could smell burning. One of the neighbours had burnt his toast. Or was it bacon? No, it was more like chicken, burnt chicken. Mr Corbet pulled a face and forgot about breakfast again. Well, he'd have to scrub as he'd just noticed smuts on his shopfront. He took up his broom with both hands to clean up that wretched mess but suddenly a flaming yellow feather fluttered down right before his staring eyes. Mr Corbet looked up and gave a start.

"Fire, fire!" shouted the chemist. "Fire! There's a phoenix! Fire!" He dropped his broom on the pavement and hustled off quickly down the road to raise the alarm. "A phoenix! A phoenix on the roof! Fire!"

* * *

Ten past six. Dawn striped the bed through the venetian blinds. A pillow on the floor. The duvet in a jumble. Crumpled sheets. Wild whispers.

As she rested her head under his chin, he stroked her hip. She rested on his warm body, five fingers nestling in the curly hair of his chest. Legs entwined, hearts snagged. She wound his hair between her thin fingers, tracing out shapes and figures and words that she didn't dare whisper to him even in this nest. His skin was burning, she thought, as her hand slipped slowly onto his nipple. He gave her thigh a squeeze. "It's time," he said and stretched himself, yawning.

"Hold me five minutes longer," she murmured to him.

He shook himself down. "No, darling," he said giving her a peck on the cheek. "It's time. I'm on duty." He kissed her before getting up. "I've got to go to work. And what would happen if your husband came back?"

"Get dressed then and I'll make you breakfast," she said, stretching out across the bed as he looked at her glowing bare breasts.

"Little minx, stop tempting me! I'll grab a sandwich on the way." He put on his trousers and zipped himself up. "And what would your huisband say if he came home after working all night to find his wife all oblivbious and washing up two mugs and two plates at daybreak?"

"The old man would forgive me because he knows I've got ... a big appetite." She smiled and turned over on the bed. He hadn't yet put on his shirt. He grabbed him and pulled on his belt buckle. Slowly she started to unzip him again.

* * *

The phoenix was burning up. It was burning with rage and squealed like anything. Its nest was nothing but cinders. And clouds of ash rose up around the bird and it tried to protect itself against the pebbles thrown from down below in the street by a crowd of townsfolk. Every time it was struck by a pebble, it lost a flaming feather and was stunned in a shower of sparks and smuts. The phoenix stamped its feet in its cinder nest, shaking its flaming head, and cast a look of fire, first from one eye then the other at the vengeful mob below.

Children continually targeted stones at it. Girls ran relays, carrying scoops of pebbles and gravel in their skirts. One small boy had a catapult. He aimed and fired a small lump at the phoenix. The lump hit the bird's right wing with enough force to extinguish half the feathers. The phoenix wailed with pain as the embers of its feathers were spread around it, scorching the roof.

And the alarm bells were still ringing.

* * *

She was burning. She was burning with passion, and squealing. Her bed was nothing but tatters. And clouds of musk rose up around the lovers. Every time he kissed her, she was stunned in a shower of sparks and smuts. As she stamped her feet, her legs writhing, she shook her flaming head. As he pumped, he cast looks of fire at her. He continually targeted her whilst she wailed with pleasure. His clothes were spread around them on the scorched bed.

Then he heard bells ringing. Twenty past six.

Liam Renouf is a young student who wrote this poem to perform at the Jersey Eisteddfod. It was well received, and has been taken up by other young performers.

Liam Renouf

La Salle dé Bain, *2008* (Jèrriais)

As-tu lavé tes mains?
Nânnîn
Tchi saligaud!
As-tu lavé ta fache?
Nânnîn
Tchi saligaud!
As-tu dêmélé tes g'veux?
Nânnîn
Tchi saligaud!
As-tu brîngi tes dents?
Nânnîn
Tchi saligaud!
As-tu lavé driéthe tes ouothelles?
Nânnîn
Tchi saligaud! Tu'es sale coumme d'la pé d'crapaud!

The Bathroom, *2008*

Have you washed your hands?
No.
What a mucky pup!
Have you washed your face?
No.
What a mucky pup!
Have you combed your hair?
No.
What a mucky pup!
Have you brushed your teeth?
No.
What a mucky pup!

Have you washed behind your ears?
No.
What a mucky pup! You're as filthy as a toad's skin!

This extract comes from a light-hearted science fiction short story by Tony Scott Warren. The quarterly Jèrriais literary magazine *Les Nouvelles Chroniques du Don Balleine* sets a theme for each issue to encourage writers to contribute new writing. The Spring 2006 issue had the future as its theme, and Tony Scott Warren produced a tale of derring-do in space. From Viking ships to spaceships, the Normans have come a long way.

Tony Scott Warren

From À tchiques années-leunmiéthe d'ichîn..., *2006* (Jèrriais)

La nièrcheu pathaîssait être en vie, au mains tchique sorte d'vie mais pas comme j'avêmes janmais rencontré d'vant. Auprès tchiques minnutes à l'analyser, i' fut évident qué ch'tait eune manniéthe dé nouage dé tchèrbon en forme d'touothâle galactique. Fliottant en espace, i' rôdait ichîn et là à mangi l'ponsi entre l's êtailes, et s'i' y'avait d'tchi muchi dans l'hâsi d'espace, comme par exempl'ye un navithe spatial, chenna donnit un gout d'èrva-s'y au fricot.

S'lon not' compiuteu, i' pathaîssait qu'i' nos avait prîns l'frais, viyant qu'not' navithe a attrapé bein des mios d'poussiéthe dans sa cliôsée d'gravité – i' n'y'a pas fort d'machinnes à netti les navithes dans not' quartchi d'espace! Chu nièr monstre avait idée – si "idée" est l'bouôn mot pour les pensées d'un nouage – d'happer eune bouochie d'ponsi, et i' nos chassait à bride avalée! Lé pus grand dangi pour nous 'tait qu'i' pouôrrait avaler not' navithe – et les deux d'nous étout en même temps! Pour dé mé, jé n'avais autchun d'si d' finni mes jours comme soupé pouor un nouage.

"Tch'est qu'j'allons faithe, Cap'taine?" jé d'mandis. I' m'dit, "Fistuthe – j'n'ai janmais 'té attatchi par un nouage d'vant. Êprouvons à lanchi des fîsées!" Dans un înstant deux d'ieux fûtent env'yées, mais même qu'i' fûssent sus l'bouon trajectouaithe, i' pâssîtent à travèrs l'nouage; d'aut's saluettes fûtent env'yées sans autchun êffet, et bétôt l'armémént 'taient presqu' êchoué. "Gâdé-ouelle! J'allons faithe sèrvi nos rayons d'forche! Ch'est la dreine chance!" dit l'Cap'taine. Pour les faithe sèrvi, i' fallait dêtouônner toutes choses tchi n'taient pon essentielles à maîn-t'nîn la vie. J'app'yis sus l' bouton, et l'navithe fit eune sécouêthie tèrribl'ye. Pouor tchiques minnutes les cieux 'taient illeunminnés par des longues colonnes d'leunmiéthe tchi jouaient sus la fache d'la nièrcheu. À la fîn nos batt'ties 'taient presqu' viédes, mais rein n'avait changi, sauf qué l'nouage pathaîssait mârri et appréchait d'nous quédaine. "Tch'est qu'j'allons faithe à ch't heu?" jé r'fis.

From **Several light-years from here,** *2006*

The blackness seemed to be alive, at least alive in some way but unlike anything we'd ever met before. After analysing it for a few minutes, it was clear that it was a type of galactic spiral carbon cloud. Floating in space, it roamed here and there eating dust between the stars, and if there was something hidden in the space clutter, like for example a spaceship, that would only make the snack tastier.

According to our computer, it seemed that it had picked up our scent, as our ship had caught up many dust particles in its gravity field – there aren't many ship-leaning machines in our quadrant of space! This black monster intended – if a cloud's thoughts can include intentions – to grab a snack of dust, and it was chasing us at breakneck speed! The greatest danger for us was that it might swallow our ship – and us two along with it! As for me, I didn't have the slightest wish to end my days as a cloud's dinner.

"What are we going to do, captain?" I asked. He said, "What can we do – I've never been attacked by a cloud before. Let's try launching missiles!" In an instant two of them were sent off, but even though they were on the right trajectory, they went through the cloud; more volleys were sent off to no effect, and soon we were almost out of weapons. "Blimey! We'll use use our force beams! It's the last chance!" said the Captain. To use them, it was necessary to turn off everything that wasn't needed for life support. I pressed the button, and the ship underwent a terrible shaking. For a few minutes the heavens were lit up by long columns of light which played across the face of the darkness. At last our batteries were almost empty, but nothing had changed, except that the cloud seemed angry and was approaching us quickly. "What are we going to do now?" I asked again.

The most recent piece in this collection is also the last one – and, of course, it's the donkey who insists on the last bray. From Wace, through the revivalists of the nineteenth century and the resisters under occupation, Channel Island writers have insisted on the value of their languages and literatures and looked to preserve them. This poem, written in 2010 by Yan Marquis, restates this perennial concern.

Yan Marquis

Note Lingo, *2010* **(Guernesiais)**

> Vou véyie bian k'note viaer lingo
> possède des adret noblles rachaenes.
> Nou soulait l'oui, et pus d'aen mot,
> partout l'île, li et sa cousaene!
> Mais daove les chàngements d'tems, i vint
> enn aote ki a naom angllectin.

Nou pourrait plleurai les chàngements,
et la gràND paerte k'il aont amnaie,
terrous pâlànt du bouan viaer tems;
mais note lingo s'en va durai
acouore aen ptit. Il est têtu!
Coume l'érague, chu titre, a valu.

Biau ké moli nou l'ot acouore
à tchique bord – parfeis es racouoins:
ch'est énne affaire, ma fé, d'ête pour!
Faot daon ké nou lé dvise, au mouoin
chaeu ki peuve, et k'nou diche au sian
ki l'apprend, brâment, 'tu fais bian!'

Mais sav-ou k'tout lingo vivànt
chànge, et chu k'y a d'pus vou veyie:
Nou dit k'ch'est d'maeme pour lé pur sàng!
Lé naote, vey-ou, chànge, a chàngi,
et chàngera. Lé progrès viant:
lingo ki n's'adapte poui vaot rian!

Et vchin l'akvaeure: Mesdames, Messiûs,
files et mousses, faot daon m'écoutai:
j'vous dmànde dé terrous faire d'vote mus,
à toutes occassiaons d'éprouvai
pour ké l'lingo seit mis en dvànt
et ké tout sache: "Il est vivànt!"

Our Lingo, *2010*

As you well know, our old lingo
is really nobly rooted:
It used to be heard, with more than single word,
all around the island, it and its cousin!
But with changing times, came
another, called English.

We could lament the changes
and the great loss that they brought about,
going on and on about the good old days;
But our lingo is going to last
a little longer yet. It's stubborn!
Just like the species that has earned this title.

Although not as strong as it was, we can still hear it
hereabouts – sometimes in secluded places:
but, really, the thing is, it needs your support!
We must therefore speak it, at least
anyone that can, and tell anyone
who's learning, really, "you're doing great!"

But you know all living lingos
change, and, you know, what's more:
they say that it's the same for the thoroughbred!
Ours, you see, changes, has changed,
and will change. Progress arrives:
a lingo that doesn't adapt is useless!

And here's the moral of my tale: Ladies, Gentlemen,
girls and boys, listen to what I'm saying:
I'm asking you to always do your best,
at any opportunity to try
to promote the lingo
and let everyone know: "It's alive!"

Biographies

Philippe Asplet (1818-1893, Jersey) Wrote as 'Flip' and 'L'Anmin Flippe'. Philippe Asplet was a politically engaged writer, tackling political scandals and election shenanigans in satirical verses he wrote for newspapers, including the short-lived satirical journal *La Lanterne Magique*. Many of his pieces are concerned with the Parish of Trinity where he lived for many years. He was a friend and strong supporter of Victor Hugo and the proscrits in Jersey, and came into conflict in his post of Centenier with the Lieutenant-Governor who took exception to his association with such troublemakers in exile. His poems make little claim to polished literary style, but can be fierce in mocking the powerful in the language of the ordinary people.

Nicholas Bott was born in Alderney in 1797, but lived much of his life in Jersey, and is the only self-professed poet of Auregnais that we know of – although he wrote in Guernesiais and Jèrriais, sometimes somewhat Gallicised, as well.

Denys Corbet (1826-1909, Guernsey) Wrote as 'Le Rimeux d'la Fouarêt' and 'Bad'lagoule'. Author of *Les Feuilles de la Forêt* (1871), *Les Chànts du Draïn Rimeux* (1884), and a series of annual booklets *Le Jour de l'an* (1874-1877). Denys Corbet was a schoolmaster and journalist, with a sideline in paintings of livestock. He also served as Constable in the parish of Forest. Collaborated on the French language newspaper *Le Bailliage* and contributed many prose articles in Guernesiais. His epic poem 'L'Touar de Guernesy' is the most substantial individual literary creation in Guernesiais.

George William de Carteret (1869-1940, Jersey) Wrote as 'Caouain' and 'G. W. de C.' He wrote occasional poetry, mostly to be performed at the annual Jersey Eisteddfod from 1912 onwards, but is best known for his weekly Jèrriais newspaper column of comment and political gossip written in the character of 'Lé

Caouain' (the owl), a disreputable bird who supposedly lived above the newspaper offices and flew round the parish halls to eavesdrop on meetings and bring back amusing stories and rumours for the readers. He was a farmer from Saint Peter, and served as secretary of the Jersey Farmers Union and as Military Vingtenier for the West of Jersey.

Alice de Faye (1849-1925, Jersey) Wrote as 'Livonia' (from the name of the family home, Livonia Cottage, a name which recalled maritime trading links with the Baltic). Alice de Faye was the younger sister of Mathilde de Faye.

Mathilde de Faye (1846-19??, Jersey) Wrote as 'Georgie'. The de Faye sisters represent a strand of writing that is more urban, more concerned with commerce, shops and fashion, than many of the male writers of their time. While still showing concerns for family, they depict a changing social world.

Marie De Garis (1910-2010, Guernsey) Marie De Garis was born in Saint Pierre du Bois and lived there for all but five years of her life – the five years of German occupation. Her greatest achievement was the *Dictiounnaire Angllais-Guernesiais*, of which the first edition was published in 1967. Her collection of Guernsey folklore and other writings helped to restore a scholarly basis to Guernesiais literature that had perhaps been lacking since George Métivier. She was awarded the M.B.E. in 1999, and her 100th birthday was an occasion marked by public recognition in Guernsey. She died a few weeks after passing her centenary.

Sir Arthur de la Mare (1914-1994, Jersey) Wrote as 'Un Vièr Trintais'. From a farming family in Trinity, the author left Jersey for a career in the British diplomatic service. Having served, amongst others, as Ambassador to Thailand, he retired to Jersey and took over the vacancy of the weekly newspaper column in Jèrriais that had not been regulary filled since the death of 'George d'la Forge'. His articles, in his distinctive Trinity dialect, displayed an unusual mix of rural conservatism and global cosmopolitanism.

Edward Gavey (1848-1919, Jersey) Headmaster of the Jersey Home for Boys. Wrote articles and short stories in English on historical themes, using Jèrriais for colour.

Thomas Alfred Grut (1852-1933, Guernsey) Wrote as 'T.A.G.' amongst others. Contributed stories and articles to *La Gazette de Guernesey* and the *Star*, some of which were collected in 1927 in a volume entitled *Des lures guernesiaises*.

Nicolas Guilbert (1826-1900, Guernsey) A farmer from Castel and friend of Denys Corbet. Nico Guilbert is often quoted by Métivier in his *Dictionnaire franco-normand*, in part due to his rather rich vocabulary. Two of his poems were republished in *Patois Poems of the Channel Islands*, but his work has never been collected together. In common with his contemporaries his style is Romantic and celebrates rural life and the virtues of farming the land.

Florence Mary Hacquoil (1902-1988, Jersey) Wrote as 'F.M.H.' Born in Saint Brelade, but brought up in Saint Ouen, Florence Hacquoil spent many years as a schoolteacher in Saint Brelade. Many of the poems that she wrote were intended for children and for recitation at the Jersey Eisteddfod.
in *Des Poêmes en Guernésiais*, 1999.

Geraint Jennings (born 1966, Jersey) Artist, illustrator and teacher. As one of the team at L'Office du Jèrriais, the Jèrriais promotion agency, he has designed the Jèrriais teaching materials for schools. Twice winner of the Grand Prix for a short story in Norman, and recognised in other writing competitions, he has written for commissions, and some of his pieces have been chosen as set texts for the Jersey Eisteddfod. In politics, he has served as an elected member of the municipality of the Parish of Saint Helier for a number of years.

David Jones (active 1960s, Wales) Journalist from Wales. Came to Jersey in the 1960s and worked for *Jersey Topic* magazine. He cast an outsider's affectionate eye on Island life.

Philippe Langlois (1817-1884, Jersey) Wrote as 'St. Louorenchais' and 'P.L'. He trained as a doctor and was a founder member of La Société Jersiaise. He was elected Deputy for his native parish of Saint Lawrence and was later elected Jurat.

Edward Le Brocq (1877-1964, Jersey) He edited the *Jersey Critic* before the Second World War, in which Ph'lip and Merrienne, his bantering and bickering old couple from Portinfer in Saint Ouen, first appeared. Edward Le Brocq edited the *Morning News* and contributed weekly columns by Ph'lip until that newspaper's closure in 1949. Ph'lip and Merrienne transferred to *Les Chroniques de Jersey* in 1950, appearing regularly until that newspaper closed in 1959. From 1960 until Edward Le Brocq's death in 1964 Ph'lip and Merrienne continued their weekly domestic wrangling and political and social commentary in the *Evening Post*.

Helier Le Cheminant (1918-1983, Guernsey) A grower, who wrote for the appreciation of God's creation, and the quirkiness of the people within it, Helier Le Cheminant used the pseudonym 'Helier d'Rocquoine', and wrote song lyrics, including some translations.

George F. Le Feuvre (1891-1984, Jersey) Wrote as 'George d'la Forge' and 'Bouanhomme George'. 'George d'la Forge' was born in Saint Ouen, the son of a blacksmith. His parents emigrated to Canada in 1901, leaving George in Jersey with his grandparents. He left school at 14 to work for a solicitor. In 1914 he was appointed Commis Vicomte for the Police and Petty Debts Courts, and in 1916 he left for the war front, seeing action on the Somme. During his war service, he met up with his brothers, two of whom were serving in the Canadian armed forces. Widowed by the 1918 flu epidemic, he rejoined his family in Canada in 1919. He served three years as a civil servant in Canada before seeking his fortune in the United States. He became a United States citizen in 1933 and took a comfortable retirement in 1946 when he returned temporarily to Jersey. He turned down an offer to take over the editorship of *Les Chroniques de Jersey*, but contributed a regular Jèrriais column. He was founding secretary of L'Assembliée d'Jèrriais, and subsequently settled into a pattern of spending part of the year in Jersey and the rest of his time in North America or travelling around the world. From 1965, following the death of Edward Le Brocq, he took up the reins of providing a regular column for the *Jersey Evening Post* (and its sister digest, the *Jersey Weekly Post*, which kept expatriate Jersey people in touch with their native Island). In 1983, the *Jersey Evening Post* marked the 900th 'lettre' from 'Bouanhomme George'. He was awarded the Prix Littéraire du Cotentin in 1974 for the first of his collections of columns, *Jèrri Jadis* (1973). A further collection, *Histouaithes et Gens d'Jèrri*, followed in 1976.

Augustus Asplet Le Gros (1840-1877, Jersey). Wrote as 'A.A.L.G.' His premature death cut short an active life. He was elected Constable of Saint Peter, and later Jurat. He was a founder member and first secretary of La Société Jersiaise, and secretary of the Royal Jersey Agricultural and Horticultural Society. His poetry in Jèrriais, whether light-hearted or serious, is always heartfelt. He published a series of annual collections of Jèrriais (and Guernesiais) literature titled *La Nouvelle Année* (which inspired Denys Corbet to produce similar collections in Guernsey) and started work on a Jèrriais dictionary.

Esther Le Hardy (1807-1881, Jersey) Wrote as 'Nenné Caton'. A poet and playwright from Saint Lawrence, she was a friend and kinswoman of Philippe Langlois. A pointed satirist and the most important female writer in Jèrriais of the nineteenth century.

Peter Le Lacheur (born 1967, Guernsey) A worker in the finance sector, Pierre Le Lacheur is a language enthusiast from Saint Pierre du Bois and a founder member of the language promotion organisation 'Les Ravigotteurs'. He is to our knowledge the youngest native speaker of Guernesiais.

Frank Le Maistre (1910-2002, Jersey) Wrote under many pseudonyms, including 'Marie la Pie' and 'F.L.M.' Frank Le Maistre left school in 1927 and went to work as a lawyer's clerk. In 1931 he joined the staff of the States Farm, a job which involved travelling round the Island, inspecting farms and talking to farmers. This enabled him to carry out his passion for collecting words and expressions in the different dialects of Jèrriais – a study that was to end up with the publication of the *Dictionnaire Jersiais-Français* in 1966. From 1933 until the early stages of the German occupation, he contributed a column to *Les Chroniques de Jersey* under the name of 'Marie la Pie' (supposedly a chattering magpie, as a counterpart to G. W. de Carteret's owl). He was a moving force behind the foundation of L'Assembliée d'Jèrriais in 1951 and edited its quarterly publication, the *Bulletîn d'Quart d'An* from 1952 to 1977. He was a close friend of 'George d'la Forge' and between them they did much to establish a stable Jèrriais orthography. In 1967 he was awarded the Prix Littéraire du Cotentin, and other honours followed including a fellowship of the Royal Academy of Uppsala, Commandeur dans l'Ordre des Arts et des Lettres, Membre de l'Académie des Arts, Sciences et Belles Lettres de Caen, Médaille de Bronze of the Centre Nationale de la Recherche Scientifique, and Officier dans l'Ordre des Palmes Académiques. He was awarded the OBE in 1976, and after the award of an honorary doctarate by the University of Caen, he became popularly known as 'Dr. Frank'.

J.J. Le Marquand (1915-1975, Jersey) John James Le Marquand, known to every-one as 'J.J.' was a farmer from Saint Ouen. He wrote playlets and other pieces in Jèrriais during the Occupation to keep up morale, and to cock a snook at the Germans. He was elected Deputy of Saint Ouen in the post-war election of 1948 under the reformed constitution, and was first elected Senator in 1951. He decided to study law in 1960, qualified as an advocate, and returned to political life on the Senatorial benches in 1966.

Henry W. Le Ray (1865-1934, Guernsey) A former school teacher, who in 1892 set up a company which exported products grown in the Guernsey horticutural industry. He was a keen promoter of football in Guernsey, but 'Guernesey ill'a chinquànte ans, Guernesey aniet, et Guernesey dans chinquànte ans' is his only known surviving literary work.

Stan Le Ruez (1901-1985, Jersey) Wrote as 'S.P. Le Ruez'. Born in Saint Mary, Stan Le Ruez spent his working life in banking and lived in Saint Saviour. On his retirement in 1966 he entered politics and won a by-election for Deputy in Saint Helier in 1967. In the 1969 general election he stood for Deputy in his home parish and represented Saint Saviour until standing down at the 1978 election. Stan Le Ruez wrote short plays for the annual Eisteddfod.

James Charles Le Touzel (1828-1917, Jersey) Noted as a young talent by Abraham Mourant in the first anthology of Jèrriais poetry in 1865, J. C. Le Touzel disappeared from the literary scene in Jersey when he emigrated to North America in his twenties. Nicholas Bott translated at least one of his poems into Guernesiais for circulation in Guernsey.

Tam Lenfestey (Thomas Lenfestey – 1818-1885, Guernsey) A farmer from Les Fontaines, Castel. Author of *Le Chant des Fontaines* (1875, poems in Guernesiais, French and English). Called the 'bard of rustic life' in Guernsey.

Edwin John Luce (1881-1918, Jersey) Wrote as 'Elie'. E. J. Luce was born in Saint Lawrence. He was an industrious reporter for *La Nouvelle Chronique de Jersey*, becoming its editor, and then editor of the merged newspaper *Les Chroniques de Jersey* formed by the merger of *La Nouvelle Chronique de Jersey* and *La Chronique de Jersey* in 1917. He produced a stream of topical prose and verse in the newspaper columns, as well as poems and song lyrics for evening entertainments. He could turned his hand with equal facility to lyrical and domestic subjects, and was encouraging to other writers – especially his older friend Jean Picot. He was active in the establishment of a Jèrriais section of the Jersey Eisteddfod, and wrote plays and organised drama performances in the vernacular. His early death as a victim of the 1918 flu epidemic was a great loss to the development of Jèrriais literature.

Philippe William Luce (1882-1966, Jersey) Wrote as 'Ph'lippe dé La Golarde'. Born in La Rue de la Golarde in Saint Lawrence, P. W. Luce was the brother of E. J. Luce. He emigrated to Canada in 1902 and pursued a career in journalism, working for the *Winnipeg Telegram*, and the *Daily News* and *Vancouver Herald* in British Columbia. He continued to send poems back to Jersey, and in 1940 he set up the Vancouver Channel Islands Society to raise money for evacuees. He wrote playlets, sketches and other material for the émigré community in British Columbia.

Thomas Henry Mahy (1862-1936, Guernsey) Wrote as 'T.H.M.' Contributed many poems to *La Gazette de Guernesey*, a collection of which was published as *Dires et pensées du Courtil Poussin* in 1922.

Henri Luce Manuel (1818-1875, Jersey) Signed himself 'L.' He was born in Saint Helier and occupied a number of positions within the Parish administration: Constable's Officer, Churchwarden and Procureur du Bien Public. He served as Parish Registrar, and themes of birth and death are not uncommon in his poetry. He published two small collections of poetry and a play in verse.

Sir Robert Pipon Marett (1820-1884, Jersey) Wrote as 'Laelius'. He studied law, and also edited the newspaper *La Patrie*, in which he published some of his poetry. He was elected Constable of Saint Helier, then was appointed successively Solicitor-General, and Attorney-General and ended his life as Bailiff of Jersey. A social reformer, as may be imagined from the wry sympathy of the social observations in his poetry, the quantity of his literary output fell off as his political career advanced. A fire at his home in Saint Brelade in 1874 which destroyed his library and papers was a tragic loss for Jèrriais literature. The domesticity of his poems particularly appealed on the Norman mainland and they have been reprinted and circulated there long after his death.

Yan Marquis (born 1968, Guernsey) Language enthusiast and a founder member of the language promotion organisation 'Les Ravigotteurs'. He learnt Guernesiais as a second language from close family and friends and has since become involved in its teaching and promotion. In 2008 he moved from a career in IT to become Guernsey's first Language Support Officer employed by the States of Guernsey.

Thomas Martin (1839-1921, Guernsey) By trade a carpenter and later road surveyor. Served as Douzenier in the parish of Saint Martin. Produced unpublished Guernesiais translations of the Bible, the plays of Shakespeare, the Corneille brothers, Voltaire and Molière as well as Longfellow's 'The Spanish Student'.

George Métivier (1790-1881, Guernsey) Wrote as 'Un Câtelain'. Also known as Georges Métivier. Called during his lifetime Guernsey's national poet, the Guernsey Burns and the Guernsey bard. Author of *Rimes guernesiaises* (1831), *Fantaisies guernesiaises* (1866) and the *Dictionnaire franco-normand* (1870), as well as a translation of the Gospel of Matthew. Métivier influenced Alfred Rossel and others in the Cotentin active in the renaissance of Norman literature on the mainland. His standardisation of Guernesiais spelling influenced the work of Fernand Lechanteur in devising a standard orthography for mainland Norman. In 1883 a posthumous collection *Poésies guernesiaises et françaises* was published. He studied medicine at Edinburgh University, but abandoned thoughts of a career as a doctor for a devotion to literature. His experiences in Scotland encouraged his inspiration by Robert Burns; the populist French poet and lyricist Pierre-Jean de Béranger was also among his influences, as were Jacques Jasmin, the Occitan poet and forerunner of Mistral and Félibrige, and William Barnes, the Dorset dialect poet and philologist. Among his adaptations and translations is a version of a poem by Henry Luce Manuel.

Philippe Le Sueur Mourant (1848-1918, Jersey) Wrote as 'Bram Bilo' and 'Piteur Pain', as well as other supposed members of the Bilo and Pain families. Born in Saint Saviour, he emigrated to Newfoundland in his youth, returning to Europe later with a career in merchant shipping based in Lorient, Brittany. He returned to Jersey in the 1880s to take over the family farm. In 1889 he burst onto the literary scene with a series of letters to a newspaper *La Nouvelle Chronique de Jersey* in the character of Bram Bilo (Abraham Billot), an unsophisticated but pompous ex-Centenier from Saint Ouen. The letters were an immediate popular success, were republished in booklet form, and became classics. Further stories followed. The author, while continuing to contribute in Jèrriais to *La Nouvelle Chronique de Jersey*, started to contribute in French, under the pen-name 'Samuel' to

a rival newspaper *La Chronique de Jersey*. He later launched a new series of characters, the Pain family, in the English-language *Morning News*.

Marjorie Ozanne (1897-1973, Guernsey) A teacher, who also ran a noted bird-
hospital, Marjorie Ozanne contributed plays to the Guernsey Eisteddfod and stories to the *Guernsey Evening Press*.

Amelia Perchard (born 1921, Jersey) Writes as 'A.L.P.' From Saint Martin, Amelia
Perchard has produced many poems, often for the Jersey Eisteddfod for which she
has written many short plays. Some of her pieces have been published in Jèrriais
magazines.

Charles Picot (1840-1921, Jersey) Wrote as 'C. du Mont', and (it is believed) 'Jan
de la Maze'. Charles Picot was born in Trinity, and after working as a teacher
trained for the priesthood. After serving in positions in England and Jersey, he
spent many years in Guernsey where he was friends with Denys Corbet. Corbet
wrote an elegy on the death of the Rev. Picot's daughter in 1889. He returned to
Jersey where he served as chaplain to the hospital and the prison before retiring.

Jean Picot (1846-1922, Jersey) A farmer who turned to literature in retirement
following an accident, writing as 'J.P.', Jean Picot is a writer who is concerned with
entertaining his readership, rather than striving for high literary style or purity of
form. He translated some of Robert W. Service's poems, as well as other works. His
Jèrriais versions of Douglas Jerrold's stories for *Punch* – *Mrs. Caudle's Curtain Lectures* –
may have influenced Edward Le Brocq's conversations between Ph'lip and
Merrienne. Jean Picot struck up a friendship with E. J. Luce and literary exchanges
and banter between the two of them appeared in the newspapers until E. J. Luce's
untimely death.

Liam Renouf (born 1995, Jersey) As a teenager, one of the youngest competitors
to have written and performed his own poetry at the Jersey Eisteddfod. He is the
youngest contributor to this collection, and the coolest.

Alfred Rossel (1841-1926, Cherbourg) First author of the mainland revival of
Norman literature in the Cotentin peninsula. He wrote poems and popular songs,
sold as broadsheets, from 1872 onwards. An edition of his collected works was
published in 1913. His song 'Sus la mé' ('At sea') is sung as a regional anthem in the
Cotentin, and is also sung in the Islands.

Tony Scott Warren (born 1949, England) Tony's father, a doctor, moved his family to Jersey where Tony grew up in Saint Brelade. He worked for many years at
Channel Television, where he produced occasional programmes in the vernaculars

of the Islands, before moving into the teaching and promotion of Jèrriais, heading up L'Office du Jèrriais.

Jean Sullivan (John Sullivan – 1813-1899, Jersey) Wrote as 'J.S.' and 'Omega'. A journalist, antiquarian and pamphleteer. An indefatigable producer of patriotic and topical poetry, he claimed royal patronage and received permission to translate Queen Victoria's *More Leaves from the Highlands* into Jèrriais. This project, like so many of his grand schemes, was never brought to fruition.

Ted Syvret (born 1936, Jersey) A farmer from Saint Ouen, Ted has, since retirement, become involved with the teaching of Jèrriais to new generations in schools. He has also been a regular contributor to La Lettre Jèrriaise on the radio.

Joan Tapley (born 1932, Jersey) Writes as J. T. From the Rondel family of Saint John. Joan Tapley taught Jèrriais at evening classes for many years and has been involved in the Jersey Eisteddfod, writing poems, stories and plays for performance.

Michael Vautier (born 1934, Jersey) Born in Saint Ouen, he moved out of his native parish in 1937. From 1952 until 1989 he farmed in Trinity, where he still lives, contributing Jèrriais poems and stories for publication, and researching Channel Islands genealogy.

Brian Vibert (born 1937, Jersey) Born into a Saint Ouen farming family, Brian studied languages and became a teacher. He ended his career as headmaster of Victoria College in Jersey. He resigned from teaching to work as a Lay Pastor. His activities in Jèrriais have involved being President of Le Don Balleine, writing newspaper articles, contributing to La Lettre Jèrriaise, and leading church services.

Wace (12th century, Jersey) Wace was born in Jersey, probably between 1090-1110, and studied in Caen and later France. He returned to Caen some time prior to 1135 where he worked until the mid-1160s when he was appointed to a prebend in Bayeux. As a 'clerc lisant' he seems to have been some sort of professional writer, but not necessarily in holy orders. He died some time after 1174. His two great verse works are the 'Roman de Brut', essentially an adaptation of Geoffrey of Monmouth's Latin account of British history, and the 'Roman de Rou', a history of the Dukes of Normandy. The 'Roman de Brut' introduced new motifs into Arthurian literature, including the Round Table, and served as the basis for Layamon's thirteenth-century Middle English 'Brut'. Despite Wace's claim to have composed many vernacular works, only three other poems are known to us: lives of Saint Nicholas and Saint Margaret of Antioch and a poem on the Immaculate Conception.

Bibliography

Vernacular Texts

Bram Bilo, P Le Sueur Mourant, Jersey

Des lures guernesiaises, T. A. Grut, 1927

Deustrès Histouèthes pour Rithe par Bram Bilo, P Le Sueur Mourant, Jersey, 1890

Dires et Pensées du Courtil Poussin, T. H. Mahy, 1922

En Sercq: Compte-rendu d'la Visite des St.-Ouennais, le Lundi 22 Août 1910, E. J. Luce 1910

Enne annaïe à la campagne, Le Campagnard, 1970/1971

Eune Collection Jèrriaise, Jersey, 2007

Fantaisies guernesiaises, George Métivier, 1866

Feuilles de la forêt, Denys Corbet, 1871

Folklore of Guernsey, Marie De Garis, 1975

Guernesey ill'a chinquante ans, Guernesey aniet, et Guernesey dans chinquante ans, Henry W. Le Ray, Guernsey Eisteddfod, 1925

Histouaithes et Gens d'Jèrri, George F. Le Feuvre, 1976

Jèrri Jadis, George F. Le Feuvre, 1973

Là, i n'y a pas d'gniet, Le Campagnard, 1970/1971

Le Chant des Fontaines, Tam Lenfestey, 1875

Le Découvrément de la Statûe d'la Raînne Victôria en Jêrri, 1890

Les Chants du draïn rimeux, Denys Corbet, 1884

Oeuvres complètes, Alfred Rossel, 1913

Piéche et 'R'citâtions, E.J. Luce, Jersey, 1913

Poësies guernesiaises et françaises, Georges Métivier, 1883

Rimes et Poësies Jersiaises, A. Mourant, Jersey, 1865

Rimes Guernesiaises, George Métivier

The Collected Works of Marjorie Ozanne, 1897-1973, ed. Ken Hill

The Patois Poems of the Channel Islands, J.L. Pitts, Jersey, 1883

The Patois Poems of the Channel Islands, J.L. Pitts, Jersey, 1885

The Roman de Rou, Wace, trans. Glyn S. Burgess, Jersey, 2002
Wace's Roman de Brut. A History of the British. Text and Translation, Weiss, Judith,
    Exeter, 2006.

Periodical publications
Bulletîn d'Quart d'An, L'Assembliée d'Jèrriais, Jersey (1952-1977)
Les Chroniques du Don Balleine (1979-1987)
Les Nouvelles Chroniques du Don Balleine (1989-)
Le Jour de l'An, ed. Denys Corbet (1874-1877)
La Nouvelle Année, ed. A. A. Le Gros, Jersey (1868-1875)
Guernsey Magazine
Jersey Topic
Syllabuses of the Jersey Eisteddfod
Festive anthologies of La Fête Nouormande

Newspapers
Guernsey
L'Indépendance
La Gazette de Guernesey
Le Bailliage
Guernsey Evening Press

Jersey
La Gazette de l'Île de Jersey
La Gazette de Césarée
La Chronique de Jersey
La Nouvelle Chronique de Jersey
Les Chroniques de Jersey
La Patrie
La Lanterne Magique
Evening Post (from 1967, *Jersey Evening Post*)
Morning News
Deutsche Inselzeitung

Almanacs
La Chronique de Jersey
La Nouvelle Chronique de Jersey
Les Chroniques de Jersey

Other texts
A Century of Roundels and other poems, Algernon Swinburne,

A Hobble through the Channel Islands in 1858; or, the Seeings, Doings and Musings of one Tom Hobbler, during a four months' residence in those parts, Edward T. Gastineau, 1860

A Sketch of the History and Present State of the Island of Jersey, Thomas Lyte, 1808

An Account of the Island of Jersey, the greatest of the Islands remaining to the Crown of England of the Ancient Duchy of Normandy, Philippe Falle, 1694

An Account of the Island of Jersey, W. Plees, 1817

Balleine's History of Jersey, Marguerite Syvret and Joan Stevens, 1998

Caesarea, Jean Poingdestre, c.1670

Carette of Sark, John Oxenham, 1907

Dame of Sark, Sibyl Hathaway, 1961

Encyclopaedia Britannica, 1876

Fields, Factories and Workshops, Prince Peter Kropotkin, 1912

General View of the Agriculture and Present State of the Islands on the coast of Normandy, subject to the Crown of Great Britain, Thomas Quayle, 1815

Guide du voyageur à Jersey, A. Desmoulins, Jersey 1875

History of the Kings of Britain, Geoffrey of Monmouth

Holinshed's Chronicles, Raphael Holinshed

In Peirson's Days, E. Gavey 1902

Jersey: An Isle of Romance, Blanche B. Elliott, 1923

Journal, John Wesley

L'Archipel de la Manche, C. Vallaux, Paris, 1913

L'Archipel de la Manche, Victor Hugo, 1883

La Normandie inconnue, F.-V. Hugo, 1857

Les Contemplations, Victor Hugo, 1856

Les Travailleurs de la mer, Victor Hugo, 1866

Methodism in the Channel Islands, R. D. Moore, 1952

Passio Sancti Helerii

Poly-Olbion, Michael Drayton, 1612

Rambles among the Channel Islands, Jean Louis Armand de Quatrefages de Bréau, 1857

Redstone's Guernsey and Jersy Guide, Louisa Lane Clarke, 1843

The Battle of the Strong, Sir Gilbert Parker, 1898

The Channel Islands, Henry D. Inglis, 1835

The Days I Knew, Lillie Langtry

The Island of Alderney... being a companion and guide for the traveller, Louisa Lane Clarke, 1851

Literary and linguistic studies

A Brief History of Jèrriais, Nicol Spence, Jersey, 1993

Balleine's History of Jersey, Marguerite Syvret and Joan Stevens, 1998

Customs, Ceremonies & Traditions of the Channel Islands, Raoul Lemprière, 1976

Des Filles, une sorcière, Dame Toumasse et quelques autres, R. J. Lebarbenchon, Azeville

George d'La Forge, Guardian of the Jersey Norman Heritage: A Study of the Life and Writings of George Francis Le Feuvre (1891–1984), Annette Torode, 2003

Georges Métivier: le Poète Nationale de Guernesey, Eugène Chatelain, 1877

Guernsey Folk Lore, Sir Edgar MacCulloch, 1903

Jèrriais – Jersey's Native Tongue, Mari C. Jones, 2003

Jersey Folk Lore, J. H. L'Amy, Jersey, 1859

Jersey: ses antiquités, M. De La Croix, Jersey, 1859

La Grève de Lecq, Roger Jean Lebarbenchon, 1988

La Normandie dialectale, R. Lepelley, Caen, 1999

La Normadie Traditionelle, Fernand Lechanteur, 1985

Maistre Wace: A Celebration, ed. Glyn S. Burgess and Judith Weiss, 2006

The German Occupation of the Channel Islands, Charles Cruikshank, 1975

The Guernsey dialect names of birds, fishes and insects, &c., E. D. Marquand, reprint from the Transactions, for 1904, of the Guernsey Society of Natural Science and Local Research, 1908

The Guernsey Norman French Translations of Thomas Martin: A Linguistic Study of an Unpublished Archive, Mari C. Jones, Leuven 2008

The Triumph of the Country: the rural community in nineteenth-century Jersey, John Kelleher, 1994

Dictionaries

Dictionnaire de patois Normand, Henri Moisy, 1887

Dictionnaire Franco-Normand, George Métivier (1870)

Dictionnaire Jersiais-Français avec Vocabulaire Français-Jersiais, Frank Le Maistre, 1966

Dictionnaire Norman-Français, J.-P. Bourdon, A. Cournée & Y. Charpentier, 1993

Dictionnaithe Angliais-Jèrriais, 2008 (second edition)

Dictionnaithe Jèrriais-Angliais, 2008

Dictiounnaire Angllais-Guernésiais, Marie De Garis, first edition 1967, third edition 1982

English-Jersey Language Vocabulary, Albert L. Carré, 1972

Le Parler Normand entre Caux, Bray et Vexin, Francis Yard, 1998